Privacy in Practice

Privacy is not just the right to be left alone, but also the right to autonomy, control, and access to your personal data. The employment of new technologies over the last three decades drives personal data to play an increasingly important role in our economies, societies, and everyday lives. Personal information has become an increasingly valuable commodity in the digital age.

At the same time, the abundance and persistence of personal data have elevated the risks to individuals' privacy. In the age of Big Data, the Internet of Things, Biometrics, and Artificial Intelligence, it is becoming increasingly difficult for individuals to fully comprehend, let alone control, how and for what purposes organizations collect, use, and disclose their personal information. Consumers are growing increasingly concerned about their privacy, making the need for strong privacy champions ever more acute.

With a veritable explosion of data breaches highlighted almost daily across the globe, and the introduction of heavy-handed privacy laws and regulatory frameworks, privacy has taken center stage for businesses. Businesses today are faced with increasing demands for privacy protections, ever-more complex regulations, and ongoing cybersecurity challenges that place heavy demands on scarce resources. Senior management and executives now acknowledge privacy as some of the biggest risks to the business.

Privacy, traditionally, has existed in a separate realm, resulting in an unintentional and problematic barrier drawn between the privacy team and the rest of the organization. With many regulatory frameworks to consider, building an all-encompassing data privacy program becomes increasingly challenging. Effective privacy protection is essential to maintaining consumer trust and enabling a robust and innovative digital economy in which individuals feel they may participate with confidence.

This book aims at helping organizations in establishing a unified, integrated, enterprise-wide privacy program. This book is aiming to help privacy leaders and professionals to bridge the privacy program and business strategies, transform legal terms and dead text to live and easy-to-understand essential requirements which organizations can easily implement, identify and prioritize privacy program gap initiatives and promote awareness and embed privacy into the everyday work of the agency and its staff.

Security, Audit and Leadership Series

Series Editor Dan Swanson, Dan Swanson and Associates, Ltd.,
Winnipeg, Manitoba, Canada

The Security, Audit and Leadership Series publishes leading-edge books on critical subjects facing security and audit executives as well as business leaders. Key topics addressed include Leadership, Cybersecurity, Security Leadership, Privacy, Strategic Risk Management, Auditing IT, Audit Management and Leadership.

Agile Enterprise Risk Management: Risk-Based Thinking, Multi-Disciplinary Management and Digital Transformation
Howard M. Wiener

Information System Audit: How to Control the Digital Disruption
Philippe Peret

Agile Audit Transformation and Beyond
Toby DeRoche

Mind the Tech Gap: Addressing the Conflicts between IT and Security Teams
Nikki Robinson

CyRM^{SM}: Mastering the Management of Cybersecurity
David X Martin

The Auditor's Guide to Blockchain Technology: Architecture, Use Cases, Security and Assurance
Shaun Aghili

Artificial Intelligence Perspective for Smart Cities
Vahap Tecim and Sezer Bozkus Kahyaoglu

Teaching Cybersecurity: A Handbook for Teaching the Cybersecurity Body of Knowledge in a Conventional Classroom
Daniel Shoemaker, Ken Sigler and Tamara Shoemaker

Cognitive Risk
James Bone and Jessie H Lee

Privacy in Practice: Establish and Operationalize a Holistic Data Privacy Program
Alan Tang

For more information about this series, please visit: https://www.routledge.com/Internal-Audit-and-IT-Audit/book-series/CRCINTAUDITA

Privacy in Practice
Establish and Operationalize a
Holistic Data Privacy Program

Alan Tang

CRC Press
Taylor & Francis Group
Boca Raton London New York

CRC Press is an imprint of the
Taylor & Francis Group, an **informa** business

First edition published 2023
by CRC Press
6000 Broken Sound Parkway NW, Suite 300, Boca Raton, FL 33487–2742

and by CRC Press
4 Park Square, Milton Park, Abingdon, Oxon, OX14 4RN

© 2023 Alan Tang

CRC Press is an imprint of Taylor & Francis Group, LLC

Library of Congress Cataloging-in-Publication Data
Names: Tang, Alan, (Information Security), author.
Title: Privacy in practice: establish and operationalize a holistic data
    privacy program/Alan Tang.
Description: First edition. | Boca Raton : CRC Press, 2023. | Series: Security, Audit and
    Leadership Series | Includes bibliographical references.
Identifiers: LCCN 2022041629 (print) | LCCN 2022041630 (ebook) | ISBN 9781032125466
    (hardback) | ISBN 9781032125473 (paperback) | ISBN 9781003225089 (ebook)
Subjects: LCSH: Data protection. | Computer security. | Privacy, Right of. |
    Internet—Security measures.
Classification: LCC HF5548.37. T36 2023 (print) | LCC HF5548.37 (ebook) |
    DDC 658.4/78—dc23/eng/20220914
LC record available at https://lccn.loc.gov/2022041629
LC ebook record available at https://lccn.loc.gov/2022041630

ISBN: 978-1-032-12546-6 (hbk)
ISBN: 978-1-032-12547-3 (pbk)
ISBN: 978-1-003-22508-9 (ebk)

DOI: 10.1201/9781003225089

Contents

PART 1   *Privacy Basics and Landscape*

PART 2   *Business Impact and a Holistic Framework*

PART 3   *Privacy Governance*

PART 4   Privacy Operations

PART 5　High-Risk Business Scenarios

PART 6 *Data Breach Handling and DPA Cooperation*

Foreword 1

Do you wish to kick-off an effective privacy program but are lost on where and how to start? This book is for you.

I first heard Dr. Alan Tang speak in Macau during the Asia Pacific Privacy Assembly forum in 2019 and was immediately impressed by his profound insights about data privacy and its implications for today's organizations. I learned much about the upcoming China data protection law when he discussed how the law came to be and its impact on companies operating within its reach. I also remember how he spoke knowledgeably about the societal, economic, and technological contexts of data privacy and protection. For someone coming from "industry", his grasp of data privacy's origins and contemporary issues and the fervor and flair he evangelized privacy's different and sometimes difficult aspects are marvelous.

I was excited that he finally put his thoughts and passion into writing to come up with this book. What I find remarkable about *Privacy in Practice* is the scope and breadth of Mr. Tang's knowledge on how to come up with an effective, holistic, and practical privacy program and the usefulness with which he presented it. Now, this is important. With the exponential growth of data privacy as a top-level concern, knowing how and where to start a practical privacy program is vital. But equally important, too, is ensuring that the materials are helpful in the real world.

I have seen the explosion of resources and references on establishing privacy programs useful for company DPOs and practitioners worldwide. But nothing comes close to an all-in-one "how to build a privacy program toolkit" than this book. I would know because as the first Privacy Commissioner of the Philippines, which is considered a newly formed volcano in data privacy, I never ceased to develop on my own and search for literature and references helpful for our companies to build their privacy programs.

After reading this book, I could say that the range of topics Dr. Alan Tang covered under one title, and the details he put are exceptional and presently unmatched. I confess that I have started using his manuscript as a reference in my work.

Dr. Tang has a nose for presenting what should genuinely matter for global privacy practitioners when building a holistic and operational privacy program. Contexts behind frameworks are vital to understanding where privacy legislations are based, where regulators are coming from and where future regulation is headed.

In this book, Dr. Tang will bring you back to where it all started. He laid the foundations of privacy principles brick by brick, how they developed slowly over time, and tracked how they spread all over the globe. His mastery of the critical privacy frameworks, sectoral rules, and laws that cast their influence worldwide shown in the book. That is why this book provides the answers to where most, if not all, of today's privacy developments stand. With Dr. Tang handholding you throughout your reading, he's handing you both a magnifying glass and a pair of binoculars as tools to chart an effective privacy program.

I learned a lot reading this book. As head of a DPA, I got to keep up with the rapid pace of privacy developments globally. A regulator's worst fear is being stumped when faced with tricky questions about global trends, practices, and cross-border privacy rules from company data protection officers and data subjects. I discovered Dr. Tang's book to be an excellent reference and useful as a map to help the reader navigate a privacy world that has become more complex. With this book as your handy companion, you will never be intimidated by privacy permutations that challenge even us, regulators.

As an elected member of the Global Privacy Assembly executive committee in 2019–2020, I had ringside seats on privacy development globally. I have witnessed the dramatic rise of more jurisdictions adopting privacy laws and starting their regimes. During that period, record fines were set in the EU, Canada, and the US, as more DPAs have stepped up in enforcing their privacy laws.

Notable, too, are the maturation of larger jurisdictions like Brazil and China. In Asia, there's the anticipation of more populous countries like India and Indonesia finally approving their privacy laws. Meanwhile, more established jurisdictions like New Zealand, Hong Kong, and Singapore have amended their laws to introduce more stringent measures to protect personal data.

All these are proof that the global data privacy momentum will not diminish. And with the patchwork of data privacy laws that have sprung up in recent years, finding your way around and steering your company away from business risks that now include hefty fines and penalties are becoming more challenging.

Your goal is to position your organization to be trusted by your clients, partners, customers, and importantly, by regulators. There is a single pathway, and that journey starts by implementing an effective privacy program to prove that your company deserves that trust.

You are fortunate to be holding on to Dr. Tang's book as your manual for building your privacy program. This book is a veritable toolbox for companies aiming to jumpstart their privacy program. It is a must-read and must-keep for company CEOs and members of the Board Directors and a companion for data protection officers and practitioners who wish to contribute to their companies' bottom line by treating data privacy and protection as a competitive differentiator.

The rules on personal data have changed but continue to develop at an unprecedented pace. As a result, you can rarely find the answers to many global privacy questions especially how to build a holistic and operational privacy program in one book. Fortunately, this book has finally arrived.

Raymund Enriquez Liboro
Former and First Privacy Commissioner for Philippines
August 1, 2022

Foreword 2

When Alan told me that he didn't set out to write a beach book, I think he forgot for a moment where I was sitting. Like so many folks in recent times, the two of us had not spoken in person for at least a few years and were having a video call to discuss this text. I looked out the window and chuckled.

Bermuda is a small place, and you often have a glimpse of a bay or the open ocean or can hear the crashing of waves on the volcanic rocks. To a certain extent, every book here becomes a beach book, whether it wants to or not.

As the first Privacy Commissioner for Bermuda, I have embraced this reality, turning to seaside analogies and nautical themes to explain the varied issues of privacy, data, and technology ethics. For example, we have designed a "Mid-Atlantic Privacy Compass" to describe our regulatory philosophy, and one of our office's key programs is a "P.I.N.K. Sandbox" to match our rose-colored beaches.

Alan's "Privacy in Practice" is most certainly not a beach book – nor should it be. The privacy and data protection issues confronted each day by anyone using a computer are not breezy. They are fundamental to the functioning of our communities.

Privacy helps our political structures to function by protecting freedoms of assembly and secret ballots. It enables our economies by helping us trust one another in online or other marketplaces where we do not know the other party. As we all are shown more and more "personalized content" and advertisements, we can see how data usage and privacy choices shape the information we receive – privacy supports the very integrity of our minds and decision-making. Protecting personal information against misuse is essential to maintaining our autonomy and self-determination. Hardly stuff to make you relax and fall asleep in the sun.

These issues are complex and changing quickly with each cycle of technological innovation or each new application for uses of information. As a regulator that is focused on proactive and constructive engagement with organizations to find mutual, win-win solutions, I firmly believe that the best way to protect individuals from the harm caused by misuse of their personal information is by convincing organizations, or "controllers," that it makes business sense to do so. Our own office has a running series we call "Privacy Means Business" to highlight how the practical application of data protection and data management programs can make organizations more efficient and profitable, all while better protecting their customers or employees.

Part of the task of privacy and data protection regulators is to make compliance with relevant laws easy – but thanks to the diversity of possible uses of data, that task is easier said than done. Here is where Alan comes in with the text you now hold. To tackle the challenging and unique issues that each organization faces, you need precisely the kind of checklists, refreshers, and quick reference tools you will find in these pages. This desk reference can be digested in bite-sized chunks, or searched, to find condensed explanations and briefings to give you the answers you need in the course of your work.

This book will not lull you to sleep like the sound of waves washing onto the shore – it will awaken you to the complexity of the rights and responsibilities created by legal regimes from around the world.

With that said, it may just help you relax after all to know that you have it, if needed, in your desk drawer.

Alexander White
Privacy Commissioner for Bermuda
10 July 2022

Preface

Privacy is not just the right to be left alone, but also the right to autonomy, control, and access to your personal data.

The employment of new technologies over the last three decades drives personal data to play an increasingly important role in our economies, societies, and everyday lives. In the digital age, various political, economic, social, and private activities of human civilization are linked or mapped to the digital space, or even directly realized in a digital manner, which will inevitably generate a massive data scale. Many of our traditional face-to-face interactions, such as banking, shopping, and social connections, are now taking place online. Personal information has become an increasingly valuable commodity in the digital age. According to the estimation of Statista, an international authoritative statistical agency, the global data volume has reached 47 zettabytes in 2020, and it is expected to reach 2,142 zettabytes by 2035.[1] The exponential explosion of data has become a strategic production factor in the digital age.

At the same time, the abundance and persistence of personal data have elevated the risks to individuals' privacy. In the age of Big Data, the Internet of Things, Biometrics, and Artificial Intelligence, it is becoming increasingly difficult for individuals to fully comprehend, let alone control, how and for what purposes organizations collect, use, and disclose their personal information. While more knowledge may lead to undeniable economic and social benefits, the availability of data and specialized analytics that are capable of linking seemingly anonymous information can paint an accurate picture of our private lives. The general public is much savvier about their data protection rights than they used to be. Consumers are growing increasingly concerned about their privacy, making the need for strong privacy champions ever more acute. The risks underline the need for more effective protection of privacy.

With a veritable explosion of data breaches highlighted almost daily across the globe, and the introduction of heavy-handed privacy laws and regulatory frameworks, privacy has taken center stage for businesses. Data protection laws exist to balance the rights of individuals to privacy and the ability of organizations to use data for their business. Data protection laws provide important rights for data subjects and the enforcement of such rights. Many data protection laws and regulations (i.e., EU GDPR) impose significant fines indicating the increasing importance of data protection as the value of personal data increases and the processing becomes even more sophisticated.

Businesses today are faced with increasing demands for privacy protections, ever-more complex regulations, and ongoing cybersecurity challenges that place heavy demands on scarce resources. Data privacy is increasingly on the tip of our tongues, regardless of company size or industry. Executives are increasingly concerned about data breaches. Senior management and executives now acknowledge privacy as some of the biggest risks to the business. With impending regulatory frameworks looming, business leaders find themselves scrambling to ensure that all bases are covered when it comes to data privacy. Privacy, traditionally, has existed in a separate realm, resulting in an unintentional and problematic barrier drawn between the privacy team and the rest of the organization. With many regulatory frameworks to consider, building an all-encompassing data privacy program becomes increasingly challenging.

Effective privacy protection is essential to maintaining consumer trust and enabling a robust and innovative digital economy in which individuals feel they may participate with confidence. Organizations that understand this and embrace a culture of privacy are those that will be most successful in this digital age.

This book is intended for the following audience from small, medium, large, and international organizations.

- Chief Privacy Officer/Privacy Officer
- Data Protection Officer
- Privacy professionals
- Chief Security Officer/Security Officer
- Risk Officer
- Business Leaders
- Professionals who want to gain knowledge in the privacy space

This book aims at helping organizations in establishing a unified, integrated, enterprise-wide privacy program that guides business units through providing privacy protection, maintaining privacy integrity, and offering protection measures during product development. This book is aiming to help privacy leaders and professionals to:

- Bridge the privacy program and business strategies. Demonstrate an understanding of the goals and strategies of the organization, and how the privacy program can support the business. Extend the privacy program beyond the privacy team or organizational function.
- Transform legal terms and dead text to live and easy-to-understand essential requirements which organizations can easily implement.
- Engage with business departments in an understanding of the scope of privacy within the context of the organization and build an environment that places privacy ownership in the hands of the business.
- Identify and prioritize privacy program gap initiatives. Establish and operationalize an actionable privacy program roadmap.
- Leverage privacy as a competitive advantage in streamlining how customer data flows through the organization. Shift the organization's view of privacy as the enemy of efficiency and innovation.
- Promote awareness and embed privacy into the everyday work of the agency and its staff.

Acknowledgments

Writing a book is way harder than I thought and more rewarding than I could have ever imagined.

I would not be able to get my work done without the continual support and vision of my friend Dan Swanson who initiated this book effort, encouraged, and guided me all the way through the entire process. I am so grateful to have had Gabriella Williams, my editor from CRC Press, to organize, review, and edit my book professionally and patiently.

A very special thanks to my mentor Chris Yau who is always there to help and guide me whenever I need him the most. I would admit that my career was largely inspired by his professionalism, generosity, and enthusiasm. I also appreciate the professional guidance and suggestions I received from my friend Gary Xu throughout the journey.

It is absolutely my honor and privilege to have the opportunity to cross paths with Mr. Alexander White, Privacy Commissioner for Bermuda and Mr. Raymund Liboro, former and first Privacy Commissioner, Philippines. I learned a lot from them, as always. I am grateful to have these two commissioners review my book and provide insightful and concreate suggestions to improve the structure and content of my book. I am filled with gratitude that Mr. White and Liboro wrote the foreword for me using their precious weekends.

Finally, I would like to acknowledge with appreciation, the support and love of my family—my wife Katherine, my daughter Elizabeth, and my son Edward. They all kept me going, and this book would not have been possible without them.

Author

 **Dr. Alan (Chang Long) Tang** is currently a Principal Research Director with Info-Tech Research Group. Dr. Tang has extensive experience devoted to privacy and security practices. He specializes in establishing and operationalizing risk-based and actionable privacy frameworks and programs in alignment with global privacy laws, regulations, and standards such as GDPR, CCPA/CPRA, PIPEDA, PIPL, LGPD, GAPP, ISO 27701, and NIST PF, etc. He believes in simplifying, automating, and scaling privacy controls to enable business growth.

Dr. Tang has firsthand experience in implementing an enterprise-wide, unified privacy framework and program for a Fortune 50 international company. The privacy framework has been implemented in 50+ countries through three phases. He has a strong history of working with business leaders in a wide range of privacy-related domains such as privacy strategy and roadmap, PIA and DPIA, privacy policies and procedures, privacy-by-design in SDLC, data subject rights assurance, data retention, data disclosure and sharing, data cross-border transfer, data security protection, privacy awareness training, data breach handling, etc.

Dr. Tang earned a PhD in information security and an MBA. Alan also holds numerous privacy and security designations including FIP, CIPP/E, CIPP/US/C, CIPM, CIPT, CISSP, CISA, PMP, and previously ISO27001LA and PCI DSS QSA.

About Info-Tech Research Group

Info-Tech Research Group is one of the world's leading information technology research and executive coaching firms, proudly serving over 30,000 IT professionals. The company produces unbiased and highly relevant research to help CIOs and IT leaders make strategic, timely, and well-informed decisions. For 25 years, Info-Tech has partnered closely with IT leaders to provide them with everything from actionable tools to analyst guidance, ensuring they deliver measurable results for their organizations.

Effective, results-driven research and expertise

IT leaders face mounting pressure to be business partners in driving their organization's success. That's where Info-Tech comes in. Info-Tech helps IT leaders:

1. Build a data-driven IT strategy
2. Manage and improve core IT processes
3. Use AI and digital tools to drive IT-led innovation
4. Select, manage, and optimize their technology portfolio
5. Understand and capitalize on industry insights and trends
6. Train and develop their IT leadership team

Icons Used in This Book

Throughout this book, I use various icons to draw your attention to specific information—here's a description of what they mean:

 Case Study: I use this icon to provide relevant and detailed analysis of court cases or enforcement cases by the data protection authorities.

 Example: When you see this icon, you know that it highlights real-life examples.

 Questions and answers: Sometimes I provide my answers to commonly asked questions.

 Guide and Recommendations: When you see this icon, you will see Info-Tech's practical approach regarding privacy and data protection practices.

Part 1

Privacy Basics and Landscape

This Part Covers the Following Topics:

- Privacy and Data Protection Key Concept
- A Brief History of Privacy
- Privacy Models and Common Principles
- Main Privacy Laws and Regulations
- Main Privacy Frameworks, Certifications and Codes of Conduct

DOI: 10.1201/9781003225089-1

1 Privacy Concept and a Brief History

This chapter is intended to help readers grasp the basic definitions of privacy, understand the brief history of privacy and be able to speak the privacy language.

This chapter covers the following topics:

- *Definition of privacy and data protection*
- *Definition of personal data*
- *Definition of sensitive personal data*
- *Timeline of privacy development*

1.1 NARRATIVES OF PRIVACY AND DATA PROTECTION

Culture Dependence

Privacy concepts and laws are culture dependent. People from different countries with diverse cultural backgrounds may have different views, interpretations, and perspectives on what is privacy. Privacy and data protection should not be studied without considering specific cultural, social, technological, and historical circumstances.

Professor Irwin Altman outlined his privacy regulation theory in *The Environment and Social Behavior* (1975) that privacy regulation theory has to do with the fact that people have different privacy standards at different times and in different contexts. For example, your definition of what constitutes "private information" in your relationship with your spouse is different than in your relationship with your children, and it's also different with your boss and coworkers.[2]

Since time immemorial, all cultures, all over the world, have had some understanding of privacy as a concept. Some codified it into laws, while others integrated it with religious beliefs. Privacy has been, and remains, the subject of rigorous academic study. Anthropology, sociology, psychology, history, and other disciplines have been looking into the concept and developing their definitions and models to describe Privacy.

Definitions of privacy have evolved over time, and our understanding of the concept is constantly changing. It is paramount that we understand not only privacy as a concept but privacy in context.

Privacy is not only about one individual

One of the commonly misunderstood facts is that your personal information implies that you are the only concerned party when it comes to sharing it. Privacy is as collective as it is personal. For instance, your DNA and other biometric data also carry substantial information about your family members, and their health and disease information.

Influential Narratives of Privacy

Although there is no one universally agreed definition of privacy, there are some representative narratives that influence and shape the landscape of privacy legislation and court cases as illustrated in Table 1.1.

In 1888, Thomas Cooley wrote in *A Treatise on the Law of Torts or the Wrongs Which Arise Independent of Contract* that people had a right to be let alone. Samuel D. Warren and Louis D. Brandeis elaborated on this concept in their seminal 1890 article in the Harvard Law Review, "The Right to Privacy." They argued that the common law's protection of property rights was moving

DOI: 10.1201/9781003225089-2

TABLE 1.1

Examples of the Definitions of Privacy

Narrative	Source
"A right to be let alone."	Thomas Cooley, A Treatise on the Law of Torts or the Wrongs Which Arise Independent of Contract (P16 and P29), 1888
	Samuel Warren and Louis Brandeis, Harvard Law Review, 1890
"No one shall be subjected to arbitrary interference with his privacy, family, home, or correspondence."	Article 12, United Nations Universal Declaration of Human Rights, 1948
"The right to respect for one's private and family life, home, and correspondence."	Article 8, European Convention on Human Rights, 1950
"The claim of individuals, groups, or institutions to determine for themselves when, how, and to what extent information about them is communicated to others."	Alan Westin, Privacy and Freedom, 1968

toward the recognition of a right to be let alone. Their article inspired some state courts to begin interpreting the civil law of torts to protect a right of privacy.

Three years after the end of the World War II, the UN Universal Declaration of Human Rights was proclaimed on December 10, 1948, in Paris, set forth milestone standards for the treatment of all people. It has influenced European data protection laws and standards. Article 12 of the declaration is the focus on protecting people's private and family life, home, and correspondence. Everyone has the right to the protection of the law against such interference or attacks. The right to freedom of expression is set out in Article 19 (Right to free speech). And Article 29 (2) addresses that the rights are not absolute, and a balance should be struck.

The European Convention on Human Rights (ECHR, formally the Convention for the Protection of Human Rights and Fundamental Freedoms) is an international treaty to protect human rights and fundamental freedoms in Europe. Article 8 (Right to respect for private and family life) sets forth the principles listed to follow. Article 10 (Freedom of speech) protects the rights of freedom of expression and to share information and ideas across national boundaries; Article 10 (2) promotes balance between Article 8 and 10.

- Everyone has the right to respect for his/her private and family life, his/her home, and his/her correspondence.
- There shall be no interference by a public authority with the exercise of this right except such as is in accordance with the law and is necessary in a democratic society in the interests of national security, public safety, or the economic well-being of the country, for the prevention of disorder or crime, for the protection of health or morals, or for the protection of the rights and freedoms of others.

Different Aspects of Privacy

Although privacy can be defined in many ways, four main areas of privacy are of particular interest regarding data protection and privacy laws and practices: information privacy, bodily privacy, territorial privacy, and communications privacy[3] as described in Table 1.2. The distinction between these four types of privacy provides useful vehicle for making academic analysis, however, in many cases, individual's privacy interests could overlap.

In general, there are three actors that can intrude on an individual's privacy rights as listed in Table 1.3.[4]

TABLE 1.2
Four Types of Privacy

Type of privacy	Description
Information privacy	As defined by Alan F. Westin in *Privacy and Freedom* in 1968 that information privacy is "the claim of individuals, groups, or institutions to determine for themselves when, how, and to what extent information about them is communicated to others."
	Examples of information privacy include identity documents (i.e., passports, driver's license), education and employment history, bank statements and financial transactions, family status, marriage status, trade union membership, etc.
Communications privacy	Communication privacy focuses on the protection of communication means, including email, postal mail, telephone conversations, fax, and other forms of communication behavior and means of communication.
Bodily privacy	Bodily privacy focuses on the protection of a person's physical existence and integrity from intrusion or offense. A person who deliberately physically infringes on the privacy of another person or his personal or interests is liable to the other person for infringement of his privacy if the intrusion is offensive to a reasonable person. Such intrusion or offense may take the form of a body scan and search, a blood test, or any form of genetic testing.
Territorial privacy	Territorial privacy focuses on the protection of people's physical environment and surrounding from others' invasion. The concept of the environment has evolved beyond home to include a broader notion such as workplace and public space, etc. Invasion of personal territorial privacy may take the form of video or audio monitoring and surveillance, physical search of the facility, etc.

TABLE 1.3
Three Actors That Might Intrude Individual's Privacy

Actor	Perspective	Description
Other individuals	Individual vs. other individuals	Protect an individual's privacy from intrusion from other individuals, such as a colleague, friend, neighbor, family member, random stranger, hacker, etc.
Organizations	Individual vs. organizations	Protect an individual's privacy from the intrusion from organizations or entities that can collect, use, and share personal data about an individual usually by providing products or services.
States	Individual vs. states	Protect an individual's privacy from intrusion from his or her own state or a foreign state that might monitor and track individual's behavior.

Figure 1.1 illustrates the high-level relationship among various aspects such as types of privacy and intrusion actors.

Privacy and Data Protection

The terms "privacy" and "data protection" are often used interchangeably. To me, there are some slight differences between privacy and data protection just like the two sides of a coin as shown in Figure 1.2. When you look at it, it represents different perspectives.

- From a data subject perspective, it is more about his or her rights, controllability, and assurance of privacy.
- From an organization (i.e., data controller or processor) perspective, it is more of the data protection side that requires and demonstrates the accountability to properly manage and protect personal data, such as the rules and safeguards applied under various laws and regulations to personal data.

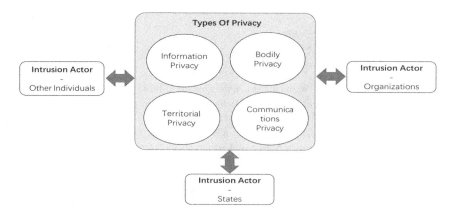

FIGURE 1.1   Relationship among types of privacy and intrusion actors.

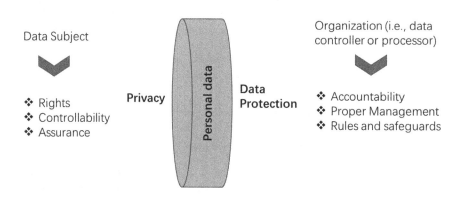

FIGURE 1.2   Privacy vs. data protection.

TABLE 1.4

Key Differences between Privacy and Confidentiality

	Privacy	Confidentiality
Focus	**Individuals**	**Data**
Attribute	Privacy is a right of a people or group of people.	Confidentiality is a property of data, any data, not just personal data.
Essential meaning	Privacy is personal choice. Privacy is a right to control access across a person's physical, decisional, informational, and dispositional dimensions.	Confidentiality is a professional obligation. Confidentiality is an agreement between the persons to maintain the secrecy of sensitive information and documents.
Protection	Protect an individual's personal information, space, body, and communications from intrusion from other individuals, organizations, and states.	Protect data from unauthorized access.

Privacy and Confidentiality

Privacy is mainly about people's rights and expectations. Confidentiality, on the other hand, is all about data. Table 1.4 illustrates the key differences.

1.2 PERSONAL DATA AND SENSITIVE PERSONAL DATA

1.2.1 PERSONAL DATA

Personal Data Definitions

You might have noticed that the definition of personal data varies from jurisdiction to jurisdiction in terms of the terms, nature, coverage, and scope. For instance, some regulations use personal data, however, other regulations use personal information. In this book, "personal data" and "personal information" will be deemed as the same and used interchangeably. Examples are listed in Table 1.5.

In a situation that an organization is operating in more than one jurisdiction that have different definitions of "personal information (data)" and "sensitive personal information", the agreed definitions should be adequate and consistent to reflect all legal contexts.

Core Elements of Personal Data

As illustrated by various definitions mentioned previously, most of the personal data definitions are substantially similar and cover the following four aspects as defined by the GPDR article 4(1).

TABLE 1.5

Examples of Personal Data Definition

Region	Regulation/Standard	Definition
EU	General Data Protection Regulation (GDPR)	Personal data means any information relating to an identified or identifiable natural person ("data subject"); an identifiable natural person is one who can be identified, directly or indirectly, in particular by reference to an identifier such as a name, an identification number, location data, an online identifier or to one or more factors specific to the physical, physiological, genetic, mental, economic, cultural or social identity of that natural person.
US	Gramm-Leach-Bliley Act (GLBA)	Non-public Personal Information means personally identifiable financial information.
US	The Health Insurance Portability and Accountability Act (HIPAA)	PHI is any individually identifiable health information in any form. "Health information" means relating to any past, present, or future health condition or to health care or to payment for health care.
US	Family Educational Rights and Privacy Act of 1974 (FERPA)	Personally Identifiable Information: The term includes, but is not limited to— (a) The student's name (b) The name of the student's parent or other family members (c) The address of the student or student's family (d) A personal identifier, such as the student's social security number, student number, or biometric record (e) Other indirect identifiers, such as the student's date of birth, place of birth, and mother's maiden name (f) Other information that, alone or in combination, is linked or linkable to a specific student that would allow a reasonable person in the school community, who does not have personal knowledge of the relevant circumstances, to identify the student with reasonable certainty (g) Information requested by a person who the educational agency or institution reasonably believes knows the identity of the student to whom the education record relates
US	The California Privacy Rights Act of 2020 (CPRA)	"Personal information" means information that identifies, relates to, describes, is reasonably capable of being associated with, or could reasonably be linked, directly or indirectly, with a particular consumer or household. Personal information includes, but is not limited to, the following if it identifies, relates to, describes, is reasonably capable of being associated with, or could be reasonably linked, directly or indirectly, with a particular consumer or household.

(Continued)

TABLE 1.5 (Continued)

Region	Regulation/Standard	Definition
US	Colorado Consumer Protection Act	(I) Personal information means a Colorado resident's first name or first initial and last name in combination with any one or more of the following data elements that relate to the resident, when the data elements are not encrypted, redacted, or secured by any other method rendering the name or the element unreadable or unusable: (A) Social security number (B) Driver's license number or identification card number (C) Account number or credit or debit card number, in combination with any required security code, access code, or password that would permit access to a resident's financial account (II) Personal information does not include publicly available information that is lawfully made available to the general public from federal, state, or local government records or widely distributed media
US	Connecticut Data Breach Law	Connecticut defines personal information as "an individual's first name or first initial and last name in combination with any one, or more, of the following data: (1) Social Security number [although Nevada specifically excludes the last four digits as PI]; (2) driver's license number or state identification card number; or (3) account number, credit or debit card number, in combination with any required security code, access code or password that would permit access to an individual's financial account."
US	DOJ Order 0904	Personally Identifiable Information: Information that can be used to distinguish or trace an individual's identity, such as name, social security number, or biometric records, alone, or when combined with other personal or identifying information that is linked or linkable to a specific individual, such as date and place of birth or mother's maiden name. DOJ information: Information that is owned, produced, controlled, protected by, or otherwise within the custody or responsibility of DOJ, including, without limitation, information related to DOJ programs or personnel. It includes, without limitation, information (1) provided by, generated by, or generated for DOJ, (2) provided to DOJ and in DOJ custody, and/or (3) managed or acquired by a DOJ contractor in connection with the performance of a contract. National security information: Information that has been determined (pursuant to Executive Order 12958 as amended by Executive Order 13292, or any successor order, or by the Atomic Energy Act of 1954, as amended) to require protection against unauthorized disclosure and is marked to indicate its classified status.
China	Personal Information Protection Law	Personal information is all kinds of information, recorded by electronic or other means, related to identified or identifiable natural persons, not including information after anonymization handling.
Canada	Personal Information Protection and Electronic Documents Act	Personal information means information about an identifiable individual.
Bermuda	Personal Information Protection Act 2016	Personal information means any information about an identified or identifiable individual.
Global	ISO/IEC 27018:2014(E)	Personally identifiable information (PII): any information that (a) can be used to identify the PII principal to whom such information relates, or (b) is or might be directly or indirectly linked to a PII principal.
US	NIST SP800–122	Personally Identifiable Information (PII) is any information about an individual maintained by an agency, including (1) any information that can be used to distinguish or trace an individual's identity, such as name, social security number, date and place of birth, mother's maiden name, or biometric records; and (2) any other information that is linked or linkable to an individual, such as medical, educational, financial, and employment information.

Region	Regulation/Standard	Definition
China	GB/T 35273–2020	Personal information: any information that is recorded, electronically or otherwise, that can be used alone or in combination with other information to identify a natural person or reflect the activity of a natural person.
North America	NERC (North American Electric Reliability Corporation)	Personnel Information that identifies or could be used to identify a specific individual, or reveals personnel, financial, medical, or other personal information. Source: NERC Employee Code of Conduct
US	FERC (The Federal Energy Regulatory Commission)	Personally Identifiable Information includes information that is personal in nature, and which may be used to identify you (e.g., social security numbers, birthdates, and phone numbers). Source: FERC Administrative Policies
Japan	APPI	Previously, the APPI defined personal information as only the name, address, and date of birth. The amended APPI seeks to be more comprehensive by including any "personal identifier code", referring to biometric information (e.g., DNA sequences, fingerprints, facial appearance), specific identifier numbers (e.g., passport and driver's license, resident cards, "My Number"), other IDs uniquely assigned to an individual (e.g., health care cards, credit cards), and any codes the PPC might designate in the future as being equivalent to the prior categories. Note that for now, unlike the European General Data Protection Regulation (GDPR), the APPI only includes codes assigned to individuals, not to devices (e.g., IP addresses, mobile subscription identification numbers).

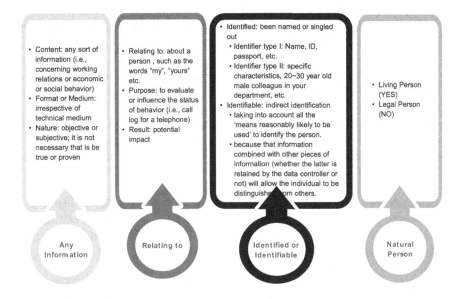

FIGURE 1.3 Four aspects of personal data.

Personal data is:

- **any information**
- **relating to**
- **an identified or identifiable**
- **natural person**

Figure 1.3 summarizes these four aspects providing a further explanation to help readers understand what each aspect entails.

Article 29 working party provides further information and context that I summarize next to help readers in making decisions on whether a piece of information is personal data.[103]

1) **Any information:** is understood to be literal. Information could be anything from a person's name to her location.
   - Content: the concept of personal data includes data providing any sort of information. The term "personal data" includes information touching the individual's private and family life, but also information regarding whatever types of activity are undertaken by the individual, like that concerning working relations or the economic or social behavior of the individual.
   - Format or medium: irrespective of the technical medium; information is available in whatever form, be it alphabetical, numerical, graphical, photographic, or acoustic, for example. It includes information kept on paper, as well as information stored in computer memory by means of binary code, or on a videotape, for instance.
   - Nature: objective or subjective; it doesn't need to be true or proven.
2) **Relating to:** refers to the information's purpose and impact on someone's privacy rights. Its juxtaposition with other content is also important. For example, a job title would not necessarily relate to a person, but a job title combined with a name likely would.
   - Content: Information "relates" to a person when it is "about" that person, and this has to be assessed in the light of all circumstances surrounding the case.
   - Purpose: taking into account all the circumstances surrounding the precise case, with the purpose to evaluate, treat in a certain way or influence the status or behavior of an individual. (i.e., call log for a telephone)
   - Result: data can be considered to "relate" to an individual because their use is likely to have an impact on a certain person's rights and interests, taking into account all the circumstances surrounding the precise case. It should be noted that it is not necessary that the potential result be a major impact. It is sufficient if the individual may be treated differently from other persons as a result of the processing of such data.
3) **Identified or identifiable:** "Identified" means that an individual person has been named or singled out—for example, by specific characteristics. And, as stated in Recital 26 of the GDPR, "Identifiable" refers to indirect identification, taking into account all the "means reasonably likely to be used" to identify the person.
   - Directly
   - Indirectly: In cases, where prima facie the extent of the identifiers available does not allow anyone to single out a particular person, that person might still be "identifiable" because that information combined with other pieces of information (whether the latter is retained by the data controller or not) will allow the individual to be distinguished from others (page 13).
4) **Natural person**: As stated in the GDPR, information must relate to a "natural person" for it to be considered personal data, which means that the information must be about a living, breathing person who is living. It doesn't include data in relation to "legal persons" (that is, corporations or other organizations with a separate legal status) or data in relation to public authorities. Figure 1.4 demonstrates the definition of natural person.

- Deceased Person
  - EU members take different approaches with respect to deceased persons:
    - Countries with regulations that do not cover personal data about deceased persons: Austria, Belgium, Bulgaria, Croatia, Cyprus, Finland, Germany, Greece, Lithuania, Luxembourg, Malta, the Netherlands, Norway, Poland, and Romania.
    - Countries with regulations that have limited obligations: the Czech Republic, Denmark (10Y after), Estonia (10Y/20Y-Minor), France, Hungary (5Y), Iceland

Further Information about Natural Person

	Unborn	Natural Person	Deceased Person	Sole traders/ Freelancers	Legal Person (i.e. Inc., Ltd.)
GDPR	Depends on the general position of national legal systems	√ Living person	✕ Generally, GDPR does not apply to deceased person but allow derogations	√	✕ Generally, GDPR does not apply to legal person but allow derogations
Other Examples		**Bermuda PIPA 2016:** Not applicable to an individual that has been in existence for at least 150 years	**Bermuda PIPA 2016:** Not applicable to an individual who has been dead for at least 20 years		

FIGURE 1.4 Definition of natural person.

(5Y or longer if confidential), Ireland (health data applies), Portugal (genetic data and health data apply).

- In terms of data subject rights request, Bulgaria, Hungary, Italy, Portugal, Slovakia, and Spain have each granted specific rights to heirs or family members of deceased persons, with respect to the processing of the deceased person's personal data (e.g., a deceased person's heirs may have the right to enforce the rights of access, rectification, or erasure, on behalf of that deceased person).
  - In Hungary, close relatives of the deceased or a person appointed by the data subject during his or her lifetime have the right to exercise data subject rights on behalf of the deceased.
  - In Italy, an agent of the deceased data subject can exercise data subjects on behalf of the deceased data subject.
  - In Spain, heirs or executors of the deceased data subject are entitled to exercise certain data subject rights (namely the right of access, the right of erasure and the right of rectification).
  - French law allows for data subjects to provide instructions for the management of their personal data after their death.
- Unborn children: The extent to which data protection rules may apply before birth depends on the general position of national legal systems about the protection of unborn children.
- Legal persons: As the definition of personal data refers to individuals (i.e., natural persons) information relating to legal persons is in principle not covered by the Directive, and the protection granted by it does not apply. However, certain data protection rules may still indirectly apply to information relating to businesses or to legal persons, in a number of circumstances.
- Sole traders: Data relating to sole traders (that is, people who run a business but not through a separate legal entity), employees, partners, and directors (where the information relates to them as individuals) may be personal data. For example, an employee's name within a corporate email address (such as paulsmith@xyz.com) will still be personal data, but the content of work emails will not necessarily be their personal data unless it "relates" to them or has an impact upon them.

 Example: Systems IDs and passwords

- Self-selected system usernames are considered personal data. GDPR Article 4 articulates that "personal data" means any information relating to an identified or identifiable natural person ("data subject"); an identifiable natural person is one who can be identified, directly or indirectly, in particular by reference to an identifier such as a name, an identification number, location data, an online identifier or to one or more factors specific to the physical, physiological, genetic, mental, economic, cultural or social identity of that natural person.

- In real-life practices, if you are allowed to select a system username, you may decide to use your public Twitter handle as your username. You may mention your Twitter ID on your Facebook or Google+ page or LinkedIn profile. Self-selected system usernames should be considered personal data because a site owner will not know if a person's self-selected usernames are the same as their public username.
- Regarding password, as a stand-alone data item, it does not belong to personal data. However, in actual business scenarios, account numbers and passwords are generally processed and treated together, that is, account numbers and passwords are usually treated together as personal data.

 Example: IP addresses

An IP address is a unique address identifying a device connected to the Internet or a local network. A series of digits separated by periods—such as 123.45.67.89—can be either static or dynamic.

- Static IP address: A static IP address, manually configured, doesn't change. Static IP addresses are personal data when it comes to the user using the device to which the IP address has been assigned.
- Dynamic IP address: A dynamic IP address is automatically configured and assigned every time when a computing device is connected to a network. As such, it is temporary and changes. Dynamic IP addresses may be personal data under certain circumstances.

If a dynamic IP address can be combined with other data by the data controller or other interested parties—data held by the Internet service provider, such as, for example, the time of the connection and the pages that were visited—the address could be regarded as personal data.

 Case Study: EU court decision—dynamic IP address, October 2017[5]

Dynamic IP addresses if they combine with other information could identify a person, and are considered personal data.

EU JUDGMENT OF THE COURT (Second Chamber)—19 October 2016. The Court of Justice of the European Union held that while Internet service providers assign dynamic IP addresses to users, website owners maintain records of using dynamic IP addresses to access their networks. Dynamic IP alone is not enough to identify a website user, but it can be combined with other data from the internet service provider to identify the user. Therefore, even if legal means are required to identify the data subject, dynamic IP addresses still meet the requirements for personal data in the EU Personal Data Protection Directive—identifiable and therefore personal data.

 Case Study: US Virginia—License plate, 2018

The Supreme Court of Virginia ruled that a lawsuit challenging a police department's practice of keeping data from automated license plate readers for a year can move forward.

The year before, a judge dismissed a case filed by the American Civil Liberties Union in Fairfax County, ruling that a license plate doesn't contain personal information.

But the state's highest court reversed that ruling and sent the case back down to Circuit Court to determine whether the record-keeping process provides police with a "readily made" link to the vehicle's owner.

The court said if that link exists, then storage of the data is not exempt from Virginia's Government Data Collection and Dissemination Practices Act because the police "collected and retained personal information without any suspicion of criminal activity."

1.2.2 SENSITIVE PERSONAL DATA

Some personal data which are, by their nature, particularly sensitive in relation to fundamental rights and freedoms merit specific protection as the context of their processing could create high or significant risks to fundamental rights and freedoms. Therefore, it requires a higher standard of protection. The risk to the rights and freedoms of natural persons, of varying likelihood and severity, may result from personal data processing which could lead to physical, material, or non-material damage, in particular: where the processing may give rise to discrimination, identity theft or fraud, financial loss, damage to the reputation, loss of confidentiality of personal data protected by professional secrecy, unauthorized reversal of pseudonymization, or any other significant economic or social disadvantage.

Similar to the definitions of personal data, there is no universally agreed definition for sensitive personal data. While most privacy laws and regulations use the term "sensitive personal information", GDPR does not specially call out sensitive personal data, but the article (9) articulates special categories of personal data.

In general, sensitive personal data is a type of personal data that:

- **Personal data revealing . . .**
  - ✓ Racial/ethnic origin, political opinions, religious/philosophical beliefs, trade union membership
- **For the purpose of uniquely identifying a natural person**
  - ✓ Genetic data
  - ✓ Biometric data
- **Data concerning . . .**
  - ✓ Health, sex life, sexual orientation
- Note: Under the HR circumstance, the listing of spouses only reveals marital status not sex life.
- **Data relating to . . .**
  - ✓ Criminal convictions, offenses, security measures

Table 1.6 lists some exemplar definitions of sensitive personal information.

Relationship diagram

Based on GDPR, I built a relationship diagram illustrating different types of personal data with various sensitivity as shown in Figure 1.5.

1.3 TIMELINE OF PRIVACY DEVELOPMENT

The social concept of privacy is rooted in some of the oldest religions, texts, and cultures. Culturally, privacy is mentioned in early developed societies from classical Greece to ancient China. For example, privacy is recognized in the Bible, Jewish law, Quran, and the Analects.

TABLE 1.6
Examples of Sensitive Personal Data Definition

Region	Regulation/ Standard	Definition
EU	General Data Protection Regulation (GDPR)	Special categories of personal data: personal data revealing racial or ethnic origin, political opinions, religious or philosophical beliefs, or trade union membership, and the processing of genetic data, biometric data for the purpose of uniquely identifying a natural person, data concerning health or data concerning a natural person's sex life or sexual orientation.
France	Data Protection Act & Implementing Decree	Collecting data about a person's health and sex life and data that directly or indirectly reflect a person's racial, political, philosophical, religious views or trade union membership is prohibited.
Germany	Federal Data Protection Act	Race, political opinions, religious and philosophical beliefs, union membership, health, and sexuality.
US	CPRA (The California Privacy Rights Act of 2020)	"Sensitive personal Information" means (1) personal information that reveals (A) a consumer's social security, driver's license, state Identification card, or passport number; (B) a consumer's account log-in, financial account, debit card, or credit card number. In combination with any required security or access code, password, or credentials allowing access to an account; (C) a consumer's precise geolocation; (D) a consumer's racial or ethnic origin, religious or philosophical beliefs, or union membership; (E) the contents of a consumer's mall, email, and text messages, unless the business is the Intended recipient of the communication; (F) a consumer's genetic data; and (2)(A) the processing of biometric Information for the purpose of uniquely identifying a consumer; (B) personal Information collected and analyzed concerning a consumer's health; or (C) personal Information collected and analyzed concerning a consumer's sex life or sexual orientation. Sensitive personal Information that is "publicly available" pursuant to paragraph (2) of subdivision (v) of Section 1798.140 shall not be considered sensitive personal Information or personal information.
US	Gramm-Leach-Bliley Act (GLBA)	Non-public Personal Information means personally identifiable financial information.
US	Colorado Privacy Act	"Sensitive data" means: (a) personal data revealing racial or ethnic origin, religious beliefs, a mental or physical health condition or diagnosis, sex life or sexual orientation, or citizenship or citizenship status. (b) genetic or biometric data that may be processed for the purpose of uniquely identifying an individual; or (c) personal data from a known child.
China	GB/T 35273–2020	Personal sensitive information: Once leaked, illegally provided, or abused, personal information may endanger personal and property safety and easily lead to damage to personal reputation, physical and mental health, or discriminatory treatment.
Australia	Privacy Act	Race, political opinions, political group membership, religious beliefs, philosophical beliefs, union membership, sexual orientation, criminal records, health information, genetic information, biometric information, and biometric templates.
Japan	Guidelines for the Protection of Personal Information in the Financial Sector	There is no definition of sensitive personal data in the Japanese Personal Data Protection Law, but the "Guidelines for the Protection of Personal Information in the Financial Sector" stipulates that the scope of sensitive personal data includes: political opinions, religious beliefs, trade union membership, race, family origin, legal residence, medical records, sex life, criminal records.
Argentina	Personal Data Protection Act 2000	Sensitive data: Personal data revealing racial and ethnic origin, political opinions, religious, philosophical, or moral beliefs, labor union membership, and information concerning health conditions or sexual habits or behavior.

Region	Regulation/ Standard	Definition
Bermuda	Personal Information Protection Act 2016	"Sensitive personal information" means any personal information relating to an individual's place of origin, race, color, national or ethnic origin, sex, sexual orientation, sexual life, marital status, physical or mental disability, physical or mental health, family status, religious beliefs, political opinions, trade union membership, biometric information, or genetic information.

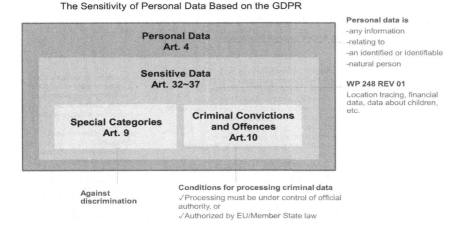

FIGURE 1.5 The sensitivity of personal data based on the GDPR.

From a privacy development timeline perspective, I think there are four main periods. The timeline that is described in Figure 1.6 illustrates the development of privacy from concept, social, and regulation development perspectives.

- Pre-Contemporary (1300s~1870s)
- Privacy 1.0: From Concept to Declaration (1880s~1950s)
- Privacy 2.0: From Principles to Regulations (1960s~2000s)
- Privacy 3.0: From Obligations to Advantages (2010s~Now)

1.3.1 PRE-CONTEMPORARY

The legal protection of privacy rights has a far-reaching history. It began in England in 1361 with the Justices of the Peace Act. This act included provisions calling for the arrest of "peeping Toms" and eavesdroppers.

In 1765, British Lord Camden struck down a warrant to enter and seize papers from a home and, in so doing, wrote,

> we can safely say there is no law in this country to justify the defendants in what they have done; if there was, it would destroy all the comforts of society, for papers are often the dearest property any man can have.

Parliamentarian William Pitt shared this view, writing that

> the poorest man may in his cottage bid defiance to all the force of the Crown. It may be frail: its roof may shake; the wind may blow through it; the storms may enter; the rain may enter—but the King of England cannot enter; all his forces dare not cross the threshold of the ruined tenement.

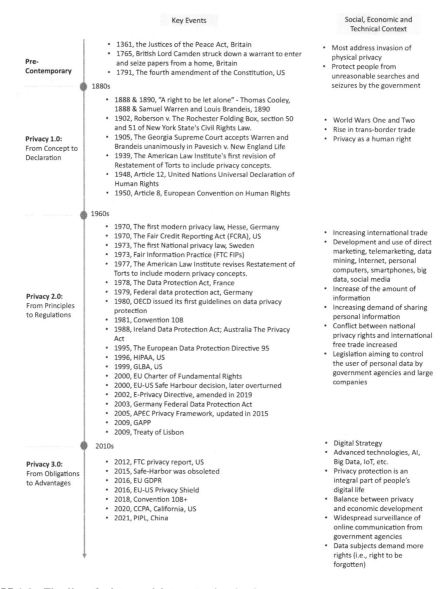

FIGURE 1.6 Timeline of privacy and data protection development.

In the following centuries, other European countries advanced more particularized privacy protections. The Swedish Parliament enacted the Access to Public Records Act in 1776, requiring that information held by the government be used for legitimate purposes. In 1858, France prohibited the publication of private facts, with violators of the prohibition subject to strict fines.

In the United States, the fourth amendment holds: The right of the people to be secure in their persons, houses, papers, and effects, against unreasonable searches and seizures, shall not be violated, and no warrants shall issue, but upon probable cause, supported by oath or affirmation, and particularly describing the place to be searched.

1.3.2   PRIVACY 1.0: FROM CONCEPT TO DECLARATION

In 1888, Thomas M. Cooley, justice, and later Chief justice of the Michigan Supreme Court, writes: "A Treatise on the Low of Torts or the Wrongs Which Arise Independently of Contract."

On December 15, 1890, two years after Cooley's writings, two brilliant young lawyers, Samuel D. Warren and Louis D. Brandeis, published in the Harvard Law Review an article titled "The Right to Privacy." Louis D. Brandeis eventually becomes a Supreme Court Justice. In 1902, Roberson v. The Rochester Folding Box Company antiprivacy judgment gave rise to sections 50 and 51 of New York State's Civil Rights Law. In 1939, The American Law Institute's first revision of Restatement of Torts included privacy concepts. The first modern international privacy law appeared in 1948, as Article 12 of the Universal Declaration of Human Rights. It was proclaimed on December 10 in Paris, with the wounds of the Second World War still fresh. It is a powerful document, drafted by representatives from all over the world hoping for a fresh, and less bloody start. In 1950, The European Convention on Human Rights is adopted, including Article 8, an expanded right to privacy.

Universal Declaration of Human Rights (^{UD}HR) December 10, 1948.

- Non-binding instrument, UDHR setup set forth milestone standards for the treatment of all people.
- It has influenced European data protection laws and standards.
- **Article 12** (Right to privacy)—No one shall be subjected to arbitrary interference with his privacy, family, home, or correspondence, nor to attacks upon his honor and reputation. Everyone has the right to the protection of the law against such interference or attacks.
- The right to freedom of expression is set out in Article 19 (Right to free speech).
- Article 29 (2) (Balance) addresses that the rights are not absolute, and a balance should be struck.

European Convention on Human Rights (ECHR, enforced in 1953)

- It is an international treaty to protect human rights and fundamental freedoms, which can be enforced by the European Court of Human Rights in Strasburg. All Council of Europe member states have ratified the convention. It is one of the key documents for enforcing fundamental human rights in Europe and worldwide.
- **Article 8** (Privacy)—Right to respect for private and family life: Everyone has the right to respect for his private and family life, his home, and his correspondence.
- Article 10 (Freedom of speech), which protects the rights of freedom of expression and to share information and ideas across national boundaries.
- Article 10 (2) (Balance), which promotes balance between Articles 8 and 10.

Social, Economic and Technical Context:

- World War One and Two
- Rise in trans-border trade

1.3.3 PRIVACY 2.0: FROM PRINCIPLES TO REGULATIONS

In 1970, The first modern privacy law was in Hesse, Germany. In 1973, The first national privacy law was in Sweden. Sweden passed the Data Act ("Datalagen," 1973), considered to be the first national data protection law. This law, which was fairly conservative by today's standards, governed how personally identifiable information was processed in computerized registers; it established a data protection authority with the ominous name "The Data Inspection Board," which would issue permits before a new personal data register could operate and determine specific conditions for its operation. The law has since been superseded by the European General Data Protection Regulation. Fair Information Practice (FTC FIPs) was initially proposed and named by the US Secretary's Advisory Committee on Automated Personal Data Systems in a 1973 report, "Records, Computers, and the Rights of Citizens", issued in response to the growing use of automated data systems containing information about individuals. The central contribution of the Advisory Committee was the development of a code of fair information practice for automated personal data systems. The Privacy Protection Study Commission also may have contributed to the development of FIPs principles in its 1977 report, Personal Privacy in an Information Society. FIPs are the main reference of many other privacy protection frameworks such as Convention 108, OECD, etc. In 1977, The American Law Institute again revised the Restatement of Torts to include modern privacy concepts.

In 1980, The Organization for Economic Cooperation and Development (OECD) issued its first guidelines on data privacy protection. The OECD guidelines are recommendations from governments to multinational enterprises on responsible business conduct. They are guidelines for the protection of privacy and transborder flows of personal data. It is aimed to enable data flows and protect personal data. This membership extends outside of Europe and is not legally binding. The principles introduced were data quality principle, purpose specification, collection limitation, use limitation, openness, individual participation, security safeguards, and accountability. The guidelines were updated in 2013.

In 1981, The Council of Europe adopted Treaty 108: Convention for the protection of individuals with regard to automatic processing of personal data. The convention 108 or Council of Europe Convention is for the protection of individuals regarding the automatic processing of personal data.

In the late 1980s, difficulties with Convention 108 were becoming apparent. Only a small number of states had ratified it, and even those had adopted a fragmented approach. In the 1990s, the European Commission proposed the introduction of a dedicated directive. The principles contained in Convention 108 were used as a benchmark for the EU Data Protection Directive (95/46/EC). Operationally, the Directive set out general data protection principles and obligations, requiring EU member states to transpose and implement them.

From the 1970s to 2010, the globalization of the world economy and e-commerce has grown exponentially. The wide adoption and application of direct marketing, telemarketing, data mining, the Internet, personal computers, smartphones, big data, and social media raised a huge amount of privacy concerns. The capability to access data and share data from anywhere, on any device and at any time increased users' privacy risks. The enforcement of data privacy laws has picked up. In Europe, data protection authorities have increased their audit activities and issued fines.

Social, Economic, and Technical Context:

- The increase in international trade
- Development and use of direct marketing, telemarketing, data mining, Internet, personal computers, e-commerce, smartphones, etc.
- The increase in the amount of information
- Increasing demand for sharing personal information
- Conflict between national privacy rights and international free trade increased
- Legislation aiming to control the use of personal data by government agencies and large companies

1.3.4 PRIVACY 3.0: FROM OBLIGATIONS TO ADVANTAGES

Since 2013, former US spy contractor Edward Snowden's revelations about widespread surveillance of online communication have reverberated in recent years, sparking an international conversation on digital privacy.

In 2014, the European Union Court of justice ruled that EU law grants EU citizens "the right to be forgotten" from search engines.

Countries are embracing broader digital strategies (i.e., Industry 4.0), which make privacy protection an integral part of people's digital life. Protecting the privacy and the rights and freedoms of individuals without creating any barriers to trade and allowing the uninterrupted flow of personal data across national frontiers. At the same time, the Snowden case (2013) reminded us of individuals' privacy rights are facing tremendous threats from government surveillance.

Social, Economic, and Technical Context:

- Digital Strategy
- Industry 4.0
- Advanced technologies, AI, Big Data, IoT, etc.
- Proliferation of social media
- Privacy protection is an integral part of people's digital life
- Widespread surveillance of online communication from government agencies
- Data subjects demand more rights (i.e., right to be forgotten)

2 Legal Systems, World Models, and Landscape

This chapter is intended to help readers explore the current landscape with respect to legal systems in various regions, world models for data protection as well as global privacy regulations.

This chapter covers the following topics:

- *Legal systems in the EU, US, and China*
- *Three types of models for data protection*
- *Worldwide privacy regulation landscape*
- *Privacy laws in main jurisdictions*
- *Sector-specific privacy regulations*

2.1 LEGAL SYSTEMS

Jurisdiction is important because if a court does not have jurisdiction over a case, it does not have the legal authority to pass judgment on the case. For a court to make a binding judgment on a case, it must have both subject matter jurisdiction (the power to hear the type of case) as well as personal jurisdiction (the power over the parties to the case).

Conflicts between laws or legal provisions: A law or legal enactment of a lower level that conflicts with one of a level above is deemed to be invalid to the extent of the conflict. This process is essential to prevent overlaps and clashes between and among laws. Whether there is conflict will be determined by a court.[6]

2.1.1 EU Legal System

Knowing the differences[7] among various types of legislation, such as EU Regulations, Directives, Decisions, Recommendations, and Opinions, is very important for every privacy professional working and/or operating in the field.

2.1.2 US Legal System

There are many sources of law in the United States as illustrated in Figure 2.1 and Table 2.2.[104]

TABLE 2.1
Types of Legislations

Legislation	Description
Regulations	A "regulation" is a binding legislative act. It must be applied in its entirety across the EU. For example, when the EU wanted to make sure that there are common safeguards on goods imported from outside the EU, the Council adopted a regulation.
Directives	A "directive" is a legislative act that sets out a goal that all EU countries must achieve. However, it is up to the individual countries to devise their own laws on how to reach these goals. One example is the EU consumer rights directive, which strengthens rights for consumers across the EU by, for example, eliminating hidden charges and costs on the Internet and extending the period under which consumers can withdraw from a sales contract.

(Continued)

DOI: 10.1201/9781003225089-3

TABLE 2.1   (Continued)

Legislation	Description
Decisions	A "decision" is binding on those to whom it is addressed (e.g., an EU country or an individual company) and is directly applicable. For example, the Commission issued a decision on the EU participating in the work of various counter-terrorism organizations. The decision related to these organizations only.
Recommendations	A "recommendation" is not binding. When the Commission issued a recommendation that EU countries' law authorities improve their use of videoconferencing to help judicial services work better across borders, this did not have any legal consequences. A recommendation allows the institutions to make their views known and to suggest a line of action without imposing any legal obligation on those to whom it is addressed.
Opinions	An "opinion" is an instrument that allows the institutions to make a statement in a non-binding fashion, in other words without imposing any legal obligation on those to whom it is addressed. An opinion is not binding. It can be issued by the main EU institutions (Commission, Council, Parliament), the Committee of the Regions and the European Economic and Social Committee. While laws are being made, the committees give opinions from their specific regional or economic and social viewpoint. For example, the Committee of the Regions issued an opinion on the clean air policy package for Europe.

TABLE 2.2
Source of Legislations in the US

Source of legislation	Description
Constitution	The "Constitution" is the supreme law of the land. The fundamental legal document in the United States and each of the individual states is their constitutions.
Federal Statutes—Acts	An "Act" is a law that has been passed. Act vs. Bill: The difference is that a bill is a proposed law that has not been passed yet, and.
State Statutes—Acts	By State Legislature/General Assembly/General Court/Legislative Assembly
Treaty	Treaties to which the United States is a party are equivalent in status to Federal legislation. Treaty is reserved for an agreement that is made "by and with the Advice and Consent of the Senate".
Executive Order	An executive order is a directive issued by the President of the United States that manages operations of the federal government and has the force of law. Executive Orders do not require Congressional approval to take effect, but they have the same legal weight as laws passed by Congress.
Regulation/Rule	Federal or state agencies. Most regulations are developed and enacted through a rule-making process, which includes public input. State agencies hold open meetings and public hearings, allowing citizens to participate in the creation of regulations.
Ordinance	An ordinance is a law passed by a municipal government. A municipality, such as a city, town, village, or borough. The power of municipal governments to enact ordinances is derived from the state constitution or statutes or through the legislative grant of a municipal charter.
Common Law	Common law is a subset of case law and refers to laws that have developed over time—as opposed to a single case—from judicial decisions, often drawing from social customs and expectations. Examples of privacy-related common law are doctor/patient and attorney/client privilege.
Precedent	Case law refers to final decisions made by judges in court cases. Common law is a subset of case law and refers to laws that have developed over time. There are types of Precedents, binding precedents, and persuasive precedents.
Consent Decree	A consent decree is an agreement between two parties in which the offending party agrees to cease illegal activity, although often without admitting wrongdoing.

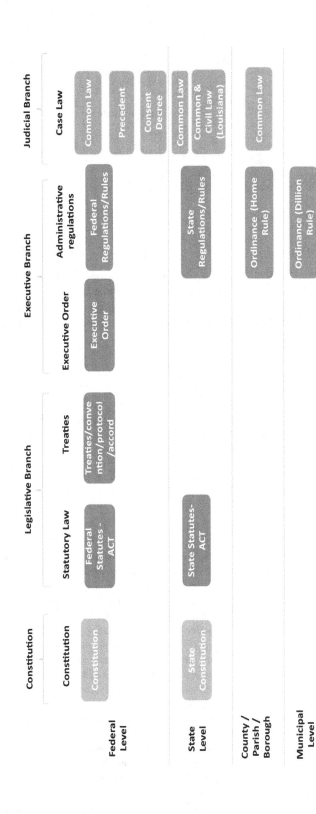

FIGURE 2.1 Legislation structure in the US.

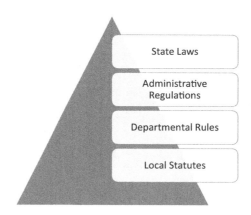

FIGURE 2.2   Privacy vs. data protection.

2.1.3   CHINA'S LEGAL SYSTEM

China's legal system covers laws that fall under seven categories and four different levels. The seven categories are the Constitution and Constitution-related, civil, and commercial, administrative, economic, social, and criminal laws and the law on the lawsuit and non-lawsuit procedures. The four different levels are state laws, administrative regulations, departmental rules, and local statutes, as shown in Figure 2.2.

2.2   WORLD MODELS FOR DATA PROTECTION

Over time, various data protection models that exist around the world today have been developed. Different countries choose to protect information in different ways. In addition, the model chosen depends on your privacy perspective. Table 2.3 provides a summary of some of today's most common privacy models include a comprehensive, sectoral framework and a self-regulatory model.

TABLE 2.3
Three Data Protection Models

Model	Examples	Description
The Comprehensive Model	Privacy laws and regulations enacted in jurisdictions such as the EU, Canada, China, Brazil, etc.	These laws apply to the collection, use and distribution of personal information **in all sectors**. In general, countries that have enacted comprehensive data protection legislation have civil servants or agencies responsible for overseeing enforcement.
The Sectoral Model	US HIPAA, US GLBA, US FERPA, etc.	This framework protects personal data by enacting laws that target **specific industries**. For example, various laws define behavior and specify the level of data protection required for personal health information, consumer finance transactions, credit records, etc. Sectoral legislation is often used as a complement to broader legislation to provide more specific protection for specific types of personal data.
Self-Regulatory Model	ISO 27701, ISO/IEC 27018 Luxembourg, Luxembourg GDPR-CARPA, PCI-DSS, etc.	The term "self-regulation" refers to different approaches to privacy protection. The self-regulatory model requires companies to adhere to **codes of conduct or standards** set by industry or independent data protection agencies. The two main issues associated with code practices established by companies and industry associations are adequacy and enforcement.

2.3 DATA PROTECTION LEGISLATION GLOBAL LANDSCAPE

2.3.1 WORLDWIDE LANDSCAPE

As more and more social and economic activities take place online, the importance of privacy and data protection is increasingly recognized. Of equal concern are the collection, use, and sharing of personal information with third parties without notice or consent of consumers. 137 out of 194 countries have put in place legislation to secure the protection of data and privacy. Africa and Asia show different levels of adoption, with 61 and 57%, respectively, of countries there having adopted privacy legislation. The share in the least developed countries is only 48%.[8]

- 71% of countries have legislation
- 9% of countries have draft legislation
- 15% of countries have no legislation
- 5% of countries have no data available

Figure 2.3 illustrates some representative data protection and privacy laws and regulations. For instance, EU GDPR, Canada PIPEDA, US HIPAA, GLBA, California CCPA, Brazil LGPD, Japan APPI, Australia Privacy act, South Africa Protection of Personal Information Act, and so on.

2.3.2 PRIVACY LAWS IN MAIN JURISDICTIONS

This section provides an overview of privacy laws and regulations in some of the main jurisdictions across the globe such as the EU, US, Canada, China, Russia, Brazil, Argentina, South Africa, etc.

2.3.2.1 List of Data Privacy Laws in Main Jurisdictions

Figure 2.4 provides a high-level summary of Data Protection and Privacy Regulations for the EU region.

Figure 2.5 provides a high-level summary of Data Protection and Privacy Regulations for the United States.

The IAPP maintains an up-to-date table of US privacy legislation status as shown to follow. My strong recommendation is to consult this resource frequently.

As of May 19, 2022, five states (California, Virginia, Colorado, Utah, Connecticut) have enacted consumer privacy laws as listed in Table 2.4.

Figure 2.6 provides a high-level summary of Data Protection and Privacy Regulations for Canada.

Figure 2.7 provides a high-level summary of Data Protection and Privacy Regulations for Russia.

Figure 2.8 provides a high-level summary of Data Protection and Privacy Regulations for China.

Figure 2.9 provides a high-level summary of Data Protection and Privacy Regulations for New Zealand.

Figure 2.10 provides a high-level summary of Data Protection and Privacy Regulations for Argentina.

Figure 2.11 provides a high-level summary of Data Protection and Privacy Regulations for Brazil.

Figure 2.12 provides a high-level summary of Data Protection and Privacy Regulations for South Africa.

2.3.2.2 One-Pagers

To help readers quickly grasp the essential requirements of some prevalent privacy laws and regulations, I summarized the following privacy laws and regulations into one-pagers and attached them as appendixes. The sections that follow will focus on EU GDPR, US CCPA/CPRA, China PIPL, and Canada PIPEDA.

Appendix A: EU GDPR One-Pager Summary
Appendix B: EU ePrivacy One-Pager Summary
Appendix C: FTC Act Section 5

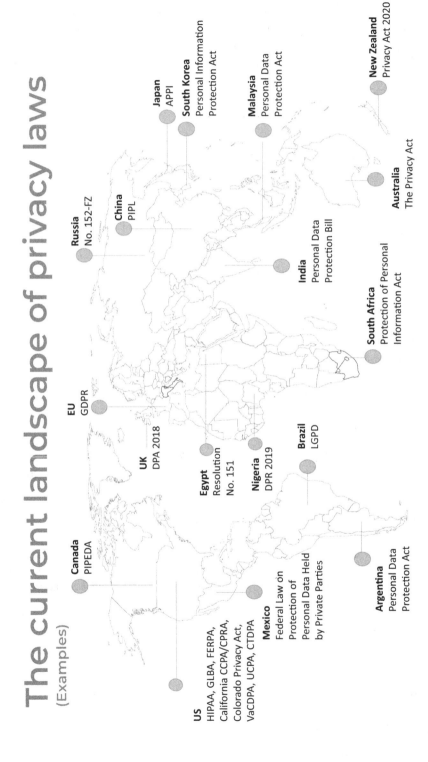

FIGURE 2.3 Landscape of worldwide privacy laws.

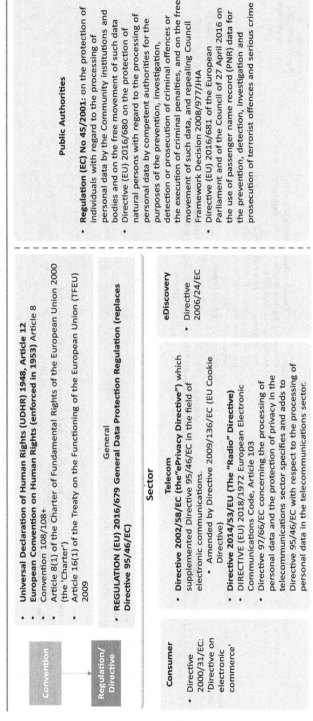

EU Data Protection and Privacy

Convention

- **Universal Declaration of Human Rights (UDHR) 1948, Article 12**
- **European Convention on Human Rights (enforced in 1953)** Article 8
- Convention 108/108+
- Article 8(1) of the Charter of Fundamental Rights of the European Union 2000 (the 'Charter')
- Article 16(1) of the Treaty on the Functioning of the European Union (TFEU) 2009

Regulation/ Directive

General

- **REGULATION (EU) 2016/679 General Data Protection Regulation (replaces Directive 95/46/EC)**

Sector

Consumer

- Directive 2000/31/EC: 'Directive on electronic commerce'

Telecom

- **Directive 2002/58/EC (the"ePrivacy Directive")** which supplemented Directive 95/46/EC in the field of electronic communications.
  - Amended by Directive 2009/136/EC (EU Cookie Directive)
- **Directive 2014/53/EU (The "Radio" Directive)**
- DIRECTIVE (EU) 2018/1972 European Electronic Communications Code, Article 103
- Directive 97/66/EC concerning the processing of personal data and the protection of privacy in the telecommunications sector specifies and adds to Directive 95/46/EC with respect to the processing of personal data in the telecommunications sector.

eDiscovery

- Directive 2006/24/EC

Public Authorities

- **Regulation (EC) No 45/2001:** on the protection of individuals with regard to the processing of personal data by the Community institutions and bodies and on the free movement of such data
- Directive (EU) 2016/680 on the protection of natural persons with regard to the processing of personal data by competent authorities for the purposes of the prevention, investigation, detection or prosecution of criminal offences or the execution of criminal penalties, and on the free movement of such data, and repealing Council Framework Decision 2008/977/JHA
- Directive (EU) 2016/681 of the European Parliament and of the Council of 27 April 2016 on the use of passenger name record (PNR) data for the prevention, detection, investigation and prosecution of terrorist offences and serious crime

FIGURE 2.4 EU data protection and privacy.

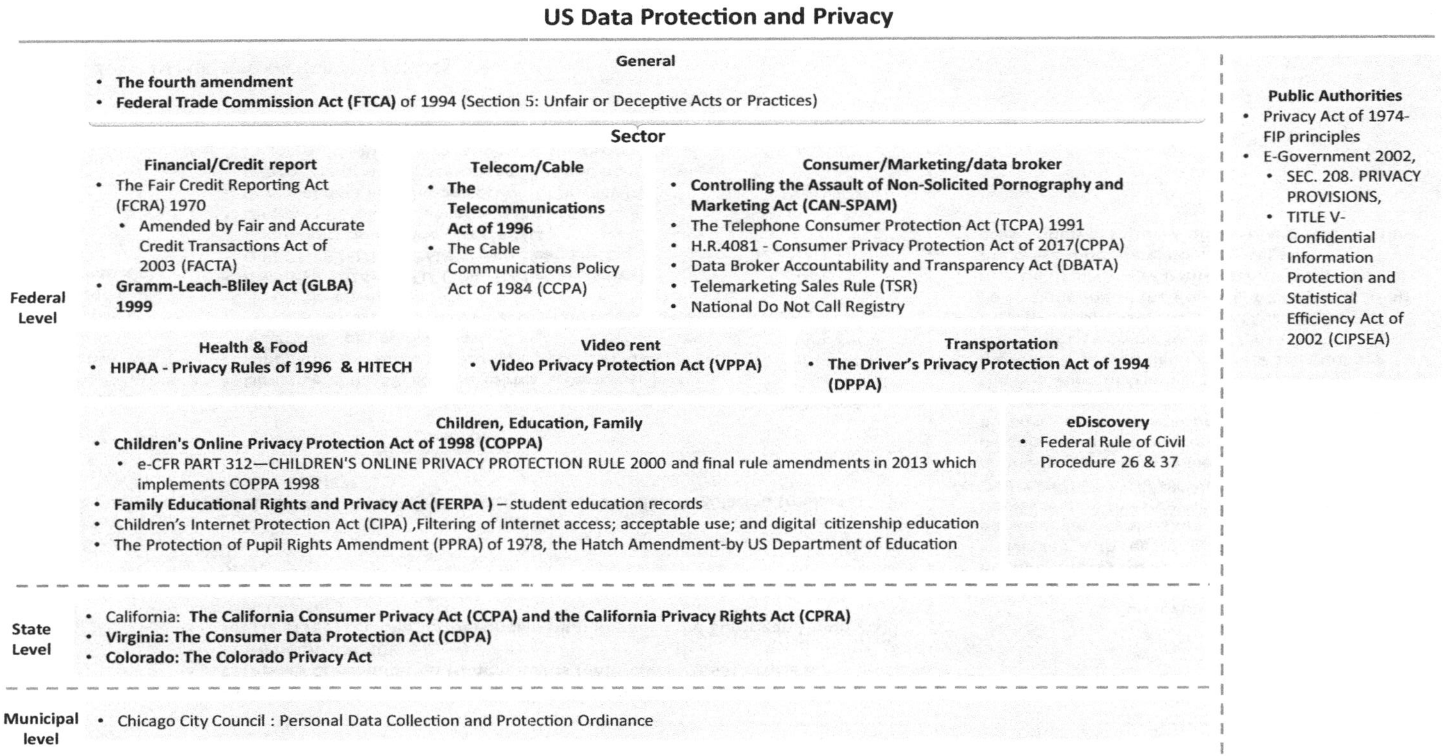

US Data Protection and Privacy

General

Federal Level

- **The fourth amendment**
- **Federal Trade Commission Act (FTCA)** of 1994 (Section 5: Unfair or Deceptive Acts or Practices)

Sector

Financial/Credit report
- The Fair Credit Reporting Act (FCRA) 1970
  - Amended by Fair and Accurate Credit Transactions Act of 2003 (FACTA)
- **Gramm-Leach-Bliley Act (GLBA)** 1999

Telecom/Cable
- **The Telecommunications Act of 1996**
- The Cable Communications Policy Act of 1984 (CCPA)

Consumer/Marketing/data broker
- **Controlling the Assault of Non-Solicited Pornography and Marketing Act (CAN-SPAM)**
- The Telephone Consumer Protection Act (TCPA) 1991
- H.R.4081 - Consumer Privacy Protection Act of 2017(CPPA)
- Data Broker Accountability and Transparency Act (DBATA)
- Telemarketing Sales Rule (TSR)
- National Do Not Call Registry

Health & Food
- HIPAA - Privacy Rules of 1996 & HITECH

Video rent
- Video Privacy Protection Act (VPPA)

Transportation
- **The Driver's Privacy Protection Act of 1994 (DPPA)**

eDiscovery
- Federal Rule of Civil Procedure 26 & 37

Children, Education, Family
- **Children's Online Privacy Protection Act of 1998 (COPPA)**
  - e-CFR PART 312—CHILDREN'S ONLINE PRIVACY PROTECTION RULE 2000 and final rule amendments in 2013 which implements COPPA 1998
- **Family Educational Rights and Privacy Act (FERPA)** – student education records
- Children's Internet Protection Act (CIPA), Filtering of Internet access; acceptable use; and digital citizenship education
- The Protection of Pupil Rights Amendment (PPRA) of 1978, the Hatch Amendment-by US Department of Education

Public Authorities
- Privacy Act of 1974- FIP principles
- E-Government 2002, SEC. 208. PRIVACY PROVISIONS, TITLE V- Confidential Information Protection and Statistical Efficiency Act of 2002 (CIPSEA)

State Level
- California: **The California Consumer Privacy Act (CCPA) and the California Privacy Rights Act (CPRA)**
- Virginia: **The Consumer Data Protection Act (CDPA)**
- Colorado: **The Colorado Privacy Act**

Municipal level
- Chicago City Council : Personal Data Collection and Protection Ordinance

FIGURE 2.5 US data protection and privacy.

TABLE 2.4

US State Privacy Laws

State	Statute/Bill	Law Name	Date into Law	Effective Date
California	CCPA	California Consumer Privacy Act	June 28, 2018	Jan. 1, 2020
	Proposition 24	California Privacy Rights Act	November 3, 2020	Jan. 1, 2023
Colorado	SB 190	Colorado Privacy Act	July 8, 2021	July 1, 2023
Virginia	SB 1392	Virginia Consumer Data Protection Act	March 2, 2021	Jan. 1, 2023
Utah	SB 227	Utah Consumer Privacy Act	March 24, 2022	Dec. 31, 2023
Connecticut	SB 6	An Act Concerning Personal Data Privacy and Online Monitoring	May 10, 2022	July 1, 2023

Canada Data Protection and Privacy

General
- The **Canadian Charter of Rights and Freedoms** (Section 7): Everyone has the right to life, liberty and security of the person **Federal Trade**

Federal Level

Private Sector
- **PIPEDA 2000** cover all provinces except for BC, AB, and Quebec listed below
  - the Digital Privacy Act 2018 amends PIPEDA and a new data breach reporting and notification provisions.
- Bill S-4
- Breach of Security Safeguards Regulations: SOR/2018-64

Public Authorities
- **Privacy Act 1983**
- **Directive on Privacy Impact Assessment**
  - all proposals and new programs that raise privacy issues.
- Any substantial redesign of an existing program or service
- Directive on Privacy Practices

Sector

Finance	Consumer	Healthcare
The Bank Act	CASL- Canada's anti-spam legislation	The Genetic Non-Discrimination Act (GNDA)

Provincial level

Alberta
- Personal Information Protection Act in Alberta ("Alberta PIPA")

British Columbia
- the Personal Information Protection Act in British Columbia ("BC PIPA")

Quebec - first private-sector privacy law passed in Canada
- the Act Respecting the Protection of Personal Information in the Private Sector in Quebec ("the Quebec Act")

Healthcare (Laws from New Brunswick, Newfoundland and Labrador and Ontario are substantially similar to PIPEDA)
11 – except Nunavut and Quebec
- In Alberta, the Health Information Act (HIA) came into force on April 25, 2001
- In British Columbia, E-Health (Personal Health Information Access and Protection of Privacy) Act came into force on November 7, 2008
- In Manitoba, the Personal Health Information Act (PHIA) came into force on December 11, 1997
- In New Brunswick, the Personal Health Information Privacy and Access Act (PHIPAA) was proclaimed in force on September 1, 2010
- In Newfoundland and Labrador, the Personal Health Information Act (PHIA) came into force on April 1, 2011
- In Nova Scotia, the Personal Health Information Act (PHIA) came into force on June 1, 2013
- In Northwest Territories, the Health Information Protection Act (HIA) came into force on October 1, 2015
- In Ontario, the Personal Health Information Protection Act of 2004 (PHIPA) came into force on November 1, 2004
  - In 2016, the Health Information Protection Act (HIPA) was introduced. It amended Ontario's PHIPA*
- In Prince Edward Island, the Health Information Act (HIA) came into force July 1, 2017
- In Saskatchewan, the Health Information Protection Act (HIPA) came into force on September 1, 2003
- In Yukon, the Health Information Privacy and Management Act (HIPM) came into force on August 31, 2016

12 (Except Nunavut)- the provinces passed one combined law applicable to both topics rather than two separate, referring laws.
- Alberta's Freedom of Information and Protection of Privacy Act (FIPPA) came into force on October 1, 1995
- British Columbia's Freedom of Information and Protection of Privacy Act (FOIPPA) came into force in 1996
- Manitoba's Freedom of Information and Protection of Privacy Act (FIPPA) came into force on February 17, 1999
- New Brunswick's Right to Information and Protection of Privacy Act (RTIPPA) came into force June 19, 2009
- Newfoundland and Labrador's Access to Information and Protection of Privacy Act (ATIPPA) came into force on June 1, 2015
- Northwest Territories/Nunavut's Access to Information and Protection of Privacy Act (ATIPP) came into force on December 31, 1996
- Nova Scotia's, Freedom of Information and Protection of Privacy Act (FOIPOP) came into force in July 1, 1994
- Ontario's Freedom of Information and Protection of Privacy Act (FIPPA) came into effect on January 1, 1988
- Prince Edward Island's Freedom of Information and Protection of Privacy Act FOIPP) came into effect November 1, 2002
- Quebec's Act Respecting Access to Documents Held by Public Bodies and the Protection of Personal Information came into force in 1983
- Saskatchewan's Freedom of Information and Protection of Privacy Act (FOIP) came into effect April 1, 1992
- Yukon's Access to Information and Protection of Privacy Act (ATIPP) came into force April 29, 1996

FIGURE 2.6 Canada data protection and privacy.

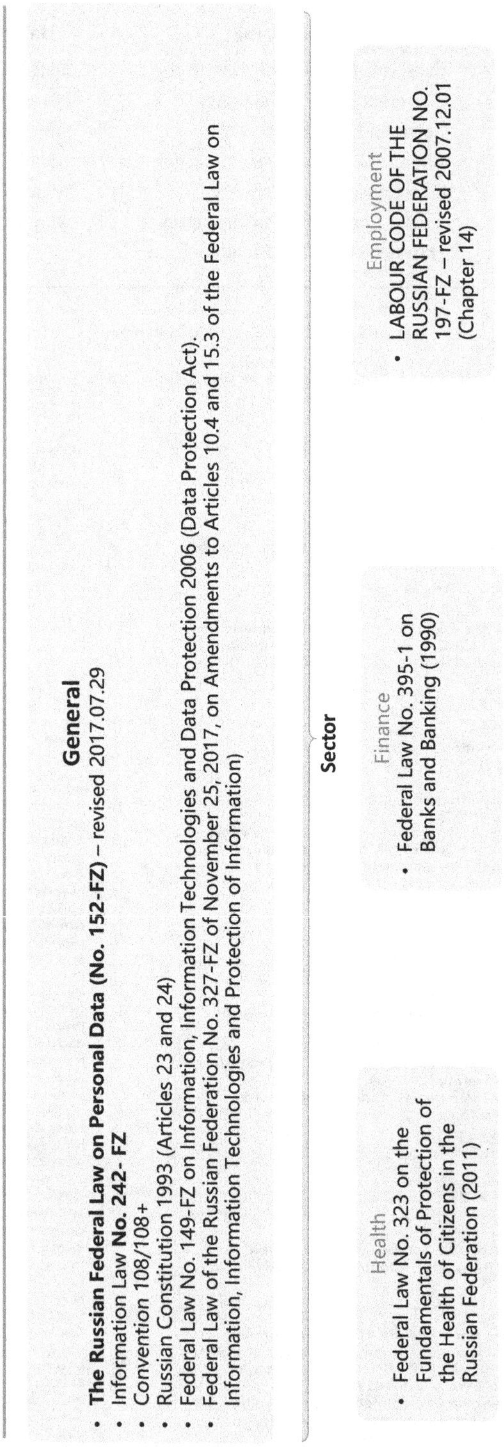

Russia Data Protection and Privacy

General

- **The Russian Federal Law on Personal Data (No. 152-FZ)** – revised 2017.07.29
- Information Law **No. 242- FZ**
- Convention 108/108+
- Russian Constitution 1993 (Articles 23 and 24)
- Federal Law No. 149-FZ on Information, Information Technologies and Data Protection 2006 (Data Protection Act).
- Federal Law of the Russian Federation No. 327-FZ of November 25, 2017, on Amendments to Articles 10.4 and 15.3 of the Federal Law on Information, Information Technologies and Protection of Information)

Sector

Health
- Federal Law No. 323 on the Fundamentals of Protection of the Health of Citizens in the Russian Federation (2011)

Finance
- Federal Law No. 395-1 on Banks and Banking (1990)

Employment
- LABOUR CODE OF THE RUSSIAN FEDERATION NO. 197-FZ – revised 2007.12.01 (Chapter 14)

FIGURE 2.7   Russia data protection and privacy.

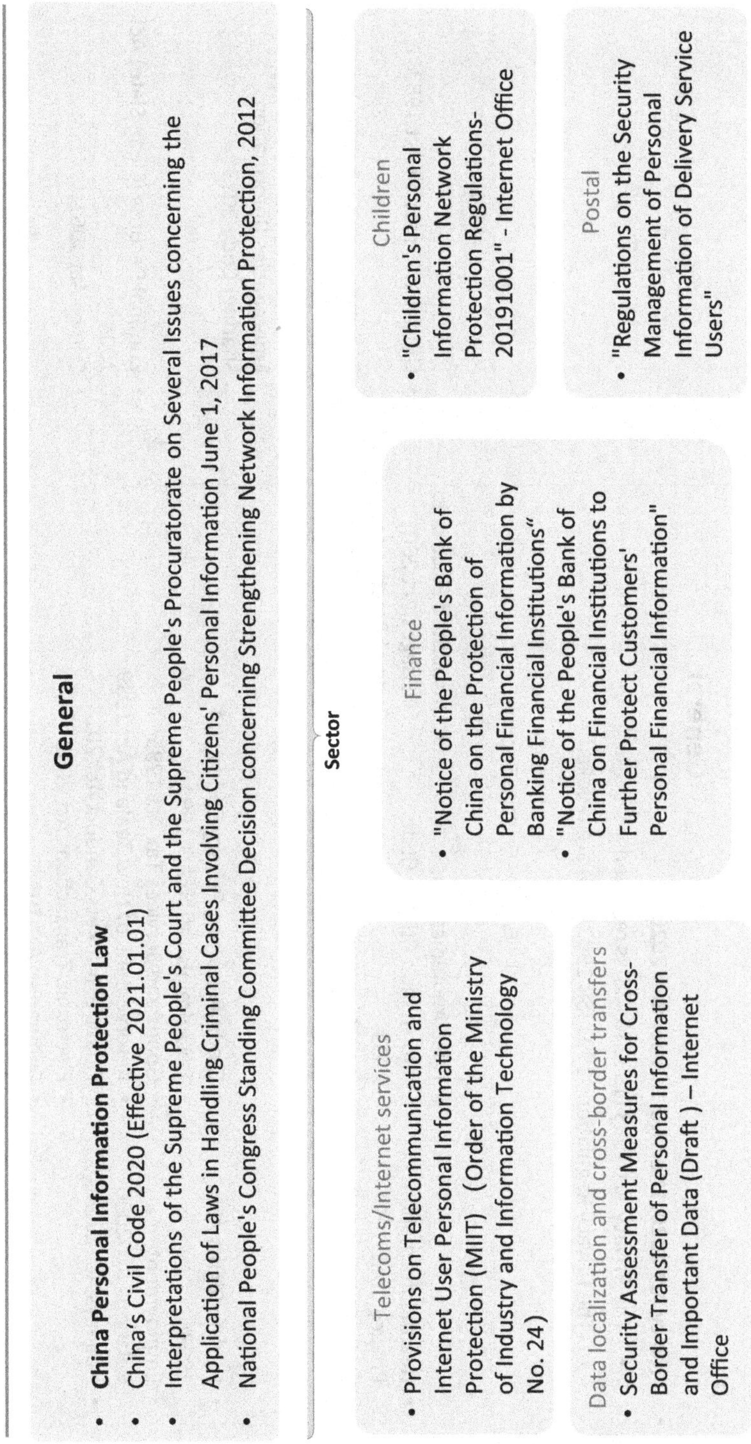

China Data Protection and Privacy

General

- **China Personal Information Protection Law**
- China's Civil Code 2020 (Effective 2021.01.01)
- Interpretations of the Supreme People's Court and the Supreme People's Procuratorate on Several Issues concerning the Application of Laws in Handling Criminal Cases Involving Citizens' Personal Information June 1, 2017
- National People's Congress Standing Committee Decision concerning Strengthening Network Information Protection, 2012

Sector

Telecoms/Internet services
- Provisions on Telecommunication and Internet User Personal Information Protection (MIIT) (Order of the Ministry of Industry and Information Technology No. 24)

Data localization and cross-border transfers
- Security Assessment Measures for Cross-Border Transfer of Personal Information and Important Data (Draft) – Internet Office

Finance
- "Notice of the People's Bank of China on the Protection of Personal Financial Information by Banking Financial Institutions"
- "Notice of the People's Bank of China on Financial Institutions to Further Protect Customers' Personal Financial Information"

Children
- "Children's Personal Information Network Protection Regulations- 20191001" - Internet Office

Postal
- "Regulations on the Security Management of Personal Information of Delivery Service Users"

FIGURE 2.8   China data protection and privacy.

New Zealand Data Protection and Privacy

General

Privacy Act 2020, Effective 1 December 2020

- The Privacy Act 1993 (1993 No 28) is repealed
  - The Privacy Regulations 1993 (SR 1993/149) are revoked

Sector

Health

- Health Information Privacy Code 1994 ('the Health Code')

Employment

- Human Rights Act 1993;
- Employment Relations Act 2000
- Holidays Act 2003

Telco

- Telecommunications Information Privacy Code 2003
- Harmful Digital Communications Act 2015

Finance

- Credit Reporting Privacy Code 2004
- Tax Administration Act 1994
- Goods and Services Tax Act 1985
- Reserve Bank of New Zealand Act 1989
- Financial Markets Conduct Act 2013
- Electronic Transactions Act 2002
- Companies Act 1993

Consumer/Marketing

- Unsolicited Electronic Messages Act 2007
- Code of Practice for Direct Marketing in New Zealand

Public Sector

- Official Information Act 1982
- Superannuation Schemes Unique Identifier Code 1995
- Civil Defence National Emergencies (Information Sharing) Code 2013

Justice/Criminal

- Criminal Records (Clean Slate) Act 2004
- Crimes Act 1961

FIGURE 2.9   New Zealand data protection and privacy.

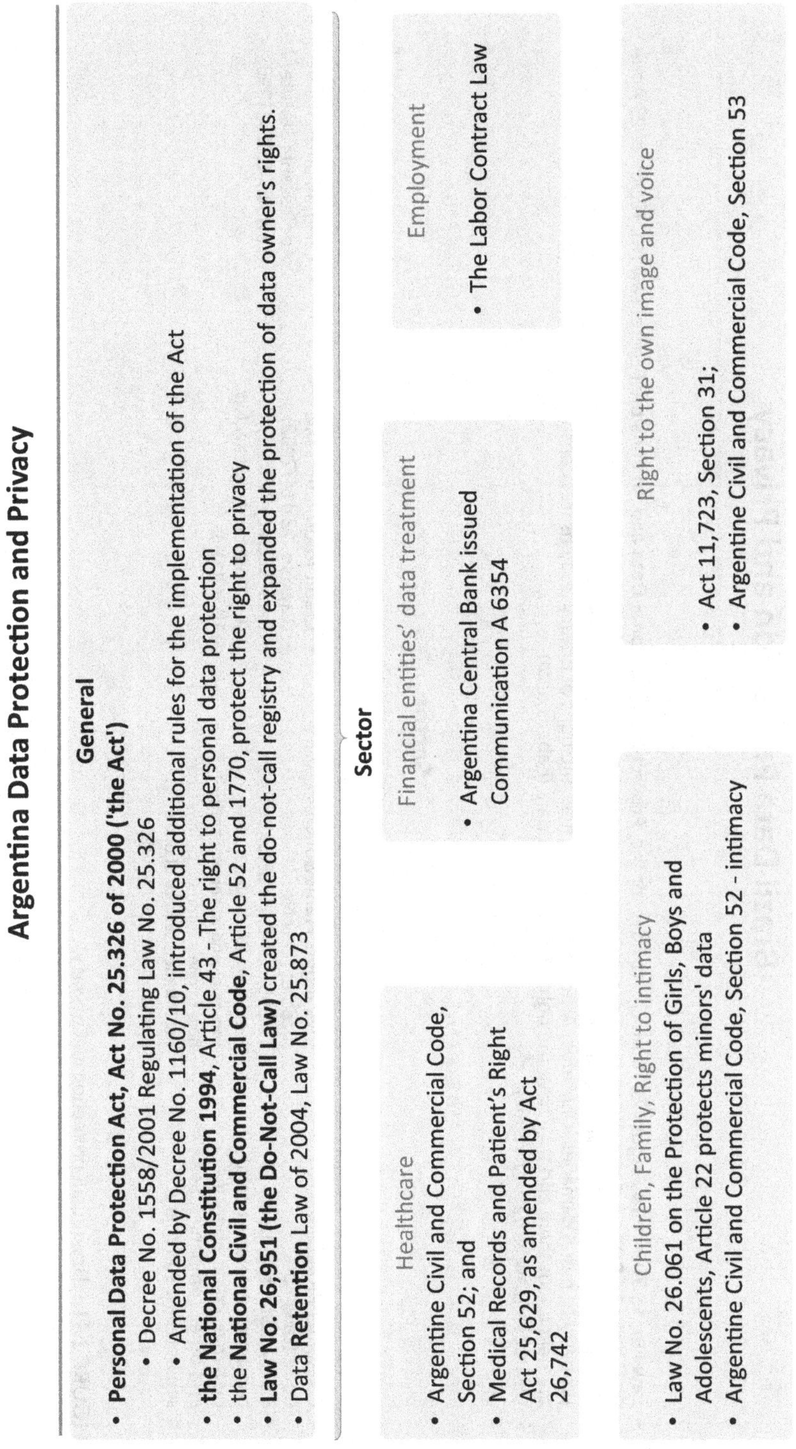

Argentina Data Protection and Privacy

General

- **Personal Data Protection Act, Act No. 25.326 of 2000 ('the Act')**
  - Decree No. 1558/2001 Regulating Law No. 25.326
  - Amended by Decree No. 1160/10, introduced additional rules for the implementation of the Act
- **the National Constitution 1994**, Article 43 – The right to personal data protection
- **the National Civil and Commercial Code**, Article 52 and 1770, protect the right to privacy
- **Law No. 26,951 (the Do-Not-Call Law)** created the do-not-call registry and expanded the protection of data owner's rights.
- Data **Retention** Law of 2004, Law No. 25.873

Sector

Financial entities' data treatment

- Argentina Central Bank issued Communication A 6354

Employment

- The Labor Contract Law

Healthcare

- Argentine Civil and Commercial Code, Section 52; and
- Medical Records and Patient's Right Act 25,629, as amended by Act 26,742

Children, Family, Right to intimacy

- Law No. 26.061 on the Protection of Girls, Boys and Adolescents, Article 22 protects minors' data
- Argentine Civil and Commercial Code, Section 52 – intimacy

Right to the own image and voice

- Act 11,723, Section 31;
- Argentine Civil and Commercial Code, Section 53

FIGURE 2.10 Argentina data protection and privacy.

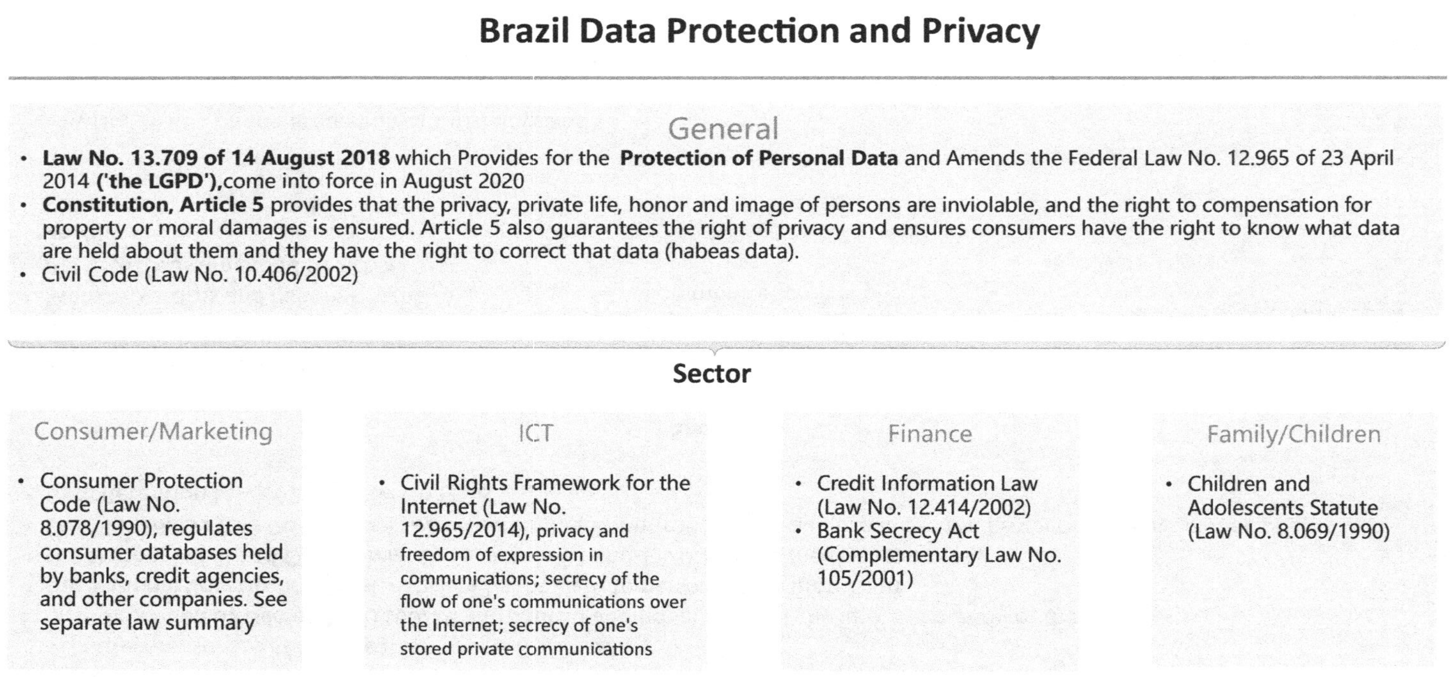

Brazil Data Protection and Privacy

General

- **Law No. 13.709 of 14 August 2018** which Provides for the **Protection of Personal Data** and Amends the Federal Law No. 12.965 of 23 April 2014 (**'the LGPD'**).come into force in August 2020
- **Constitution, Article 5** provides that the privacy, private life, honor and image of persons are inviolable, and the right to compensation for property or moral damages is ensured. Article 5 also guarantees the right of privacy and ensures consumers have the right to know what data are held about them and they have the right to correct that data (habeas data).
- Civil Code (Law No. 10.406/2002)

Sector

Consumer/Marketing

- Consumer Protection Code (Law No. 8.078/1990), regulates consumer databases held by banks, credit agencies, and other companies. See separate law summary

ICT

- Civil Rights Framework for the Internet (Law No. 12.965/2014), privacy and freedom of expression in communications; secrecy of the flow of one's communications over the Internet; secrecy of one's stored private communications

Finance

- Credit Information Law (Law No. 12.414/2002)
- Bank Secrecy Act (Complementary Law No. 105/2001)

Family/Children

- Children and Adolescents Statute (Law No. 8.069/1990)

FIGURE 2.11   Brazil data protection and privacy.

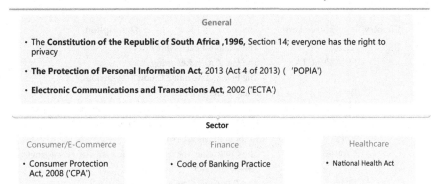

FIGURE 2.12 South Africa data protection and privacy.

Appendix D: US HIPAA One-Pager Summary
Appendix E: US GLBA One-Pager Summary
Appendix F: US FERPA One-Pager Summary
Appendix G: US COPPA One-Pager Summary
Appendix H: US FACTA One-Pager Summary
Appendix I: California CCPA One-Pager Summary
Appendix J: Canada PIPEDA One-Pager Summary
Appendix K: Canada Anti-Spam Law One-Pager Summary
Appendix L: China PIPL One-Pager Summary
Appendix M: China Data Security Law One-Pager Summary
Appendix N: Australia Privacy Act One-Pager Summary
Appendix O: New Zealand Privacy Act 2020 One-Pager Summary
Appendix P: Brazil LGPD One-Pager Summary
Appendix Q: Argentina PDPA One-Pager Summary

2.3.3 SECTOR SPECIFIC LAWS

There are many privacy and data protection laws and regulations which are intended to manage privacy risks in certain sectors such as finance, healthcare, and education, as illustrated in Table 2.5.

TABLE 2.5

Examples of Sector Privacy Laws and Regulations

Sector	Country	Privacy Law	Description
Healthcare	US	HIPAA	The Health Insurance Portability and Accountability Act
		HITECH	The Health Information Technology for Economic and Clinical Health Act
		GINA	The Genetic Information Nondiscrimination Act of 2008
	Canada	Provincial Healthcare	Ontario Personal Health Information Protection Act of 2004
		Privacy Laws	BC Personal Health Information Access and Protection of Privacy Act
		GNDA	The Genetic Non-Discrimination Act

(Continued)

TABLE 2.5   (Continued)

Sector	Country	Privacy Law	Description
Finance	US	GLBA	The Gramm-Leach-Bliley Act
		FCRA/FACTA	The Fair Credit Reporting Act
			The Fair and Accurate Credit Transactions Act
		BSA	Bank Secrecy Act
		DODD-FRANK	Dodd-Frank Wall Street Reform and Consumer Protection Act
		FDCPA	Fair Debt Collection Practices Act
		RFPA	Right to Financial Privacy Act
Marketing	US	CAN-SPAM	The Controlling the Assault of Non-solicited Pornography and Marketing Act
		TCPA	The Telephone Consumer Protection Act
		TSR	Telemarketing Sales Rules
	Canada	CASL	Canada's Anti-Spam Law
Education	US	FERPA	Family Educational Rights and Privacy Act
		PPRA	The Protection of Pupil Rights Amendment
Telecom/Internet	US	COPPA	Children's Online Privacy Protection Act
		Telecom Act	The Telecommunications Act
		Cable Act	The Cable Television Privacy Act
	China	Internet User Protection	Provisions on Telecommunication and Internet User Personal Information Protection
Workplace	US	ADA	American with Disabilities Act
		ADEA	Age Discrimination in Employment Act
		EPPA	Employee Polygraph Protection Act
		ERISA	Employee Retirement Income Security Act
		FLSA	Fair Labor Standards Act
		FMLA	Family and Medical Leave Act
		IRCA	Immigration Reform and Control Act
		NLRA	National Labor Relations Act
		SCA	Stored Communications Act
		WPA	Whistleblowers Protection Act

3 GDPR, CCPA/CPRA, PIPL and PIPEDA

This chapter is intended to provide a high-level introduction to prevalent privacy regulations across the globe such as EU GDPR, US CCPA/CPRA, China PIPL, etc. to equip readers with the necessary knowledge needed to kick off a privacy program.

This chapter covers the following topics:

- *EU GDPR*
- *US CCPA/CPRA*
- *China PIPL*
- *Canada PIPEDA*

3.1 EU GDRP

GDPR stands for General Data Protection Regulation and is the new European Union Regulation set to replace the Data Protection Directive 95/46/EC (DPD). It involves the protection of personal data and the rights of individuals. This complex regulation is composed of 11 chapters, 99 articles (which dictate the compliance requirements), 173 recitals (which provide context to the articles), and 88 pages.

It seeks to unify data protection legislation across Europe. It aims to ease the flow of personal data across the 28 EU member states before Brexit. It was approved by the EU Parliament on April 14, 2016, and takes effect after a two-year transition period; unlike a Directive it does not require any enabling legislation to be passed by the government. It has been in force since May 2018.

The GDPR not only applies to organizations located within the EU but it will also apply to organizations located outside of the EU if they offer goods or services to, or monitor the behavior of, EU data subjects. It applies to all companies processing and holding the personal data of data subjects residing in the European Union.

3.1.1 SEVEN PRINCIPLES

Lawfulness, fairness, and transparency: Personal data shall be processed lawfully, fairly, and in a transparent manner in relation to the data subject.

Purpose limitation: Personal data shall be collected for specified, explicit, and legitimate purposes and not be further processed in a manner that is incompatible with those purposes.

Data minimization: Personal data shall be adequate, relevant, and limited to what is necessary with respect to the purposes for which they are processed. The organization shall apply anonymization or pseudonymization to personal data, if possible, to reduce the risks to the data subjects concerned.

Accuracy: Personal data shall be accurate and, where necessary, kept up to date; reasonable steps must be taken to ensure that personal data that are inaccurate, having regard to the purposes for which they are processed, are erased or rectified in a timely manner.

Storage period limitation: Personal data shall be kept for no longer than is necessary for the purposes for which the personal data are processed.

Integrity and confidentiality: Considering the state of technology and other available security measures, the implementation cost, and the likelihood and severity of privacy risks, use appropriate technical or organizational measures to ensure appropriate security of personal data, including protection against accidental or unlawful destruction, loss, alteration, unauthorized access to, or disclosure.

Accountability: Data controllers shall be responsible for and be able to demonstrate compliance with the principles outlined previously.

3.1.2   GDPR vs. Directive 95/46/EC

GDPR made some substantial improvements to the Data Protection Directive 95/46/EC as shown in Table 3.1.

TABLE 3.1

Comparison between the GDPR and Data Protection Directive 95/46/EC

		Data Protection Directive 95/46/EC	GDPR
Human rights		Over rotated rights—absolute rights	Balance of rights: Privacy is a fundamental right but not an absolute right
Immediately applicability		Places obligations on member states	Directly applicable and enforceable as law
		Is transposed into 28 national laws in the EU	Provides one set of data protection rules for all
		Differs across member states	Allows member states a degree of tailoring
Territorial Scope	Extra-territorial applicability	EU territorial applicability	Expands territorial scope and is applicable under two scenarios; 1) when processor or controller is established in the Union, and 2) when processor or controller is not established in the Union.
Requirements	Special categories of personal data	Racial or ethnic origin, political opinions, religious or philosophical beliefs, trade-union membership, and the processing of data concerning health or sex life.	Two new categories, biometric and genetic data have been added under GDPR. Racial or ethnic origin, political opinions, religious or philosophical beliefs, or trade-union membership, and the processing of genetic data, biometric data for the purpose of uniquely identifying a natural person, data concerning health or data concerning a natural person's sex life or sexual orientation shall be prohibited.
	Consent	GDPR articulates what is considered valid consent: Freely given, specific, informed, and unambiguous indication.	
	Data protection principles	Five principles: • Fairly and lawfully • Purpose Limitation • Data Minimization • Accuracy • Storage Limitation	Two principles were added and one extended • Lawfulness, Fairness, and Transparency • Purpose Limitation • Data Minimization • Accuracy • Storage Limitation • Integrity and Confidentiality • Accountability

		Data Protection Directive 95/46/EC	GDPR
	Data subject rights	Compared with Directive 95/46/EC, GDPR enriches the rights enjoyed by data subjects, as follows: In terms of categories, the GDPR stipulates eight rights of data subjects: the right to know, the right to access, the right to rectification, the right to erasure (the right to be forgotten), the right to restrict processing, the right to data portability, the right to object, and the right not to be subject to automated decision-making; Compared with Directive, it adds the right to be forgotten and the right to portability. In addition to adding the right to portability, the GDPR also adds more data subject rights: In terms of the right to know, the requirement to inform data subjects of DPO contact information, legitimate interests, facts and protection mechanisms for cross-border transfers, data retention periods or principles, right to complain, existence and logic of automated decision-making, new purposes, data sources (not when obtained from the data subject). In terms of access rights, the data subject has the right to request the controller to provide the data storage period or principle, the existence of data subject rights, the right to complain, the protection mechanism for cross-border transfer, and the right to request a copy. Regarding the right to erasure, the Directive only states that the data subject has the right to request the deletion of data that is not processed in accordance with the directive. Processing, illegal processing, deletion as required by law, deletion of minors' data, etc., and add notification to other data controllers to delete links and copies when the data is disclosed. In terms of the right to restrict processing, the Directive only states that the data subject has the right to request the blocking of data that does not meet the requirements of the directive. The GDPR clarifies the situation in which the data subject has the right to request the restriction of processing: during the period of questioning the accuracy, the data is illegally processed, and the data subject requests the restriction of processing no longer necessary but necessary for litigation, during the period of verifying whether other interests take precedence because the data subject refuses the processing based on legitimate interests.	
	Data processor	DPD fixes liability on controllers but leaves out processors.	GDPR includes both. Data processors have direct compliance obligations.
	Records of processing activities	Not specified under DPD	Data controllers and processors all save records of data processing activities.
	DPIA	Not specified under DPD	Data protection impact assessment has become part of a legal requirement in the GDPR.
	Cross-border data transfers	The restrictions on cross-border data transfer remain unchanged under the GDPR, and more cross-border transfer compliance mechanisms are provided.	
	Data breach notification	Not specified under DPD	Notify supervisory authorities and data subjects of a data breach within 72 hours.
Enforcement	Penalties	Not specified under DPD	Can be fined up to 4% of annual global turnover or €20 million (whichever is greater).
	One-Stop-Shop (ME)	Not specified under DPD	The supervisory authority of the main establishment of a company can act as the lead authority to uniformly implement law enforcement.
New organization		Formed the Article 29 working party	Forms the European Data Protection Board (EDPB)

3.1.3   LEGAL EFFECT OF GDPR RECITALS

A recital is a formal statement appearing in a legal document such as a deed that is preliminary in nature. It provides an explanation of the reasons for the transaction. The role of recitals is fundamentally "scene-setting" in nature and does not automatically form part of the legally binding agreement between the contracting parties.

GDPR is EU law. An authoritative legal interpretation of "GDPR Recitals" is provided in a document published by the Committee on Legal Affairs of the European Parliament (also known as "JURI"). The document is called "General Principles of EU Administrative Procedural Law: In-depth Analysis" (the "Analysis") which was completed in June 2015.

One of the objectives of the Analysis is given in the Executive Summary, which reads: "The Analysis puts forward drafting proposals for the general principles of EU administrative procedural law to be included in the Recitals of a draft Regulation on EU Administrative procedures". As follows is an excerpt of the **Analysis** that succinctly defines the legal effect of recitals in EU regulations:

As far as general principles of EU administrative procedural law are concerned, there are two options for "codification" in the framework of a Regulation on EU administrative procedures: first to try and formulate all relevant principles in articles of the operative part of the Regulation or, second, to use the recitals of the proposed Regulation. There are several legal technical and expediency reasons that lead to favor of the second solution.

On the other hand, placing the principles in the recitals has the advantage that, while not being in themselves binding, they are a demonstration of the legislature's interpretation of principles. The courts are not directly bound by the relevant wording, but they may use the recitals to choose a specific orientation in interpretation—as demonstrated by the case-law of the EU Courts—or to identify a specific concept to be a "general principle of EU law".

In conclusion, recitals may be perceived as legally inconsequential. However, when a dispute arises over legal interpretation, recitals may be brought into play as an aid to interpretation by a judge/arbitrator who is tasked with deciphering an ambiguous legal provision.

3.2   US CCPA/CPRA

The California Consumer Privacy Act of 2018 (CCPA 2018) and CCPA Regulations were signed into law on June 28, 2018, and came into effect on January 1, 2020.

California Privacy Rights Act (CPRA) Initiatives AKA "CCPA 2.0", the passage of Proposition 24 in California on November 3, 2020. It takes effect in January 2023.

3.2.1   IMPORTANCE OF CPRA

The CPRA would modify CCPA rules by:

- Further clarifying the definition of "sale" as related to consumer data.
- Creating a "limited exception" to deletion and access rights.
- Exempting an increasing number of small businesses from the law.
- Creating a new category of personal information on "sensitive data."
- Allowing consumers to correct inaccurate information.
- Extending the "look-back" period for consumer access to the information collected about them.
- Placing new obligations on service providers.
- Importantly, if passed, the CPRA would establish a new data protection agency to regulate and enforce.

A couple of CCPA/CPRA requirements are different from other privacy laws and regulations.

- Limit the Use of My Sensitive Personal Information: Provide a clear and conspicuous link on the business's internet homepage(s), titled "Limit the Use of My Sensitive Personal Information".
- Sale of personal data: Provide a clear and conspicuous link on the business's Internet homepage(s), titled "Do Not Sell or Share My Personal Information" (CCPA/CPRA).

3.2.2 GDPR vs. CCPA vs. CPRA

The CCPA, CPRA and GDPR draw some differences in various areas as shown in Table 3.2.

TABLE 3.2

Comparison among GDPR, CCPA, and CPRA

Category	Domain	GDPR	CCPA	CPRA
Scope	Effective date	5/25/2018	1/1/2020	1/1/2023
	Covered entities	Controllers and processors	Businesses	Businesses
	Protected individuals	Data subjects	Consumers	Consumers
	Children protection	✓	✓	✓
	Employee covered	✓	✗	✗
	Restrictions on sensitive data	✓	✗	✓
	Lawful bases to process personal data	✓	✗	✗
Data subject rights/ Individual rights	Right to be informed	✓	✓ (Right to notice)	✓ (Right to notice)
	Right of access	✓	✓ (Right to know)	✓ (Expanded Right to know, beyond 12-month look-back)
	Right to rectification	✓	✗	✓ (New, Right to Correct Information)
	Right to erasure	✓	✓	✓ (Modified Right to Delete, pass requirements to third parties)
	Right of restriction of processing	✓	✗	✗
	Right to data portability	✓	✓	✓ (Expanded Right to Data Portability, transmit data to another entity)
	Right to object	✓	✓ (Right to Opt-out, Do Not Sell)	✓ (Expand Right to Opt-out to both selling and sharing)
	Right not to be subject to automated individual decision-making, including profiling	✓	✗	✓ (New, Right to Opt-Out of Automated Decision-Making Technology) (New, Right to Access Information About Automated Decision-Making)

(Continued)

TABLE 3.2 (Continued)

Category	Domain	GDPR	CCPA	CPRA
	Right to Opt-in	✓ (Consent as a legal basis)	✓ (Children's PD and Financial incentives programs)	✓ (Strengthened Opt-In Rights for Minors, wait 12 months before re-asking, Financial incentives programs)
	Right to Limit Sensitive Personal Information Processing	✓ (Article 9)	✗	✓ (new)
	Right to communication about PD breach	✓ (Art. 33)	✓ (Leverage state's general breach notification statutes)	✓ (Leverage state's general breach notification statutes)
	Right to compensation/ award damages	✓	✓ (non-encrypted or non-redacted PI)	✓ (non-encrypted or non-redacted PI)
	Right to Non-Discrimination/Right not to be subject to discrimination for the exercise of rights	✓ (Inferred Art. 5, 13, 22)	✓	✓
Obligations	Privacy notice	✓	✓	✓
	Privacy by design and default	✓	✗	✓
	Processors/third-party management	✓	✓	✓
	Records of processing activities (i.e., data inventory)	✓	✗	✓
	DSR assurance and handling	✓	✓	✓
	Separate links required for DO NOT SELL, DO NOT SHARE, LIMIT USE OF SENSITIVE PERSONAL DATA	✗	✓	✓
	Appropriate security technical and organizational measures	✓	✓	✓
	Data breach notification	✓	✓	✓
	Data protection impact assessment	✓	✗	✗
	Data protection officer required	✓	✗	✗
	Cross-border transfers limitation	✓	✗	✗
Enforcement	Dedicated supervisory authority	✓	✗	✓
	Administrative/Civil fines	✓	✓	✓
	Private rights of action	✓	✓	✓

3.3 CHINA PIPL

Personal Information Protection Law (PIPL) was formally passed on August 20, 2021, Beijing Time, and became effective on November 1, 2021.

The China Personal Information Protection Law (PIPL) applies to all organizations that

1) Process activities within Chinese territory
2) Are outside Chinese territory, if the processing activity:
   - Offering goods or services to individuals within Chinese territory
   - Engaging in analysis or evaluation of behaviors of individuals within Chinese territory

PIPL vs. GDPR

Although PIPL is similar to GDPR to a certain extent, it does differ from the GDPR in several ways. The following is a high-level summary of those areas.

Lawful basis: Unlike GDPR and many other privacy regulations, the PIPL does not provide "legitimate interests" as a lawful basis for processing personal information. The "legitimate interests" lawful basis is broadly used in business scenarios such as employment environment, etc.

Data subject rights: The PIPL provides similar rights to data subjects in terms of personal information processing. Unlike GDPR's requirement to respond to requests within one month with possibly another two-month extension, the PIPL only vaguely requires organizations to respond to the requests in a timely manner rather than providing a specific timeline for responding.

The PIPL and GDPR draw some similarities with respect to data subject rights as shown in Table 3.3.

Cross-border data transfer: Although, both GDPR and PIPL are trying to stipulate the requirements from three aspects: adequacy decisions, appropriate safeguards, and derogations/other situations. The key differences are as follows.

- Adequacy decisions
  - Firstly, GDPR's mechanism worked very well and encouraged more countries (i.e., Japan and South Korea) to join the mix. Although the PIPL doesn't articulate a clear path for adequacy recognition, the intention (article 38) is to require organizations outside China to have the same level of data protection, which is similar to what the GDPR requires.

TABLE 3.3
Data Subject Rights under the GDPR and PIPL

Rights under the GDPR	Rights under the PIPL
Right to information	√
Right to access	√
Right to correction/rectification	√
Right to erasure	√
Right to object to and restrict the processing of an individual's data	√
Right to data portability	√ (but needs to satisfy conditions stipulated by the Cyberspace Administration of China)
Right not to be subject to automated decision-making	√
Right to withdraw consent	√
Right to lodge a complaint with the regulator	√

- Secondly, the PIPL shows the willingness of and opens the door for participation in mutual recognitions regarding cross-border transfers, as demonstrated by article 38 that China will respect and adhere to relevant provisions of participated international treaties and agreements.
- Thirdly, based on the principle of equality and reciprocity (article 41), China strongly objects that any country or region adopts discriminatory prohibitions, restrictions, or other similar measures against China in terms of personal information protection, China may take corresponding measures based on actual conditions (article 43).
- Appropriate safeguards
  - Firstly, it seems the PIPL is following the GDPR to provide various paths for organizations to facilitate the cross-border transfer scenarios, such as standard contractual clauses, and certification, etc.
  - Secondly, there are slight differences between GDPR and PIPL. On the one hand, the PIPL does not have BCR and Code of Conduct as valid mechanisms. The GDPR does not require security reviews for critical information infrastructure operators which PIPL requires. Security reviews are intended to give the authorities more control over the critical information infrastructure operators.
- Derogations/Other Situations
  - The GDPR provides clearly defined scenarios for derogations in terms of personal data cross-border transfers, such as consent, etc. However, the PIPL leaves room for future interpretation; article 38(4) stipulates that cross-border transfer is permitted if it meets the requirements of "Laws, administrative regulations or other conditions stipulated by the national cybersecurity and informatization department".

The PIPL and GDPR draw some differences and similarities with respect to cross-border data transfers as shown in Table 3.4.

TABLE 3.4

Cross-Border Data Transfers under the GDPR and PIPL

	GDPR	PIPL
Adequacy	Adequacy decisions need to be reviewed every four years. • The European Commission has so far recognized Andorra, Argentina, Canada (commercial organizations), Faroe Islands, Guernsey, Israel, Isle of Man, Japan, Jersey, New Zealand, Switzerland, and Uruguay as providing adequate protection. • On June 28, 2021, the Commission adopted two adequacy decisions for transfers of personal data to the United Kingdom, under the General Data Protection Regulation (GDPR) and the Law Enforcement Directive (LED) respectively. • On June 16, 2021, the Commission launched the procedure for the adoption of an adequacy decision for transfers of personal data to South Korea under the General Data Protection Regulation.	**Not defined** If any country or region opposes any discriminatory prohibition, restriction or other similar measures against the People's Republic of China in terms of personal information protection, the People's Republic of China may take corresponding measures against the country or region based on actual conditions.
Appropriate safeguards	Legally binding and enforceable instrument	In accordance with relevant provisions of participated international treaties and agreements
	Binding Corporate Rules (BCR)	**Not defined**
	Standard Contractual Clauses	Standard Contractual Clauses
	Code of conduct	**Not defined**
	Certification	Certification

	GDPR	**PIPL**
	Security Reviews—Not required	Security Reviews by National Cyberspace Administration departments (*note: this is required for Critical information infrastructure operators and personal information processors that process personal information up to the number prescribed by the national cyberspace administration. The personal information should be stored in China.*)

Derogations/ Other Situations	• Explicitly consented
	• Necessary for the conclusion or performance of a contract
	• Necessary for important reasons of public interest
	• Establishment, exercise, or defense of legal claims
	• Protect the vital interests of the data subject or of other persons
	• The transfer is made from a register which according to Union or Member State law is intended to provide information to the public and which is open to consultation either by the public in general or by any person who can demonstrate a legitimate interest, but only to the extent that the conditions laid down by Union or Member State law for consultation are fulfilled in the particular case.
	• If the data processing activity is based on legitimate interest, the transfer can still proceed if all the following conditions are met.
	  • Only if the transfer is not repetitive
	  • Concerns only a limited number of data subjects
	  • Is necessary for the purposes of compelling legitimate interests which are not overridden by the interests or rights and freedoms of the data subject
	  • Shall inform the supervisory authority of the transfer
	  • Shall inform the data subject of the transfer and on the compelling legitimate interests pursued
		Meet conditions set forth by laws and regulations

Data localization: This is the area where the GDPR and PIPL differ significantly. The GDPR does not require data localization. However, the PIPL clearly and deliberately articulates Critical Information Infrastructure (CII) operators shall store personal information collected and generated within China. The detail is outlined in article 40 that "Critical information infrastructure operators and PI processors that process PI up to the number prescribed by the national cybersecurity and informatization department shall store PI collected and generated within China."

3.4   CANADA PIPEDA

PIPEDA applies to private-sector organizations across Canada that collect, use or disclose personal information in the course of commercial activities.

The law defines a commercial activity as any particular transaction, act, or conduct, or any regular course of conduct that is of a commercial character, including the selling, bartering, or leasing of donor, membership, or other fundraising lists.

Alberta, British Columbia, and Quebec have their own private-sector privacy laws that have been deemed substantially similar to PIPEDA. Organizations subject to a substantially similar provincial privacy law are generally exempt from PIPEDA with respect to the collection, use, or disclosure of personal information that occurs within that province.

Ontario, New Brunswick, Nova Scotia, Newfoundland, and Labrador have also adopted substantially similar legislation regarding the collection, use, and disclosure of personal health information.

Amendment in 2015

In 2015, PIPEDA was amended by the passage of the Digital Privacy Act (DPA). The DPA introduced new provisions that are aimed at improving PIPEDA, including the following:

- Breach Notification and Record-Keeping Requirements
  - Organizations will be subject to mandatory notifications to the OPC of any breach of security safeguards involving personal information. For breaches where there is a "real risk of significant harm to individuals," the requirement also mandates notification to individuals.
  - Organizations will also be required to keep a record of all breaches involving personal information and provide a copy to the OPC upon request. Organizations that knowingly fail to report to the OPC or notify affected individuals of a breach that poses a real risk of significant harm, or knowingly fail to maintain a record of all breaches, could face fines of up to $100,000.
- Updated definitions
  - Personal information has been updated to mean information about an identifiable individual. Business contact information has been updated to include any information that is used to communicate or facilitate communication with an individual in relation to their employment, business, or profession, such as the individual's name, position name or title, work address, work telephone number, work fax number, or work electronic address.
- Update to Consent
  - Investigations/fraud detection and prevention. Organizations may now disclose personal information without consent to another organization in certain circumstances. However, it must be reasonable to expect that disclosure with the knowledge or consent of an individual would compromise the investigation or the ability to prevent, detect or suppress the fraud.
  - Business transactions. Organizations can use and disclose personal information without consent in connection with business transactions provided certain conditions are met. PIPEDA defines business transactions and includes, for example, the sale of a business, a merger, or the lease of a company's assets.
  - Witness statements in insurance claims. Personal information can be collected, used, and disclosed in witness statements without consent where "necessary to assess, process, or settle an insurance claim."
  - Identifying injured, ill, and deceased; communicating with next of kin. Organizations will be allowed to disclose personal information without consent to a government institution, individual's next of kin, or authorized representative if it is necessary to identify an individual who is injured, ill or deceased. If the individual is alive, the individual must be informed in writing that the disclosure took place. Information can also be disclosed to a government institution that has requested the information, identified its lawful authority to obtain the information, and indicated that the disclosure is requested for the purpose of communicating with the next of kin or authorized representative of an injured, ill, or deceased person.
  - Financial abuse. Organizations can disclose personal information without consent to a government institution or an individual's next of kin or authorized representative when they have reasonable grounds to believe the individual "has been, is or may be the vic-

tim of financial abuse." Disclosures may also be made (1) for the purpose of preventing or investigating the abuse and (2) only if it is reasonable to expect that the disclosure with the knowledge or consent of an individual would compromise the ability to prevent or investigate the abuse.

- Employment relationships in federally regulated workplaces. Consent is not required for the collection, use or disclosure of personal information where necessary to establish, manage or terminate an employment relationship. The organization must, however, inform individuals in advance that their personal information could be collected, used, or disclosed for such purposes.
- Personal information produced in the course of employment, business, or profession. Personal information produced by an individual during an individual's employment, business or profession may be collected, used, or disclosed without the individual's consent if such collection, use, or disclosure is consistent with the purpose for which the information was produced.
- Compliance Agreements
  - The OPC may enter into compliance agreements aimed at ensuring organizations comply with PIPEDA. These agreements are reached in situations where the OPC believes, on reasonable grounds, that an organization has committed, is about to commit, or is likely to commit an act or omission that could constitute a contravention of PIPEDA or a failure to follow a recommendation in Schedule I to the act.
  - Under a compliance agreement, an organization agrees to take certain actions to bring itself into compliance with PIPEDA. Entering into a compliance agreement would preclude the OPC from commencing or continuing a court application under PIPEDA with respect to any matter covered by the agreement.
  - If an organization fails to live up to commitments in an agreement, the OPC could, after notifying the organization: (1) apply to the court for an order requiring the organization to comply with the terms of the agreement, or (2) commence or reinstate court proceedings under PIPEDA, as appropriate.
- Public Interest Disclosures

PIPEDA's confidentiality provisions continue to apply, but the scope of what can be disclosed in the public interest has been broadened. The OPC may now make public any information that comes to its knowledge in the performance or exercise of its duties or powers under the PIPEDA if it deems that doing so is in the public interest. Previously, this discretion applied only to information "relating to the personal information management practices of an organization."

4 Privacy Best Practices, Standards, and Certifications

This chapter is intended to help readers have a full picture of global privacy frameworks, and principles, as well as the connections and links among them; To enable readers to have a concrete understanding of how those frameworks are different from each other and why.

This chapter covers the following topics:

- *Prevalent Privacy Frameworks*
- *Relationship tree for privacy frameworks and regulations*
- *Data protection certifications*
- *Data protection codes of conducts*

4.1 PREVALENT PRIVACY FRAMEWORKS

As privacy laws spread to other countries in Europe, international institutions took up privacy with a focus on the international implications of privacy regulation. In 1980, the Council of Europe adopted a Convention for the Protection of Individuals with regard to Automatic Processing of Personal Data At the same time, the Organization for Economic Cooperation and Development (OECD) proposed similar privacy guidelines in the OECD Guidelines on the Protection of Privacy and Transborder Flows of Personal Data. The OECD Guidelines, Council of Europe Convention, and European Union Data Protection Directive relied on FIPs as core principles. All three organizations revised and extended the original US statement of FIPs, with the OECD Privacy Guidelines being the version most often cited in subsequent years.

The following lists some of the more prevalent privacy and data protection frameworks and standards.

- Convention 108/108+ (1980/2018)
- OECD Principles (1980)
  - By 1980, and with data processing blindly obeying Moore's Law, the Organization for Economic Cooperation and Development (OECD) issued the first international guidelines on data privacy protection. It is in these guidelines that the world first gets a glimpse of what's to come in the years ahead. Terms such as "Data Controller" and "Data Subject" are introduced and defined, along with the concept of transborder data flows. The OECD guidelines are recommendations from governments to multinational enterprises on responsible business conduct. The guidelines were updated in 2013. They are guidelines for the protection of privacy and transborder flows of personal data. It is aimed to enable data flows and protect personal data. This membership extends outside of Europe and is not legally binding.
- Australian Privacy Principles (APPs) from Privacy Act 1988
- New Zealand Privacy Act 1993
- FTC Fair Information Practice Principles (1995, 1998)
- Canada Standards Association (CSA) Model Code 1996
- Resemble OECD principles, Incorporated into PIPEDA
- FTC Fair Information Practice Principles (1995, 1998)
- AICPA/CICA GAPP Principles (2003, 2006, 2009)

DOI: 10.1201/9781003225089-5

- The Generally Accepted Privacy Principles (GAPP) is a framework intended to assist Chartered Accountants and Certified Public Accountants in creating an effective privacy program for managing and preventing privacy risks. The framework was developed through joint consultation between the Canadian Institute of Chartered Accountants (CICA) and the American Institute of Certified Public Accountants (AICPA) through the AICPA/CICA Privacy Task Force. GAPP's ten principles are listed in Appendix C for your reference.
- APEC Principles (2005)
- BCR (2008,2017, 2018)
- PbD Principles (2010)
  - The 7 Foundational Principles of Privacy by Design is authored by former Information and Privacy Commissioner of Ontario Ann Cavoukian. These principles guide on applying the seven foundational principles of privacy by design.
- ISO/IEC 29100:2011 Privacy framework (2011)
- White House Green Paper (2012)
- GDPR Principles (2016)
- The GSMA Mobile Privacy Principles (2016)

4.2 PRIVACY FRAMEWORKS, REGULATIONS, AND THE RELATIONSHIP

Most of the time, the privacy regulations and frameworks are not created out of the thin air. They usually stem from existing principles with modifications to some extent. Figure 4.1 illustrates the relationship among some of the most prevalent regulations and frameworks.

4.3 CERTIFICATIONS AND CODES OF CONDUCT

There are many and various privacy and data protection standards available for organizations to follow. Organizations need to plan and manage certification and CoC audit and attestation schedule and execution in accordance with approved and applicable guidelines. Prior to embarking on the use of these instruments, it is essential that your organization considers its pros and cons. Organizations should identify and choose the appropriate data protection standards to comply with considering the business operational needs, such as marketplace, data cross-border transfers, and so on.

Similar to the GDPR, this book does not define "certification mechanisms, seals or marks" and uses the terms collectively.

4.3.1 BENEFITS OF PRIVACY CERTIFICATIONS COCS

Demonstration of accountability

Under some privacy and data protection regulations (i.e., GDPR), adherence to approved codes of conduct (CoCs) or approved certification mechanisms may be used as an element by which to demonstrate compliance with the data protection obligations. The certification mechanisms support controllers and processors to be able to demonstrate necessary compliance with the privacy laws and regulations (i.e., GDPR) by proving greater visibility and credibility. It also supports individuals to quickly evaluating the protection levels required for daily processing operations.

- GDPR Art. 24.3: Adherence to approved codes of conduct as referred to in Article 40 or approved certification mechanisms as referred to in Article 42 may be used as an element by which to demonstrate compliance with the obligations of the controller (24.3).
- GDPR Art. 25.3: An approved certification mechanism pursuant to Article 42 may be used as an element to demonstrate compliance with the requirements set out in paragraphs 1 and 2 of this Article.

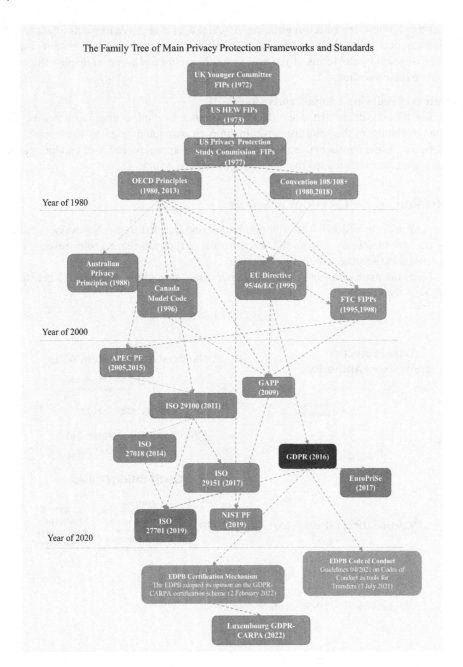

FIGURE 4.1 The family tree of main privacy protection frameworks and standards.

Support business growth

Cisco's report[9] finds that privacy has become a major business imperative and a critical component of customer trust for organizations around the world. And for the second year in a row, 90% of the respondents said they would not buy from an organization that does not properly protect its data, and 91% indicated that external privacy certifications are important in their buying process.

Self-regulation and assessment

Organizations with robust privacy programs can expect privacy certifications and CoCs as an additional tool to validate their privacy compliance. Also, certifications and attestations provided by third parties are a robust way of self-regulation. A seal program requires its participants to abide by codes of information practices and adhere to some variation of monitoring to ensure compliance. Companies that abide by the terms of the seal program are then allowed to display the program's privacy seal on their websites.

Consideration of reducing administrative fines
GDPR Article 83 articulates that when deciding whether to impose an administrative fine and deciding on the amount of the administrative fine in each individual case due regard shall be given to a list of factors in the regulation, including adherence to approved codes of conduct pursuant to Article 40 or approved certification mechanisms pursuant to Article 42.

4.3.2   Key Roles in the Certification Scheme

Although the roles of the National Accreditation Bodies and Data Protection Supervisory Authorities vary from country to country, Figure 4.2 demonstrates a typical scenario with respect to setting forth the certification scheme within a jurisdiction.

Table 4.1 lists the main tasks and powers of supervisory authorities in relation to certification in accordance with the GDPR.[10]

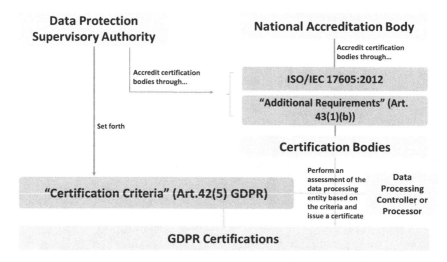

FIGURE 4.2   Key elements of a GDPR certification program.

TABLE 4.1

Main Tasks and Powers of Supervisory Authorities

	Provisions	Requirements
Tasks	Article 43(6)	Requires the supervisory authority to make public the criteria referred to in Article 42(5) in an easily accessible form and transmit them to the Board.
	Article 57(1)(n)	Requires the supervisory authority to approve certification criteria pursuant to Article 42(5).
	Article 57(1)(o)	Provides that where appropriate (i.e., where it issues certification), it shall carry out a periodic review of certification issued in accordance with Article 42(7).
	Article 64(1)(c)	Requires the supervisory authority to communicate the draft decision to the Board, when it aims to approve the criteria for certification referred to in Article 42(5).

	Provisions	Requirements
Powers	Article 58(1)(c)	Provides that the supervisory authority has the power to carry out reviews of certification pursuant to Article 42(7).
	Article 58(2)(h)	Provides that the supervisory authority has the power to withdraw or order the certification body to withdraw certification or order the certification body not to issue certification.
	Article 58(3)(e)	Provides that the supervisory authority has the power to accredit certification bodies.
	Article 58(3)(f)	Provides that the supervisory authority has the power to issue certification and approve certification criteria.
	Article 58(3)(e)	Provides that the supervisory authority has the power to accredit certification bodies.
	Article 58(3)(f)	Provides that the supervisory authority has the power to issue certification and approve certification criteria.

Questions and Answers

Are "codes of conduct" mandatory or voluntary?

In general, codes of conduct are voluntary for organizations to comply with. The following two guidelines articulate further details.

- EDPB Guidelines 1/2019 on Codes of Conduct: "Codes of conduct" GDPR codes are voluntary accountability tools that set out specific data protection rules for categories of controllers and processors.
- UK ICO: Codes of Conduct: Codes of conduct are voluntary accountability tools, enabling sectors to identify and resolve key data protection challenges in their sector with assurance from ICO that the code, and its monitoring, are appropriate.

Questions and Answers

Are "certifications" mandatory or voluntary?

In general, certifications are voluntary for organizations to comply with. The following two guidelines articulate further details.

- Guidelines 1/2018 on certification: The GDPR does not introduce a right to or an obligation of certification for controllers and processors; as per Article 42(3), certification is a voluntary process to assist in demonstrating compliance with the GDPR.
- UK ICO: Certification: Applying for certification is voluntary.

Questions and Answers

Does GDPR privacy certification mean GDPR compliant?

Getting GDPR certified does NOT mean GDPR compliant.

Firstly, GDPR Article 42 articulates that the certification shall be voluntary and available via a process that is transparent, and more importantly, a certification pursuant to this Article does not reduce the responsibility of the controller or the processor for compliance with this Regulation and is without prejudice to the tasks and powers of the supervisory authorities which are competent pursuant to Article 55 or 56.

Secondly, EPDB Guidelines 1/2018 says on page 5 that "Since certification does not prove compliance in and of itself but rather forms an element that can be used to demonstrate compliance, it should be produced in a transparent manner." Also, it says on page 5 that "A data controller or processor may have been awarded certificates for a specific processing operation and yet find itself infringing the Regulation."

Last but not least, CNIL Privacy Seal informs the public that the procedure or product proposed corresponds to the requirements of the Data Protection Authority. In this, CNIL mentioned that it plays the role of a confidence indicator. It does not aim to exempt its holders from administrative formalities.

4.3.3   MAIN PRIVACY CERTIFICATIONS AND CoCs

There are many Privacy Certifications and Codes of Conduct (CoC) that organizations can leverage to help to establish their privacy and data protection programs. For instance, there are more than 16,000 organizations have achieved the JIPDEC PrivacyMark. One thing is worth noting, although HIPAA is one of the most prevalent privacy-related regulations in the US, there's no official program for organizations to become compliant, receive a "HIPAA Certified" badge, and be done with it.

Table 4.2 lists 21 Representative Privacy Certifications and CoCs.[11]

TABLE 4.2

Examples of Privacy and Data Protection Relevant Certifications and CoCs

Certification Type	Geographical Coverage	Sector	Functional Scope	Type	Validity
ISO/IEC 27701:2019 Security techniques—Extension to ISO/IEC 27001 and ISO/IEC 27002 for privacy information management—Requirements and guidelines www.iso.org/standard/71670.html	International	Any	Management system certification	Voluntary	3 years
ISO/IEC 27018:2019 Information technology—Security techniques—Code of practice for protection of personally identifiable information (PII) in public clouds acting as PII processors www.iso.org/standard/76559.html	International	Cloud service providers	Management system certification	Voluntary	3 years
EU—Binding Corporate Rules (BCR) cooperation procedure https://ec.europa.eu/info/law/law-topic/data-protection/international-dimension-data-protection/binding-corporate-rules-bcr_en#:~:text=Binding%20corporate%20rules%20(BCR)%20are,group%20of%20undertakings%20or%20enterprises.	EU	Any	Management system	Voluntary	valid until amended, replaced or repealed, if necessary, by supervisory authorities
EU—EU Cloud Code of Conduct approved by the Beglian Data Protection Authority in May 2021 https://eucoc.cloud/en/about/about-eu-cloud-coc	EU	Cloud Service Provider (CSPs)	Management systems	Voluntary	1 year
EU—Code of Conduct for Cloud Infrastructure Services Providers (CISPE)	EU	Cloud Infrastructure Services Providers	Management systems	Voluntary	3 years

Certification Type	Geographical Coverage	Sector	Functional Scope	Type	Validity
Luxembourg GDPR-CARPA certification Luxembourg becomes the first country to introduce a certification mechanism according to the GDPR criteria. The National Data Protection Commission (CNPD) has adopted its certification mechanism GDPR-CARPA on 13th May 2022. GDPR-CARPA is the first certification mechanism to be adopted on a national and international level under the GDPR (General Data Protection Regulation). https://cnpd.public.lu/fr/actualites/national/2022/06/conference-certification.html	Luxembourg	Any	Data processing activities	Voluntary	3 years
UK BSI—BS 10012 Personal Information Management System www.bsigroup.com/en-GB/BS-10012-Personal-information-management/	International	Any	Management system	Voluntary	3 years
CNIL Label -Safebox www.cnil.fr/en/privacy-seals	France	Data storage	Product	Voluntary	3 years
CNIL—ASIP Santé—Authorization procedure dedicated to processors storing personal health data https://esante.gouv.fr/offres-services/hds/liste-des-herbergeurs-agrees	France	Health data hosting	Processes	Mandatory	3 years
Germany—European Privacy Seal (EuroPriSe) www.euprivacyseal.com/EPS-en/Home	International	Any	Products and services	Voluntary	2 years
Germany—Datenschutzaudit beim ULD www.datenschutzzentrum.de/audit/	Germany—State of Schleswig-Holstein	Public bodies	Data processing and personal information management system	Voluntary	3 years
Germany—ePrivacy—ePrivacyseal EU/DE/CH www.eprivacy.eu/en/customers/awarded-seals/	EU, Germany, Switzerland	Any	Data processing and personal information management system	Voluntary	2 years
Germany—ePrivacy—ePrivacyApp Health/HS www.eprivacy.eu/en/customers/awarded-seals/	EU, Germany, Switzerland	Any/Healthcare	Product/Mobile Application	Voluntary	until any changes are made
Italy—ISDP 10003 Data Protection Certification https://in-veo.com/en/certification/isdp-10003-2020-data-protection	International	Any	Processes	Voluntary	3 years
Netherlands—Privacy Audit Proof www.privacy-audit-proof.nl/	The Netherlands	Any	Data Processing	Voluntary	1 year
US—iKeepSafe FERPA/COPPA/CSPC/ATLIS https://ikeepsafe.org/certifications/	US	Education	Products and processes	Voluntary	1 year

(Continued)

TABLE 4.2 (Continued)

Certification Type	Geographical Coverage	Sector	Functional Scope	Type	Validity
US—TRUSTArc APEC CBPR https://trustarc.com/consumer-info/ privacy-certification-standards/	APEC	Any	Processes	Voluntary	1 year
US—TRUSTArc APEC PRP	APEC	Any	Processes	Voluntary	1 year
US—TRUSTArc APEC Children's Privacy Assessment Criteria	APEC	Any	Processes	Voluntary	1 year
Canada—PECB MS Privacy by Design Certification https://gpsbydesigncentre.com/privacy-by-design-certification/#:~:text=PECB%20 MS%20offers%20certification%20 services,set%20forth%20in%20our%20 standard.	International	Any	Products and processes	Voluntary	3 years
China—Data Security Management Certification Requirements for data and cyber certification are scattered in all three China major data and cyber laws, i.e., the PIPL, DSL and CSL.	China	Any	Management system and processes	Voluntary	3 years
Japan—JIPDEC PrivacyMark System https://privacymark.org/	Japan	Any private entities	Management system	Voluntary	2 years
Payment Card Industry Data Security Standard (PCI DSS)	International	Organizations that processing credit card information	Systems and processes	Mandatory	1 year

Part 2

Business Impact and a Holistic Framework

This Part Covers the Following Topics:

- Privacy Program Drivers and Challenges
- A Unified Privacy Framework
- Privacy Program Assessment
- Privacy Initiatives Prioritization and Roadmap
- Privacy Program Metrics and Tools

DOI: 10.1201/9781003225089-6

5 Data Protection Drivers and Challenges

This chapter is intended to provide readers with the facts and numbers in making the business case to the leadership team to get their buy-in for privacy initiatives.

This chapter covers the following topics:

- *Privacy Balanced Scorecard*
- *Financial Impact and Criminal Charges*
- *Internal Process Optimization and Customers Satisfaction*
- *Learning and Growth*
- *Main Challenges and Obstacles*

5.1 PRIVACY BALANCED SCORECARD

Cisco, a worldwide leader in IT and networking, published a "Data Privacy Benchmark Study" in 2022. Cisco's study[9] finds that privacy is mission-critical, as 90% consider privacy a business imperative. And the survey showed privacy investment continues to rise and organizations see a high return on investments from privacy spending. And over 60% of respondents felt they were getting significant business value from privacy, especially when it comes to reducing sales delays, mitigating losses from data breaches, enabling innovation, achieving efficiency, building trust with customers, and making their company more attractive.

Noncompliance impact isn't just the number of administrative fines. The violation of privacy law could have a direct and indirect impact. For instance, under the GDPR, organizations could get administrative fines of up to 4% of global annual turnover. One of the biggest fines issued so far was that the Luxembourg DPA issued Amazon €350 million in 2021 because Amazon's behavioral analysis and targeted advertising practices lacked valid consent from its users. Violation of privacy laws could easily damage an organization's reputation. Business processes and operations could be put on hold by Data Protection Authorities (DPAs) even if the business could be closed. For instance, Analytica was shut down due to a violation of privacy laws. An organization could also get into lawsuits due to collective actions and claims. Last but not least, breach of privacy laws could end up with jail time; in Greece, it might lead to 20 years imprisonment time.

An effective privacy program has a range of benefits that needs to be presented to decision-makers and stakeholders to gain the resources and support required to operate effectively. Buy-in from decision-makers and stakeholders will ensure that the privacy program is allocated appropriate resources, privacy is embedded within the agency's culture and employees within your organization support the privacy program and are aware of their role within it. Figure 5.1 depicts the privacy value proposition balanced scorecard which is a convenient vehicle to communicate the impact of noncompliance or the benefits of an organization's privacy program to stakeholders.

DOI: 10.1201/9781003225089-7

FINANCIAL/ CRIMINAL CHARGES
- Avoid hefty regulatory fines which could be up 20 million Euros or to 4% of the global revenue whichever is greater in some jurisdictions (i.e. EU)
- Avoid criminal charges
- Avoid data breach related cost
- Reduce the premium of cyber insurance policy

CUSTOMERS
- Greater transparency boosts customers' trust and confidence
- Satisfying contractual requirements
- Enhanced reputation through demonstrating data protection compliance

INTERNAL PROCESS
- Privacy risks are reduced through effective privacy management program
- Compliance with applicable laws to avoid disruption of business operations and legal challenges, etc.
- Alignment with business strategy and Establishing competitive advantages

LEARNING & GROWTH
- Enhance data protection awareness level
- Better staff engagement
- Staff are confident when handling personal information

FIGURE 5.1   Privacy balanced scorecard.

5.2   FINANCIAL IMPACT AND CRIMINAL CHARGES

Avoid hefty administrative fines
Under the GDPR, there are the following two tiers of administrative fines.

- 20 million or 4% (whichever is higher) of global revenue for both controller and processor for infringements of
  - Basic principles
  - Data subjects' rights
  - International data transfers
  - Obligations of member state law adopted under Chapter IX (Provisions relating to specific processing situations)
  - Non-compliance with a supervisory authority's order
- 10 million or 2% (whichever is higher) of global revenue for both controller and processor for infringements of most other obligations

To the current date (November 29, 2022), Table 5.1 lists the highest fines under the GDPR.[12]

TABLE 5.1
Highest Imposed Fines under the GDPR

#	Country	Date of Decision	Imposed Fine [€]	Controller/ Processor	Quoted Art.	Type
1	LUXEMBOURG	2021-07-16	746,000,000	Amazon Europe Core S.à.r.l.	Unknown	Non-compliance with general data processing principles
2	IRELAND	2022-09-05	405,000,000	Meta	Article 8	The fine is aimed at Instagram's violation of children's privacy, including its publication of kids' email addresses and phone numbers.

#	Country	Date of Decision	Imposed Fine [€]	Controller/ Processor	Quoted Art.	Type
3	IRELAND	2022-11-28	265,000,000	Meta	Article 25	Meta was €265 million by the Irish Data Protection Commission (DPC) following a data breach that saw the personal details of about 533 million of Facebook users published online back in 2019.
4	IRELAND	2021-09-02	225,000,000	WhatsApp Ireland Ltd.	Art. 5 (1) a) GDPR, Art. 12 GDPR, Art. 13 GDPR, Art. 14 GDPR	Insufficient fulfillment of information obligations
5	FRANCE	2021-12-31	90,000,000	Google LLC	Art. 82 loi Informatique et Libertés	Insufficient legal basis for data processing
6	FRANCE	2021-12-31	60,000,000	Facebook Ireland Ltd.	Art. 82 loi Informatique et Libertés	Insufficient legal basis for data processing
7	FRANCE	2021-12-31	60,000,000	Google Ireland Ltd.	Art. 82 loi Informatique et Libertés	Insufficient legal basis for data processing
8	FRANCE	2019-01-21	50,000,000	Google LLC	Art. 13 GDPR, Art. 14 GDPR, Art. 6 GDPR, Art. 5 GDPR	Insufficient legal basis for data processing
9	GERMANY	2020-10-01	35,258,708	H&M Hennes & Mauritz Online Shop A.B. & Co. KG	Art. 5 GDPR, Art. 6 GDPR	Insufficient legal basis for data processing
10	ITALY	2020-01-15	27,800,000	TIM (telecommunications operator)	Art. 5 GDPR, Art. 6 GDPR, Art. 17 GDPR, Art. 21 GDPR, Art. 32 GDPR	Insufficient legal basis for data processing
11	ITALY	2021-12-16	26,500,000	Enel Energia S.p.A	Art. 5 (1) a), d) GDPR, Art. 5 (2) GDPR, Art. 6 (1) GDPR, Art. 12 GDPR, Art. 13 GDPR, Art. 21 GDPR, Art. 24 GDPR, Art. 25 (1) GDPR, Art. 30 GDPR, Art. 31 GDPR, Art. 130 (1), (2), (4) Codice della privacy	Insufficient legal basis for data processing
12	UNITED KINGDOM	2020-10-16	22,046,000	British Airways	Art. 5 (1) f) GDPR, Art. 32 GDPR	Insufficient technical and organizational measures to ensure information security
13	UNITED KINGDOM	2020-10-30	20,450,000	Marriott International, Inc	Art. 32 GDPR	Insufficient technical and organizational measures to ensure information security
14	ITALY	2022-02-10	20,000,000	Clearview AI	Art. 5 (1) a), b), e) GDPR, Art. 6 GDPR, Art. 9 GDPR, Art. 12 GDPR, Art. 13 GDPR, Art. 14 GDPR, Art. 15 GDPR, Art. 27 GDPR	Non-compliance with general data processing principles

(Continued)

TABLE 5.1   (Continued)

#	Country	Date of Decision	Imposed Fine [€]	Controller/ Processor	Quoted Art.	Type
15	IRELAND	2022-03-15	17,000,000	Meta Platforms Ireland Limited	Art. 5 (2) GDPR, Art. 24 (1) GDPR	Insufficient technical and organizational measures to ensure information security
16	ITALY	2020-07-13	16,700,000	Wind Tre S.p.A.	Art. 5 GDPR, Art. 6 GDPR, Art. 12 GDPR, Art. 24 GDPR, Art. 25 GDPR	Insufficient legal basis for data processing
17	ITALY	2020-11-12	12,251,601	Vodafone Italia S.p.A.	Art. 5 (1), (2) GDPR, Art. 6 (1) GDPR, Art. 7 GDPR, Art. 15 (1) GDPR, Art. 16 GDPR, Art. 21 GDPR, Art. 24 GDPR, Art. 25 (1) GDPR, Art. 32 GDPR, Art. 33 GDPR	Non-compliance with general data processing principles
18	GERMANY	2021-01-08	10,400,000	notebooksbilliger.de	Art. 5 GDPR, Art. 6 GDPR	Insufficient legal basis for data processing
19	AUSTRIA	2021-09-28	9,500,000	Austrian Post	Unknown	Unknown
20	ITALY	2019-12-11	8,500,000	Eni Gas e Luce	Art. 5 GDPR, Art. 6 GDPR, Art. 17 GDPR, Art. 21 GDPR	Insufficient legal basis for data processing
21	SPAIN	2021-03-11	8,150,000	Vodafone España, S.A.U.	Art. 28 GDPR, Art. 24 GDPR, Art. 44 GDPR, Art. 21 LSSI, Art. 48 (1) b) LGT, Art. 21 GDPR, Art. 23 LOPDGDD	Insufficient fulfillment of data subject's rights
22	AUSTRIA	2022-01-14	8,000,000	REWE International AG	Unknown	Unknown

In jurisdictions other than the EU, we are also seeing hefty fines issued by the regulators. For instance, the US Federal Trade Commission (FTC) slapped Facebook with a $5 billion fine and penalized Equifax $575 million in 2019.

Avoid criminal charges

Table 5.2 illustrates some examples of criminal charges in various jurisdictions.

TABLE 5.2
Examples of Criminal Charges

Region	Years (highest imprisonment)	Country	Associated Laws and Regulations
Europe	20 Years	Greece	If the unlawful acts caused endangerment of democratic functions or national security, they are punishable with imprisonment of a term of 5 to 20 years and a pecuniary penalty of up to €300,000.
	6 Years	Italy	Article 167-bis: unlawful communication and disclosure of personal data object of processing on large scale is punished with imprisonment from 1 to 6 **years**.
	5 Years	France	According to the Criminal Code, up to **5 years** imprisonment and fines of up to €300,000 for individuals, or €1.5 million for companies.

Region	Years (highest imprisonment)	Country	Associated Laws and Regulations
		Ireland	Up to €250,000 and/or imprisonment for a maximum term of **5 years.**
		Bulgaria	If considerable damage has been caused or other serious consequences have occurred, the punishment may include imprisonment of up to **5** years.
		Cyprus	Up to 5 years. If a person is convicted for an offense under points (g) to (j) and such offense hinders the interests of the State or raises risks for the seamless operation of Government or threatens national security, a sentence of 5 years of imprisonment and/or a fine of €50,000 may be imposed.
	4 Years	Portugal	Imprisonment for up to 4 years, in addition to a fine of up to €240,000.
		Turkey	1~4 years
	3 Years	Germany	Transferring personal data of a large number of people to a Third Party without authorization (where the personal data was not previously publicly available), or otherwise making such data accessible for commercial purposes, is punishable with imprisonment of up to **3 years** or a fine.
		Poland	Noncompliant data processing of a special category of personal data is subject to a fine, imprisonment, or imprisonment of up to three years. • Maximum 2 years of imprisonment for processing personal data without legal basis or proper authorization • Maximum 3 years of imprisonment for processing special categories of personal data without legal basis or proper authorization • Maximum 2 years of imprisonment for obstruction of an audit by the supervisory authority
		Iceland	Under the Data Protection Act, an individual may be sentenced to up to **3 years** of prison for an especially serious breach of the Data Protection Act. The representative of a legal entity, or its employees, can be sentenced to prison in addition to being subject to an administrative fine. A DPO, or an employee of the DPA, who violates obligations of secrecy can be sentenced to up to one year of imprisonment or, in special circumstances, up to **3 years**.
		Croatia	3 years. A legal entity may face fines for criminal offenses up to HRK 8 million (approx. €1 million).
	1 Year	Austria	1 year, or with a fine of up to 720 day-fines (daily rate between €4 and €5,000)
		Finland	1 year, Under the Criminal Code
		Luxembourg	Article 51: Anyone who knowingly prevents or hinders, in any manner whatsoever, the performance of the tasks incumbent on the CNPD, is punished by imprisonment of 8 days to **1 year** and a fine of 251 to 125,000 euros or one of these penalties only.
		Liechtenstein	Up to one year, or a fine of up to 360 day-fines.
	6 Months	Denmark	Imprisonment for a term not exceeding 6 months.
		Malta	A fine of between €1,250 and €50,000 and/or a 6-month imprisonment
	No defined specific terms of imprisonment	Slovakia	Criminal act no. 300/2005 Coll. Shall be liable to a term of imprisonment.
		Estonia	The following breaches are subject to potential criminal penalties: • the unlawful disclosure of personal data by a person subject to a confidentiality obligation arising from the law. • the unlawful disclosure of, or the enabling of illegal access to, sensitive personal data, or data concerning the commission of or falling victim to an offense before:

(Continued)

TABLE 5.2 (Continued)

Region	Years (highest imprisonment)	Country	Associated Laws and Regulations
			• a public court hearing • making a decision in the matter of the offense • termination of the court proceedings in the matter • the illegal use of another person's identity.
		Latvia	The Latvian Criminal Law imposes criminal liability for the following offenses:
			• Illegal activities involving personal data, where these activities have caused substantial harm. • A controller or a processor who carries out the aforementioned activities for the purposes of vengeance, acquisition of property or blackmail. • A person influencing a controller, a processor or a data subject using violence, threats, abuse of trust, bad faith, or deceit in order to perform illegal activities involving personal data.
Asia Pacific	1 Year	Japan	Up to 1 year
North America	10 years	US-GLBA	Level 1: Up to 5 years imprisonment Level 2: Involving more than $100,000 in a 12-month period
			• Double fine • 10 years

Avoid data breach related cost

An effective privacy program will allow an organization to identify and mitigate its privacy risks and avoid data breaches and loss. A privacy program will not eliminate all breaches, but it can decrease the risk of a breach, reduce the number of breaches and improve how an organization responds to a breach.

If an organization has a tested privacy incident response plan, it will allow the organization to contain a breach more quickly and better mitigate the impact of the breach by lessening the loss. In 2019 the global average time to identify a breach was 206 days and the average time to contain a breach was 73 days, totaling 279 days. In 2018, CompariTech carried out a report finding that, in the long term, organizations that have suffered data breaches financially underperformed.

Table 5.3 lists the data breaches/leakage incidents that involve more than 100 million data records.

TABLE 5.3
High-Profile Data Breaches

#	Company	Number of Records	Types of Data	Date of Report
1	CAM4	10.88 billion	First and last names, email addresses, password hashes, country of origin & sign-up dates, gender preference & sexual orientation, device information, language, usernames and chat logs, payment logs with card type and currency, transcripts of email correspondence, correspondence with other users and CAM4 support, token information, IP addresses, fraud & spam logs	March 2020

#	Company	Number of Records	Types of Data	Date of Report
2	Advanced Info Service (AIS-Thailand)	8.3 billion	DNS queries, real-time internet records anyone with access to the database can identify the user's websites or apps they used and can paint a picture of what a person does on the Internet	May 2020
3	Yahoo	3 billion	Names, email addresses, telephone numbers, encrypted or unencrypted security questions and answers, dates of birth, and hashed passwords	October 2017 (breach occurred around August 2013)
4	Aadhaar (data subjects: Indian citizens)	1.1 billion	Names, unique 12-digit identity numbers, bank details, photographs, thumbprints, retina scans	March 2018
5	BlueKai (Oracle)	Estimated about billions of records	Names, home addresses, email addresses, and sensitive users' web browsing activity	June 2020
6	Whisper	900 million (many of data subjects involved children)	User's stated age, ethnicity, gender, hometown, nickname and any membership in groups, many of which are devoted to sexual confessions and discussion of sexual orientation and desires users' last submitted post, many of which pointed back to specific schools, workplaces and residential neighborhoods	March 2020
7	First American Financial Corp	885 million	Bank account records, social security numbers, wire transactions, other mortgage paperwork	May 2019
8	Verifications.io	763 million	Email addresses, names, phone numbers, IP addresses, dates of birth and genders	February 2019
9	LinkedIn	700 million (impacts 92% of LinkedIn users)	Email addresses, full names, phone numbers, physical addresses, geolocation records, LinkedIn username and profile URL, personal and professional experience/background, genders, other social media accounts and usernames	June 22, 2021
10	Sina Weibo	538 million records	Real names, site usernames, gender, location	November 2020
11	Facebook	533 million (people from 106 countries)	Phone numbers, full names, locations, email addresses, and biographical information	April 2019
12	Yahoo	500 million	Names, email addresses, phone numbers, hashed passwords, birth dates, and security questions and answers	September 2016
13	Starwood (Marriott)	500 million	Names, contact information, passport number, Starwood Preferred Guest numbers, travel information, and credit and debit card numbers, and expiration dates	November 2018
14	Estée Lauder	440 million	Emails, IP addresses and internal logs/reference documents	January 2020
15	Adult Friend Finder	412.2 million	Names, email addresses and passwords	October 2016
16	MySpace	360 million	Owner's listed name, username, and birthdate	June 2013
17	Broadvoice	350 million	Names, phone numbers and call transcripts	October 2020

(Continued)

TABLE 5.3   (Continued)

#	Company	Number of Records	Types of Data	Date of Report
18	Microsoft	250 million	Records contained plain text data including customer email addresses, IP addresses, geographical locations, descriptions of the customer service and support claims and cases, Microsoft support agent emails, case numbers and resolutions, and internal notes that had been marked as confidential.	January 2020
19	Exactis	340 million	Phone numbers, home, and email addresses, interests, and the number, age, and gender of their children	June 2018
20	Twitter	330 million	Passwords	May 2018
21	Wattpad	268 million	Email address and password combinations	July 2020
22	NetEase	234 million	Email addresses and plain text passwords.	October 2015
23	Sociallarks	200 million	Names, phone numbers, email addresses, profile descriptions, follower and engagement data, locations, LinkedIn profile links, connected social media account login names	January 2021
24	Deep Root Analytics (data subjects: US voters)	200 million	Names, addresses and birthdates	Jun 2017
25	Court Ventures (Experian)	200 million	Credit card numbers and social security numbers	Oct 2013
26	LinkedIn	165 million	Accounts, passwords	June 2012
27	Dubsmash	162 million	Email addresses, usernames and DBKDF2 password hashes	December 2018
28	Adobe	152 million	Internal ID, username, email, encrypted password and password hint in plain text	October 2013
29	MyFitnessPal (Under Armour)	150 million	Email addresses, IP addresses and login credentials such as usernames and passwords stored as SHA-1 and bcrypt hashes (the former for earlier accounts, the latter for newer accounts)	February 2018
30	Equifax	148 million	Names, home addresses, phone numbers, dates of birth, social security numbers, and driver's license numbers, credit card information of approximately 209,000 consumers	September 2017
31	eBay	145 million	Names, email addresses, physical addresses, phone numbers and dates of birth	February/March 2014
32	Canva	137 million	Email addresses, names, usernames, cities and passwords stored as bcrypt hashes	May 2019
33	Heartland Payment Systems	134 million	Credit cards	March 2008
34	Apollo	126 million	Names, email addresses, place of employment, roles held and location	July 2018
35	Badoo	112 million	Email addresses and PII such as names, birthdates and passwords stored as MD5 hashes	July 2013

#	Company	Number of Records	Types of Data	Date of Report
36	Capital One	106 million	Credit card data, names, addresses, ZIP codes, phone numbers, email addresses, birthdates and self-reported income, customer credit scores, credit limits, balances, payment history, and contact information	March 2019
37	Evite	100 million	Names, email addresses, passwords, and IP addresses	February, 2019
38	Quora	100 million	Names, email addresses, encrypted passwords, user accounts linked to Quora and public questions and answers posted by users	December 2018

5.3 INTERNAL PROCESS OPTIMIZATION

Privacy risk reduction and Compliance with laws

Violation of privacy regulations could end up with business processes and operations being put on hold or shut down by Data Protection Authorities (DPAs). An effective privacy program is the best way to facilitate compliance with all applicable privacy laws. Privacy legislation provides a baseline of privacy practice by setting out how agencies can collect, use, disclose, store, and provide access to personal information. Complying with applicable privacy laws reduces the likelihood of misuse or unauthorized disclosure of personal information held by an organization.

Violation of privacy regulations could end up in getting into lawsuits due to collective actions and claims. GDPR makes it considerably easier for data subjects to bring civil claims against data controllers and against data processors. The data subject doesn't have to have suffered financial loss or even any material damage, such as loss of or destruction of goods or property, and can claim for nonmaterial damage, such as distress and hurt feelings. In addition, data subjects have the right to require a consumer protection body to exercise rights and bring claims on their behalf. This isn't quite the same as the ability to bring class actions, but it increases the risk of group claims. Data subjects can now bring civil claims against data controllers for infringements of their data subject rights. So, if, for example, you don't respond appropriately to a data subject's right request or if you experience a data breach that affects the data subject's personal data, you could find yourself on the receiving end of a civil claim. As you may have noticed in recent high-profile data breaches, such as the British Airways data breach in 2019, data protection lawyers are placing advertisements encouraging victims of data breaches to join group actions against the data controller. A civil claim against you would not only damage your reputation further but would also cost a significant amount of time and money to defend the claim.

Alignment with business strategy and establishing competitive advantages

Strong data protection capability can be your competitive advantage. Being privacy-compliant can improve customer retention rates and loyalty. By embracing the privacy laws and regulations and showing your customers, prospects, and employees that you care about the protection of their personal data, you gain a competitive advantage.

Stephen Warwick wrote an article on February 3, 2022, mentioning "Since Apple's privacy update went into effect in late April 2021, these four social media companies (Meta, Snap, Twitter, and Pinterest) have erased a combined $278 billion in market value."

Another example would be that Porsche is strategically developing the issue of data protection to deliver commercial and enhanced customer experience results. Porsche considers the digital self-determination of its customers to be of the utmost importance to ensure the company's success in the digital age. The entire automotive industry is in the midst of a far-reaching change process on the data highway. This has also had an impact on the types of privacy hitherto used in the corporate environment. To meet the new demands, the sports car manufacturer has anchored the strategic orientation of privacy, with a focus on products and customers, as a separate strategic area in its Corporate Strategy 2030. The cornerstones of Porsche's new privacy strategy, "Privacy—Accelerating Dreams & Innovation", were recently approved by the Executive Board, which means that the strategy will be taken into account in the future development of products and services.[13]

Elizabeth Denham, the UK information commissioner, summed up this idea nicely:

> Accountability encourages an upfront investment in privacy fundamentals, but it offers a payoff down the line, not just in better legal compliance, but a competitive edge. There is a real opportunity for organizations to present themselves on the basis of how they respect the privacy of individuals and over time this can play more of a role in consumer choice.

5.4   CUSTOMERS SATISFACTION

Increased customer trust and confidence

The data privacy program is about creating a trustworthy organization. Effective privacy protection is essential to maintaining consumer trust and enabling a robust and innovative digital economy in which individuals feel they may participate with confidence. Organizations that understand this and embrace a culture of privacy are those that will be most successful in this digital age. By having an effective privacy program, an organization will foster this trust and confidence, reduce the number of complaints, and be an exemplary corporate citizen.

These challenges are taking place amidst a backdrop of considerable social concern about the control of personal information. A survey conducted by the Office of the Privacy Commissioner (OPC) in 2016 revealed that 92% of Canadians are concerned that they are losing control of their personal information, with 57% responding that they were "very concerned".

The unauthorized disclosure of personal information and loss of privacy can have devastating impacts on customers such as:

- Financial fraud
- Identity theft
- Unnecessary costs in personal time and finances
- Destruction of property
- Harassment
- Reputational damage
- Emotional distress
- Physical harm

The general public is much savvier about their data protection rights than they used to be. The introduction of the GDPR garnered a lot of publicity due to the increased sanctions. Supervisory authorities ran various awareness campaigns to ensure that data subjects were aware of their rights. Certain high-profile cases, such as the Facebook and Cambridge Analytica cases and the British Airways data breach case, have received broad coverage in the media.

This savviness has led to an increase in the number of complaints from data subjects whose personal data hasn't been processed in accordance with the GDPR. Data subjects are lodging complaints both directly to the data controller and to supervisory authorities. A report by the Data & Marketing Association and Axciom entitled "Data privacy: What the consumer really thinks" showed that individuals from around the world are, in the vast majority, quite concerned about how their personal data is used and protected.[14] If you aren't compliant with the GDPR, you're showing your prospects, customers, and employees that you aren't concerned about the protection of their personal data.

If customers have trust and confidence in an organization, they'll be more likely to engage with the organization and receive the services they need. If you don't comply with the privacy laws and regulations, you are likely to lose the trust of your customers and prospects. When they don't trust you, they don't want to buy from you or otherwise do business with you. For instance, British Airways sent an email to all of its customers to assure them that they could trust British Airways with their personal data. But just a couple of months later, British Airways suffered a large data breach that compromised the financial details of 185,000 customers, details that were sold on the dark web. As a result of this data breach, the share price of IAG (British Airways' parent company) decreased by 5.8% (equivalent to a loss of £350M).

5.5 LEARNING AND GROWTH

Engagement with privacy and security within organizations has not kept pace with the increasing demands from regulations. As a result, organizations often find themselves saying they support privacy and security engagement but struggling to create behavioral changes in their staff.

You need to develop a defined structure for privacy and security in the context of your organization to:

- Align your business goals and your security and privacy strategy to obtain support from your senior leadership team
- Enhance data protection awareness level
- Promote staff engagement
- Listening to your employees' concerns regarding their information
- Boosted employee confidence
- Measure adherence to requirements using metrics

5.6 MAIN CHALLENGES AND OBSTACLES

Organizations are facing various challenges with respect to establishing and operationalizing a privacy program, as follows:

- Staff are not adequately trained to handle personal information
- The organization does not understand where personal information is stored and processed
- Privacy risks are not associated with new products, services, or processes
- Privacy risks are not associated with material changes to existing products, services, or processes
- Personal information is retained longer than is necessary for the business purpose
- More personal information is collected than is required for the business purpose
- Third-party providers do not handle personal information appropriately
- Personal information is used or disclosed in an unauthorized manner
- Privacy-related inquiries are not appropriately handled
- Personal information is inadequately secured
- Privacy processes do not operate as intended
- Privacy-related incidents are not responded to appropriately
- The organization does not learn from patterns of privacy-related incidents

The sections to follow focus on the five challenges that impede organizations to build a robust and productive privacy program.

Build a comprehensive privacy program

Creating comprehensive, organization-wide data protection and privacy strategy continues to be a major challenge for data protection and privacy officers and privacy specialists. Compliance with data protection and privacy regulations is a challenging and complex task, which only becomes tougher as governments create and revise their national standards. DPOs and privacy professionals face not just these constantly shifting externalities, but considerable internal organizational challenges as well. In this report, we examine the challenges faced by these data protection and privacy officers, along with their priority goals in 2020 and their expected approach to achieve them.

Resource and Budget

Based on the CPO Magazine report "Data Protection & Privacy Officer Priorities 20202", 7% named getting budget and available resources as the organization's No. 1 challenge. 57% of organizations have an annual budget of no more than $250,000 for data protection and privacy. 76% of organizations have fewer than 10 employees in roles focused on data protection and privacy.

In the early and middle stages of spinning up a data protection and privacy program, the main challenge for data protection and privacy officers is a lack of budget and resources. These same organizations are also facing significant challenges in obtaining support from the executive ranks, compared to those with a higher level of program maturity.

The demand for privacy professionals is increasing. The IAPP's 2017 study estimated that GDPR regulatory requirements would create at least 75,000 data protection officer (DPO) positions worldwide. In May 2019, one year after the GDPR terms became active, there were estimated to be 500,000 organizations with registered DPOs in the European Economic Area (EEA) alone.

It's important to ensure that the decision-makers understand what's required to implement and manage a successful privacy program. Most of a program's resources would generally be allocated across three areas: people, process, and technology. An organization's privacy team needs to have enough staff who are appropriately skilled. The composition of the team will vary depending on the organization's context, size, and risk profile. The resources should be appropriately and sufficiently assigned to support the required privacy processes, such as establishing data inventories conducting risk assessments, and implementing appropriate controls.

Privacy-aware culture and cross-functional collaboration

While a robust privacy program and controls, coupled with other disciples such as cybersecurity, are of significant value, ultimately an organization must shift to take a proactive stance on privacy and data protection. This requires that principles and behaviors that promote privacy are embedded in the operational seams of how the organization runs on a daily basis and are supported from both the top-down and bottom-up. A culture of privacy and data protection starts with employees and members of the organization being fully engaged with how this discipline promotes their own success and the overall performance of the organization.

Based on the CPO Magazine report "Data Protection & Privacy Officer Priorities 20202", 49% have made governance of data processing and the formation of a privacy-aware culture a top priority. Larger organizations are more likely to have problems implementing policies and measures across their various business functions (28% of those with over 1,000 employees). Large organizations with complex structures and businesses tend to require more sophisticated programs that are harder to implement and more challenging to get everyone on board.

Organizations that want to have successful data protection and privacy program need formal employee training and awareness campaigns. The best results come when these efforts get granular, down to individual responsibilities.

Companies that are most closely aligned with and intentional in positively shaping their employee privacy culture will achieve the most productivity from their employees and the easiest adoption of new technologies and data analytics in the workplace and in their products and services. Multinationals straddling differing privacy cultures across the three privacy regulatory poles will find the most difficulty rolling out technologies globally and may need to consider different regional approaches to optimize employee productivity and returns on investment.

Engagement with privacy and data protection within organizations has not kept pace with the increasing demands from regulations. As a result, organizations often find themselves saying they support privacy engagement but struggle to create behavioral changes in their staff. Employees aren't fully engaged with how privacy and data protection impact them. These barriers make this challenge difficult to address for many organizations:

- Privacy is often viewed as an inhibitor of innovation and a compliance obligation box to be ticked as opposed to competitive advantage and differentiator.
- Training modules, tests, and continuous learning are integral parts of ensuring that privacy and data protection are embedded in the organization, but they are just the beginning. Unfortunately, IT and business leaders consider them to be the core of a privacy-centric culture.
- Identifying indicators by which to measure an organization's employee engagement with privacy is challenging at the best of times.

Integration of privacy, security, and data governance

Privacy, security, and data governance are three different but closed intertwined disciplines.

Security is necessary for privacy, but not sufficient. A common assumption is that security and privacy are one and the same. Security's role is to protect and secure assets, of which confidential data—especially personal data—is a large focus. The consequences of a personal data breach can be severe, including the loss of customer trust and potential regulatory consequences. As a result, we often think of how we use security to protect data.

But that is not equivalent to privacy. Privacy must be thought of as a separate function. While there will always be ties to security in the ways it protects data, privacy starts and ends with the focus on personal data. Beyond protection, privacy extends to understanding why personal data is being collected, what the lawful uses are, how long it can be retained, and who has access to it.

While many data protection incidents stem from a security weakness, and many security incidents have privacy consequences, there are also many privacy incidents that are a class of their own. There are major GDPR and CCPA violations that have nothing to do with security indeed.

Information Governance underpins good data compliance, records management, information classification, confidentiality, procedural controls and so much more.

Table 5.4 describes some key differences among privacy, security, and data governance.

TABLE 5.4

Key Differences among Privacy, Security, and Data Governance

	Privacy Management	Security Management	Data Governance
Subject	Privacy is concerned with an individual's fundamental rights and ability to control the use of personal information.	Cybersecurity often focusses on the protection and security of the information and information systems from unauthorized attacks and against threats.	Ensuring the use of data and information complies with organizational policies, standards and strategy including regulatory, contractual, and business objectives.
Assurance objectives/ Different principles:	• Lawfulness, fairness, and transparency • Purpose limitation • Data minimization • Accuracy • Storage limitation • Integrity and confidentiality • Accountability	• Confidentiality • Integrity • Availability • Resilience • Accountability (i.e., non-repudiation, Traceability)	• Quality • Accessibility • Utility

(Continued)

TABLE 5.4   (Continued)

	Privacy Management	Security Management	Data Governance
Professional practices:	10 domains (GAPP)	14 main domains (ISO 27001 Annex A)	IMBOK
	• Management • Notice • Choice and consent • Collection • Use, retention, and processing • Access • Disclosure to third parities • Security for privacy • Quality • Monitoring and enforcement	• Information security policies • Organization of information security • Human resource security • Asset management • Access control • Cryptography • Physical and environmental security • Operations security • Communications security • System acquisition, development, and maintenance • Supplier relationships • Information security incident management • Information security aspects of business continuity management • Compliance	• six "knowledge" areas • Information technology • Information system • Business information • Business process • Business benefit • Business strategy • Four "process" areas • Projects • Business change • Business operations • Performance management • Create/Collect • Store • Use/Process • Share/Transfer • Preserve/Archive • Dispose
Different team:	Normally led by Legal team or compliance team	Normally led by cybersecurity team or IT team	Normally led by business functions and IT team

6 Unified Data Protection Framework

This chapter is intended to help readers be equipped with a structured privacy framework that provides a systematic approach in terms of principles, technical and organizational measures to guide the privacy professional through privacy management.

This chapter covers the following topics:

- *Common privacy principles*
- *Obligations for data controllers and processors*
- *A unified privacy framework*
- *A list of privacy control objectives and sets*

6.1 COMMON DATA PROTECTION PRINCIPLES

There are many privacy regulations, frameworks, and standards worldwide that set forth data protection basic principles. Table 6.1 lists out some of the most influential principles covered by various regulations and frameworks that are represent widely accepted concepts.

TABLE 6.1
Influential Privacy and Data Protection Principles

Regulation/Framework	Principles
Convention 108/108+ (1980/2018)	Duties of the Parties
	Legitimacy of data processing and quality of data
	Special categories of data
	Data security
	Transparency of processing
	Rights of the data subject
	Additional obligations
	Exceptions and restrictions
	Sanctions and remedies
	Extended protection
OECD Principles (1980)	Collection Limitation
	Data Quality
	Purpose Specification
	Use Limitation
	Security
	Safeguards
	Openness
	Individual Participation
	Accountability

(Continued)

DOI: 10.1201/9781003225089-8

TABLE 6.1   (Continued)

Regulation/Framework	Principles
Australian Privacy Principles (APPs) from Privacy Act 1988	Open and transparent management of personal information
	Anonymity and pseudonymity
	Collection of solicited personal information
	Dealing with unsolicited personal information
	Notification of the collection of personal information
	Use or disclosure of personal information
	Direct marketing
	Cross-border disclosure of personal information
	Adoption, use or disclosure of government related identifiers
	Quality of personal information
	Security of personal information
	Access to personal information
	Correction of personal information
New Zealand Privacy Act 1993	Purpose of collection of personal information
	Source of personal information
	Collection of information
	Manner of collection of personal information
	Storage and security of personal information
	Access to personal information
	Correction of personal information
	Accuracy of personal information to be checked before use
	Agency not to keep personal information for longer than necessary
	Limits on use of personal information
	Limits on disclosure of personal information
	Unique identifiers
FTC Fair Information Practice Principles, (1995, 1998)	Notice/Awareness
	Choice/Consent
	Access/Participation
	Integrity/Security
	Enforcement/Redress
Canada Standards Association (CSA) Model Code-1996	Accountability
	Identifying Purposes
Resemble OECD principles, Incorporated into PIPEDA	Consent
	Limiting Collection
	Limiting Use, Disclosure, and Retention
	Accuracy
	Safeguards
	Openness
	Individual Access
	Challenging Compliance
FTC Fair Information Practice Principles, (1995, 1998)	Notice/Awareness
	Choice/Consent
	Access/Participation
	Integrity/Security
	Enforcement/Redress
AICPA/CICA GAPP Principles (2003, 2006, 2009)	Management
	Notice
	Choice and Consent
	Collection
	Use, Retention and Disposal
	Access

Regulation/Framework	Principles
	Disclosure to Third Parties
	Security for Privacy
	Quality
	Monitoring and Enforcement
APEC Principles (2005)	Preventing Harm
	Notice
	Collection Limitation
	Uses of Personal Information
	Choice
	Integrity of Personal Information
	Security Safeguards
	Access and Correction
	Accountability
BCR (2008,2017, 2018)	Transparency, fairness, and lawfulness
	Purpose limitation
	Data minimization and accuracy
	Limited storage periods
	Processing of special categories of personal data
	Security
	Restriction on transfers and onward transfers
PbD Principles (2010)	Proactive not Reactive; Preventative not Remedial
	Privacy as the Default Setting
	Privacy Embedded into Design
	Full Functionality—Positive-Sum, not Zero-Sum
	End-to-End Security—Full Lifecycle Protection
	Visibility and Transparency—Keep it Open
	Respect for User Privacy—Keep it User-Centric
ISO/IEC 29100:2011 Privacy framework (2011)	Consent and choice
	Purpose, legitimacy, and specification
	Collection limitation
	Data minimization
	Use, retention, and disclosure limitation
	Accuracy and quality
	Openness, transparency, and notice
	Individual participation and access
	Accountability
	Information security
	Privacy compliance
White House Green Paper (2012)	Control
	Transparency
	Respect for Context
	Security
	Access and Accuracy
	Focused
	Collection
	Accountability
GDPR Principles (2016)	Lawfulness, fairness and transparency
	Purpose limitation
	Data minimisation
	Accuracy
	Storage period limitation
	Integrity and confidentiality
	Accountability

(Continued)

TABLE 6.1   (Continued)

Regulation/Framework	Principles
The GSMA Mobile Privacy Principles (2016)	Openness, transparency, and notice
	Purpose and use
	User choice and control
	Data minimization and retention
	Respect user rights
	Security
	Education
	Children and adolescents
	Accountability and enforcement

Although the principles within each privacy framework vary to some degree, the following list summarizes the top 10 most common privacy principles across the globe.

- Lawfulness, fairness, and transparency
- Purpose limitation
- Data minimization
- Storage period limitation
- Accuracy
- Security
- Disclosure to third parties
- Cross-border data transfer
- Data subject rights assurance
- Accountability

 Questions and answers

What is the difference between Privacy by Design vs. Privacy by Default?

Privacy-by-design is the philosophy that requires embedding privacy requirements into the early stage of product/process development, and ensuring privacy is built-in not an add-on.

You can consider privacy-by-default as a part of the privacy-by-design concept. Basically, privacy-by-default means an organization product's initial settings are placed in the best interest of the consumers not the organization. For instance, marketing cookies should be disabled by default on the website.

6.2   UNIFIED DATA PROTECTION FRAMEWORK

A privacy program framework is a master plan and implementation roadmap that provides the structure of privacy principles, technical and organizational measures to guide the privacy professional through privacy management and prompts them for the details to determine all privacy-relevant decisions for the organization.

Executive management and boards need a structured framework for overseeing the organization's data and privacy management. They should have a clear understanding of data and privacy regarding the balance between risk and strategy. Data and privacy issues should be understood and addressed in a proactive versus reactive manner. As the world continues to undertake significant policy changes with the resultant increases in data privacy obligations, an effective approach to data privacy is creating a compliance program and approach that meets the data privacy requirements of today and the future.

Senior executives and directors should question not only how the company's compliance processes meet current data privacy regulations but also whether they are flexible enough to meet future such obligations. This approach is not as hard as it seems, as most global privacy laws follow common principles that can be addressed in a consistent framework.

The purpose of a privacy program extends beyond compliance with the privacy laws, regulations, and Principles. A privacy program should also consider an organization's wider obligations and build trust with the individuals whose personal information they collect and hold. The main scope of a privacy program is the activities that enable managing the full lifecycle of personal information from collection to deletion. Understanding stakeholder expectations and the wider context that an agency operates within are important to governing a privacy program effectively.

GDPR Art. 25 stipulates that

taking into account the state of the art, the cost of implementation and the nature, scope, context, and purposes of processing as well as the risks of varying likelihood and severity for rights and freedoms of natural persons posed by the processing, the controller shall, both at the time of the determination of the means for processing and at the time of the processing itself, implement appropriate technical and organizational measures, such as pseudonymization, which are designed to implement data-protection principles, such as data minimization, effectively and to integrate the necessary safeguards into the processing in order to meet the requirements of this Regulation and protect the rights of data subjects.

An effective privacy program ensures compliance, but simply being compliant does not mean you have an effective privacy program. A robust privacy and data protection control framework enables you to test once, attest many. A robust privacy control framework provides a set of common controls which can be mapped to various compliance requirements, allowing you to satisfy multiple obligations by implementing a single control.

Instead of reactively checking the compliance boxes based on a set of governing laws, develop a privacy framework that proactively anticipates while staying in scope of the needs of your organization.

Figure 6.1 is a visual representation of my Privacy Framework which provides a clear path toward proactive privacy management which is pro-privacy, non-invasive, and pro-consumer. By developing a flexible and customized data privacy program, your organization significantly strengthens its ability to recover from data privacy incidents and reduces its overall risk of exposure.

 ## Guide and Recommendations

One practical privacy framework example is from Info-Tech Research Group (Info-Tech). Figure 6.2 is a visual representation of Info-Tech's Privacy Program Methodology which consists of 12 data protection domains. The methodology includes high-level governance items as well as more tactically defined areas.

Info-Tech's privacy framework will supplement the comprehensive model listed in Figure 6.1. Info-Tech's framework is beneficial for organizations that want to roll out their privacy programs in a condensed and cost-effective manner.

 ## Case Study—Google Buzz

FTC Charged Deceptive Privacy Practices in Googles Rollout of Its Buzz Social Network.

In March 2011, the FTC charged that Google Buzz social networking service had violated its own privacy policies. Google was charged that it used deceptive tactics and violated the privacy promises that were provided to its consumers in 2010. Two things are noteworthy and might serve as lessons learned to organizations.

- This consent decree was the first in which the company agreed to implement a "comprehensive" privacy program. The term "comprehensive" signals that the FTC believes privacy should be fully integrated with product development and implementation.
- To enforce the comprehensive privacy program clause, Google agreed to undergo independent third-party privacy audits on a biannual basis.

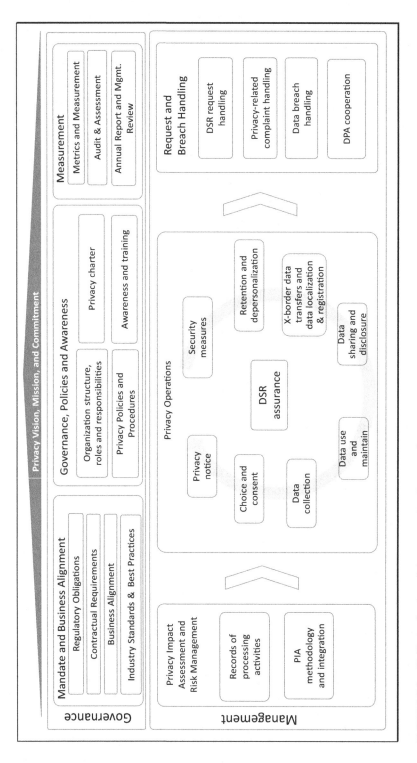

FIGURE 6.1   Unified privacy and data protection framework.

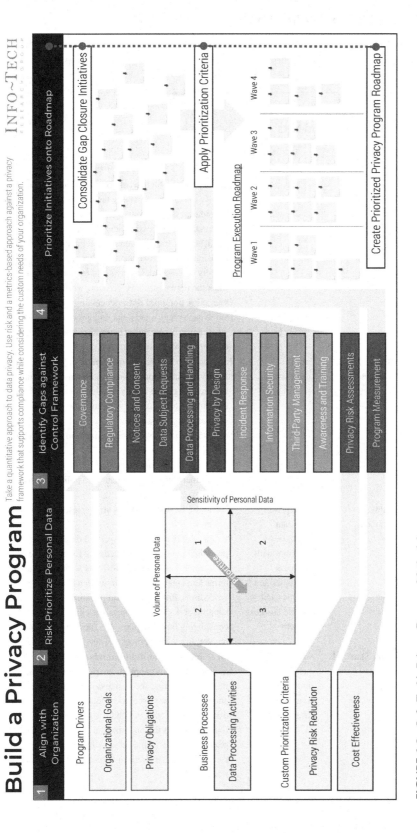

FIGURE 6.2 Info-Tech's Privacy Program Methodology

6.3   DATA PROTECTION OBJECTIVES AND CONTROLS

Table 6.2 lists out the correspondent privacy control domains, control groups, control objectives and control sets based upon the privacy framework discussed in the previous section.

TABLE 6.2
Privacy Control Objectives and Sets

Domain	Control Group	Control Objective	Control Set
Privacy Mandate and Business Alignment	Regulatory Obligations	Comply with applicable laws and regulations	**Identify applicable jurisdictions and legal obligations** Identify the jurisdictions in which the entity operates in accordance with the business' nature, and purposes of the personal data processing activities, etc. Identify and document applicable privacy-related laws, regulations, directives, decisions, scope, associated requirements, and possible penalty of violating the laws and regulations. Monitor and track the regulatory developments within those jurisdictions. **Determine personal data processing roles** Define each entity's personal data processing role based on whether the organization determines the purpose and means of data processing activities.
	Contractual Requirements	Fulfill contractual requirements	**Incorporate customer requirements** Identify and incorporate data protection contractual requirements from legally binding documents (i.e., agreements or contracts) with customers into the privacy program. **Incorporate privacy-related condition of cyber insurance policy** Identify and incorporate data protection contractual requirements from cyber insurance policy into the privacy program.
	Business Alignment	Align privacy and data protection program with business strategies and policies and enable business growth	**Be consistent with business strategies, objectives, and policies** Review and identify privacy-related requirements from existing published policies and procedures. Establish the privacy and data protection program consistent with the requirements, terms and languages that are written in current policies and procedures. Privacy program planning should consider, support, and enable business strategies and growth considering business plans (i.e., new products, new marketplaces, new processes, new business units).
	Industry Standards and Best Practices	Adherence to selected industry standards and frameworks	**Select and follow suitable standards** Identify and choose appropriate privacy protection standards to follow considering the business needs with respect to additional privacy protection controls, privacy principles, certifications, codes of conduct, seal programs, cross-border transfers, etc. If the organization has decided to comply with selected industry standard(s) or framework(s), ensure the privacy program is built in alignment with that standard(s) or framework(s).

Domain	Control Group	Control Objective	Control Set
Governance, Policies and Awareness	Privacy governance charter	Establish right-sized privacy governance structure and set forth enterprise-wide principles and requirements for privacy and data protection practices	**Establish an overarching privacy governance charter** Create and publish enterprise-wide internal-facing privacy governance charter that establishes the right-sized privacy governance structure and sets forth enterprise-wide principles and requirements for privacy and data protection practices.
	Key roles and responsibilities	Streamline and align with privacy program activities, roles, and responsibilities among business stakeholders	**Privacy Program Ownership** Designate the ownership who oversees the privacy and data protection practices and be ultimately responsible for the privacy program. Personal information controller/handlers shall disclose the methods of contacting privacy program owners and report the contact to the corresponding data protection authorities. **Designate an independent privacy protection role if required or necessary** The organization should designate a Data Protection Officer (DPO) if required by law or necessary for the business operations. **Designate a representative if required or necessary** Designate a writing Data Processing Representative (Representative) if required by law or necessary for the business operations. Note: Some privacy regulations (i.e., PIPL Article 3(2), GDPR Article 3(2)) require organizations to designate a writing representative.
		Agree on collaborative responsibilities across the organization	**Coordinate and Define Cross-Functional Responsibilities** Usually, a privacy program is a collaboration effort among cross-functional teams. Coordinate, define and assign clear lines of responsibilities to build and effectively manage the program. Note: Without defined responsibilities, privacy initiatives can easily fall between the cracks and issues may not be handled effectively. One of the techniques to define and socialize privacy program cross-functional roles and responsibilities is to leverage the RACI (Responsible, Accountable, Consulted, Informed) chart.

(Continued)

TABLE 6.2   (Continued)

Domain	Control Group	Control Objective	Control Set
	Policies and Procedures	Establish privacy and data protection policies and procedures	**Privacy policies and procedures** Organizations should establish and operationalize adequate and proper privacy policies and procedures to manage privacy and data protection practices. Policies and procedures may cover the following aspects (Not an exhaustive list).
			• Notice • Choice and consent • Collection • Use, retention, and disposal • Data subject rights • Disclosure to third parties • Security for privacy including data breach handling • Monitoring and enforcement
	Privacy awareness and training	Establish privacy protection culture and promote awareness program across the enterprise	**Privacy Awareness and Training** Roll out regular privacy awareness training program to employees, contractors, interns, etc. The organization should ensure:
			• The workforce is informed and trained on its roles and responsibilities. • Senior executives understand their roles and responsibilities. • Privacy personnel who are responsible for protecting the privacy and security of personal information meet adequate professional qualifications and have received needed training. • Third parties (e.g., service providers, customers, partners) understand their roles and responsibilities.
			Acknowledge and commit to comply with privacy protection policies Require employees to acknowledge and commit to comply with requirements written in the data privacy policies as part of the new employee onboarding process or annual policy review and acknowledgment protocol.
Privacy Impact Assessment and Risk Management (PIARM)	Personal data processing inventory and data flows	Understand the business processes via establishing and maintaining an up-to-date personal data processing inventory and data flows	**Definition of "personal information" and "sensitive personal information"** Formally define the term of "personal information" and "sensitive personal information" within the organization. In a situation that an organization is operating in more than one jurisdiction that have different definitions of "personal information (data)" and "sensitive personal information", the agreed definitions should be adequate and consistent to reflect all legal context.

Domain	Control Group	Control Objective	Control Set
	PIA Methodology and Integration	Establish and embed PIA into business processes and product development lifecycle (PDLC)	**Personal data processing inventory** A data processing inventory is the foundation of further privacy risk assessment and mitigation. An organization should establish and maintain an up-to-date data processing inventory as records of data processing. A data processing inventory usually includes elements such as name of business processes, types of personal information processed, purposes of processing, legal basis of processing, etc. **Personal data flows** A robust privacy protection program should cover end-to-end data flows to avoid missing any uncontrolled risks with respect to internal transferring of personal data. Establish and maintain up-to-date data flows among business processes and/or IT systems to reflect the actual personal data lifecycle. Note: Personal data should only be shared with relevant internal business processes or recipients for the purposes specified in the privacy notice. Personal data flow is also an effective vehicle to record internal personal data sharing activities. **PIA Methodology** Organizations should establish a consistent process for privacy impact assessment. The content of the personal information protection impact assessment shall include the following core aspects. Whether or not the personal information handling purpose, handling method, etc., are lawful, legitimate, and necessary; The influence on individuals' rights and interests, and the security risks; Whether protective measures undertaken are legal, effective, and suitable to the degree of risk. **Business Process Privacy Risk Management** Organizations should perform privacy impact assessments for existing business processes to assess and mitigate privacy and data protection risks. Organizations should ensure new initiatives or processes will take privacy risks into considerations at an early stage, for instance integrating PIA into project management practices, etc. **PDLC Privacy-by-Design** If the organization undertakes product or system development work that might involve personal data processing, the organization should integrate privacy-by-design into the PDLC phases such as requirement analysis, design, development, testing, deployment, and operations, etc.

(Continued)

TABLE 6.2   (Continued)

Domain	Control Group	Control Objective	Control Set
Privacy Operations	Privacy notice	Inform data subjects before or at the time when personal data is obtained	**Privacy notice required** Privacy notice should be provided before or at the time when personal data is obtained from data subjects (i.e., customers, employees). A privacy notice usually consists of the following sections (not an exhaustive list): • The identity and contact of the organization • Types of personal data will be collected and processed • The purposes and methods of data processing • How the personal data will be used and shared • How the personal data is being stored and data retention period • Cross-border transfer mechanisms • Security protection of the personal data • Data subjects' rights and the ways to exercise the rights
		Be transparent with the organization's data processing practices	**Appropriate manner of transparency** The privacy notice should be provided in an appropriate manner. The privacy notice must be concise, transparent, intelligible, and easily accessible. **The way privacy notice is delivered** Normally privacy notice should be in "writing" or by other means, including where appropriate, by "electronic means", where requested by the data subjects it may be provided orally.
		Provide accessibility to data subjects	**Accessibility** Privacy notice should be easy for data subjects to find and query any time. A mechanism should be provided for data subjects to easily download the privacy notice.
		Date the privacy notice	**Effective date** Assert the commitment to privacy by providing an effective date for privacy notice. Privacy notice should be provided with an effective date. Note: In addition to providing the effective date, it is also a common practice for organizations to provide a change log of their privacy notices or links to their previous versions of privacy notices.
		Update or notify data subjects of the changes of privacy notice or remind data subjects of its availability	**Changes of the privacy notices** If the privacy notice changes, data subjects should be informed with the updated privacy notice. The changes could result from various aspects such as the change of data types or processing purposes, etc. **Reminder of the availability of privacy notice** As required by some privacy regulations, data subjects should be reminded of the availability of its privacy notice, as well as how to obtain a copy of it on a regular basis.

Domain	Control Group	Control Objective	Control Set
	Lawful Basis and Consent	Ensure data processing activities are lawful	**Lawfulness of processing** All data processing activities should have proper legal basis. It is prohibited to handle personal information in misleading, swindling, coercive, or other such ways. No business units or individuals may illegally collect, use, process, or transmit other persons' personal information, or illegally sell, buy, provide, or disclose other persons' personal information, or engage in personal information handling activities harming national security or the public interest.
		Obtain data subject's consent if it is the lawful basis	**Obtainment of consent** If consent is the suitable lawful basis, an organization must obtain an individual's valid consent for the collection, use or disclosure of the individual's personal information. The individual's consent must be obtained at or before the time of the collection of the personal information. **Consent to changes** Data subjects must be notified of the privacy notice changes and consent should be re-obtained if necessary. If privacy notice changes, the organization should instruct data subjects to view the changes and re-obtain their consent if needed.
		Ensure the consent is valid	**Validity of Consent** Consent should be freely given, specific, informed, and unambiguous or explicit. Note: Silence, pre-ticked boxes or inactivity should not constitute consent. User inactivity within a long period of time cannot be regarded as consent. **Separate and explicit consent needed in certain circumstances** When processing personal data might pose substantial risk to data subjects, separate and explicit consent is needed for certain scenarios with examples listed as follows (NOT an exhaustive list). <ul><li>Data subjects are minors (need to obtain consent from parents): China—less than 14 years old; GDPR—less than 16 years old</li><li>Processing of special categories of data/sensitive personal data</li><li>Automated individual decision-making, including profiling</li><li>Direct marketing purposes</li><li>Sale of personal data</li><li>Image collection or personal identity recognition in public venues</li><li>Processing publicly available information that might pose substantial impact to the data subject</li><li>Involving data transfers to third countries</li><li>Etc.</li></ul>

(Continued)

TABLE 6.2   (Continued)

Domain	Control Group	Control Objective	Control Set
		Keep of the records and evidence of consent	**Records of consent** Where processing is based on consent, the data handler/controller shall be able to demonstrate that the data subject has consented to processing of his or her personal data. Consent choice should be recorded and show that who consented, when they consented, what they were told, how they consented, etc. Note: In some jurisdictions (i.e., United States, Canada), telemarketers are required to keep track of the "Do Not Call Registry".
		Ensure data subjects have the right and mechanisms to withdraw their consent	**Withdraw of Consent** Data subjects have the right to withdraw their consent at any time. The organization should provide the proper mechanisms for data subjects to withdraw their consent. The effort to withdraw consent is equal to that of providing consent. Organizations should cease collection, use and disclosure of personal data after data subjects withdraw their consent. Note: The withdrawal of consent should not affect the lawfulness of processing based on consent before its withdrawal.
	Data collection	Ensure data collection methods are lawful, fair, and transparent.	**Lawfulness of Collection** Collecting and processing personal data only with proper legal basis. Do not collect personal data that is prohibited by laws and regulations. **Fairness of Collection** Personal data should be collected in a fair way that does not involve behaviors such as intimidation, deceiving, or cheating, etc.
		Limit the collection only necessary to satisfy the corresponding purposes	**Purpose limitation** Personal data can only be collected for specified, explicit and legitimate purposes that articulated in the privacy notice. Personal data beyond the purposes cannot be collected.
		Data minimization	**Data minimization** Only collect data adequate, relevant, and limited to what is necessary in relation to the purposes for which they are processed.
		Ensure data collection from third parties complies with applicable laws	**Collection From Third Parties** The organization should undertake due diligence to ensure that third parties from whom personal information is collected are reliable sources and the collection is done fairly and lawfully. The organization needs to establish and implement proper controls (i.e., contractual obligation) to manage the risks of collecting (i.e., purchasing) data from third parties.

Domain	Control Group	Control Objective	Control Set
	Data use and maintain	Limit data use to the intended purposes only	**Data use purpose limitation** Only use personal data for the purposes specified in the privacy notice provided to the data subjects. If the collected data needs to be used for purposes not listed in the privacy notice, the controller either needs to conduct purpose compatibility test to ensure the new purposes are compatible with the informed purposes in the privacy notice, to re-obtain user consent before using them for new purposes and in new scenarios.
		Limit data access based on need-to-know principle	**User access and restrictions on display** Users' access to personal data should be granted based on need-to-know basis. Formal identity and access management policy, procedures should be put into place to manage personnel's access controls. Design and implement technical solutions to enforce and monitor the usage and processing of personal data. Where display of personal data on an interface (such as display screen and paper) is involved, the personal data Controller should take measures such as de-identification to process the to-be-displayed personal data, so as to reduce the risk of personal data leakage during the display. **System access** Access to systems functions or APIs should be authorized and monitored based on business needs. Establish policy for authorization to be evaluated and obtained before a system calls functions or APIs or performs operations on user data, such as reading content.
		Ensure the accuracy and integrity of personal data	**Accuracy and Integrity** Ensure personal data is accurate, relevant, up-to-date and complete.
		Log, monitor and audit personal data operations	**Operations Logging** Systems that collect and process personal data must log operators' personal data operations (i.e., access, change) to keep the audit trails that demonstrate how data is being accessed and used in the organization.
	Data Sharing and Transfer	Manage the risks of data sharing	**Necessity, Purpose and Legal Basis of data sharing and transfer** Unless otherwise specified in laws and regulations or authorized by the data subject, the organization should not make personal information public. The organization can only disclose personal information to a Third Party for the purposes specified in the privacy notice after the consent of the data subject is obtained. The organization should establish and execute the policy and processes to manage the necessity, purpose, legal basis of personal data sharing or transfer to external recipients.

(Continued)

TABLE 6.2   (Continued)

Domain	Control Group	Control Objective	Control Set
		Controller to processor data transfer: Ensure the data processor provides adequate protection to the personal data	**Data processor/entrusted personal management-pre-contract due diligence check** The organization should perform due diligence check from privacy protection perspective before selecting a service or product provider. Personal data is disclosed only to third parties who have the capability to protect personal data complying with applicable regulations, the organization's privacy protection policies and requirements. **Data processor/entrusted personal management-Data Processing Agreement (DPA)** A legally binding data processing agreement (DPA) should be established between the organization and the processor. The DPA can be a standalone document or part of the master agreement or contract. Usually, a DPA should cover the following components (not an exhaustive list). • Defined the data processing roles • Defined contract processing • Processing instructions • Sub-processor management • Security controls • Data breach notifications • Data Secrecy • Data subject request (DSR) handling obligations • Compliance demonstration support • Cross-border transfer • Termination of Service • Liability and indemnity **Data processor/entrusted personal management—Post-contract checks and monitoring** Company should establish processes to assess (i.e., go-live checks, audits) whether the processor has implemented effective control measures to meet terms of the DPA and the processor is able to continue to meet terms of the DPA. **Data processor/entrusted personal management— Termination of contract** When the entrustment relationship is terminated, the organization should put in place a formal transition-out process to ensure the data processor can no longer access the personal data such as data deletion and access de-provisioning, etc.
		Agree on the rights and obligations of each controller	**Controller to controller data transfer** Two data controllers (i.e., joint-controllers or two independent controllers) should establish an agreement to set forth the rights and obligations of each controller. The agreement should not influence an individual's rights to demand any one personal information controller perform under this Law's provisions.

Domain	Control Group	Control Objective	Control Set
		The accountabilities and duties of data protection should be carried on	**Data Transfer due to mergers, acquisitions or dissolutions** Personal information controllers shall, where it is necessary to transfer personal information due to mergers, separations, dissolution, declaration of bankruptcy, and other such reasons, notify individuals about the receiving party's name or personal name and contact method. The receiving party shall continue to fulfill the personal information handler's duties. Where the receiving side changes the original processing purposes or methods, they shall notify the individual again.
	Data cross-border transfers and data localization	Implement proper cross-border data transfer mechanism	**Cross-border data transfer mechanism** Cross-border data transfer obligations are subject to the law of the country or region where the business is carried out. Establish proper cross-border data transfer strategy and mechanism (i.e., Standard Contractual Clauses, BCR) based on the regulatory requirements and business needs. Based on the defined cross-border data transfer mechanism, the IT systems usually need to be designed in the way (i.e., location of datacenters and servers) in alignment with the cross-border transfer mechanisms. Personal data processing operations (i.e., staffing, and technical support operations) also need to align with defined cross-border data transfer mechanism.
		Comply with data localization obligations within each jurisdiction	**Data Localization** Identify and document the data localization obligations for the jurisdictions that the organization is operating in. Design and implement IT systems that satisfy the data localization requirements. Note: the PIPL Article 40 requires that "Critical information infrastructure operators and personal information handlers handling personal information reaching quantities provided by the State cybersecurity and informatization department shall store personal information collected and produced within the borders of the People's Republic of China domestically. Where they need to provide it abroad, they shall pass a security assessment organized by the State cybersecurity and informatization department; where laws or administrative regulations and State cybersecurity and informatization department provisions permit that security assessment is not conducted, those provisions are to be followed."
	Data retention and depersonalization	Only retain personal data required for fulfilling the intended purposes	**Data retention schedule** The organization should establish a data retention schedule that aligns with applicable laws and regulations within each jurisdiction in which an organization operates. Retain personal data only within the time frame needed for reasonable business purposes. Note: Personal data shall not be kept or archived indefinitely "just in case", or if there is only a small possibility that it will be used. The retention period also shall not be shorter than the applicable statutory minimum retention period.

(Continued)

TABLE 6.2   (Continued)

Domain	Control Group	Control Objective	Control Set
		Secure de-identify or delete personal information	**Data depersonalization** The organization needs to execute the data retention schedule to de-identify or delete personal data after it reaches the retention period, or the data is no longer necessary for the purposes for which the personal data are processed Note: A good data retention and depersonalization program can also help to prevent personal data loss, theft, abuse, or unauthorized access, etc.
		Manage privacy risks when discontinuing business operations	**Privacy risks associated with discontinuance of operation by data controllers** The data controllers shall, in the case of discontinuance of operation of a product or service that processes personal information, implement controls to manage privacy-related risks (not an exhaustive list). a) Stop collecting personal data in a timely fashion. b) Notify data subjects of the discontinuance of operation by sending a notice to each of them or through a public notice. c) Delete or anonymize the personal data they hold.
		Comply with legal hold and eDiscovery obligations	**Legal hold and eDiscovery** Legal hold and eDiscovery obligations should be considered and integrated into the data retention and depersonalization program, schedule, and process.
	Security protection of personal data	Classify and categorize personal data to get proper protection	**Data classification and Categorization** Personal information shall be properly identified, categorized, and classified considering factors such as legal implications, nature and purpose, sensitivity, criticality to business operations, and potential impact to data subjects if disclosed to unauthorized personnel. Organizations should establish an appropriate data classification scheme to facilitate the data classification.
		Implement proper and reasonable security technical and organizational measures	**Security Technical and Organizational Measures (TOMs)** Organizations shall implement appropriate technical and organizational measures using a risk-based approach to ensure the confidentiality, integrity, availability, and resilience of personal data based on the data classification scheme. Typical security measures might include the following controls (not an exhaustive list). • Information security policies • Organization of information security • Human resource security • Asset management • Access control • Cryptography • Physical and environmental security • Operations security • Communications security • System acquisition, development, and maintenance • Supplier relationships • Information security incident management • Information security aspects of business continuity management • Compliance

Domain	Control Group	Control Objective	Control Set
	Data Subject Rights Assurance	Ensure service or product equipped with capability to fulfill data subject rights	**Data subject rights assurance** Organizations should design the services, products or processes that are equipped with the capability to fulfill data subject rights.
Request, Complaint and Data Breach Handling	DSR request handling	Respond to data subject right requests in a timely manner	**DSR Requests Handling** Organizations should establish and operationalize a process to handle data subject right requests from external and internal data subjects. Usually, the process covers the considerations such as intake triage, identity verification, fulfill the requests, response to data subjects, case closure, etc.
	Complaint and Dispute handling	Address privacy-related Inquiries, Complaints, and Disputes from internal and external stakeholders properly	**Internal Whistleblowing process** Organizations should establish a process to address privacy-related inquiries, complaints, and disputes from internal and external stakeholders. Organizations need to appoint designated contact in handling complaints or inquires. Organizations should incorporate lessons learned from problematic data actions. **Dispute and Lawsuit Handling** Organizations should establish a process to address privacy-related inquiries, complaints, and disputes from internal and external stakeholders. Organizations need to appoint designated contact in handling complaints or inquires. Organizations should incorporate lessons learned from problematic data actions. **Privileged information Protection** Organizations should always protect privileged information such as attorney-client privilege etc. during the communication with both internal and external personnel.
	Data breach handling	Handle data breaches properly to minimize the impact	**Data breach handling process** Organizations should establish a consistent data breach handling process that includes the handling requirements, procedure, responsibilities throughout various phases such as preparation, detection, investigation and triage, containment, eradication and recovery, reporting, improvements, etc. Different jurisdictions may pose very different legal obligations to organizations with respect to data breach reporting to data protection authorities and data subjects. The organization should identify, document, and maintain corresponding requirements in each jurisdiction in which the organization operates. When it is required to notify either the data protection authorities or data subjects, usually the organization should include the following content (not an exhaustive list). • The types of personal data impacted, causes, and possible harm caused by the leak, distortion, or loss that occurred or might have occurred. • The mitigation measures taken by the personal information handler and measures individuals can adopt to mitigate harm. • Contact method of the personal information handler.

(Continued)

TABLE 6.2 (Continued)

Domain	Control Group	Control Objective	Control Set
			Data breach drills Organizations should conduct regular data breach drills to evaluate the effectiveness of data breach handling process and make updates and improvements accordingly.
	Data Protection Authority (DPA) Cooperation	Identify concerned DPAs in applicable jurisdictions	**Identification of concerned DPAs and their guidelines** Organizations should identify concerned data protection authorities (DPAs) in applicable jurisdictions and document the contact information. Also, organizations should monitor and follow the guidelines published by DPAs. Note: DPAs may have different powers (i.e., investigative powers, corrective powers, authorization, and advisory powers) in different jurisdictions.
		Establish an internal procedure to guide cooperation with DPAs	**Cooperation with DPAs** Organizations should establish and implement an internal procedure with respect to response to DPAs' inquiries and/or investigations. The procedure may include setting up a contact point (i.e., liaison) and protocols of proper interactions with the DPAs. Note: some organization may also build ongoing communication channels with DPAs.
Measurement and Improvement	Privacy program measurement	Evaluate the effectiveness of the privacy program	**Privacy program measurement** The effectiveness of the privacy program and controls should be monitored and assessed via methods such as setting the privacy metrics, etc. to guide the improvement. Note: Some organizations may also evaluate the privacy program using maturity level models (i.e., Initial/Ad hoc, Developing, Defined, Managed and Measured, Optimized)
	Privacy-related audits and assessments	Plan and execute privacy-related audits and assessments activities	**Administrative process** Privacy-related audits and assessments should be properly planned (i.e., scheduled), executed and managed. Audits and assessments may include internal driven or external driven (i.e., certifications, attestations) effort. Note: Organizations may integrate privacy-related audits and assessments into the enterprise schedule.
		Manage and close the identified findings	**Findings and gaps** Findings and gaps from the audits and assessments should be formally documented, solutioned, and prioritized. The proposed mitigating controls should be resourced, implemented, and monitored throughout the risk mitigation process.
	Privacy risk and compliance management review	Review the overall privacy and data protection compliance stance and undertake improvements	**Privacy risk and compliance management review** The organization's Senior Leadership Team (SLT) should be presented, on a regular basis (i.e., once a year), with the privacy program compliance status report, perform management review of the posture and risks, and provide guidance and resource for the improvement. If problems are identified, remediation plans are developed and implemented.

7 Privacy Program Assessment and Roadmap

This chapter is intended to help readers undertake a holistic approach to assess the privacy compliance gap, propose actionable solutions, and formulate a sound and feasible privacy implementation plan and roadmap.

This chapter covers the following topics:

- *Key tenets of implementing a privacy program*
- *A phased approach to implementation*
- *Maturity assessment and gap initiatives*
- *Privacy program roadmap*

7.1 KEY TENETS

It is not easy to establish a unified, enterprise-wide privacy framework. It is much harder to implement and operationalize one. The following tenets focus on the impetus for the privacy program's creation, establishment, and operations to enable business growth and the values enshrined in privacy laws.

It is beyond just compliance.

Accountability is not merely a tick-the-box exercise. Instead of reactively checking the compliance boxes based on a set of governing laws, develop a privacy framework that proactively anticipates while staying within the scope of the needs of your organization.

You need to consider how to demonstrate your accountability dependent on your circumstances. Privacy needs to be part of the planning of any new or updated product, service, system, or process. Privacy considerations should help drive the design rather than being bolted on at the end to address a few privacy risks.

The Privacy by Design approach is characterized by proactive rather than reactive measures. It anticipates and prevents privacy-invasive events before they happen. PbD does not wait for privacy risks to materialize, nor does it offer remedies for resolving privacy infractions once they have occurred. It aims to prevent them from occurring. In short, Privacy by Design comes before the fact, not after.

Privacy is dynamic. Fit privacy to your organization.

Respect the data protection and privacy rights of customers and employees by avoiding unnecessary or unjustified data processing activities. Design and implement privacy controls that strike the best balance between meeting regulatory obligations and minimizing operational disruption. Be selective with metrics. Choose to implement only metrics that are relevant to the business context. Make understanding compliance requirements as easy as possible for stakeholders and avoid using jargon whenever possible.

Design flexible depersonalization governance processes and solutions to address volatile legal and business environments. Take a process vs. system-based approach to assessing personal data as it flows throughout the organization. Evaluate our state of compliance on an ongoing basis and iterate as needed to ensure our posture accurately reflects the business' defined risk tolerance.

Privacy doesn't live in isolation. Make it operational.

Contextualize privacy for your organization by involving the business units from day one. By assigning ownership and flexibility to business units in how they weave privacy into their day-to-day, privacy becomes part of operational design and structure. Review, revise, and reprioritize.

DOI: 10.1201/9781003225089-9

Speaking the same language: Sell privacy to the business by speaking a language they understand. IT and InfoSec leaders need to see privacy as more than just compliance, but as a driver of business efficiency. Sell privacy to the business by speaking a language they understand. IT and InfoSec leaders need to see privacy as more than just compliance, as a driver of business efficiency.

A good privacy program takes time.

It is important to understand that privacy compliance is an ongoing effort. Leverage the iterative process embedded in each phase to prioritize privacy initiatives based on value and risk and support the rollout through customized metrics.

7.2   A PHASED APPROACH

Due to the restraints of resources, it is reasonable for organizations to execute privacy initiatives using a phased approach.

In general, there are five basic steps in developing and operating a solid privacy program.

- The first step is to answer fundamental questions, such as why you need a privacy program, who is responsible for which privacy activities, the scope of data processing activities, etc.
- The second step is to understand your privacy program status and where you want to be, basically the gap. You need to know what personal data you collect and for what purposes, etc., and perform a thorough gap assessment to provide you with the visibility which will guide your strategy and priorities.
- The third step is to design and prioritize privacy controls. Organizations need to propose privacy controls based on the gap analysis, prioritize privacy controls based on cost, effort, risk, and business alignment, set dates for the launch and execution of privacy initiatives, and assign ownership for initiatives.
- The fourth step is to implement and operationalize the privacy controls proposed.
- Last but not least, organizations need to measure the effectiveness of the privacy controls and make continuous improvements.

Table 7.1 illustrates some of the main phases of establishing a privacy program.

TABLE 7.1

Main Phases of Establishing a Privacy Program

Phase	Activities
Phase 1 Understand your environment	1. Collect legal obligations (i.e., laws, regulations, etc.)
	2. Collect contractual requirements
	3. Determine which industry standard to comply with
	4. Understand privacy program accountability and responsibilities
	5. Define the scope data processing activities
Phase 2 Conduct a gap analysis	6. Perform PIA and identify privacy risks or compliance gap
Phase 3 Design and prioritize privacy controls	7. Design privacy controls based on the gap analysis
	8. Prioritize privacy controls based on cost, effort, risk, and business alignment
	9. Set firm dates for launch and execution of privacy initiatives
	10. Assign ownership for initiatives
Phase 4 Implement and operationalize	11. Implement and operationalize the privacy controls proposed
Phase 5 Measure and improve	12. Establish a set of metrics for the Data Privacy Program
	13. Conduct internal and/or external audits if necessary
	14. Achieve privacy and security certification if necessary
	15. Submit the DPO report to the executive team as planned

7.3 MATURITY ASSESSMENT AND GAP INITIATIVES

Privacy Maturity Models (PMM) are recognized methods by which organizations can systematically measure their progress against established privacy benchmarks. The PMM provides entities with a useful and effective means of assessing their privacy program against a recognized maturity model and has the added advantage of identifying the next steps required to move the privacy program ahead. The PMM can also measure progress against both internal and external benchmarks. Further, it can be used to measure the progress of both specific projects and the entity's overall privacy initiative.

The PMM can be used to provide:

- Agreement on the Privacy Maturity assessment criteria
- The status of privacy initiatives and maturity of the entity's privacy program
- A comparison of the organization's privacy program among business or geographical units, or the enterprise as a whole
- Assessment over time and the progress made

This book's privacy maturity model is based on the Capability Maturity Model (CMM) which serves the foundation for many other maturity models across the globe. The PMM uses five maturity levels as follows.

In developing the PMM, each organization's personal information privacy practices may be at various levels, whether due to legislative requirements, corporate policies, or the status of the organization's privacy-related initiatives. Also, based on an organization's approach to risk, not all privacy initiatives would need to reach the highest level on the maturity model.

Table 7.3 summarizes the PMM assessment domains and control groups.

TABLE 7.2
Definition of Privacy Maturity Models (PMMs)

	PMM Level	Description
1	Ad hoc	Privacy program and activities are reactive. Lack of awareness and governance. Lacking strategic vision, the program is less effective and less responsive to the needs of the business.
2	Developing	Procedures or processes are generally informal, incomplete, and inconsistently applied. The privacy program tends to rely on the talents of individuals. A plan is in place and in the process of execution.
3	Defined	Policies, procedures, and processes are fully documented and implemented and cover all relevant aspects.
4	Quantitatively Managed	Robust privacy program governance and metrics management processes are in place. Reviews are conducted to assess the effectiveness of the controls and drive privacy and data protection decisions.
5	Optimized	Individual data protection controls are optimized using key performance indicators (KPIs) that continually measure service effectiveness and efficiency. Regular review and feedback are used to ensure continuous improvement towards optimization of the given process. Automation is used to drive the efficiency of the processes.

TABLE 7.3
PMM Assessment Domains and Control Groups

Domain	Control Group	Control Objective
Privacy Mandate and Business Alignment	Regulatory Obligations	Comply with applicable laws and regulations
	Contractual Requirements	Fulfill contractual requirements
	Business Alignment	Align privacy and data protection program with business strategies and policies and enable business growth
	Industry Standards and Best Practices	Adherence to selected industry standards and frameworks

(Continued)

TABLE 7.3   (Continued)

Domain	Control Group	Control Objective
Governance, Policies and Awareness	Privacy governance charter	Establish right-sized privacy governance structure and set forth enterprise-wide principles and requirements for privacy and data protection practices
	Key roles and responsibilities	Streamline and align with privacy program activities, roles and responsibilities among business stakeholders
		Agree on collaborative responsibilities across the organization
	Policies and Procedures	Establish privacy and data protection policies and procedures
	Privacy awareness and training	Establish privacy protection culture and promote awareness program across the enterprise
Privacy Impact Assessment and Risk Management (PIARM)	Personal data processing inventory and data flows	Understand the business processes via establishing and maintaining an update-to-date personal data processing inventory and data flows
	PIA Methodology and Integration	Establish and embed PIA into business processes and product development lifecycle (PDLC)
Privacy Operations	Privacy notice	Inform data subjects before or at the time when personal data is obtained
		Be transparent with organization's data processing practices
		Provide accessibility to data subjects
		Date the privacy notice
		Update or notify data subjects of the changes of privacy notice or remind data subjects of its availability
	Lawful Basis and Consent	Ensure data processing activities are lawful
		Obtain data subject's consent if it is the lawful basis
		Ensure the consent is valid
		Keep of the records and evidence of consent
		Ensure data subjects have the right and mechanisms to withdraw their consent
	Data collection	Ensure data collection methods are lawful, fair, and transparent
		Limit the collection only necessary to satisfy the corresponding purposes
		Data minimization
		Ensure data collection from third parties comply with applicable laws
	Data use and maintain	Limit data use to the intended purposes only
		Limit data access based on need-to-know principle
		Ensure the accuracy and integrity of personal data
		Log, monitor, and audit personal data operations
	Data Sharing and Transfer	Manage the risks of data sharing
		Controller to processor data transfer: Ensure the data processor provide adequate protection to the personal data
		Agree on the rights and obligations of each controller
		The accountabilities and duties of data protection should be carried on
	Data cross-border transfers and data localization	Implement proper cross-border data transfer mechanism
		Comply with data localization obligations within each jurisdiction
	Data retention and depersonalization	Only retain personal data required for fulfilling the intended purposes
		Secure de-identify or delete personal information
		Manage privacy risks when discontinuing business operations
		Comply with legal hold and eDiscovery obligations
	Security protection of personal data	Classify and categorize personal data to get proper protection
		Implement proper and reasonable security technical and organizational measures
	Data Subject Rights Assurance	Ensure service or product equipped with capability to fulfill data subject rights

Domain	Control Group	Control Objective
Request, Complaint and Data Breach Handling	DSR request handling	Respond to data subject right requests in a timely manner
	Complaint and dispute handling	Address privacy-related inquiries, complaints, and disputes from internal and external stakeholders properly
	Data breach handling	Handle data breaches properly to minimize the impact
	Data Protection Authority (DPA) Cooperation	Identify concerned DPAs in applicable jurisdictions
		Establish an internal procedure to guide cooperation with DPAs
Measurement and Improvement	Privacy program measurement	Evaluate the effectiveness of the privacy program
	Privacy-related audits and assessments	Plan and execute privacy-related audits and assessments activities
		Manage and close the identified findings
	Privacy risk and compliance management review	Review the overall privacy and data protection compliance stance and undertake improvements

TABLE 7.4

Examples of High-Level Assessment Results

	Current Maturity Level	Target Maturity Level	Highest Level
Privacy Mandate and Business Alignment	1.5	4	5
Governance, Policies and Awareness	1	4	5
Privacy Impact Assessment and Risk Management (PIARM)	2	4	5
Privacy Operations	1.5	4	5
Request, Complaint, and Data Breach Handling	2	4	5
Request, Complaint, and Data Breach Handling	2	4	5
Measurement and Improvement	1.5	4	5

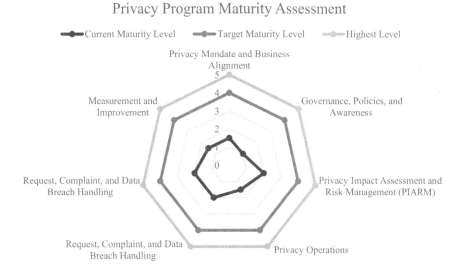

FIGURE 7.1   Privacy program maturity assessment chart.

Based on the maturity assessment, an organization can generate a dashboard and provides its senior leadership team with the level of information the leaders need to make privacy and data protection decisions as shown in Tables 7.4 and 7.5 and Figures 7.1 and 7.2.

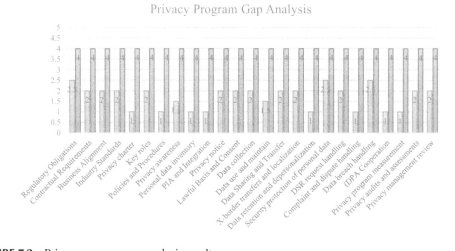

FIGURE 7.2   Privacy program gap analysis results.

TABLE 7.5
Examples of Detailed Assessment Results

Control Group	Current Maturity Level	Target Maturity Level
Regulatory Obligations	2.5	4
Contractual Requirements	2	4
Business Alignment	2	4
Industry Standards	2	4
Privacy charter	1	4
Key roles	2	4
Policies and Procedures	1	4
Privacy awareness	1.5	4
Personal data inventory	1	4
PIA and Integration	1	4
Privacy notice	2	4
Lawful Basis and Consent	2	4
Data collection	2	4
Data use and maintain	1.5	4
Data Sharing and Transfer	2	4
X-border transfers and localization	2	4
Data retention and depersonalization	1	4
Security protection of personal data	2.5	4
DSR request handling	2	4
Complaint and dispute handling	1	4
Data breach handling	2.5	4
DPA Cooperation	1	4
Privacy program measurement	1	4
Privacy audits and assessments	2	4
Privacy management review	2	4

7.4   PRIVACY PROGRAM ROADMAP

After identifying all the gap initiatives mentioned previously, you need to prioritize those initiatives and build an actionable roadmap to set coherent goals for where your organization wishes to get to with its privacy practices. A privacy roadmap lays out the goals of the organization's privacy program and how it will accomplish those goals. These goals will work well if they are coupled with objectives that are targeted and make sense in the context of the agency's overall privacy stance and risk profile rather than being generic or overly broad.

A privacy roadmap should

- be aligned with the organization's overall strategy
- state privacy goals to promote a privacy culture and improve privacy practices within the organization
- be owned by a member of the senior leadership team
- identify key stakeholders
- the initiatives should be prioritized and planned by all stakeholders in a collaborative manner based on cost, effort, risk, and business alignment
- set dates for launch and execution of privacy initiatives
- be reviewed, revised, and reprioritized accordingly to reflect the latest developments

There are many ways to prioritize gap initiatives. In general, the following aspects should be considered:

- Level of alignment with business: how these initiatives support the business strategy and goals
- Level urgency: how soon an initiative should be completed
- Estimated cost and effort: the level of initial and ongoing cost and effort to complete the initiatives
- Status: what is the current progress in terms of implementing the initiatives
- Leadership engagement: whether a particular initiative needs leadership approval etc.

Table 7.6 illustrates some factors that can be used to prioritize privacy initiatives.

TABLE 7.6
Examples of Prioritization Factors

#	Initiatives	Alignment with Business	Urgency	Estimated Cost and Effort	Status	Leadership Engagement
1	Finalize the privacy program governance structure and define the key roles and responsibilities	High	High	Low	Working In Progress	Yes
2	Embed privacy requirement language of the contracts	High	Medium	Medium	Almost Done	No
3	Establish a standard guide for implementing PET solutions	Medium	Low	High	Not Started	No

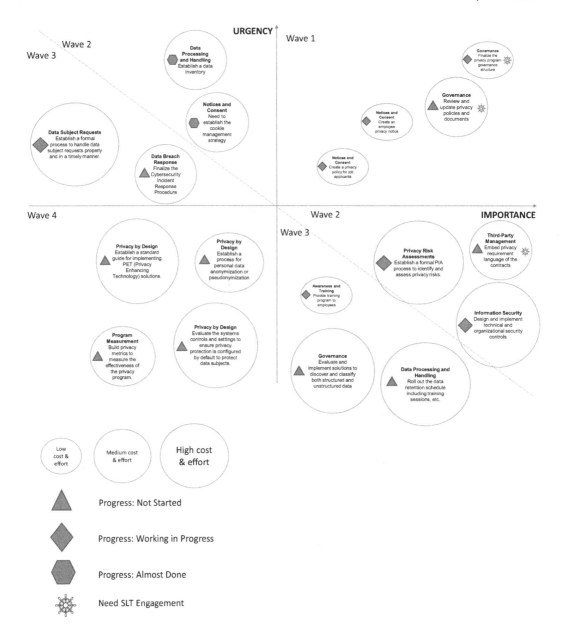

FIGURE 7.3   Privacy effort prioritization map.

Figure 7.3 illustrates the prioritization map based on the input from Table 7.6.

Figure 7.4 provides an example of a privacy program roadmap with various phases, initiatives, and timetable of execution.

Figure 7.5 provides an example of a privacy program plan based on the previous roadmap with owners defined for each initiative.

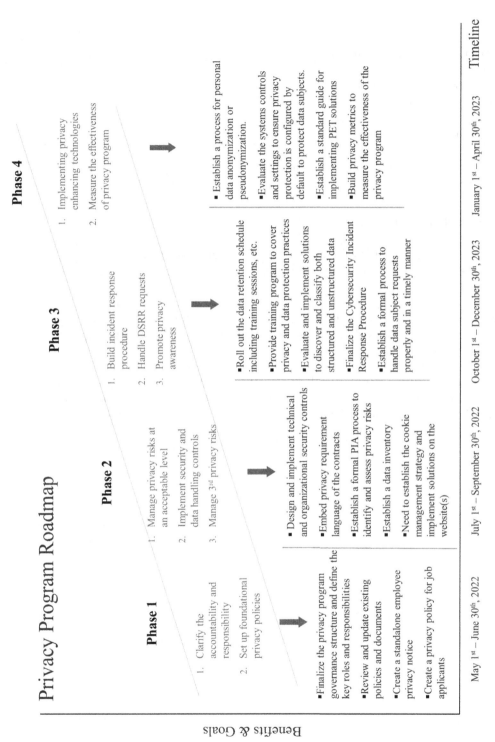

FIGURE 7.4 Privacy effort roadmap.

Privacy Program Roadmap

Phase 1

1. Clarify the accountability and responsibility
2. Set up foundational privacy policies

- Finalize the privacy program governance structure and define the key roles and responsibilities
- Review and update existing policies and documents
- Create a standalone employee privacy notice
- Create a privacy policy for job applicants

May 1st – June 30th, 2022

Phase 2

1. Manage privacy risks at an acceptable level
2. Implement security and data handling controls
3. Manage 3rd privacy risks

- Design and implement technical and organizational security controls
- Embed privacy requirement language of the contracts
- Establish a formal PIA process to identify and assess privacy risks
- Establish a data inventory
- Need to establish the cookie management strategy and implement solutions on the website(s)

July 1st – September 30th, 2022

Phase 3

1. Build incident response procedure
2. Handle DSRR requests
3. Promote privacy awareness

- Roll out the data retention schedule including training sessions, etc.
- Provide training program to cover privacy and data protection practices
- Evaluate and implement solutions to discover and classify both structured and unstructured data
- Finalize the Cybersecurity Incident Response Procedure
- Establish a formal process to handle data subject requests properly and in a timely manner

October 1st – December 30th, 2023

Phase 4

1. Implementing privacy enhancing technologies
2. Measure the effectiveness of privacy program

- Establish a process for personal data anonymization or pseudonymization.
- Evaluate the systems controls and settings to ensure privacy protection is configured by default to protect data subjects.
- Establish a standard guide for implementing PET solutions
- Build privacy metrics to measure the effectiveness of the privacy program

January 1st – April 30th, 2023

Timeline

Benefits & Goals

Initiative	Owner	2022												2023			
		J	F	M	A	M	J	J	A	S	O	N	D	J	F	M	A
Build privacy program governance structure	John Smith					██	██										
Define the roles and responsibilities	Harry Hughes	██	██	██	██	██		██	██	██	██	██	██	██	██	██	██
Establish a data inventory	Ron Dias								██	██	██						
Embed privacy requirement language of the contracts	Sarah Granger		██	██	██	██	██	██	██	██				██	██	██	██
Establish DSR procedure	Peter Jones													██	██	██	██

FIGURE 7.5   Privacy program implementation plan.

Guide and Recommendations

Organizations that utilize Info-Tech's privacy program framework can generate a gap analysis chart as shown in Figure 7.6 to demonstrate the maturity assessment gaps for their privacy programs.

In addition to the gap analysis tool, Info-Tech also provides a holistic approach, as shown in Table 7.7, to help organizations prioritize gap initiatives based on various factors such as initial cost, ongoing cost, initial staffing, ongoing staffing, alignment with business, and privacy risk reduction.

Info-Tech also established a cost and effort estimates tool to provide estimation of the cost and effort associated with implementing and maintaining a privacy program as shown in Table 7.8, which can help organizations to calculate and communicate the financial aspects with key stakeholders.

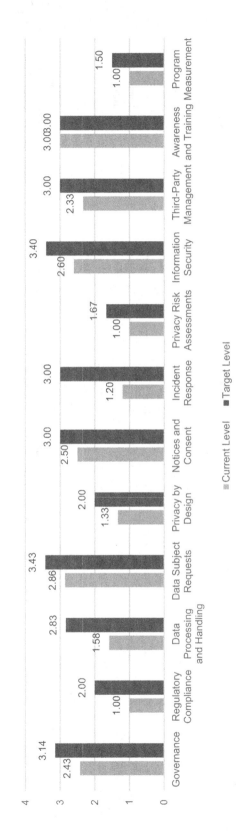

FIGURE 7.6 Info-Tech's Gap Analysis Tool

TABLE 7.7
Info-Tech's Gap Initiative Prioritization Approach

Cost and Benefit to Your Organization on Average

		Manufacturing Example	Retail Example	Healthcare Example	Financial Services Example
Initial Cost	High	>$50,000	>$100,000	>$50,000	>$100,000
	Medium	$3,000-$50,000	$10,000-$100,000	$7,500-$50,000	$10,000-$100,000
	Low	<$3,000	<$10,000	<$7,500	<$10,000
	Zero	$ -	$ -	$ -	$ -
Ongoing Cost (Annual)	High	>$10,000	>$20,000	>$10,000	>$50,000
	Medium	$600-$10,000	$2,000-$20,000	$1,500-$10,000	$5,000-$50,000
	Low	<$600	<$2,000	<$1,500	<$5,000
	Zero	$ -	$ -	$ -	$ -
Initial Staffing in Hours	High	>160 Hours	>40 Hours	>24 Hours	>240 Hours
	Medium	40-160 Hours	8-40 Hours	8-24 Hours	80-240 Hours
	Low	<40 Hours	<8 Hours	<8 Hours	<80 Hours
	Zero	0 Hours	0 Hours	0 Hours	0 Hours
Ongoing Staffing (Hours/Week)	High	>20 Hours	>8 Hours	>4 Hours	>20 Hours
	Medium	2-20 Hours	2-8 Hours	2-4 Hours	2-20 Hours
	Low	<2 Hours	<2 Hours	<2 Hours	<2 Hours
	Zero	0 Hours	0 Hours	0 Hours	0 Hours
Alignment With Business	High	Required by key contract	Directly supports audit requirement or key contract	Directly supports patient requirements or availability	Directly addresses a regulatory or prior audit requirement, or directly supports key corporate strategy (such as benefitting member experience).
	Medium	Indirectly supports key contract, or directly supports corporate/IT strategy	Indirectly supports audit requirement, key contract, or corporate/IT strategy	Indirectly supports patient requirement or business impact initiative	Indirectly supports regulatory/audit or directly supports key contract or corporate/IT strategy.
	Low	Other	Other	Other	Other
Privacy Risk Reduction	High	Directly improves customer, compliance, or legal risk	Causing regulatory consequences of >$100,000	Directly reduces patient or compliance risk (i.e. directly reduces possibility of a breach)	Directly reduces compliance risk (i.e. directly reduces possibility of a breach)
	Medium	Indirectly improves customer, compliance, or legal risk	Causing regulatory consequences of $20,000-$100,000	Implements nonexistent control	Implements nonexistent control
	Low	Foundational compliance control/visibility improvement	Causing regulatory consequences of <$20,000	Foundational privacy best practice	Foundational privacy best practice

TABLE 7.8
Info-Tech's Cost Estimation Tool

| Wave | Count of planned initiatives | INITIAL IMPLEMENTATION | | ONGOING ANNUAL | | ROUGH 4-YEAR TOTAL | |
		Total wave COST ($)	Total wave EFFORT (FTE)	Total wave COST ($)	Total wave EFFORT (FTE)	Total wave COST ($)	Total wave EFFORT (FTE)
0	2	$ 200,000.00	0.96	$ 15,500.00	0.05	$ 254,250.00	1.14
1	14	$ 87,500.00	2.28	$ 96,500.00	0.99	$ 425,250.00	5.70
2	12	$ 155,000.00	1.66	$ 31,000.00	1.22	$ 263,500.00	5.94
3	6	$ 5,000.00	1.66	$ -	1.20	$ 5,000.00	5.85
4	4	$ 77,500.00	0.36	$ -	0.16	$ 77,500.00	0.91
Total	38	$ 525,000.00	6.92	$ 143,000.00	3.61	$ 1,025,500.00	19.53

8 Privacy Program Management Metrics and Tools

This chapter is intended to help readers establish and operate a data protection metrics program and understand the current landscape and features of privacy program management tools.

This chapter covers the following topics:

- *Privacy program metrics*
- *Privacy audits and assessments*
- *Annual report and management review*
- *Privacy program management tools*

8.1 MEASUREMENT AND IMPROVEMENT

Program measurement helps to gauge the efficacy of privacy procedures, demonstrate compliance, increase privacy awareness, reveal gaps, and provide a basis for any improvements to the privacy program. Effective program measurement provides confidence to an organization's senior leaders and other important stakeholders that the expected privacy outcomes and benefits are being achieved.

8.1.1 PRIVACY PROGRAM METRICS

The effectiveness of the privacy program and controls should be monitored and assessed via methods such as setting the privacy metrics, etc. to guide the improvement. Some organizations may also evaluate the privacy program using maturity level models (i.e., Ad hoc, Developing, Defined, Managed, Optimized).

Metrics are a useful tool to communicate the current state of an organization's privacy practices and the effectiveness of its privacy program. Effective metrics add value by reflecting the current business environment and forecasting for the future. Metrics can facilitate discussions with senior leaders, other business units and stakeholders. Using metrics can also advance the maturity of an organization's privacy program and operations.

There are different metrics for different audiences based on their level of interest, influence, and responsibility. An organization will need to consider what metrics will best facilitate the achievement of their desired privacy goals and outcomes. Metrics can be used in the following aspects:

- Trending
- Privacy program return on investment (ROI)
- Privacy program maturity level
- Resource utilization

General principles for setting up metrics

- **Establish the connection:** Align with enterprise strategy and goals and be reflective of the relevant indicators. Select metrics that make sense for the group you're reporting up to and ensure that the metrics are business-relevant and support strategic initiatives and the direction of the organization. You can also use privacy metrics to gain buy-in for your privacy program.

DOI: 10.1201/9781003225089-10

- **Focus on your own organization:** Don't focus on industry benchmarks for privacy. Your privacy requirements will be unique and continue to evolve over time. Be selective with your own metrics. Choose to implement only metrics that are relevant to your environment.
- **Repeatable and integration:** A good metric is easy to understand and repeatable. Use the language of your business unit champions as you create a metrics program that they can understand and integrate.
- **Make it operational:** Metrics take your privacy program from static documentation to a functional operation. Ensure that each task populated within the privacy program roadmap is supported by corresponding metrics.

Examples of privacy program metrics

Table 8.1 illustrates some examples of privacy program metrics.

If you want to make the metrics operational, you also need to define some of the key attributes to each of the KPIs, such as the audience, frequency, KPI target, owner, source, etc. as shown in the following example in Table 8.2.

TABLE 8.1
Examples of Privacy Program Metrics

Privacy Domain	Privacy KPI
Privacy Notice and Consent	% of data collection processes that don't provide privacy notices
	% of data collection processes that reply on consent don't obtain valid consent
Data Subject Requests	Number of data subject requests received (monthly, quarterly, yearly)
	Number of DSRs un-responded vs. responded
	Number of different types of DSRs (i.e., access, aectication, deletion)
	% of DSRs responded within the required timeframe
	Average days to fulfill DSRs
Privacy Risk Assessments & Privacy by Design	% of projects that include PIA and PbD during planning phase
	% of processes within the organization that include PIA and PbD
	Number of risks identifed but not mitigated
Data Breach Response	Average cost of a data breach
	Number of data breaches tracked (origin, org. unit, project, security level)
	Mean time to resolve the data breach response cases
Third-Party Management	% of data processing agreements in place for external vendors
	% high-risk vendors in full compliance
Awareness and Training	% of staff completed privacy training
	Avg. privacy training score for key roles
	% of privacy personnel with privacy certification

TABLE 8.2
Metrics Implementation Considerations

Privacy Domain	Privacy KPI	KPI Target	Audience	Frequency	Owner	Source
Privacy Notice and Consent	% of data collection processes that don't provide privacy notices	0%	ELT team	Quarterly	Privacy Officer	Audits on external-facing websites and products
	% of data collection processes that rely on consent don't obtain valid consent	0%	ELT team	Monthly	Privacy Officer	Audits on external-facing websites and products

Privacy Domain	Privacy KPI	KPI Target	Audience	Frequency	Owner	Source
Data Subject Requests_	Number of data subject requests received	-	ELT team	Bi-weekly	Privacy Officer	Web portal and DSAR handling system
	Number of DSRs un-responded vs. responded	0 un-responded 100 responded	ELT team	Bi-weekly	Privacy Officer	Web portal and DSAR handling system
	% of DSRs responded within the required timeframe	100%	ELT team	Bi-weekly	Privacy Officer	Web portal and DSAR handling system
	Average days to fulfill DSRs	Maximum 30 days	ELT team	Bi-weekly	Privacy Officer	Web portal and DSAR handling system
Privacy Risk Assessments & Privacy by Design_	% of projects that include PIA and PbD during the planning phase	100%	ELT team	Per project	Privacy Officer, Business Managers	Privacy program management system
	% of processes within the organization that include PIA and PbD	100%	ELT team	Per department	Privacy Officer, Business Managers	Privacy program management system
	Number of risks identified but not mitigated	0	ELT team	Per PIA	Privacy Officer, Business Managers	Privacy program management system
Data Breach Response_	The average cost of a data breach	-	ELT team	Quarterly	Privacy Officer, Security Officer	Ticket management system
	Number of data breaches tracked (origin, org. unit, project, security level)	-	ELT team	Quarterly	Privacy Officer, Security Officer	Ticket management system
	Mean time to resolve the data breach response cases	24 hours	ELT team	Quarterly	Privacy Officer, Security Officer	Ticket management system
Third-Party Management_	% of data processing agreements in place for external vendors	100%	ELT team	Monthly	Privacy Officer, Vendor Management Team	3rd party management system
	% high-risk vendors in full compliance	100%	ELT team	Monthly	Privacy Officer, Vendor Management Team	3rd party management system
Awareness and Training_	% of internal staff and external contractors/partners completed privacy and security training	95%-100%	ELT team	Monthly	Privacy Officer, HR	LMS
	The % pass rate of the privacy and security training	100%	ELT team	Monthly	Privacy Officer, HR	LMS

8.1.2 Privacy Audits and Assessments

The purpose of a privacy audit is to determine the degree to which technology, processes and people comply with privacy policies, and practices.

There are three types of audits:

- Internal self-evaluation (first party)
- Supplier audit (second party)
- Independent audit (third party)

Privacy-related audits and assessments should be properly planned (i.e., scheduled), executed, and managed. Audits and assessments may include internal driven or external driven (i.e., certifications, attestations) efforts. Organizations may integrate privacy-related audits and assessments into the enterprise schedule.

Findings and gaps from the audits and assessments should be formally documented, solutioned, and prioritized. The proposed mitigating controls should be resourced, implemented, and monitored throughout the risk mitigation process.

If applicable, organizations should plan and manage certification audit and attestation schedules and execution for industry standards (i.e., ISO 27701, EuroPriSe) and industry frameworks/principles (i.e., APEC CBPR).

8.1.3 Annual Report and Management Review

To ensure the technical and organizational measures are implemented and maintained properly, the DPO/CPO of the organization should establish a mechanism to produce regular (normally once a year) data protection reports to organization's top management team.

The organization's Senior Leadership Team (SLT) should be presented, on a regular basis (i.e., once a year), with the privacy program compliance status report, perform management review of the posture and risks, and provide guidance and resource for the improvement. If problems are identified, remediation plans are developed and implemented.

Those measures shall be reviewed and updated where necessary in alignment with changes in regulatory and business requirements. For each jurisdiction in which the entity operates, the effect on privacy requirements from changes in the following factors is identified and addressed:

- Legal and regulatory
- Contracts, including service-level agreements
- Industry requirements
- Business operations and processes
- People, roles, and responsibilities
- Personal data collected and processed
- Adherence to data protection principles
- Personal data collection and usage practices
- Data retention and de-identification practices
- Data sharing practices
- DSR assurance and handling practices
- Security controls
- Data breach handling practices
- Cross-border transfers
- Vendor privacy risk management
- Technology

8.2   PRIVACY PROGRAM MANAGEMENT TOOLS

Based on the CPO Magazine report "Data Protection & Privacy Officer Priorities 20202", 20% are making new privacy technology implementation a priority only after privacy programs have matured.

There is a broader range of technology options on the market. The first International Association of Privacy Professionals (IAPP) technology report was released in 2017 and the most recent version was released in 2021. Privacy tech has undergone a paradigm shift over the past five years, affecting everything from the development of privacy tech tools to the attitude toward privacy tech vendors. When the IAPP released the inaugural "Privacy Tech Vendor Report" in 2017, the IAPP identified 44 vendors for the first report. The number was always expected to go up. Since 2017, the privacy landscape underwent a metamorphosis. The emergence of the California Consumer Privacy Act, Brazilian General Data Protection Law and other privacy laws around the world have forced organizations to adhere to a new array of compliance requirements, and in response, the demand for privacy tech grew exponentially. Each year, the report has chronicled the rise of privacy tech vendors in the marketplace. The IAPP has identified 365 privacy tech vendors in 2021.[15]

I summarized the 11 core functions that might be relevant to organizations' privacy operations needs as listed in Table 8.3.

TABLE 8.3
Privacy Management Tool Core Functions

Feature	Description
Personal Data Discovery	It is the feature that identifies and classifies personal data that the organization processes, transmits, stores, and uses. It also provides capabilities to identify high-risk or sensitive data elements collected by the organization.
Website Scanning and Cookie Management	Checks your organization's website to determine cookies, beacons, other trackers are embedded to help ensure compliance with various cookie laws and other regulations.
Data Flow and Mapping	Manual or automated solutions help organizations determine data flows throughout your organization. Tracks an organization's various data flows and provides clear path of data in and outside of the organization.
Data Inventory and Privacy Risk Management	Provides automation and consolidation of specific tasks associated with data privacy program, including PIAs/DPIAs/risk assessments, vendor risk assessments, Transfer Impact Assessments (TIAs), Record of Processing or data inventory.
Consent Management	Helps organizations collect, track, demonstrate, manage user's consent. Provides mechanisms for collecting, storing, and validating data subject consent has been obtained as a part of data collection practices.
Data Subject Request Management	Supports and manages the data subject request process, including the intake, verification, and response processes.
User Access Monitoring	Tracks and monitors internal access to personal data processed, transmitted, used, and stored by the organization.
Breach Response Support	Helps companies respond to data breach by providing information to relevant stakeholders of what was compromised and what notification/obligations must be met.
De-identification/ Pseudonymity	Techniques to ensure personal data is not associated with a specific data subject and reduce risk of privacy infringement.
Communications	Facilitates safe and compliant communications within internal team. Provides mechanisms for efficient, secure, and compliant communications within internal team.
Privacy Regulatory Database	Extensive, usually automated, information on latest privacy laws worldwide. Library or database that includes real-time updates on privacy laws and regulatory changes across jurisdictions.

Part 3

Privacy Governance

This Part Covers the Following Topics:

- Identification of Data Protection Legal Obligations
- Document Data Protection Business Expectations
- Privacy Program Governance Organizational Structure
- Privacy Program Roles and Responsibilities
- Privacy Policies and Procedures
- Privacy Awareness, Training, and Engagement

DOI: 10.1201/9781003225089-11

9 Data Protection Legal Mandate and Business Requirements

This chapter is intended to provide readers with a systematical and structured approach to understand the mandate, nature, scope, context, purpose, and type of personal data processing within the organizations.

This chapter covers the following topics:

- *Identify privacy compliance scope, either territorial or material*
- *Determine personal data processing roles and obligations*
- *Build a connection between data protection and business strategy and objectives*

9.1 IDENTIFY LEGAL OBLIGATIONS

Privacy protection starts with knowledge. Organizations need to know their privacy obligations and understand what is expected of them to comply with the law.

An organization should identify the jurisdictions in which it operates in accordance with business' nature and the purposes of the personal data processing activities, etc. It should monitor and track the regulatory developments within those jurisdictions. The organization should identify and document applicable privacy-related laws, regulations, directives, decisions, scope, associated requirements, and possible penalty of violating the laws and regulations.

The organization should properly identify and document the material scope and territorial scope to evaluate the applicability of a specific privacy law.

9.1.1 HOUSEHOLD ACTIVITIES

Most privacy regulations do not apply to the processing of personal data by a natural person in the course of a purely personal or household activity.

Personal or household activities could include correspondence and the holding of addresses, or social networking and online activity undertaken within the context of such activities. Despite the difficulty, the then-EU Article 29 Working Party (Art. 29 WP) has developed a set of basic criteria that shall be used in determining whether or not particular processing is being done for personal or household purposes. None of these criteria are, in themselves, necessarily determinative. However, a combination of these factors shall be used to determine whether particular processing falls within the scope of personal or household processing.

- Is the personal data disseminated to an indefinite number of persons, rather than to a limited community of friends, family members or acquaintances?
- Is the personal data about individuals who have no personal or household relationship with the person posting it?
- Does the scale and frequency of the processing of personal data suggest professional or full-time activity?
- Is there evidence of a number of individuals acting together in a collective and organized manner?
- Is there the potential adverse impact on individuals, including intrusion into their privacy?

 **Case Study**

Bodil Lindqvist v. Aklagarkammaren I Jonkoping, December 6 20[16]

Mrs. Lindqvist was a catechist in the parish of Alseda (Sweden). In 1998 Mrs. Lindqvist made a homepage on the Internet for the conformation so it would help them access the information they might need. She requested the administrator of the Swedish church's website to set up a link between the church's website and her homepage. On her website, there was information about herself and 18 of her colleagues in the parish. This had their first names and, in some cases, their full names. She had descriptions of the jobs held by her colleagues and their hobbies. She had descriptions of their family circumstances, telephone numbers, and other matters were mentioned. She said about one colleague who had injured her foot and was on half-time on medical grounds.

The European court of justice judged that this case does not fall within the category of exclusion. The publication was not completely for personal or household use. Mrs. Lindqvist was fined SEK 4000. She did not inform her colleagues of the existence of these pages, and she hadn't obtained consent. She also hadn't notified the datainspektionen (supervisory authority for the protection of electronically transmitted data) of her data.

9.1.2   AN ESTABLISHMENT

Some privacy regulations (i.e., GDPR) articulate the obligations for an establishment within the jurisdiction.

There's no definition of establishment within the GDPR, but Recital 22 suggests that it implies the "effective and real exercise of activity through stable arrangements. The legal form of such arrangements, whether through a branch or a subsidiary with a legal personality, is not the determining factor in that respect."

The concept of establishment must be interpreted broadly. If you have any presence in an EU member state, whether it's a single representative such as an employee or agent, you need to carefully consider whether you have an establishment in that EU member state.

- The fact that the non-EU entity responsible for the data processing does not have a branch or subsidiary in a Member State does not preclude it from having an establishment there within the meaning of EU data protection law.
- GDPR Recital 225 clarifies that an "establishment implies the effective and real exercise of activities through stable arrangements. The legal form of such arrangements, whether through a branch or a subsidiary with a legal personality, is not the determining factor in that respect."
- the CJEU (the Weltimmo v. NAIH case) ruled that the notion of establishment extends to any real and effective activity—even a minimal one—exercised through stable arrangements.

The legal form of such establishment (e.g., branch, subsidiary etc.) is not the determining factor. The formalist approach whereby organizations are considered to be established solely in the place in which they are registered is not the correct approach. There is a 3-pronged test:

  (i)   Is there an exercise of real and effective activity—even a minimal one?
 (ii)   Is the activity through stable arrangements?
(iii)   Is personal data processed in the context of the activity?

Case Study

Weltimmo v. Hungarian Data Protection Authority (NAIH), 2015[17]

Weltimmo was incorporated in Slovakia, and its business was advertising properties on its website. The target market, however, was Hungary, with Hungarian properties being featured and the text of the adverts on the website being written in Hungarian. Complaints were made to the NAIH because properties weren't being removed when requested. Weltimmo argued that the NAIH did not have jurisdiction to take action against it because it was incorporated in Slovakia.

The Court of Justice of the European Union (CJEU) confirmed that the place of incorporation wasn't a deciding factor, and that the presence of a single representative may be sufficient to have an establishment within a certain territory if that representative acts with a sufficient degree of stability. The Court also considered these circumstances:

- The website was solely targeted at Hungarians
- Weltimmo had a representative in Hungary who represented Weltimmo in administrative and legal proceedings
- Weltimmo had a bank account in Hungary for recovery of debts
- Weltimmo used a letterbox in Hungary for the management of day-to-day business matters
- The court commented that the nationality of the data subjects was irrelevant

Case Study

Facebook Fan Pages 2018[18]

Facebook Germany is responsible for promoting and selling advertising space and carries on activities addressed to persons residing in Germany. Given that a social network such as Facebook generates a substantial part of its income from advertisements posted on the web pages set up and accessed by users and given that Facebook's establishment in Germany is intended to ensure the promotion and sale in Germany of advertising space that makes Facebook's services profitable, the activities of that establishment must be regarded as inextricably linked to the processing of personal data at issue in the main proceedings. Consequently, such treatment must be regarded as being carried out in the context of the activities of an establishment of the controller.

Case Study

Google Spain v. AEPD 2014[19]

An "establishment" exists where an organization engages in the effective and real exercise of activity through stable arrangements in an EU Member State. It is not required that the processing be carried out by the establishment itself. The processing of personal data by the not-established controller suffices if it is "carried out in the context of the activities" of the establishment. In this case, the activities of the search engine and those of its establishment in the Member State are inextricably linked since the activities relating to the advertising space constitute the means of rendering the search engine economically profitable and that engine is the means enabling those activities to be performed.

9.1.3   Extra-Territorial Effect

Some of the privacy regulations (i.e., GDPR) have extra-territorial effects. Those privacy regulations apply to entities established outside the jurisdiction under certain circumstances such as offering goods or services to data subjects within the jurisdiction, monitoring data subjects within the jurisdiction, etc. **To better facilitate the discussions, the following content of this section is provided in the context of GDPR compliance.**

Offering goods or services

To determine what is meant by offering goods or services to data subjects "in the Union", account should be taken of recital 23 of the GDPR which states as follows:

Recital (23) In order to ensure that natural persons are not deprived of the protection to which they are entitled under this Regulation, the processing of personal data of data subjects who are in the Union by a controller or a processor not established in the Union should be subject to this Regulation where the processing activities are related to offering goods or services to such data subjects irrespective of whether connected to a payment. In order to determine whether such a controller or processor is offering goods or services to data subjects who are in the Union, it should be ascertained whether it is apparent that the controller or processor envisages offering services to data subjects in one or more Member States in the Union. Whereas the mere accessibility of the controller's, processor's, or an intermediary's website in the Union, of an email address or other contact details, or the use of a language generally used in the third country where the controller is established, is insufficient to ascertain such intention, factors such as the use of a language or a currency generally used in one or more Member States with the possibility of ordering goods and services in that other language, or the mentioning of customers or users who are in the Union, may make it apparent that the controller envisages offering goods or services to data subjects in the Union.

There must be sufficient connecting factors to the EU territory and to the targeting of individuals in the EU. Therefore, the mere fact of being the service provider of the app on the phones of Asian customers visiting temporarily a country within the EU would not, in the absence of other factors showing an intention of the service provider to provide its services in one or more Member States in the EU, in itself constitute a sufficient factor to make such provision of services to those dedicated customers fall within the scope of the GDPR.

A report shows a number of high-profile US news websites owned by Tronc and Lee Enterprises were "temporarily unavailable in Europe". Affected sites included the New York Daily News, Chicago Tribune, LA Times, Orlando Sentinel, and Baltimore Sun.[20] However, just because your website is accessible by data subjects within EU countries doesn't mean that the GDPR applies to you.

The following factors are considered in determining whether the GDPR applies to your organization.

- Your text is in an EU language
- You're displaying prices in an EU currency
- You've enabled the ability for people to place orders in EU languages
- You make references to the country of EU users or customers
- You have advertisements directed to people within EU member states
- You display telephone numbers with international codes
- You're using a domain of the European member state (for example,. de or. eu)
- You mention clients or customers in European member states

This isn't an exhaustive list—all circumstances need to be considered.

Monitoring EU citizens

Another situation in which non-EU organizations can fall within the scope of the GDPR is when they are monitoring the behavior of individuals inside the Union. The EDPB does not consider that any online collection or analysis of personal data of individuals in the EU would automatically count as "monitoring". It will be necessary to consider the controller's purpose for processing the data and, in particular, any subsequent behavioral analysis or profiling techniques involving that data. The EDPB takes into account the wording of Recital 24, which indicates that to determine whether processing involves monitoring of a data subject behavior, the tracking of natural persons on the Internet, including the potential subsequent use of profiling techniques, is a key consideration.

- Behavioral advertisement
- Geo-localization activities, in particular for marketing purposes
- Tracking through wearable and other smart devices
- Online tracking through the use of cookies or other tracking techniques such as fingerprinting
- Personalized diet and health analytics services online
- CCTV
- Market surveys and other behavioral studies based on individual profiles
- Monitoring or regular reporting on an individual's health status

Practical advice for US companies

Organizations seeking to ensure that the GDPR does not apply to them must avoid giving the impression that they do offer goods or services to users in the EU. This can be accomplished by:

- Removing the top-level domain names of EU member states from the organization's website, e.g., "de."
- Not offering services to EU users on websites or via marketing materials.
- Removing all EU countries from website address fields or similar drop-down menus.
- Not using EU member state languages.
- Not referring to individuals in an EU member state in order to promote goods and services; e.g., if the organization's website talks about German customers who use the related products.
- Not allowing users hosted in the EU to sign up for services.
- Not offering shipments to the EU or payment in euros.
- Including disclaimers on the landing page of the organization's website stating that neither products nor services are envisaged as being offered to users in the EU.
- Not entering direct contractual relationships with EU end users/customers.

9.2 PERSONAL DATA PROCESSING ROLES AND OBLIGATIONS

9.2.1 RELATIONSHIP AMONG DATA PROCESSING ROLES

As discussed in Chapter 7, a data controller is a natural or legal person, public authority, agency, or other body that alone or jointly with others determines the purposes and means of the processing. A data processor is a natural or legal person, public authority, agency, or other body that processes personal data on behalf of a controller.

Joint controllers are two or more controllers who together determine the purposes and means of processing—and therefore share the responsibilities of the data controller. If two or more separate organizations collect and use data for a common purpose, they are joint controllers. Note that they don't need to be processing the data at the same time or in equal parts. As joint controllers, you share the obligations placed on data controllers under the GDPR in respect of the data set that you jointly control. You need to decide which of the joint controllers is responsible for complying with each of the data controller's obligations, especially regarding data protection rights.

Some privacy laws have defined roles for both data controllers and data processors. However, some privacy laws only have one defined role. Table 9.1 lists some examples of jurisdictions with

TABLE 9.1

Data Processing Roles in Various Jurisdictions

Type	Jurisdiction/Law	Defined Roles
Two roles	EU, South Korea, Mexico	Data Controller & Data Processor
	Russia	Operator & Operator's Assignment
	Hong Kong	Data User & Data Processor
	US—CCPA	Business & Service Provider
	US—HIPAA	Covered Entities & Business Associates
One role	China	Data Controller
	Japan	Principal
	US—other regulations, Canada, Singapore	Organization
	Australia	Entity
	New Zealand	Agency

various defined roles. For more details regarding the roles in the data processing chain, please see Chapter 19.

9.2.2 DETERMINE THE DATA PROCESSING ROLE

Although various laws and regulations might have slightly different definitions for data controller and data processor, the core principles to define the roles are quite similar.

In general, a data controller is:

- A natural or legal person, public authority, agency, or other body
- That alone or jointly with others determines the purposes and means of the processing

A data processor is:

- A natural or legal person, public authority, agency, or other body
- That processes personal data on behalf of a controller

As data controller and data processor have different obligations under privacy regulations. An organization should define its personal data processing role based on whether the organization determines the purpose and means of data processing activities.

Also in some cases, personal information handlers may need to take on further accountabilities. For instance, the China PIPL Article 58 articulates that personal information handlers providing important Internet platform services, that have a large number of users, and whose business models are complex shall fulfill the following obligations:

- Establish and complete personal information protection compliance systems and structures according to State regulations, and establish an independent body composed mainly of outside members to supervise personal information protection circumstances.
- Abide by the principles of openness, fairness, and justice; formulate platform rules; and clarify the standards for intra-platform product or service providers' handling of personal information and their personal information protection duties.
- Stop providing services to product or service providers on the platform that seriously violate laws or administrative regulations in handling personal information.
- Regularly release personal information protection social responsibility reports and accept society's supervision.

Main criteria

It is not up to you to decide whether your organization is a controller or processor. It is depending on the fact of what your organization does with the data. Purposes and Means are the key considerations.

To determine whether you are a data controller you need to ascertain which organization decides:

- To collect the personal data in the first place and the legal basis for doing so
- Which items of personal data to collect (i.e., the content of the data)
- The purposes the data are to be used for
- Which individuals to collect data about
- Whether to disclose the data and if so, who to
- How long to retain the data or whether to make non-routine amendments to the data.

Within the terms of the agreement with the data controller, and its contract, a data processor may decide:

- What IT systems or other methods to use to collect personal data
- How to store the personal data
- The method for ensuring a retention schedule is adhered to
- The means used to delete or dispose of the data
- The detail of the security surrounding the personal data
- The means used to transfer personal data from one organization to another
- The means used to retrieve personal data about certain individuals.

Opinion 1/2010 on the concepts of "controller" and "processor", ARTICLE 29 DATA PROTECTION WORKING PARTY

- When it comes to assessing the <u>determination of the purposes and the means with a view to attribute the role of the data controller</u>, the crucial question is therefore to which level of details somebody should determine purposes and means in order to be considered as a controller.
- It can also be said that determining the purposes and the means amounts to determining respectively the <u>"why" and the "how"</u> of certain processing activities. In this perspective, and taking into account that both elements go together, there is a need to provide guidance about which level of influence on the "why" and the "how" may entail the qualification of an entity as a controller.
- Determination of the "purpose" of processing is reserved to the "controller". <u>Whoever makes this decision is therefore (de facto) controller</u>. The determination of the "means" of processing can be delegated by the controller, as far as technical or organizational questions are concerned. Substantial questions which are essential to the core of lawfulness of processing are reserved to the controller. A person or entity who decides e.g., on how long data shall be stored or who shall have access to the data processed is acting as a "controller" concerning this part of the use of data, and therefore has to comply with all controller's obligations.
- <u>"Means" does not only refer to the technical ways of processing personal data, but also to the "how" of processing</u>, which includes questions like "which data shall be processed", "which third parties shall have access to this data", "when data shall data be deleted", etc.
- Determination of the "means" <u>therefore includes both technical and organizational questions</u> where the decision can be well delegated to processors (e.g., "which hardware or software shall be used?") and essential elements that are traditionally and inherently reserved to the determination of the controller, such as "which data shall be processed?", "for how long shall they are processed?", "who shall have access to them?", and so on.

- Therefore, two basic conditions for qualifying as a processor are on the one hand <u>being a separate legal entity with respect to the controller</u> and on the other hand <u>processing personal data on his behalf</u>. This processing activity may be limited to a very specific task or context or maybe more general and extended.

Common misunderstandings
The manager is the controller

- Not the manager, but the legal entity is the controller
- But information security-wise, he is the "data owner"

The employee is the processor

- An employee is never the processor, but he/she processes data

There can only be one controller

- There can be multiple controllers for the same processing, in most cases each for a part of the processing.

An organization can either be the controller or the data processor. It can't be both.

- Yes and no to this statement. You can be a data controller and a data processor at the same time for different processing activities, although you cannot be a controller and a processor in relation to the same processing activities. For example, if your business is a cloud hosting provider, you would be a data controller in relation to the contact data (personal data) about each of your clients, and you would be a data processor in relation to the personal data contained within the content that you are hosting for your clients.

 Example: Financial transactions—joint controllers

ARTICLE 29 DATA PROTECTION WORKING PARTY; Opinion 1/2010 on the concepts of "controller" and "processor"
Let's take the case of a bank, which uses a financial messages carrier in order to carry out its financial transactions. Both the bank and the carrier agree on the means of processing financial data. The processing of personal data concerning financial transactions is carried out at a first stage by the financial institution and only at a later stage by the financial messages carrier. However, even if at the micro level each of these subjects pursues its own purpose, at the macro level the different phases and purposes and means of processing are closely linked. In this case, both the bank and the message carrier can be considered joint controllers.

A travel agency—controller or Joint controller

ARTICLE 29 DATA PROTECTION WORKING PARTY; Opinion 1/2010 on the concepts of "controller" and "processor"
Case 1: A travel agency sends personal data of its customers to the airlines and a chain of hotels, with a view to making reservations for a travel package. The airline and the hotel confirm the availability of the seats and rooms requested. The travel agency issues the travel documents and vouchers for its customers. In this case, **the travel agency, the**

airline, and the hotel will be three different data controllers, each subject to the data protection obligations relating to its own processing of personal data.

Case 2: The travel agency, the hotel chain, and the airline decide to set up an internet-based common platform in order to improve their cooperation with regard to travel reservation management. They agree on important elements of the means to be used, such as which data will be stored, how reservations will be allocated and confirmed, and who can have access to the information stored. Furthermore, they decide to share the data of their customers in order to carry out integrated marketing actions. In this case, the travel agency, the airline, and the hotel chain will have joint control on how personal data of their respective customers are processed and will therefore be joint controllers with regard to the processing operations relating to the common internet-based booking platform. However, each of them would still retain sole control with regard to other processing activities, e.g., those relating to the management of their human resources.

Transfer of employee data to tax authorities—two separate controllers

ARTICLE 29 DATA PROTECTION WORKING PARTY; Opinion 1/2010 on the concepts of "controller" and "processor"

Company XYZ collects and processes the personal data of its employees with the purpose of managing salaries, missions, health insurance, etc. However, a law also imposes an obligation on the company to send all data concerning salaries to the tax authorities, to reinforce fiscal control.

In this case, even though both company XYZ and the tax authorities process the same data concerning salaries, the lack of shared purpose or means with regard to this data processing will result in qualifying the two entities as two separate data controllers.

Barristers—independent/separate controllers

ARTICLE 29 DATA PROTECTION WORKING PARTY; Opinion 1/2010 on the concepts of "controller" and "processor"

A barrister represents his/her client in court, and in relation to this mission, processes personal data related to the client's case. The legal ground for making use of the necessary information is the client's mandate. However, this mandate is not focused on processing data but on representation in court, for which activities such professions have traditionally their own legal basis. Such professions are therefore to be regarded as independent "controllers" when processing data in the course of legally representing their clients.

9.2.3 Obligations

Table 9.2 lists of the key obligations for data controllers and data processors (not an exhaustive list).

9.3 PRIVACY IN ALIGNMENT WITH BUSINESS

An organization should align its privacy program with business objectives and goals.

Align with Business Strategies

The privacy program and controls should be consistent with business strategies, objectives, and policies. Organizations should review and identify privacy-related requirements from existing published policies and procedures. Organizations need to establish a privacy and data protection program consistent with the requirements, terms, and languages that are written in current policies

TABLE 9.2

Key Obligations for Data Controllers and Data Processors

Obligations for BOTH data controllers and data processors

- Establish risk-based and appropriate technical and organizational measures
- Demonstrate compliance
- Establish records of processing activities
- Implement personal data security measures
- Establish proper international data transfer mechanisms
- Designate a representative if needed
- Appoint a DPO if needed
- Cooperation with the supervisory authority
- Adhere to codes of conduct (Voluntary)
- Adhere to the certification process and requirements (Voluntary)

Obligations for data controllers	**Obligations for data processors**
• Protect the rights of the data subjects	• Process personal data, only adhere to instructions from the controller (Article 29)
• Establish data protection policies	
• Ensure data protection by design and by default	• Contract stipulations or clauses defined in DPA (Article 28.1, 28.3)
• Performa data protection impact assessment	
• Manage processors properly	• Shall use only sub-processors authorized by the controller (Article 28.1) and sub-processor management (Article 28.4)
• Notify personal data breach to the supervisory authority and data subjects if necessary	
	• Notification to the controller: personal data breach (Article 33.2) and infringe this Regulation (Article 28.3.h)

and procedures. Privacy program planning should consider, support, and enable business strategies and growth considering business plans (i.e., new products, new marketplaces, new processes, new business units).

Identify Contractual Requirements

Organizations need to identify and incorporate data protection contractual requirements from legally binding documents (i.e., agreements or contracts) with customers into the privacy program.

Incorporate privacy-related conditions of cyber insurance policy

Organizations need to identify and incorporate data protection contractual requirements from cyber insurance policy into the privacy program.

 Guide and Recommendations

Organizations that follow Info-Tech's privacy program methodology and tools can utilize its research or guided implementation services to identify compliance obligations and contractual requirements. You can leverage the 12 domains and subsequent privacy controls as you work to right-size Info-Tech's Privacy Framework for your organization.

You can use Info-Tech's *Privacy Framework Tool*, review each privacy control, and determine the current organizational maturity based on the five-point CMMI scale below. Capture any relevant comments, as required.

- Initial/Ad hoc
- Developing
- Define and Documented
- Managed and Measurable
- Optimized

The table below shows a fraction of Info-Tech's *Privacy Framework Tool that maps key privacy controls (i.e. Notices and Consent) with various privacy laws and regulations (i.e. GDPR, CCPA/CPRA, Virginia CDPA, Colorado Privacy Act).*

Domain	Privacy Control	GDPR	CCPA	CPRA	Virginia Consumer Data Protection Act
Notices and Consent	A privacy notice has been created to notify data subjects and other interested parties of how personal data is being used. The privacy notice is provided to data subjects at the point of data collection.	Privacy Notice Art.12,13,14	Privacy Notice Article 2. NOTICES TO CONSUMERS	Privacy Notice SEC. 4. Section 1798.100	Controllers shall provide consumers with a reasonably accessible, clear, and meaningful privacy notice. If a controller sells personal data to third parties or processes personal data for targeted advertising, the controller shall clearly and conspicuously disclose such processing, as well as the manner in which a consumer may exercise the right to opt out of such processing. § 59.1–574. Data controller responsibilities; transparency.
	Consent is captured when collecting personal data by offering data subjects an opt-in or opt-out option. Consent is captured when sharing and/or disclosing data by offering data subjects an opt-in or opt-out option. Consent is captured when using data by offering data subjects an opt-in or opt-out option. There is a process for data subjects to withdraw their consent. The effort to withdraw consent is equal to that of providing consent.	Consent – Needs to be collected from all data subjects in some form, whether or not collection was done via a third party. Can also be withdrawn at any point and should be done so easily. Art.7,8	Consent needs to be collected from the data subject, meaning this does not apply to data collected from third parties. CCPA is specific in that it requires an opt out of the sale of personal data. § 999.305. Notice at Collection of Personal Information § 999.330. Minors Under 13 Years of Age	Consent needs to be collected from the data subject, meaning this does not apply to data collected from third parties, though they are bound by the processing agreement with the first party and must comply with data-deletion requests. CPRA is specific in that it requires an opt out of the sale of personal data. SEC. 13. Section 1798.135	Not process sensitive data concerning a consumer without obtaining the consumer's consent, or, in the case of the processing of sensitive data concerning a known child, without processing such data in accordance with the federal Children's Online Privacy Protection Act (15 U.S.C. § 6501 et seq.). § 59.1–574. Data controller responsibilities; transparency.

(Continued)

(Continued)

Domain	Privacy Control	GDPR	CCPA	CPRA	Virginia Consumer Data Protection Act
	There is a consent management process that collects individual consent and tracks it in a repository. There is a process to track valid consent for marketing and sales communications. There is a process to collect consent for website tracking technologies (such as cookies).				

Info-Tech Insight

The Info-Tech's best-practice framework will force you to re-evaluate your current operations and understand how to integrate privacy. To gain the most benefits from your privacy program, review and understand which domains are most critical to your operations and which you will want to put the most focus on. This will ensure that this framework works for you and builds a privacy program around your organization's specific requirements

10 Governance Structure and Responsibilities

This chapter is intended to help an organization establish proper privacy and data protection governance structure and defined roles and responsibilities across the enterprise.

This chapter covers the following topics:

- *Personal data protection governance structure*
- *Primary roles and accountability*
- *Cross-functional teams and responsibilities*

10.1 DATA PROTECTION GOVERNANCE STRUCTURE

Privacy program governance enables an organization to set its program direction and manage its operations to achieve its intended outcomes. It also ensures strategic objectives are connected to the daily operations of an organization in assigning roles, setting expectations, granting power, and verifying performance.

Privacy doesn't live in isolation. While there may be one individual or group designated to manage the privacy program, privacy is everyone's responsibility. Employees will have to perform the necessary actions such as limiting their personal data collection or anonymizing data. The success of the program will rely on everyone understanding how to put privacy first. By assigning ownership and flexibility to your business units in how they weave privacy into their day-to-day, privacy becomes part of operational design and structure.

Good governance requires:

- Clear purpose for the privacy program
- Defined roles and responsibilities
- Accountability
- Transparency
- Risk management
- Reporting, monitoring, and assurance
- Continuous improvement.

There are three types of privacy governance structure: centralized, decentralized, and hybrid. However, there is no one-size-fits-all solution with respect to the privacy program governance structure. A successful privacy program will be structured in a way that best fits the needs of your organization. Minimize disruption to ensure a successful adaptation and launch.

Right-size your privacy governance structure. Look at your current organizational and governance setup and see which structure fits best. Consider the following when building out your privacy organizational structure.

- Determine where ownership of the privacy program will be.
  - Common choices are a dedicated privacy team or the Legal, Information Security, and/or HR departments.
  - Decide whether a privacy officer is necessary in your organization—some regulations recommend it.

DOI: 10.1201/9781003225089-13

- Review your current organizational structure to decide which model would be best for your privacy practices: centralized, distributed, or hybrid.
  - Review the previous examples for how this could be structured. Be mindful that you can set up this structure based on your own unique requirements, for example, two different groups can share ownership of the entire privacy program.
- Select and document the appropriate governance structure. Make note of significant changes that will need to occur to facilitate implementation of the governance structure.

Table 10.1 illustrates the advantages and disadvantages of the following three governance models: centralized governance model, decentralized governance model, and hybrid governance model.

TABLE 10.1
Three Models of Privacy Program Governance

Model	Description	Pros	Cons
Centralized governance model	The centralized governance model has a dedicated data protection team that directs all other departments related to the management of personal data. The centralized model facilitates the idea that one group is entirely responsible for propagating privacy throughout the organization.	• Responsibility and accountability are clearly defined. In a centralized model, one team or one person remains responsible for privacy-related issues. • Streamlined processes and procedures for the entire organization. • Centrally track privacy initiatives and compliance to better track compliance. • Establishing a dedicated privacy team usually indicates leadership support for the program.	• This structure can create bureaucratism that slows response times to certain privacy issues. • Other groups may lack accountability because they feel that the privacy team handles everything related to privacy.
Decentralized governance model	In the decentralized model, we find that it is the responsibility of each department to create and shape their privacy practices. This can be done with the help of privacy stewards assigned within each group. These individuals work with their team to integrate data protection into their business processes.	• In a distributed organization, the level of organizational structure is reduced. • Privacy professionals can take advantage of departmental or business unit expertise and integrate data protection more seamlessly. • Delegation of decision-making power to lower levels. This helps roll out the projects and improves the change management within your organization.	• Compliance tracking can be difficult. Lack of centralized privacy tracking and reporting can quickly fail to demonstrate regular compliance. • Different views on what privacy means for each group can lead to inconsistent processes and standards. • Processes or procedures could be duplicated many times, wasting resources.
Hybrid governance model	This hybrid scheme combines the best of centralized and decentralized structures. Centralized data protection for tracking and reporting purposes, business unit data protection champions tasked with obtaining ownership from business units.	• Assign key individuals (i.e., Chief Privacy Officer) responsible for privacy-related issues • Establish policies and instructions to other parts of the organization • The local business units will then adhere to and support the enterprise-wide policies and directions.	• Finding a dedicated privacy expert to fill the entire team can be difficult.

Organizations that are identified as having adopted a hybrid privacy governance model report shorter sales delays (4.6 weeks) when compared against organizations that employ either a fully centralized (9.8 weeks) or decentralized model (7.1 weeks)[21]

Privacy and Data Protection Committee

In some cases, the privacy governance could end up with establishing a privacy and data protection committee. However, please keep in mind a committee is not always the best solution for some organizations. Whether a committee is needed depends on the specific business context.

A data protection committee is usually chaired by a senior leadership member and staffed with leaders, privacy advocates, and champions from various business departments.

10.2 THE CHIEF PRIVACY OFFICER

An organization should designate the owner who oversees the privacy and data protection practices and be ultimately responsible for the privacy program. The privacy program owner exercises the highest authority within an organization to ensure that privacy obligations are met and complied with within the organization. The actual title of the privacy ownership may vary significantly from organization to organization. For instance, some organizations designate a Chief Privacy Officer (CPO) as the owner, while organizations designate a Chief Legal Counsel as the owner.

Personal information controller/handlers shall disclose the methods of contacting the privacy program owner and report the contact to the corresponding data protection authorities.

Some privacy regulations (i.e., PIPL Art. 52) require organizations to designate a personal information protection owner in certain circumstances such as processing a large amount of personal information. Here is an example, according to GB/T 35273–2020 Information security technology—Personal information (PI) security specification (section 11), an organization that meets any of the following conditions shall set up a full-time post and a department dedicated to PI security work:

- Main business involves the processing of PI, and the number of employees exceeds 200.
- Processes the PI of more than 1,000,000 individuals or is estimated to process the PI of more than 1,000,000 individuals.
- Processes the sensitive PI of more than 100,000 individuals.

If not already mandated by governing privacy laws, consider appointing a privacy officer to formalize privacy ownership in the organization.

10.2.1 KEY RESPONSIBILITIES

As a Chief Privacy Officer, you play a vital role in promoting strong privacy governance and capability in your organization. This helps to build customer confidence that your organization is respecting and protecting personal information.

Figure 10.1 provides some of the prevalent jobs and responsibilities of a typical CPO and help you to navigate through various CPO mandates.

10.2.2 THE POSITION

One of the most frequently asked questions is where the CPO should report to.

Traditionally, data privacy began as a legal requirement for the vast majority of companies. As a result, reporting to the General Counsel has been the typical placement for the privacy organization.

Privacy Governance Structure	Privacy Compliance, Documentation and Measurement	Privacy Impact Assessments	Record of Data Processing Activities
Privacy Notices, Choice and Consent	Data Retention Policy and Schedule	Vendor Privacy Requirements	Security Technical and Organizational Measures
Cross-Border Transfers	Data Subject Requests, Inquires and Complaints Handling	Data Breach Handling	Privacy Awareness and Training

FIGURE 10.1 Jobs and responsibilities of a typical CPO.

However, things are changing. I have seen a few different reporting structures for CPOs based on organizations' unique business needs and culture.

- Privacy Department
  - In the most privacy-mature organizations, a dedicated privacy function exists that heads up all privacy initiatives.
  - This does involve coordinating with all other relevant departments, but privacy is centrally managed by one group.
- Legal, Compliance, Audit
  - In many organizations without a dedicated privacy team, it often falls to Legal, Compliance, and/or Audit to take the privacy mantle.
  - Since many privacy programs are being driven by the increase of privacy regulations, these groups often become huge proponents of implementing privacy within the organization.
- InfoSec or IT
  - Privacy can also be owned by the security team. Many still think of security and privacy as being the same thing and it is not uncommon to conflate these two functions into one team.
  - However, it is worth noting again that these two are different and many privacy initiatives go beyond security controls.
- Human Resources
  - Occasionally the HR department will take on the privacy program.
  - This is the case for organizations that do not have a dedicated legal counsel and where most personal data held by the organization is that of the employees.

For some organizations, it still might make good sense for the privacy program to stay in Legal. Here are some characteristics of companies drawing that conclusion:

- The company is in a regulated industry such as financial services or healthcare, where the primary privacy strategy is sustaining compliance.
- The company is a multinational facing a substantial amount of privacy legal determinations, such as what to do about the EU GDPR, the new China Personal Information Protection Law, and India's impending privacy bill, etc.
- The company employs a strong CPO who is also an attorney.

Also, the legal team might take different roles in terms of managing the privacy program as listed here.

- *Legal advisory*: acting as the company's privacy counsel, providing ad hoc advice to corporate and business functions.
- *Regulatory compliance*: operating as an oversight function, holding corporate and business functions accountable to programmatic controls.
- *Privacy operations support*: performing repeatable privacy processes such as data-subject rights requests and privacy impact assessments, and aligning staff to dedicated businesses or functions such as data, digital, and IT.

10.3   THE INDEPENDENT DATA PROTECTION OFFICER (DPO)

If it is required by law or necessary for business operations, an organization should designate a Data Protection Officer (DPO).

10.3.1   LEGAL REQUIREMENTS OF DESIGNATING A DPO

Some privacy regulations (i.e., GDPR) may require organizations to designate a data protection officer (DPO) that is an independent oversight role. For instance, GDPR Art. 37 requires an organization to designate a DPO in the following circumstances.

- The processing is carried out by a public authority or body, except for courts acting in their judicial capacity.
- The core activities of the controller or the processor consist of processing operations which, by virtue of their nature, their scope, and/or their purposes, require regular and systematic monitoring of data subjects on a large scale.
- The core activities of the controller or the processor consist of processing on a large-scale special categories of data pursuant to GDPR Article 9 and personal data relating to criminal convictions and offenses referred to in GDPR Article 10.

Table 10.2 lists some of the jurisdictions that have DPO requirements.[22]

10.3.2   DPO's DESIGNATION, POSITION AND TASKS

It is the fact that different privacy regulations set forth different requirements for DPO's designation, position and tasks. For this book's discussion purpose, the following list shows key considerations under the GDPR.

- **The DPO is (Art. 37)**
  - ✓ Staff member or contractor
  - ✓ Professional and expert in relevant legal requirements
  - ✓ Easily accessible
    - Located within the European Union
    - On the same site or hotline as the employees who need access to them
  - ✓ Publish the contact details of the DPO and communicate them to the supervisory authority
    - Postal address
    - Email address or dedicated phone number
    - Hotline
    - Note: The DPO's name is not necessary

TABLE 10.2

Examples of Jurisdictions with DPO Requirements

Jurisdiction	Associated Regulation	Relevant Article/Section	Requirements	Applicability
EU member states (wording)	The General Data Protection Regulation (GDPR)	Article 37–39	Designate a Data Protection Officer (DPO).	Data controllers
United States (other regulations)	Health Insurance Portability and Accountability Act (HIPAA)	Section 164.530(a)(1)	Designate a Privacy Official (PO).	Covered Entities (Ces) or the health care components • Health plans • Health care providers • Health care clearinghouses
China	Personal Information Protection Law (PIPL)	Article 52	Appoint personal information protection officers, to be responsible for supervising personal information handling activities as well as adopted protection measures, etc.	Personal information handlers that handle personal information reaching quantities provided by the State cybersecurity and informatization department shall appoint personal information protection officers, to be responsible for supervising personal information handling activities as well as adopted protection measures, etc.
Russia	The Federal Law No. 152-FZ	Article 18	The appointment of a person as responsible for organizing the processing of personal data by the operator being a legal entity.	Covered operators
Brazil	Lei Geral de Proteção de Dados Pessoais—LGDP	Article 41	Appoint a Data Protection Officer (DPO) *Note: Not Independent supervision, more of a compliance position handling both internal and external endeavors.*	Data controllers
Canada	Personal Information Protection and Electronic Documents Act (PIPEDA)	Schedule 1, 4.1 Principle 1	Designate an individual or individuals who are accountable for the organization's compliance.	Covered entities

- **DPO Position (Art. 38)**
    - ✓ Report to highest management level
        - Such independence requires that the DPO reports to the highest levels of management. This is important because it will prevent messages from getting attenuated before reaching management.

✓ Independent:
  • **Does not receive any instructions regarding the exercise of those tasks.** The enterprise shall not attempt to direct the DPO in their tasks, for example in terms of what the preferred results would be, how to investigate complaints, whether to consult supervisory authorities, and how to interpret laws.
  • **And must not be punished or dismissed for carrying out these tasks.** Punishment refers to withheld or delayed promotion, barriers in career development and benefits, and warnings.
  • The DPO is not personally responsible for non-compliance. While this language mitigates the risk of enforcement against a DPO directly by a data protection authority, it does not necessarily protect a DPO from liability to the company arising from his or her error or negligence.
✓ Can be part-time—no conflict of interests
  • The Information Commissioner of Slovenia addresses DPO appointment under GDPR: The Information Commissioner ("Commissioner") addressed, on April 20, 2018, the appointment of a data protection officer (DPO) by organizations under the General Data Protection Regulation (Regulation (EU) 2016/679) (GDPR). The Commissioner considered recent notifications of DPO appointments, highlighting the importance of appointing an independent DPO who acts as an auditor with regard to personal data. In particular, any person deciding on the means and processing of personal data, such as a director, a member of the board, or a legal representative cannot be appointed as a DPO due to a conflict of interest.
✓ Protected against unfair dismissal
✓ Be bound by secrecy or confidentiality
• **Controller/Processor must (Art. 38)**
  ✓ Involve DPO in timely manner
    • Facilitate communication with and involvement of the DPO in all issues related to personal data protection. Controllers and processors should involve DPOs in all personal data protection matters.
    • Reasons why any suggestions from the DPO are not adopted should be recorded.
    • If data leakage occurs, the DPO must be consulted.
  ✓ Provide resources
    • (1) Support from senior management; (2) time; (3) official internal communication of the DPO's account/channel; (4) financial resources and staff; (5) HR, legal, IT, and security support; (6) continuous training; (7) information on established teams and respective responsibilities.
  ✓ Provide access to personal data and processing operations
  ✓ Help the DPO maintain expert knowledge of topics and issues related to personal data protection.
  ✓ Ensure that the DPO is not put in a situation that is a conflict of interest, such as a position that requires determining the purposes and means of processing personal data.
• **Tasks DPO (Art. 39)**
  ✓ Inform/advise
    • The DPO is not personally responsible for non-compliance
  ✓ Monitor compliance (such as assignment of responsibilities, awareness-raising and training of staff involved in processing operations, and the related audits)
  ✓ Provide advice regarding DPIA
  ✓ Cooperate with DPA
    • Language skills
  ✓ Contact person for DPA and data subjects
    • Risk-based performance of tasks

- **DPO in practice**
  - DPO Charter
    - ✓ Reporting line
    - ✓ Powers
    - ✓ Protection
  - DPO job grading
    - ✓ Must be able to effectively discuss privacy issues with leadership
  - DPO resources
    - ✓ Must have own budget
    - ✓ May need own staff with specific competencies
  - Group DPO possible
    - ✓ Language skills
    - ✓ Must be available for all covered controllers/processing entities

Case Study—Spain AEPD v. Glovo, 2020

Spain AEPD: A Data Protection Committee can't be the substitute for a DPO, June 10, 2020

The Spanish Agency for Data Protection has fined Glovo 25,000 euros for not having a protection delegate data as established in article 37 of the General Data Protection Regulation. This is the first company sanctioned for this matter in Spain.

Glovo is the first company in Spain sanctioned for this matter after two claims filed in May and November of 2019 with the body in charge of data protection in Spain. Glovo alleges that it is exempt from the obligation of having a data protection delegate and that, in any case, it has a Data Protection Committee that carries out the functions of a single person. The AEPD indicates as proven facts in its resolution that the home delivery platform did not have a data protection officer at the time of making the inquiries and claims to be exempt from the obligation. It has also been found that Glovo has appointed a data protection officer at the beginning of the year, days after the sanctioning process began, according to the document made public. The sanction includes as an aggravating circumstance that Glovo carries out personal data treatment "on a large scale", although this concept is not clearly defined.

Taking into account everything exposed and the current legislation, the Spanish Data Protection Agency imposed a fine of 25,000 euros on Glovo for an infringement of Article 37 of the General Data Protection Regulation, which includes the obligation to appoint a data protection delegate under certain assumptions, typified in article 83.4 of the RGPD, which regulates the general conditions for the imposition of administrative fines.

The sanction includes as an aggravating circumstance that the platform carries out a treatment of personal data "on a large scale due to the number of clients it has." Although the resolution does not indicate what that number is, nor does the RGPD make it clear. The resolution of the AEPD is not firm and there is both an appeal for reversal and contentious-administrative appeal before the National Court.

10.3.3 LEGAL RISKS OF BEING A DPO

Data protection officers may have tremendous job security under Article 38(3) of the European Union's General Data Protection Regulation, but the job may also come with hidden risks. In some

TABLE 10.3
Examples of DPOs' Personal Liability

Jurisdiction	Description
Hong Kong	Regulation: The Personal Data (Privacy) Ordinance (PDPO)
	Civil liability: Subject to subsection (4), an individual who suffers damage by reason of a contravention:
	(a) of a requirement under this Ordinance.
	(b) by a data user; and
	I which relates, whether in whole or in part, to personal data of which that individual is the data subject, shall be entitled to compensation from that data user for that damage.
	Criminal liability: A person who, either alone or jointly or in common with other persons, controls the collection, holding, processing or use of the data. If the data is provided for gain, to a fine of $1,000,000 and to imprisonment for 5 years.
	Penalty Imprisonment: Up to 5 years
Singapore	Regulation: The Personal Data Protection Act (PDPA)
	Civil liability: "Where an offense under this Act committed by a body corporate is proved
	(a) to have been committed with the consent or connivance of an officer; or
	(b) to be attributable to any neglect on his part . . ."
	Criminal liability: "The officer as well as the body corporate shall be guilty of the offense and shall be liable to be proceeded against and punished accordingly."
	Penalty Imprisonment: 1–3 years
Malaysia	Regulation: Personal Data Protection Act 2010 ("PDPA")
	Criminal liability: "Was in any manner or to any extent responsible for the management of any of the affairs of the body corporate or was assisting in such management— (a) may be charged severally or jointly."
	Penalty Imprisonment: Up to 2 years
Philippines	Regulation: Republic Act No. 10173 (the Data Privacy Act)
	Civil/Criminal liability: The penalty shall be imposed upon the responsible officers, as the case may be, who participated in, or by their gross negligence, allowed the commission of the crime.
	Penalty Imprisonment: 6 months—7 years

countries, DPOs—or their equivalent under local law—may be held personally liable for failing to comply with local privacy law.

Table 10.3 lists some examples of Personal Liability for Privacy and Data Protection Officers.[23]

10.4 DESIGNATING A REPRESENTATIVE

An organization should designate a writing Data Processing Representative (Representative) if required by law or necessary for the business operations.

Some privacy regulations (i.e., GDPR, PIPL) may require organizations to designate a writing representative in certain circumstances such as processing of special data in a large scale.

GDPR Article 27: Where Article 3(2) applies, the controller or the processor shall designate in writing a representative in the Union.

- Where Article 3(2) applies, the controller or the processor shall designate in writing a representative in the Union (27.1).
- The obligation laid down in paragraph 1 of this Article shall not apply to: (a) processing which is occasional, does not include, on a large scale, processing of special categories

of data as referred to in Article 9(1) or processing of personal data relating to criminal convictions and offenses referred to in Article 10, and is unlikely to result in a risk to the rights and freedoms of natural persons, taking into account the nature, context, scope and purposes of the processing; or (b) a public authority or body (27.2).

- The representative shall be established in one of the Member States where the data subjects, whose personal data are processed in relation to the offering of goods or services to them, or whose behavior is monitored, are (27.3).
- The representative shall be mandated by the controller or processor to be addressed in addition to or instead of the controller or the processor by, in particular, supervisory authorities and data subjects, on all issues related to processing, for the purposes of ensuring compliance with this Regulation (27.4).
- The designation of a representative by the controller or processor shall be without prejudice to legal actions which could be initiated against the controller or the processor themselves (27.5).

PIPL Article 53: Personal information handlers outside the borders of the People's Republic of China, as provided in Article 3, Paragraph 2, of this Law, shall establish a dedicated entity or appoint a representative within the borders of the People's Republic of China to be responsible for matters related to the personal information they handle, and are to report the name of the relevant entity or the personal name of the representative and contact method, etc., to the departments fulfilling personal information protection duties and responsibilities.

The primary responsibilities of the Representative under the GDPR are:

- The Representative represents the data controller or data processor with respect to their obligations under the GDPR and has primarily a passive role, with the following two main responsibilities.
- The Representative is mandated by the data controller or data processor to receive correspondence from the supervisory authorities and data subjects on all issues related to the processing of personal data. The Representative must also make available to the supervisory authority, at their request, the Article 30 processing records of the data controller or data processor.
- The Representative may be fined if they fail to fulfill their obligations under the GDPR. Recital 81 of the GDPR states that "the designated Representative should b. subject to enforcement proceedings in the event of noncompliance by the data controller or data processor." This statement seems to suggest that the Representative can be liable for the noncompliance of the data controller or data processor. Guidance from the European Data Protection board (EDPB) suggests that this is the case.

 Case Study: Regional Court of the Hague v. WhatsApp, 2016

No processing without representation

WhatsApp Inc. and the Dutch Data Protection Authority (*Autoriteit Persoonsgegevens*) have been fighting over the question of whether WhatsApp has to appoint a representative in the Netherlands. On November 22 the Regional Court of the Hague took its decision against WhatsApp.

WhatsApp Inc., the US-American company behind the internationally well-known instant messaging app, and the Dutch Data Protection Authority have been fighting over the question of whether WhatsApp, which so far does not have any offices in the European Union, has to appoint a representative in the Netherlands.

Should WhatsApp fail to appoint a representative in the Netherlands it will potentially have to face penalty payments of €10,000.00 per day up to a maximum of €1M.

10.5 CROSS-FUNCTIONAL RESPONSIBILITIES

A privacy program is NOT one person or one department's job. It is a collaborative effort across the entire organization. It's Everyone's Job. The privacy program must include multiple stakeholders for it to be successful. It's integral to assign clear lines of ownership to build and effectively manage the program.

Identifying decision-makers and communicating the importance of an effective privacy program is an important part of managing a privacy program. Don't assume that everyone in the room has the same level of understanding of the regulatory environment or the complexity of the undertaking. There will invariably be different levels of privacy knowledge among your various stakeholders.

Getting buy-in from an organization's senior leaders is vital for obtaining the resources required to manage the privacy program and embedding privacy within the organization's culture. A privacy program also requires support from a range of teams within the agency, including, among others:

- Legal
- IT/Information security
- Data governance/Information management
- Risk and assurance
- Project management office
- Product research and development
- Human resources
- Finance
- Procurement
- Customer relationship
- Communications
- Lines of business

Without defined responsibilities, privacy initiatives can easily fall between the cracks and issues may not be handled effectively. One of the techniques to define and socialize privacy program cross-functional roles and responsibilities is to leverage the RACI (Responsible, Accountable, Consulted, Informed) chart.

- Accountable: the buck stops here; the position with yes/no authority
- Responsible: the doer; the position working on the activity
- Consulted: in the loop; the position involved prior to decision or action
- Informed: keep in the picture; the position that needs to know of the decision or action

The RACI chart will help clearly define each organizational team's roles and accountabilities. Leverage this tool to identify and understand the owners of the data privacy program within the organization, across the different work units. Figure 10.2 illustrates an example of defined data protection roles and responsibilities among cross-functional teams.

RACI CHART EXAMPLE

Program Tasks	Privacy Officer	Director of IT	Information Security Officer	General Counsel	Leadership Team	HR	Finance and Accounting	Business Teams
Build the privacy organizational structure	A	R	R	C	C	R	C	I
Establish a data inventory	A	C	C	C	I	R	R	R
Establish a privacy risk assessment process and perform PIAs	A	C	R	C	I	R	R	R
Create relevant privacy notices/policies	A	C	C	R	C	C	C	R
Where necessary, develop and manage a consent process for data subjects	A	R	C	R	I	I	I	C
Build personal data classification and handling process	C	R	A	C	I	C	C	R
Establish and execute data retention policy and schedule	A	R	R	C	C	C	C	R
Implement proper cybersecurity controls to protect personal data	C	R	A	C	I	C	C	R
Establish an incident response process to manage data breaches	R	R	A	C	I	C	C	R

R – Responsible, A – Accountable, C – Consulted, I – Informed

FIGURE 10.2 RACI chart example.

11 Privacy Policies and Procedures

This chapter is intended to provide readers with a systematic and structured approach to establish and implement privacy policies and procedures.

This chapter covers the following topics:

- *Privacy documentation structure*
- *Privacy mission statement*
- *Privacy charter*

11.1 PRIVACY DOCUMENTATION STRUCTURE

Organizations should establish and operationalize adequate and proper privacy policies and procedures to manage privacy and data protection practices. Some privacy regulations (i.e., GDPR, HIPAA, GLBA) have explicit requirements of establishing privacy and security policies within an organization. Although some privacy regulations might not specifically articulate the policy requirements, it is essential and fundamental to build the privacy policies to govern the privacy practices within the organization.

The purpose of a data protection policy is to explain to employees what can and cannot be done with data they are handling and to outline the consequences of a policy violation. Data protection policies should be used where proportionate in relation to processing activities. Also, compliance with your own privacy policy is not the same as complying with applicable privacy regulations. Your policy cannot authorize conduct otherwise prohibited by the law.

Depends on each organization's legal obligations and business context, the need for the privacy policies and procedures various. Figure 11.1 shows an example of a typical structure of privacy policies and procedures. And Table 11.1 describes the main purposes for each document. Please note that it is not an exhaustive list. Also, organizations don't have to implement all these policies and procedures.

11.2 PRIVACY MISSION STATEMENT

In general, a privacy and data protection mission statement usually covers the following aspects.

- The value the organization places on privacy
  - Complying with laws, regulations, and industry standards
  - Lowering risk solutions/reducing risks
  - Avoiding an incident of data loss
  - Sustaining market value and reputation
  - Supporting business commitment and objectives to stakeholders, customers, partners, and vendors
  - Competitive advantages by building trust
- Desired organizational objectives (Legal, culture, and customer expectations)
- Strategies to achieve intended outcomes
- Clarification of the roles and responsibilities

DOI: 10.1201/9781003225089-14

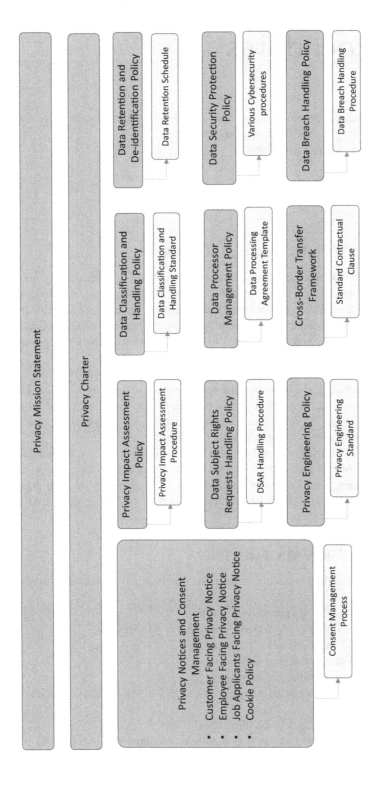

FIGURE 11.1   An example of privacy policy and procedure structure.

TABLE 11.1
Main Purposes for Each Document

Document Type	Main Purposes
Privacy Mission Statement	A privacy mission statement concisely communicates an organization's approach to privacy to all stakeholders. It's an important component that lays the groundwork for the rest of the privacy program and should align with the organization's broader purpose.
Privacy Charter	A privacy policy is an internal document addressed to staff that clearly states how personal information will be handled, stored, and transmitted to meet an organization's needs and all applicable laws.
Customer Facing Privacy Notice	A customer-facing privacy notice is an external statement addressed to anyone whose personal information is handled by an organization. A privacy notice must be provided when an organization collects personal information from an individual.
Employee Facing Privacy Notice	An employee-facing privacy notice is an internal statement addressed to employees whose personal information is handled by an organization. A privacy notice must be provided when an organization collects personal information from an employee.
Job Applicants Facing Privacy Notice	A job-applicant facing privacy notice is a statement addressed to job applicants whose personal information is handled by an organization. A privacy notice must be provided when an organization collects personal information from a job applicant.
Cookie Policy	A cookie policy states a list of cookies an organization uses on the websites and explains briefly what cookies are and informs users why an organization uses cookies.
Consent Management Process Procedure	Consent management gives data subjects appropriate control over their personal data and how it is collected, used, and shared. A consent management procedure is needed to ensure that an organization meets its obligations for obtaining and managing the specific, informed, and unambiguous consent of data subjects for their personal data to be processed by the organization.
Privacy Impact Assessment Policy	A privacy impact assessment policy sets forth the requirements for privacy risk assessment and mitigation.
Privacy Impact Assessment Procedure	A privacy impact assessment procedure helps an organization to identify, evaluate, and mitigate privacy risks efficiently and in compliance with the privacy regulations applicable to that organization.
Data Classification and Handling Policy	A data classification and handling policy defines the classification scheme and outlines the expected data handling requirements throughout the lifecycle of data based on its value, location, and level of protection.
Data Classification and Handling Standard	A data classification and handling standard defines how data is identified, classified, labeled, and properly handled and protected in accordance with its importance and potential impact on an organization.
Data Retention and De-identification Policy	A data retention and de-identification policy outlines the data retention and de-identification requirement in alignment with laws and regulations.
Data Retention Schedule	A data retention schedule defines the length of time that data is retained so that the organization eliminates data that no longer requires storage, security, and resources.
Data Subject Right Requests Handling Policy	A Data Subject Rights Requests Handling Policy defines the roles, responsibilities, and requirements for handling data subject rights requests.
Data Subject Right Requests Handling Procedure	A Data Subject Rights Requests Handling Procedure sets forth the steps, standards, and criteria throughout the process of handling data subject rights requests.
Data Processor Management Policy	A Data Processor Management Policy articulates the requirements that an organization must only use data processors that provide sufficient guarantees of their abilities to implement the technical and organizational measures necessary to meet the requirements of privacy regulations.

(Continued)

TABLE 11.1   (Continued)

Document Type	Main Purposes
Data Processing Agreement Template	A Data Processing Agreement Template establishes an agreement on the roles and responsibilities within the framework of the listed data protection principles between the data controller and the data processor.
Data Security Protection Policy	A Data Security Protection Policy sets forth the requirements to protect the confidentiality, integrity, and availability of personal data.
Various Cybersecurity Procedures	Depending on an organization's context, various cybersecurity procedures might be needed to protect personal data, such as identity and access control management, network security management, etc.
Privacy Engineering Policy	A Privacy Engineering Policy sets forth the requirements to ensure that privacy considerations are integrated into the product/process/software design.
Privacy Engineering Standard	A Privacy-by-Design Standard provides methodologies, tools, and techniques to ensure systems provide acceptable levels of privacy.
Cross-Border Transfer Framework	A Cross-Border Transfer Framework establishes proper cross-border data transfer mechanisms in accordance with applicable privacy laws and regulations.
Standard Contractual Clause	The purpose of Standard Contractual Clauses (SCCs) is to ensure compliance with the requirements of privacy laws (i.e., GDPR) with regard to the processing of personal data and the free movement of such data for the transfer of personal data to a third country.
Data Breach Handling Policy	A Data Breach Handling Policy sets forth roles, responsibilities, and requirements for handling data breach incidents.
Data Breach Response Procedure	A Data Breach Response Procedure defines the steps of detection, analysis, containment, eradication, recovery, and post-incident activity.

To follow are some examples of privacy mission statements.

Australian Bankers Association

From 21 December 2001, the ABA has considered itself bound by the private sector provisions (other than the credit reporting provisions) of the Privacy Act 1988 ("Privacy Act").

Our policy is to comply with those provisions of the Privacy Act and that includes telling you about the ABA's policies for handling personal information that we may collect, hold, use or disclose for the purposes of our functions and activities.

Citibank

Our goal is to maintain your trust and confidence when handling personal information about you. Our Online Privacy Statement describes how we may collect, use and share information you provide when you visit this website, receive our emails or interact with advertisements we have on third-party websites.

US Immigration and Customs Enforcement (ICE)

The Office's mission is to ensure the integrity and usability of the agency's records and data, and that individual privacy is protected.

US Veterans Affairs

The mission of VA Privacy Service is to preserve and protect the Personally Identifiable Information (PII) of Veterans, their beneficiaries, and VA employees by promoting a culture of privacy awareness and maintaining the trust of those we serve.

Ireland, Office of the Data Protection Commissioner

Our Mission is to protect the individual's right to privacy by enabling people to know, and to exercise control over how their personal information is used, in accordance with the Data Protection Acts, 1988 & 2003.

Hong Kong, The office of the Privacy Commissioner for Personal Data (PCPD)

Our mission is to secure the protection of privacy of the individual with respect to personal data through promotion, monitoring and supervision of compliance with the Ordinance.

Hong Kong Trade Development Council

We respect your privacy, and we promise:

- to implement computer, physical and procedural safeguards to protect the security and confidentiality of the personal data we collect
- to limit the personal data collected to the minimum required to provide services requested by you
- to permit only our properly trained, authorized employees to access personal data
- not to disclose your personal data to external parties unless you have agreed, we are required by law, or we have previously informed you.

11.3 PRIVACY CHARTER

A mature privacy program usually creates and establishes an enterprise-wide internal-facing privacy governance charter that sets forth the right-sized privacy governance structure and articulates enterprise-wide principles and requirements for privacy and data protection practices.

The following list illustrates the core components of a typical privacy charter.

- Purpose: Describe the purpose of this policy and emphasize the importance of privacy and data protection to the organization
- Scope: Describe the applicability of this policy in terms of employees and vendors, contractors, or entities (i.e., subsidiaries)
- Terms and definitions: Definitions for core terms such as personal data, Sensitive Personal Data, Data Subject, Consent, Data Controller, Data Processor, Data Processing, etc.
- Basic principles: Sets forth basic principle for privacy and data protection, such as lawfulness, fairness and transparency, purpose limitation, data minimization, accuracy, storage period limitation, integrity and confidentiality and accountability, etc.
- Organization and Responsibilities: Articulate ownership of the privacy program and high-level roles and responsibilities among various business units
- Privacy practice—notification: Use reasonable endeavors to notify Data Subjects of the types of Personal Data collected, the purposes of the Processing, Processing methods, the Data Subjects' rights with respect to their Personal Data, and organization's security measures to protect Personal Data
- Privacy practice—Choice and consent: Personal Data collection should be based on the data subject's consent, or other lawful grounds, and a record of such consent or authorization must be retained
- Privacy practice—Data collection: Collect the least amount of Personal Data as possible based on purpose relevancy and necessity. If Personal Data is collected from a third party, the organization should try to ensure that the Personal Data is collected legally
- Privacy practice—Data use: The use purposes and methods of Personal Data should be consistent with the information contained in the privacy notice. Access to and Processing of Personal Data should be controlled

- Privacy practice—Accuracy, integrity, and relevance: Organization should maintain the accuracy, integrity and relevance of Personal Data based on the Processing purpose
- Privacy practice—Data retention and disposal: Personal Data shall be kept for no longer than is necessary for the purposes for which the Personal Data are Processed. Personal data should be securely deleted or de-identified after it reaches its data retention period
- Privacy practice—Disclosure to third parties: Ensure that the supplier or business partner will provide security measures to safeguard Personal Data that are appropriate to the risks associated with the Personal Data
- Privacy practice—Cross-border transfer of Personal Data: Employ appropriate mechanisms for cross-border transfer of personal data
- Privacy practice—Data security and data breach: Security mechanisms designed to protect Personal Data shall be used to prevent Personal Data from being stolen, misused, or abused, and prevent Personal Data against leakage. Personal data breach should be handled and reported timely and properly.
- Privacy practice—Data subject rights: Organization should provide Data Subjects with a reasonable access mechanism to enable them to access their personal data, and allow them to update, rectify, erase, or transmit their personal data, etc. if appropriate or required by law
- Complaints: Procedure or mechanism for employees to submit privacy-related complaints
- Non-compliance: Process or protocols to handle violations of the policy

12 Privacy Awareness, Training, and Engagement

This chapter is intended to provide readers with a holistic approach to conduct privacy awareness and training and prompt data protection awareness and enhance the capability of privacy professionals across the enterprise.

This chapter covers the following topics:

- *Challenges and key considerations*
- *Awareness-raising approaches*
- *Role-based awareness and training program*

12.1 CHALLENGES AND KEY CONSIDERATIONS

A privacy-centric culture relies on employees' understanding and engaging with relevant disciplines. They must be able to contextualize how privacy applies to their roles and responsibilities. An organization's privacy program activities bring its privacy strategy to life and embed privacy into the everyday work of the agency and its staff.

Some privacy regulations (i.e., GDPR) explicitly require organizations to establish awareness-raising and training programs. For instance, GDPR Art. 39 states:

> to monitor compliance with this Regulation, with other Union or Member State data protection provisions and with the policies of the controller or processor in relation to the protection of personal data, including the assignment of responsibilities, awareness-raising and training of staff involved in processing operations, and the related audits.

Privacy and data protection are heavy-hitting items that all organizations, regardless of size, location, or industry, are considering with extreme care. The media is regularly peppered with stories of large-scale breaches, ransomware attacks, and incidences of insider threats that wreak havoc on organizations' internal operations, external perspectives and customer bases, and overall brand reputations.

While a robust privacy and data protection program and controls are of significant value, ultimately an organization must shift to take a proactive stance on privacy. This requires that principles and behaviors that promote privacy are embedded in the operational seams of how the organization runs on a daily basis and are supported from both the top-down and bottom-up. A culture of privacy starts with employees and members of the organization being fully engaged with how these two disciplines promote their own success and the overall performance of the organization.

Engagement with privacy and data protection within organizations has not kept pace with the increasing demands from regulations. As a result, organizations often find themselves saying they support privacy and data protection engagement but struggle to create behavioral changes in their staff.

Driving engagement with privacy and data protection within organizations is a challenge because:

- Privacy is often viewed as a cost and an inhibitor of innovation and a compliance obligation box to be ticked as opposed to competitive advantage and differentiator.
- Employees aren't fully engaged with how privacy and security impact them. Based on MediaPRO's report[24], 61 to 66% of surveyed employees are unsure of whether or not the GDPR, CCPA, PCI DSS, and FERPA apply to their organization.

- Training modules, tests, and continuous learning are integral parts of ensuring that privacy and data protection are embedded in the organization, but they are just the beginning.
- Leadership teams see privacy and data protection as something that's handled elsewhere.
- Organizations don't know how to measure engagement with privacy and data protection.

While rolling out regular privacy awareness training programs to employees, contractors, interns, etc., the organization should ensure:

- Develop a defined structure for privacy and data protection in the context of your organization.
- Senior executives understand their roles and responsibilities.
- Align your business goals and your privacy strategy to obtain support from your senior leadership team.
- The workforce is informed and trained on its roles and responsibilities.
- Privacy personnel who are responsible for protecting the privacy and security of personal information meet adequate professional qualifications and have received needed training.
- Third parties (e.g., service providers, customers, partners) understand their roles and responsibilities.
- Measure adherence to requirements using metrics.

Some organizations may also want to provide customized training to various business units based on the nature of the business processes as well as enhanced knowledge training to privacy professionals.

 Case Study

ICO vs. FLYBE, 2014
    In November 2014, FLYBE Aviation reported a data security incident to the ICO. A temporary employee of FLYBE sent a scanned copy of the employee's passport to his personal mailbox. The worker was in charge of the "air side pass" where FLYBE employees are required to pass inspections and then work at different airports.
    The ICO investigation found:

- FLYBE did not provide personal data protection training to all employees handling personal data, including this temporary worker in this case.
- FLYBE's data protection policy was insufficient and did not provide sufficient advice on what personal information the company collects, stores, and protects.
- In this case, the temporary worker's job resulted in access to a large amount of employee personal data, including passports, banking information, and possibly criminal records (for background check purposes). The ICO was concerned that temporary workers in "air side pass" jobs have access to so much personal information that they should be subject to the same background checks as permanent employees.

The ICO requires FLYBE to:
    Revise its privacy policy on the storage and use of personal data to reflect the different kinds of information that FLYBE processes, including how this information is protected.

- Ensure that employees are aware of FLYBE's information on the storage and use of personal data.
- Regular employees and temporary employees who process personal data should be trained on how to properly handle personal data before processing personal data and should be updated every year. Training needs to be monitored and recorded.
- Reasonable steps must be taken to ensure the reliability of temporary employees who have access to personal data and, when appropriate, the same background checks as regular employees.
- Other appropriate Security measures to protect personal data from unlawful processing, accidental loss, and destruction.

12.2 AWARENESS RAISING APPROACHES

Training and awareness are the foundation of an organization's privacy program. An effective training program includes privacy training for all staff at induction and regular intervals thereafter, as well as providing customized privacy training for staff who deal with large amounts of sensitive personal information.

Training activities may include:

- Classroom training
- Online learning
- Workshops
- Newsletters
- Booklets and flyers
- Posters
- Campaigns (for example, Privacy Week).

Examples

Figure 12.1 provides an example of privacy awareness training course outline.

INTRODUCTION
THE IMPORTANCE OF PRIVACY PROTECTION
- Enforcement Case Study
- Preventing Harm
- Legal Compliance
- Contractual Compliance
KEY DEFINITIONS
- Identifying Personal Data
- Sensitive Personal Data
COLLECTING PERSONAL DATA
- Lawful Basis
- Consent
- Data Minimization
PROCESSING PERSONAL DATA
- Data Quality
- Limited Access
- Confidentiality
- Purpose Specification
- Data Retention

INDIVIDUAL RIGHTS
- Notice and Transparency
- Access and Correction
- Right to Erasure
- Right to Data Portability Restriction, Objection, Withdrawing Consent
SHARING PERSONAL DATA
- International Transfers of Personal Data
- Sharing Personal Data with Third Parties
- Sharing Personal Data Internally
SECURITY AND DATA BREACH HANDLING
- Security Safeguards
- Data Incidents
ACCOUNTABILITY
- Our Responsibilities
- Personal Data Refers to Real People
- Privacy by Design
- Contacting the Privacy Office
CONCLUSION

FIGURE 12.1 Privacy awareness training course outline example.

12.3   ROLE-BASED AWARENESS AND TRAINING PROGRAM

Effective privacy and compliance help drive consumer confidence. Good data privacy practices can give you a competitive advantage through transparency. Buy-in from the top for privacy and data protection is a lot easier if you can directly link the impact of employees' privacy and data protection engagement to business objectives. A business-aligned privacy and data protection program ensures executive and employee support.

A one-size-fits-all approach to privacy and data protection won't work: Engagement requires relevant training and awareness for each department or business group within the organization.

The role of organizational structure in privacy and data protection is to enable cross-functional collaboration and engagement. Gauging effective privacy and data protection will look different at each level of the organization's structure such as the executive team, the leadership team, the privacy specialists, and employees.

Your executive team will take accountability and ownership for both the positive and less-than-positive outcomes of your privacy program performance. This level of accountability will not be shared evenly across all employees of the organization, but responsibility still exists across all levels; it is, in fact, the key requirement for privacy and security engagement to succeed organizationally.

Each employee has a different role, responsibility, and level of accountability with respect to privacy and data protection. Align your privacy engagement enablers in a manner that considers the role and function that the individual fulfills. Certain enablers will align more closely with specific organizational groups. For example, the Executive Scorecard will heavily align with the Executive team, somewhat align with the Leadership team, and likely not be relevant for the Specialist and Foundations groups.

Table 12.1 illustrates the mapping between the enablers and various levels of stakeholders.

TABLE 12.1
Enablers and Various Levels of Stakeholders

	Privacy Policies	Procedures and Standards	Awareness and Training	Metrics and Dashboard	Engagement and Involvement
Senior Leadership Team (SLT)	Privacy charter Organization-wide policies	N/A	SLT level awareness/ one-pagers	SLT/boardroom dashboard	Sponsor for budget and resource approval
Business Heads	Business specific policies (i.e., research, production, marketing, sales)	Business relevant operation procedures	Business specific and related awareness and training courses	Business enablement metrics and dashboard	Business heads as owners Champions from business units
IT Leaders	IT specific policies (i.e., email communication)	IT relevant operation procedures	IT specific and related awareness and training courses	IT related metrics and dashboard	CIO as owner Champions from IT department
HR Leaders	HR specific policies (i.e., recruiting, employee management)	HR relevant operation procedures	HR specific and related awareness and training courses	HR related metrics and dashboard	HR leader as owner Champions from HR department
Privacy and Security Professionals	Privacy and security management policies	Privacy and security operations	In-depth training Certifications	Operational metrics (i.e., DSR counts and on-time response rate)	Core team
Employees	General policy (i.e., acceptable use policy)	N/A	Annual employee awareness course	N/A	Engaged

	Policies	SOPs	Expert Groups/ Incentives	Training Modules	Awareness Programs	Scorecard
Executive	Enterprise-wide policies		Owner/ sponsor		Executive awareness	Executive scorecard
Business Leadership	Business-related policies	Business-related SOPs	Champions	Business-related training	Business awareness	Business leadership scorecard
Specialist	Security and privacy mgmt. policies	Security and privacy mgmt. SOPs	Core team	Profession-related training		
Foundations	Daily job-related policy		Incentive program		Employee awareness	

Info-Tech Insight

To truly take hold, privacy and security engagement must be supported by senior leadership, aligned with business objectives, and embedded within each of the organization's operating groups and teams.

 ### Guide and Recommendations

Each employee has a different role, responsibility, and level of accountability with respect to privacy and security. Organizations that follow Info-Tech's research of "Embed Privacy and Security Culture Within Your Organization" can align their privacy and security engagement enablers in a manner that takes into account the role and function that the individual fulfills. Certain enablers will align more closely with specific organizational groups. For example, the Executive Scorecard will heavily align with the Executive team, somewhat align with the Leadership team, and likely not be relevant for the Specialist and Foundations groups. Please see the examples below.

 ### Case Study

FCC v. AT&T, 2015
   AT&T data breach fined $25M by FCC on April 8, 2015.
   AT&T's call centers in Mexico, Colombia, and the Philippines violated consumer privacy. Employees of three locations have unauthorized access to consumers' names, phone numbers, Social Security numbers, and other account-related information to obtain AT&T cell phone unlock codes and provide this information to a third party, which holds a large number of stolen or second-hand phones require this information to unlock the phone. Because AT&T failed to take effective measures to avoid such behaviors and failed to notify the FCC in a timely manner after the customer's proprietary network information was leaked, the FCC fined AT&T $25M.

Part 4

Privacy Operations

DOI: 10.1201/9781003225089-16

13 Privacy Impact Assessment (PIA)

This chapter is intended to help readers to establish and operationalize a privacy impact assessment process to identify and mitigate privacy risks at an acceptable level.

This chapter covers the following topics:

- *Definition of privacy impact assessment*
- *PIA vs. DPIA vs. PbD*
- *PIA legal obligations and industry guidelines*
- *Core components of a PIA report*
- *When a PIA is needed*
- *PIA process*

13.1 WHAT IS A PIA

A privacy impact assessment (PIA) is a systematic assessment of a business or project that identifies the impact that the project might have on the privacy of individuals and sets out recommendations for managing, minimizing, or eliminating those impacts.

The object of a privacy risk assessment (PIA) is to identify problems and risks and find the proper solutions or controls to manage privacy risks. In other words, a PIA is to prevent rather than put out fires. PIA process can help organizations incorporate data protection considerations into organizational planning and demonstrate compliance to supervisory authorities. Privacy impact assessments are most effective when aligned or integrated with an organization's overall risk management approach.

Some privacy regulations (i.e., GDPR) requiring a data controller shall, prior to the processing, carry out an assessment of the impact of the envisaged processing operations on the protection of personal data. For instance, GDPR Art. 35 states that a data protection impact assessment shall in particular be required in the case of:

(a) A systematic and extensive evaluation of personal aspects relating to natural persons which is based on automated processing, including profiling, and on which decisions are based that produce legal effects concerning the natural person or similarly significantly affect the natural person;

(b) Processing on a large scale of special categories of data referred to in Article 9(1), or of personal data relating to criminal convictions and offenses referred to in Article 10; or

(c) A systematic monitoring of a publicly accessible area on a large scale.

Organizations should establish a consistent process for privacy impact assessment. An organization's privacy impact assessment provides a snapshot of its current privacy risks and how it will manage them as an organization. A privacy impact assessment will allow an organization to:

- identify privacy risks
- identify potential mitigations
- prioritize resources to areas of greatest risk
- identify opportunities for improvement

Each PIA will vary depending on the nature and extent of personal information that is involved in a business process or project. However, there are some general principles that consistently apply to PIAs.

A PIA:

- Needs to consider the privacy risks and mitigation strategies for a business process or project, it's not just a basic compliance check.
- Should be done at a stage that is early enough for it to influence how the business process or project proceeds (for example, at the planning and design or business case stage).
- Should evolve with a business process or project (an effective PIA will contemplate privacy risks that might arise if a project expands in scale or scope; when the project changes, the PIA should be revisited and updated)
- Should incorporate feedback on privacy risks from stakeholders that might be interested or affected by a business process or project.
- Will map how information is collected as part of a project, and once it is collected, how the information will flow (who can access it, how it will be stored, what it will be used for, and so on).
- Should identify any privacy issues and suggest ways that the privacy risks can be managed, minimized, or eliminated (using the information flow map).

Privacy impact assessments should be prepared in consultation with the appropriate business units and external stakeholders.

For instance, when an organization conducts a PIA, it should:

- Seek advice from the CPO/DPO.
- When appropriate, seek the views of data subjects or their representatives on the intended processing.
- Consultation with the supervisory authority when the PIA/DPIA indicates a high risk to data subjects that are not mitigated.

13.2   PIA VS. DPIA VS. PBD

The term Privacy Impact Assessment (PIA) is often used in other contexts to refer to the same concept of Data Protection Impact Assessment (DPIA). Therefore, basically, they are the same thing as described in ICO and Deloitte's guidelines. In this book, the term PIA will be used interchangeably with DPIA.

- *ICO-Preparing for the General Data Protection Regulation (GDPR): 12 steps to take now*
  - *Page 10 "Note that where a PIA (or DPIA as the GDPR terms it) indicates high-risk data processing, you will be required to consult the ICO to seek its opinion as to whether the processing operation complies with the GDPR."*
- *Deloitte—The General Data Protection Regulation: Long-awaited EU-wide data protection law finalized*
  - *In the section of PIAs "The DPIA resembles Privacy Impact Assessments (PIAs) that many organizations already execute regularly."*

Privacy by Design (PbD) is a methodology. The core idea is to proactively consider privacy protection. The objective is to avoid or minimize privacy risks with respect to business management and operations.

The implementation of the PbD methodology should not only be included in the research and development process but also in the entire life cycle of the product. PIA, as a method of privacy risk assessment, is introduced into the process of PbD landing R&D process as a tool for risk identification.

13.3 LEGAL OBLIGATIONS AND INDUSTRY GUIDELINES

Table 13.1 lists some examples of regulatory requirements regarding privacy impact assessment from various privacy laws and regulations.

Many countries have developed and published PIA guidelines including the EU, US (different sectors have their own PIA guides, DHS, HHS, DISA, etc.), UK, Canada, Australia, Dutch, etc. Table 13.2 lists some examples of guidelines from various jurisdictions.

TABLE 13.1
Examples of Regulatory Requirements Regarding Privacy Impact Assessment

Region	Privacy Regulation	Related Section and Description
EU	GDPR	Article 35 Data protection impact assessment (a PIA) is mandatory for data controllers in the following situations: 1) Where there is a systematic and extensive evaluation of personal aspects relating to natural persons, which is based on automated processing, including profiling, and on which decisions are based that produce legal effects concerning the natural person or similarly significantly affect the natural person 2) Processing on a large scale of sensitive personal data and personal data relating to criminal convictions and offenses 3) Systematic monitoring of a publicly accessible area on a large scale.
US	E-Government Act of 2002	SEC. 208. Privacy Provisions The E-Government Act of 2002, Section 208, establishes the requirement for agencies to conduct privacy impact assessments (PIAs) for electronic information systems and collections. A) IN GENERAL. An agency shall take actions described under subparagraph (B) before— (i) developing or procuring information technology that collects, maintains, or disseminates information that is in an identifiable form; or (ii) initiating a new collection of information that— (I) will be collected, maintained, or disseminated using information technology; and (II) includes any information in an identifiable form permitting the physical or online contacting of a specific individual, if identical questions have been posed to, or identical reporting requirements imposed on, 10 or more persons, other than agencies, instrumentalities, or employees of the Federal Government.
Mexico	FEDERAL LAW ON THE PROTECTION OF PERSONAL DATA HELD BY PRIVATE PARTIES	Article 39(X) Carry out studies of the impact on privacy prior to the implementation of new types of processing of personal data or material modification of existing types of processing.
Canada	Directive on Privacy Impact Assessment takes effect on April 1, 2010. Requires all government institutes to conduct PIA.	
UK	There is no statutory requirement for any organization to complete a PIA. However, central government departments have been instructed to complete PIAs by Cabinet Office.	
Dutch	As of September 1st, 2013, in the Netherlands, a new rule applies to ICT proposals initiated by the national-level government entities (Ministries, etc.): ICT project proposals must now include a Privacy Impact Assessment (PIA).	

TABLE 13.2
PIA Guidelines

Region	Guideline
EU	• PIAF Deliverable D1—A Privacy Impact Assessment Framework for data protection and privacy rights • PIAF—Recommendations for a privacy impact assessment framework for the European Union, November 2012
US	• NIST SP800—122 Guide to Protecting the Confidentiality of Personally Identifiable Information (PII) • DHS—PIA Guide 2010 • DHS—Handbook for Safeguarding Sensitive Personally Identifiable Information 2012 • DoD PIA Guide 2008 • DISA PIA Guide • SEC—PRIVACY IMPACT ASSESSMENT (PIA) GUIDE 2007
UK	• ICO—Preparing for the General Data Protection Regulation (GDPR) 12 steps to take now • ICO—Conducting privacy impact assessments code of practice (Does not specify either Data Controller or Data Processor) • ICO—Privacy Impact Assessment Handbook v2.0
Canada	• Directive on Privacy Impact Assessment Appendix C—Core privacy impact assessment • Office of the Information and Privacy Commissioner of Alberta, Privacy Impact Assessment Requirements for Use with the Health Information Act
Australia	• Australian Government Office of the Australian Information Commissioner—Guide to undertaking privacy impact assessments 2014 • The Australian Privacy Commissioner (OPC) PIA Guide 2004 • The Victorian Privacy Commissioner (OVPC) PIA Guide
New Zealand	• Office of the Privacy Commissioner—PIA handbook • Office of the Privacy Commissioner—Privacy Impact Assessment (PIA) Toolkit
Dutch	• PIA model

13.4 CORE COMPONENTS OF A PIA REPORT

The PIA report is a living document intended to identify risks and identify measures and is therefore never "finished". It is not an in-control statement or management statement about compliance.

In general, a PIA report should cover the following areas and identify specific components or actions taken or to be taken to meet each area's requirements.

- Systematic description of the personal data processing operations
  - Collection authority
  - Types of personal data
  - Data subjects involved
  - Duration of the data processing
- The lawful basis and purposes of the processing
- Assessment of the necessity and proportionality of the processing operations in relation to the purposes
- Assessment of the risks to the rights and freedoms of data subjects
  - Of the data processing itself: data collection, use, retention, accuracy, disclosure, security, cross-border transfers, etc.
  - In case of a data breach
  - Potential risks/harm for data subjects and the influence on individuals' rights and interests

- Privacy risk mitigating measures: protective measures undertaken are legal, effective, and suitable to the degree of risk.
  - Measures envisaged addressing the risks, including safeguards, security measures, and mechanisms to ensure the protection of personal data
  - Address the risks
  - Demonstrate compliance with privacy Regulations
- Discuss with stakeholders (if possible)
  - Prior consultation DPA where risks found in PIA cannot be mitigated
- Document PIA results
- Periodic evaluation

13.5   TRIGGER OF A PIA

Organizations should perform privacy impact assessments for existing business processes to assess and mitigate privacy and data protection risks. Organizations should ensure new initiatives or processes will take privacy risks into consideration at early stages, for instance, integrating PIA into project management practices, etc.

13.5.1   HIGH-RISK DATA PROCESSING SCENARIOS

In general, a PIA process should cover high-risk data processing scenarios that the processing is likely to entail a significant risk or harm to the rights and freedoms of natural person.

An interference with privacy means an organization has breached someone's privacy and they have suffered harm as a result. Privacy harms can be abstract and hard to imagine. Harm can be actual or anticipated (meaning the consequence has not yet happened).

Businesses must consider not only the harms of unintended or unauthorized uses of data, but also the harms of intended uses of the data, including screening, scoring, and other forms of algorithmic decision-making. Businesses must also account for the full range of harms that can result from the processing and misuse of personal information.[25]

The concept of "significant harm" includes any harm that may cause—physical, emotional, or material damage to data subjects. Examples are listed as follows.

- Bodily harm
- Humiliation
- Discrimination
- Damage to reputation or relationships
- Loss of employment, business, or professional opportunities
- Financial loss
- Significant economic or social disadvantage
- Identity theft or fraud
- Inability to exercise rights (including but not limited to privacy rights)
- Inability to access services or opportunities
- Loss of control over the use of personal data
- Loss of confidentiality

Table 13.3 lists DPIA guidelines from some of the European Economic Area (EEA) member states.

Based on the analysis of all guidelines mentioned previously, I summarize a list of high-risk data processing activities in Table 13.4 (not an exhaustive list).

TABLE 13.3

DPIA Guidelines from (EEA) Member States

EEA Member State	DPIA List	EDPB Comments
Austria	Whitelist from the Austrian Data Protection Authority	Opinion 1/2018 Austrian SAs DPIA List
Belgium	Blacklist & whitelist from the Belgian Privacy Commission	Opinion 2/2018 Belgium SAs DPIA List
Bulgaria	Списък на видовете операции по обработване на лични данни, за които се изисква извършване на оценка за въздействие върху защитата на данните съгласно чл. 35, пар. 4 от Регламент (ЕС) 2016/679 https://iapp.org/media/pdf/resource_center/bulgaria_blacklist.pdf	Opinion 3/2018 Bulgaria SAs DPIA List
Croatia	https://iapp.org/media/pdf/resource_center/croatia_blacklist.pdf	Opinion 25/2018 Croatia SAs DPIA List
Cyprus	https://iapp.org/media/pdf/resource_center/cyprus_blacklist.pdf	
Czech Republic	https://iapp.org/media/pdf/resource_center/czech_blacklist.pdf	Opinion 4/2018 Czech Republic SAs DPIA List
Denmark	www.datatilsynet.dk/media/6928/draft-danish-dpia-list.pdf	Opinion 24/2018 Denmark SAs DPIA List
Estonia	https://iapp.org/media/pdf/resource_center/estonia_blacklist.pdf	Opinion 6/2018 Estonia SAs DPIA List
Finland	https://tietosuoja.fi/en/list-of-processing-operations-which-require-dpia	Opinion 8/2018 Finland SAs DPIA List
France	Blacklist from the CNIL https://iapp.org/media/pdf/resource_center/france_blacklist.pdf	Opinion 9/2018 France SAs DPIA List
Germany	Blacklists from German DPAs	Opinion 5/2018 Germany SAs DPIA List
Greece	www.gdpr-awareness.eu/files/GDPR-Article-35-DPIA-List.EN.pdf	Opinion 7/2018 Greece SAs DPIA List
Hungary	Blacklist from the Hungarian data protection authority	Opinion 10/2018 Hungary SAs DPIA List
Ireland	Blacklist from the Data Protection Commission https://iapp.org/media/pdf/resource_center/irish_dpc_blacklist.pdf	Opinion 11/2018 Ireland SAs DPIA List
Italy	Blacklist from the Italian Data Protection Authority	Opinion 12/2018 Italy SAs DPIA List
Latvia	https://iapp.org/media/pdf/resource_center/latvia_blacklist.pdf	Opinion 14/2018 Latvia SAs DPIA List
Lithuania	www.ada.lt/go.php/eng/List-of-data-processing-operations-subject-to-the-requirement-to-perform-data-protection-impact-assessment/1	Opinion 13/2018 Lithuania SAs DPIA List
Luxembourg	https://cnpd.public.lu/en/professionnels/obligations/AIPD.html	Opinion 26/2018 Luxembourg SAs DPIA List
Malta	https://idpc.org.mt/en/Pages/dpia.aspx	Opinion 15/2018 Malta SAs DPIA List
Netherlands	https://iapp.org/media/pdf/resource_center/dutch_final_dpia.pdf	Opinion 16/2018 Netherlands SAs DPIA List
Poland	Blacklist from Poland's DPA https://iapp.org/media/pdf/resource_center/poland_blacklist.pdf	Opinion 17/2018 Poland SAs DPIA List
Portugal	Blacklist from Portugal's National Commission for Data Protection	Opinion 18/2018 Portugal SAs DPIA List
Romania	https://privacyone.ro/2018/11/20/romanian-dpa-adopts-dpia-list/	Opinion 19/2018 Romania SAs DPIA List

EEA Member State	DPIA List	EDPB Comments
Slovakia	www.dataprotection.gov.sk/uoou/sites/default/files/ list_of_processing_operations_which_are_subject_to_ the_requirement_for_dpia.pdf	Opinion 21/2018 Slovakia SAs DPIA List
Slovenia	www.ip-rs.si/fileadmin/user_upload/Pdf/Ocene_ucinkov/ SI_DPIA_list_35-4_35-6_Slovenia_revised_21dec2018_ OBJAVA_ZA_WEB.pdf	Opinion 27/2018 Slovenia SAs DPIA List
Spain	www.twobirds.com/en/news/articles/2019/spain/ spanish-data-protection-agency-publishes-list-of- processing-operations	Opinion 6/2019 on the draft list of the competent supervisory authority of Spain regarding the processing operations subject to the requirement of a data protection impact assessment
Sweden	www.datainspektionen.se/globalassets/dokument/beslut/ list-regarding-data-protection-impact-assessments.pdf	Opinion 20/2018 Sweden SAs DPIA List
United Kingdom	Blacklist from the Information Commissioner's Office	Opinion 22/2018 United Kingdom SAs DPIA List
Norway	www.datatilsynet.no/globalassets/global/regelverk/ veiledere/dpia-veileder/dpialist280119.pdf	https://iapp.org/media/pdf/resource_ center/edpb_opinion_2019_02.pdf
Iceland	www.dataprotection.ie/sites/default/files/uploads/2018-11/ Data-Protection-Impact-Assessment.pdf	Opinion 7/2019 on the draft list of the competent supervisory authority of Iceland regarding the processing operations subject to the requirement of a data protection impact assessment
Liechtenstein	www.datenschutzstelle.li/application/files/7515/4028/5547/ DPIA_List_Liechtenstein_finalversion_ENG_20181023.pdf	https://iapp.org/media/pdf/resource_ center/edpb_opinion_2019_01.pdf

TABLE 13.4
Examples of High-Risk Data Processing Activities

Processing	Description
Processing special categories of personal data	Involves the special categories of personal data defined in GDPR, Article 9. Personal data relates to the following types of special categories of personal data: • Racial or ethnic origin • Political opinions • Religious or philosophical beliefs • Trade union membership • Genetic and biometric data (for the purpose of uniquely identifying a natural person) • Health • Sexual behavior and/or sexual orientation
Data relating to criminal convictions or offenses	Processing of personal data relating to criminal convictions and offenses. For example, data about criminal allegations, proceedings, or convictions; processing activities that are further transferred to law enforcement agencies; whistleblowing system.
Data processed on a large scale	The following factors should be particularly considered when determining whether the processing is carried out on a large scale. One common example is your organization processing personal data from customers (data subjects). Also consider: • The number of data subjects concerned, either as a specific number or as a proportion of the relevant population • The volume of data and/or the range of different data items being processed • The duration, or permanence, of the data processing activity • The geographical extent of the processing activity

(Continued)

TABLE 13.4   (Continued)

Processing	Description
Evaluation or scoring	Includes profiling and predicting, especially from "aspects concerning the data subject's performance at work, economic situation, health, personal preferences or interests, reliability or behavior, location or movements." Example: a company building behavioral (or marketing) profiles based on usage or navigation on its website, gathering public social media data for generating profiles, and processing economic situation data.
Employee monitoring	Processing is used to observe, monitor, or control employees, including data collected through networks or "a systematic monitoring of a publicly accessible area." "Employee" is one of the nine main criteria of data concerning vulnerable data subjects and covers aspects concerning the data subject's performance at work. It is suggested that a DPIA would be required if the criteria of vulnerable data subjects and systematic monitoring were met. Example: information security monitoring
Tracking and monitoring	This processing involves tracking an individual's geolocation or behavior, including but not limited to the online environment. Further examples include: • Social networks and software applications • Hardware/software offering fitness/lifestyle/health monitoring • IoT devices, applications, and platforms • Web and cross-device tracking (excluding cookies) • Eye-tracking (for example, using eye-tracking to determine users' attention distribution on web pages) • Processing location data of employees • Wealth profiling—the identification of high net-worth individuals for the purposes of direct marketing
Deployment and modification of a public CCTV surveillance system	The WP29 interprets "publicly accessible area" as being any place open to any member of the public, e.g., a piazza, shopping center, street, marketplace, train station, or public library. It is recommended that data protection impact assessments are carried out when: • Cameras are added to systems • The positions of cameras are changed • Whole or parts of systems are upgraded • New systems are installed
Matching or combining datasets	One example: originating from two or more data processing operations performed for different purposes and/or by different data controllers in a way that would exceed the reasonable expectations of the data subject.
Data concerning vulnerable data subjects	Vulnerable data subjects are in any case where an imbalance in the relationship between the positions of the data subject and controller can be identified. Vulnerable data subjects may include children (they are considered as not able to knowingly and thoughtfully oppose or consent to the processing of their data), employees, the elderly, patients, and other more vulnerable segments of the population requiring special protection (people experiencing mental illness, asylum seekers, etc.).
Whether to make decisions that may greatly affect data subjects	This refers to when the processing in itself "prevents data subjects from exercising a right or using a service or a contract." This includes processing operations that aim at allowing, modifying, or refusing data subjects' access to a service or entry into a contract. For example, using automated decision-making to decide whether to provide service to the data subjects.
Disclosure to recipients other than the organization's affiliates	Whether to disclose to recipients other than the organization's affiliates.
Cross-border transfer	Whether cross-border transfer exists. (Note: The cross-border transfer in this point refers specifically to the scenarios where personal data will be transferred outside EU/EEA scope, which is considered a high-risk activity.)

Questions and answers

What is the definition of large scale?

While the GDPR does not define what constitutes large-scale processing, the WP29 has previously recommended in its guidelines WP243 on data protection officers (DPOs) that the following factors, in particular, be considered when determining whether the processing is carried out on a large scale:

- the number of data subjects concerned—either as a specific number or as a proportion of the relevant population
- the volume of data and/or the range of different data items being processed
- the duration, or permanence, of the data processing activity
- the geographical extent of the processing activity

Ireland DPIA guide—Examples of large-scale processing include:

- a hospital (but not an individual doctor) processing patient data
- tracking individuals using a city's public transport system
- a supermarket chain tracking real-time location of its customers
- an insurance company or bank processing customer data
- a search engine processing data for behavioral advertising
- a telephone or internet service provider processing user data

Note: Individual professionals processing patient or client data are not processing on a large scale.

Info-Tech Insight

Structure drives success: take a process vs. system-based approach to assessing personal data as it flows throughout the organization.

Fit privacy to the business: Contextualize privacy for your organization by involving the business units from day 1 and collect requirements that promote cross-collaboration.

Guide and Recommendations

Organizations that follow Info-Tech's privacy program methodology and tools can utilize its DPIA threshold assessment tool to assess how much private data will be affected by planned processing activities. This tool provides a threshold assessment function to help organizations determine whether a light or full DPIA is needed. The threshold assessment questionnaire is listed below.

- Does this processing strongly resemble another data processing activity for which a DPIA has already been performed?
- Do you have a lawful basis for this processing activity?
- Is consent the lawful basis (e.g. marketing communications)?
- What kind of data will you be processing?
- Do you have a lawful basis for processing personal data?
- Will you be processing data of vulnerable persons?
- Will you be processing biometric and/or genetic data?
- Will personal data from multiple sources/databases be combined, compared, or matched?

- Is personal data obtained without the knowledge of the Data Subject?
- Will you be tracking the Data Subject's geolocation or behavior in an offline or online capacity?
- Has the data you plan to collect already been made publicly available?
- Will you be processing any type of data on a large scale?
- Will you be processing personal data on a large scale?
- Will you be systematically monitoring a publicly accessible area?
- Will this large-scale processing likely make it more difficult for Data Subjects to exercise their rights?
- Will you be profiling or using automated decision making?
- Do you have a lawful basis for processing data via automated decision making?
- Will profiling be conducted on a large scale?
- Will this profiling or automated decision making be used to make decisions about a Data Subject's access to a service, opportunity, or benefit?
- Will the choices, behavior, or circumstance of the Data Subject be affected in a significant and noticeable way?
- Is this profiling or automated decision making systematic?
- Will this processing involve new technologies or existing technologies used in a new way?
- Will EU personal data be moved outside of the EU borders?

13.5.2 PRIVACY BY DESIGN

Organizations should integrate privacy by design and by default into the business processes to ensure data protection principles are followed and data subjects' rights are protected. If the organization undertakes product or software development work that might involve personal data processing, the organization should integrate privacy-by-design into the PDLC phases such as requirement analysis, design, development, testing, deployment, operations, etc.

In addition, I would recommend organizations embed PIA into business processes and product development lifecycle as demonstrated in Figure 13.1.

Privacy protective features should be designed into a system, rather than bolted-on later. You should start early to ensure that project risks are identified and appreciated before the problems become embedded in the design. You should commence a PIA as part of the project initiation phase (or its equivalent in whichever project method the organization uses). If the project is already under way, start today, so that any major issues are identified with the minimum possible delay.

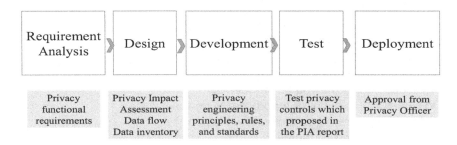

FIGURE 13.1   PIA in business processes and product development lifecycle.

The quality attributes required to improve privacy in design include:

- Identifiability: the extent to which an individual can be identified within a system
- Network centricity: the extent to which personal information remains local to the client
- Availability: the need to ensure that information is available to satisfy business needs
- Integrity: the extent that the system maintains a reliable state, including the quality of the data being free from error:
  - Accuracy: whether information is correct and free from errors
  - Completeness: whether there is any missing information
  - Currency: whether the information is up to date
- Mobility: the extent to which a system moves from one location to another
- Predictability: aims to enable reliable assumptions about a system, particularly its data and the processing of that data by all stakeholders
- Manageability: refers to the ability to granularly administer personal information, including modification, disclosure, and deletion

Table 13.5 lists the key differences between Privacy by Design and Privacy by Default.

 Example: Google Buzz

An example of how the accountability principle has been interpreted arose when, on February 9, 2010, Google Inc. released Google Buzz, a social networking tool that automatically draws upon contact information from a user's Gmail account, adding certain contacts as "followers" and thereby revealing potentially sensitive user information. By February 12, 2010, one blogger had already posted a complaint stating that the automatic follow feature had exposed information about her current location and workplace to an abusive ex-husband. The privacy commissioner, along with privacy officers from nine other nations, sent an open letter to Google's CEO calling on the company to correct its inadequate privacy protection system. In essence, the data protection commissioners from around the world called on Google and all large social media companies to be more accountable for the information they control.

TABLE 13.5

Key Differences between Privacy by Design and Privacy by Default

Privacy by Design	Privacy by Default
Data privacy must be embedded into the design and overall lifecycle of any technology, to provide safeguards on personal data.	• Is to ensure that only personal data that is necessary to achieve your specific purpose is processed. Things to consider:
Things to consider when reviewing business processes, products, or services are:	• Adopt default privacy settings on systems
• Using a new way of storing data	• Be transparent with your customers and employees on data processing activities and practices
• Engaging a third party to manage and maintain an IT system	• Only process data that is proportionate to the purpose
• Transferring data to a new third party	• Provide information and options to individuals to exercise their rights
• New or changing business process	
• New product offering	
• New use of existing data to improve a product or service	

13.5.3 PRIVACY BY DEFAULT

90% of users will usually follow the indicated default. System functions and features that might cause users privacy concerns should be disabled by default and should be not enabled unless permissions are granted by users.

Functions involving user privacy protection should be set to protect privacy by default. Insecure settings may incur user privacy disclosure or other losses. The privacy should be protected by default, not requiring users to perform extra operations. Comply with the customer's requirement or industry practice if the customer requires otherwise or the product settings are already compliant with industry conventions. In scenarios where the customer requires otherwise, submit the customer's requirement to the requirement management process (e.g., submitting a contract to the contract review process).

The Article 29 Working Party of the EU proposes in WP223 Opinion 8/2014 on the Recent Developments on the Internet that, to prevent location tracking, device manufacturers should limit device fingerprinting by disabling wireless interfaces when they are not used or should use random identifiers (such as random MAC addresses to scan Wi-Fi networks) to prevent a persistent identifier from being used for location tracking.

Mainstream industry vendors (such as Samsung and Apple) forbid the recorder function during phone calls.

As stipulated in section 5.3.1 in the Chinese communications industry standard Technical Requirements for Security Capability of Smart Mobile Terminal, third-party apps should obtain users' opt-in consent before invoking the sensitive functions of MITs.

As stipulated in section 5.3.1 in the Chinese communications industry standard Technical Requirements for Security Capability of Smart Mobile Terminal, MIT operating systems should provide user data protection functions.

Some notable examples are listed as follows regarding privacy by default.

- GPS is disabled by default on a mobile phone. When any app needs to use location information, a dialog box will be displayed to ask the user whether to enable GPS.
  - Example: A weather and clock app does not use user locations by default. A user can enable the use of location for a better experience and disable it on the configuration page at any time. Upon the first use of this app, a message will be displayed to obtain users' consent for using their locations.
- The automatic synchronization and backup function for user data, such as contacts, photos, and short messages, is disabled by default in phones. Users can enable the function on the configuration page or back up data manually.
- Home appliances: Listening mode disabled by default for Alexa, etc.
- If a product allows mute photo taking, the muting option must be provided and not enabled by default (photo taking is not mute by default). Muting can be exploited for secret photo-taking. Industry specifications in Japan and South Korea require that products sold in these countries must not provide the mute photo-taking function (completely forbidding). The function can be provided in other countries only after Legal Affairs Dept thinks that the function complies with local laws after assessment.
- Do not enable the recorder during phone calls. If a local recorder is enabled during phone calls, both parties' calls can be recorded. If not appropriately designed, this function may breach user privacy. We should align with the industry and forbid the recorder during phone calls.

13.6 PIA PROCESS

Figure 13.2 illustrates an example of a privacy impact assessment process and Table 13.6 describes seven steps as well as the key considerations throughout the process.

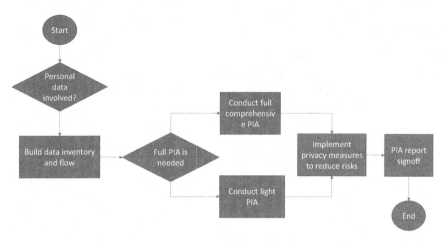

FIGURE 13.2 An example of a privacy impact assessment process.

TABLE 13.6

Seven Steps and Key Considerations

Step	Operation	Key Consideration
1. Identify whether personal data is involved	Determine whether a business process collects, and processes personal data based on your organization's definition.	The definition of personal data should be formally established within your organization.
2. Establish a data inventory and/or a data flow	Establish the data inventory and data flow for this business process.	The data inventory normally should cover the following components: (a) the name and contact details of the controller and, where applicable, the joint controller, the controller's representative, and the data protection officer (b) the purposes of the processing (c) a description of the categories of data subjects and the categories of personal data (d) the categories of recipients to whom the personal data have been or will be disclosed including recipients in third countries or international organizations (e) where applicable, transfers of personal data to a third country or an international organization, including the identification of that third country or international organization (f) where possible, the envisaged time limits for erasure of the different categories of data (g) where possible, a general description of the technical and organizational security measures
3. Determine whether a full PIA is needed	Assess whether a business process will pose high privacy risks to the data subjects and your organization.	You can reference the list of high-risk data processing activities listed in the previous section.

(Continued)

TABLE 13.6   (Continued)

Step	Operation	Key Consideration
4. Risk assessment	Based on the result of 3, carry out either a full PIA or a light PIA to assess privacy risks.	When identifying privacy risks, you should assess privacy risks throughout the information life cycle: • Collection • Storage and security • Use • Access and correction • Disclosure • Retention • Disposal Having identified the privacy risks, an organization will need to understand the: • possible consequences • likelihood of each risk occurring to assign a rating to each risk. An organization's risk and assurance team should establish a risk rating matrix that can be used to assess privacy risks. In addition to establishing the consequence and likelihood of a risk, calculating the cost of the risk actualizing can be a useful exercise to communicate the severity of the risk.
5. Risk mitigation	Propose countermeasures and implement risk mitigation methods appropriate to the risk levels.	Having rated the privacy risks, an organization will need to determine its response to each of the identified risks. Common responses include: • Avoid/eliminate—reducing the probability of the risk eventuating to zero. • Mitigate—reducing the consequence and/or likelihood of the risk. • Accept—accepting the risk and its consequences. When deciding which response to adopt, consider the feasibility of the mitigation, the cost of the mitigation, and the cost of remedying any harm caused to individuals. Different organizations will manage privacy risks differently depending on their risk appetite.
6. Document and sign off on PIA results	Record all activities and evidence and sign off on the PIA report.	The PIA report should be fully communicated and signed off.
7. Monitor and update	Monitor the changes and update the PIA report accordingly	The ongoing effectiveness of privacy risk assessment requires monitoring, reviewing, and updating. The consequences and/or likelihood of privacy risks may change over time depending on factors both internal and external to an organization. The effectiveness of the mitigations of the risks may also change over time and an agency may need to reconsider risks that were previously accepted.

14 Record of Processing Activities

This chapter is intended to help readers establish a data inventory to record personal data processing activities in a compliant and systematic manner.

This chapter covers the following topics:

- *Visibility of data processing activities*
- *Data inventory core components*
- *Process-driven data inventory*

14.1 VISIBILITY OF DATA PROCESSING ACTIVITIES

Structure drives success. A data processing inventory is the foundation of further privacy risk assessment and mitigation. A data inventory identifies the personal information an organization handles as it moves across the organization's systems and is an important component of an effective privacy risk assessment.

A good privacy program starts with knowledge. An organization should establish and maintain an up-to-date data processing inventory as records of data processing.

The data processing inventory can help organizations fulfill regulatory needs (e.g., GDPR Art. 30). The record of data processing takes a dynamic and comprehensive approach to mapping data's flow throughout an organization. It acts as a document that demonstrates an organization's accountability and awareness of how personal data is leveraged. This document inventories the full set of processes in which personal data is collected and processed by the organization.

The following are examples from some privacy-related regulations.

GDPR Records of processing activities (Art. 30)
Each controller and, where applicable, the controller's representative, shall maintain a record of processing activities under its responsibility. That record shall contain all the following information:

(a) the name and contact details of the controller and, where applicable, the joint controller, the controller's representative, and the data protection officer.
(b) the purposes of the processing.
(c) a description of the categories of data subjects and the categories of personal data.
(d) the categories of recipients to whom the personal data have been or will be disclosed including recipients in third countries or international organizations.
(e) where applicable, transfers of personal data to a third country or an international organization, including the identification of that third country or international organization and, in the case of transfers referred to in the second subparagraph of Article 49(1), the documentation of suitable safeguards.
(f) where possible, the envisaged time limits for erasure of the different categories of data.
(g) where possible, a general description of the technical and organizational security measures as referred to in Article 32(1).

HIPAA

Disclosures or access (both authorized and unauthorized) of their PHI during the past 6 years, so you must log non-TPO of disclosures of PHI whether intentional or accidental.

Identifies gaps in the organization's data processing activities, and highlights data processing activities with a high degree of risk due to:

DOI: 10.1201/9781003225089-18

- Sensitivity of data stored
- Retention periods
- Vendor agreements
- Documentation of procedures around processing activities

 Questions and answers

What is the application of derogation provided by Art. 30 (5)?
The derogation provided by Article 30(5) is not absolute. There are three types of processing to which it does not apply. These are:

- Processing that is likely to result in a risk to the rights and freedoms of data subjects.
- Processing that is not occasional.
- Processing that includes special categories of data or personal data relating to criminal convictions and offenses.

WORKING PARTY 29 POSITION PAPER on the derogations from the obligation to maintain records of processing activities pursuant to Article 30(5) GDPR.

- The WP29 underlines that the wording of Article 30(5) is clear in providing that the three types of processing to which the derogation does not apply are alternative ("or") and the occurrence of any one of them alone triggers the obligation to maintain the record of processing activities.

14.2 DATA INVENTORY CORE COMPONENTS

A data processing inventory usually includes elements such as name of business processes, types of personal information processed, purposes of processing, legal basis of processing, etc.

A robust privacy protection program should cover end-to-end data flows to avoid missing any uncontrolled risks with respect to internal transferring of personal data. Establish and maintain up-to-date data flows among business processes and/or IT systems to reflect the actual personal data lifecycle.

Note: Personal data should only be shared with relevant internal business processes or recipients for the purposes specified in the privacy notice. Personal data flow is also an effective vehicle to record internal personal data sharing activities.

Take GDPR as an example: GDPR's article 30 about records of processing requires a data inventory should cover the following core components.

1) For a data controller
- Name, contact details of controller
- Name contact details representative and DPO (*)
- Purposes of processing
- Process should be established, or system should be implemented to ensure personal data processing activities have appropriate legal basis and records kept properly.
    - Legitimate interests: Demonstrate Processing is necessary for the purposes of the legitimate interests pursued by the controller or by a third party, except where such interests are overridden by the interests or fundamental rights and freedoms of the data subject which require protection of personal data, in particular where the data subject is a child.

- Categories of personal data, data subjects and recipients
- Transfers to non-EEA countries, incl. safeguards taken (*)
- Time limits for erasure (per category of data), if possible
- Description of security measures (if possible)
- (*) where applicable

2) For a data Processor

- Name, contact details processor
- Name, contact details of each controller
- Name contact details representative and DPO (*)
- Categories of processing
- Transfers to non-EEA countries, incl. safeguards taken (*)
- Description of security measures (if possible)
- (*) where applicable

 Example

Table 14.1 provides a data inventory example which was used by some organizations.

 Questions and answers

How often should I review or update the data inventory?

It is a living document. You should keep this inventory up to date. Technically, this should be integrated into the privacy impact assessment process, which should trigger the refresh or modifications. Otherwise, it should be reviewed regularly (annually, bi-annually) based on upon specific business context.

TABLE 14.1
Example of a Data Inventory

Component	Description
Business process that collects and processes personal data	*Describe the business process and the processing activities*
Source of collection	*Describe where the personal data is collected from, for instance, whether personal data is collected directly from the data subject or purchased from a third party*
Personal data type	*Describe what categories of personal data are collected*
Lawful basis	*Describe what's the lawful basis of the collection (i.e., consent, performance of a contract, legal obligation, etc.)*
Purposes of collecting and using personal data	*Describe the purposes and specific scenarios of collecting and using personal data*
Systems the data is stored in	*Describe where the personal data is stored*
Whether to disclose to the 3rd parties	*Describe whether personal data needs to be disclosed to third parties*
Country the personal data resides	*Describe which country personal data is stored*
Whether the data is transferred to third countries	*Describe whether the organization needs to cross-border transfer personal data*
What is the retention period of the personal data	*Describe how long it will be stored*
Security measures	*Describe the technical and organizational security measures that have been put in place to protect the personal data*
Business owner/contact	*Describe who/which department is the business owner of the personal data listed*

14.3   PROCESS-DRIVEN DATA INVENTORY

Based on my experience, the most cost-effective manner to establish and maintain a data inventory is to build the data inventory categorized and grouped by the business processes. Also, it is critical to determine the appropriate level of granularity with your processing activities.

Table 14.2 lists some exemplar business processes in a few business operation domains: HR, Finance, and Legal/Compliance.

TABLE 14.2
Examples of Business Processes

Business Operation	Exemplar Process
HR	Attract
	• Passive talent pool management
	Recruit
	• Application
	• Assessment
	• Standard background check
	• Health Check
	• Criminal record
	• Drug testing
	• Onboard
	• Offer and Onboarding
	• Payroll/Compensation
	• Benefits enrollment and administration
	• Perform and grow
	• Basic information updates
	• Time and attendance
	• Performance evaluation
	• Employee survey
	• Affirmative action reports
	• Exit/Off-boarding
	• Investigations and employee disciplinary
	• Termination
	• Retirement plans and management
	Alumni
Finance	• Planning & Forecasting
	• Financial Close & Consolidation
	• Financial Analysis and Reporting (management, statutory, disclosure)
	• Billing, Orders, and credit
	• Expense management (i.e., reimbursement)
	• Payroll processing
	• Authorized signatories
	• Compliance Regulatory Reporting (Taxation)
	• Investment appraisal
Legal/Compliance	• Document review (Agreement, Contract, MNDA/NDA)
	• Business advice (Business operations, Board-Level advice)
	• Complaint handling (internal and external)
	• Internal discovery and disciplinary Actions
	• Attorney-Client Privileged Content
	• Liaison with local law enforcement
	• Outside Counsel

15 Privacy Notice

This chapter is intended to help readers identify privacy risks associated with the transparency principle and create compliant privacy notices.

This chapter covers the following topics:

- *Privacy notice basics*
- *Types of privacy notices*
- *Fairness and transparency*
- *Core components of a privacy notice*
- *Key considerations of providing privacy notices*

15.1 PRIVACY NOTICE BASICS

A privacy notice is a mechanism of being transparent to data subjects.

To ensure that personal data are processed fairly and lawfully, controllers must provide the certain minimum information to data subjects, regarding the collection and further processing of their personal data. A privacy notice is a statement made to a data subject that describes how the organization collects, uses, retains, and discloses personal data. A privacy notice is sometimes referred to as a privacy statement, a privacy policy, or a fair processing statement.

The purpose of a privacy notice is to ensure individuals are aware of the way their data is processed and to help them understand what data is being collected, why, how it's being used, etc. Individuals should know who is collecting their personal information, how it's being used, and to whom it is disclosed. This is so they have the information necessary to exercise meaningful control over an organization's use of their personal information. At the time of or before collecting personal data through products, services, or marketing activities, an organization must reasonably endeavor to notify data subjects of the types of personal data collected, the purposes of the processing, the processing methods, the data subjects' rights with respect to their personal data, and the organization's security measures to protect personal data. Your privacy notice explains your commitment to the data subject. Make sure it's accessible at the beginning of all data collection activities.

 Example

Different organizations use different terms referring to the privacy notice. Some organizations prefer the term "privacy notice", while others prefer "privacy statement" or "privacy policy" or even other terms. Table 15.1 lists various terms used by some organizations.

Taking GDPR as an example, the key articles in relation to transparency in the GDPR, as they apply to the rights of the data subject, are found in Chapter III (Rights of the Data Subject). Article 12 sets out the general rules which apply to: the provision of information to data subjects (under Articles 13–14); communications with data subjects concerning the exercise of their rights (under Articles 15–22); and communications in relation to data breaches (Article 34).

Article 12 requires that the information or communication in question must comply with the following rules:

- it must be <u>concise, transparent, intelligible,</u> and <u>easily accessible</u> (Article 12.1)
- <u>clear and plain language</u> must be used (Article 12.1); the requirement for clear and plain language is of particular importance when providing information to children (Article 12.1)

DOI: 10.1201/9781003225089-19

TABLE 15.1

Examples of Privacy Notice, Policy, or Statement

	Privacy Policy	Privacy Statement	Privacy Notice	Historical Versions	List of Changes	Only Up-to-Date Version
AIA privacy policy	✓					✓
Alibaba privacy policy	✓					✓
Amazon's privacy notice			✓		✓	
Apple policy	✓					✓
Cisco privacy statement		✓		✓		
CVS pharmacy privacy policy	✓					✓
Disney privacy policy	✓					✓
Facebook data policy	✓					✓
Forbes privacy statement		✓				✓
Google privacy policy	✓			✓		
HPE		✓				✓
IAPP privacy notice			✓			✓
IBM privacy statement		✓		✓		
ICO (UK) privacy notice			✓		✓	
JD.com privacy policy	✓			✓		
LinkedIn privacy policy	✓				✓	
Microsoft policy statement		✓			✓	
Netflix privacy statement		✓				✓
Oracle general privacy policy	✓			✓		
Salesforce privacy statement		✓				✓
Samsung	✓					✓
Tencent privacy policy	✓					✓
Tiktok privacy policy	✓					✓
T-Mobile privacy notice			✓			✓
Twitter	✓			✓		

- it must be <u>in writing</u> "*or by other means, including where appropriate, by electronic means*" (Article 12.1); where requested by the data subject it may be provided <u>orally</u> (Article 12.1), and
- it generally must be provided <u>free of charge</u> (Article 12.5)

Where personal data have not been obtained from the data subject directly. For example, data is obtained from public channels, or shared by or purchased from other companies. Privacy notice should be provided within a reasonable period after obtaining the data.

Notice to data subjects may not be required when personal data is legitimately obtained from public channels if (i.e., GDPR requirement, applicable to Europe):

1) Data subject has already known it.
2) It is impossible to notify data subjects or doing so will require disproportionate effort or incur huge costs.
   Note: One case from Poland DPA demonstrated that mailing to 6 million data subject is not considered disproportionate effort or incurring huge costs.
3) Data collection complies with the laws and regulations of the EU or its Member States, and sufficient security protection measures are provided.

Case Study

Swedish DPA vs. Klarna Bank—lack of information on processing of customer data on company website.[26]

On March 29, 2022, the Swedish DPA fined Klarna Bank €727,070 for lack of information on processing of customer data on company website. The Swedish Data Protection Authority imposed the fine on the company because the information on the processing of customer data it had provided via its website did not comply with the requirements of the GDPR. Klarna had adjusted its data protection practices several times during the course of the investigation. The identified misconduct dates back to spring 2020.

The authority found that information on the purpose and legal basis of the processing of personal data was completely missing for one service. Similarly, Klarna did not provide any information on whether data was transferred to countries outside the EU or EEA. Other information was incomplete or incorrect. This concerned information regarding the transfer of data to Swedish and foreign credit agencies and regarding the recipients of various categories of data. Furthermore, Klarna had not properly informed the data subjects about their rights (including the rights to deletion, data portability and objection).

15.2 TYPES OF PRIVACY NOTICES

According to industry best practices, a privacy statement should be provided in all scenarios where personal data is collected online or offline, a website is hosted by or on behalf of the company, or software collects or transfers personal data to the company.

Some regulations set forth prescriptive requirements for the content that should be included in the privacy notice, such as PIPL Article 17, and GDPR Articles 12 and 13, etc. It is also common for organizations to create separate privacy notices for various business products/services, with examples listed as follows:

- Separate notices for different types of data subjects such as external customers, internal employees, job applicants, etc.
  - Employee Privacy Notice: This Privacy Notice doesn't need to be posted on your website and should be provided to employees whenever they become employees (or as soon thereafter as is possible). This should include the same information as contained in your wider Privacy Notice but only what's relevant to your employees.
  - Candidate Privacy Notice: You should also provide job applicants with a Privacy Notice. It should not be the same as your employee Privacy Notice, because you won't be processing the data in the same way as set out in the employee Privacy Notice until they become employees. Again, the Privacy Notice should set out the same information as in your general Privacy Notice, but only what's relevant to candidates.
- Separate notices for different products or services. For a company that offers a wide range of products, the privacy notices for each product can be incorporated into the overall privacy notice or provided separately. For instance, Google provides different privacy notices for YouTube and Chrome.
  - If an organization has more than one product or service that collects personal data for different purposes, each product or service should have its own privacy notice. The privacy notices for each product can either be provided separately or included in the overarching privacy notice with product-specific notice provided.
- Separate notices for different regions. For instance, some organizations provide different privacy notices for EU and California, etc.

- If the company's product or service collects and processes different types of personal data in different regions in a significant way that one privacy notice can't cover all scenarios, or the local laws (CCPA, etc.) have specific requirements that can't be addressed in one unified privacy notice, separate and customized privacy notices should be provided in the operating regions.

15.3   FAIRNESS AND TRANSPARENCY

Notice should be provided at the time when personal data are obtained where personal data are collected from the data subject. Notice should be provided in a timely manner where personal data have not been obtained from the data subject. Data subjects must be notified of the updates of privacy statements.

The information should be provided in a concise, transparent, intelligible, and easily accessible form, using clear and plain language, in particular for any information addressed specifically to a child.

15.3.1   FAIRNESS

Being transparent by providing a privacy notice is an important part of fair processing. You can't be fair if you are not being honest and open about who you are and what you are going to do with the personal data you collect. However, this is only one element of fairness. Providing a privacy notice does not by itself mean that your processing is necessarily fair. You also need to consider the effect of your processing on the individuals concerned.

The main elements of fairness include:

- Using information in a way, such as proportionate and not excessive, that people would reasonably expect. This may involve undertaking research to understand people's expectations about how their data will be used.
- Thinking about the impact of your processing. Will it have unjustified adverse effects on them?
- Being transparent and ensuring that people know how their information will be used. This means providing privacy notices or making them available, using the most appropriate mechanisms. In a digital context this can include all the online platforms used to deliver services.

15.3.2   TRANSPARENCY

An organization should be transparent with its data processing practices.

The privacy notice should be provided in appropriately. The privacy notice must be concise, transparent, intelligible, and easily accessible.

1) Concise communication
Under WP260 rev.01 Paragraph 8, "Concise communication" manner means that:
- Data controllers should present the information/communication efficiently and succinctly in order to avoid information fatigue.
- In an online context, the use of a layered privacy statement/notice will enable a data subject to navigate to the particular section of the privacy statement/notice that they want to immediately access rather than having to scroll through large amounts of text searching for particular issues.
- This information should be clearly differentiated from other non-privacy-related information such as contractual provisions or general terms of use.

- Note: In the EU, EULA (civil law) and the privacy notice are two separate documents.
- The following items if applicable should be presented clearly and separately from any other information:
- Personal data type
- Special categories of personal data
- Cookie (Directive 2002/58/EC) (for instance, France CNIL stipulates that the validity period of the consent for cookies is 13 months.)
- Legal basis
- Legitimate interest
- Public interest
- Purpose
- Profiling
- Direct marketing purposes

2) Clear and plain language

Clear and plain language must be used (i.e., GDPR Article 12.1); the requirement for clear and plain language is of particular importance when providing information to children (i.e., GDPR Article 12.1).

Under WP260 rev.01 Paragraph 12 & 13, the requirement for clear and plain language means that:

- Information should be provided in as simple a manner as possible, avoiding complex sentence and language structures.
- It should not be phrased in abstract or ambivalent terms or leave room for different interpretations. In particular, the purposes of, and legal basis for, processing personal data should be clear.
- The information should be concrete and definitive.

3) Intelligible

Under WP260 rev.01 Paragraph 9, "intelligible" means that: it should be understood by an average member of the intended audience. Intelligibility is closely linked to the requirement to use clear and plain language.

An accountable data controller will have knowledge about the people they collect information about, and can use this knowledge to determine what that audience would likely understand. For example, a controller collecting the personal data of working professionals can assume its audience has a higher level of understanding than a controller that obtains the personal data of children. If controllers are uncertain about the level of intelligibility and transparency of the information and effectiveness of user interfaces/notices/policies etc., they can test these, for example, through mechanisms such as user panels, readability testing, formal and informal interactions, and dialogue with industry groups, consumer advocacy groups, and regulatory bodies, where appropriate, amongst other things. The following two points are abstracted from the guide "Tilburg University: The Concept of 'Clear and Plain Language' in the GDPR".

- Knowledge Level—adults or children; general public or expert academics
- Language Type—The notice content is in a language required by local laws in some jurisdictions such as France, Italy, Spain, Slovakia (it should be in a language the data subject speaks), etc.
- Note: GDPR was published in 26 languages.
- With over 7,000 languages spoken in the world, how can it be possible to provide a Privacy Policy in every language? It probably isn't possible. For practical reasons, a common school of thought is to provide a translated copy of your Privacy Policy for each language your website is written in. This is a conservative and easily managed approach.

4) Easily accessible

An organization should provide access to data subjects. The privacy notice should be easy for data subjects to find and query at any time. A mechanism should be provided for data subjects to easily download the privacy notice.

Under WP260 rev.01 Paragraph 11: The "easily accessible" element means that:

The data subject should not have to seek out the information; it should be immediately apparent to them where and how this information can be accessed. For example, by providing it directly to them, by linking them to it, by clearly signposting it or as an answer to a natural language question (for example in an online layered privacy statement/notice, in FAQs, by way of contextual pop-ups which activate when a data subject fills in an online form, or in an interactive digital context through a chatbot interface, etc. These mechanisms are further considered subsequently, including in paragraphs 33 to 40).

* Different business scenarios
* Online
* Mobile App
* Offline
* Telephone or in-person

Normally privacy notice should be in "writing "or by other means, including where appropriate, by "electronic means", where requested by the data subjects it may be provided orally.

1) For example, a link to the privacy policy needs to be provided at the bottom of the website for easy queries. Marketing emails also need to provide a link to the privacy statement.

2) A link to the notice can be provided in a system or application, or the notice can be printed on the maintenance work order and warranty card. For example, providing copies of XX (Product Name) Privacy Notice, Statement About XX (Product Name) and Privacy, User Agreement, and other legal documents in **Settings > About** for user query at any time.

There are a few further ways to enhance the transparency of a privacy notice.

1) Layered privacy notices

A layered privacy notice contains increasingly detailed notices. Article 29 Working Party has endorsed the use of up to three layers, so long as the total meets legal requirements. The top layer contains the short notice—just the key elements, including links that provide the user with the option to read more details. Links may also connect the user to specific portions of the notice, allowing them to navigate quickly. The second and third layers may contain a condensed notice followed by a full notice, or a full notice followed by FAQs and additional links.

2) Just-in-time notices

A "just-in-time" notice is delivered at or right before a user accepts a service or product, helping to facilitate meaningful choice. An organization may also give just-in-time notice when previously collected data is to be used for a new purpose.

3) Standardized icons

Recital 60 of the GDPR endorses the use of standardized icons within privacy notices to communicate required information. The challenge will be to design icons readable by humans and computers that accurately reflect the meaning of abstract, complex messages, such as, "No personal data are retained in the unencrypted form". Successful use of standardized icons could help controllers incorporate visualization, where appropriate, into privacy notices-one of the requirements of the GDPR's transparency principle. Recital 166 delegates decisions about the development of standardized icons to the European Commission.

 **Case Study**

France—CNIL vs. Google: 2019

In January 2019, CNIL proposed a €50 million fine following complaints from two organizations, noyb.eu (the European Center for Digital Rights or None of Your Business) and LQDN (La Quadrature du Net)

Based on the inspections carried out, the CNIL's restricted committee responsible for examining breaches of the Data Protection Act observed two types of breaches of the GDPR.

A violation of the obligations of transparency and information—GOOGLE

- First, the restricted committee notices that the information provided by GOOGLE is not easily accessible to users.
  - Indeed, the general structure of the information chosen by the company does not enable it to comply with the Regulation. Essential information, such as the data processing purposes, the data storage periods, or the categories of personal data used for the ads personalization, are excessively disseminated across several documents, with buttons and links on which it is required to click to access complementary information. The relevant information is accessible after several steps only, implying sometimes up to 5 or 6 actions. For instance, this is the case when a user wants to have complete information on his or her data collected for personalization purposes or the geo-tracking service.
- Moreover, the restricted committee observes that some information is not always clear or comprehensive.
  - Users are not able to fully understand the extent of the processing operations carried out by GOOGLE. But the processing operations are particularly massive, and intrusive because of the number of services offered (about twenty), the amount and the nature of the data processed and combined. The restricted committee observes in particular that the purposes of processing are described in a too generic and vague manner, and so are the categories of data processed for these various purposes. Similarly, the information communicated is not clear enough so that the user can understand that the legal basis of processing operations for the ads personalization is consent, and not the legitimate interest of the company. Finally, the restricted committee notices that the information about the retention period is not provided for some data.

A violation of the obligation to have a legal basis for ads personalization processing.

The company GOOGLE states that it obtains the user's consent to process data for ads personalization purposes. However, the restricted committee considers that the consent is not validly obtained for two reasons.

- First, the restricted committee observes that the users' consent is not sufficiently informed.
  - The information on processing operations for the ads personalization is diluted in several documents and does not enable the user to be aware of their extent. For example, in the section "Ads Personalization", it is not possible to be aware of the plurality of services, websites, and applications involved in these processing operations (Google search, YouTube, Google home, Google maps, Playstore, Google pictures . . .) and therefore of the amount of data processed and combined.

- Then, the restricted committee observes that the collected consent is neither "specific" nor "unambiguous".
  - When an account is created, the user can admittedly modify some options associated with the account by clicking on the button "More options", accessible above the button "Create Account". It is notably possible to configure the display of personalized ads.
  - That does not mean that the GDPR is respected. Indeed, the user not only has to click on the button "More options" to access the configuration, but the display of the ads personalization is moreover pre-ticked. However, as provided by the GDPR, consent is "unambiguous" only with a clear affirmative action from the user (by ticking a non-pre-ticked box for instance). Finally, before creating an account, the user is asked to tick the boxes "I agree to Google's Terms of Service" and "I agree to the processing of my information as described above and further explained in the Privacy Policy" in order to create the account. Therefore, the user gives his or her consent in full, for all the processing operations purposes carried out by GOOGLE based on this consent (ads personalization, speech recognition, etc.). However, the GDPR provides that the consent is "specific" only if it is given distinctly for each purpose.

 Case Study

Poland's first GDPR fine—violation of notification obligations, 2019

On March 26, 2019, the chairman of the Polish data protection enforcement agency issued Poland's first penalty ticket for violating the GDPR, with a fine of 943,000 Polish zloty (about 220,000 euros).

The sanctioned company (the "Company") obtained personal information about 6 million people from public sources, primarily the Central Electronic Register ("Central Electronic Register") and information on economic activity. The company processes such public source information for commercial purposes. However, as the data controller, the company has not informed the relevant data subjects of the data processing activities it is carrying out on the personal data of the data subjects. Therefore, the data subjects were not informed of these processing activities, and therefore cannot raise the right to object to processing or exercise other data subject rights. The Polish data protection enforcement authority considered this a very serious violation that affected the rights and freedoms of data subjects.

After the investigation, the company, as the controller, only notified the data subject of the email address in its possession by emailing the information disclosure obligation required by Article 14 of the GDPR. For the rest of the data subjects involved, the company said that it did not inform these data subjects due to the high cost, and only displayed the terms of their relevant information on its official website to complete the notification.

The Polish data protection law enforcement agency found out that the company has the mailing addresses and phone numbers of all the data subjects involved in the case. The Polish data protection law enforcement agency believed that the "excessive cost" described by the company was just an excuse for not fulfilling its statutory obligations, and the company should fulfill its information disclosure obligations to all data subjects through the contact information of the individuals involved in the case through these mailing addresses.

In addition, the Polish data protection enforcement authority believed that the company's violation of the GDPR in this information disclosure obligation was subjective and intentional: the company knew that the controller has the obligation to disclose information under the GDPR and the obligation to directly inform the relevant data subjects. When imposing a fine, the law enforcement agency also duly considered that the company did not take any measures to stop the infringement, nor did it announce that it would stop the infringement.

15.4   CORE COMPONENTS OF A PRIVACY NOTICE

Most privacy and data protection regulations require that privacy notices contain certain information. For instance, under the GDPR, the requirements are as follows.

Where personal data relating to a data subject are collected from the data subject, the controller shall, at the time when personal data are obtained, provide the data subject with all of the following information.

- the identity and the contact details of the controller and, where applicable, of the controller's representative (13.1.a)
- the contact details of the data protection officer, where applicable (13.1.b)
- the purposes of the processing for which the personal data are intended as well as the legal basis for the processing (13.1.c)
- where the processing is based on point (f) of Article 6(1), the legitimate interests pursued by the controller or by a third party (13.1.d)
- the recipients or categories of recipients of the personal data, if any (13.1.e)
- where applicable, the fact that the controller intends to transfer personal data to a third country or international organization and the existence or absence of an adequacy decision by the Commission, or in the case of transfers referred to in Article 46 or 47, or the second subparagraph of Article 49(1), reference to the appropriate or suitable safeguards and the means by which to obtain a copy of them or where they have been made available (13.1.f).

In addition to the information referred to in 13.1, the controller shall, at the time when personal data are obtained, provide the data subject with the following further information necessary to ensure fair and transparent processing:

- the period for which the personal data will be stored, or if that is not possible, the criteria used to determine that period (13.2.a)
- the existence of the right to request from the controller access to and rectification or erasure of personal data or restriction of processing concerning the data subject or to object to the processing as well as the right to data portability (13.2.b)
- At the latest at the time of the first communication with the data subject, the right referred to in 21.1 (public interest and legitimate interest, including profiling) and 21.2 (direct marketing purposes) shall be explicitly brought to the attention of the data subject and shall be presented clearly and separately from any other information (21.4)
- where the processing is based on point (a) of Article 6(1) or point (a) of Article 9(2), the existence of the right to withdraw consent at any time, without affecting the lawfulness of processing based on consent before its withdrawal (13.2.c)
- the right to lodge a complaint with a supervisory authority (13.2.d)
- whether the provision of personal data is a statutory or contractual requirement, or a requirement necessary to enter a contract, as well as whether the data subject is obliged to provide the personal data and of the possible consequences of failure to provide such data (13.2.e)

- the existence of automated decision-making, including profiling, referred to in Articles 22(1) and (4) and, at least in those cases, meaningful information about the logic involved, as well as the significance and the envisaged consequences of such processing for the data subject (13.2.f).

Another example would be the Quebec Bill 64:

Anyone who collects personal information from the person concerned on behalf of a public body must, when the information is collected and subsequently on request, inform that person

(1) of the name of the public body on whose behalf the information is collected.
(2) of the purposes for which the information is collected.
(3) of the means by which the information is collected.
(4) of whether the request is mandatory or optional.
(5) of the consequences for the person concerned or for the third person, as the case may be, for refusing to reply to the request or, if applicable, for withdrawing consent to the release or use of the information collected pursuant to an optional request; and
(6) of the rights of access and correction provided by law.

If applicable, the person concerned is informed of the name of the third person collecting the information on behalf of the public body and of the possibility that the information could be released outside Québec.

On request, the person concerned is also informed of the personal information collected from him, the categories of persons who have access to the information within the public body, the duration of the period of time the information will be kept, and the contact information of the person in charge of the protection of personal information.

Core components

A privacy notice should be provided before or at the time when personal data is obtained from data subjects (i.e., customers, employees). A privacy notice usually consists of the following sections in Table 15.2 (not an exhaustive list):

Effective date and updates

A privacy notice should be provided with an effective date. In addition to providing the effective date, it is also a common practice for organizations to provide a change log of their privacy notices or links to their previous versions of privacy notices. If the privacy notice changes, data subjects should be informed of the updated privacy notice. The changes could result from various aspects such as the change of data types or processing purposes, etc.

15.5   KEY CONSIDERATIONS OF PROVIDING PRIVACY NOTICES

Just because something is simple (you know what to do) doesn't mean it's easy to do. Being fair and transparent in the privacy notice is the same thing.

The privacy notice should be provided to data subjects in an appropriate and timely manner. The privacy notice should cover all legal requirements and be easy to find and understand. Your organization should consider the following questions:

- Is notice provided before or at the time of personal data collection?
- If the data is not obtained directly from the user, has notice been provided in a timely manner as required by governing legislation (e.g., GDPR)?
- Is the notice provided in writing or by other means, including electronic means? (When requested by the data subject, the information may be provided orally, provided the identity of the data subject is proven by other means.)

TABLE 15.2

Core Components of a Privacy Notice

	Core Component	Description
1	The identity of the organization	Describe the entity and its affiliates who collect and process personal data.
2	What personal data do we collect and why we collect this personal data	List service functions and types of personal data collected from users, purposes of personal data processing as well as the legal basis for the processing, etc. • Service functions and types of personal data collected from users • Purposes of personal data processing as well as the legal basis for the processing • Incl. which legitimate interests (if applicable) • Present possible consequences for users' rejection of data collection in the privacy notice. For example, if this option is not consented to, the app may be forcibly logged out, or some functions cannot be implemented.
3	How we collect your personal data	Articulate the ways the organization collects data from data subjects, such as personal data knowingly and actively "provided by" the data subjects or personal data generated by and collected from the activities of users, by virtue of the use of the service or the device, etc. • Personal data knowingly and actively "provided by" or "created by" the data subject such as account data (e.g., mailing address, username, password, phone number, payment information) submitted via online forms • Personal data generated by and collected from the activities of users, by virtue of the use of the service or the device • Personal data we observed • Personal data we collect from other sources • Personal data we derive • Technologies used: For instance, we might use various technologies to collect and store information, including cookies, pixel tags, local storage, such as browser web storage or application data caches, databases, and server logs.
4	Cookie and similar technologies	Describe the types of cookies used, the purposes of the cookies, and how users can control the cookie settings.
5	How we use the personal data	Describe the ways the organization will use and share personal data.
6	How personal data is shared with processor or sub-processors	Illustrate how the organization will ensure its vendors will protect the transferred personal data properly.
7	How we store your personal data	Describe personal data storage location, the retention period of personal data, etc.
8	Cross-border transfer of your personal data	Articulate the mechanisms such as Standard Contractual Clauses (SCC), etc.
9	How we protect your data	Describe the technical and organizational measures taken to protect personal data.
10	Children's personal data	Define the age of a child and describe measures of safeguarding the personal data of children.
11	Your data subjects' rights	Describe the rights that data subjects are entitled to have, and the ways data subject can exercise their rights. • For instance, right of access, rectification, and deletion of personal data, right to restriction or rejection of personal data processing, and right to data portability, object to automated decision-making (including identification analysis and user profiling), etc. • Data subjects' right to withdraw their consent at any time, data subjects' right to complain to supervisory authorities, and possible consequences to data subjects, etc.
12	Contact details	List the contact details of the Privacy Officer or the DPO (if any).

- Does the notice cover legally required information (e.g., types of collected data, application scope, retention period, storage location, data controller, and DPO's contact information)?
- Does each product or service that collects personal data for different purposes have its own privacy notice (or an overarching notice that includes product-specific information)?
- Does each region that has unique regulations or collects data in a significantly different way have its own notice?
- Are privacy notices easy to find and can they be queried by users at any time?
- Is there a mechanism that allows users to easily download the notice (e.g., as a PDF)?
- Is the notice in the languages required by local laws?
- Is the notice in clear and plain language (i.e., is it concise, transparent, intelligible, and in an easily accessible form)?

16 Lawful Basis

This chapter is intended to help readers establish and implement mechanisms to ensure personal data processing activities have appropriate legal basis and records are kept properly.

This chapter covers the following topics:

- *Common lawful basis*
- *Performance of a contract*
- *Legal obligation*
- *Vital interest*
- *Public interests*
- *Legitimate interests*
- *Consent*

16.1 COMMON LAWFUL BASIS

All data processing activities should have proper legal basis. Most privacy and data protection regulations require organizations (i.e., data controllers) define proper lawful basis at or before collecting personal data from data subjects.

An organization must choose which ground it is relying on to process the data before it starts the processing. Swapping lawful grounds after the organization has chosen one is difficult to justify, so be certain about the lawful ground before processing the data. If the circumstances relating to the processing have genuinely changed, the organization may be able to rely on a new ground for processing, but that organization must first inform the data subject.

The GDPR articulates that processing shall be lawful only if and to the extent that at least one of the following applies:

(a) the data subject has given consent to the processing of his or her personal data for one or more specific purposes.

(b) processing is necessary for the performance of a contract to which the data subject is party or to take steps at the request of the data subject prior to entering a contract.

(c) processing is necessary for compliance with a legal obligation to which the controller is subject.

(d) processing is necessary to protect the vital interests of the data subject or of another natural person.

(e) processing is necessary for the performance of a task carried out in the public interest or in the exercise of official authority vested in the controller.

(f) Processing is necessary for the purposes of the legitimate interests pursued by the controller or by a third party, except where such interests are overridden by the interests or fundamental rights and freedoms of the data subject which require protection of personal data, in particular where the data subject is a child.

China's PIPL (Article 13) articulates that personal information handlers may only handle personal information where they conform to one of the following circumstances:

- Obtaining individuals' consent.
- Where necessary to conclude or fulfill a contract in which the individual is an interested party, or where necessary to conduct human resources management according to lawfully formulated labor rules and structures and lawfully concluded collective contracts.

DOI: 10.1201/9781003225089-20

- Where necessary to fulfill statutory duties and responsibilities or statutory obligations.
- Where necessary to respond to sudden public health incidents or protect natural persons' lives and health, or the security of their property, under emergency conditions.
- Handling personal information within a reasonable scope to implement news reporting, public opinion supervision, and other such activities for the public interest.
- When handling personal information disclosed by persons themselves or otherwise already lawfully disclosed, within a reasonable scope in accordance with the provisions of this Law.
- Other circumstances provided in laws and administrative regulations.

Table 16.1 lists six common lawful bases.

TABLE 16.1
Six Common Lawful Bases

Lawful Basis	Description	Examples
Legal obligation	Processing is necessary for compliance with a legal obligation to which the controller is subject.	Examples: 1. Collecting SSN for social security purposes 2. Sharing salary information with tax authorities for tax reporting 3. Statutory warranty services 4. Legal assistance Note: under the GDPR, this option is meant to be interpreted narrowly. It applies to legal obligations required by EU and member state laws only. It does not include legal obligations of contracts or those of third countries (outside of the EU)

Performance of a contract	Processing is necessary for the performance of a contract to which the data subject is a party or to take steps at the request of the data subject prior to entering a contract	Examples:
		1. HR-related cases
		  • Collecting and using bank information for processing employee salary
		  • Attendance, performance, benefit, service, training, etc.
		2. Customer-related cases
		  • A customer may purchase a product or service from an organization. For that product or service to be delivered to the right person, the organization must collect the right address and contact information.
		3. Managing civil contracts with non-employees (individual contractors)/channel partners/solution partners.

Legitimate interest	Processing is necessary for the purposes of the legitimate interests pursued by the controller or by a third party, except where such interests are overridden by the interests or fundamental rights and freedoms of the data subject.	Examples: 1. Sharing personal data within a group of undertakings or institutions affiliated to a central body for administrative purposes 2. Preventing fraud 4. Ensuring network and information security, including preventing unauthorized access to electronic communications networks and stopping damage to computer and electronic communication systems 5. CCTV monitoring 6. Audit and investigation 6. Responding to legal proceedings 7. Reporting possible criminal acts or threats to public security to a competent authority

Lawful Basis	Description	Examples
Consent	An individual has given consent to the processing of his or her personal data for a specific purpose.	Examples: 1. Collect personal data during usage of products, websites, and applications, etc. Personal information might include email address, phone number, profile picture, birthday, gender, etc. 2. Collect consumer's personal data for marketing purposes. In the HR context: *Freely given consent will be difficult to prove because of the unequal distribution of power between the employer and employee. However, under some local labor laws, employers are obligated to get consent from employees to process their personal data. And if collecting and processing special categories of data, an employer must rely on explicit consent or an obligation under employment law.*
Vital interests	Processing is necessary to protect the vital interests of the data subject or of another natural person.	Examples: 1. Cases of humanitarian emergencies, in particular in situations of natural and man-made disasters.
Public interest	Processing is necessary for the performance of a task carried out in the public interest or in the exercise of official authority vested in the controller	Examples: 1. Administration of justice 2. Research and statistical purposes, such as census

16.2   PERFORMANCE OF A CONTRACT

Article 6(1)(b) of the GDPR states that "processing shall be lawful if the processing is necessary for the performance of a contract to which the data subject is party or in order to take steps at the request of the data subject prior to entering into a contract."

The lawful processing ground of contractual necessity relates only to contracts an organization enters with the data subject. Here are some examples:

- When an organization enters a contract with a customer: If that organization requires certain data from the customer so that the organization can provide services to the customer such as their name, address, email address, and financial details, the organization should rely on this ground for processing such personal data.
- When an organization needs to fulfill an order: If that organization requires certain data to be processed so that the organization can fulfill the order for the services or products, such as body measurements to make tailored suits, the organization should rely on this ground for the processing.
- When an organization needs to deliver an order: Similarly, if that organization needs a name and address to send goods to a data subject, the organization's lawful grounds for processing is a contractual necessity because the organization requires this information to perform the contract.
- When an organization is paying its employees: To comply with that organization's obligations regarding employment contracts to pay employees, that organization will need to process certain personal data relating to employees, such as their name, address, and payment details.

The second part of this ground for processing is when an organization needs to "take steps at the request of the data subject prior to entering into a contract." An example is when a data subject has asked for a quote, but the contract hasn't yet been entered.

16.3   LEGAL OBLIGATION

Article 6(1)(c) of the GDPR states that processing shall be lawful if processing is necessary for compliance with a legal obligation to which the data controller is subject.

Recital 45 of the GDPR states that the processing should have a basis in EU or member state law—that is, that the legal obligation emanates from a law passed at the level of either the EU or an individual country. Laws passed in countries outside the EU don't apply.

This ground applies to statutory or common-law obligations, but not to contractual obligations. The legal obligation lawful basis doesn't require a legal obligation to process—rather the overall purpose is to comply with a legal obligation an organization is subject to.

Here are some examples:

- Sharing employee data with the tax authorities
- Processing data under money laundering regulations
- Disclosing data because of a court order

It is worth noting that if an organization processes data to follow an EU or member state legal obligation, the data subject cannot generally exercise its right to erasure, right to data portability, or right to object to processing.

16.4   VITAL INTERESTS

Article 6(1)(d) of the GDPR provides a lawful basis for processing where "processing is necessary in order to protect the vital interests of the data subject or of another natural person."

Recital 46 defines "vital interests" as being "an interest which is essential for the life of the data subject or that of another natural person." This clarifies that this ground for processing is available only in life-or-death situations and when the processing is necessary for the data subject's survival. This is likely to be the case only in emergency situations, such as when the data subject is so ill that they cannot consent to the processing.

Recital 46 goes on to state that processing under this ground should take place only where the processing cannot be based on another lawful basis.

Recital 46 further anticipates that this ground can be used not just for saving the life of an individual but also on a larger scale, referring to processing being necessary for "humanitarian purposes, including for monitoring epidemics and their spread," referring also to natural and manmade disasters.

16.5   PUBLIC INTERESTS

Article 6(1)(e) of the GDPR provides a lawful basis for processing when "processing is necessary for the performance of a task carried out in the public interest or the exercise of official authority vested in the controller." Unless an organization can exercise official authority, this ground for processing isn't relevant to that organization. Member states may implement their legislation to specify what constitutes public interest.

The UK provided some guidance in Part 2, Chapter 2 of the Data Protection Act of 2018. Public interest matters include the ones listed here:

- The administration of justice
- The exercise of a function of either House of Parliament

- The exercise of a function conferred on a person by an enactment or rule of law
- The exercise of a function of the Crown, a Minister of the Crown, a government department, or
- An activity that supports or promotes democratic engagement

Case Study

Uzun v. Germany, September 2, 2010[27]

The applicant, suspected of involvement in bomb attacks by a left-wing extremist movement, complained in particular that his surveillance via GPS and the use of the data obtained thereby in the criminal proceedings against him had violated his right to respect for private life.

The Court held that there had been no violation of Article 8 of the Convention. The GPS surveillance and the processing and use of the data thereby obtained had admittedly interfered with the applicant's right to respect for his private life. However, the Court noted, it had pursued the legitimate aims of protecting national security, public safety, and the rights of the victims, and of preventing crime. It had also been proportionated. GPS surveillance had been ordered only after less intrusive methods of investigation had proved insufficient, had been carried out for a relatively short period (some three months), and had affected the applicant only when he was travelling in his accomplice's car. The applicant could not therefore be said to have been subjected to total and comprehensive surveillance. Given that the investigation had concerned very serious crimes, the applicant's surveillance by GPS had thus been necessary in a democratic society.

Case Study

Hambardzumyan v. Armenia, December 5, 2019[27]

The applicant alleged that the police had not had a valid court warrant to place her under secret surveillance during a criminal investigation. She complained in particular about the covert surveillance and its subsequent use in the criminal proceedings against her.

The Court held that there had been a violation of Article 8 of the Convention, finding that the surveillance measure used against the applicant had not had proper judicial supervision and had not been "in accordance with the law" within the meaning of the Convention. It noted in particular that the warrant had not been specific enough about the person who was the object of the surveillance measure, vagueness which was unacceptable when it came to such a serious interference with the right to respect for private and family life as secret surveillance. Furthermore, the warrant had not listed the specific measures that were to be carried out against the applicant. The Court held, however, that there had been no violation of Article 6 (right to a fair trial) of the Convention in the applicant's case, finding that the use of the secretly taped material had not conflicted with the requirements of fairness guaranteed by Article 6 § 1.

16.6   LEGITIMATE INTERESTS

Article 6(1)(f) of the GDPR gives you a lawful basis for processing when

processing is necessary for the purposes of the legitimate interests pursued by the controller or by a Third Party except where such interests are overridden by the interests or fundamental rights and freedoms of the data subject which require protection of personal data, in particular where the data subject is a child.

Both historically and continuing up to the present, the legal ground of Legitimate Interests has been misused and misapplied for processing personal data to the benefit of data controllers and to the detriment of data subjects. The legitimate interest of the controller or a third party has often been used as a safety net in the absence of another legitimate basis for processing personal data, and while it may still prove a more realistic option than consent, it should be used with caution.

- It cannot be used for processing special categories of personal data. Consent is required.
- It cannot be used for processing personal data about Children unless the organization is a public authority. Consent from the holder of parental responsibility
- Data subjects' fundamental rights and freedoms have not been compromised.
- Demonstration that it is a legitimate interest for the controller or the Third Party and the processing of the personal data is necessary for the legitimate interest.

An organization needs to demonstrate processing is necessary for the purposes of the legitimate interests pursued by the controller or by a third party, except where such interests are overridden by the interests or fundamental rights and freedoms of the data subject which require protection of personal data, in particular where the data subject is a child.

Recitals 47 to 49 of the GDPR state that a legitimate interest can be to:

- Network and information security: Ensure network and information security, which could include processing to prevent unauthorized access to networks, prevent malicious code distribution, stop denial-of-service (DoS) attacks
- Fraud prevention
- Detection or prevention of criminal acts or threats to public security: Disclose information about criminal acts or security threats to the authorities
- Certain countries, such as Italy, are more prescriptive about what constitutes legitimate interests, so check each relevant jurisdiction.

3-Step Legitimate Interest Assessment (LIA)

Legitimate interests are often a condition relied upon by the data controllers to process personal data, but data controllers have to be careful to rely on legitimate interests in the right context.

Each time an organization intends to rely on legitimate interests for processing personal data, it is a good idea to complete an LIA form and keep it on record. Retaining a record will help evidence compliance with an organization's accountability obligations.

The 3-step Legitimate Interests Assessment test includes the following aspects: legitimate purpose, necessity and proportionality, and balancing of interests.

1) Legitimate purpose

The first part of a Legitimate Interests Assessment should be a legality and purpose test, in which an organization determines whether it has a legitimate interest to conduct the processing. A legitimate interest simply means that the processing is done for the purpose of an interest that isn't unlawful or unethical.

A wide range of interests may be legitimate interests. The interests can be an organization's or its third party's, and they can relate to that organization's business interests or benefits for society as a whole or part. The interests don't need to meet a certain standard, but if they aren't compelling, the rights and freedoms of the data subject will more easily override these interests when the organization carries out the balancing test

The organization's Privacy Notice must clearly and transparently inform the data subject not only that it is processing their personal data based on legitimate interests but also why the legitimate interest the organization identified is in fact legitimate.

Questions an organization might need to ask during the legality and purpose test:

- Why do you want to process the data
- What benefit do you expect to receive from processing the data
- Whether any third parties benefit from your processing of the data
- Whether there are any wider public interests in your processing of the data
- How important are the benefits to you and/or the Third Party and/or the public are
- What the impact would be if you didn't proceed with the processing
- Whether the processing will comply with data protection and other applicable laws
- Whether the processing will comply with applicable industry codes of practice or guidelines
- Whether there are any ethical issues with the processing

2) Necessity and proportionality

The second part of the LIA form is the Necessity test, in which an organization determines whether the processing is necessary to achieve its legitimate interests, whether the organization must conduct this processing to achieve the purposes. Necessary in this test doesn't mean that the processing itself must be essential, but it must be targeted and proportionate. In other words, the method of processing must not exceed what is necessary to achieve the organization's purposes.

To perform a Necessity test is to work out whether the processing of personal data is necessary for the pursuit of an organization's commercial or business objectives. That doesn't necessarily mean indispensable, but it's more than ordinary, useful, reasonable, and desirable.

Probably the easiest question to ask is this: "is there another way to achieve the identified interest?"

To answer this question, an organization is looking at the processing here and asking itself whether a less intrusive way of processing the information would achieve the goal. If the processing isn't necessary, the organization can't rely on legitimate interest as a lawful basis.

Things to consider when an organization performs the necessity test:

- The processing will help you achieve your purpose
- The processing will help a Third Party achieve its purpose
- The processing is reasonable and proportionate to achieve the purpose
- You can achieve the purpose without the processing
- You can achieve the purpose by processing less data or processing the data in a less intrusive way

3) Balancing of interests

The third and final part of the test is the Balancing test, in which an organization determines the impact of the processing on the data subject's interests, rights, and freedoms.

A balancing test ensures that the rights and freedoms of the data subject have been evaluated and that their interests don't override the organization's legitimate interest. This evaluation should always be conducted fairly and in an unbiased way.

An organization should document the balancing test, including its thought process on it in case the organization is ever challenged over the use of legitimate interests as a lawful ground of processing. An organization must decide whether it has satisfied the Balancing test for each category of data subjects and each processing and each purpose. In carrying out the Balancing test, consider these factors:

- The nature of the personal data:
  - The more sensitive or private the data and the more vulnerable the individual, the more likely the data subject's rights and freedoms will be at risk.
  - If it's special-category data, an organization needs to give more weight to protecting the rights and freedoms of the data subject. The nature of an organization's interest as a data controller.

- Evaluate if the data processing activities will process:
  - Special-category data, such as medical data or data relating to religious beliefs
  - Criminal-offense data
  - Data that people consider to be private, such as financial information
  - Children's data
  - The data of vulnerable individuals such as the elderly or mentally challenged. Also consider the effect that an organization's chosen method of processing and frequency of any communication might have on more vulnerable individuals—ads targeted at people who are struggling financially, for example, or gamblers or alcoholics.
  - Data about people in the context of their personal lives or private lives, for example, personal finance data
- The reasonable expectations of the data subject
  - Would or should they expect the processing to take place? If they would, the impact of the processing is likely to have already been considered and accepted. If they have no expectations, the impact is greater and is given more weight in the Balancing test.
  - An organization needs to consider whether people will expect it to use its data in a fair way consider the following aspects:
    - The organization's status in comparison to the data subject: Is the organization in a dominant position?
    - The ways in which the data is processed: Does it involve profiling or data mining, publication, or disclosure to a large number of people? Is the processing on a large scale?
    - You have an existing relationship with the data subject.
    - You used the data subject's data in the past.
    - You collected the data directly from the data subject.
    - You have explained the data processing and its purposes by providing a Privacy Notice to data subjects when you collected their data, for example.
    - You collected the data from a Third Party and, if so, what they told the individual about how the data would be used
    - You have any direct feedback on the expectations of data subjects, such as from market research or consultation.
    - The data was collected recently or long ago. If an organization collected the data long ago and the data subject hasn't since heard from the organization, receiving marketing literature out of the blue, for example, may not be expected.
    - Any changes in technology or otherwise would mean that you're processing the data in ways the data subject wouldn't expect.
    - The purpose for the processing and the method of processing is obvious and likely to be understood by your data subject.
    - Any particular circumstances would mean that the data subjects would or would not expect the processing.
    - Any imbalance exists in the relationship between you and the data subject so that you have power over the data subject.
- The likely impact on the data subject
  - Consider both positive and negative impacts.
    - Will there be any harm to the data subject as a result of the processing?
    - What is the likelihood of the impact on the data subject and its severity?
  - In thinking about the likely impact the processing will have on the data subject consider whether the processing may
    - Result in any risk to the rights and freedoms of your data subjects
    - Result in any physical harm to the data subjects

- Result in any financial loss, identity theft, or fraud
- Result in any loss of control by the data subject over their personal data
- Result in any significant economic or social disadvantage (such as reputational damage, discrimination, or loss of confidentiality)
- Adversely impact data subjects exercising their individual rights (privacy rights or any other rights)
- Adversely impact data subjects accessing services or opportunities
- Add value to a product or service that the data subject uses

Right to object

Data subjects have the right to object to the processing on the grounds of legitimate interests. If somebody objects to an organization's processing on the grounds of legitimate interests, the organization must stop that processing unless it can either:

- Demonstrate compelling, legitimate grounds for the processing that override the interests, rights, and freedoms of the data subject
- Show that the processing is for the establishment, exercise, or defense of legal claims

If an organization receives an objection to processing personal data for direct marketing purposes from a data subject, the organization must stop processing that personal data as soon as you receive an objection. It has no exemptions or grounds to refuse that right.

 Case Study

Google Spain—2014

Legitimate interest requires balancing the interest of the controller and third-party with the interest of the data subject. In this case, having regard to the sensitivity of the data subject's private life to information contained in announcements and the fact that the initial publication occurred 16 years earlier, the data subject has established that the links should be removed.

16.7   CONSENT

16.7.1   Obtaining Consent

Where the processing is based on consent, the controller must obtain an individual's valid consent for the collection, use, or disclosure of the individual's personal information and shall be able to demonstrate that the data subject has consented to the processing of his or her personal data.

As stipulated in GDPR Articles 6, 7, and 14, data subjects' explicit consent must be obtained for the collection and processing of their personal data. The data controller should prove that the data processing has been consented to by the data subjects, and the data is processed in compliance with laws. Data subjects have the right to withdraw their consent at any time.

According to GDPR Recital 32, consent should be given by a clear affirmative act establishing an indication of the data subject's agreement to the processing of personal data relating to him or her.

Consent must be given by the data subject with the conditions met: informed, specific, freely given, and Unambiguous. The individual's consent must be obtained at or before the time of the collection of the personal information.

The Article 29 Working Party of the EU proposes in *WP202 Opinion 02/2013 on apps on smart devices* that, the right of freedom means that a user is entitled to determine whether to accept or reject the processing of personal data concerning him or her. Therefore, if an app needs to process personal data, users must have the right to decide whether to accept or reject the processing. During app installation, the UI should not only provide the "agree" option, but also "cancel", "stop installation", or other similar options.

As stipulated in Article 29 Working Party of the EU proposes in *WP223 Opinion 8/2014 on the on Recent Developments on the Internet*, since wearable "connected things" are likely to replace existing items that provide usual functionalities, data controllers should offer an option to disable the "connected" feature of the thing and allow it to work as the original, unconnected item (i.e., disable the smart watch or glasses connected functionality). The Working Party has already specified that data subjects should have the possibility to "continuously withdraw (their) consent, without having to exit the" service provided.

It is also stipulated in WP223 Opinion 8/2014 that IoT device manufacturers must provide granular choices when granting access to applications. The granularity should not only concern the category of collected data, but also the time and frequency at which data are captured.

Implied consent vs. explicit consent

Table 16.2 provides a couple of examples showing the differences between implied and explicit consent.

TABLE 16.2

Differences between Implied and Explicit Consent

Country/Law	Implied Consent (opt-out)	Explicit	Exception
GDPR	X	All scenarios if consent is the lawful basis	Other lawful bases
Canada/PIPEDA	When the personal information being collected is innocuous and the purpose of the collection straightforward	When the personal information is sensitive, explicit, and documented, means of obtaining consent, such as opt-in options, are required	a) the collection is clearly in the interests of the individual and consent cannot be obtained in a timely way. b) it is reasonable to expect that the collection with the knowledge or consent of the individual would compromise the availability or the accuracy of the information and the collection is reasonable for purposes related to investigating a breach of an agreement or a contravention of the laws of Canada or a province. c) it is contained in a witness statement and the collection is necessary to assess, process or settle an insurance claim. d) it was produced by the individual in the course of their employment, business or profession and the collection is consistent with the purposes for which the information was produced. e) the collection is solely for journalistic, artistic or literary purposes. f) the information is publicly available and is specified by the regulations. g) the collection is made for the purpose of making a disclosure. i) under subparagraph (3)(c.1)(i) or (d)(ii) 41 or ii) that is required by law.

Case Study

Luxembourg DPA v. Amazon, 2021
Amazon faces a €350 million fine in Luxembourg
Following the Google case (€50 million fine by French DPA in 2019) and the H&M case (€35 million fine by the German DPA in 2020), Amazon could face by far the largest privacy fine (€350 million) by Luxembourg's data-protection commission. The details are not clear yet as the decision hasn't been finalized. From publicly available information, it seems related to Amazon's behavioral analysis and targeted advertising practices and lack of consent of its users.
Based on Amazon's 2020 annual revenue ($386.1 billion), there is a chance the fine might be increased after the draft decision being circulated among 26 DPAs.
2) What this fine says about GDPR enforcement
A) The published EU DPAs' enforcement cases and the 29 WP opinion WP 253 provide guidance regarding the deciding factors on an appropriate fine.
Top privacy practice areas (based on DPAs' annual reports and enforcement cases)

- Notification and effective consent
- Personal data security protection
- Data subject rights assurance
- Cross-border transfer
- Data Breach Notification

Top business practice areas (based on DPAs' annual reports and enforcement cases)

- Privacy concerns brought by new technologies (i.e., big data/AI)
- Digital marketing
- Internal Employee management
- Privacy for social network
- Privacy for health care data

B) EU is taking a tougher stance
It is questioned by the European Parliament and some non-profit organizations that the pace to issue administrative fines for the on-file cases in one member state might be too slow.

16.7.2 Conditions for Consent

Consent is a common basis used to legitimately process personal data. Consent is likely to be the appropriate ground where your organization wants to offer a real choice to people—for example, whether they want to receive your marketing emails.

Where the processing is based on consent, the controller shall be able to demonstrate that the data subject has consented to the processing of his or her personal data.

Under the GDPR (i.e., Art. 4 and 7), the following additional conditions shown in Table 16.3 must be met to use this option.

Case Study

FTC v. Apple, 2014
Apple was asked by the FTC to return $32.5M to the user because it did not obtain the user's consent to charge in-app fees.

TABLE 16.3
Conditions for Consent

Condition	Description
Freely given	The data subject must be able to choose to give or not. Freely given means that the data subject is free to choose whether to give consent without any detriment and has genuine choice and control over what personal data they provide. • Consent obtained by way of duress or coercion doesn't constitute valid consent. • If the relationship has a power imbalance (such as during employment or during processing by a public authority), proving that consent is freely given is difficult. • When assessing whether consent is freely given, utmost account shall be taken of whether, inter alia, the performance of a contract, including the provision of a service, is conditional on consent to the processing of personal data that is not necessary for the performance of that contract. • Incentivizing consent is possible. If you offer money-off/discount vouchers for subscribing to an email marketing list, for example, this would still be valid consent. If, however, the data subject suffers a detriment or is unfairly penalized as a result of not providing consent, the consent that were obtained aren't valid. An example of a detriment is charging higher prices for a service if the data subject refuses to consent to their data being shared with third parties. • If consent are bundled so that a data subject can only consent to all of the processing, this consent isn't valid because the consent hasn't been freely given—perhaps the data subject wanted to sign up for one type of processing but was forced to sign up for another as well, because the consent were bundled.
Specific	The consent must be given for a specific purpose. If you're processing personal data for multiple purposes, you must obtain consent for each purpose. • It should refer clearly and precisely to the scope and the consequences of the data processing (WP29 opinion). • If another purpose arises, the controller may be required to obtain additional consent. • You should regularly review your processing in consideration of your stated purpose and, if you notice any "purpose creep," obtain fresh consent if the new purposes are not compatible with the original purposes.
Informed	You must provide the data subject with all necessary information about the processing at the point that the person provides consent. • This must be in a form and in a language that's easy to understand. Language that's likely to confuse will invalidate consent. • Subjects must be informed, at least, of the controller's identity, the purpose for processing, and Information about how processing may affect data subjects. • If you're sharing the data with any third parties who are relying on that consent, the identities of those third parties must also be named. • A third party may be able to provide consent on behalf of another person, but you need to ensure that they're duly authorized to do so. If a third party is providing consent, the data subject still needs to be fully informed about the processing and the purposes by way of a Privacy Notice.
Unambiguous or explicit	For consent to be valid, there must be no doubt about the data subject's wishes. If there is any uncertainty about whether the data subject has consented. the presumption is that they have not consented. • Clearly distinguishable from other matters, in an intelligible and easily accessible form, using clear and plain language. • You should ensure that the consent is separate from other terms and conditions so that it isn't buried in lots of legalese. • Unambiguous indication of wishes. • This requires positive, affirmative action, such as checking opt-in or choosing technical settings for web applications. • A pre-ticked box is not valid consent: Silence, pre-ticked boxes, and inactivity do not qualify as unambiguous indications of a data subject's wishes. • As easy to withdraw as to give consent • Consent can always be withdrawn, so if you need the data for the stated purposes, it's always wise to rely on other lawful grounds for processing where possible. Or in other words, if the data subject withdraws their consent and you would try to continue processing the data under a different lawful ground, consent isn't the appropriate grounds for the processing.

On January 15, 2014, because Apple failed to inform parents when they entered the password that they agreed to in-app purchases by entering the password and failed to inform parents that Apple would keep the password for 15 minutes, and during these 15 minutes, children may make purchases without entering a password. Since March 2011, at least tens of thousands of consumers have complained that children have made in-app purchases without parental authorization, resulting in economic losses for parents, which has been identified by the FTC Constitutes "unfair conduct affecting commerce" in violation of Part 5 of the Federal Trade Commission Act. The FTC requires Apple to return $32.5M to users.

 Case Study

South Korea, 2016
In the Supreme Court Decision 2016Do13263, decided on April 7, 2017, the Supreme Court invalidated the consent obtained from data subjects because the defendant had collected personal information under circumstances that made it difficult for data subjects to clearly understand what they had consented to, even though the consent they had provided satisfied formalities prescribed by law, i.e., the notice was provided in font size of 1mm.

16.7.3 SEPARATE CONSENT

When the processing of personal data might pose substantial risk to data subjects, separate and explicit consent is needed for certain scenarios.

Table 16.4 lists some examples (note: this is NOT an exhaustive list).

 Example

App A can work only after GPS is enabled. If a user starts App A, GPS should be disabled by default, and the user should be prompted to enable GPS (with a message containing a shortcut for users to enter the configurations menu). App A cannot enable GPS and use related services without users enabling GPS themselves.

 Example

Product S provides the online upgrade function. User's confirmation (such as OK or Upgrade later) is required and user's consent must be obtained before starting the upgrade process.

 Example

System S provides a function of restoring factory settings. Users' app data should also be deleted when restoring factory settings. Design should allow explicit notification to users that their data will be deleted upon restoring, and data can be deleted only after users give their consent.

16.7.4 RECORDS OF CONSENT

Most privacy laws and regulations (i.e., GDPR Article 7) require a data controller shall be able to demonstrate that the data subject has consented to the processing of his or her personal data. In

TABLE 16.4
Examples of Scenarios That Need Separate Consent

Scenario	Description
Data subject	Data subjects are minors (need to obtain consent from parents) For instance, Chinese laws define a child as someone who is less than 14 years old; GDPR defines define a child as someone who is less than 16 years old.

Personal data type	• **Processing of special categories of data/Sensitive personal data**. By default, sensitive personal data of data subjects is not collected. If the collection of the user's sensitive personal data is necessary, the user's **explicit consent** must be obtained.
	• Users' explicit consent must be obtained before collecting, using, or disclosing their special categories of data. (Russia requires written consent.)
	• Processing of sensitive personal data needs to be executed based on the laws and regulations in the target delivery country. (The laws of the EU or its member states may prohibit the processing of preceding personal data, regardless of whether data subjects' explicit consent is obtained.)
	• HIPAA: Authorization for CE—needed for the scenarios not permitted
	  • Psychotherapy notes
	  • Marketing purposes
	  • Sale of PHI
	• **Cookie** (GDPR article 21.4, Directive 2002/58/EC/DIRECTIVE 2009/136/EC) (for instance, France CNIL stipulates that the validity period of the consent for cookies is 13 months.)
	• Communications secrecy (ePrivacy)
	• Location-based services (ePrivacy)

Legal basis	• Legitimate interest • Public interest
Purpose	• **Automated individual decision-making, including profiling.** Systems that provide user profiling should provide a mechanism to **object** from such profiling. • If a system performs profiling based on personal data stored in the system, there must be a mechanism to opt out from such profiling. Ensure that data subjects' personal data is no longer processed after they withdraw their consent. If the processing cannot be stopped immediately for justified reasons, for example, a long computing period, the processing must be stopped before the next period starts. • **Direct marketing purposes (GDPR article 21.2, 21.3 & ePrivacy)**. The data subject shall have the right to **object** at any time to the processing of his/her personal data for direct marketing purposes. • If a user chooses to opt out of marketing activities, their contact details cannot be used for marketing. • You must not make it difficult for data subjects to opt out, for example, by asking them to complete a form or confirm in writing forms. When marketing information is sent to data subjects, the data subjects must be provided with a way to opt out, and the opt-out way is recommended to be consistent with the opt-in way as much as possible. For email marketing, you should provide a valid opt-out email address or a hypertext link, so the data subjects can opt out by sending an email to this mail address or clicking the link. • If personal data is used for marketing, use profiling, or surveys, the data controller must provide a mechanism to obtain data subjects' explicit consent and allow them to withdraw their consent anytime. • **Data transfers to third countries** when there **is no adequacy decision or appropriate safeguard** (GDPR Article 49). • **Image collection or personal identity recognition in public venues.** • The installation of image collection or personal identity recognition equipment in public venues shall occur as required to safeguard public security and observe relevant State regulations and clearly indicating signs shall be installed. Collected personal images and personal distinguishing identity characteristic information can only be used for the purpose of safeguarding public security; it may not be used for other purposes, except where individuals' separate consent is obtained. • **Sale of personal data**. It should be consented to or authorized by data subjects. • The CCPA requires covered organizations to put up "DO NOT SELL MY BUTTON" on their websites. • Processing publicly available information that might pose a substantial impact on the data subject.

Scenario	Description
	• Personal information controllers may, within a reasonable scope, process personal information that has already been made public by the person themselves or otherwise lawfully, except where the person clearly refuses. Personal information controllers processing already disclosed personal information, where there is a substantial impact on individual rights and interests, shall obtain personal consent in accordance with the provisions of this Law.
	• **Recommendation:** First-time Internet connection
	• If the application software running on the data subject's system needs an Internet connection, the data controller must inform the data subject before connection and provide a mechanism to obtain the data subject's consent. User consent must be obtained before the first Internet connection for operations consuming user traffic to prevent it from being suspected of maliciously consuming user traffic.
	• Before connecting to the Internet, application software must provide users with dialog boxes, so data subjects can decide whether to agree to the Internet connection. To avoid excessive prompts that may upset users, it is advised to obtain user consent before the first Internet connection and provide users with options of allowing automatic programmatic Internet connection since then or choosing Internet connection every time.
	• If the product does not have a UI, product materials should tell users that programs will be connected to the Internet. As in the equipment vendor scenario, the product team should design a mechanism to inform data subjects and obtain their consent.
	• **Recommendation:** User consent must be obtained before personal data is transferred to personal computers or other similar equipment or transferred out of the equipment.
	• Information is stored on a user device (i.e., data or software download, etc.).
	• System or configurations are modified on a user device (software upgrade, etc.).
	• Data is deleted from a user device (i.e., restoring data needs deleting data first).
	• Data is copied from a user's device.
	• Setting or reading cookies on data subjects' systems.
	• **Recommendation:** Transfer of error reports
	• Prior to the transfer of error reports that may contain personal data out of user systems, the data controller and equipment vendor must notify the users and obtain their consent.
	• Before an error report on the program crash is sent, users must be given the possibility to opt in so users can decide whether to agree on report sending. Products without any UI should provide the explicit statement in materials.
	• If the equipment vendor provides the function of transferring error reports that may contain personal data out of data subjects' systems, the product team should design a mechanism to notify data subjects and obtain their consent.

some jurisdictions (i.e., US, Canada), telemarketers are required to keep track of the "Do Not Call Registry".

The evidence of consent should be recorded and show who provided the consent, when they consented, what they were told, how they provided the consent, etc. If complaints are lodged or investigations begin down the line, an organization needs to demonstrate this evidence. The organization should keep records of the following consent-related information as listed in Table 16.5.

16.7.5 CONSENT TO CHANGES

GDPR Article 13 and Article 14 provide that where the data controller intends to further process the personal data for a purpose other than that for which the personal data were collected, the controller shall provide the data subject prior to that further processing with information on that other purpose.

Data subjects must be notified of the privacy notice changes and consent should be re-obtained if necessary. If privacy notice changes, the organization should instruct data subjects to view the changes and re-obtain their consent if needed.

TABLE 16.5
Records of Consent Management

Item	Description
Who consented	Such as name or another online identifier (username for example)
When they consented	The date on which the consent was given
What they were told about the processing	Details that were provided at the time about the processing and the purposes
How they consented	For example, in writing or by submitting data into an online sign-up form for a newsletter subscription
Whether they subsequently withdrew consent	Whether the person has withdrawn consent and, if so, on what date. You can accomplish documenting the details of the processing and the purposes that were provided at the time of the processing by referring to your Privacy Notice that was in force at the time. Keep notes of how Privacy Notices are amended over time so that you know which version was shown to each data subject. This can be as low-tech as keeping a hard copy file of Privacy Notices and writing the dates on the top from when and until when they were effective.

   Example

If a privacy statement for a device app changes, a dialog box is displayed when the user uses the app, notifying that the privacy statement has been changed and the user needs to give consent to the new privacy statement before using the app.

16.7.6 WITHDRAWAL OF CONSENT

An organization should ensure data subjects have the right and mechanisms to withdraw their consent.

Some examples of legal obligations regarding consent withdrawal include the following.

- GDPR Article 7 provides that the data subject shall have the right to withdraw his or her consent at any time. It shall be as easy to withdraw as to give consent.
- US (CAN-SPAM) requires that upon receipt of a subscription request, the subscription must be completed within 10 working days.

Keep the following aspects in mind as you consider how to enable data subjects to withdraw consent:

- The data subject shall have the right to withdraw his or her consent at any time.
  - A data subject must not suffer any detriment by withdrawing their consent. If the data subject suffers, the consent is invalid.
  - A Third-Party can withdraw consent on behalf of a data subject. You must, however, satisfy yourself that the Third-Party has the authority to do so. This may cause difficulties where data subjects use automated software tools for unsubscribing.
- The organization should provide the proper mechanisms for data subjects to withdraw their consent.
  - The data subject should be provided with a mechanism to withdraw or modify the consent or privacy settings at any time with respect to the data collected from or generated by users through using products or services.
  - The organization should test the withdrawal/subscription mechanisms to ensure it does what it intended to do.

- There is no set time limit that dictates how long consent is valid. However, you need to monitor consent and refresh them where necessary depending on the context, including data subjects' expectations and how often you email them. For example, if you haven't emailed people for a long time, you may need to obtain fresh consent. If in doubt, the UK's supervisory authority, the ICO recommends refreshing consent every two years. You should also consider contacting data subjects regularly (every six months, for example), to remind them of their right to withdraw consent.
- The effort to withdraw consent is equal to that of providing consent.
  - For example, if you have obtained consent via a tick box on a website, the data subject must be able to withdraw consent online rather than, say, write a letter to withdraw consent.
  - Marketing emails provide the un-subscription method. The un-subscription must be free of charge and easy to execute without requiring additional information. The un-subscription link must be attached to the pushed emails. If the data subject chooses to opt out of marketing campaigns, his/her personal data (such as the mobile number and email address) can no longer be used for marketing and marketing-aimed profiling. The un-subscription must be free of charge. Users are not required to provide additional information (except email addresses and opt-out method preferences) to unsubscribe to marketing emails. The opt-out method must be easy to execute, such as by replying to an email or accessing a web page link.
- The withdrawal of consent shall not affect the lawfulness of processing based on consent before its withdrawal.
  - If you rely on consent as your lawful grounds for the processing, you need to inform data subjects of their right to withdraw consent. The place to do this is in your Privacy Notice.
- Organizations should cease collection, use, and disclosure of personal data after data subjects withdraw their consent.
  - When consent is withdrawn, you must stop processing the data immediately. Where this isn't possible, it must be stopped as soon as possible. If the processing cannot be stopped immediately for justified reasons, for example, a long computing period, the processing must be stopped before the next period starts. Such withdrawal applies only to the future, not to the processing that took place in the past when data was collected legitimately. Processing in the past cannot be simply annulled. However, the data controller should delete such data if there is no other legal basis justifying the further storage of the data.
  - After data subjects withdraw their consent, products must not collect users' personal data. For example, cookies need to be collected for user behavior analysis and marketing emails. If a data subject withdraws the consent to such collection, the data controller must stop collecting user cookies and analyzing previously collected user cookies to send marketing emails. Products should provide a deletion guide based on actual service scenarios for cookies collected prior to withdrawal.
  - If products provide user account deregistration, deletion of users' personal data should be sufficiently considered after deregistration. If products provide an account retention period to allow users to activate their accounts again, processing of users' personal data should be stopped, and users' personal data should be deleted after the retention period.
  - If a data subject withdraws consent, you don't necessarily need to delete all their data. For example, if a data subject opts out of email marketing (effectively withdrawing consent to you for processing their data to send email marketing), you can properly

keep this data on a suppression list (so that you have a record of the data subject's opting out).

- If you need to retain data for legal or auditing purposes, you can do so, but at the point of obtaining the consent, you must be upfront with the data subject about your intentions to continue to process the data for certain purposes.

17 Data Collection

This chapter is intended to help readers mitigate privacy risks by minimizing personal data collecting using a proper lawful basis and having legitimate purposes while enabling business operations.
This chapter covers the following topics:

• *Lawfulness and Fairness*
• *Purpose Limitation*
• *Data Minimization*

17.1 LAWFULNESS AND FAIRNESS

Organizations should ensure data collection methods are lawful, fair, and transparent. Organizations should collect and process personal data only with a proper legal basis and not collect personal data that is prohibited by laws and regulations.
Lawfulness:

a. Collect and process personal data with a proper legal basis.
b. Do not collect personal data that is prohibited by laws and regulations.
c. Do not obtain personal data from unauthorized channels.
d. Collection from third parties: Ensure data collection from third parties complies with applicable laws.
   • The organization should undertake due diligence to ensure that third parties from whom personal information is collected are reliable sources and the collection is done fairly and lawfully. The organization needs to establish and implement proper controls (i.e., contractual obligation) to manage the risks of collecting (i.e., purchasing) data from third parties.
   • There are several ways an organization can manage the risks. For instance, the organization can perform due diligence before establishing a relationship with a third-party data provider. The organization can review the privacy policies, collection methods, and types of consent of third parties before accepting personal information from third-party data sources. Also, the organization can sign and enforce legally binding contracts that include provisions requiring personal information to be collected fairly and lawfully and from reliable sources.

Fairness:
Personal data should be collected in a fair way and does not involve behaviors such as intimidation, deceiving, cheating, etc.

a. Do not deceive or mislead personal data subjects into providing their personal data. Such as do not conceal the personal data collection function provided by the products or services.
b. Do not force or intimidate personal data subjects to provide their personal data.
   • For instance, do not conceal the personal data collection function provided by the products or services.
c. Fairness also means that you should only use personal data in ways that data subjects would reasonably expect. This is particularly important when you are relying on the lawful ground of legitimate interests to process the data.

DOI: 10.1201/9781003225089-21

d. Provide proper security controls as needed to protect personal data collected by the
   organization.

Note: Lack of security controls could be deemed unfair. For instance, in the Finance sector, if the
PCI-DSS standard is not implemented, it could be deemed unfair.

 Examples

A smartphone product provides corresponding privacy statements near features in product materials. However, in the introduction of one feature, only the IMSI, IMEI, phone
number, IP address, and MAC address are listed, while some personal data with a high
impact such as user longitude and latitude location and HTTP packets (may contain personal data such as usernames and session IDs) are not described when they are collected
by the feature. This is questioned by customers.

17.2   PURPOSE LIMITATION

Organizations should only collect adequate, relevant, and limited to what is necessary regarding the
purposes for which they are processed.

GDPR Article 5(1)(b) requires that personal data shall be collected for specified, explicit, and
legitimate purposes and not further processed in a manner that is incompatible with those purposes.

According to PART I of SCHEDULE 1 The Data Protection Principles in the UK Data Protection
Act 1998, personal data shall be obtained only for one or more specified and lawful purposes and
shall not be further processed in any manner incompatible with that purpose or those purposes.

The first thing an organization needs to do when collecting data is to identify the specific purpose for which the data is being processed. For instance, collecting employee bank information for
payment processing purposes, collecting customer email addresses for marketing materials about
your services, etc.

Organizations need to understand the technology the organization uses to grow the business
and, in the process, how the organization plans to use and/or leverage the data it collects for protection, marketing, business development, monetization, and other purposes. Specifically, they should
understand the business purpose of collecting information from customers; how the collection process and the use of data are being communicated to customers; what the organization is doing with
the information it collects; the risks arising from how data is collected, maintained, and stored; and
how those risks are being managed.

If you want to use this data for another purpose that you did not previously inform the data subject about, such as sharing their data with third parties so that the third party can market to them,
this is a new purpose—and is outside the scope of your original purpose.

You may process personal data for an additional purpose only if one of the following statements
applies:

- The additional purpose is compatible with the original purpose
- You obtain consent to process the personal data for the new purpose
- Further processing is required for a task carried out in the public interest
- Further processing is for archiving purposes in the public interest, scientific or historical
  research purposes, or statistical purposes.

This principle creates challenges for organizations to describe their purposes in ways that are precise enough to provide valuable information to individuals but broad enough to include potential
future purposes, so they don't need to obtain consent every time they identify a new use for personal

information. This principle often leads organizations to state purposes for use in a broad manner. The natural tendency to be as vague and as broad as possible will, however, be criticized by regulators if the organization is ever investigated and if the broad explanation of the purpose leaves individuals guessing about the real purpose motivating the collection.

 Example

Purposes of collecting and processing Social Security Numbers (SSNs) in the education sector in Florida (US)

In compliance with Florida State Statute 119.071(5), students should be aware that education organizations collect and use social security numbers (SSNs) if specifically required by law to do so or if necessary for the performance of their duties and responsibilities. Table 17.1 lists some of the exemplar purposes of collecting and processing SSNs from students.

TABLE 17.1

Examples of Purposes of Collecting and Processing SSNs from Students

Data Processing Domain	Purpose	Statute or Regulation
Registrar	SSNs are collected from students for inclusion on official transcripts and for business purposes in accordance with parameters outlined by the US Department of Education. SSNs are reported to the state of Florida as required by state reporting requirements for postsecondary institutions.	Florida Statue 119.071 (5)
Admissions	Federal legislation related to the American Opportunity Tax Credit requires that all postsecondary institutions report student SSNs to the Internal Revenue Service.	Hope/Lifetime Tax Credit uses are authorized by 26 USC 6050S and Federal Register, June 16, 2000/IRC Section 25A. Florida Statue 119.071 (5) Tracking uses are authorized by SBE Rule 6A-10955(3)(e); 1008.386, F.S. and the General Education Provisions Act (20 USC 1221(e-1))
Financial Aid	The Federal Department of Education requires students to submit their SSN when completing the federal application for student aid. SSNs are collected to coordinate and verify eligibility and disbursement requirements for federal, state, and institutional aid programs.	Higher Education Act of 1965, as amended, Sections 441–448, 483 and 484(p), 20 USC 1091(p), 20 USC 1078–2(f); Code of Federal Regulations, 34 CFR 668.32(i) and 668.36; 38 USC 3471
Financial Services	SSNs are collected for reporting requirements related to administering student employee wages and benefits. When a student is employed by an education organization, SSNs are collected and maintained on the Internal Revenue Service required W4 form and reported on the IRS required W2 form. SSNs are collected for the verification of student direct deposit requests for wages as allowed by FS119.71(2)(a) and FS 119.71(6)(c).	Internal Revenue Code, sections 3402(f)(2)(A), 6109, and 6051(a)(2); FS119.71(2)(a) and FS 119.71(6)(c)

(Continued)

TABLE 17.1   (Continued)

Data Processing Domain	Purpose	Statute or Regulation
Human Resources	SSNs are collected for employment eligibility and reported to IRS and the Social Security Administration, including for W-4s and I-9s.	26 USC 6051 and 26 CFR 31.6011 (b)-2, 26 301.6109–1 and 31.3404(f)(2)-1 and FS 119.071(5) (a) 6
Continuing Education	Because of Florida State Education Reporting requirements, students who enroll in Continuing Education and Corporate Training classes are required to submit SSNs.	Florida Statue 119.071 (5)

17.3   DATA MINIMIZATION

Organizations should only collect data necessary for the services in compliance with the data minimization principle. Data minimization dictates that you identify the minimum amount of personal data necessary to achieve the purposes you communicated to the data subject and not process any further data than is necessary for those purposes.

You may process only personal data that is adequate, relevant, and limited to what is necessary to accomplish the purposes for which it is processed. It's also important for organizations to understand whether the organization needs all the information it collects. You therefore first need to understand why you need that data—that is, you need to know the specific purpose of the processing.

Organizations often think about how to practically handle the dichotomy of "minimizing data capture to protect privacy" and "maximizing the knowledge of the organization to provide better services", or simply, **how much data is too much data.**

Questions to ask yourself before collecting and processing the personal data:

1) Is personal data necessary for business purposes?
   a. For example, when a product processes user's payment results, user account's credit card and balance information which is not required for auditing should not be stored in system logs. Besides, users' credit card information should not be stored in plain text in the database, and a system administrator should not be able to directly view users' credit card information. Once such information is leaked, great risks will be brought to users' financial security.
   b. Another example, hotels should not ask a guest to provide the license plate number for their car if the guest is not going to use the hotel parking lot.
   c. You cannot collect data that isn't necessary now just in case you might need it in the future or because it might become useful to you.
2) Can we only process parts of personal data instead of the entire set of personal data?
   a. For instance, to reimburse employees' annual health check fees in the HR context, an organization only needs evidence that an employee has done the check and paid the fee. A detailed health check report is not needed for reimbursement purposes.
3) Is the encrypted or anonymized data useful in the business context?
   a. Organizations can use data minimization technologies and align with best practices of the business, such as personal data generalization, anonymization, and differential privacy technology.

It is very challenging to get it right from the very beginning. Fortunately, there is some guidance we can follow to determine what data can be collected in some business scenarios.

New Chinese Provisions Define the "Necessary" Personal Information Mobile Apps Can Collect

Four departments of the Chinese government have jointly issued a regulation, which will take effect on May 1, 2021, that sets forth new provisions for personal data collection through mobile apps. The National Law Review reports: "Under the Provisions, 'necessary personal information' is defined as personal information that is necessary for the regular operation of mobile applications ('apps'), (i.e., personal information without which apps could not provide their intended basic functions)."

Article 5 of the regulation explicitly lays out 39 app categories of varying functions and services, including

- Map navigation
- Ride-hailing
- Instant messaging
- Online shopping
- Payments
- Short video
- Livestream
- Mobile games

As an example of category-specific definitions, within map navigation, only location, departure, and destination information are considered necessary information under this regulation.

Follow this regulation's guidance closely if your organization operates mobile apps in China. Because it is the first of its kind in its scope and prescriptive measures, authorities will likely be more focused on this regulation's enforcement.

18 Data Usage and Maintenance

This chapter is intended to help readers ensure personal data only be used for the purposes speci-fied in the privacy notice and based on the data minimization principle.

This chapter covers the following topics:

- *Data use purpose limitation*
- *Access control*
- *Accuracy and integrity*

18.1 DATA USE PURPOSE LIMITATION

Personal data must be used for the purposes specified in the privacy notice and based upon the data minimization principle. The purposes, methods, and retention period of personal data should be con-sistent with the information contained in the notice to data subjects or authorizations by data subjects.

Organizations should maintain the accuracy, integrity, relevance, and completeness of personal data based on the processing purpose. Security mechanisms designed to protect personal data shall be used to prevent personal data from being stolen, misused, or abused, and prevent personal data from leakage. Reasonable steps must be taken to ensure that personal data that is inaccurate, having regard to the purposes for which they are processed, is erased or rectified.

Personal data should be anonymized to realize irreversible de-identification if appropriate or, if appropriate, aggregate data, such as statistical or research results that do not identify an individual, should be used. The personal data processing principles do not apply to anonymized data and aggre-gate data as they are not personal data.

Access to and processing of personal data should be controlled, with encryption or other meth-ods used to help ensure the ongoing confidentiality, integrity, availability, and resilience of process-ing systems.

Where the processing for a purpose other than that for which the personal data have been col-lected is not based on the data subject's consent or relevant privacy laws which constitute a neces-sary and proportionate measure to safeguard the rights and freedom of data subjects, the controller shall, to ascertain whether processing for another purpose is compatible with the purpose for which the personal data are initially collected, take into account, inter alia:

Purpose Compatibility Test

Organizations can only use personal data for the purposes specified in the privacy notice provided to the data subjects. If the collected data needs to be used for purposes not listed in the privacy notice, the controller either needs to conduct a purpose compatibility test to ensure the new pur-poses are compatible with the informed purposes in the privacy notice, or to re-obtain user consent before using them for new purposes and in new scenarios.

The purpose compatibility test should consider the following aspects illustrated in Table 18.1.

 Case Study

Bundeskartellamt prohibits Facebook from combining user data from different sources, 2019

The Bundeskartellamt imposed on Facebook far-reaching restrictions in the process-ing of user data on February 7, 2019. According to Facebook's terms and conditions

TABLE 18.1

Purpose Compatibility Test Considerations

Aspect	Description
Nature of data	The nature of the personal data, in particular, whether special categories of personal data are processed, or whether personal data related to criminal convictions and offenses are processed.
Reasonable expectation	Any link between the purposes for which the personal data have been collected and the purposes of the intended further processing. An additional question to ask: • Do we have a legal basis for the new purpose?
The way data processed	The context in which the personal data have been collected, in particular, regarding the relationship between data subjects and the controller. An additional question to ask: • Do we need all of the data for the new purpose according to the data minimization principle?
The impact	The possible consequences of the intended further processing for data subjects.
Safeguards	The existence of appropriate safeguards, which may include encryption or pseudonymization. Additional questions to ask: • Are the security measures sufficient for the new processing? • Do all persons who currently have access to the data really need to have access under the new purpose?

users have so far only been able to use the social network under the precondition that Facebook can collect user data also outside of the Facebook website on the Internet or smartphone apps and assign these data to the user's Facebook account. All data collected on the Facebook website, by Facebook-owned services such as e.g., WhatsApp, Instagram, and on Third-Party websites can be combined and assigned to the Facebook user account.

The authority's decision covers different data sources:

(i) Facebook-owned services like WhatsApp and Instagram can continue to collect data. However, assigning the data to Facebook user accounts will only be possible subject to the users' voluntary consent. Where consent is not given, the data must remain with the respective service and cannot be processed in combination with Facebook data.

(ii) Collecting data from Third-Party websites and assigning them to a Facebook user account will also only be possible if users give their voluntary consent.

If consent is not given for data from Facebook-owned services and third-party websites, Facebook will have to substantially restrict its collection and combining of data. Facebook is to develop proposals for solutions to this effect.

18.2 ACCESS CONTROL

Organizations should limit personal data access based on the need-to-know principle. Users' access to personal data should be granted based on a need-to-know basis. Formal identity and access management policy, and procedures should be put into place to manage personnel's access controls. Organizations should design and implement technical solutions to enforce and monitor the usage and processing of personal data.

System access

It is recommended that IT systems be used to manage the O&M permissions of databases and application system hosts, including applying for, approving, allocating, and revoking permissions, recording the mappings between accounts and employees, and managing audit logs of operators. In a system that provides O&M and operation management for multiple services, personal data management permissions for different services must be isolated.

Access to systems functions or APIs should be authorized and monitored based on business needs. Establish policy for authorization to be evaluated and obtained before a system calls functions or APIs or performs operations on user data, such as reading content. A security protection mechanism must be provided for these interfaces, such as those for IMSI reading, calling, voice recording, photo-taking, and shot message sending and receiving. Otherwise, malware may use these interfaces to obtain user privacy or intervene in users' freedom of communications.

User access and restrictions on display

Where the display of personal data on an interface (such as a display screen and paper) is involved, the personal data Controller should take measures such as de-identification to process the to-be-displayed personal data, so as to reduce the risk of personal data leakage during the display.

Operations Logging

Organizations should log, monitor, and audit personal data operations. Systems that collect and process personal data must log operators' personal data operations (i.e., access, change) to keep the audit trails that demonstrate how data is being accessed and used in the organization.

For instance, Under HIPAA, if an entity processes PHI data, access to the PHI should be retained for at least 6 years. Disclosures or access (both authorized and unauthorized) of their PHI during the past 6 years should be recorded, so you must log non-TPO of disclosures of PHI whether intentional or accidental.

Operations may be logged at the management plane, such as personal data export operations. Audit trails and logs can be assigned to individual users, to understand which individuals are accessing personal data.

 Example

A system logs administrators' personal data operations, including the time of operation, administrators' usernames or IDs, sources (e.g., IP addresses or hostnames) of operations, types of operations (query, access, modification, deletion, upload, download, import, export, etc.), operation description (e.g., changing the CRM_USERNAME field of a user), and operating results.

18.3 ACCURACY AND INTEGRITY

An organization should ensure the accuracy, integrity, and completeness of personal data. Please see the following examples of definitions of "Accuracy" in Table 18.2.

An opinion isn't inaccurate just because the data subject doesn't agree with it. If the opinion was based on facts that were incorrect, the opinion might also be incorrect and should be revised based on the accurate facts.

You should take every reasonable step to ensure that the personal data is accurate and, where necessary, kept up to date. In this context, measures mean that you should develop processes in your business to ensure that the data is accurate—not just during the collection process but for all of the processing.

TABLE 18.2

Examples of Definitions of "Accuracy"

Jurisdiction/ Regulation	Description
UK/Data Protection Act of 2018	Accuracy means the personal data isn't incorrect or factually misleading.

Canada/CPPA (draft)	**Accuracy of information**
	(1) An organization must take reasonable steps to ensure that personal information under its control is as accurate, up-to-date, and complete as is necessary to fulfill the purposes for which the information is collected, used, or disclosed.
	Extent of accuracy
	(2) In determining the extent to which personal information must be accurate, complete, and up to date, the organization must take into account the individual's interests, including
	    (a) whether the information may be used to make a decision about the individual.
	    (b) whether the information is used on an ongoing basis.
	    (c) whether the information is disclosed to third parties.
	Routine updating
	(3) An organization is not to routinely update personal information unless it is necessary to fulfill the purposes for which the information is collected, used, or disclosed.

19 Personal Data Sharing

This chapter is intended to help readers establish an end-to-end vendor privacy management process to properly manage the risks of personal data sharing with external stakeholders as well as purchasing personal data from data brokers.

This chapter covers the following topics:

- *The necessity of personal data sharing*
- *Data processing chains*
- *End-to-end vendor management*
- *Purchasing data from data brokers*

19.1 NECESSITY OF PERSONAL DATA SHARING

An organization should properly manage the risks of personal data sharing. Business leaders need to understand where the critical data resides, and how it is being managed, within the supply chain and among third-party providers. These leaders know that the process can be outsourced but the risks cannot. Therefore, privacy and data issues arising with any outside data processors of personally identifiable information still go back to the source for ultimate responsibility. That means the organization and its brand are ultimately liable for damages should any third party experience a data breach.

Vendor security risk management is a growing concern for many organizations. Whether suppliers or business partners, we often trust them with our most sensitive data and processes. More and more regulations require vendor security risk management, and regulator expectations in this area are growing. Many organizations know that they need to secure their supply chain but struggle with finding the right level of due diligence.

It is critical to ensure all third parties are operating with the same privacy standards and maintaining data in compliance with the sourcing organization's policies. Third-party risk management is critical, especially with data management. It affects the entire value chain. Organizations failing to perform effective third-party risk management could face serious brand-eroding data and compliance issues.[28]

Here are some key considerations with respect to personal data sharing:

- **Lawful basis:** Unless otherwise specified in the laws and regulations or authorized by the data subject, the organization should not make personal information public.
  - For instance, HIPAA and COPPA forbid disclosures of covered information to third parties, unless there is opt-in consent, or a different exception applies. The Gramm-Leach-Bliley Act (GLBA) forbids disclosures to third parties unless the individual has not opted out or a different exception applies.[29]
  - Data sharing and disclosure should be consented to by users or have an appropriate legal basis and have compatible purposes.
  - If the privacy statement does not notify data subjects that their data will be provided to a third party, they can be notified before the first transfer or each transfer, and their consent should be obtained before their data is transferred to a third party. User-friendly UIs and operation options should be provided for data subjects, and notifications can be displayed using more than a dialog.[30]
- **Purpose limitation:** The organization can only disclose personal information to a Third Party for the purposes specified in the privacy notice after the consent of the data subject is obtained.

- **Data Sharing Governance:** The organization should establish and execute the policy and processes to manage the necessity, purpose, and legal basis of personal data sharing or transfer to external recipients.
  - Transferring personal data to external recipients should be justified, documented, and monitored.
- **End-to-End Data Processor Management:** The organization shall only engage with third parties who provide substantially the same protection of the personal information as that which the organization is required to provide under privacy laws.
  - When an organization authorizes a supplier or business partner to process personal data on behalf of the organization, it should seek to ensure that the supplier or business partner will provide security measures to safeguard personal data that are appropriate to the risks associated with the personal data.
  - The supplier or business partner should only process personal data to carry out its contractual obligations to the organization or upon instruction, and not for any other purpose.[31]

There is quite a range of privacy and data protection laws and regulations which are illustrated in the Table 19.1.

TABLE 19.1
Examples of Obligations Regarding Personal Data Sharing

Privacy Regulation/ Standard	Related Clause or Section	Requirement Regarding Data Sharing
General Data Protection Regulation (GDPR)[32][33]	Article 28 (1)	Where the processing is to be carried out on behalf of a controller, the controller shall use only processors providing sufficient guarantees to implement appropriate technical and organizational measures in such a manner that processing will meet the requirements of this Regulation and ensure the protection of the rights of the data subject.
	Article 46 (1)	In the absence of a decision pursuant to Article 45(3), a controller or processor may transfer personal data to a third country or an international organization only if the controller or processor has provided appropriate safeguards, and on the condition that enforceable data subject rights and effective legal remedies for data subjects are available.
HIPAA[34][35]	§164.308(b)(1)	Business associate contracts and other arrangements. A covered entity may permit a business associate to create, receive, maintain, or transmit electronically protected health information on the covered entity's behalf only if the covered entity obtains satisfactory assurances, in accordance with §164.314(a), that the business associate will appropriately safeguard the information. A covered entity is not required to obtain such satisfactory assurances from a business associate that is a subcontractor.
	§164.308(b)(2)	A business associate may permit a business associate that is a subcontractor to create, receive, maintain, or transmit electronically protected health information on its behalf only if the business associate obtains satisfactory assurances, in accordance with §164.314(a), that the subcontractor will appropriately safeguard the information.
	§164.308(b)(3)	Implementation specifications: Written contracts or other arrangements (required). Document the satisfactory assurances required by paragraph (b)(1) or (b)(2) of this section through a written contract or other arrangements with the business associate that meets the applicable requirements of §164.314(a).

Privacy Regulation/ Standard	Related Clause or Section	Requirement Regarding Data Sharing
New York Department of Financial Services Cybersecurity Requirements[36]	500.11(a)	Each Covered Entity shall implement written policies and procedures designed to ensure the security of Information Systems and Nonpublic Information that are accessible to, or held by, Third-Party Service Providers. Such policies and procedures shall be based on the Risk Assessment of the Covered Entity and shall address to the extent applicable: (1) the identification and risk assessment of Third-Party Service Providers. (2) minimum cybersecurity practices required to be met by such Third-Party Service Providers in order for them to do business with the Covered Entity. (3) due diligence processes used to evaluate the adequacy of cybersecurity practices of such Third-Party Service Providers. (4) periodic assessment of such Third-Party Service Providers based on the risk they present and the continued adequacy of their cybersecurity practices.
	500.11(b)	Such policies and procedures shall include relevant guidelines for due diligence and/or contractual protections relating to Third-Party Service Providers including to the extent applicable guidelines addressing: (1) the Third-Party Service Provider's policies and procedures for access controls, including its use of Multi-Factor Authentication as required by section 500.12 of this Part, to limit access to relevant Information Systems and Nonpublic Information. (2) the Third-Party Service Provider's policies and procedures for use of encryption as required by section 500.15 of this Part to protect Nonpublic Information in transit and at rest. (3) notice to be provided to the Covered Entity in the event of a Cybersecurity Event directly impacting the Covered Entity's Information Systems or the Covered Entity's Nonpublic Information being held by the Third-Party Service Provider; and (4) representations and warranties addressing the Third-Party Service Provider's cybersecurity policies and procedures that relate to the security of the Covered Entity's Information Systems or Nonpublic Information.
North Carolina— Statewide security and privacy standards[37]	§ 143B-1376. (a)	The State CIO shall be responsible for the security and privacy of all State information technology systems and associated data. The State CIO shall manage all executive branch information technology security and shall establish a statewide standard for information technology security and privacy to maximize the functionality, security, and interoperability of the State's distributed information technology assets, including, but not limited to, data classification and management, communications, and encryption technologies. The State CIO shall review and revise the security standards annually. As part of this function, the State CIO shall review periodically existing security and privacy standards and practices in place among the various State agencies to determine whether those standards and practices meet statewide security, privacy, and encryption requirements. The State CIO shall ensure that State agencies are periodically testing and evaluating information security controls and techniques for effective implementation and that all agency and contracted personnel are held accountable for complying with the statewide information security program. The State CIO may assume the direct responsibility of providing for the information technology security of any State agency that fails to adhere to security and privacy standards adopted under this Article.

(Continued)

TABLE 19.1 (Continued)

Privacy Regulation/ Standard	Related Clause or Section	Requirement Regarding Data Sharing
	§ 143B-1376. (b)	The State CIO shall establish standards for the management and safeguarding of all State data held by State agencies and private entities and shall develop and implement a process to monitor and ensure adherence to the established standards. The State CIO shall establish and enforce standards for the protection of State data. The State CIO shall develop and maintain an inventory of where State data is stored. For data maintained by non-State entities, the State CIO shall document the reasons for the use of the non-State entity and certify, in writing, that the use of the non-State entity is the best course of action. The State CIO shall ensure that State data held by non-State entities is properly protected and is held in facilities that meet State security standards. By October 1 each year, the State CIO shall certify in writing that data held in non-State facilities is being maintained in accordance with State information technology security standards and shall provide a copy of this certification to the Joint Legislative Oversight Committee on Information Technology and the Fiscal Research Division.
	§ 143B-1376. (c)	Before a State agency can contract for the storage, maintenance, or use of State data by a private vendor, the agency shall obtain the approval of the State CIO. (2015–241, s. 7A.2(b); 2019–200, s. 6(f).)
OSFI Cybersecurity Guidelines (Canada)[38]	4.25	The FRFI considers cyber security risk as part of its due diligence process for material outsourcing arrangements and critical IT service providers, including related subcontracting arrangements.
	4.26	Contracts for all material outsourcing arrangements and critical IT service providers include the provision for safeguarding the FRFI's Information.
NIST 800–53 R4[39] [40]	SA-12	The organization protects against supply chain threats to the information system, system component, or information system service by employing organization-defined security safeguards as part of a comprehensive, defense-in-breadth information security strategy.
	SA-12 (2)	The organization conducts a supplier review prior to entering into a contractual agreement to acquire the information system, system component, or information system service.
	SA-12 (5)	The organization employs organization-defined security safeguards to limit harm from potential adversaries identifying and targeting the organizational supply chain.
	SA-12 (8)	The organization uses all-source intelligence analysis of suppliers and potential suppliers of the information system, system component, or information system service.
NIST Cybersecurity Framework	ID-SC-1	Cyber supply chain risk management processes are identified, established, assessed, managed, and agreed to by organizational stakeholders
	ID.SC-2	Suppliers and third-party partners of information systems, components, and services are identified, prioritized, and assessed using a cyber supply chain risk assessment process.
	ID.SC-3	Contracts with suppliers and third-party partners are used to implement appropriate measures designed to meet the objectives of an organization's cybersecurity program and Cyber Supply Chain Risk Management Plan.
	ID.SC-4	Suppliers and third-party partners are routinely assessed using audits, test results, or other forms of evaluations to confirm they are meeting their contractual obligations.
PCI DSS 3.2[41]	12.8	Maintain and implement policies and procedures to manage service providers with whom cardholder data is shared, or that could affect the security of cardholder data, as follows:

Privacy Regulation/ Standard	Related Clause or Section	Requirement Regarding Data Sharing
	12.8.1	Maintain a list of service providers, including a description of the service provided.
	12.8.3	Ensure there is an established process for engaging service providers including proper due diligence prior to engagement.
	12.8.4	Maintain a program to monitor service providers' PCI DSS compliance status at least annually.
	12.8.5	Maintain information about which PCI DSS requirements are managed by each service provider and which are managed by the entity.
ISO 27002:2013[42]	15.1.1	Information security policy for supplier relationships
	15.1.2	Addressing security within supplier agreements
	15.1.3	Information and communication technology supply chain
	15.2.1	Monitoring and review of supplier services
	15.2.2	Managing changes to supplier services

19.2   DATA PROCESSING CHAINS

The data processing activities might involve various roles throughout the data life cycle. Figure 19.1 demonstrates the relationship among those roles with associated data-sharing agreements that are needed to manage data protection risks.

Joint Controllers

Two data controllers (i.e., joint controllers or two independent controllers) should establish an agreement to set forth the rights and obligations of each controller. The agreement should not influence an individual's rights to demand any one personal information controller perform under this Law's provisions.

GDPR requirements:

- If you're sharing data with a joint controller, Article 26 of the GDPR states that there must be an "arrangement" in place between the data controllers. Article 26 does not necessarily require a written agreement. However, having a written agreement in place to evidence the arrangement is best practice and helps to demonstrate accountability.

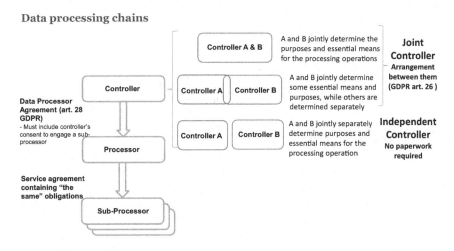

FIGURE 19.1   Roles associated with data processing chains.

- Article 26 of the GDPR states that the joint controllers shall "in a transparent manner" determine their respective responsibilities for compliance—in particular, in relation to the provision of information to data subjects and the exercise of data subject rights. The exception to this is where EU law or national law of any EU member state sets out the respective responsibilities. Regardless of the nature of the arrangement and the division of responsibilities between the joint controllers, a data subject may exercise their rights against each of the joint controllers.

China's PIPL requirements:

- Article 20: Where two or more personal information handlers jointly decide on personal information handling purpose and handling method, they shall agree on the rights and obligations of each. However, the agreement does not influence an individual's rights to demand any one personal information handler perform under this Law's provisions.
- Where personal information handlers jointly handling personal information harm personal information rights and interests, resulting in damages, they bear joint liability according to the law.

For a joint controller Data Sharing Agreement, you need to include these two elements:

- Specify each party's responsibilities for compliance with the GDPR
- A designated contact point: You may want to consider designating a contact point for data subjects, and include the points specified for a controller-to-controller Data Sharing Agreement.

It would be good practice to include these elements too:

- An obligation on each party to comply with data protection
- A description of the data that's being shared and whether it's sensitive data
- An obligation on each party to provide assistance to the other in the event of a data subject exercising their rights
- Provisions for data retention
- Provisions about onward transfers of the data to a third party
- A description of the security that's in place to protect the data
  - An obligation to inform the other party of any data breach
  - Agreement on how to deal with any investigation by a supervisory authority
- A mutual indemnity for each party to reimburse the other for any loss suffered as a result of the other's actions or inactions

Independent Controllers

If you, as a data controller, are sharing personal data with another independent data controller, the GDPR doesn't specifically require an arrangement or agreement. Nonetheless, I would recommend setting up an arrangement between the two Independent Controllers to clarify the roles and minimize the data protection risks.

Controller to Processor

Processing by a processor shall be governed by a contract or other legal act under Union or Member State law, that is binding on the processor with regard to the controller and that sets out the subject matter and duration of the processing, the nature, and purpose of the processing, the type of personal data and categories of data subjects and the obligations and rights of the controller. That contract or other legal act shall stipulate, in particular, that the processor:

(a) processes the personal data only on documented instructions from the controller, including with regard to transfers of personal data to a third country or an international organization, unless required to do so by Union or Member State law to which the processor is subject; in such a case, the processor shall inform the controller of that legal requirement before processing, unless that law prohibits such information on important grounds of public interest.

(b) ensures that persons authorized to process the personal data have committed themselves to confidentiality or are under an appropriate statutory obligation of confidentiality

(c) takes all measures required pursuant to Article 32

(d) respects the conditions referred to in paragraphs 2 and 4 for engaging another processor

(e) taking into account the nature of the processing, assists the controller with appropriate technical and organizational measures, insofar as this is possible, for the fulfillment of the controller's obligation to respond to requests for exercising the data subject's rights laid down in Chapter III

(f) assists the controller in ensuring compliance with the obligations pursuant to Articles 32 to 36 taking into account the nature of processing and the information available to the processor

(g) at the choice of the controller, deletes or returns all the personal data to the controller after the end of the provision of services relating to processing, and deletes existing copies unless Union or Member State law requires the storage of the personal data

(h) makes available to the controller all information necessary to demonstrate compliance with the obligations laid down in this Article and allow for and contribute to audits, including inspections, conducted by the controller or another auditor mandated by the controller.

Data Processor to Sub-processors
The processor shall not engage a sub-processor without the prior written authorization of the controller. Also, the same data protection obligations must be imposed on that sub-processor by way of a contract or other legal act; however, the initial processor will remain fully liable if the sub-processor fails to fulfill its data protection obligations.

Where a processor engages another processor for carrying out specific processing activities on behalf of the controller, the same data protection obligations as set out in the contract or other legal act between the controller and the processor shall be imposed on that other processor by way of a contract or other legal act, in particular providing sufficient guarantees to implement appropriate technical and organizational measures in such a manner that the processing will meet the requirements of privacy regulations. Where that other processor fails to fulfill its data protection obligations, the initial processor shall remain fully liable to the controller for the performance of that other processor's obligations.

19.3   END-TO-END VENDOR MANAGEMENT

The processor and any person acting under the authority of the controller or of the processor, who has access to personal data, shall not process those data except on instructions from the controller unless required to do so by applicable privacy laws and regulations.

It is clear that supply chain data breaches are on the rise based on the following statistics according to Ponemon Institute (2018):

- 61% of organizations experienced a data breach caused by their supply chain in 2018, an increase from 56% in 2017.
- Only 29% of organizations believe a third-party vendor would notify them of a data breach.
- Only 28% of organizations believe they will be notified when a third-party shares data with its vendors along the supply chain.

Many organizations know that they need to secure their supply chain but struggle with finding the right level of due diligence. An efficient and effective assessment process can only be achieved when all stakeholders are participating. An end-to-end third-party privacy risk management process should be established to protect the shared data. Effective vendor privacy risk management is an end-to-end process that includes assessment, risk mitigation, and periodic re-assessments.

TABLE 19.2
Main Phases for a Data Protection Risk Management Process

Phase	Activities
Pre-Contract	• Categorize vendors
	• Perform due diligence check
Signing of Contract	• Sign the data processing agreement
Execution of Contract	• Monitor privacy controls
	• Check or audit as needed
Termination of Contract	• Delete or return data
	• Deprovision access

Table 19.2 lists the four main phases for an end-to-end vendor data protection risk management process.

19.3.1 RISK-BASED MANAGEMENT

Data protection evaluations and assessments that are too onerous will lead to vendors who refuse to bid for your business, driving the business to bypass your assessment process.

Your organization needs to understand the right level of data protection due diligence for vendor management to achieve business goals and compliance obligations.

Also, it is recommended to categorize organization outsourcing services into different criticality levels and design vendor evaluation and risk treatment control respectively.

Table 19.3 illustrates a high-level strategy for managing vendor-related data protection risks based on the service criticality levels.

TABLE 19.3
Service Risk Level Criteria and Vendor Management Requirements

Service Risk Level Criteria			Vendor Risk Management Requirement
Tier I Critical Risk Service	Meet two of the following three criteria. • The vendor will process highly sensitive personal data, such as personal data revealing racial or ethnic origin, political opinions, religious or philosophical beliefs, or trade union membership, genetic data, biometric data, data concerning health, or data concerning a natural person's sex life or sexual orientation. • The vendor processes a large volume (i.e., more than 100,000) of personal data. • The outsourced process/ activity is mission-critical to the organization.	Violation of privacy regulatory requirements could cause critical business disruption, huge administrative fines, significant reputation damage, or a large scale of lawsuits.	Vendors in the tier 1 category will receive the most comprehensive advanced assessment. • Screening stage • Perform full-blown due diligence assessment • Vendor's policies, procedures, and standards • Attestation- SOC2 Type2, ISO27701/27001, etc. • Technical security assessments—passive (SSL, DNS, data breach search) and proactive (Pen Test, Vulnerability assessment, etc.) • Conduct data breach search • Contract signing stage • Sign a data processing agreement (DPA) • Contract execution stage • Carry out regular **on-site** audits • Attestation reports • Contract termination stage • Delete personal data and de-provision access

Service Risk Level Criteria			Vendor Risk Management Requirement
Tier II High-Risk Service	Meet one of the following three criteria. • The vendor will process highly sensitive personal data, such as personal data revealing racial or ethnic origin, political opinions, religious or philosophical beliefs, or trade union membership, genetic data, biometric data, data concerning health, or data concerning a natural person's sex life or sexual orientation. • The vendor processes a large volume (i.e., more than 100,000) of personal data. • The outsourced process/activity is mission-critical to the organization.	Violation of privacy regulatory requirements could cause moderate business disruption, administrative fines, or some level of reputation damage.	Vendors in the tier 2 category will receive a less comprehensive assessment than those in tier 1. • Screening stage- • Perform full-blown due diligence assessment • Attestation—SOC2 Type2, ISO27701/27001, etc. • Contract signing stage • Sign a data processing agreement (DPA) • Contract execution stage • Carry out **remote audits** • Attestation report • Contract termination stage • Delete personal data and de-provision access
Tier III Routine Risk Service	The vendor will process a fair amount of non-sensitive personal data. The outsourced process/activity is supporting main business functions and operations.	Violation of privacy regulatory requirements could cause a controllable negative impact on the organization.	Vendors in the tier 3 category will receive a less comprehensive assessment than those in tier 2. • Screening stage • Perform full-blown due diligence assessment • Contract signing stage • Sign a data processing agreement (DPA) • Contract termination stage • Delete personal data and de-provision access
Tier IV Low Risk Service	The Vendor will process only a small amount of non-sensitive personal data. The outsourced process/activity is non-essential to the organization's business operations.	Violation of privacy regulatory requirements could cause very limited to no impact on the organization.	Vendors in the tier 4 category will receive a less comprehensive assessment than those in tier 3. • Screening stage • Perform **light version** due diligence assessment • Contract signing stage • Sign a data processing agreement (DPA) • Contract termination stage • Delete personal data and de-provision access

19.3.2 PRE-CONTRACT

Personal data is disclosed only to third parties who have the capability to protect personal data by complying with applicable regulations, organization's privacy protection policies, and requirements. The organization should perform due a diligence check from a privacy protection perspective before selecting a service or product provider.

Table 19.4 provides an exemplar evaluation checklist that organizations can use as a reference to build their checklists.

TABLE 19.4
Evaluation Questionnaire

Domain	Evaluation Questionnaire
Regulatory obligations	Does your organization identify and document applicable privacy-related laws and regulations as well as associated requirements within the jurisdictions in which your organization operates?
	Is there a mechanism in place to monitor and track the developments of laws, regulations, and official guidelines in those jurisdictions?
Key roles and responsibilities	Does your organization designate the owner who oversees the privacy and data protection practices and is ultimately responsible for the privacy program?
	Does your organization make the privacy program ownership's contact available to internal employees and external data subjects?
Policies and procedures	Does your organization establish and publish a set of privacy policies and procedures that are necessary to manage the privacy program?
	If so, do those policies and procedures cover the following aspects (not an exhaustive list)?
	• Notice
	• Choice and consent
	• Collection
	• Use, retention, and disposal
	• Data subject rights
	• Disclosure to third parties
	• Security for privacy including data breach handling
	• Monitoring and enforcement
Privacy awareness and training	Does your organization establish and roll out a regular (i.e., annual) privacy awareness and training program for employees, senior leaders, privacy professionals, etc.?
	If so, is there a mechanism in place to evaluate the effectiveness of the awareness and training program?
Personal data processing inventory and data flows	Does your organization establish and maintain an up-to-date data processing inventory as records of data processing activities?
	If so, does the data processing inventory include core elements such as the name of business processes, types of personal information processed, purposes of processing, legal basis of the processing, security controls, retention period, etc.?
	Does your organization establish and maintain up-to-date data flows among business processes and/or IT systems to reflect the actual personal data lifecycle?
Privacy notice	Does your organization provide appropriate privacy notice before or at the time when personal data is obtained from data subjects (i.e., customers, employees)?
	If so, does the privacy notice consist of the following core sections (not an exhaustive list)?
	• The identity and contact of the organization
	• Types of personal data to be collected and processed
	• The purposes and methods of data processing
	• How the personal data will be used and shared
	• How the personal data will be stored and the data retention period
	• Cross-border transfer mechanisms
	• Security protection of the personal data
	• Data subjects' rights and the ways to exercise the rights
Lawful basis and Consent	Does your organization require all data processing activities to have a proper legal basis? And require that no business units or individuals may illegally collect, use, process, or transmit other persons' personal information, illegally sell, buy, provide, or disclose other persons' personal information, or engage in personal information handling activities harming national security or the public interest?
	If so, does your organization define the lawful basis based on the applicable laws and regulations?

Domain	Evaluation Questionnaire
	If consent is the suitable lawful basis of a particular data processing activity, does your organization require that valid consent must be obtained at or before the time of the collection of the personal information?
	Note: Personal information handlers may not refuse to provide products or services on the basis that an individual does not consent to the handling of their personal information or rescinds their consent, except where handling personal information is necessary for the provision of products or services.
Data collection	Does your organization collect personal data in a fair way and not involve behaviors such as intimidation, deceiving, cheating, etc.?
	Does your organization only collect personal data for specified, explicit, and legitimate purposes articulated in the privacy notice?
	Does your organization only collect the adequate, relevant, and limited type of personal data that is necessary in relation to the purposes for which they are processed?
	Does your organization establish and implement proper controls to manage the risks of collecting (i.e., purchasing) data from third parties? For instance, your organization needs to undertake due diligence to ensure that third parties from whom personal information is collected are reliable sources and that the collection is done fairly and lawfully.
Data use and maintain	Does your organization only use personal data for the purposes specified in the privacy notice provided to the data subjects?
	If the collected data needs to be used for purposes not listed in the privacy notice, does your organization conduct a purpose compatibility test to ensure the new purposes are compatible with the informed purposes in the privacy notice?
	Does your organization grant users access to personal data only based on a need-to-know basis?
	If the personal data needs to be displayed on the screen or printed on paper, does your organization take measures such as de-identification to process the to-be-displayed personal data, so as to reduce the risk of personal data leakage during the display?
	Does your organization implement a mechanism to ensure personal data is accurate, up-to-date, and complete?
	Does your organization log operators' personal data operations (i.e., access, change) to keep the audit trails that demonstrate how data is being accessed and used in the organization?
Data sharing and transfer	Does your organization implement a mechanism to review, evaluate and verify the necessity, purpose, and legal basis before personal data is shared and transferred outside the organization?
	Does your organization notify data subjects about the name or personal name of the recipient, their contact method, the handling purpose, handling method, and personal information categories, and obtain separate consent from the data subjects?
Data cross-border transfers and data localization	Does your organization conduct personal information cross-border transfers?
	If so, does your organization establish a proper cross-border data transfer strategy and mechanism (i.e., Standard Contractual Clauses) based on the regulatory requirements and business needs? Are the IT systems designed in the way (i.e., location of datacenters and servers) in alignment with the cross-border transfer mechanisms? Do personal data processing operations (i.e., staffing and technical support operations) align with defined cross-border data transfer mechanisms?
Data retention and depersonalization	Does your organization establish a data retention schedule that aligns with applicable laws and regulations within each jurisdiction in which an organization operates?
	Does your organization execute the data retention schedule to de-identify or delete personal data after it reaches the retention period, or the data is no longer necessary for the purposes for which the personal data are processed?
Security protection of personal data	Does your organization establish an appropriate data classification scheme to facilitate the data classification, categorization, and identification considering factors such as legal implications, nature and purpose, sensitivity, criticality to business operations, and potential impact on data subjects if disclosed to unauthorized personnel?

(Continued)

TABLE 19.4 (Continued)

Domain	Evaluation Questionnaire
	Does your organization implement appropriate technical and organizational measures (TOMs) using a risk-based approach to ensure the confidentiality, integrity, availability, and resilience of personal data?
	Typical security measures might include the following controls (not an exhaustive list).
	• Information security policies
	• Organization of information security
	• Human resource security
	• Asset management
	• Access control
	• Cryptography
	• Physical and environmental security
	• Operations security
	• Communications security
	• System acquisition, development, and maintenance
	• Supplier relationships
	• Information security incident management
	• Information security aspects of business continuity management
	• Compliance
Data Subject Rights Assurance	Does your organization design the services, products or processes that are equipped with the capability to fulfill data subject rights?
	Does your organization use personal information to conduct automated decision-making?
	If so, does your organization guarantee the transparency of the decision-making and the fairness and justice of the handling result?
PIA Methodology and Integration	Does your organization establish a consistent process for privacy impact assessment including the criteria for privacy risk identification, evaluation, treatment, etc.?
	If so, does the PIA process cover high-risk data processing scenarios that might impose a significant risk to data subjects? Examples of high-risk data processing activities are listed as follows (not an exhaustive list).
	• Processing special categories of personal data
	• Data relating to criminal convictions or offenses
	• Data processed on a large scale
	• Data concerning vulnerable data subjects
	• Automated profiling, evaluation, scoring, or decision making
	• Employee monitoring
	• Tracking & monitoring
	• Matching or combining datasets
	• Deployment and modification of a public CCTV surveillance system
	• Whether to make decisions that may greatly affect data subjects
	• Cross-border transfer
DSR request handling	Does your organization establish and operationalize a process to handle data subject right requests from external and internal data subjects?
Data breach handling	Does your organization establish a consistent data breach handling process that includes the handling requirements, procedure, and responsibilities throughout various phases such as preparation, detection, investigation and triage, containment, eradication and recovery, reporting, improvements, etc.?
	Does your organization document and maintain the requirement regarding whether and when to notify either the data protection authorities or data subjects?
	Does your organization conduct regular (i.e., annual) data breach drills to evaluate the effectiveness of the data breach handling process and make updates and improvements accordingly?

19.3.3   Signing of Contract

A legally binding data processing agreement (DPA) should be established between the organization (the data controller) and the processor. The DPA can be a standalone document or part of the master agreement or contract. Usually, a DPA should cover the following components as listed in Table 19.5 (not an exhaustive list).

As a data processor, an organization needs to ensure the outsourced data processing activities have a proper lawful basis and adhere to data protection principles articulated in privacy and data protection regulations.

TABLE 19.5
Core Components of a DPA

	Core Component	Description
1	Defined the data processing roles	Define the roles and responsibilities such as data controller, data processor, etc.
2	Defined contract processing	The DPA shall define the types of personal data and purposes of the data processing (contract processing). This is usually accomplished by using an annex, such as: • What processing will take place • Purposes of the data processing • Type of personal data and whether the data includes any special categories of data • Type of data subjects • Duration
3	Processing instructions	The data processor shall process personal data in accordance with documented instructions from the data controller.
4	Sub-processor	The data processor shall obtain the controller's approval to engage sub-processors. The data processor shall ensure the sub-processor(s) have the level of data protection in accordance with data protection laws.
5	Security controls	The data processor shall implement appropriate security technical and organizational measures (TOMs).
6	Data breach notification and handling	Define the timeframe of a data breach notification from the data processor to the data controller, as well as the handling process.
7	Data secrecy and staff awareness and training	Ensure the secrecy/confidentiality of personal data transferred to the data processor. Outline awareness and training in relation to the handling and processing of personal data.
8	Data subject request	Define the processor's role in supporting the data controller in fulfilling DSR handling obligations.
9	Compliance demonstration	The data processor will make available to the data controller all information requested by the data controller to demonstrate compliance with data protection laws.
10	Audit and Inspection rights	The data controller should have the rights and may audit and inspect data processors' compliance with their obligations under this Data Processing Agreement or applicable data protection laws.
11	Cross-border transfer	Proper mechanisms should be implemented to facilitate data cross-border transfer activities.
12	Termination of Service	On termination of services, the data processor shall return, destroy, or permanently erase all personal data transferred from the data controller.
13	Liability and indemnity	In a contract with a third party, clearly state that privacy risks and losses incurred by the third party shall be borne by the third party and that the data controller will not be held liable.

Questions and answers

How to establish proper liability and indemnity between a data controller and data processor?

If the data processor agrees to take on certain liability by providing warranties and indemnity in the Data Processing Agreement, it will want to make sure this liability is capped in some way and not unlimited. This may be a difficult negotiation with the data controller pushing for a liability cap that's as high as possible.

In general, in high-value, complex transactions, data controllers typically require a higher cap for liabilities for data protection than for the general indemnities under the service agreement (a "super cap" or an "enhanced liability" cap). One way of approaching the negotiation is to look at the risks involved. Both the data controller and data processor need to look at the following factors:

- The sensitivity of the data: The more sensitive, the higher the liability cap.
- The type and complexity of the processing: In particular, whether the processing operations are commoditized or designed specifically just for the data controller.
- The number of data subjects involved: The more data subjects involved, the higher the liability cap.
- The price being paid for the services: The price may go up if you insist on a high liability cap.
- The term of the contract: The longer the contract, the higher the liability cap over the lifetime of the contract.
- The due diligence already carried out on the processor: This includes whether any past incidents have occurred, such as data breaches, and how advanced their security systems are.
- The history between the data controller and the data processor and the reputation of the processor. Any sub processors involved, and their reputation and the due diligence carried out on them.

 Case Study

Spain AEPD v. Vodafone España, S.A.U., May 2021

The Spanish DPA fined Vodafone €100,000 for not ensuring that the processor they contracted with had implemented and continued to implement appropriate technical and organizational measures to ensure compliance with the GDPR.

A data subject filed a complaint with the Spanish DPA (AEPD) against Vodafone as they received a phone call with commercial purposes from the company after signing up for the Robinson list. The AEPD launched an investigation and discovered that the call had been made by Xfera Móviles, who acted on behalf of Vodafone on marketing activities (as a processor, as determined by the DPA). Xfera alleged that there had been an error when filtering the phone numbers of the Robinson list.

The DPA concluded that there had been a violation of Article 28 GDPR due to the lack of diligence of Vodafone in ensuring that the processor they contracted with had implemented and continued to implement appropriate technical and organizational measures to ensure compliance with the GDPR.

Case Study

Germany—ICANN vs. EPAG, May 2018

This is the first GDPR court case. The German Bonn State Court directly invoked the GDPR "data minimization" and other principles to make a judgment, which is the first practice so far in an effective judicial process that the GDPR is used as a basis.

EPAG (the data processor), in the process of fulfilling the DPA with ICANN (the data controller), believes that the collection of certain non-essential information violates the "data minimization principle" in the GDPR, lacks a legal basis, and refuses to perform the contract.

ICANN (data controller) filed an application with the court asking the court to compel EPAG (data processor) to continue to collect this type of personal data in accordance with the DPA.

Court decision: The controller is unable to prove that the data is necessary for its operations and rejects the data controller's request for the data processor to collect such data in accordance with principles such as GDPR "data minimization".

19.3.4 EXECUTION OF CONTRACT

Company should establish processes to assess (i.e., go-live checks, audits) whether the processor has implemented effective control measures to meet terms of the DPA and the processor is able to continue to meet terms of the DPA.

The following aspects listed in Table 19.6 should be considered.

19.3.5 TERMINATION OF THE CONTRACT

When the entrustment relationship is terminated, the organization should put in place a formal transition-out process to ensure the data processor can no longer access the personal data such as data deletion and access de-provisioning, etc.

TABLE 19.6

Key Considerations for Execution of Contracts

Aspect	Consideration

Monitoring and audit	Monitor/audit the performance and SLA and security requirements from service providers.
	• Cadence: annually, quarterly, etc.
	• Methods
	  • Attestation (SOC2 Type2, ISO27001 certification, etc.): The Third Party verifies whether its behavior meets the entity's requirements based on the internal audit report or other processes.
	  • Questionnaire/checklist from the organization/entity: The Third Party answers the questionnaire about their personal information protection behavior.
	  • An Internal audit report from the service provider

Managing changes	Manage changes (scope, purposes) and update accordingly • In case the data processor no longer meets the security/privacy requirements, or • There is a contract/scope change

19.4   PURCHASING PERSONAL DATA FROM DATA BROKERS

In June 2017, the employees of an Apple partner (located in China) used Apple's internal system to illegally query and modify the personal information of Apple mobile phones and obtained the personal information such as the names and mobile phone numbers of Apple mobile phone users through the serial number and identification code information of the Apple mobile phone received from other places. They illegally obtained 200,000 records and sold them, involving more than 50 million yuan, and 20 employees involved were arrested.

Some privacy and data protection laws and regulations (i.e., CCPA/CPRA) set forth explicit requirements for organizations to provide a clear and conspicuous link on the business's Internet homepage(s), titled "Do Not Sell or Share My Personal Information".

Table 19.7 lists some of the key aspects that organizations should check before they purchase data from data brokers.

TABLE 19.7
Key Privacy Considerations for Purchasing Data

Domain	Risk	Corresponding Measures
Lawful basis	Fail to demonstrate a proper lawful basis	It simply requires all processing of personal data to be lawful, which can be achieved by demonstrating one of six lawful purposes: • The processing of personal data is for legitimate interests pursued by the data controller. • Processing has been consented to by the data subject. • Processing is of vital interest to the data subject. • Processing is in the interest of the public. • Processing is required for the performance of a contract. • Processing is required to comply with a legal obligation. 1. If you are using bought-in lists and are sending an email to a named person, you must do so on the basis of Legitimate Interests and your company must have conducted a Legitimate Interests Assessment. Your email must contain a link to your privacy policy and your Legitimate Interests Assessment. 2. Only use the list if all the people on the list specifically consented to receive that type of message from you.
Accountability	Your list broker's assurance of valid consent is not enough	Under GDPR, it's the data buyer's responsibility to carry out due diligence on the broker to make sure: The data is current; The broker has permission from the individual to pass their data onto you; The individual's consent for your type of planned marketing is valid; The consent is recent enough to still be valid;
Transparency	Fail to notify the data subjects	Strict attention to the GDPR requires that all of the following information be communicated to the data subject: • Where you obtained the information from and whether your source is publicly accessible • The categories of personal information processed (e.g., name, address, email, employer, etc.) • A brief explanation of the purpose for which you obtained the person's information • The applicable legal basis for your processing • Your identity and contact information, along with the identity and contact information of your EU representative and your Data Protection Officer

Domain	Risk	Corresponding Measures
		• The identification of any recipients, or categories of recipients, of the personal information you are processing; if any recipient is located outside of the EU, you must also identify the legal basis for transferring information to it • Your retention period, or, if there is none set, the criteria for determining the storage period, for the personal data • A summary of the data subject's rights under the GDPR • A description of any automated decision-making (e.g., profiling) that will be based on the personal information collected, including the logic and significance of the consequences of such processing
Accuracy	The data provided by the broker is not up to date	Check whether the data you are using is the newest version of your broker regularly. The frequency depends on the speed of data decay.
Choice and Consent	Don't have an option for data subjects to object to your data processing. It's not easy enough for data subjects to object and stop your further e-marketing.	You must ensure there is an option for the addressee to remove himself or herself from the list. If you are using email addresses your email must contain a mechanism whereby the person can opt out of receiving any further e-marketing communications from you.
Vendor Risk	Your broker does not comply privacy laws and regulations (i.e., GDPR)	Conduct due diligence on your broker and their data. Ask for a data sample and assurance that the rest of the list is compiled in the same way.
Security	The transfer methods of data from the broker and you are not safe	Require your broker to use secure data transfer methods, such as cloud-based bespoke applications or lead delivery portals that require access through a username and password.

20 Data Residency and Cross-Border Transfers

This chapter is intended to provide readers with visibility into various legal obligations on cross-border data transfers and local data storage to identify and mitigate associated privacy risks.
This chapter covers the following topics:

- *Residency requirements and transfer restrictions*
- *Different perspectives of "transfer"*
- *EU/GDPR cross-border transfer framework*
- *EU–US personal data transfers*
- *APEC CPEA, CBPR, and PRP*
- *A six-step approach*

20.1 RESIDENCY REQUIREMENTS AND TRANSFER RESTRICTIONS

Cross-border data transfer obligations are subject to the law of the country or region where the business is carried out. An organization should establish a proper cross-border data transfer strategy and mechanism (i.e., Standard Contractual Clauses, BCR) based on the regulatory requirements and business needs. Based on the defined cross-border data transfer mechanism, the IT systems usually need to be designed (i.e., location of data centers and servers) in alignment with the cross-border transfer mechanisms. Personal data processing operations (i.e., staffing and technical support operations) also need to align with defined cross-border data transfer mechanisms.

As a company operating globally, the organization transfers and processes data worldwide. Countries worldwide impose different requirements for data cross-border transfer and data residency (such as no limitation, conditional limitation, or a prohibition against transfers of certain types of Personal Data out of the country).

Data residency is also called data localization in a certain context. Cisco's report[43] finds that 92% of survey respondents said this data localization had become an important issue for their organizations. But it comes at a price—across all geographies, 88% said that localization requirements are adding significant cost to their operation. Organizations need to comply with data residency obligations within each jurisdiction. Organizations need to identify and document the data localization obligations for the jurisdictions in which the organization is operating.

General Principles for Cross-Border Transfers

If an organization transfers personal data across different jurisdictions which impose different data protection requirements, the organization should establish a proper cross-border data transfer mechanism in accordance with applicable privacy laws and regulations.

- Countries worldwide impose different requirements for the cross-border transfer of personal data (such as no limitation, conditional limitation, or a prohibition against transfers of certain types of personal data out of the country).
- Organizations should monitor the regulation of cross-border transfers of personal data. Before transferring personal data out of a country, every entity should consult the corresponding data protection officer (DPO) or Legal Affairs Dept.
- The entity receiving the personal data should comply with the basic principles of personal data processing in this policy to provide an adequate level of privacy protection.

There are three general principles to consider with respect to personal data cross-border transfers:

- Have the proper lawful basis to process the personal data
- Provide notification to the data subject before the transfer
    - Intent to transfer personal data internationally
    - Existence or absence of an adequacy decision or appropriate safeguards
- Implement proper data cross-border transfer mechanisms

Restrictions and Requirements
Table 20.1 lists some of the jurisdictions that impose restrictions and requirements on cross-border transfers and data residency.

 Example

Microsoft 365 Services[105]—Where your Microsoft 365 customer data is stored
Where EU data is stored
According to the articles on the Microsoft's website as listed next, Table 20.2 lists the locations that EU data is stored by various Microsoft products.

- https://docs.microsoft.com/en-us/microsoft-365/enterprise/o365-data-locations?view=o365-worldwide
- https://docs.microsoft.com/en-us/microsoft-365/admin/services-in-china/parity-between-azure-information-protection?preserve-view=true&view=o365–21vianet

20.2   DIFFERENT PERSPECTIVES OF "TRANSFER"

It is worth noting that there are different perspectives with respect to the definition of "transfer". The scope of transfer is not harmonized with privacy and data protection regulations.
    For instance, under the EU GDPR, the transfer may happen by

- Sending personal data outside of the EU: For example, when a data controller within the EU sends names and email addresses to a digital marketing agency outside of the EU
- Making personal data accessible outside of the EU: Remote access from a third country (for example, in support situations) and/or storage in a cloud situated outside the EEA offered by a service provider, is also considered to be a transfer under the GDPR.

However, under the New Zealand Privacy Act 2020, using offshore cloud providers or other agents to store or process your data is not treated as a disclosure under principle 12 of the Privacy Act 2020, so long as the agent or cloud provider is not using that information for their own purposes.

 Case Study

C-101/01, LINDQUIST, 2003
    The publication on the internet does not constitute a transfer, as an internet user would have to connect to the internet and personally carry out the necessary actions to consult those pages where:

(i) the internet pages did not contain the technical means to send that information automatically to people who did not intentionally seek access; and,
(ii) the internet page is stored with his/her hosting provider in that or another Member State.

TABLE 20.1

Examples of Cross-Border Data Transfers Obligations

Jurisdiction	Data Type	Cross-Border Transfer	Data Residency	Description	Reference
Argentina	Personal data	Transfer restricted	N/A	The cross-border transfer generally requires the prior consent of the data subject or arranging a DTA to comply with Argentina's data protection law, if the third country does not provide an adequate level of protection. The Argentinian DPA published a Regulation on November 18, 2016, which introduces the two model contracts issued by the EU for international data transfers to countries that do not provide adequate levels of protection. The Regulation also requires notification to the DPA, within 30 days, when contracts other than those provided in the Regulation are used for an international data transfer.	Ley 25.326 de Protección de los Datos Personales 2000 (in Spanish)
Angola	Personal data	Transfer restricted	N/A	International transfers of personal data are allowed to countries with an adequate level of protection and require prior notification to the DPA. The DPA decides which countries ensure an adequate level of protection by issuing an opinion in this respect. In the case of transfers between the companies of the same group, the requirement of an adequate level of protection may be reached through the adoption of harmonized and mandatory internal rules on data protection and privacy.	Lei No. 22/11 da Protecção de Dados Pessoais de 17 de Junho (in Portuguese) (Law No. 22/11 of the Protection of Personal Data of 17 June 2011)
Australia	Personal data	Transfer restricted	N/A	Personal information may only be disclosed to an organization outside of Australia where the entity has taken reasonable steps to ensure that the overseas recipient does not breach the APPs. Personal information can be transferred out of Australia with the consent of the individual or under other conditions.	AUSTRALIAN PRIVACY PRINCIPLES (APPs)
Australia	Personal data/heath record	Transfer prohibited	Local storage	The System Operator, a registered repository operator, a registered portal operator, or a registered contracted service provider that holds records for the purposes of the My Health Record system (whether or not the records are also held for other purposes) or has access to information relating to such records, must not: (a) hold the records, or take the records, outside Australia; or (b) process or handle the information relating to the records outside Australia	MY HEALTH RECORDS ACT 2012

(Continued)

TABLE 20.1 (Continued)

Jurisdiction	Data Type	Cross-Border Transfer	Data Residency	Description	Reference
Canada	Public Sector— Personal information held by public institutions and public agencies (BC and Nova Scotia)	Transfer prohibited	N/A	Two Canadian provinces, **British Columbia and Nova Scotia**, have enacted laws requiring that personal information held by public institutions and public agencies be stored and accessed only in Canada unless one of a few limited exceptions applies. Nova Scotia: • This law sets out the rules public bodies in Nova Scotia must follow when it comes to the international disclosure of personal information. Although there are several specific exceptions, **the general rule is that personal information must be stored in Canada and accessed only in Canada unless there is consent from the individual to whom the information pertains**, or another law allows for the storage outside of Canada, or storage outside of Canada is deemed a necessity	Freedom of Information and Protection of Privacy Act (British Columbia) Personal Information International Disclosure Protection Act (Nova Scotia)
	Private Sector— Personal data	Transfer restricted	N/A	**PIPEDA:** Canada does not prohibit cross-border transfer, but organizations remain liable for information they transfer outside of the country. And before transferring data outside Canada, an organization must ensure that it is able to meet its obligations under Canadian law by using contractual means to require the recipient to provide comparable protection for the information. **PIPA Alberta:** specifically requires a transferring organization to include the countries outside Canada and the purposes, and **special notice** is needed. **Quebec Privacy Act:** requires that an organization must take reasonable steps to ensure that personal information transferred to service providers outside Quebec will not be used for other purposes and will not be communicated to third parties without consent. In some circumstances, health information laws prohibit personal information from being disclosed outside of a province or Canada Things to consider: Before transferring personal information, assess the risks to the integrity, security, and confidentiality of the data outside of Canada—this may require avoiding transfers to certain countries or transferring sensitive information	Personal Information Protection and Electronic Documents Act Personal Information Act Alberta ('PIPA Alberta') An Act Respecting the Protection of Personal Information in the Private Sector ('Quebec Privacy Act')

Country	Data type	Transfer status	Storage	Description	Law
China	Personal data	Transfer restricted	Local storage	Obtain contractual commitments from any service provider (including affiliated companies) so that the personal information will have comparable protections to the protections in Canada Inform individuals that their information may be sent to another country and may be accessed by the courts, law enforcement, and national security authorities under local laws (which may be different than the laws in Canada) Cross-border transfers should satisfy one of the following conditions: 1) Standard Contractual Clauses 2) Security Reviews by National Cyberspace Administration departments (note: this is required for **Critical information infrastructure operators and personal information processors that process personal information up to the number** prescribed by the national cyberspace administration. The personal information should be stored in China.) 3) Personal information protection certification 4) Meet conditions set forth by laws and regulations	**Personal Information Protection Law**
	Personal information—collection by **critical information infrastructure operators**	Transfer restricted	Local storage	Personal information gathered and produced by critical information infrastructure operators in the mainland territory of the People's Republic of China should be stored within the mainland territory of the People's Republic of China, and the cross-border provision of such information must be assessed by corresponding regulation organizations. Critical information infrastructure: basic information networks providing services such as public correspondence and radio and television broadcast; important information systems for important industries such as **energy, transportation, water conservation, and finance, and public service areas such as electricity, water and gas utilities, medical and sanitation service and social security; military networks and government affairs networks for state organizations at the sub-district city level and above; and networks and systems owned or managed by network service providers with massive numbers of users.**	**PEOPLE'S REPUBLIC OF CHINA CYBERSECURITY LAW**

(Continued)

TABLE 20.1 (Continued)

Jurisdiction	Data Type	Cross-Border Transfer	Data Residency	Description	Reference
	(1) Personal information (2) The data contains important data	Transfer restricted	Local storage	(1) Personal information and important data collected and generated by operators of critical information infrastructure (2) The data contains **important data** Important data refers to the data (including original data and derived data) collected and generated by the Chinese government, enterprises, and individuals within the territory that do not involve state secrets but are closely related to **national security, economic development, and public interests**. Data that may endanger national security and public interest after authorized disclosure, loss, misuse, alteration or destruction, or aggregation, integration, or analysis. (3) Personal information processors whose processing of personal information reaches **one million people** provide personal information overseas (4) Accumulatively providing personal information of more than **100,000 people** or sensitive personal information of more than **10,000** people abroad;	**Measures for Security Assessment of Data Exports (Draft)**
	Online publishing service data	N/A	Local storage	The online publishing services provider shall host the relevant servers and storage devices within the territory of the People's Republic of China.	PROVISIONS OF THE ADMINISTRATION OF ONLINE PUBLISHING SERVICES
	Internet map data	N/A	Local storage	Internet map service entities must deploy servers on which map data is stored within the territory of the People's Republic of China.	Regulation on Map Management
	Government cloud data	Transfer restricted	Local storage	Cloud computing service platforms and data centers providing services for government departments must be deployed within the territory of the People's Republic of China. Without approval, sensitive information cannot be transferred, processed, or stored outside China.	Opinions of the Office of the Central Leading Group for Cyberspace Affairs on Strengthening Cybersecurity Administration of Cloud Computing Services for Communist Party and Government Agencies
	Personal data— population health information	Transfer prohibited	Local storage	Medical health and family planning institutions shall not store population health information on, host, or rent servers outside of the territory of the People's Republic of China.	Measures for the Administration of Population Health Information

	Personal information—credit data	Transfer restricted	Local storage	Credit investigation organizations must organize, store, and process data collected within China in the territory of the People's Republic of China. When providing data to organizations or individuals outside the territory of the People's Republic of China, credit investigation organizations must comply with laws, administrative regulations, and related rules of the credit investigation industry supervision department of the State Council.	Regulation on the Administration of Credit Investigation Industry
	Personal information—personal financial information	Transfer restricted	Local storage	Personal financial information collected by financial institutions (including non-banking payment institutions) should be stored, processed, and analyzed within China. Unless otherwise specified by laws, regulations, or the People's Bank of China, financial institutions cannot provide overseas countries or regions with personal financial information about the territory of the People's Republic of China. To process cross-border business and under the authorization of the data subject, financial institutions within China shall comply with the law, regulations, and provisions of the relevant supervisory department when transferring relevant personal financial information to overseas institutions (including head office, parent company, or branch office, subsidiary and other associated instructions necessary for performing the business), and require the overseas institution keep the personal financial information received confidentially by adopting effective measures like a contract or on-site verification.	Measures for the Protection of Financial Consumers' Rights and Interests by People's Bank of China
Bosnia And Herzegovina	Personal data	Transfer restricted	N/A	Personal data may be transferred to countries where an adequate level of personal data protection is ensured. The member states of the Council of Europe Convention for the Protection of Individuals with regard to Automatic Processing of Personal Data are considered an adequate level of personal data protection. The cross-border transfer is allowed with the data subject's consent or under other necessary situations.	Law on the Protection of Personal Data (Unofficial in English) General regulations of the Personal Data Protection Agency
Colombia	Personal data	Transfer restricted	N/A	The cross-border transfer of data is prohibited unless the foreign country where the data will be transferred meets at least the same data protection standards or if the data owner has expressly and unambiguously authorized or is subject to other exceptions. The data transmission agreement must be signed by the data controller and the data processor but does not necessarily notify the data subjects.	Ley 1581 de 2012—Marco general de la protección de los datos personales en Colombia

(Continued)

TABLE 20.1 (Continued)

Jurisdiction	Data Type	Cross-Border Transfer	Data Residency	Description	Reference
Croatia	Personal data	Transfer restricted	N/A	Personal data is allowed to be transferred to countries and international organizations with an adequate level of data protection. If the European Commission has established for a particular third country that it does not provide an adequate level of data protection, the AZOP will forbid a transfer to such country. The cross-border transfer to countries without adequate level can happen also according to the data subject's consent or other exceptions.	Act on the Implementation of the General Data Protection Regulation (in Croatian: Zakon o provedbi Opće uredbe o zaštiti podataka) (the "Implementation Act")
EU & EEA	Personal data	Transfer restricted	N/A	1. No general restrictions are imposed for the cross-border transfer of personal data. (Some special restrictions may exist in some countries for sensitive personal data.) 2. Transfer outside of EU and EEA is allowed when the third country ensures an adequate level of protection. EC has issued a list of countries recognized to provide an adequate level of protection. Derogations include consent, necessary for the performance of the contract, etc. 3. Transfer to a third country that does not ensure an adequate level of protection is allowed where the controller adduces adequate safeguards, for most of the countries, the Model Clauses approved by EC are considered appropriate safeguards. 4. Prior approvals of DTA by the Data Protection Authority (DPA hereafter) is required in Austria, Belgium, Croatia, Cyprus, Estonia, France, Latvia, Lithuania, Luxembourg, Malta, and Spain. 5. Prior notifications of DTA to the DPA are required in Bulgaria, Greece, Portuguesa, and Romania. 6. For all data processing activities, data processing agreements are required between the data controller and data processor in Germany, and in several northern states, the agreements shall be submitted to the DPA. DTA is required when transferring sensitive personal data outside of Germany. 7. All DTAs must formally be submitted to the DPA for examinations. 8. Transfer of sensitive data to countries outside France is not prohibited but has to be justified. 9. All cross-border transfers require prior approvals by the Estonian Inspectorate. 10. In Spain cross-border data transfer requires prior authorization from DPA. 11. If standard transfer clauses are changed, approvals by the DPA are required in Denmark, Germany, Ireland, Poland, Slovakia, and Slovenia.	GDPR

Country	Data type	Transfer status	Local storage/requirements	Description	Law/Regulation
Germany	Government cloud service data	**Transfer prohibited**	Local storage	Protected Information (e.g., business secrets and sensitive data about the federal IT infrastructure) for any procurement or use of cloud services by the federal German administration shall be processed within the territory of Germany.	Criteria for the procurement and use of cloud services by the federal German administration
Hong Kong—China	Personal data	Transfer restricted	N/A	A data user shall not transfer personal data to a place outside Hong Kong unless the user has reasonable grounds for believing that there is in force in that place any law that is substantially similar to or serves the same purposes as this Ordinance and the consent is given and under other conditions.	THE PERSONAL DATA (PRIVACY) ORDINANCE
India	Personal data	Transfer restricted	N/A	A corporate entity may not transfer any sensitive personal information to another person or entity outside India in which jurisdictions do not maintain an equivalent level of protection as in India, unless the data subject's consent is obtained, or the transfer is necessary for the performance of the contract to which the data subject is a party.	The "Information Technology (Reasonable Security Practices and Procedures and Sensitive Personal Data or Information) Rules
India	Government email data	Transfer prohibited	Local storage	No person shall take or cause to be taken out of India any public records. In 2013, the Delhi High Court interpreted this requirement to bar the transfer of government emails outside India.	The Public Records Act of 1993
Iceland	Personal data	Transfer restricted	N/A	The transfer of personal data to a country that does not provide an adequate level of personal data protection is prohibited unless the data subject's consent is given or under other necessary situations. Transfer to an EU or EEA country or to any country which is on the EU list of the countries which ensure an adequate level of data protection is allowed.	Act No. 90/2018 on Data Protection and the Processing of Personal Data
Indonesia	Data held by Electronic System Operator for the public service	N/A	Local storage Local IT Infrastructure Requirements: data center and disaster recovery center	Electronic System Operator for the public service is obliged to put the data center and disaster recovery center in Indonesian territory.	Regulation 82 concerning "Electronic System and Transaction Operation"

(Continued)

TABLE 20.1 (Continued)

Jurisdiction	Data Type	Cross-Border Transfer	Data Residency	Description	Reference
	Data related to oil and gas activities	Transfer restricted	Local storage Local IT Infrastructure Requirements: data center and disaster recovery center	Indonesia has very specific legal requirements. Oil and gas companies that have signed a Production Sharing Contract (PSC) with the State for upstream oil and gas activities are usually required to have a data center and disaster recovery center in Indonesia and need to obtain prior ESDM approval to transfer confidential data related to their upstream oil and gas activities outside Indonesia.	
Israel	Personal data	Transfer restricted	N/A	Personal data may be transferred abroad to the extent that the laws of the country to which the data is transferred ensure a level of protection, no lesser than the level of protection of data provided for by Israeli Law; or the data subject's consent is given or an agreement to comply with the conditions governing the use of the data as applicable under Israeli Laws between the data exporter and the recipient has been concluded, or under other conditions. The receiving country is required to have a data protection level not lower than that of Israeli law, which can be guaranteed by agreeing to comply with the data protection conditions of Israeli law, or to obtain the consent of the data subject, to Convention 108 member states or countries that can receive EU data according to arrangements (such as the United States) and other exceptions. The sender must sign a data transfer agreement with the receiver to ensure that reasonable measures are taken to ensure that it will not be transferred to other third parties and other content.	Privacy Protection Act No.5741/1981 and 5752/1992
Japan	Personal data	Transfer restricted	N/A	Transfers to third parties in foreign countries except if the transfer is to (i) a receiver having a data protection system that is equivalent to the system required under The Act on the Protection of Personal Information on the Protection of Personal Information (APPI), or (ii) a receiver located in a country that is designated by the Committee as providing an adequate level of protection.	Act on the Protection of Personal Information
Lesotho	Personal data	Transfer restricted	N/A	The cross-border transfer is allowed when the recipient is subject to a code or law which upholds substantially similar principles for the reasonable processing of information to those principles found in the Act or when the data subject's consent is given, or subject to other exceptions.	Data Protection Act 2011

Country					
Macau—China	Personal data	Transfer restricted	N/A	The transfer of personal data outside Macau can only take place if the recipient country ensures an adequate level of personal data protection or pursuant to a data subject unequivocal consent with prior registration with the DPA. Transfer to a country with an adequate level of protection can be based on the explicit consent of the data subject after notifying the data protection authority, and ensuring the adequate level of data protection through a contract requires the approval of the data protection authority (there is a law enforcement case in 2017).	Personal Data Protection Act (Act 8/2005)
Madagascar	Personal data	Transfer restricted	N/A	The transfer of a data subject's personal data to a third-party country is allowed only if the country provides individuals with a sufficient level of protection or the data subject's consent is given and other necessary conditions are satisfied. Other exceptional cases need to be approved by DPA.	Law No. 2014–038
Macedonia	Personal data	Transfer restricted	N/A	Transfer of personal data out of Macedonia is allowed only if the third country in question provides an adequate level of personal data protection which will be assessed by DPA, or to the members of EU and EEA and the countries or any country which is on the EU list of the countries (also see EU & EEA in this form) which ensure an adequate level of the data protection.	The Law on Personal Data Protection 2020
Mauritius	Personal data	Transfer restricted	N/A	Personal data shall not be transferred to another country unless that country ensures an adequate level of protection for the rights of data subjects in relation to the processing of personal data unless the transfer is made on such terms as may be approved by the Data Protection Commissioner, data subject's consent is given or subject to other exceptions.	Data Protection Act 2017
Malaysia	Personal data	Transfer restricted	N/A	A data user may not transfer personal data to jurisdictions outside of Malaysia unless that jurisdiction has been pacified by the Minister, unless the data user has taken all reasonable steps and exercised all due diligence to ensure that the personal data will not be processed in a manner which, if that place were Malaysia, would contravene the DPA, or consent is given or other necessary situations.	Personal Data Protection Act 2010

(Continued)

TABLE 20.1 (Continued)

Jurisdiction	Data Type	Cross-Border Transfer	Data Residency	Description	Reference
Mexico	Personal data	Transfer restricted	N/A	The data transferer is responsible for the protection of personal data and should notify and obtain the consent of the data subject. For transfers to third parties other than subcontractors, the third party shall be provided with a privacy notice and restricted purpose. The third party shall bear the same obligations as the sender. When transferring to affiliated companies such as subsidiaries and parent companies, transferring for the benefit of the data subject according to the contract, or necessary for the performance of the contract, etc., the consent of the data subject is not required. The transfer to the data processor does not require notification or consent of the data subject but is subject to a signed agreement and certain conditions.	Federal Law on Protection of Personal Data Held by Private Parties 2010 Regulations to the Federal Law on Protection of Personal Data Held by Private Parties 2011
Montenegro	Personal data	Transfer restricted	N/A	Personal data may be transferred to countries or provided to international organizations, where an adequate level of personal data protection is ensured, on the basis of the DPA's previously obtained consent. Or maybe transferred to an EU or EEA country or to any country which is on the EU list of the countries (also see EU & EEA) which ensures an adequate level of the data protection	Law on Protection of Personal Data No. 79/2009, 70/2009, 44/2012, 22/2017
Morocco	Personal data	Transfer restricted	N/A	The transfer of a data subject's personal data to another country is allowed if the country provides a sufficient level evaluated with regards to national laws and applicable security measures or authorization by DPA is required (According to the local information, it is possible but time-consuming to abstain the authorization). Exceptions include necessary and other situations. The DPA establishes a list of states which considered to provide a sufficient level.	Act No. 09–08 on the Protection of Individuals with Regard to the Processing of Personal Data—Morocco Local legal advice
Monaco	Personal data	Transfer restricted	N/A	The transfer of data is authorized for cross-border access, storage, and processing of data only to a country with equivalent protection and reciprocity unless accepted by the data subject or other situations. A list of the countries deemed to have equivalent protection and reciprocity is listed. Parties to Convention of the Council of Europe n° 108 relating to the protection of individuals for personal data automatic processing are deemed to have the equivalent protection.	Data Protection Law n° 1.165 of December 23, 1993, modified from time to time and notably by Law n° 1.353 of December 4, 2008, and most recently by Law n°1.462 of June 28, 2018 (DPL).

Country	Data	Transfer status	Storage	Description	Regulation
New Zealand	Personal data	Transfer restricted	N/A	The Privacy Commissioner is given the power to prohibit a transfer to a third State which does not provide comparable safeguards to the Act and the transfer would be likely to lead to a contravention of the basic principles of national application set out in Part Two of the OECD Guidelines.	Privacy Act 2020, Effective 1 December 2020
Nigeria	Consumer data held by ICT companies	N/A	Local storage	ICT companies must host all subscriber and consumer data locally within the country.	Relevant Regulation: Nigeria National Information Technology Development Agency's Guidelines for Nigerian Content
	Government data held by ICT companies	Transfer restricted	Local storage	ICT companies must host government data locally within the country and shall not for any reason host any government data outside the country without express approval.	Development in Information and Communications Technology
	Personal data	Transfer restricted	N/A	An adequate level of protection is required.	
Pakistan	Personal data	Transfer restricted	N/A	Data cannot be transferred from Pakistan to a country that is not recognized by Pakistan. Pakistan currently does not recognize Israel, Taiwan, Somaliland, Nagorno Karabakh, Transnistria, Abkhazia, Northern Cyprus, Sahrawi Arab Democratic Republic, South Ossetia, and Armenia. This list may change from time to time. Data collated by, inter alia, banks, insurance firms, hospitals, defense establishments, and other "sensitive" installations/institutions cannot be transferred to any individual/body unless it is transferred with the permission of the relevant regulator or similar bodies.	The Personal Data Protection Bill 2020 ('the Bill').
Peru	Personal data	Transfer restricted	N/A	The data holder generally must abstain from making transfers of personal data if the destination country does not afford adequate protection levels, which are equivalent to those afforded by the PDPL or in international standards, with several exceptions such as consent. Adequate measures can be ensured via a written agreement.	Ley N° 29733—Ley de Protección de Datos Personales

(Continued)

TABLE 20.1 (Continued)

Jurisdiction	Data Type	Cross-Border Transfer	Data Residency	Description	Reference
Singapore	Personal data	Transfer restricted	N/A	An organization can transfer personal data overseas if it has taken appropriate steps to ensure that: (1) It complies with the data protection provisions set out in the Personal Data Protection Law in respect of the transferred personal data, if the personal data remains in its possession or under its control. (2) If the personal data is transferred to a third-party recipient in a country or territory outside Singapore, the recipient is bound by legally enforceable obligations to provide a standard of protection that is comparable to that under the Personal Data Protection Law. "Legally enforceable obligations" include any contract requiring the recipient to provide a standard of protection for the personal data transferred to the recipient that is at least comparable to the protection under the Act. Transfer overseas is also permitted when consent is given or subject to other exceptions.	PERSONAL DATA PROTECTION ACT 2012 PERSONAL DATA PROTECTION REGULATIONS 2014
South Africa	Personal data	Transfer restricted	N/A	A responsible party may not transfer personal information about data subject to the third party in a foreign jurisdiction unless: (1) the recipient is subject to a law or contract which upholds principles of reasonable processing of the information that are substantially similar to the principles contained in the PPI Act and includes provisions that are substantially similar to those contained in the PPI Act relating to the further transfer of personal information from the recipient to third parties. (2) with consent or under other situations.	Protection of Personal Information Act
Switzerland	Personal data	Transfer restricted	N/A	Personal data may be disclosed outside Switzerland: (1) if the destination country offers an adequate level of data protection. The FDPIC maintains and publishes a list of such countries. All EU and EEA countries are deemed to be adequate. (2) if data transfer agreements or other contractual clauses are concluded and notified and submitted to the FDPIC whereas mere information is sufficient if model clauses approved by the FDPIC are used. (3) subject to other exceptions.	Federal Act on Data Protection (FADP)

Country	Data type	Restriction	Local storage	Description	Law/Act
Serbia	Personal data	Transfer restricted	N/A	The cross-border transfer is allowed to a member state of the Council of Europe Convention for the Protection of Individuals with regard to Automatic Processing of Personal Data otherwise, Transfer Approval is required.	Law on Personal Data Protection N°97/08
Seychelles	Personal data	Transfer restricted	N/A	DPA may, if satisfied that the transfer is likely to contravene or lead to a contravention of any data protection principle, serve that person with a transfer prohibition notice.	Data Protection Act of 2003
South Korea	Map data	Transfer restricted	Local storage	No person shall take maps aboard without permission from the Minster of Land, Transport, and Maritime Affairs.	The Act on Land Survey Waterway Survey and Cadastral Records
	Personal data	Transfer restricted	N/A	Prior notification to data subjects and their consent is required for cross-border data transfer.	the Personal Information Protection Act (PIPA) The Act on the Promotion of IT Network Use and Information Protection (Network Act)
Russia	Personal data	N/A	Local storage	Russian citizens' personal data shall be stored within the territory, however, it's not clear in relation to the cross-border data transfer rules. At least one copy of the personal data of Russian citizens must be stored on the territory. Transfers can only be made to countries with an adequate level of protection (Roskomnadzor has published a list). Convention 108 member states can be considered to have an adequate level of protection. Exceptions for transfers to countries without an adequate level of protection include data subject consent, the performance of contracts, etc. Listed countries include Australia, Argentina, Canada, Israel, Mexico, and New Zealand. The DPA blocked LinkedIn in Russia in 2016 due to a violation of the local storage requirement.	The amendments of DATA PROTECTION ACT No. 152 FZ
KSA (Kingdom of Saudi Arabia)	Personal data	Transfer restricted	Local storage	There is no definition of personal data or specific requirements for cross-border transfer. But according to local practices, cross-border transfer of personal data is highly sensitive in KSA, and general approval by the telecommunication authorities is required which is very likely to be rejected. To avoid punishment, local server deployment within the territory of KSA is generally advised.	Local legal advice

(Continued)

TABLE 20.1 (Continued)

Jurisdiction	Data Type	Cross-Border Transfer	Data Residency	Description	Reference
Taiwan	Personal data	Transfer restricted	N/A	The DPA may restrict the international transfer of personal data by the data controller if it involves major national interests: (1) where a national treaty or agreement specifies otherwise (2) where the country receiving personal data lacks proper regulations that protect personal data and that might harm the rights and interests of the data subject, or (3) where the international transfer of personal data is made to a third country through an indirect method in order to evade the provisions of the Personal Data Protection Law.	The Personal Information Protection Act 2015 ('PDPA')
Trinidad And Tobago	Personal data	Transfer restricted	N/A	Personal information may be transferred outside of Trinidad and Tobago in which jurisdictions ensure an equivalent level of protection.	Data Protection Act 2011 (in English)
Tunisia	Personal data	Transfer restricted	N/A	The cross-border transfers need prior authorization by DPA.	Organic Act No. 2004–63
Turkey	Personal data	Transfer restricted	N/A	Without consent, the cross-border transfer is allowed to the country to which personal data will be sent shall have a sufficient level of protection or when the data controllers in Turkey and the target country have undertaken protection in writing and obtained the Data Protection Board's permission.	LAW ON PROTECTION OF PERSONAL DATA
UAE	Personal data	Transfer restricted	N/A	Data Controllers may transfer Personal Data out of the DIFC if the Personal Data is being transferred to a Recipient in the jurisdiction that has laws that ensure an adequate level of protection for that Personal Data or any other jurisdiction approved by the DPA, or with consent or under other necessary situations.	The Abu Dhabi Global Market (ADGM) Data Protection Regulations 2021 ("DPR 2021")
Ukraine	Personal data	Transfer restricted	N/A	The personal data may be transferred to foreign counterparties only on the condition of ensuring an appropriate level of protection, which includes member-states of the European Economic Area and signatories to the EC Convention on Automatic Processing of Personal Data. The list of the states ensuring an appropriate level of protection of personal data will be determined by the DPA.	On protection of Personal Data No. 2297-VI
Uruguay	Personal data	Transfer with restriction	N/A	The transfer of personal data to countries or international entities which do not provide adequate levels of protection (according to European standards) is forbidden unless consent is given or when the guarantees of adequate protection levels arise from "contractual clauses", and self-regulation systems.	La Ley 18.331 Protección de Datos Personales y Acción de Habeas Data del 11 agosto del año 2008 y el Decreto reglamentario 414/2009

United States	Government cloud service data	Transfer prohibited	Local storage	Cloud computing service providers in the governmental sectors shall store the data within the territory of the US unless otherwise approved by the DoD or its authorized parties.	Defense Federal Acquisition Regulation Supplement: Network Penetration Reporting and Contracting for Cloud Services (DFARS Case 2013-D018)
Vietnam	Data held by Internet service providers	N/A	Local storage	Some internet service providers are required to have at least one server system in Vietnam, e.g., news websites, social networks, mobile networks, game service.	The Decree on Management, Provision, and Use of Internet Services and Information Content Online (Decree 72)

TABLE 20.2

Where EU Data Is Stored by Microsoft Products

| Service name | WHERE EU DATA IS STORED | | |
	Location for Tenants Created with a Billing Address in France	Location for Tenants Created with a Billing Address in Germany	Location for Tenants Created with a Billing Address in All Other EU Countries
Exchange Online	France	Germany	European Union
OneDrive for Business	France	Germany	European Union
SharePoint Online	France	Germany	European Union
Skype for Business	European Union	European Union	European Union
Microsoft Teams	France	Germany	European Union
Office Online & Mobile	France	Germany	European Union
Exchange Online Protection	France	Germany	European Union
Intune	European Union	European Union	European Union
MyAnalytics	France	Germany	European Union
Planner	European Union	European Union	European Union
Yammer	European Union	European Union	European Union
OneNote Services	France	Germany	European Union
Stream	European Union	European Union	European Union
Whiteboard	European Union	European Union	European Union
Forms	European Union	European Union	European Union

20.3   EU/GDPR CROSS-BORDER TRANSFER FRAMEWORK

20.3.1   THE UNDERLINE LOGIC

Article 44 of the GDPR sets out the basic principles for the cross-border movement of personal data in the EU, the core of which is to ensure that in the case of cross-border transfers, the level of personal data protection provided by the GDPR is "not undermined". That said, the level of protection afforded by GDPR should follow the flow of personal data. According to the logic of the GDPR, the protection of personal data is a fundamental human right. Therefore, the protection of personal information in cross-border scenarios is mainly to protect the legitimate rights and interests of individuals, even if the data has already transferred out of the EU.

From the perspective of GDPR, there are three main changes when data flows out of the country compared with the movement of personal data within the EU:

- Firstly, the applicable laws and regulations are different after data is transferred outside of EU.
- Secondly, the channels for personal data subjects to safeguard their legitimate rights and interests have become fewer and more difficult.

Therefore, the design of the GDPR data cross-border transfer system mainly focuses on solving the previous three problems. In terms of specific system design, the GDPR stipulates a wealth of cross-border data transmission mechanisms in Chapter V.

20.3.2   SUMMARY OF ACCEPTABLE MECHANISMS

The cross-border transfer may present an additional but unavoidable risk for your organization. Use the table on the following slide to help determine which transfer mechanism best suits your needs. Be sure to consider current, planned, and future data processing/transfer activities and needs.

Table 20.3 lists some of the personal data cross-border mechanisms as well as their pros and cons.

TABLE 20.3

Pros and Cons of Common Cross-Border Mechanisms

Data Transfer Category	Data Transfer Mechanism	Benefit	Challenges
Adequacy decisions	An adequacy decision is basically a decision, made by the European Commission stating that a country is adequate for the international transfer of data. There are several factors they look at to see if the country is adequate, such as: —Respect for rule of law —Access to justice —International human rights standards —General and specific laws The European Commission has so far recognized Andorra, Argentina, Canada (commercial organizations), Faroe Islands, Guernsey, Israel, Isle of Man, Japan, Jersey, New Zealand, Republic of Korea, Switzerland, the United Kingdom under the GDPR and the LED, and Uruguay as providing adequate protection.[44]	No need to implement further mechanisms if data is being transferred to a jurisdiction that has been granted the adequacy status	Very few countries are deemed with an adequate data protection level. Adequacy decisions need to be reviewed every four years
International Agreements	EU-US Trans-Atlantic Data Privacy Framework The European Commission and the United States announce that they have agreed in principle on a new Trans-Atlantic Data Privacy Framework, which will foster trans-Atlantic data flows and address the concerns raised by the Court of Justice of the European Union in the Schrems II decision of July 2020.	Replace the invalid Privacy Shield framework A flexible framework that can meet various data transfer needs Reduce the paperwork for organizations	Not finalized yet. The teams of the US Government and the European Commission will now continue their cooperation to translate this arrangement into legal documents that will need to be adopted on both sides to put in place this new Trans-Atlantic Data Privacy Framework. For that purpose, these US commitments will be included in an Executive Order that will form the basis of the Commission's assessment in its future adequacy decision.
	EU-US Passenger Name Records (PNRs) transfer agreement	N/A	N/A

(Continued)

TABLE 20.3 (Continued)

Data Transfer Category	Data Transfer Mechanism	Benefit	Challenges
Appropriate safeguards	Standard Contractual Clauses (SCCs) This is the model clause to use. This is the most frequently used way to legitimize international data transfers to other countries considered not to provide adequate levels of protection. This was created and approved by the European Commission. The new SCCs now cover four different potential data transfer scenarios: (i) controller-to-controller (ii) controller-to-processor (iii) processor-to-processor (iv) processor-to-controller	Easy to implement No DPA approval needed	Not suitable for complex data transfers. Difficult to meet business agility. Needs a legal solution.
	Ad-hoc Contractual clauses	It gives room for individual tailoring to a company's needs	Must be authorized by the Supervisory Authorities
	Binding Corporate Rules (BCRs) This is used internally to move data within a corporation. They might use this so they can transfer data to other parts of their organization. ✓BCR–Controller ✓BCR–Processor ✓BCRs by themselves do not "authorize" all transfers automatically for all EU member states. Most of the member states still require a formal "transfer notification" which is normally granted if the BCRs have been accepted by the relevant country.	Meets business agility needs: Binding corporate rules (BCRs) are data protection policies that each group company adheres to. This helps to ensure the requisite protection for personal data, regardless of the country's data protection legislation in which the group company is established. Raises trust in the organization Doubles as the solution for Art. 24/25 GDPR Sets a high compliance maturity level Sets a high compliance maturity level	Takes time to draft/implement Requires DPA approval (scrutiny) Requires a culture of compliance Approved by one "lead" authority and two other "co-lead" authorities Takes usually between 6 and 9 months for the approval process only Needs ongoing obligation to monitor compliance with the BCRs, including regular audits and staff training
	Approved code of conduct	Raises trust in the sector Self-regulation instead of law	No code of conduct approved yet. Takes time to draft/implement Requires DPA approval Requires a culture of compliance Particular needs of the organization may not be met

	Certification Mechanisms	Raises trust in the organization	No certification schemes are available yet except for the Luxembourg GDPR-CARPA certification issued in May 2022. Risk of compliance at minimum necessary. Requires audits
Derogations	An exemption from the prohibition on transferring personal data outside the EEA. • Explicitly consented • Necessary for the conclusion or performance of a contract • Necessary for important reasons of public interest • Establishment, exercise, or defense of legal claims • Protect the vital interests of the data subject or of other persons • The transfer is made from a register that according to Union or Member State law is intended to provide information to the public and which is open to consultation either by the public in general or by any person who can demonstrate a legitimate interest, but only to the extent that the conditions laid down by Union or Member State law for consultation are fulfilled in the particular case. • If the data processing activity is based on legitimate interest, the transfer can still proceed if all the following conditions are met. • Only if the transfer is not repetitive • Concerns only a limited number of data subjects • Is necessary for the purposes of compelling legitimate interests which not overridden by the interests or rights and freedoms of the data subject • Shall inform the supervisory authority of the transfer • Shall inform the data subject of the transfer and on the compelling legitimate interests pursued	If using consent, it provides legal certainty (provided consent is valid). Transparent.	Challenge to obtain consent from data subjects. The administrative burden of managing consent (i.e., record, withdraw)

20.3.3 The New Standard Contractual Clauses (SCCs)

On June 4, 2021, the European Commission (EC) issued its revised Standard Contractual Clauses (SCCs) for data transfers to third countries.

The Structure of the Document
There are 18 clauses in total, while clause 7 is optional.

You can only add other clauses or additional safeguards, provided that they do not contradict, directly or indirectly, these clauses or prejudice the fundamental rights or freedoms of data subjects. You cannot remove existing clauses.

In the event of a contradiction between these clauses of the new SCCs and the provisions of related (other) agreements between the parties that existed at the time these clauses are agreed or entered into thereafter, these clauses shall prevail.

The new SCCs take a modular approach for clauses 8–15 and 17–18 and cover the following transfer scenarios:

- Module 1: Transfer controller to controller
- Module 2: Transfer controller to processor
- Module 3: Transfer processor to processor
- Module 4: Transfer processor to controller

Three annexes are very logical and handy in capturing essential elements.

- Annex A: List of parties
- Annex B: TOMs
- Annex C: List of sub-processors

Timetable for the New SCCs

- June 27, 2021—the new SCCs are applicable
- Sept. 27, 2021—the old SCCs (Decision 2001/497/EC & Decision 2010/87/EU) are invalid for new contracts
- Dec. 27, 2022—all SCC-based contracts need to be updated

 Questions and answers

How do the new SCCs address the Schrems II concerns?
Clause 14 reenforces the requirements that organizations should carry out and document the **Data Transfer Impact Assessments**.

 Questions and answers

What are the actionable steps for organizations to avoid interruptions of data flow?
Step 1—Identify: Inventory your current cross-border data transfer business scenarios and identify which ones are utilizing the SCC mechanism.
Step 2—Assess: Evaluate the strategy of utilizing the new and old SCCs to align with your business strategies.
Step 3—Prioritize: Prioritize transitioning of the new SCCs based on business and contract management context.
Step 4—Integrate: Embed your SCC updates within your organization's contract review and renew the lifecycle instead of creating a separate workflow.

20.3.4   Binding Corporate Rules (BCRs)

EU Working Party 29 releases recommendations on standard BCR-C and BCR-P applications (2018.04)

On April 18, 2018, the Article 29 Working Party (WP29) released "Recommendation on the Standard Application for Approval of Controller Binding Corporate Rules for the Transfer of Personal Data" for data controllers ('BCR-C') and "Recommendation on the Standard Application form for Approval of Processor Binding Corporate Rules for the Transfer of Personal Data" for data processors ('BCR-P'). In particular, the WP29 provided a template of checklist controller, and the processor can refer to and do the self-check and highlighted that the Recommendations aim to update and align its previous documentation on the matter with the General Data Protection Regulation (Regulation (EU) 2016/679) ('GDPR') and are intended to help applicants demonstrate how to meet the requirements set out in Article 47 of the GDPR. Until now, more and more companies have closed the EU BCR cooperation procedure, and are using BCR to conduct the transfer of personal data.

You can find the approved Binding Corporate Rules after 25 May 2018 using the following link.

- https://edpb.europa.eu/our-work-tools/accountability-tools/bcr_el?page=0

You can also find the pre-GDPR BCRs overview list using the following link.

- https://edpb.europa.eu/our-work-tools/our-documents/other/pre-gdpr-bcrs-overview-list-0_en

20.4   EU-US PERSONAL DATA TRANSFERS

20.4.1   Brief History and Current Status

Table 20.4 illustrates a brief history of EU-US Personal Data Transfer mechanisms.

20.4.2   Shrems II Ruling

What is the ruling
On July 16, 2020, the highest court in the European Union (EU), the Court of Justice of the European Union (CJEU), issued a landmark judgment in the case of Data Protection Commissioner v. Facebook Ireland Limited, Maximillian Schrems (Case C-311/18) (Schrems II).[45]

1) The Court of Justice of the European Union (CJEU) declared the European Commission's Privacy Shield Decision invalid on account of invasive US surveillance programs (i.e., PRISM and UPSTREAM, etc.), thereby making transfers of personal data on the basis of the Privacy Shield Decision illegal.
   - This is on the basis that the access and use of EU personal data by US authorities are not restricted in a way that, according to the court, complies with the requirements of EU law.
2) Based on the Schrems II decision (July 16, 2020), Standard Contractual Clauses (SCCs) remain valid but the Court stipulated stricter requirements for the transfer of personal data based on standard contract clauses (SCCs).

Implications for commercial data transfers
As a result of the Court's decision, EU companies can no longer legally transfer data to the US-based on the Privacy Shield framework. Companies that continue to transfer data on the basis of an invalid

TABLE 20.4
A Brief History of EU-US Personal Data Transfer Mechanisms

Mechanism	Description	Current Status

Safe Harbor	The EU Commission and the US government created the US—EU Safe Harbor Framework. On July 26, 2000, the EU Commission determined that companies participating in the Framework provide an "adequate level of protection" for EU data
	• **Numbers**
	    ✓ 4,000+ Safe-Harbor participants
	• **Enforcement**
	    ✓ US Federal Trade Commission
		Invalid.
		It was declared invalid by the European Court of Justice in October 2015.

Privacy Shield	Negotiations with European Commission result in the EU-US Privacy Shield agreement in February 2016. Companies can sign up for the EU-US Privacy Shield. The EU-US Privacy Shield was a replacement for the International Safe Harbor Privacy Principles.
	• **Self-regulatory scheme**
	    ✓ Self-certification
	    ✓ US-based companies only
	• **7 Privacy Shield Principles**
	    ✓ Notice
	    ✓ Choice
	    ✓ Accountability for onward transfers (to countries outside the European Economic Area) and vendor agreements
	    ✓ Security
	    ✓ Data integrity and purpose limitation
	    ✓ Access
	    ✓ And recourse, enforcement, and liability
	• **Additional provisions have been put in place**
	    ✓ US Ombudsman Privacy Shield
	    ✓ Recourse mechanism for noncompliance (i.e., internal compliant process, independent dispute resolution provider, department of Commerce or Federal Trade Commission, Binding arbitration)
	    ✓ Annual joint review (i.e., the European supervisory authorities, the Commission, and the Department of Commerce)
	    ✓ Limited and proportionate surveillance
	• **Numbers**
	    ✓ 5,000+ Privacy Shield participants
	• **Enforcement**
	    ✓ US Federal Trade Commission
		Invalid.
		The ECJ declared the EU-US Privacy Shield invalid on 16 July 2020.

Trans-Atlantic Data Privacy Framework	The European Commission and the United States announce that they have agreed in principle on a new Trans-Atlantic Data Privacy Framework, which will foster trans-Atlantic data flows and address the concerns raised by the Court of Justice of the European Union in the Schrems II decision of July 2020.	Principles agreed, details need to be finalized. The teams of the US Government and the European Commission will now continue their cooperation to translate this arrangement into legal documents that will need to be adopted on both sides to put in place this new Trans-Atlantic Data Privacy Framework. For that purpose, these US commitments will be included in an Executive Order that will form the basis of the Commission's assessment in its future adequacy decision.

mechanism risk a penalty of €20 million or 4% of their global turnover, pursuant to Article 83(5) (c) GDPR.

The decision has an impact on the business operations or research collaborations among entities in the EU and US. For example, about 40 clinical and observational studies collaborated between EU and US entities on risk factors and exposures for cancer have been suspended or delayed due to the EU decision.[46]

The Berlin, Hamburg, and Dutch DPAs advise halting transfers to the United States. The Berlin DPA even advises retrieving data from the United States. Many DPAs stress the need for further analysis and case-by-case assessments.[47]

- A discussion between German Data Protection Authorities (DPAs) at their joint Datensch utzkonferenz (DSK) meeting highlighted the next steps of a Schrems II Task Force: DPAs, led by Hamburg and Berlin, will begin initiating enforcement measures. The Hamburg DPA will conduct random checks on companies to determine whether or not they are in compliance with Schrems II requirements.

 Case Study

German Hamburg DPA vs. Zoom, 2021[48]

DPA Hamburg warned Senate Office regarding the use of the video conferencing tool ZOOM on August 16, 2021.

The Hamburg Commissioner for Data Protection and Freedom of Information has officially warned the Senate Chancellery of the Free and Hanseatic City of Hamburg not to use the video conferencing solution from Zoom Inc. in the so-called on-demand variant. According to the DPA this violates the GDPR, as such use involves the transfer of personal data to the United States. There is no sufficient protection for such data in the third country. This was established by the European Court of Justice in the Schrems II decision more than a year ago (C-311/18).

A data transfer is therefore only possible under very narrow conditions, which are not present in the planned use of Zoom by the Senate Chancellery according to the DPA. In this way, the data of public authority employees and external call participants will be exposed to the risk of mass surveillance in the US without any reason, against which there are no sufficient legal protection options. The EDPB has formulated requirements for transferring personal data to a third country such as the United States in accordance with the GDPR. The Hamburg DPA applies this standard to the economy as well as to public administration. The documents submitted by the Senate Chancellery on the use of Zoom indicate that these standards are NOT being met. Other legal bases, such as the consent of all those affected, are also not relevant here according to the DPA.

20.4.3 Data Transfer Impact Assessments

Based on the Schrems II decision (July 16, 2020), Standard Contractual Clauses (SCCs) remain valid, but the Court stipulated **stricter** requirements for the transfer of personal data based on standard contract clauses (SCCs).

There is a responsibility on processors and controllers to ensure that the laws of the country into which personal data is being imported do not **conflict with their ability** to provide adequate protections the data subject is granted by the General Data Protection Regulation (GDPR) and the EU Charter of Fundamental Rights (CFR).

As a Data Exporter

For **each particular** transfer of personal data, the data exporter must assess whether there are any conflicting **goals (case-by-case assessment)**.

1) Such an assessment must be made **regardless of which third country** the data importer resides in. You should **take particular care** if you plan to make a restricted transfer to the countries such as the United States, China, etc.[49]

   • US: Some state surveillance is acceptable in this context. For example, where security services must apply for a warrant before demanding personal data from a business. **Some US surveillance laws** (FISA 702, EO 12.333, and Presidential Policy Directive 28) do not meet this standard. Therefore, these surveillance laws could be a problem if you plan to use SCCs to transfer personal data to certain US companies. You'll need to consider whether you can apply additional safeguards to your restricted transfers to protect against state interference.

   • China: Your organization needs to pay extra caution regarding whether your data processors are subject to some of the Chinese laws such as the National Intelligence Law, the Anti-Terrorism Law, the Counter-espionage Law, the State Security Law, etc.

2) The assessment must, in particular, take into account both the SCCs and any access by the public authorities of that third country (by making a thorough assessment of local law provisions of importing countries) to the personal data transferred as permitted under that third country's legal system.[50]

   • As a **first step**, **know your transfers**.

      • Mapping all transfers of personal data to third countries can be a difficult exercise. Being aware of where the personal data goes is however necessary to ensure that it is afforded an essentially equivalent level of protection wherever it is processed. You must also verify that the data you transfer is adequate, relevant, and limited to what is necessary in relation to the purposes for which it is transferred to and processed in the third country.

   • A **second** step is to **verify the transfer tool your transfer relies on**, amongst those listed under Chapter V GDPR.

   • A **third step** is to **assess** if there is anything in **the law or practice of the third country** that may impinge on the effectiveness of the appropriate safeguards of the transfer tools you are relying on, in the context of your specific transfer.

      • Your assessment should be primarily focused on third country legislation that is relevant to your transfer and the Article 46 GDPR transfer tool you are relying on and which may undermine its level of protection.

      • Laws that allow common law enforcement access to **data in individualized cases and subject to the approval of a judge will be compliant with EU law**. Forms of less democratic, far-reaching access ("mass processing") or access without judicial review will be incompliant with EU law.

      • After the Schrems I judgment, in 2016, Article 29 Working Party (now EDPB) provided clear guidance on what can and what cannot be regarded as a justifiable interference to fundamental rights in a democratic society regarding data protection law (Articles 7 and 8 of the Charter). In this Working Document, the DPAs have already identified four European Essential Guarantees that should be respected in the countries where EU data are sent:

         • A. Processing should be based on clear, precise, and accessible rules
         • B. Necessity and proportionality with regard to the legitimate objectives pursued must be demonstrated
         • C. An independent oversight mechanism should exist
         • D. Effective remedies need to be available to the individual.

      • For evaluating the elements to be taken into account when assessing the law of a third country dealing with access to data by public authorities for the purpose of surveillance, please refer to the EDPB European Essential Guarantees recommendations. In particular, this should be carefully considered when the legislation governing the access to data by public authorities is ambiguous or not publicly available.

- In the absence of legislation governing the circumstances in which public authorities may access personal data, if you still wish to proceed with the transfer, you should look into other relevant and objective factors, and not rely on subjective factors such as the likelihood of public authorities' access to your data in a manner not in line with EU standards. You should conduct this assessment with due diligence and document it thoroughly, as you will be held accountable to the decision you may take on that basis.

- A **fourth step** is **to identify and adopt supplementary measures** that are necessary to bring the level of protection of the data transferred up to the EU standard of essential equivalence.

  - This step is only necessary if your assessment reveals that the third country legislation impinges on the effectiveness of the Article 46 GDPR transfer tool you are relying on or you intend to rely on in the context of your transfer.

  - You may ultimately find that no supplementary measure can ensure an essentially equivalent level of protection for your specific transfer. In those cases where no supplementary measure is suitable, you must avoid, suspend, or terminate the transfer to avoid compromising the level of protection of the personal data. You should also conduct this assessment of supplementary measures with due diligence and document it.

- A **fifth step** is to **take** any **formal procedural steps** the adoption of your supplementary measure may require, depending on the Article 46 GDPR transfer tool you are relying on.

- The **sixth and final step** will be for your organization to re-evaluate at appropriate intervals the level of protection afforded to the data you transfer to third countries and to monitor if there have been or there will be any developments that may affect it.

3) If your organization concludes that SCCs cannot provide an adequate level of data protection, and you proceed with a restricted transfer despite this, **your organization must inform your Data Protection Authority**.

As a Data Importer

- The data importer must inform the exporter of any inability to comply with the terms of the SCCs in order to allow the exporter to suspend the data transfer or terminate the SCCs.

  - In practice, data importers can **give a warranty** in relation to making the best efforts to provide the data exporter with **relevant information** in the assessment of the **third country's laws** and

  - Must **promptly** notify the data exporter if **circumstances change** which means that the data importer cannot fulfill its obligations.

- In addition, **each supervisory authority** in the exporting EU country is required to handle complaints submitted by data subjects.

  - If, in the view of the supervisory authority, the SCCs are not being complied with by the parties or cannot be complied with in the third country and there are no additional safeguards in place to ensure an "adequate level of protection," the supervisory authority is **required** to **suspend or prohibit** transfers of personal data.

Questions and answers

Is there a list of US providers that fall under these surveillance laws?[49]

There is no full list of all US providers that fall under 702 FISA (50 USC § 1881a), as all "electronic communication service providers" fall under this law. The definition of an "electronic communication service provider" can be found in 50 USC § 1881(b)(4).

At the same time, a number of companies have even published so-called "transparency reports" that list accesses under FISA. This allows us to know that these companies are definitely under a FISA order.

You can find some examples here (many other companies simply do not share such information, despite falling under FISA 702):

1. AT&T
2. Amazon (AWS)
3. Apple
4. Cloudflare
5. Dropbox
6. Facebook
7. Google
8. Microsoft
9. Verizon Media (former Oath & Yahoo)
10. Verizon

 Questions and answers

Can I simply use Article 49 GDPR for all US transfers?
The EDPB has taken the position that Article 49 may only be used for "occasional and not repetitive transfers", which limits Article 49 to individual situations where users have given explicit consent or if the transfer is strictly necessary to provide a contract (e.g., travel booking abroad).
It is worth noting that outsourcing processing operations is not strictly "necessary" to provide the contract if you could theoretically also use an EU/EEA provider or process data in-house. Controllers should also be mindful that data subjects can withdraw their consent at any time.

20.5   APEC CPEA, CBPR, AND PRP

20.5.1   THE DESIGN LOGIC

CPEA

Another cross-border enforcement cooperation effort is the Asia-Pacific Economic Cooperation (APEC) Cross-border Privacy Enforcement Arrangement (CPEA).

There are 21 Member Economies within the APEC framework including the United States; Australia; Brunei Darussalam; Canada; Chile; China; Hong Kong, China; Indonesia; Japan; Malaysia; Mexico; New Zealand; Papua New Guinea; Peru; The Philippines; Russia; Singapore; Republic of Korea; Chinese Taipei; Thailand; and Vietnam. APEC members recognize the importance of protecting information privacy and maintaining information flows between economies in the Asia-Pacific region and between APEC economies and their international trading partners.

The APEC Cross-border Privacy Enforcement Arrangement (CPEA) creates a framework for regional cooperation in the enforcement of Privacy Laws. Any Privacy Enforcement Authority

(PE Authority) in an APEC economy may participate. The APEC CPEA facilitates information sharing, promotes effective cross-border cooperation, and encourages information sharing and investigative/enforcement cooperation. There are more than 20 agencies participating in the CPEA.

CBPR

In November 2011, Under the CPEA, APEC issued a directive to declare the implementation of the Cross Border Privacy Rules System (CBPRs) which is a voluntary certification system. The system aims to facilitate barrier-free cross-border information exchange within the APEC framework.

The APEC Cross-Border Privacy Rules (CBPR) System is a government-backed data privacy certification that companies can join to demonstrate compliance with internationally recognized data privacy protections. The CBPR System implements the **APEC Privacy Framework** endorsed by APEC Leaders in 2005 and updated in 2015.

Through the CBPR System, certified companies and governments are working together to ensure that when personal information moves across borders, it is protected in accordance with the standards prescribed by the system's program requirements and is enforceable across participating jurisdictions.

The CBPR System protects personal data by requiring:[51]

- Enforceable standards
- Accountability
- Risk-based protections
- Consumer-friendly complaint handling
- Consumer empowerment
- Consistent protections
- Cross-border enforcement cooperation

PRP

PRP stands for Privacy Recognition for Processors. The PRP helps personal information processors ("processors") demonstrate their ability to provide effective implementation of a personal information controller's ("controller") privacy obligations related to the processing of personal information. The PRP also helps controllers identify qualified and accountable processors.

The APEC Cross Border Privacy Rules ("CBPR") System only applies to controllers. The limited scope of the CBPR System has resulted in a call by controllers for the development of a mechanism that will help them identify qualified and accountable processors with whom to contract. Similarly, processors in the APEC Member Economies ("APEC economies") have expressed an interest in such a mechanism, as it would enable them to demonstrate their ability to provide effective implementation of a controller's privacy requirements; including helping small and medium-sized enterprises not known outside of their economy to become part of a global data processing network.

The PRP represents the baseline requirements a processor must meet to be recognized by an APEC-recognized Accountability Agent and provide assurances with respect to the processor's privacy policies and practices.

20.5.2 CBPR Rules and Operations

The purpose of CBPRs is to ensure the realization of the nine principles in the APEC privacy framework in member economies through specific mechanisms, to provide guiding principles and standards for the protection of personal information privacy in the Asia-Pacific region, and ultimately to promote the protection of personal information in the region based on achieving barrier-free flow and promoting the development of cross-border e-commerce in the Asia-Pacific region.

In essence, the basic logic of CBPRs promoting the cross-border flow of personal data is that if different companies in different countries make a unified commitment and follow the nine personal data protection principles proposed by the APEC Privacy Framework, personal data will flow between these companies unhindered. Accordingly, since these companies use the same set of principles to protect personal data, countries participating in CBPRs can no longer use the protection of personal data as a reason to hinder the cross-border flow of personal data.

The FTC is a CPEA participant and in July of 2012, the agency was approved as the system's first privacy enforcement authority. The United States is asking Brazil to join CPEA/CBPR as a non-APEC economy in 2019.

Conditions for countries to join CBPR

- Limited to APEC member countries,
- At least one privacy enforcement agency in the country has joined the CPEA
  - There are currently 8 participating economies: USA, Mexico, Japan, Canada, Singapore, the Republic of Korea, Australia, and Chinese Taipei.
- Submit an application to join and meet CBPR certification standards (domestic laws, regulations or administrative management, etc., match CBPR requirements).
  - (1) comply with minimum requirements based on a set of commonly agreed-upon rules known as the APEC Privacy Framework. Minimum requirements include:
    - Notice
    - Collection limitation
    - Use, transfer, and disclosure of personal information
    - Choice
    - Integrity of personal information
    - Security safeguards
    - Access and correction
    - Accountability
  - (2) be verified by assessment and certification from an independent public or private sector body—an "accountability agent."

Conditions for companies to join CBPR

- The legal jurisdiction of one of the CBPR participating jurisdictions
- There is at least one accreditation agency in that jurisdiction, or the participating country declares that it agrees to use accreditation agencies in other CBPR participating jurisdictions.
- Meet CBPR certification standards, pass the certification agency compliance review, and finally pass. Many companies have joined so far, of which the majority are American companies including Apple, IBM, Cisco, and Hewlett-Packard.
- Please reference the following link for further information.
  - www.apec.org/about-us/about-apec/fact-sheets/what-is-the-cross-border-privacy-rules-system

20.5.3   PRP Rules and Operations

There are several enforcement mechanisms available across the participating APEC economies to ensure the effective oversight of processors recognized under the PRP.

These include:

- Where applicable, direct privacy enforcement authority backstop enforcement of the processor's compliance with the PRP program requirements.
- Enforcement by contract between the Accountability Agent and the processor, whereby the Accountability Agent assumes primary responsibility for enforcing the processor's compliance with the PRP program requirements.

- Government oversight over an Accountability Agent, and enforcement by the APEC Data Privacy Subgroup ("DPS") via the Joint Oversight Panel's authority to recommend to the DPS the suspension of an Accountability Agent in the event the Accountability Agent fails to perform its obligations under the Accountability Agent Recognition Criteria.
- Mechanisms that can have the effect of enforcing privacy, such as private rights of action, and third-party beneficiary rights for enforcement authorities under the contracts between the Accountability Agents and the processors.

PRP Process Overview

1) Process for Participation and Discontinuation of Participation by APEC Economies in the PRP System

To participate in the PRP System, an Economy must first satisfy the relevant conditions in 3.1 of the Charter of the APEC Cross-Border Privacy Rules and Privacy Recognition for Processors Systems Joint Oversight Panel. The Economy then nominates one or more Accountability Agents for APEC recognition or notifies the ECSG Chair of receipt of application(s) for such recognition. Once at least one Accountability Agent has been recognized in relation to that Economy, organizations will be able to commence participation in the PRP System in the Economy.

- An Economy may cease participation in the PRP System at any time by giving three months' written notice to the APEC ECSG Chair.

2) Process for Recognition of Accountability Agents

- An Economy can nominate an Accountability Agent operating within its jurisdiction for APEC recognition or, where appropriate, notify the Joint Oversight Panel that they have received a request for such recognition and submit the received application and associated documentation for consideration. In either case, the Economy should describe the relevant domestic laws and regulations which may apply to the activities of Accountability Agents operating within their jurisdiction and the enforcement authority associated with these laws and regulations. Where the Privacy Enforcement Authority of an Economy assumes the role of Accountability Agent, the nomination may be done by the Economy with a confirmation that the Privacy Enforcement Authority is a participant of the CPEA as well as a summary of how that privacy enforcement authority may enforce the PRP System requirements.
- In those instances where an Economy proposes to make use of an Accountability Agent in another participating APEC Economy to certify an applicant organization principally located within its borders, the proposing economy should notify the Joint Oversight Panel of this proposal. The proposing Economy should describe to the Joint Oversight Panel the relevant domestic laws and regulations which may apply to the activities of Accountability Agents operating within their jurisdiction and the enforcement authority associated with these laws and regulations.
- All applications for recognition will include a signed attestation by the Accountability Agent and all necessary supporting documentation as stipulated in the Accountability Agent recognition criteria.
- Upon receipt of a request for recognition pursuant to paragraphs 27 or 28, the Joint Oversight Panel will commence a review of the required documentation and request any additional information necessary to ensure the recognition criteria have been met. When the Joint Oversight Panel has completed this review process, they will issue a recommendation to APEC Economies as to whether to recognize the Accountability Agent. Economies will consider the Accountability Agent's request for recognition, considering the recommendation of the Joint Oversight Panel. Economies may consult stakeholders, such as business or civil society representatives, when considering

the Joint Oversight Panel recommendation, except regarding business proprietary information provided by the Accountability Agent. If no objections are received from Economies within a set deadline, the request will be considered to be approved by the ECSG.

3) Process for Certification of Organizations

- Applicant organizations should make use of Accountability Agents located within the jurisdiction in which the applicant organization is primarily located, or an Accountability Agent recognized previously.
- Once an applicant organization selects and contacts an eligible APEC-recognized Accountability Agent, the Accountability Agent will provide the self-assessment questionnaire to the organization for completion and will review the answers and any supporting documentation based on its assessment guidelines or make use of APEC recognized documentation and review procedures.
- The proposed application process would be iterative and allow for back-and-forth discussions between the applicant organization and the Accountability Agent.
- The Accountability Agent Recognition Criteria describe the role of Accountability Agents as follows:
  - The Accountability Agent is responsible for the self-assessment and compliance review phases of the PRP System accreditation process. Applicant organizations will be responsible for developing their privacy policies and practices and may only participate in the PRP System if these policies and practices are certified by the relevant Accountability Agent to be compliant with the requirements of the PRP System. It is the responsibility of the Accountability Agent to certify an organization's compliance with these requirements.
  - The self-assessment questionnaire and assessment guidelines are publicly available documents and prospective applicant organizations will have access to the guidelines so that they can see how their responses to the self-assessment questionnaire will be assessed. In considering how best to assist prospective applicant organizations, a recognized Accountability Agent may wish to develop additional documentation outlining their review process.

20.5.4 LIST OF PARTICIPATING JURISDICTIONS AND CERTIFICATION BODIES

Table 20.5 lists the participating jurisdictions and certification bodies for CBPR and PRP.

20.6 CHINA CERTIFICATION SPECIFICATION

The China National Information Security Standardization Technical Committee published the *Certification for Cross-Border Processing of Personal Information* in June 2022 to set forth the requirements regarding personal data cross-border transfers.

This specification requires that cross-border transferring of data should follow the following principles:

- Lawfulness, legitimacy, necessity, and good faith
- Openness and transparency
- Information quality
- Equal protection
- Clear responsibility
- Voluntary certification

I summarized the core requirements as listed:

TABLE 20.5

Participating Jurisdictions and Certification Bodies

	CBPR	PRP
Participating Jurisdictions	USA, Mexico, Canada, Japan, the Republic of Korea, Australia, Singapore, and Chinese Taipei	USA, Singapore
Certification Bodies	• Japan—JIPDEC • KOREA—Korea Internet & Security Agency • Singapore—Infocomm Media Development Authority • US • Schellman • TrustArc • NCC Group • HITRUST • BBB • Chinese Taipei—Institute for Information Industry	• Singapore—Infocomm Media Development Authority • US • Schellman • TrustArc

1) Personal information protection impact assessment

Personal information handlers who carry out cross-border activities of personal information evaluate in advance whether the activities of providing personal information overseas are legal, legitimate, and necessary and whether the protective measures taken are appropriate and effective in accordance with the degree of risk, etc.

The personal information protection impact assessment shall at least include the following matters:

- Whether the provision of personal information overseas complies with laws and administrative regulations.
- The impact on the rights and interests of data subjects, especially the impact of the legal environment and network security environment of overseas countries and regions on the rights and interests of data subjects.
- Other matters are necessary to safeguard the rights and interests of personal information.

2) Notice and Consent

Inform the data subjects about the cross-border processing of personal information and obtain the individual consent of the data subject.

3) Sign a legally binding agreement

A legally binding and enforceable document should be signed between the personal information handler and the overseas recipient who carries out cross-border processing of personal information to ensure that the rights and interests of the data subjects are fully protected. The overseas recipient shall process personal information cross-border in accordance with the processing purpose, processing method, protection measures, etc. agreed in the signed legally effective document, and shall not process personal information beyond the agreed cross-border processing.

The document should at least specify the following:

- Personal information handlers and overseas recipients who carry out cross-border processing of personal information.
  - An organization that clearly assumes the legal responsibility within the territory of the People's Republic of China.

- The overseas recipient undertakes to accept the supervision of the certification body; the overseas recipient undertakes to accept the jurisdiction of the relevant laws and administrative regulations of the People's Republic of China on personal information protection.
- Basic information on cross-border processing of personal information, including the quantity, scope, type, and sensitivity of personal information.
- The purpose, manner, and scope of cross-border processing of personal information.
- The start and end time of overseas storage of personal information and the processing method after expiration.
- Countries or regions where cross-border processing of personal information needs to be transferred.
- Measures to protect the rights and interests of data subjects; resources and measures to protect the rights and interests of data subjects.
- Compensation and disposal rules for personal information security incidents.

4) Organizational management

Person in charge of personal information protection: Both personal information handlers and overseas recipients that carry out cross-border processing of personal information should designate a person in charge of personal information protection.

The person in charge of personal information protection shall have professional knowledge of personal information protection and relevant management work experience, which shall be undertaken by members of the decision-making level of the organization. The person in charge of personal information protection shall undertake the following responsibilities:

- Clarify the main objectives, basic requirements, work tasks, and protection measures of personal information protection.
- Provide people, financial, and material resources for the organization's personal information protection work to ensure that the required resources are available.
- Guide and support relevant personnel to carry out the organization's personal information protection work to ensure that personal information protection work achieves the expected goals.
- Report the personal information protection work to the main person in charge of the organization and promote the continuous improvement of personal information protection work.

Personal information protection organizations: Personal information handlers and overseas recipients that carry out cross-border processing of personal information should set up personal information protection organizations to fulfill their obligations to protect personal information and prevent unauthorized access and personal information leakage, tampering, loss, etc. and undertake the following responsibilities in cross-border processing of personal information:

- Formulate and implement an activity plan for cross-border processing of personal information in accordance with the law.
- Organizing and conducting personal information protection impact assessments.
- Supervise the organization's processing of cross-border personal information in accordance with the cross-border personal information processing rules agreed upon by the processor and the overseas recipient.
- To receive and process requests and complaints from personal data subjects.

5) Protection of the rights and interests of data subjects

At the request of the data subject, provide a copy of the legal text that involves the rights and interests of the data subjects.

- Data subjects have the right to require personal information handlers and overseas recipients to provide copies of the legal texts involving the rights and interests of data subjects.
- Data subjects have the right to know and decide the processing of their personal information, the right to withdraw their consent to the cross-border processing of their personal information, and the right to restrict or refuse the processing of their personal information by others.
- Data subjects have the right to access, copy, correct, supplement, and delete their personal information from overseas recipients.
- Data subjects have the right to require personal information processors and overseas recipients to explain their cross-border processing rules for personal information.
- Data subjects have the right to refuse the personal information handlers to make a decision only by means of automated decision-making.
- Data subjects have the right to complain and report illegal personal information processing activities to the departments of the People's Republic of China that perform personal information protection duties.
- Data subjects have the right to initiate judicial proceedings against the handler and overseas recipient who carry out cross-border processing of personal information in the court where he or she habitually resides.

6) Incident handling

- When it is difficult to ensure the security of cross-border personal information, the cross-border processing of personal information should be suspended in a timely manner.
- If personal information is leaked, tampered with, or lost, the personal information handler and the overseas recipient shall immediately take remedial measures and notify the departments and individuals performing personal information protection duties.

20.7 A SIX-STEP APPROACH

Table 20.6 describes the six-step approach for facilitating personal data cross-border transfers.

TABLE 20.6
A Six-Step Approach for Data Cross-Border Transfers

Step	Description
1. Know your business context and data flows	Identify and map the data flow that involves cross-border transfers
2. Under legal obligations	Assess the legal obligations with respect to data residency and cross-border transfers.
3. Identify transfer mechanisms	Identify available data transfer tools such as adequacy decisions, standard contractual clauses (SCCs), binding corporate rules (BCRs), etc.
4. Implement required measures	Implement necessary supplementary controls as required by the local laws.
5. Transfer using the selected mechanism	Execute the data transfers using the selected mechanism.
6. Monitor, review, and update the mechanism	Make changes accordingly to the selected mechanism as necessary. For instance, if your organization adds another data flow from the EU to Singapore, you might need to update the SCCs accordingly.

21 Data Retention and De-Identification

This chapter is intended to help readers establish and execute an actionable data retention policy and schedule and help readers to understand personal data de-identification techniques.

This chapter covers the following topics:

- *Data retention benefits and challenges*
- *Data retention and destruction mandate*
- *Data retention key considerations*
- *Data destruction and de-identification*

21.1 DATA RETENTION BENEFITS AND CHALLENGES

An organization must not retain personal information for a period longer than necessary to fulfill the purposes described in the notice or comply with applicable laws. Personal data must be depersonalized or deleted after it reaches the retention period.

Most sector-based regulations include requirements for disposal and for how long you have to keep that information. The general standard for data retention is no longer necessary to fulfill the purpose for which the information was collected.

Here are some of the benefits of establishing a robust data retention and de-identification program:

- Reduced litigation risks, regulatory fines, and penalties by keeping information for only the length of time that is legally required.
- Improved security by protecting business-critical information, minimizing data leakage, and ensuring the availability of information when needed.
- Simplify the process for responding to data subject right requests.
- Reduced physical storage costs by balancing retention requirements with the ability to purge data that is no longer needed.

On the other side, there are many challenges organizations are facing to implement and execute data retention programs.

1) High volumes of data dispersed across multiple internal and external repositories, making it difficult to maintain visibility and control over data flows and retention obligations.
2) Business lines tend to store personal data as long as they can just in case in the future the data will be used.
   - For instance, to analyze user behavior, a Business Intelligent (BI) system collects and stores personal data on user behavior (such as the first access time, last access time, browsing, download, searching, and payment) permanently, without defining a retention period for each type of personal data based actual business needs, unless there is no sufficient storage space. This practice increases the risk of leaking users' personal data greatly and leads to significant adverse impacts.
   - Another example: A user booked an air ticket through airplane company X and provided the credit card account as the payment voucher. When the user booked another air ticket through company X again, the service personnel asked whether to use the

credit card whose last digits are xxxx again for payment. Company X did not delete the user's credit card information in a timely manner after finishing the business and stored such information without notifying the user and obtaining the user's consent, which irritated the user.

3) Business lines think "the personal data was only recently acquired/collected. The retention time is still way ahead, and we did not need to delete any data yet. We will design and implement the deletion concept in future".

4) There are no uniform retention periods on the international level.
   - Every country has its own rules and practices that can differ greatly.
   - Requirements vary for different types of information/data/record, HR, Financial, Tax, CCTV.
   - Some laws set forth minimum retention periods (i.e., tax, employment laws), while others articulate maximum retention periods (i.e., privacy laws)
   - Data retention triggers are different, such as last deposition date, determination date, etc.

5) Administrative overhead in managing a manual data-deletion process

 Case Study

The German DPA v. Deutsche Wohnen, 2021
   The German DPA fined Deutsche Wohnen (a housing rental company renting out ~160,000 apartments) 14.5 million euros for GDPR violation in August 2021. The fine was equivalent to about 1% of the company's annual revenue.
   The DPA found that Deutsche Wohnen did not have a sufficient data deletion concept and did not comply with GDPR data deletion requirements.
   The GDPR violation was discovered during an audit of the DPA in June 2019. The DPA had requested a compliant deletion concept of Deutsche Wohnen already in 2017, but the company did not implement the recommendation.
   Deutsche Wohnen argued that the storing and archiving of the tenant data was required due to tax obligations and it will challenge the DPA decision in court.

21.2   DATA RETENTION AND DESTRUCTION MANDATE

21.2.1   DATA RETENTION

The organization should establish a data retention schedule that aligns with applicable laws and regulations within each jurisdiction in which an organization operates. Retain personal data only within the time frame needed for reasonable business purposes.

Personal data shall not be kept or archived indefinitely "just in case", or if there is only a small possibility that it will be used. The retention period also shall not be shorter than the applicable statutory minimum retention period.

Beware of conflicts in your obligations. Some regulations and laws dictate that data must be retained, while others demand that data be deleted once it is no longer in active use. You may have to make a judgment call regarding what the right retention period is. This should be done in conjunction with your legal counsel.

Table 21.1 lists some examples of data retention requirements from various laws and regulations.

21.2.2   DATA DESTRUCTION

Many US states have data destruction laws. These are sometimes incorporated in data breach laws, like breach notification laws, most have common elements, including specifying to whom the law

TABLE 21.1
Examples of Data Retention Obligations

Business Scenario	Business Process	Data Retention Requirement
Recruitment	Non-successful applicants	3-year: Italy 1-year: Poland, Finland, Lithuania, China 6-month: Norway (recommendation), Denmark, UK 4-week: Netherland
	Employment eligibility verification	2-year: UK
	Recruitment and selection records (includes announcements, applications received, interview notes, tests)	5-year: Portugal
HR operations	Attendance, performance evaluation, promotions, transfers, layoffs, terminations	50-year: Romania 40-year: employee health data— No legal period for others—Switzerland 10-year: Germany, Portugal, Spain, Italy, Belgium 5-year: France 3-year: UK
	HR hotline record on HR consultations and services provided to employees	3-year
Payroll/salary/bonuses	Payroll/salary/bonuses	10-year: Portugal, Poland, Spain, Italy, Belgium 7-year: Austria, Romania, China, Malaysia 5-year: France 3-year: Luxembourg 2-year: Netherland
Business travel and reimbursement	Hotel, flight tickets, travel record, reimbursement	10-year: Spain 7-year: Austria, China 3-year: Poland (after the activity)
Insurance	Health and accident insurance	5-year: Poland
Accounting and tax documents	Accounting and tax documents	10-year: Belgium, Luxembourg, Switzerland 5-year: France, Netherlands, Slovenia, Poland, Norway
Lawsuit	Salary related	10-year: Poland (After court ruling)
	Benefit related	3-year: Poland (After court ruling)
IT system and information security monitoring	IT system and information security monitoring	7-year: Austria, China (After leave) 3-year: Poland (after leave) 1-month: Many countries
Facility Security	Visitors: Onsite visit record	6-month: Italy
	Physical access control logs	3-month: Luxembourg
	Video monitoring	1-year: Slovenia 3-month: Poland 1-month: Luxembourg 3-day: Germany (conflicting data) 7-day: Norway,
Marketing	Marketing activities	3-year: Poland 1-year: US, Austria, China, Germany, Romania, Denmark, Greece, Cyprus, Syria
	Raffle	10-year: Germany 6-year: Spain 1-year: Czech, Portugal, Switzerland, Poland, Romania, China

(Continued)

TABLE 21.1   (Continued)

Business Scenario	Business Process	Data Retention Requirement
	Customer experiment	6-year: smartphone/end device (TSMP)
		3-month: Austria, China
2C-Online registration and activities	Registration	3-month (after deregistration)
	Consumer access log information: Access logs generated when users use systems. This type of information includes IP addresses, and user IDs.	3-month
2C-Sale, promotion, order, payment and refund	Promotion	10-year: Germany, Lithuania
		2-year: Italy
	Order and order execution	5-year: Spain, China, South America, Europe
	Payment and transaction information	7-year: China, China-HK, Europe, Russia, Singapore
	Refund	10-year: Germany
2B-PO and contract (after finishing contract)	PO and contract	7-year: UK, Belgium, Portugal, Italy, Switzerland
		3-year: Poland, Austria, China, Japan
Customer relationship management (after finishing contract)	Customer relationship management	3-year:
		2-year: Syria, Slovenia, Austria, Hungary, Croatia, Denmark
Vendor and partner management (after finishing contract)	Vendor and partner management	10-year: Spain, Switzerland, Belgium, France, Netherlands
		7-year: Austria, Romania, Germany, China, UK
		6-year: Poland, Norway, Bulgaria, Spain, Czech, Denmark
		3-year: Sweden, Japan, Croatia
Service	2C-Hotline and online service	3-year: Austria, China, Romania, Poland
		2-year: Germany
	2C-diagnose, repair	3-year: Poland
		2-year: Germany, Egypt, Belgium, Austria, China, Hungary, Latvia, Lithuania, Finland
	2B-Client support, technical and professional service, etc.	3-month: Germany, Austria, Romania, UK
Training and certification	Registration, survey	5-year: Austria, China
	Training delivery	10-year: Poland (recommendation)
		7-year: Austria, China
Media relationship	Invitation, gift, activities	6-month: China, Finland, Lithuania, Latvia, Poland, Romania, Sweden

applies, which may be government and/or private businesses, the required notice, exemptions, penalties, etc.

For instance, in North Carolina, Gen. Stat. §14–113.20 and §75–60 to 66 and §132–1.10 (extended provisions to government agencies) articulate the following requirements:

- "Any business that conducts business in North Carolina and any business that maintains or otherwise possesses personal information of a resident of North Carolina."

- It requires such entities to take "reasonable measures" to safeguard against unauthorized access to personal information "in connection with or after its disposal."
- There's the phrase "reasonable measures," but in this case, North Carolina describes what it means by "reasonable measures:"
  - First, implementing and monitoring compliance with policies and procedures that require the burning, pulverizing, or shredding of papers containing personal information so that information cannot be practicably read or reconstructed.
  - Second, implementing and monitoring compliance with policies and procedures that require the destruction or erasure of electronic media and other non-paper media containing personal information so that the information cannot practicably be read or reconstructed.
  - And third, describing procedures relating to the adequate destruction or proper disposal of personal records as official policy in the writings of the business entity.
- The law allows businesses to subcontract with record destruction after due diligence, which requires reviewing an independent audit of the business' operations, reviewing references, and requiring independent certification of the business and/or personally evaluating "the competency and integrity of the disposal business."
- North Carolina exempts financial institutions subject to GLBA, health insurers or healthcare facilities subject to HIPAA, and consumer reporting agencies subject to the FCRA.
- The law does not specify damages but denies a right of public action in the absence of personal injury.

Most other state laws are essentially the same as North Carolina's although, for example,

- the Arizona law applies only to paper records
- Illinois and Utah apply only to government entities
- New York applies only to for-profit businesses
- Alaska specifically authorizes a right to private action
- California requires destruction such that records are "unreadable or undecipherable through any means"
- Massachusetts stipulates steep penalties ("not more than $100 per data subject affected, provided said fine shall not exceed $50,000 for each instance of improper disposal").

Table 21.2 lists some examples of data disposal regulations from some states in United States.[52]

TABLE 21.2
Examples of Data Disposal Regulations in US

State	Legislation	Applies to Businesses?	Applies to Government?
California	Cal. Civ. Code §§ 1798.81, 1798.81.5, 1798.84	✓	✗
Colorado	Colo. Rev. Stat. § 6–1–713	✓	✗
Virginia	Va. Code § 2.2–2009 (F)	✗	✓
Utah	Utah Code § 13–44–201	✓	✗
Florida	Fla. Stat. § 501.171(8)	✓	✗
New York	N.Y. Gen. Bus. Law § 399-H	✓	✗
Texas	Tex. Bus. & Com. Code § 72.004, § 521.052	✓	✗
Washington	Wash. Rev. Code § 19.215.020	✓	✓

Questions and answers

If there are no clear legal obligations regarding data retention periods, what is the reasonable approach to set up the proper data retention schedule?
  Usually, there are two types of scenarios regarding data retention periods.

- The first scenario: There are laws, regulations, or guidelines that specify the data retention periods, such as the examples provided in the previous table. It is straightforward. We simply follow the requirements.
- The second scenario: There are NO clear requirements from laws and regulations. This leaves a bit of room for organizations to decide "reasonable data retention periods" based on their business context. The best practice is to communicate with the owner of that data and set up a reasonable retention period with legitimate business rationale documented. There are no right or wrong decisions as long as the rationale is fairly reasonable.

 Case Study

SEC v. J.P. Morgan Securities LLC
  On December 17, 2021, the Securities and Exchange Commission announced charges against J.P. Morgan Securities LLC (JPMS), a broker-dealer subsidiary of J.P. Morgan Chase & Co., for widespread and longstanding failures by the firm and its employees to maintain and preserve written communications.
  JPMS admitted the facts outlined in the SEC's order and acknowledged that its conduct violated the federal securities laws and agreed to pay a $125 million penalty and implement robust improvements to its compliance policies and procedures to settle the matter.
  Recordkeeping and books-and-records obligations have been an essential part of market integrity and a foundational component of the SEC's ability to be an effective cop on the beat. As technology changes, it's even more important that registrants ensure that their communications are appropriately recorded and are not conducted outside of official channels in order to avoid market oversight.
  As described in the SEC's order, JPMS admitted that from at least January 2018 through November 2020, its employees often communicated about securities business matters on their personal devices, using text messages, WhatsApp, and personal email accounts. None of these records were preserved by the firm as required by the federal securities laws. JPMS further admitted that these failures were firm-wide and that practices were not hidden within the firm. Indeed, supervisors, including managing directors and other senior supervisors—the very people responsible for implementing and ensuring compliance with JPMS's policies and procedures—used their personal devices to communicate about the firm's securities business.
  JPMS agreed to the entry of an order in which it admitted to the SEC's factual findings and its conclusion that JPMS's conduct violated Section 17(a) of the Securities Exchange Act of 1934 and Rules 17a-4(b)(4) and 17a-4(j) thereunder, and that the firm failed reasonably to supervise its employees with a view to preventing or detecting certain of its employees' aiding and abetting violations. JPMS was ordered to cease and desist from future violations of those provisions, was censured, and was ordered to pay the

$125 million penalties. JPMS also agreed to retain a compliance consultant to, among other things, conduct a comprehensive review of its policies and procedures relating to the retention of electronic communications found on personal devices and JPMS' framework for addressing non-compliance by its employees with those policies and procedures.

21.3   DATA RETENTION KEY CONSIDERATIONS

Determine which laws or regulations you are currently subject to or will be obligated to comply with in the future. Review your Privacy Program to identify the laws or regulations that dictate how data containing Personally Identifiable Information (PII) should be retained or deleted. Consider planned expansion into new markets and how data sovereignty or data residency laws influence data retention rules.

Successful data retention is closely linked with security governance, compliance, and data classification. Without these guardrails, most organizations struggle to establish a reliable data retention schedule.

When deciding whether the data is still necessary, you may decide you need to delete some data but still retain other data about an individual. For example, if a data subject was a customer five years ago, you may decide that you no longer need to keep all of that data subject's details, but you might decide that you need to keep a record of the transaction in case of a legal claim or for tax records.

Data Repositories
Establish a single source of truth for your data. This will allow you to go to the source and delete the first instance of the data (as per your retention schedule), and then plan to purge the secondary, tertiary, etc. instances on a regular basis.

- Data tends to sprawl from one location to another as different stakeholders use it for different purposes. However, regardless of its location, we must adhere to the data retention schedule. Knowing where to look is half the battle.
- Use your data-flow maps to identify storage locations for every instance of your data.
- If your organization has a personal data inventory that was built and used for personal data protection purposes, you can obtain the relevant information about data repositories from the inventory.
  - A personal data inventory normally includes data elements such as personal data types, lawful basis, processing purposes, where data resides, etc.

Data archive
Taking personal data offline is, of course, not the same as deletion and, although it may reduce the risk of security breaches, by holding the personal data you are still processing it and data subject rights, and all the other principles will still apply to that personal data.

GDPR Recital 67

- Methods by which to restrict the processing of personal data could include, inter alia, temporarily moving the selected data to another processing system, making the selected personal data unavailable to users, or temporarily removing published data from a website. In automated filing systems, the restriction of processing should in principle be ensured by technical means in such a manner that the personal data are not subject to further processing operations and cannot be changed. The fact that the processing of personal data is restricted should be clearly indicated in the system.

ICO guide—Deleting personal data

- There is a significant difference between deleting information irretrievably, archiving it in a structured, retrievable manner or retaining it as random data in an un-emptied electronic wastebasket. Information that is archived, for example, is subject to the same data protection rules as "live" information, although the information that is in effect inert is far less likely to have any unfair or detrimental effect on an individual than live information.
- As to whether you need to delete backups of the personal data, the UK's ICO's guidance on this is that you need to put the personal data beyond use. The guidance states that "if it is appropriate to delete personal data from a live system, you should also delete it from any backup of the information on that system."

Legacy files

Privacy and data protection laws and regulations (i.e., GDPR) apply the same set of requirements to both frequently accessed files and legacy files. From privacy risk and compliance management perspectives, identifying what you have regarding personal data is a starting point that will lay down the groundwork for later privacy controls.

Discontinuance of Operation

Organizations need to manage privacy risks when discontinuing business operations.

Organizations shall, in the case of discontinuance of operation of a product or service that processes personal information, implement controls to manage privacy-related risks (not an exhaustive list).

a) Stop collecting personal data in a timely fashion.
b) Notify data subjects of the discontinuance of operation by sending a notice to each of them or through a public notice.
c) Delete or anonymize the personal data they hold.

 Guide and Recommendations

The best way to resolve the difficulties with building an effective data retention program is to:

- Identify your retention requirements.
- Develop a retention schedule and risk profile for your data processes and types.
- Use the above outputs to determine where the greatest risks lie, and plan to reduce them as much as possible.

By focusing on the high-risk areas, you will manage your data retention processes more efficiently.

Figure 21.1 demonstrates the logic flow to build an effective data retention plan by identifying data retention requirements (i.e. regulatory obligations, business needs and data types), establishing proper data retention governance structure (i.e. data retention policy and schedule) and enforcing the data retention program and focusing on highest risk areas.

Info-Tech Insight

Focus your efforts on data with the highest risk levels, and work towards implementing an automated process. Manual efforts will always carry the most risk.

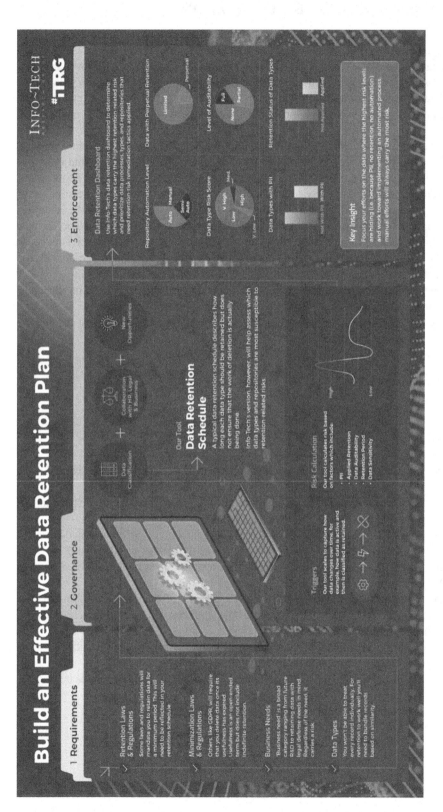

FIGURE 21.1 Info-Tech's Data Retention Blueprint Thought Model

21.4   DATA DESTRUCTION AND DE-IDENTIFICATION

An organization needs to execute the data retention schedule to de-identify or delete personal data after it reaches the retention period, or the data is no longer necessary for the purposes for which the personal data are processed. A retention schedule is necessary but having one won't ensure retention-related risks are managed effectively. Rather, the key lies in identifying risky data processes, types, and repositories and finding solutions to lower those risks. Good data retention and depersonalization programs can also help to prevent personal data loss, theft, abuse, unauthorized access, and so on.

If the stored data contains personal data, a mechanism for deleting expired data must be provided. A function should be provided to allow the data controller to configure the data retention period. If the retention period of personal data cannot be defined, a mechanism must be available to support the retention period policy. Systems should set a retention period for personal data and ensure that the retention period can be configured. If the system cannot define the retention period of personal data, it needs to provide a mechanism to support the retention period policy. For example, when a user deregisters an account, the system should delete the personal data concerning him or her. For expired personal data, the system must provide a mechanism for deleting or anonymizing the data.

Very few retention programs run on automation alone. Some manual deletion should be expected. Manual deletion is manageable provided we have a plan to deal with it.

Personal information should be destroyed using irretrievable destruction methods to ensure personal information is destroyed and can no longer be retrieved.

21.4.1   DATA DESTRUCTION

Some of the key questions to ask:

- Are your staff informed of data destruction procedures?
- Is destruction of personal information done in-house or outsourced?
    - If it is done in-house, what are the standards and tools to achieve the data destruction goals?
    - If outsourced, what steps have you taken to ensure appropriate handling of the personal information?
    - Where the Third Party has been instructed by the organization to irretrievably destroy the personal information, have steps been taken to verify that this has occurred?
    - Have steps been taken to verify the irretrievable destruction of personal stored by a Third Party on a third party's hardware, such as cloud storage?
- Has personal information contained in hard copy records that are disposed of through garbage or recycling collection been destroyed through a process such as pulping, burning, pulverizing, disintegrating, or shredding?
- Is hardware containing personal information in electronic form properly "sanitized" to completely remove the stored personal information?
- Are backups of personal information also destroyed? Are backups arranged in such a way that destruction of backups is possible?
    - If not: have steps been taken to rectify this issue in the future?
    - Has the backed-up personal information been put beyond use?
- How is compliance with data destruction procedures monitored and enforced?

Example

After a user deleted the account, the desktop cloud system deleted only the data index within the system but did not delete user data securely. Then the deleted user data space was reclaimed in a resource pool and randomly assigned to a new desktop user. This new user could use data restoring tools to scan the disks and restore the deleted personal data. The previous user's personal data was leaked.

Example

When processing user payment results, a product displays users' credit card numbers and balances in logs without any encryption or anonymization. Users' credit card information is saved in the database in plaintext, which is accessible for system administrators. Information leak will pose large risks for users' financial security.

21.4.2 ANONYMIZATION, PSEUDONYMIZATION, AND AGGREGATION

There are several important safeguards for de-identifying personal data at different levels: anonymization, pseudonymization, aggregation, and more.

- According to German *Federal Data Protection Act* (BDSG), personal data shall be collected, processed, and used, and data processing systems shall be chosen and organized in accordance with the aim of collecting, processing, and using as little personal data as possible. In particular, personal data shall be rendered anonymous or aliased as allowed by the purpose for which they are collected and/or further processed.
- GDPR Article 25 and Article 32 provide that the controller and the processor shall implement appropriate technical and organizational measures to ensure a level of security appropriate to the risk (including inter alia as appropriate the pseudonymization and encryption of personal data and the ability to ensure the ongoing confidentiality, integrity, availability and resilience of processing systems and services).

Anonymization is where the data subject is no longer identifiable and where it is not possible at any point in the future to reidentify the individual. Truly anonymized data are not considered as personal data. Therefore, anonymized data are not subject to laws and regulations on personal data protection.

Pseudonymization is intended to remove the association between a set of identifying data and the data principal. It aims at protecting personal data by hiding the identities of individuals in a dataset, e.g., by replacing one or more personal identifiers with so-called pseudonyms (and protecting the link between the pseudonyms and the initial identifiers). When applied correctly, pseudonymization hides the identity of an individual in the context of a specific dataset. It can also reduce the risk of the linkage of personal data across different data processing domains.

Data aggregation is another way to render or de-identify personal data. The aggregation of data is different from the collection of individual data, as it does not impact or expose individual consumer data.

The Techniques: Pseudonymization and anonymization methods and processes must be documented, ensuring that the specific methods being used are being implemented correctly and can be verified. If constraints need to be used during pseudonymization and anonymization for business requirements, the constraints must be minimized.

Definition
The definitions are listed in Table 21.3.

TABLE 21.3

Definitions of Data De-Identification Techniques

Term	Definition and Example	Whether It Is Still Personal Data after the Action
Anonymization	The process of rendering data into a form which does not identify individuals and where identification is not likely to take place. If at any point you can reidentify the individual, that data isn't anonymized. For data to be truly anonymized, the process must be irreversible. This book uses the broad term "anonymization" to cover various techniques that can be used to convert personal data into anonymized data.	No
Pseudonymization	The processing of personal data in such a manner that the personal data can no longer be attributed to a specific data subject without the use of additional information, provided that such additional information is kept separately and is subject to technical and organizational measures to ensure that the personal data are not attributed to an identified or identifiable natural person. To pseudonymize a data record involves taking information that can directly identify a person, such as a name or date of birth, and removing it or replacing it with artificial identifiers. Doing so enables the data to be processed or transferred without enabling the data subjects to be re-identified. It's useful in cases where the identities of the data subjects are neither required nor relevant because the data can still support other types of data analysis.	Yes
Aggregation	In general, data is displayed as totals, so no data relating to or identifying any individual is shown. However, if the sample size is too small, this may enable identification, in which case it's personal data and the privacy laws apply. For example, if you carry out an employee survey and create a report that only contains statistics such as 67% of employees were in favor of the Working from Home (WFH) policy, this in and of itself would not be personal data. However, if you continue to store (or process in any other way) the underlying data that contains the names of the employees or other identifiers of the employees, you will still be processing personal data.	Depends on the level of aggregation (EDPB opinion[53])
Re-identification	The process of analyzing data or combining it with other data with the result that individuals become identifiable. Sometimes termed "de-anonymization". This book uses the term "re-identification" to describe the process of turning anonymized data back into personal data through the use of data matching or similar techniques.	Yes

21.4.2.1 Anonymization

With regard to anonymization, if information that relates to an individual and that can identify a natural person is truly anonymized, it is no longer personal data. Data protection law does not apply to data rendered anonymous in such a way that the data subject is no longer identifiable. Fewer legal restrictions apply to anonymized data. While it's often difficult within an organization to fully anonymize the data, the anonymization of personal data is possible and can help service society's information needs in a privacy-friendly way.[54]

Table 21.4 lists some examples of the data anonymization techniques.

TABLE 21.4

Examples of the Data Anonymization Techniques

Technology	How It Works	Advantage	Disadvantage	Application Suggestion
Masking	Replaces some characters in the attribute value with fixed special characters, such as an asterisk (*). Dynamic masking: Dynamic masking rewrites data on the fly, typically using a proxy mechanism, to mask all or part of data delivered to a user. It is usually used to protect some sensitive data in applications, for example masking out all but the last digits of a credit card number when presenting it to a user.	Keeps some attribute information and the length of messages.	Has high risks; the information is easier to be identified for information holders; data cannot be restored, and much of the attribute information is lost.	Applies to anonymization of character strings, such as IMSIs and email addresses.
Truncation	Abandons the last several characters in the attribute value to ensure data fuzziness.	Keeps some attribute information.	Has high risks; the information is easier to be identified for information holders; data cannot be restored, and much of the attribute information is lost.	Applies to anonymization of character strings, such as IMSIs and MSISDNs.
Noise addition	Adds a random value to the original data.	Keeps the real original value unknown.	Distorts the original data; this method cannot be used alone, and identifiers must be deleted jointly. For data scattered within a range, a data subject can be easily identified.	Applies to digit fields that allow data distortion.
Date offset for rounding	Offsets and rounds the data, abandoning accuracy for security of the original data.	Ensure data density in time layout.	Has high risks; If a record is known, it is easy to deduct approximate values of other records.	Applies to anonymization of date fields.
Shuffling (or mixing)	Shuffles data randomly recorded in a field of a table. Complete shuffling or replacement must be ensured, with all data fields in all data sets are processed in this way. During shuffling, if data (such as phone numbers or credit card numbers) are unique and cannot be shuffled or replaced, other identifier protection measures (such as masking) must be used jointly.	Cannot restore data after random shuffling.	Cannot be used alone; identifiers have to be deleted jointly.	Applies to digit values that need to keep the sum and average values.

This following table lists some examples of using masking to anonymize some common personal data.

21.4.2.2   Pseudonymization

Pseudonymization is a way to protect data (by enhancing security). Pseudonymized data still fall in the scope of personal data. Therefore, pseudonymized data are subject to requirements for personal data processing.

Typically, there are three steps involved in a pseudonymization process.

TABLE 21.5
Examples of Data Anonymization Cases

Personal Data Type	Guide	Examples
Bank account	Display only first 6 digits and last 4 digits.	7800001234561234 → 780000******1234
Official identification number (such as the SSN, passport number, and driver license number)	Mask the birth date and last 4 digits in an identity number.	1234567890123456 → 123456***********
(Given and family) names	Display only the family name.	John Anderson → * Anderson Kevin M. Bouchard → ** Bouchard
Birth date	Display only the year.	1960–1–1 → 1960-*-*
Telephone number	Phone numbers are sensitive in countries. Only display the first three digits and last four digits.	12345678901 → 123****8901
Email address	Characters preceding the @ sign can be anonymized, and the domain names of mailboxes can be kept unchanged.	kevinsmith@xyz.com -> kev***@xyz.com
IP address	Mask last 8 bits of an IPv4 address and last 88 bits of an IPv6 address.	Mask last 8 bits of an IPv4 address: For example: 192.168.12.123 → 192.168.12.***
MAC address	Mask last four bits or use salt for hash.	01-22-33-44-7A-BC → 12-34-56-78-**-**

TABLE 21.6
Three Types of Pseudonymization Techniques

Type	Description
Deterministic pseudonymization	Always using the same pseudonym for the same data
Document randomized pseudonymization	Using the same pseudonym for the same data only within a consistent scope
Fully randomized pseudonymization	Always using a different pseudonym for the same data

Step 1: Remove names or other identifiers from a data set (by using techniques such as hashing or data masking or even something as simple as substituting numbers for names and other identifiers) so that the data can no longer be attributed to any individual,

Step 2: Keep the removed data separate from the pseudonymized data, and

Step 3: Ensure the removed data and the pseudonymized data is subject to technical and organizational measures (such as restricting access to the removed data to employees who have a need to know to perform their functions) to ensure that the pseudonymized data isn't attributed to that individual.

In general, there are three types of pseudonymization techniques as illustrated in Table 21.6.

Depending on the requirements in terms of protection, utility, scalability, etc., there are different approaches to pseudonymization that can provide equally good results, depending on the requirements in terms of protection, utility, scalability, etc. Some basic pseudonymization techniques are offset, permutation, enumeration, encryption, hash, and tokenization.

21.4.2.3 Aggregation

Business leaders should be engaged in the process of defining the activities and parameters around data aggregation. There may be different ethical considerations involved, even though the aggregated data may no longer contain PII or legally protected consumer information. Accordingly, senior management and the board should understand the organization's strategy and practices regarding data aggregation in the context of the agreed views on ethics, compliance, and the desired risk profile. Ultimately, the senior leadership team should determine the propriety of the data aggregation and usage practices the organization undertakes.

A few key questions you might need to ask before employing the data aggregation process:

- Is data aggregation the right thing to do?
- How effective is the organization's process for aggregating data in maintaining compliance with privacy laws and regulations?
- Is the personal data being scrubbed and anonymized appropriately?

22 Security of Personal Data Processing

This chapter is intended to help readers employ a holistic approach to mitigate data security risks by implementing reasonable technical and organizational measures.

This chapter covers the following topics:

- *Obligations for protecting personal data*
- *Appropriate TOMs and challenges*
- *A holistic approach to data security*

22.1 OBLIGATIONS FOR PROTECTING PERSONAL DATA

Organizations need to ensure personal data is securely protected to protect its confidentiality, integrity, and availability. Security measures should be evaluated regularly.

Many security and data protection laws and regulations set forth explicit requirements for protecting personal data in a reasonable and appropriate manner. For instance, Article 5(1)(f) of the GDPR states that personal data must be processed "in a manner that ensures appropriate security of the personal data, including protection against unauthorized or unlawful processing and against accidental loss, destruction, or damage, using appropriate technical or organizational measures."

Table 22.1 lists some of the exemplar regulations which impose data security obligations.

In general, organizations are required or expected to implement appropriate risk-based technical and organizational measures to ensure the ongoing confidentiality, integrity, and availability of personal data.

- **The controller and the processor shall provide**
  - ✓ Appropriate technical and organizational measures
- **To ensure**
  - ✓ A level of security appropriate to the risk
- **Taking into account**
  - ✓ The state of the art
  - ✓ Costs of implementation
  - ✓ The nature, scope, context, and purposes of processing
- **Including, as appropriate**
  - ✓ Pseudonymization
  - ✓ Encryption
  - ✓ Confidentiality, integrity, availability, and resilience of processing systems and services
  - ✓ Restore availability and access to personal data in a timely manner in the event of an incident
  - ✓ Regularly testing, assessing, and evaluating the effectiveness of the security measures.

DOI: 10.1201/9781003225089-26

TABLE 22.1

Examples of Data Security Obligations

Jurisdiction/ Regulation	Requirement
EU/GDPR	GDPR Article 32 requires that the data controller and processor should have the ability to restore the availability and access to personal data in a timely manner in the event of a physical or technical incident.
	GDPR Articles 33 and 34 and Recitals 86 to 88 stipulate that, the controller shall detect and document any personal data breaches, comprising the facts relating to the personal data breach, its effects, and the remedial action taken.
	As stipulated in GDPR Article 5(1)(f), Article 9, and Recital 39, personal data shall be processed in a manner that ensures appropriate security of the personal data, including protection against unauthorized or unlawful processing and against accidental loss, destruction, or damage, using appropriate technical or organizational measures.
US/FTC	FTC uses its Section 5 power (under the FTC Act) to brings actions against companies misrepresenting their information security practices (as a deceptive trade practice) or failing to provide "reasonable procedures" to protect personal information (as an unfair trade practice).
US/HIPAA and GLBA	There are federally imposed information security provisions in the healthcare and financial sectors based on HIPAA and GLBA, respectively.
US/Massachusetts 201 CMR 17(2010)	Detailed minimum standards and technical requirements are generally considered the most prescriptive in the nation.
	It establishes detailed minimum standards to "safeguard . . . personal information contained in both paper and electronic records." The law requires businesses holding "personal information," which is defined as a Massachusetts resident's name plus a sensitive data element, such as a Social Security number) to implement many a comprehensive data security program, including the following features:
	• A specific individual responsible for information security must be designated.
	• Organizations must anticipate risks to personal information and take appropriate steps to mitigate such risks.
	• Encryption of all transmitted records and files containing personal information that will travel across public networks, and encryption of all data containing personal information to be transmitted wirelessly.
	• Encryption of all personal information stored on laptops or other portable devices.
	• They must develop security program rules that include impose penalties for employees' violations of those rules.
	• The program must also prevent access to personal information by former employees, contractually obligate third-party service providers to maintain similar procedures, and restrict physical access to records containing personal information.
	• On an ongoing basis, business must monitor the effectiveness of the security program and review it at least once a year, as well as whenever business changes could impact security.
	• Finally, they must document responses to incidents.
US/California Assembly Bill 1950	California had probably one of the first data security laws that addressed in a more comprehensive manner the protection of personal information.
	It provided that organizations that held personal information of California residents had to apply reasonable security controls around that personal information.
	And they also, and this is an important concept that's growing too, they had to obligate any Third-Party processors or subcontracted agents dealing with that information, they had to contractually obligate them to have those same reasonable security protections in place.
Washington HB 1149	HB 1149 permits financial institutions to recover the costs associated with reissuance of credit and debit cards from large processors whose negligence in the handling of credit card data is the proximate cause of the breach.
	Processors can avoid this liability if they encrypt personal data earned PCI-compliant certification within one year of the breach.

Jurisdiction/ Regulation	Requirement
China/Provisions on the Protection of Children's Personal Information Online	Article 13 Network operators shall take measures such as encryption to store children's personal information to ensure information security.

22.2   APPROPRIATE TOMS AND CHALLENGES

Appropriate TOMs

 Questions and answers

Why should your organization implement appropriate security controls?

- Firstly, it is required by many laws and regulations (i.e., GDPR Art. 32). Violation of these laws and regulations could result in hefty fines.
- Secondly, it is a contractual requirement written in the controller to processor data processing agreement. Violation of contractual obligations might cause your organization business opportunities and potential reputation damage.
- Last but not the least, data subjects might launch collective actions against your organization for lack of proper security controls.

As required by the GDPR, for instance, principles relating to the processing of personal data (art. 5) and Security of processing (art. 32):

- Processed in a manner that ensures appropriate security of the personal data, including protection against unauthorized or unlawful processing and against accidental loss, destruction, or damage, using appropriate technical or organizational measures ("integrity and confidentiality").
- Considering the state of the art, the costs of implementation and the nature, scope, context, and purposes of processing as well as the risk of varying likelihood and severity for the rights and freedoms of natural persons, the controller and the processor shall implement appropriate technical and organizational measures to ensure a level of security appropriate to the risk, including inter alia as appropriate:
  - (a) the pseudonymization and encryption of personal data
  - (b) the ability to ensure the ongoing confidentiality, integrity, availability and resilience of processing systems and services
  - (c) the ability to restore the availability and access to personal data in a timely manner in the event of a physical or technical incident
  - (d) a process for regularly testing, assessing, and evaluating the effectiveness of technical and organizational measures for ensuring the security of the processing.
- In assessing the appropriate level of security account shall be taken in particular of the risks that are presented by processing, in particular from accidental or unlawful destruction, loss, alteration, unauthorized disclosure of, or access to personal data transmitted, stored, or otherwise processed.
- Adherence to an approved code of conduct as referred to in Article 40 or an approved certification mechanism as referred to in Article 42 may be used as an

element by which to demonstrate compliance with the requirements set out in paragraph 1 of this Article.

- The controller and processor shall take steps to ensure that any natural person acting under the authority of the controller or the processor who has access to personal data does not process them except on instructions from the controller unless he or she is required to do so by Union or Member State law.

Questions and answers

What level of security measures are considered appropriate?

There is no "one size fits all" solution to information security. It means that what's "appropriate" for you will depend on your own circumstances, the processing you're doing, and the risks it presents to your organization.

Before deciding what measures are appropriate, you need to assess your information risk. You should review the personal data you hold and the way you use it to assess how valuable, sensitive, or confidential it is—as well as the damage or distress that may be caused if the data was compromised.

From my perspective, the following factors, as illustrated in Figure 22.1, should be considered with respect to determining and implementing appropriate security technical and organizational measures within your organization.

Example

The US Department of Education established the Privacy Technical Assistance Center (PTAC) as a "one-stop" resource for education stakeholders to learn about data privacy, confidentiality, and security practices related to student-level longitudinal data systems and other uses of student data. The PTAC created a "Data Security Checklist"[106] to assist stakeholder organizations, such as state and local education agencies, with developing and maintaining a successful data security program. The main components of the checklist are listed in the Table 22.2.

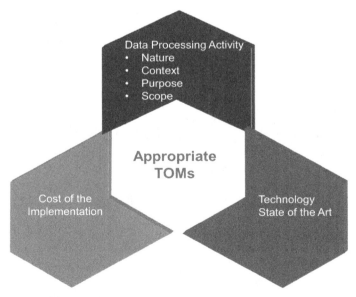

FIGURE 22.1   Key considerations of security TOMs.

TABLE 22.2
Main Components of the Security Checklist

#	Component	Description
1	Policy and governance	Develop a comprehensive data governance plan that outlines organizational policies and standards regarding data security and individual privacy protection.
2	Personnel security	Create an Acceptable Use Policy that outlines appropriate and inappropriate uses of the Internet, Intranet, and Extranet systems.
3	Physical security	Make computing resources physically unavailable to unauthorized users.
4	Network mapping	Network mapping provides a critical understanding of the enterprise (i.e., servers, routers) and its connections.
5	Inventory of assets	The inventory should include both authorized and unauthorized devices used in your computing environment.
6	Authentication	The ways in which someone may be authenticated fall into three categories: something you know, something you have, or something you are.
7	Provide a layered defense	Employ a "Defense in Depth" architecture that uses a wide spectrum of tools arrayed in a complementary fashion.
8	Secure configurations	It is a best practice not to put any hardware or software onto your network until it has been security tested and configured to optimize its security.
9	Access control	Securing data access includes requiring strong passwords and multiple levels of user authentication, setting limits on the length of data access (e.g., locking access after the session timeout), limiting logical access to sensitive data and resources, and limiting administrative privileges.
10	Firewalls and Intrusion Detection/ Prevention Systems (IDPS)	A firewall is a device designed to permit or deny network transmissions based upon a set of rules. Firewalls are frequently used to protect networks from unauthorized access while permitting legitimate communications to pass. An IDPS is a monitoring device that is designed to detect malicious activity on the network. Although some automatically take remediation action, most report suspicious activity to a central monitoring point for further analysis.
11	Automated vulnerability scanning	When new vulnerabilities (to hardware, operating systems, applications, and other network devices) are discovered, hackers immediately scan networks for these vulnerabilities.
12	Patch management	Patch management is the process of using a strategy and plan for the testing and rollout of software updates and patches on a regular basis.
13	Shut down unnecessary services	Each port, protocol, or service is a potential avenue for ingress into your enterprise. A best practice, which should be part of a secure configuration, should include shutting down all services and ports that are not required in your computing environment.
14	Mobile devices	When sensitive data are stored on servers or on mobile devices, such as laptops or smartphones, the data should be encrypted.
15	Emailing confidential data	Consider the sensitivity level of the data to be sent over the email. Emailing unprotected PII or sensitive data poses a high risk. It is recommended that organizations use alternative practices to protect transmissions of these data.
16	Incident handling	When an incident does occur, it is critical to have a process in place to both contain and fix the problem. Procedures for users, security personnel, and managers need to be established to define the appropriate roles and actions.
17	Audit and compliance monitoring	Audits are used to provide an independent assessment of your data protection capabilities and procedures.

Example

Open Web Application Security Project (OWASP) forbids the use of GET requests (URLs) for high-impact personal data and recommends the POST methods to process high-impact personal data.

Case Study

Spain AEPD v. HTTPS protocols
The Spain data protection agency AEPD policed HTTPS protocols on webpages.

HTTPS protocols are HTTP protocols with encryption. HTTPS uses Transport Layer Security to encrypt normal HTTP requests and responses, strengthening the security of HTTP websites.

In November 2020, the AEPD imposed a €1,000 fine on a company for not implementing the HTTPS protocol on its webpage (PS/00185/2020). Also, the AEPD issued a reprimand to a public authority for the same reason (H/T Gerard Espuga Torné).

In both cases, the DPA considered that the HTTP protocol in webpages does not constitute an adequate measure to protect the security of the personal data that the controller is processing (art. 32 GDPR).

Challenges for Organizations
There are some common obstacles to implementing appropriate security controls, InfoSec leaders must first understand:

- What data your organization needs to keep safe and how to enable business growth. Layer in the process of exchanging data and ensuring the secure transfer of this information while still making it accessible to the intended group of end-users, and the challenge becomes increasingly complex.
- Sensitive and high-risk data now lives in various repositories both in and out of the organization, in both on-prem and cloud environments. Security leaders need to understand where the data resides within the organization.
  - An expanding global economy brings with it an expectation of collaboration—not just internally, but between different organizations in different areas of the world. Data has become an asset, and unlike the devices to which it travels, data is not static or stationary, but dynamic and fluid in nature.
  - Throughout its lifecycle, data will live in a multitude of repositories and move through various sources. The extent of a business' data sources no longer lies within the confines of the office or primary workspace, a set of easily-controlled devices, or even a physical data center—organizations increasingly keep high volumes of sensitive, valuable data in the cloud.
- Security leaders need to be fully aware of the current compliance and regulatory obligations based on location and industry.
- Securing data is no longer as simple as implementing a singular set of controls. InfoSec leaders must also select a combination of technical and process controls that fit the business environment and reduce user friction.

Case Study

Equifax v. Adequate security controls
The Equifax data breach occurred between May and July 2017 at the American credit bureau Equifax. In September 2017, Equifax announced that an attack on its servers had

provided access to the personal information of personal data of 147.9 million Americans along with 15.2 million British citizens and about 19,000 Canadian citizens were compromised in the breach. Numerous lawsuits were filed against Equifax in the days after the disclosure of the breach.

In September 2017, the director of the Consumer Financial Protection Bureau (CFPB), authorized an investigation into the data breach on behalf of affected consumers. On July 22, 2019, Equifax agreed to a settlement with the Federal Trade Commission (FTC), CFPB, 48 US states, Washington, DC, and Puerto Rico to alleviate damages to affected individuals and make organizational changes to avoid similar breaches in the future. The total cost of the settlement included $300 million to a fund for victim compensation, $175 million to the states and territories in the agreement, and $100 million to the CFPB in fines.[45] In July 2019, the FTC published information on how affected individuals could file a claim against the victim compensation fund using the website EquifaxBreachSettlement.com.[55]

The Office of the Privacy Commissioner (OPC) of Canada also launched an investigation to determine if Equifax's information safeguards and accountability methods were sufficient under PIPEDA and whether they had obtained adequate consent for the transfer of personal information from Equifax Canada to Equifax Inc. in the United States. The OPC ultimately concluded that Equifax had failed to comply with the requirements of PIPEDA in each of these areas[56]:

- Inadequate vulnerability management—to prevent attacks through known vulnerabilities
- Inadequate network segregation—to reduce the scope of access and harm in the case of a breach
- Inadequate implementation of basic information security practices—to be able to appropriately manage the use of personal information and identify potential unauthorized use
- Inadequate breach response measures—Equifax Canada not being informed of the breach until just hours before the public announcement
- Inadequate notification to data subjects
- Inadequate data retention—Equifax held on to personal information it no longer needed for years past the five-year period mandated by its own retention policy
- Inadequate oversight
  - Lack of clarity about the scope of the information being handled by Equifax Inc.
  - Lack of clarity about roles and responsibilities
  - Lack of adequate monitoring

22.3   A HOLISTIC APPROACH FOR DATA SECURITY

A robust data security strategy must protect data through the entire data lifecycle. Data security efforts must be business-focused, with multi-layered defense, while extending to all data sources.

Secure your high-risk data also takes a multi-faceted approach to the problem that incorporates foundational technical elements, compliance considerations, and supporting processes and policies, including assessing what technical controls currently exist within the organization and considering additional controls, reviewing compliance obligations and information security frameworks (NIST, CIS) for guidance, and developing a set of data security initiatives that involve both technical and supporting procedural controls.

Organizations shall implement appropriate technical and organizational measures using a risk-based approach to ensure the confidentiality, integrity, availability, and resilience of personal data based on the data classification scheme. The ultimate security framework depends on each organization's specific business context.

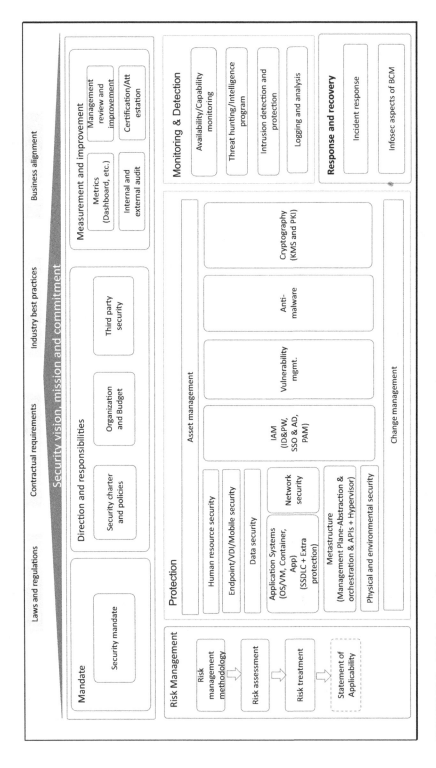

FIGURE 22.2 Unified security framework.

I created a security framework that uses a best-of-breed approach to leverage and aligns with most major security standards, including:

- ISO 27001/27002
- COBIT
- Center for Internet Security (CIS) Critical Controls
- NIST Cybersecurity Framework
- NIST SP 800–53
- NIST SP 800–171
- Factor Analysis of Information Risk (FAIRTM)

The following diagram illustrates typical security measures as food for thought an organization might need to consider.

A holistic security framework can help your organization to:

- Reduce complexity within the control environment by using a single framework to align multiple compliance regimes.
- Reduce costs and efforts related to managing IT audits through planning and preparation.
- Improve information security practices through self-assessments.
- Provide senior management with a structured framework for making business decisions on allocating costs and efforts related to cybersecurity and data protection compliance obligations.
- Reduce compliance risk.
- Enable better visibility into compliance status.

Table 22.3 provides a checklist to help an organization implement and operationalize its security program based on the aforementioned framework.

 Case Study

UK ICO v. British Airways, 2020[57]
The UK ICO fined British Airways (BA) £20M for failing to protect customers' personal data.

The attacker was believed to have potentially accessed the personal data of approximately 429,612 customers and staff. This included names, addresses, payment card numbers, and CVV numbers of 244,000 BA customers. Other details thought to have been accessed include the combined card and CVV numbers of 77,000 customers and card numbers only for 108,000 customers. Usernames and passwords of BA employee and administrator accounts as well as usernames and PINs of up to 612 BA Executive Club accounts were also potentially accessed.

An ICO investigation found the airline was processing a significant amount of personal data without adequate security measures in place. There were numerous measures BA could have used to mitigate or prevent the risk of an attacker being able to access the BA network. These include:

- Limiting access to applications, data, and tools to only personnel that are required to fulfill a user's role.
- Undertaking rigorous testing, in the form of simulating a cyber-attack, on the business' systems.
- Protecting employee and third-party accounts with multi-factor authentication.

TABLE 22.3

Security Controls Checklist

Domain	Control Group	Control Objective	Control Set
Mandate	Security mandate	Legal requirements	Checkpoint: Compliance with legal requirements. To avoid breaches of legal, statutory, regulatory, or obligations related to information security and of any security requirements.
			Checkpoint: Privacy and protection of personally identifiable information.
			Checkpoint: Regulation of cryptographic controls.
			Checkpoint: Intellectual property rights.
			Checkpoint: Protection of records.
		Contractual requirements	Checkpoint: Identification of applicable contractual requirements.
Direction and responsibilities	Security charter and policies	Scope of the ISMS	Checkpoint: The scope of ISMS is formally defined.
		Policies for information security	Checkpoint: A set of policies for information security shall be defined, approved by management, published, and communicated to employees and relevant external parties.
			Checkpoint: The policies for information security shall be reviewed at planned intervals or if significant changes occur to ensure their continuing suitability, adequacy, and effectiveness.
	Organization of information security	Organization of information security	Checkpoint: Information security roles and responsibilities. All information security responsibilities shall be defined and allocated.
			Checkpoint: Segregation of duties. Conflicting duties and areas of responsibility shall be segregated to reduce opportunities for unauthorized or unintentional modification or misuse of the organization's assets.
			Checkpoint: Contact authorities. Appropriate contacts with relevant authorities shall be maintained.
			Checkpoint: Contact special interest groups. Appropriate contacts with special interest groups or other specialist security forums and professional associations shall be maintained.
			Checkpoint: Information security in project management. Information security shall be addressed in project management, regardless of the type of the project.
	Third-party security	Supplier security policy	Checkpoint: Information security policy for supplier relationships.
		Pre-contract	Checkpoint: Due diligence
		Contract	Checkpoint: Addressing security within supplier agreements.
		During service	Checkpoint: Monitoring and review of supplier services. Organizations shall regularly monitor, review, and audit supplier service delivery.
			Checkpoint: Managing changes to supplier services.
		After-contract	Checkpoint: Transition out, data deletion and access de-provisioning

Risk Management	Risk management	Build and execute risk management process	Checkpoint: Risk management methodology
			Checkpoint: Assess the information security risks
			Checkpoint: The organization shall define and apply an information security risk treatment process
			Checkpoint: Re-assessment of security risks
			Checkpoint: Statement of Applicability
Protection	Asset management	Inventory and ownership of assets	Checkpoint: Assets associated with information and information processing facilities shall be identified and an inventory of these assets shall be drawn up and maintained.
			Checkpoint: Ownership of assets. Assets maintained in the inventory shall be owned.
		Acceptable use of assets	Checkpoint: set up acceptable rules of use of assets such as using the Internet, using for work, restrictions on software installation, etc.
		Media handling	Checkpoint: Management of removable media. Procedures shall be implemented for the management of removable media in accordance with the classification scheme adopted by the organization.
			Checkpoint: Secure disposal or reuse of equipment. All items of equipment containing storage media shall be verified to ensure that any sensitive data and licensed software have been removed or securely overwritten prior to disposal or re-use.
	Physical and environmental security	Security areas	Checkpoint: Physical security perimeter. Security perimeters shall be defined and used to protect areas that contain either sensitive or critical information and information processing facilities.
			Checkpoint: Physical entry controls. Secure areas shall be protected by appropriate entry controls to ensure that only authorized personnel are allowed access.
			Checkpoint: Securing offices, rooms, and facilities. Physical security for offices, rooms and facilities shall be designed and applied.
			Checkpoint: Protecting against external and environmental threats. Physical protection against natural disasters, malicious attacks, or accidents shall be designed and applied.
			Checkpoint: Working in secure areas. Procedures for working in secure areas shall be designed and applied.
			Checkpoint: Delivery and loading areas. Access points such as delivery and loading areas and other points where unauthorized persons could enter the premises shall be controlled and, if possible, isolated from information processing facilities to avoid unauthorized access.
			Checkpoint: Physical surveillance. Video cameras
			Checkpoint: Intruder detection and prevention/Alarm

(Continued)

TABLE 22.3　(Continued)

Domain	Control Group	Control Objective	Control Set
		Equipment and environmental security	Checkpoint: Removal of assets. Equipment, information, or software shall not be taken off-site without prior authorization. Media containing information shall be protected against unauthorized access, misuse, or corruption during transportation.
			Checkpoint: Security of equipment and assets off-premises.
			Checkpoint: Cabling security and prevention from electromagnetic radiation attack.
			Checkpoint: Equipment siting and protection.
			Checkpoint: Supporting utilities.
			Checkpoint: Equipment maintenance.
		Handling Visitors	Checkpoint: Develop procedures to previsioning access to visitors and to easily distinguish between onsite personnel and visitors, especially in areas where critical data is accessible and make sure all visitors are handled in an appropriate way.
	Network security	Network security policy	Checkpoint: Network security policy
		Network segmentation	Checkpoint: Segregation in networks/FW: Groups of information services, users and information systems shall be segregated on networks to different trust levels/tiered zones.
		Internal network access control (SDN)	Checkpoint: NAC-Network access control
		Protect wireless network and connections	Checkpoint: Segment and protection of wireless networks and connections.
		Teleworking Policy	Checkpoint: A policy and supporting security measures shall be implemented to protect information accessed, processed, or stored at teleworking sites.
		Internet content control	Checkpoint: Internet content control
		Information transfer	Checkpoint: Information transfer policies and procedures. Formal transfer policies, procedures and controls shall be in place to protect the transfer of information using all types of communication facilities.
Host/application (SDL + Extra protection)		Security requirements	Checkpoint: Information security requirements analysis and specification
		Design	Checkpoint: Threat modeling
			Checkpoint: Security technical architecture
		Development	Checkpoint: Separation of development, testing, and operational environments.
			Checkpoint: Secure development environment Control.
			Checkpoint: Access control to program source code.
			Checkpoint: Secure system engineering principles
			Checkpoint: Security test integrated with unit testing, and functional tests

Test		Checkpoint: SAST
		Checkpoint: DAST
		Checkpoint: General vulnerability scan
		Checkpoint: Pen Test
	Release	Checkpoint: Protection of test data. Test data shall be selected carefully, protected, and controlled.
		Checkpoint: Operational environment security such as secure configurations, etc.
		Checkpoint: Final security review
	Outsourced development	Checkpoint: Outsourced development. The organization shall supervise and monitor the activity of outsourced system development.
	Extra application protection	Checkpoint: Web Security
		Checkpoint: Email Security
		Checkpoint: DNS Security
Data security	Information classification and handling	Checkpoint: Classification of information. Information shall be classified in terms of legal requirements, value, criticality and sensitivity to unauthorized disclosure or modification.
		Checkpoint: Labeling of information. An appropriate set of procedures for information labeling shall be developed and implemented in accordance with the information classification scheme adopted by the organization.
		Checkpoint: Handling of assets. Procedures for handling assets shall be developed and implemented in accordance with the information classification scheme adopted by the organization.
	Apply encryption to protect data	Checkpoint: Protect data as rest
		Checkpoint: Protect data in motion
		Checkpoint: Protect data in use
	Comprehensive Data Loss Prevention	Checkpoint: Should cover data life cycle including creation, use, store, disclosure, and disposal.
	Privacy and protection of personally identifiable information	Checkpoint: Anonymization
		Checkpoint: Pseudonymization
		Checkpoint: Information retention and disposal
		Checkpoint: Build an appropriate eDiscovery process to handle eDiscovery requests to meet the legal requirements.

(Continued)

TABLE 22.3 (Continued)

Domain	Control Group	Control Objective	Control Set
	Endpoint/VDI/Mobile security	Endpoint/VDI/Mobile policy	Checkpoint: A policy and supporting security measures shall be adopted to manage the risks introduced by using mobile devices.
		Endpoint threat protection	Checkpoint: Technical side. Should consider the following basic functionality for the endpoint protection tools:
		VDI security	Checkpoint: Physical Side
			Checkpoint: VDI security protections
		Mobile device management	Checkpoint: MDM
	Human resource security	Prior to employment (clean background)	Checkpoint: Screening. Background verification checks on all candidates for employment shall be carried out in accordance with relevant laws, regulations and ethics and shall be proportional to the business requirements, the classification of the information to be accessed and the perceived risks.
			Checkpoint: Terms and conditions of employment. The contractual agreements with employees and contractors shall state their and the organization's responsibilities for information security.
		During employment (clean behaviors)	Checkpoint: Management responsibilities. Management shall require all employees and contractors to apply information security in accordance with the established policies and procedures of the organization.
			Checkpoint: Information security awareness, education, and training. All employees of the organization and, where relevant, contractors shall receive appropriate awareness education and training and regular updates in organizational policies and procedures, as relevant for their job function.
			Checkpoint: Disciplinary process. There shall be a formal and communicated disciplinary process in place to act against employees who have committed an information security breach.
		Termination and change of employment (clean assets and permission)	Checkpoint: Termination or change of employment responsibilities.
	IAM (ID&PW, SSO & AD, PAM)	Access control policy	Checkpoint: An access control policy shall be established, documented, and reviewed based on business and information security requirements.
			Checkpoint: User registration and de-registration. Formal user registration and de-registration process shall be implemented to enable the assignment of access rights.
		User, Identity, and entitlement management	Checkpoint: User access provisioning. A formal user access provisioning process shall be implemented to assign or revoke access rights for all user types to all systems and services.
			Checkpoint: Review of user access rights. Asset owners shall review users' access rights at regular intervals.
			Checkpoint: Removal or adjustment of access rights. The access rights of all employees and external party users to information and information processing facilities shall be removed upon termination of their employment, contract, or agreement, or adjusted upon change.

Authentication and Credentials	Checkpoint: Management of secret authentication information of users. The allocation of secret authentication information shall be controlled through a formal management process.
	Checkpoint: Secure log-on procedures. Where required by the access control policy, access to systems and applications shall be controlled by a secure log-on procedure.
	Checkpoint: Password management system. Password management systems shall be interactive and shall ensure quality passwords.
	Checkpoint: Use MFA as needed.
Access Management	Checkpoint: Information access restriction. Access to information and application system functions shall be restricted in accordance with the access control policy.
Privileged access management	Checkpoint: Management of privileged access rights. The allocation and use of privileged access rights shall be restricted and controlled.
	Checkpoint: Use of privileged utility programs. The use of utility programs that might be capable of overriding system and application controls shall be restricted and tightly controlled.
User Responsibilities	Checkpoint: Use of secret authentication information. Users shall be required to follow the organization's practices in the use of secret authentication information.
	Checkpoint: Unattended user equipment. Users shall ensure that unattended equipment has appropriate protection.
	Checkpoint: Clear desk and clear screen policy. A clear desk policy for papers and removable storage media and a clear screen policy for information processing facilities shall be adopted.
Technical vulnerability management	Checkpoint: Management of technical vulnerabilities. Information about technical vulnerabilities of information systems being used shall be obtained in a timely fashion, the organization's exposure to such vulnerabilities evaluated and appropriate measures taken to address the associated risk.
Cryptographic controls	Checkpoint: Policy on the use of cryptographic controls. A policy on the use of cryptographic controls for the protection of information shall be developed and implemented.
Cryptography (KMS, CA)	Checkpoint: Key management. A policy on the use, protection and lifetime of cryptographic keys shall be developed and implemented throughout the whole lifecycle.
Protection from malware	Checkpoint: Detection, prevention, and recovery controls to protect against malware shall be implemented, combined with appropriate user awareness.
Anti-malware	

(Continued)

TABLE 22.3 (Continued)

Domain	Control Group	Control Objective	Control Set
Monitoring & Detection	Availability/Capability monitoring	Availability/Capability monitoring	Checkpoint: The use of resources shall be monitored, tuned and projections made of future capacity requirements to ensure the required system performance.
	Intrusion detection and protection	Intrusion detection and protection	Checkpoint: Intrusion detection and protection. Checkpoint: Anti-DDOS solution. Checkpoint: File integrity solution
	Logging and analysis	Clock synchronization Control	Checkpoint: The clocks of all relevant information processing systems within an organization or security domain shall be synchronized to a single reference time source.
		Event logging	Checkpoint: Event logs recording user activities, exceptions, faults, and information security events shall be produced, kept, and regularly reviewed.
		Event analysis	Checkpoint: event analysis.
		Protection of log information	Checkpoint: Logging facilities and log information shall be protected against tampering and unauthorized access.
Response and recovery	Incident response	Incident management procedure	Checkpoint: Create a formal security incident handling process.
	Infosec aspects of BCM	Information security continuity	Checkpoint: Planning information security continuity. The organization shall determine its requirements for information security and the continuity of information security management in adverse situations (e.g., during a crisis or disaster). Checkpoint: Implementing information security continuity. The organization shall establish, document, implement and maintain processes, procedures, and controls to ensure the required level of continuity for information security during an adverse situation. Checkpoint: Verify, review, and evaluate information security continuity. The organization shall verify the established and implemented information security continuity controls at regular intervals to ensure that they are valid and effective during adverse situations.
		Backup plan	Checkpoint: Information backup. Backup copies of information, software and system images shall be taken and tested regularly in accordance with an agreed backup policy.
		Redundancies	Checkpoint: Network Hierarchy and redundancy. Branches and network devices associated with IP Range Checkpoint: Host and application redundancy

Measurement and improvement	Metrics (Dashboard, etc.)	Monitoring and measurement results	Checkpoint: metrics
	Internal and external audit	Internal audit program	Checkpoint: Integrate security audit into internal audit program.
		External audit program	Checkpoint: Integrate security audit into external audit program.
	Certification/ Attestation	Certification/Attestation	Checkpoint: Manage certification and attestation activities.
	Management review and improvement	Management review and improvement	Checkpoint: Management review process
			Checkpoint: improvement process

Case Study

UK ICO v. Marriott International, 2020[58]

The UK ICO fined Marriott International 18.4 million GBP for violations of the EU GDPR related to its 2018 data breach. The ICO's investigation found that Marriott did not implement proper technical and organizational measures to protect personal data processed in their systems. Marriott estimated that 339 million guest records worldwide were affected following a cyber-attack in 2014 on Starwood Hotels and Resorts Worldwide Inc.

In 2014, an unknown attacker installed a piece of code known as a "web shell" onto a device in the Starwood system giving them the ability to access and edit the contents of this device remotely. This access was exploited in order to install malware, enabling the attacker to have remote access to the system as a privileged user. As a result, the attacker would have had unrestricted access to the relevant device, and other devices on the network to which that account would have had access.

The personal data involved differed between individuals but may have included names, email addresses, phone numbers, unencrypted passport numbers, arrival/departure information, guests' VIP status, and loyalty program membership number.

Case Study

Singapore PDPC v. Flight Raja Travels, 2018[59]

The Personal Data Protection Commission ('PDPC') issued, on June 11, 2018, its decision against Flight Raja Travels Singapore Pte. Ltd., for breach of the protection obligation under Section 24 of the Personal Data Protection Act 2012 (PDPA), which requires organizations to establish reasonable security arrangements to protect personal data from unauthorized disclosure ("the Decision"). The Decision outlines that a complainant, while using the booking system of Flight Raja Travels, was able to access passport numbers, booking ID, flight details, and booking dates of other users. Until December 2016 the booking system was accessed by users through Flight Raja Travels' login browser via its website, it then introduced a mobile application for users to access the booking system. The PDPC found that Flight Raja Travels had failed to test the effects of access through the mobile application with the existing access through the website, which resulted in the disclosure of users' personal information.

The PDPC ordered Flight Raja Travels to assess its mobile application, discover and remedy any risk to personal data from the changes made to introduce the new mobile application function, create a report of the assessment, as well as action taken in response. In addition, Flight Raja Travels was required to put in place procedures and processes to manage the risks to the personal data in its possession or control when making changes to its applications by implementing testing procedures and documenting the tests conducted.

Part 5

High-Risk Business Scenarios

This Part Covers the Following Topics:

- PbD in Marketing Practices
- Workforce Data Protection
- Protection of Children's Data
- PbD For AI Solutions

DOI: 10.1201/9781003225089-27

23 PbD in Marketing Practices

This chapter is intended to help readers understand how digital marketing works, the privacy implications associated with marketing activities as well as how to build privacy by design into the marketing processes.

This chapter covers the following topics:

- *Main marketing channels*
- *Consumer expectations and privacy implications*
- *Legal obligations and enforcement status*
- *Marketing technology and initiatives*
- *Privacy-enabled marketing practices*
- *Online marketing and cookies*
- *Email marketing*
- *Telemarketing*

23.1 MAIN MARKETING CHANNELS

Online marketing has many names. You may have heard it called online advertising, digital marketing, web advertising, and so on. In short, it's a form of marketing that uses the Internet to spread a message about an organization's brand, services, and products. Methods include email, social media, display advertising, and more. Advertisers want to show adverts to individuals who are likely to buy their product, and individuals want to see adverts that are relevant to them. Behind it stands a complex web of data processing involving the profiling, tracking, auctioning, and sharing of personal data.

Table 23.1 describes some of the categories.

 Case Study

French CNIL v. Vectaury, 2018

In October 2018, the French CNIL warned Vectaury on notice to cease the processing of personal data because it had not gained valid consent to the data processing activities and had not been transparent about using real-time bidding as part of its profiling strategy. Vectaury claimed it had implemented the IAB Consent Framework, but CNIL said that the consent was not informed, not specific, and not given by affirmative action.

23.2 CONSUMER EXPECTATIONS AND PRIVACY IMPLICATIONS

People are caring about their privacy

People's privacy online is more important than ever. In the minds of consumers, data protection expectations for marketing are high. Consumers are more comfortable sharing their data when they understand what's in it for them. When people trust the ethics of a company, and have positive and enduring relationships, they are more comfortable sharing data. There is a social pressure; a concern that people will be judged as naive if they do not show concern, even when they cannot pinpoint why or what it is they should be worried about. This can lead to feelings of guilt or shame that they are not doing more to change this.

DOI: 10.1201/9781003225089-28

TABLE 23.1

Main Marketing Channels

Category	Description
Display Advertising	Display advertising is the use of banner ads in graphical or text form that appear in specifically designated areas of a website or social media platform.
Online Behavioral Advertising (OBA)	Online behavioral advertising involves tracking consumers' online activities, across sites and over time in order to deliver advertisements targeted to their inferred interests. Behavioral advertisers often use sophisticated algorithms to analyze the collected data, build detailed personal profiles of users, and assign them to various interest categories.
Real-Time Bidding (RTB)	RTB is the process by which the digital ads we see every day are curated. For each ad, an auction takes place milliseconds before it is shown in an app or browser.
Affiliate Marketing	In affiliate marketing, you market other organizations' products or services in return for a percentage of the price paid by the customer. You aren't sharing your customers' or prospects' data with the Third-Party organization, but rather are emailing your customers and prospects about the products and services of a Third Party and including a link to their website or landing page for the particular promotional offer.
Telemarketing— Automated calling	An automated calling system automatically calls a telephone number and then plays a prerecorded message when the call is answered. This doesn't include the automated calling of telephone numbers to facilitate a live call once the individual answers the telephone.
Offline Marketing	Offline marketing, sometimes referred to as traditional marketing, is any marketing that doesn't occur on the Internet. Types include face-to-face prospecting and networking, events, exhibitions, referrals, postal marketing, non-automated calls, etc.

The Data Privacy Study[60] shows that almost all the participating internet users aged 20–65 (95%) were overall unwilling to provide certain personal information to an online company.

There is also a contradiction supported by the "Data Privacy Study": while almost all the participating internet users aged 20–65 (95%) were overall unwilling to provide certain personal information to an online company, five in seven (71%) had done so in practice, when it was necessary to complete a purchase or receive a service.[61]

People also take actions to protection their online privacy as shown in Ipsos's report as follows.[62]

- 74% of participants agreed "I control who sees my posts (photos/videos) when using social networks"
- 73% of participants agreed "I delete cookies/my browsing history"
- 70% of participants agreed "I switch off geolocation when I don't use it"
- 58% of participants agreed "I use search engines to search for information about me that is available online"

As discussed in UK Information Commissioner's Opinion: Data protection and privacy expectations for online advertising proposals[107], Table 23.2 lists some of the key issues found by the UK ICO with respect to marketing privacy practices.

Privacy Implications and Risks

On the one hand, security and privacy compliance will be a key pre-requisite consideration in any marketing technology deployment or re-deployment. IT should exercise due diligence by participating and ensuring proper security and compliance adherence to support design requirements versus being brought in after decisions have already been made. Ensure compliance processes are adhered to as new go-to-market strategies are developed. Besides privacy laws impacting processes, client trust must be maintained by ensuring their data is kept secure and private. Compliance processes

TABLE 23.2

Key Issues Regarding Marketing Privacy Practices

Domain	Issues
Transparency and choice	Data processing activities are complex, and organizations do not provide sufficient clarity about the processing. • For instance, Fingerprinting, which combines very specific information about someone's browser or device (i.e., screen resolution settings) is often used to covertly identify and track individual users without providing them a means to opt out, and is done without first obtaining advanced permission. Collection of invalid consent due to design choices and lack of clear and comprehensive information about the purpose of use of cookies and similar technologies. The use of non-essential cookies is often justified by the "legitimate interests" of the organization.
Lawful basis	Illegal processing of personal data through the use of legitimate interest cookies and similar techniques. Organizations cannot show how to properly perform a legitimate interest balancing test and take appropriate safeguards.
Data collection—data minimization	There is no assessment of what data is needed to achieve the goal, as all data is otherwise perceived to be useful.
Profiling	Abusive use of profiling and data that is imbalanced, intrusive, and unfair in relation to its intended purposes.
Third-party risks	Multiple parties are involved in the supply chain. There is a lack of clarity about roles and responsibilities. In addition, the complex data supply chains make it unclear who processes personal data and how that process meets data protection requirements.
Information Security	Data subjects have no confidence about the security of their personal data once it is collected, stored, and processed.
Data retention	Inconsistent retention periods among various departments mean that different retention periods may apply. The rationale for retention periods that do exist is unclear.

should be carefully planned in collaboration with IT, legal, and marketing departments. Damage to a client's brand image damages the Marketing & Advertising agency's brand as well.

On the other hand, getting privacy right can be the differentiator between a good and a bad experience for a consumer and is therefore vital for the future of any business. For marketers, while there are great rewards to being privacy-first, the consequences of getting it wrong are correspondingly troubling. Brands who don't give privacy the attention it deserves risk losing the trust and respect of their customers.

Table 23.3 illustrates some of the main privacy risks to individuals.[63]

People need reassurance through honesty and clarity

People have a sense of what ethical marketing should involve, but they don't always see these expectations reflected by brands. This leads to disengagement and skepticism, which brands can counter by applying some basic principles of honesty and clarity.

Given people's general lack of awareness and understanding, the mechanisms that companies use to communicate about data privacy need to be clear and reassuring. There is a low-level feeling that brands could be tricking people into sharing their data. This is especially the case when people feel they are forced to submit data to access a company's offer.[64] People claim to prefer to buy from companies that are honest about what personal data they collect and why. This is especially true of people who are skeptical overall—who are more likely to purchase from brands they perceive to be honest.[62]

Privacy also presents a set of rapidly changing challenges to CMOs. Changing people's attitudes and perceptions towards personalization can make a difference. Brands should focus on building

TABLE 23.3
Main Privacy Risks to Individuals

Privacy Risks to Individuals	Description
Lack of visibility and control	Individuals may not be able to exercise their rights because they are unaware that the practices the organization is employing to process their personal data.
Targeting	Extensive data processing can profile an individual's behavior, preferences, and attitudes, and can make inferences in ways that the individual cannot reasonably expect.
Data leakage	The amount, confidentiality, scope, and number of organizations involved in processing personal data increase the risk of personal data breaches.
Data overuse or misuse	When data collected for one purpose is reused or misused for another purpose that is incompatible with the original purpose of collection (for example, by another entity to which the data was disclosed).

trust and consider how they communicate around privacy. Where participants have more positive attitudes towards data sharing, privacy, and personalization, they find ads more relevant.

- An ageing approach to privacy and the frequency with which people encounter bad marketing practices, has led to a general skepticism toward brands' data-handling behaviors. This skepticism, coupled with rapid technological changes, measurement challenges, and a constantly evolving regulatory environment, has marketers struggling to navigate a landscape that previously served them very well.
- A key tenet of marketing is that the better you understand your customers, the better you can market to them. This applies as much to their purchasing habits as it does their privacy needs. To gain a solid foothold in an era of shifting sands, marketers need to uncover more about people's attitudes to privacy so they can proactively exceed expectations.
- Marketing & Advertising agencies need to consider the fact that changing end-consumer behaviors will impact their client's business one way or another.
- When Internet users see personalized marketing, they can often view it as mysterious, confusing, or even unethical. For those people to see value in marketing, they need to feel that their data has been used wisely and ethically, and that brands are using it to provide them with individual benefit.

The Information Commissioner's Office (ICO) and CMA joint statement of May 2021 outlined that the interest of consumers is best served when the objectives of both competition and data protection are achieved.[65]

23.3   LEGAL OBLIGATIONS AND ENFORCEMENT STATUS

The rapid emergence and expansion of online services that now function on a global scale have posed substantial new challenges to governments and regulatory authorities around the world. As a result, governments and regulatory authorities are having to think hard about the rules and laws that apply to the digital economy and its business models, including how they should be enforced, and where interventions can be made most effectively.

Table 23.4 lists some of the existing privacy and data protection regulations related to marketing operations.

TABLE 23.4
Examples of Data Protection Regulations Related to Marketing Operations

Region/Regulation	Requirement
EU-GDPR	GDPR Right to object (21) Where personal data are processed for direct marketing purposes, the data subject shall have the right to object at any time to processing of personal data concerning him or her for such marketing, which includes profiling to the extent that it is related to such direct marketing (21.2). Where the data subject objects to the processing for direct marketing purposes, the personal data shall no longer be processed for such purposes (21.3). According to EU DIRECTIVE 2002/58/EC (the ePrivacy Directive), using cookies for legitimate purposes must notify users of the purposes of the processing and their rights to refuse such processing. Cookies can be exempted from the requirement if the cookie is used for communication transmission, or if the cookie is strictly necessary to provide the service explicitly requested by the subscriber or user.
UK	The Data Protection Act 2018. This sets out three separate data protection regimes: general processing (Part 2—the UK GDPR), law enforcement processing (Part 3), and intelligence services processing (Part 4). The UK GDPR sits alongside the DPA 2018. It is a UK law that came into effect on January 1st, 2021 and is based on the EU GDPR with some changes to make it work more effectively in the UK context. The Privacy and Electronic Communications Regulations 2003 (as amended) (PECR) provides more specific rules than the UK GDPR in a number of areas such as cookie use.
US-Federal	The federal CAN-SPAM Act of 2003 (*Controlling the Assault of Non-Solicited Pornography and Marketing Act of 2003*) generally regulates commercial email messages. A commercial email message must contain, among other things, a clear and conspicuous identification that the message is an advertisement, an opt-out notice and method for opting out, and a valid physical postal address of the sender. The law also prohibits certain deceptive acts and practices involving emails. FTC Telemarketing Sales Rule (TSR)—Do Not Call Provisions • The Federal Trade Commission (FTC) first issued its TSR in 1995, implementing the Telemarketing and Consumer Fraud and Abuse Prevention Act. It has since amended the TSR in 2003, 2008, and 2010. • The Telemarketing Sales Rule requires telemarketers to make specific disclosures of material information; prohibits misrepresentations; sets limits on the times telemarketers may call consumers; prohibits calls to a consumer who has asked not to be called again; and sets payment restrictions for the sale of certain goods and services. • The do not call provisions of the TSR cover any plan, program, or campaign to sell goods or services through **interstate phone calls**. • This includes calls by telemarketers who solicit consumers, often on behalf of third-party sellers. It also includes sellers who provide, offers to provide, or arrange to provide goods or services to consumers in return for some type of payment as part of a telemarketing transaction. National Do Not Call Registry—Covers both interstate and intrastate telemarketing calls. The Telephone Consumer Protection Act TCPA 1991 was updated in 2012 to address robocalls.
US-State	The California Consumer Privacy Act (CCPA) treats cookies as personal information and requires that data collection practices are communicated to the consumer but does not require a cookie banner. However, users must have the option to opt out. The California Privacy Rights Act (CPRA) expands the provisions in CCPA to include third-party data collection via advertising cookies. Users must be able to opt out. The Colorado Privacy Act (CPA) and the Virginia Consumer Data Protection Act (VDCPA) allow consumers a right to opt out of profiling "in furtherance of decisions that produce legal or similarly significant effects concerning the consumer." Both require data protection assessments for targeted advertising, the sale of personal information, and profiling.
Canada-CASL	National Do Not Call Registry

(Continued)

TABLE 23.4   (Continued)

Region/Regulation	Requirement
China	Personal Information Protection Law

Under the Personal Information Protection Law ("PIPL", Effective November 1, 2021), personal information refers to various kinds of information related to identified or identifiable natural persons recorded in electronic or other forms.

If a cookie is useful for the purpose of analysis, performance improvement, or social as well as advertising purposes, then express, clear, and withdrawable consent must be obtained.

Algorithm Regulation

The Provisions on the Management of Algorithmic Recommendation on Internet Information Services

- Effective on March 1, 2022
- apply to the use of algorithmic recommendation technology to provide internet information services within PRC

Algorithmic recommendation technology

- Generation and synthesis, e.g., virtual reality, automated content generation, AI-written news
- Personalized recommendation, e.g., content recommendation (i.e., short-video platform), e-commerce recommendation (i.e., online shopping)
- Sequence refinement, RTB, search results ranking
- Search filter, e.g., Baidu
- Dispatching-and decision making, e.g., delivery service, transporting service

Transparency and explainability

- inform users of the circumstances of the algorithmic recommendation services
- disclose the algorithmic recommendation service's basic principles, intended purposes, main operation mechanisms
- Provide an explanation of where algorithmic recommendation services may cause major impacts on user's rights and interests

User Rights

- provide users with options NOT targeting their individual characteristics
- provide users with convenient options to close algorithmic recommendation services
- provide users with functions for selecting or deleting user labels used in algorithmic recommendation services that target their personal traits
- No unreasonable differentiation based on users' preferences, habits or other characteristics
- portals for user appeals and public complaints
- Specific protection measures for vulnerable user groups (i.e., children, elderly people)

(Advertising Law of the People's Republic of China, 2015

Provisions on the Administration of Communication Short Message Service, 2015)

Singapore-PDPA	Cookies are not specifically regulated per se in Singapore.

Depending on the type of information collected, the use of cookies in Singapore may be subject to regulation under the data protection laws of Singapore (PDPA) to the extent that such cookies are used to collect, use, or disclose an individual's personal data.

"Personal data" under the PDPA refers to data about an individual who can be identified from that data or from that data and other information to which the organization has or is likely to have access.

The PDPC has issued a number of advisory guidelines (not legally binding)

Where an organization's use of cookies does not involve the collection of personal data, for example, session cookies which collect and store technical data to facilitate website video playback, the organization does not need to obtain consent under the PDPA.

Where consent is required, it may be deemed to have been given under certain circumstances

- deemed consent by conduct
- deemed consent by contractual necessity
- deemed consent by notification

If personal data is used for behavioral targeting, the individual's consent is required. The PDPC has NOT issued any enforcement decisions specifically in relation to cookies.

Region/Regulation	Requirement
South Korea-PIPA	Under the PIPA, Online Service Providers are required to include matters regarding the installation of applications that automatically collect personal data (e.g., cookies) and the methods on how to avoid such installation in the privacy policy.
	There is no statutory provision explicitly requiring business entities to obtain consent to collect cookies online. However according to the Guideline on Minimum Collection of Personal Information issued by the Ministry of the Interior and Safety in charge of the PIPA in 2018, if the information is collected through cookies is necessary for the provision of services (such as to ease the entry and navigation of the website), the purpose, items collected, and retention period shall be disclosed in the privacy policy. If personal information not directly related to the provision of services (such as for marketing) is collected through cookies it can only be done with the consent of the data subject.
Brazil-LGPD	The Brazilian General Data Protection Law (LGPD) entered into force on September 18, 2020.
	The LGPD imposes purpose-based limitations on processing personal data.
	• Consent is generally needed to collect personal data for targeting or tracking purposes.
	• The LGPD establishes specific requirements for the means of obtaining consent.

23.4 MARKETING TECHNOLOGY AND INITIATIVES

Digital marketing technology adoption has exploded, increasing marketing budgets and campaign frequency. IT must prepare for digital marketing requirements by improving digital marketing technology, processes, and human capital.

Driving efficiencies around current and new technologies will require current process reviews. New technologies such as AI, marketing automation, and predictive analytics will be introduced into the infrastructure, and all will require process alignment or process reinvention.

The data from IAPP Global Privacy Summit 2022 shows that there are more than 8,000 solutions available in the marketing technology space with categories being broken down listed as follows.

- 1969 in social
- 1926 in content
- 1258 in data
- 1314 in sales
- 922 in AdTech

Technologies used in online advertising, and the way they are deployed, have the potential to be highly privacy-intrusive.

Recent years have seen a limiting of the ways in which their users are tracked by online services. Examples include:

Industry entities including browser manufacturers are working together in order to carry out initiatives that seek to limit the ways in which their users are tracked by online services and shift towards less intrusive tracking and profiling practices. This may be both to protect those individuals but also to provide differentiation in the market.

Table 23.5 lists some of the tech initiatives. This is not an exhaustive summary.

Questions and answers

Whether "Google Advertising ID" ("GAID") or Apple IDFA is personal data under the GDPR?

Google created GAID (and Apple created "IDFA" (i.e., Identifier For Advertising) for the purposes of identifying unique devices. GAID and IDFA are online identifiers

TABLE 23.5
Examples of Marketing Tech Initiatives

Tech Initiative	Description
Browser privacy enhancement	Apple
	Apple introduced Intelligent Tracking Prevention (ITP) into Safari in June 2017. Apple states that ITP now blocks third-party cookies (TPCs) by default.
	Microsoft
	Edge includes a tracking prevention feature based on the Disconnect list. By default, it blocks trackers from sites the user has not visited. This intends to fulfill Microsoft's "browser privacy promise"[66]
	Brave Software
	The Brave browser automatically blocks online adverts and tracking by default and incorporates protections against fingerprinting.[67]
	Mozilla
	Firefox incorporates several tracking protections such as Enhanced Tracking Protection (ETP), Total Cookie Protection (TCP), and Enhanced Cookie Clearing (ECC).[68] The ETP function includes a disconnect list. It blocks social media trackers and cross-site tracking cookies.
	DuckDuckGo
	The DuckDuckGo browser extension and mobile app will show users a Privacy Grade rating (A-F) when the users visit a website. This rating lets users see at a glance how protected users are, dig into the details to see who is trying to track the users, and learn how DuckDuckGo enhanced the underlying website's privacy measures.
Surveillance advertising	FTC-Surveillance Advertising Petition
	On December 27, 2021, the FTC published a "Petition for Rulemaking to Prohibit Surveillance Advertising" that it received from Accountable Tech. The Petition requests that the FTC exercise its unfair methods of competition authority to initiate a rulemaking that prohibits "surveillance advertising."
	Per the Petition, surveillance advertising is when an information or communication platform collects personal data and targets advertisements at users, based on that personal data, "as they traverse" the Internet. The Petition also contemplates that tracking users and building data profiles may be subject to regulation.
	The Petition focuses on the actions of "dominant firms" but seeks a broad prohibition of "surveillance advertising" that may apply to firms of all sizes. The FTC accepted comments on the Petition, but the outcome is unclear at the moment.
	Congress: Banning Surveillance Advertising Act
	Rep. Anna Eshoo (D-CA), Rep. Jan Schakowsky (D-IL), and Sen. Cory Booker (D-NJ) introduced H.R.6416, the "Banning Surveillance Advertising Act," in January 2022.
	Notably, the Act would:
	• Prohibit advertisers from targeting ads based on personal information that the advertiser has purchased or obtained from another person;
	• Prohibit advertisers from targeting ads based on personal information that identifies an individual as a member of a protected class; and
	• Create a private right of action and establish damages for violations of the Act.
	The Act reflects the growing legislative interest in the advertising industry.
Advertising identifiers Use of advertising identifiers to provide more transparency to individuals about online tracking	Apple's Identifier for Advertising (IDFA)
	• IDFA (iOS "cookie") goes opt-in
	Google Android reducing access to Google Advertising ID (GAID)
	• The Advertising ID on Android will be replaced by a string of zeros when an individual opts out of personalized advertising

Tech Initiative	Description
Cross-Site/App Tracking Restriction	Apple: **App Tracking Transparency** (ATT) framework • Series of structured notices and consent gating data collection on iOS, effective April 2021 • ATT requires apps to present individuals with an "authorization request" when they collect data, and share data with other organizations (e.g., for tracking that individual across different online services or accessing the IDFA) • Opt-in rate 37% in US, 46% globally (as of April 2022) Google Analytics 4 (GA4) GA4 is the next generation of Google Analytics. GA4 is a new property designed for the future of measurement: • Collects both website and app data to better understand the customer journey • Uses events instead of session-based data • Includes privacy controls such as cookieless measurement, and behavioral and conversion modeling • Predictive capabilities offer guidance without complex models • Direct integrations to media platforms help drive actions On July 1, 2023, standard Universal Analytics properties will no longer process data. You'll be able to see your Universal Analytics reports for a period of time after July 1, 2023. However, new data will only flow into Google Analytics 4 properties. Google Privacy Sandbox (GPS) intends to replace the use of third-party cookies (TPCs) and other forms of cross-site tracking with alternative technologies for enabling targeted advertising (and the measurement of advertising). The GPS has three key goals:[69] • Replacing functionality served by cross-site tracking • Turning down TPCs • Mitigating workarounds

User preferences and identifiers	The Transparency and Consent Framework (TCF)
	The TCF is developed by IAB Europe. It aims to communicate an individual's preferences between online services and other participants within the advertising data supply chain.
	• Ad-supported digital media and RTB companies highly dependent on TCF
	Consent rates are high (70%+)
	• Disruption and limitation for consumers
	• Huge ecosystem with uneven implementation
	• Belgian DPA has ruled against the TCF
	  • TCF team drafting required remediation action plan
	  • ADP's feedback on the action plan will be pivotal for the future of TCF
	  • TCF will have 6 months to implement the action plan
	Global Privacy Control (GPC)
	GPC is a proposed specification that will allow individuals to notify online services of their privacy preferences. It can take the form of a setting within a browser or an extension that an individual can install. When enabled, it sends a signal communicating the individual's preferences about the sale or sharing of their data to each site. It shares similarities with the historic Tracking Preference Expression specification ("Do Not Track" or DNT).
	• Supported by Firefox, Brave, DuckDuckGo, etc.
	• EU/UK relevance
	Advanced Data Protection Control (ADPC)
	ADPC is developed by the RESPECTeD Project, formed by the Sustainable Computing Lab at the University of Vienna and the non-profit organization Nyob.eu. It is Managed by NOYB and the Sustainable Computing Lab at Vienna University. It "aims to empower users to protect their online choices in a human-centric, easy and enforceable manner". It also intends to support publishers and service providers to comply with applicable law, including data protection.[70]
	• Technical standard to manage and automate EU consent decisions for the user
	• Potential compatibility with TCF, CMPs, etc.
	• Meant to specifically address cookie banners

like cookies. Based on the GAID, Google creates anonymous user profiles in order to deliver targeted advertising to Android users. Online identifiers that are associated with online browsing history like GAID are often going to be personal data under the GDPR, although a context-specific analysis always applies, unless and until it is proved that the data subject is not directly or indirectly identifiable and cannot be singled out. For example, if a controller has two databases—database A contains lots of personal data plus the GAID, while database B just contains the GAID as the key and lots of "marketing" assessments. Even if two databases are separated, since they both belong to the controller, it is still possible for the controller to connect the data and recognize individuals by indirect means. So, GAID here is much more likely to be regarded as personal data and should be protected in compliance with the GDPR.

23.5 PRIVACY-ENABLED MARKETING PRACTICES

The future of marketing is shifting to the collection of First-Party data that a company owns and controls, so the company is able to efficiently and effectively reach the audience on its own paces and terms. It means more companies will need to collect this information directly from their customers, and properly store and manage it.

- Marketing leaders who put privacy and data protection as a high priority and focus on exceeding customer expectations, rather than just meeting legal requirements, can increase value, gain trust, and gain competitive advantage.
- Marketers should take a systemic approach and consider the data protection practices, as illustrated in Figure 23.1, when designing new marketing experiences. Individuals' interests, rights, and freedoms should sit behind any design proposal. Market participants should consider how they will evidence their assessment of this during the design of their products, services, and applications.
- People expect a sense of control. Organizations need to go beyond just compliance and make it manageable. When people feel they lack control over their personal data, they can become skeptical of digital marketing. Marketers should provide the mechanisms that customers need to manage their privacy.

Be transparent and meaningful

Organizations should be clear about which data an organization uses to deliver their experiences. The Ipsos Global Trends online survey shows that 73% of internet users aged 16–74 globally are concerned about how the information collected about them when they go online is used.[63]

Brands can have a more positive impact by making a point of reassuring customers about how their data is being used, and by making it easier for people to recall what they agreed to share. Those who consciously agree to share their data are more positive about ads presented to them and find them more relevant.

Organizations should be transparent about how and why personal data is processed across the ecosystem and who is responsible for that processing.

- Provide sufficient processing information. You need to provide sufficient information about the processing before a data subject is asked to consent. Provide a list of third parties with whom the data is being shared. You must provide the list to the data subject in a clear and easily accessible way before the data subject is asked to decide whether to consent. Allow different purposes of the processing be consented to individually, as with parties with whom data will be shared. The default should always be no consent.
- Cover all grounds. Regardless of whether the collection is active or passive, all collected personal data must be disclosed to the data subject. Organizations should articulate the specific purposes for processing personal data and demonstrate how this is fair, lawful,

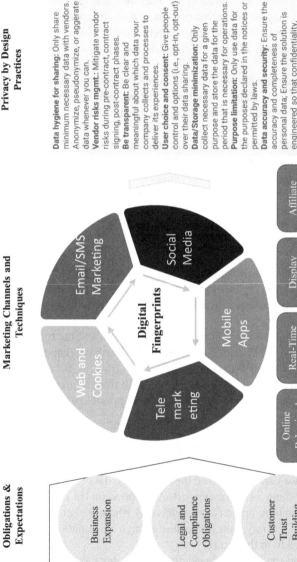

Obligations & Expectations

Business Expansion

Legal and Compliance Obligations

Customer Trust Building

Marketing Channels and Techniques

Digital Fingerprints

Email/SMS Marketing

Social Media

Web and Cookies

Mobile Apps

Tele mark eting

Online Behavioral Advertising

Real-Time Bidding

Display Advertising

Affiliate Marketing

Privacy by Design Practices

Data hygiene for sharing: Only share minimum necessary data with vendors. Anonymize, pseudonymize, or aggerate data whenever you can.
Vendor risks mgmt.: Mitigate vendor risks during pre-contract, contract signing, post-contract phases.
Be transparent: Be clear and meaningful about which data your company collects and processes to deliver its experiences.
User choice and consent: Give people control and options (i.e., opt-in, opt-out) over their data sharing.
Data/Storage minimization: Only collect necessary data for a given purpose and store the data for the period that is necessary for operations.
Purpose limitation: Only use data for the purposes declared in the notices or permitted by laws.
Data accuracy and security: Ensure the accuracy and completeness of personal data; Ensure the solution is engineered so that confidentiality, integrity and availability are built-in.
Data subject request: Be responsive to data subject requests within the required timeframe.

Objectives

Getting privacy right can be the differentiator between a good and a bad experience for a consumer and is therefore vital for the future of any business.

- Business enablement and growth
- Reduce privacy risks and enhance data protection posture
- Be compliant and avoid hefty fines or business disruptions
- Enhance customer trust relationship
- More efficient and strongest ROI

FIGURE 23.1 Privacy by design for marketing key considerations.

and transparent, and articulate the benefits from the user's perspective as well, considering their reasonable expectations.

- Make it meaningful. When people see value in exchange, they are more likely to engage and share the personal data that brands need to make future exchanges more valuable. Despite the apparent complexity of this field and the inherent tensions that have been uncovered, marketers can take simple steps to increase consumer confidence and make people feel positive about the value a brand can offer.

User choice and control

Digital markets are competitive, giving users a genuine choice over the service, product, or provider they prefer. When people understand their personal data sharing and have proper control over it, they feel more positive about tailored advertising and are more likely to find it relevant. Only 3% of respondents believe they have complete control of the disclosure and removal of their data online.[62] Where peoples claim to feel they have control over their data, this leads to both a more positive emotional response to ads, as well as people finding them more relevant. For example, people with lower levels of control only deemed 18% of ads relevant, but for those with high levels of control, this rose to 43%.[62]

People are three times more likely to react positively to advertising and twice as likely to find it relevant when they feel a greater sense of control over how their data is used online. Awareness of how data is used online, as well as overall confidence in a digital environment, also drive relevance.[62]

Meaningful user choice and control are fundamental both to robust data protection and effective competition. Organizations should give people control over their data sharing and make it **manageable**. The rights of citizens to privacy in relation to their personal data are protected so that they have appropriate control over their data and can make meaningful choices over whether and for what purposes it is processed. Where individuals are given meaningful choice and control in a competitive digital economy, "privacy" itself may increasingly become an area in which businesses compete for new customers.

- Choice architecture and default settings are designed in a way that reflects users' interests.
- Ensure the solution allows organizations that use it to obtain freely given, specific, informed, and unambiguous consent from individuals, and that consent is as easy to withdraw as it is to give.
  - Individuals must be offered the ability to receive adverts without tracking, profiling, or targeting based on personal data, e.g., contextual advertising that does not require any tracking of user interaction with content.
  - Organizations must allow the data subject to opt out from all marketing activities. You must comply with the request to opt out as soon as possible and without charge to the data subject.
- Where individuals choose to share their data, they must have meaningful control and the ability to fully exercise their information rights.
- Market participants should evidence high privacy, no tracking by default option, and demonstrate how user choice can be exercised throughout the data lifecycle.
- Organizations need to main a suppression list. A suppression list is a list of personal data about data subjects who have opted out of marketing where, rather than deleting the data subject's personal data entirely, you retain just enough information to ensure that their preferences are adhered to in the future.
  - If a data subject opts out from receiving direct marketing messages, you must not email them any direct marketing messages or ask them by email to opt in. Numerous large fines have been levied on data controllers who have sent direct marketing emails to data subjects who have previously opted out.

Data minimization and Purpose limitation
Organizations should only collect the necessary information for a given purpose.

- Consider whether the outcomes can be achieved without using personal data at all.
- If the solution requires personal data, you need to ensure the solution processes the minimum amount of data necessary to achieve its purposes. You also need to explain why, as well as the steps are taken to identify and mitigate risks and ensure that new risks are not introduced.
- Process data for the minimum amount of time necessary.

The design of the proposals must clearly articulate the specific purposes for processing personal data and demonstrate how this is fair, lawful, and transparent. Personal data should be limited to what is needed to achieve the purpose.

- Market participants should assess the necessity and proportionality of this processing in the context of those purposes and demonstrate how their proposals uphold the integrity of the purpose limitation principle.
- The solution must be designed so that an organization using it can identify a specific, explicit, and legitimate purpose for the processing activities.
- Use the least privacy intrusive approach possible to achieve the purpose.
- Ensure the solution avoids augmenting, matching or combining personal data without strong justification, transparency and control.
- Inform individuals about these purposes (whether the data is obtained directly from them or not).
  - An organization must explain to the data subject in the Privacy Notice, who you are and specify that you plan to use the personal data for marketing purposes. You also need to notify the data subject if you plan to disclose the data to third parties, especially if you share or sell the data for the Third Party to market to the data subject.
- Ensure that if they plan to process personal data for purposes other than those originally specified, the new use is fair, lawful, and transparent.
  - You can't use the personal data for any purposes other than the ones for which you have notified the data subject. If you have collected the data for purposes other than marketing you cannot decide to start marketing to the data subject, because that's a different purpose.

Responsible sharing
The supply chain involves multiple parties. Data protection law enables fair and proportionate data sharing. Users have more control over their personal data and can make meaningful decisions over whether to withhold access to it or share it with others. For instance, organizations should not sell customer data.

Data security
Ensure the solution is engineered so that confidentiality, integrity, and availability are built-in. Apply appropriate security techniques to secure the data at rest, data in use and, data-in-transit.

Accuracy: You must ensure that personal data is accurate and kept up to date. If your marketing list is outdated and doesn't accurately reflect a data subject's preferences for marketing, it's in breach of the GDPR.

One of the key challenges is that individuals have no guarantee about the security of their personal data once it is processed.

When collecting personal data online, remember security obligations. Consider using a secure online form—for example, a form whose submitted data is encrypted.

The solution should demonstrate how it reduces tracking vectors and addresses re-identification risks.

Data Subject Rights Assurance

Ensure the solution allows individuals to exercise their rights, whether by browsers, software settings or applications. Demonstrate how it considers the user journey at all aspects of design and development.

The solution must enable organizations that use it to demonstrate that it is a targeted and effective way to achieve their purpose, and the benefits to the organizations are not disproportionate to any risk to privacy rights.

It must also assist those organizations in demonstrating they cannot reasonably achieve the purpose using a less intrusive method, and that they are able to justify any impact on individuals.

Accountability

There must be accountability across the full lifecycle of the processing and supply chain, with transparency about how and why personal data is processed across the ecosystem and who is responsible for that processing. This must be transparent to the user. Market participants should evidence how accountability will work across the supply chain.

The marketing practices should address existing privacy risks and consider any new risks they introduce as far as practicable. Market participants should evidence how they identify privacy risks in their proposals and how they mitigate them

 Guide and Recommendations

Organizations that follow Info-Tech's *Privacy by Design for Digital Marketing* blueprint can utilize its digital marketing *privacy readiness assessment tool* to determine organizations' current readiness level with respect to digital marketing practices. The readiness assessment tool example is provided below.

	Core Component	**Description**
Privacy Notice (external-facing notice and employee notice)	The identity of the organization	Describe the entity and its affiliates who collect and process personal data.
	What personal data you collect and why you collect this personal data	List the service functions and types of personal data collected from users, purposes of personal data processing as well as the legal basis for the processing, etc.
	How you collect personal data	Articulate the ways the organization collects data from data subjects, such as personal data knowingly and actively "provided by" the data subjects or personal data generated by and collected from the activities of users, by virtue of the use of the service or the device, etc.
	How you use the personal data	Describe the ways the organization will use and share personal data.
	How personal data is shared with the processor or sub-processors	Illustrate how the organization will ensure its vendors will protect the transferred personal data properly.
	How you store personal data	Describe the personal data storage location(s), retention period of personal data, etc.
	Cross-border transfer of personal data	Articulate the mechanisms used such as Standard Contractual Clauses (SCC), etc.
	How you protect personal data	Describe the technical and organizational measures taken to protect personal data.
	Data subjects' rights	Describe the rights that data subjects are entitled to and the ways data subjects can exercise their rights.
	Contact details	List the contact details of the organization's Privacy Officer or the DPO (if any).

	Core Component	Description
Privacy Impact Assessment	Evaluation of whether personal data is involved	Determine whether a business process collects and processes personal data based on your organization's definition.
	Establishment of a data inventory and/or a data flow	Build a data inventory using the Info-Tech's *Data Process Mapping Tool*. Establish the data flow for this business process.
	Determination of whether a full DPIA is needed	Assess whether a business process will pose high privacy risks to the data subjects and your organization based on the criteria defined.
	Risk assessment	Carry out either a full DPIA or a light DPIA to assess privacy risks using consistent criteria such as Info-Tech's *Data Protection Impact Assessment Tool*.
	Risk mitigation	Propose countermeasures and implement risk mitigation methods appropriate to the risk levels.
	Document and sign off on DPIA results	Record all activities and evidence and sign off on the DPIA report.
Data Classification and Handling	A data classification policy has been established and implemented	A data classification policy should include the following elements: – Purpose – Scope – Definitions and roles – Policy – Policy compliance – Related policies, procedures, and standards – Revision history
	A data classification and handling standard has been established and implemented	A data classification and handling standard should include the following elements: – Classification levels – Data handling requirements – Sample electronic disclaimers and statements – Sample physical disclaimers and statements – Related documents – Revision history
Data Retention and De-identification	A data retention policy has been established and implemented	A data retention policy should include the following elements: – Definitions – Policy statements – Exceptions – Governing laws and regulations – Non-compliance actions
	A data retention schedule has been established and implemented	A data retention schedule should include the following elements: – All data retained – Retention requirements in applicable jurisdictions – Disposition – Accountability/ownership – Purpose of processing – Classification

(Continued)

(Continued)

Core Component		Description
Third Party Privacy Management	Pre-contract: due diligence check	Perform internal and external due diligence. Personal data shall be disclosed only to third parties who have the capability to protect personal data according to the privacy protection policy of the entity or other specific guidelines/requirements.
	Signing of contract: data processing agreement	A data processing agreement (DPA) should cover the following elements:

A data processing agreement (DPA) should cover the following elements:

– Defined the data processing roles (including data controller, data processor, business and service providers, etc.)
– Defined contract processing: The DPA shall define types of personal data and the purposes of the data processing (contract processing), usually by using an annex.
– Processing instructions: The data processor shall process personal data in accordance with documented instructions from the data controller.
– Sub-processor: The data processor shall obtain the controller's approval to engage sub-processors. The data processor shall ensure the sub-processor(s) have the level of data protection that's in accordance with data protection laws.
– Security: The data processor shall implement appropriate security technical and organizational measures (TOMs).
– Data breach: Data breach notifications.
– Data secrecy and staff awareness and training.
– Data subject request (DSR): DSR handling obligations.
– Compliance demonstration: The data processor shall make available to the data controller all information requested by the data controller to demonstrate compliance with data protection laws.
– Compliance audit and investigation: The data processor shall assist and co-operate with audits or investigations initiated by the data controller or data protection authorities.
– Cross-border transfer: Proper mechanisms should be implemented to facilitate the data cross-border transfer activities.
– Termination of service: Upon termination of the services the data processor shall return, destroy, or permanently erase all personal data transferred from the data controller.
– Liability and indemnity: In the contract with a third party, state clearly that privacy risks and losses incurred by the third party shall be borne by the third party and the data controller will not be held liable.

Core Component		Description
	Post-contract: continuous monitoring and regular check or audit	The data processor shall make available to the data controller all information requested by the data controller to demonstrate compliance with data protection laws.
		The data processor shall assist and co-operate with audits or investigations initiated by the data controller or data protection authorities.
	Termination of contract: data deletion, access deprovisioning	Termination of service: On termination of the services the data processor shall return, destroy, or permanently erase all personal data transferred from the data controller.
Cross-Border Transfer Mechanism	Document of the evaluation and decision of which cross-border transfer mechanism is suitable for your organization	Based on your business scenarios, a formal analysis of various cross-border transfer mechanisms should be performed, documented and approved.
	If standard contractual clauses (SCCs) is chosen, the steps outlined in the "Description" column (column D) should be followed.	**Step 1 – Identify:** Inventory your current cross-border data transfer business scenarios and identify which ones are using the SCC mechanism.
		Step 2 – Assess: Evaluate the strategy of using the new and old SCCs to align with your business strategies.
		Step 3 – Prioritize: Prioritize transitioning to the new SCCs based on your business and contract management context.
		Step 4 – Integrate: Embed your SCC updates within your organization's contract review and renew lifecycle instead of creating a separate workflow.
DSAR Handling	Handling the DSAR intake	Handle the triage and assign the case to the proper team.
	Verifying the identity of the requestor	Verify the identity of the requestor.
	Sending confirmation to the data subject	Send a manual or automated message of acknowledgement to the data subject upon receiving the DSAR.
	Gathering and collecting requested information	The person who's responsible for collecting information works with the organization to collect the requested information.
	Responding to the DSAR	The person who's responsible responds to the DSAR.
	Closing the request	Formally close the request.
Data Breach Handling	Incident response plans have been created for personal data breaches	The data breach handling process can be a separate document or integrated into the security incident response process.
	Notification requirements have been identified for breaches and incorporated in response plans	Ensure the data breach notification requirements are identified for all applicable jurisdictions.
Program Measurement	Metrics have been established for the privacy program	Metrics and KPIs are established for various stakeholders.
	Privacy metrics communicated	Privacy metrics are communicated to the relevant stakeholders, which can include senior management, the legal department, and external auditors.

23.6   ONLINE MARKETING AND COOKIES

Online advertising enables advertisers to reach individuals with their products and brands while helping organizations to generate income to fund their online services. Online data collection can be categorized as either active or passive. The active collection is of personal data submitted by the data subject. The collection is voluntary and may be through registration forms, transaction forms, online profiles on social networking sites, and account settings.

Data subjects are less likely to be aware of passive collection of their personal data because it is typically collected automatically. Methods include web server logs, cookies, web beacons, proxies, analytics of application or website use, and third-party data (such as a broker list). The profiles created about individuals were extremely detailed and repeatedly shared. They were enriched with information gathered from other sources. Sometimes, this profiling was disproportionate, intrusive, and unfair, and in many cases, individuals were unaware it was taking place.

Data protection regulators have issued over 90 enforcement orders relating to cookie compliance. Large fines for cookie non-compliance have been issued against Google (€150M) and Facebook (€60M). It continues to be an important focus for CNIL enforcement with particular focus on ease of withdrawing consent/rejecting cookies. Similar regulatory focus exists in Germany, the Netherlands, and Belgium.

23.6.1   ONLINE TRACKING

The term "tracking" is defined by the World Wide Web Consortium (W3C) as "The collection of data regarding a particular user's activity across multiple distinct contexts, and the retention, use, or sharing of data derived from that activity outside the context in which it occurred."[71]

Table 23.6 lists some of the common online identifiers.

From a data protection perspective, online tracking is a term that describes or refers to different processing activities, undertaken by different means, for different purposes. A variety of organizations can undertake it, from single businesses to large corporate entities.

Online tracking may include many of the activities referred to in the previous provisions, depending on the circumstances of any implementation and intended purposes, such as:

- Collection
- Use

TABLE 23.6
Common Online Identifiers

Identifier	Description
Account handle	This term refers to one of the social media usernames. Social media handles are enough to identify an individual without referring to their real name.
Device fingerprint	Information about specific properties of the device. The information typically includes the MAC address, operating system used, screen resolution, installed fonts, etc. and can be used to track the device.
Cookie	This is a small text file that a web server delivers to a web browser to create web pages tailored to the user. Cookies can be used to track users' behavior on a single site or across different sites.
Pixel tag	These are small image files (also called clear GIFs or web beacons) loaded through a web page that can cause websites to place and read cookies They can trigger the collection of information, such as a person's IP address, the time the person viewed the pixel, and what browser the person is using. The biggest difference between a cookie and a pixel is who is trying to track you, a third-party ad tool, or the website itself.
Advertising ID	A user-resettable ID is assigned by a device or operating system. When sent to advertisers and other third parties, this ID helps advertising services because it can be used to track how the person uses applications.

- Disclosure by transmission
- Dissemination or otherwise making available
- Alignment or combination

In principle, online tracking can therefore be considered as processing activities involving the monitoring of individuals' actions, especially over a period (including the behavior, location or movements of individuals and their devices), in particular to:

- Build profiles about them
- Take actions or decisions concerning them
- Offer goods and services to them
- Evaluate the effectiveness of services they use
- Analyze or predict their personal preferences, behaviors, and attitude

23.6.2 COOKIES

Cookies are small pieces of data sent from a website and stored locally on a user's computer while the user is browsing. They can be deleted by the user. The cookie itself contains at least the following information: (a) an ID that is 18 characters long and unique to the individual's browser and (b) the date, time, and duration of the individual's visit to the "COOKIED" website.

Cookies allow web servers to keep track of the end user's browser activities and connect individual web requests into a session. Cookies can also be used to prevent users from needing authorization for every password-protected page they access during a session by recording that they have successfully supplied their usernames and passwords already.

Example uses of cookies:

- Storing items in an online shopping cart.
- Recording pages visited in the past for targeted advertising.
- Remembering login information to reduce the need to sign in on every visit.
- Remembering previously entered information, such as a user's name, address, and phone number on web forms.
- Video streaming and volume setting preferences selected in the past.

Cookies help generate a smoother user experience, but they also have privacy implications. Some cookies (including third-party cookies) track, store, and share direct personal data or data that can be connected with an individual in order to provide targeted advertising.

GDPR requires websites to ask for explicit consent from users before using cookies. The following must be available on the website:

- A pop-up box/banner notification clearly informing the user that cookies are being used with options to opt in and opt out within that box/banner. The notification itself cannot limit website functionality.
- A separate cookie policy (linked from the pop-up notification) providing specific details for users to understand cookie use and associated user rights. To meet EU requirements, this cookie policy must be separate from the Privacy Notice.

Some countries have defined a validity period for the consent to use cookies. For example, according to the CNIL in France, the user's consent shall be considered valid for a maximum of 13 months. Upon the expiration of this period, the user's consent must be obtained again.

noyb.eu filed 422 complaints with ten EU data protection authorities.[72] This came after it had sent written warnings and draft complaints to more than 500 companies on May 31, 2021. NOYB focused on 8 key areas where the cookie banners were lacking. The biggest issue was making the revocation of consent as easy as giving consent.[72] Only 18% of the companies added such an option (a "reject" button) to their website.

23.6.2.1   Cookie Types

Not all cookies are created for the same purposes. Some are used to remembering your website preferences (such as your language choices) or login details, enabling you to use and log in to that site easier. Other cookies enable organizations to track your behavior on your browser, for example, so that they can target you for more relevant online advertising.

Table 23.7 explains the different types of cookies.

Depending on who places the cookie on your browser, cookies may be referred to as "first-party" (if they are placed by the website that is visited) or "third party" (if they are placed by a party other than the visited website).

- First-party cookie: First-party cookies are directly stored by the website (or domain) you visit. These cookies allow website owners to collect analytics data, remember language settings, and perform other useful functions that provide a good user experience.
  - Example: On an e-commerce website, facilitates logins to that site or for the advertising purposes of that website.
- Third-party cookie: When a cookie is installed on a user's computer by or on behalf of a third-party marketer, the cookie's ID will be matched when the user later visits a website that is part of the marketer's network, thus allowing the marketer to place a specific ad on the website being viewed by the user. The cookie permits data regarding browsing history

TABLE 23.7
Four Types of Cookies

Varieties of Cookies		Example Purposes
Essential Cookies	Essential Cookies or Strictly Necessary Cookies, Required Cookies	These cookies are necessary for the website to function and generally cannot be disabled. They enable user navigation around the website. They are usually set in response to actions made by visitors which amount to a request for services, such as setting privacy preferences, logging in, or filling in forms. Visitors can set browsers to block or alert about these cookies, but some parts of the site will not then work.
Non-Essential Cookies	Functional or Personalization Cookies	These cookies are used to tailor or customize the website to provide enhanced features and content. They are based on how users have used the website previously and set up other customizations, such as remembering language preferences, choice of playlists, favorite content, geolocation, and more to help you find new content based on what you've looked at before.
	Performance Cookies	These cookies collect information on how users interact with the website. These cookies are often collected for statistical and measurement purposes. They help organizations to know which pages are the most and least popular and see how visitors move around the site. They provide data on which pages users visit, how often, errors encountered, and other information to help improve user experience.
	Marketing Cookies, or Targeting Cookies, Advertising Cookies	These cookies are used to provide information about user interaction with the website content. They deliver relevant, user-dependent advertised content, as well as track the effectiveness of ad campaigns on third-party websites and email. These cookies are used by third-party partners that may remember web browsing activity and know your demographics (such as age and location).

to be recorded and saved to better predict a user's interests and develop a more accurate marketing profile of the user.

- Example: Used by advertisers to track you across multiple websites.

Table 23.8 illustrates the key differences between first-party cookies and third-party cookies.[73]

In addition, depending on how long the cookies will stay on your device, they may be referred to as "session cookies" which are also known as in-memory, transient, or nonpersistent cookies if they are deleted when a session ends, or "persistent cookies" if they remain longer.

- Session cookies: Session cookies are cookies that last for a session. A session starts when you launch a website or web app and ends when you leave the website or close your browser window. Session cookies contain information that is stored in a temporary memory location which is deleted after the session ends.
  - Example: A shopping cart on an e-commerce site that remembers the products or services you add to the cart, which remain when you load a new page
- Persistent cookies: Some cookies remain on your computer but expire on a specific date or after a set period. Some cookies have no expiration date, so, unless individuals remove them themselves, the cookies will remain on their computers in perpetuity.
  - Example: Tracks your behavior online so that advertisers can send targeted ads.

There is another type of cookie called "Secure Cookie" that can be transmitted only by way of an encrypted connection (such as HTTPS) making the cookie less vulnerable to being hacked. Cookies that collect special category data, such as where the browsing of health websites is being tracked, should be especially concerned to ensure that the cookie is secure.

23.6.2.2   DPA Guidance

Many data protection regulators have issued guidance with respect to cookies and similar tracking technologies. A few examples are listed as follows.

EDPB

On May 4, 2020, the European Data Protection Board (EDPB) updated guidelines (Guidelines 05/2020) around online consent to be compliant with the GDPR. One of the updated guidelines provided clarification on the validity of consent as provided by data subjects when interacting with cookie walls.

- Two recommendations were provided:
  - service providers cannot prevent data subjects from accessing a service on the basis that they do not consent; and

---

TABLE 23.8
Key Differences between First-Party Cookies and Third-Party Cookies

	Who Places the Cookies	Purposes	Who Has Access to the Cookies	Browser Support
First-Party Cookies	Placed by the website you visit	Provide user experience for that specific website	Accessible by the website that places the cookies	All browsers support first-party cookies
Third-Party Cookies	Deployed by a third party other than the visited website	Track web users across many different sites, allowing ads to follow you around the web and develop a more accurate marketing profile of the user	Accessible by any site that loads and runs the codes from the third party that places the cookies	Some browsers block third-party cookies

- "cookie walls" are not permitted: access to services and functionalities must not be made conditional on the consent of users to the placement of cookies or similar technologies on their terminal equipment.
- Most importantly, the Guidelines provide that consent within cookie walls cannot be considered freely given. Additionally, scrolling or swiping through a webpage, or similar actions do not constitute a clear or affirmative action. Thus, unambiguous consent has not been obtained, and there is no way for the user to withdraw consent in a way that was as easy as granting it.
- Ultimately, the EDPB clearly states cookie walls are illegal and not a valid way to obtain user consent of individuals inside the EU.

France

The Commission nationale de l'informatique et des libertés (CNIL), France's data protection authority, published new information on March 18, 2021 to clarify its guidelines on cookies and tracking technologies originally published on September 17, 2020. These new guidelines seek to account for the GDPR's definition of consent and are meant to clarify expectations in advance of the second phase of implementation, effective April 2, 2021.

These clarification documents outline how the CNIL will apply sanctions in response to violations of the GDPR, and they offer best practices for organizations seeking to obtain user consent for cookies and other tracking data. Although the clarification is not formally binding, it provides additional information for organizations in their use of cookies and the granularity of consent organizations must obtain as well as additional details regarding consent methods, cookie banner content, withdrawal of consent, consent exceptions, and other aspects of cookie management.

The CNIL highlighted the following principles and recommendations as it relates to cookie walls:

- Continued browsing with the cookie banner can no longer be considered a valid form of user consent, and consent validity requires a clear positive action
- Users should have easy access to manage their cookie preferences and withdraw their consent at any time, and companies should implement this through a static cookie icon as a best practice
- Cookie walls, are likely to undermine the freedom of users to consent; therefore, while CNIL does not ban cookie walls, it highlights that the lawfulness of cookie walls must be assessed on a case-by-case basis
- While the CNIL does not outwardly ban cookie walls, they admit it's not the best option for gaining consent.

UK

In July 2019, the UK Information Commissioner's Office published its new guidance on the use of cookies and other internet-tracking technologies.

Germany

In March 2019, the German conference of supervisory authorities published guidance on internet tracking. Note there is also additional German state-level guidance. For instance, Berlin DPA suggested that services like Google Analytics may only be used with consent.

Spain

In November 2019, the Spanish data protection authority, the Agencia Española de Protección de Datos, published its guidance on the use of cookies and other internet-tracking technologies.

Netherlands

On March 7, 2019 the Dutch Privacy Authority stated that websites should stay accessible when tracking cookies are declined.

If you are looking for specific guidance with respect to various cookie types, Figure 23.2 provides a high-level view of whether consent is needed for essential cookies, functional cookies, performance cookies, and marketing cookies.

Table 23.9 outlines the respective differences and similarities among guidance from various countries.

		UK ICO	France CNIL	Spain DPA	Dutch DPA	German DPA
Essential	Essential Cookies	X Do not need consent	X Do not need consent	X Do not need consent	X Do not need consent	X Do not need consent
Non-essential	Functional Cookies / Performance Cookies	Need consent	Need consent	Need consent	X Do not need consent	X Do not need consent
	Marketing Cookies	Need consent	Need consent	Need consent	Need consent	Need consent

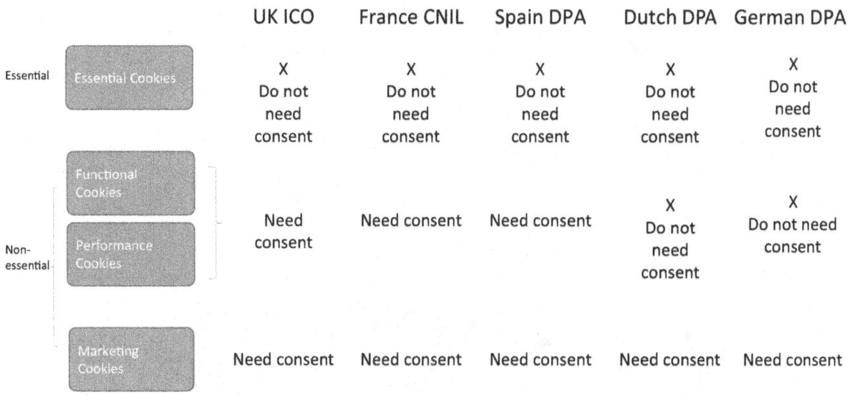

FIGURE 23.2   Different requirements for cookie settings in different jurisdictions.

TABLE 23.9

Differences and Similarities among Guidance from Various Countries

	Covered Technologies	Implied Consent	Identification of Parties	Cookie Walls	Analytic Cookies	Consent Validity for Cookies
France	Rules are applicable to all types of technologies, including cookies, pixels, etc. that store or access information on the user's device.	If consent is required, users must give specific, freely given and unambiguous consent before the respective activity commences. Scrolling or swiping through a webpage, or similar actions do not constitute a clear or affirmative action.	In order for consent to be informed, the user must be able to identify all parties processing their data.	The revised October 2020 guidelines no longer provide a blanket prohibition of cookie walls. Cookie walls should be reviewed and analyzed on a "case by case" basis.	(1) requires consent for analytic cookies and (2) by derogation accepts that certain types of analytic cookies can be regarded as "strictly necessary"	6 months
UK				Cookie wall is "unlikely to be valid."	Need consent	Not specified
Germany				Not allowed	No consent required unless they lead to a transfer of personal data to a third party.	Not specified
Spain				Allowed as long as the user is informed about it.	Need consent	24 months

23.6.2.3 Proper Cookie Settings

Figure 23.3 shows various cookie setting practices and which ones are not recommended and which ones are considered generally accepted practices.

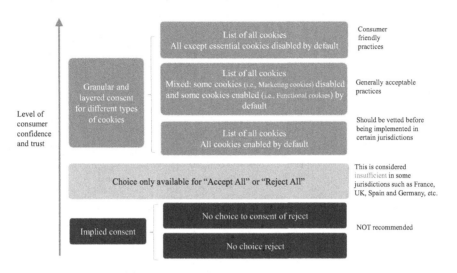

FIGURE 23.3 Generally acceptable practices for cookie settings.

 Case Study

France CNIL v. Google Analytics, February 2022
    CNIL Concludes that EU-US Data Transfer via Google Analytics is Illegal
    Following the decisions made by EDPS (January 5, 2022) and Austrian DPA (January 12, 2022) regarding Google Analytics, the CNIL rejects the risk-based approach and emphasizes that the supplementary measures put in place by Google are insufficient because "they do not exclude the possibility of access to personal data by US government agencies". The CNIL concludes that the data of Internet users is transferred to the United States via Google Analytics in violation of Article 44 of the GDPR. The CNIL ordered the website manager to bring this processing into compliance with the GDPR, if necessary, by ceasing to use the Google Analytics functionality (under the current conditions) or by using a tool that does not involve a transfer outside the EU. These 3 cases are just a fraction of the 101 complaints filed by NOYB in the 27 EU Member States and the 3 other European Economic Area (EEA) states. We are expecting more cases to be issued. The CNIL specifically notes it acts in cooperation with all EU/EEA DPAs in this matter.
    Google Analytics Universal isn't compliant with many regulations that are currently in place. All organizations who are subject to the GDPR and using Google Analytics must review their cookie strategies, policies, and settings immediately and mitigate the compliance risks accordingly. If using Google Analytics, marketers should set up GA4 if they haven't already.

 Case Study

France CNIL v. Google Ireland Limited, December 2020
    CNIL sanctioned 60 million euros against GOOGLE LLC and 40 million euros against GOOGLE IRELAND LIMITED.

The restricted committee, the CNIL body responsible for imposing sanctions, noted a few violations of Article 82 of the Data Protection Act as listed here.

1) A deposit of cookies without prior collection of the user's consent
   - When a user went to the google.fr page, several cookies pursuing an advertising purpose were automatically placed on their computer without any action on their part.
   - As this type of cookie cannot be placed without the user having expressed his consent, the restricted committee considered that the companies had not complied with the requirement provided for by article 82 of the Data Protection Act and the prior collection of the consent before the deposit of non-essential cookies.

2) A lack of information for users of the google.fr search engine
   When a user went to the google.fr page, an information banner was displayed at the foot of the page, bearing the following words "Reminder concerning Google's confidentiality rules" in front of which appeared two buttons entitled "Me call back later" and "Consult now".
   - This banner did not provide the user with any information relating to cookies that had already been placed on his computer, upon arrival on the site. This information was also not provided to him when he clicked the "Consult now" button.
   - The restricted committee, therefore, considered that the information provided by the companies did not allow users residing in France to be previously and clearly informed about the deposit of cookies on their computer nor, consequently, of the objectives of these cookies and the means made available to them as to the possibility of refusing them.

3) The partial failure of the "opposition" mechanism
   - When a user deactivated the personalization of ads on Google search using the mechanism made available to him from the "Consult now" button, one of the advertising cookies remained stored on his computer and continued to read information intended for the server to which it is attached.
   - The restricted committee considered that the "opposition" mechanism put in place by the companies was partially faulty, in violation of article 82 of the Data Protection Act.

 Case Study

France CNIL v. Amazon Europe Core, December 2020
   CNIL sanctioned 35 million euros against Amazon Europe Core.
   The restricted committee, the CNIL body responsible for pronouncing sanctions, noted two violations of article 82 of the Data Protection Act:
   1) A deposit of cookies without obtaining the user's consent
   The limited group noted that when an Internet user went to one of the pages of the amazon.fr site, a large number of cookies for advertising purposes were instantly placed on his computer, that is to say before the user performs any action. However, the restricted committee recalled that this type of cookies, not essential to the service, could only be placed after the Internet user has expressed his consent. It considered that the fact of placing cookies concomitantly on arrival on the site was a practice that, by nature, was incompatible with prior consent.
   2) A lack of information for users of the amazon.fr site

First of all, the restricted training noted that in the case of an Internet user who went to the amazon.fr site, the information provided was neither clear nor complete.

It considered that the information banner displayed by the company, in this case, "By using this site, you accept our use of cookies to provide and improve our services. Find out more", contained only a general and approximate description of the purposes of all the cookies placed. In particular, it considered that upon reading this banner, the user was not able to understand that the cookies placed on his computer had the main objective of showing him personalized advertisements. It also noted that the banner did not indicate to the user either that he has the right to refuse these cookies or the means at his disposal for this purpose.

Then, the restricted committee noted that the failure of the company to meet its obligations was even more manifest in the case of users who went to the amazon.fr site after having clicked on an ad published on another website. She stressed that in this case, the same cookies were placed without any information delivered to Internet users.

Case Study

Spanish DPA vs. MyHeritage, January 2022

Spanish DPA fined MyHeritage €16,000 for unlawful use of non-essential cookies and lacking information in the policy.

The information contained in the privacy policy, which has been updated and expanded, does not meet all the requirements of Article 13 of the GDPR according to the DPA. It was noted that there is no information on the possibility of exercising the right of portability and the right to limit processing. Likewise, the right of data subjects to file a complaint with the supervisory authority was also not indicated.

On the website itself, technically unnecessary cookies had been used directly when the page was accessed without the corresponding consent of the users. This DPA stated that, when accessing the homepage of the website, (first layer), without performing any action on it and without rejecting cookies, the website uses not strictly necessary cookies, both own and third party. In addition, on the homepage, the banner does not inform the webpage visitor sufficiently.

Furthermore, the cookie policy did not contain any information about what cookies were used exactly.

23.6.3   RISK MITIGATION PLAN

You need to follow a three-step approach to assess and mitigate your online marketing privacy risks as described here.

Step one: Assess your cookies
You need to assess and understand the following factors:

- What are cookies
- What types of cookies are being used
- Why the cookies are being used
- How long do the cookies remain (for example, is it a session cookie that only lasts for the browsing session or a persistent cookie that lasts beyond the session and if so, what is the expiry date)
- Who serves the cookie—whether it is a first-party or third-party cookie
- How to refuse the cookie later
- Contact information

Step two: Writing your cookie policy

You can provide information about cookies in your Privacy Notice. However, data controllers commonly have a separate Cookie Policy that specifies which cookies they're using.

Usually, a cookie policy should cover the aspects which are previously mentioned.

Step three: Post cookie policy and configure consent settings

The data controller should provide a technical mechanism or platform for data subjects to manage cookie preferences and give or withdraw consent before setting or reading cookies from data subjects' systems (for marketing or advertisement) unless it is allowed by laws.

If a website sets a cookie on user devices to analyze user behavior for marketing, advertisement, or surveys rather than providing basic services, user consent must be obtained before the cookies are set. No cookie can be used before users give their consent.

23.7 EMAIL MARKETING

Under the ePrivacy Directive, Table 23.10 lists some examples regarding opt-in and opt-out requirements for email marketing activities to new customers in various European Countries.

TABLE 23.10

Examples of Opt-In and Opt-Out Requirements

Country	Email	
	B-to-C (Sending marketing emails to new consumers)	B-to-B (Sending marketing emails to new business contacts addresses)
	Opt-in 👍 Opt-out 👎	
Austria	👍	👍
Bulgaria	👍	👍
		Note: In addition, the organization should always observe whether a legal entity is entered in the public register of entities that do not wish to receive unsolicited email commercial communications.
Croatia	👍	👍
Cyprus	👍	👍
Czech Republic	👍	👍
Denmark	👍	👍
Finland	👍	👎
Greece	👍	👍
Hungary	👍	👍
Latvia	👍	👎
Lithuania	👍	👍
Norway	👍	👍
Poland	👍	👍
Romania	👍	👍
Serbia	👍	👍
Slovakia	👍	👍
Slovenia	👍	👎
		Note: If the business contact address was published by the legal person as its contact email address.
Sweden	👍	👎
		Note: The marketing material is deemed to be relevant to the business representative's professional role and employment.

Email Marketing Privacy Considerations

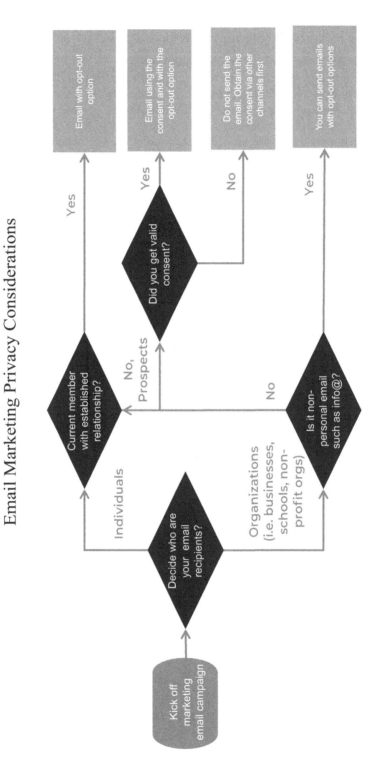

FIGURE 23.4 Email Marketing Privacy Considerations.

Figure 23.4 illustrates the steps an organization can follow to design its email campaign strategy and operations.

*Please note, Under the EU ePrivacy Directive, the opt-out mechanism can only be used if the scenario meets the following criteria.

- Context of a sale
- Content is about similar products/services
  - ✓ The similar products and services exemption provided by the ePrivacy Directive only applies to marketing contacts with whom
    - (i) there has already been a sale
    - (ii) carried out by the same legal entity that obtained the individual's details
    - (iii) limited to similar products and services of that entity, and
    - (iv) to an individual who has not objected to the use of the email address for direct marketing via email, and
    - (v) who was offered an opt-out when his/her details were first obtained and then every time the details are used for direct marketing.
- Opt-out is offered at the collection

**You can obtain consent in one of the following ways:

- By telephone (note: not an automatic telephone dialer, it must be a manual call)
- By mail (physical mail not electronic mail)
- If there is a software/app interface with the data subject, you can update the privacy statement and obtain consent by updating the software/app
- Other creative ways (cannot use email, fax, automated calling machines)

Figure 23.5 shows the general practice for organizations to obtain consent from consumers.

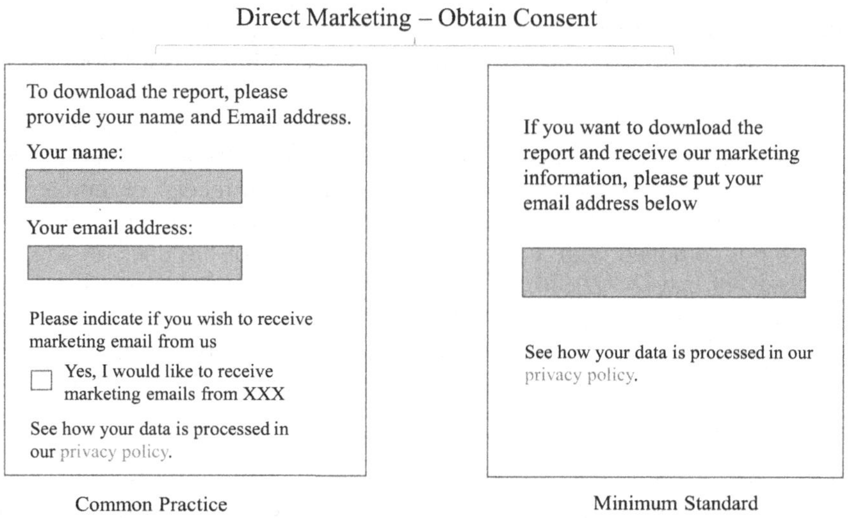

Direct Marketing – Obtain Consent

To download the report, please provide your name and Email address.

Your name:

Your email address:

Please indicate if you wish to receive marketing email from us

☐ Yes, I would like to receive marketing emails from XXX

See how your data is processed in our privacy policy.

Common Practice

If you want to download the report and receive our marketing information, please put your email address below

See how your data is processed in our privacy policy.

Minimum Standard

FIGURE 23.5 Direct marketing consent practices.

 **Case Study**

UK ICO vs. Everything DM Ltd, 2018

The ICO fined Everything DM Ltd £60.000 for sending 1.42 million emails without the correct consent on September 6, 2018. Everything DM, direct marketing specialists based in the UK, acquired lists of email addresses, and sent emails on behalf of its clients for a fee.

When the ICO investigated, it found that while some data subjects had consented to receive emails from unspecified "partners" and/or "Third-Party companies," the consent wasn't valid because neither Everything DM nor the third-party clients on whose behalf Everything DM was sending emails had been specifically named in that consent. In addition, the emails gave the impression they were sent by the clients directly, but Everything DM sent the emails.

Steve Eckersley, ICO director of investigations, said, "Firms providing marketing services to other organizations need to double-check whether they have valid consent from people to send marketing emails to them. Generic third-party consent is not enough, and companies will be fined if they break the law."

The consent for data processing should be obvious, prominent, and not bundled with other terms and conditions. So, if you're collecting personal data at the same time, you're selling a product or service or otherwise need to incorporate terms and conditions, you must have separate tick boxes for accepting terms and conditions.

 Case Study

Greece HDPA v. OTE, Cosmote, Wind, and Vodafone, 2018

HDPA fined OTE, Cosmote, Wind, and Vodafone €150,000 each for unsolicited communications.

The Hellenic data protection authority (HDPA) announced, on October 18, 2018, that it had fined Wind Hellas Telecommunications SA, Vodafone-Panafon Hellenic Telecommunications Company SA, Hellenic Telecommunications Organization SA (OTE) and Cosmote Mobile Telecommunications SA €150,000 each for unsolicited communications.

The HDPA noted that it had received a large number of complaints by individuals who had been contacted for direct marketing purposes, despite being included in the opt-out registers. Furthermore, the HDPA highlighted that upon receipt of the complaints, it had conducted investigations and issued warnings to cease such communications, which were not complied with, leading to the imposition of the fines, in accordance with Article 10 of Law 2472/1997 on the Protection of Individuals with Regard to the Processing of Personal Data, and Article 11 of Law 3471/2006 on the Protection of Personal Data and Privacy in the Electronic Telecommunications Sector.

23.8   TELEMARKETING

Telecommunications involves very important privacy issues. One set of privacy telecommunications issues concerns specific communications channels and methods such as telemarketing, electronic mail, and faxes.

If telephone solicitation is a main market channel of your business, then you must be mindful of any applicable do-not-call rules. No person or company shall initiate any telephone solicitation to residential consumers whose telephone numbers are on the do-not-call registry.

More Effective Cold Calling: Cold calling a farm area with many of the owners listed on the do-not-call registry can be disheartening, but it may also be a blessing in disguise. Your advertising efforts may ultimately be more effective if you don't call people who have indicated they dislike receiving telemarketing calls. Ultimately, what matters the most is not how many people you have to call, but how well you handle each call. Although cross-checking your call list with the do-not-call registry may be cumbersome and time-consuming, your advertising efforts may ultimately be more effective if you no longer call people who have chosen to go on the do-not-call registry. Whether your call list gets shorter or not, the important thing is to make every call count.

Change Marketing Practices: marketers may be able to alter some of their current marketing practices to fall within one of the do-not-call exemptions.

23.8.1   EU ePrivacy

Under the ePrivacy, Table 23.11 lists some examples regarding opt-in and opt-out requirements for telemarketing activities from various European Countries.

 Case Study

Italian DPA v. Sky Italia, 2021
    Sky Italia was ordered to pay nearly €3.3 million by Italy's data protection authority Garante for allegedly misusing customer data to make unwanted promotional phone calls. The decision of the DPA came at the end of an investigation launched

TABLE 23.11

Examples Regarding Opt-In and Opt-Out Requirements

| | Telemarketing (marketing calls made with human intervention) | | | |
| | B-to-C | | B-to-B | |
Country	Marketing Calls Made to Consumers	Government List Screening Required? (in addition to your own "do not call list")	Marketing Calls Made to Business Contacts	Government List Screening Required? (in addition to your own "do not call list")
	Opt-in 👍 Opt-out 👎 Yes✓ No ✗			
Austria	👍	✗	👍	✗
Bulgaria	👍		👍	✗
Croatia	👎	✓	👎	✗
Cyprus	👍	✗	👍	✓
Czech Republic	👍	✗	👍	✗
Denmark	👍	✓	👎	✓
Finland	👎	✓	👎	✗
Greece	👎	✓	👎	✓
Hungary	👎	✓	👎	✓
Latvia	👎	✗	👎	✗
Lithuania	👍	✗	👍	✗
Norway	👎	✓	👎	✓
Poland	👍		👍	✗
Romania	👎	✗	👎	✗
Serbia	👍	✗	👍	✗
Slovakia	👍	✗	👍	✗
Slovenia	👎	✗	👎	✗
Sweden	👎		👎	

following dozens of reports and complaints from people who complained of receiving unwanted phone calls, made to promote the services offered by Sky, both directly and through the call centers of other companies.

Many critical issues were encountered, in particular the making of promotional calls without information and consent, and using unverified lists acquired from other companies. Contrary to Sky's opinion, the consent given by users to communicate their data to third parties to the company supplying the lists did NOT authorize it to use the names for promotional purposes.

In order to correctly carry out the activity of telemarketing, Sky, at the beginning of the telephone call, would have had to provide the user with its own informative report explaining also the origin of the data and—only after having obtained the consent—to proceed with the commercial proposal.

23.8.2   US Telemarketing Rules

23.8.2.1   US Federal Level Rules

23.8.2.1.1   Do Not Call Rules

American consumers strongly object to unwanted and uninvited telemarketing calls to their homes. In December 2002, the FTC ordered the implementation of a national **do not call provision** in TSR. the provisions only apply to **interstate** telephone calls (i.e., calls made across state lines) (16 C.F.R. § 310.2(cc)).

- The do not call provisions of the TSR cover any plan, program, or campaign to sell goods or services through interstate phone calls. This includes calls by telemarketers who solicit consumers, often on behalf of third-party sellers. It also includes sellers who provide, offer to provide, or arrange to provide goods or services to consumers in return for some type of payment as part of a telemarketing transaction.

In July 2003, the FCC enacted new do-not-call requirements for both **interstate and intrastate telemarketing** calls. The National Do Not Call Registry is a list of phone numbers from consumers who have indicated their preference to limit the telemarketing calls they receive. The registry is managed by the Federal Trade Commission (FTC), the nation's consumer protection agency. It is enforced by the FTC, the Federal Communications Commission (FCC), and state officials. According to the FCC, these federal rules set a minimum standard "by operation of general conflict preemption law," and therefore "**supersede** all less restrictive state do-not-call rules". The do-not-call rules prohibit, among other things, any person or entity from initiating a telephone solicitation to a residential or cell phone registered on the national do-not-call registry, unless an exemption.

The area codes in the National Do Not Call Registry cover the 50 states, the District of Columbia, Puerto Rico, US Virgin Islands, Guam, North Mariana Islands, American Samoa, and toll-free numbers (500, 800, 866, 877, 880, 881, 882, and 888). The do not call provisions do not cover calls from political organizations, charities, telephone surveyors, or companies with which a consumer has an existing business relationship.[74]

The following are the exemptions to the FCC do-not-call rules:

- Written permission
  - Checking the do-not-call registry is not required for a telephone call made to someone who has given prior express invitation or permission to call. This permission must be evidenced by a signed, written agreement to be contacted by this caller at a specified telephone number (47 C.F.R. § 64.1200(c)(2)(ii)).

- The consumer's consent must be explicit and, in the writing, and a marketer's request for such consent must be "clear and conspicuous," not hidden in fine print or pre-checked on a website. The FTC has taken a particularly hard line on sweepstakes entry forms, which it views as having been used to deceptively obtain consumers' consent.
- Established business relationships
  - The FCC defines an "established business relationship" as "a prior or existing relationship formed by a voluntary two-way communication between a person or entity and a residential subscriber with or without an exchange of consideration, on the basis of" one of the following.
    - Existing customers: The consumer's purchase or business transaction with the entity within the last 18 months; or
    - Prospects: The consumer's inquiry or application regarding the entity's products or services within the last three months.
  - An established business relationship with a particular company does not extend to affiliated companies unless the consumer would reasonably expect them to be included given the nature and type of goods or services offered by the affiliate and the identity of the affiliate.
  - There is no established business relationship if either party previously terminated the relationship.
  - Furthermore, a caller must honor the consumer's request to be placed on the caller's company-specific do-not-call list (discussed subsequently), even if the parties continue to do business together.
- Personal relationships
  - A "personal relationship" means any family member, friend, or acquaintance of the telemarketer making the call.
- Tax-exempt nonprofit organizations
  - Nonprofits (i.e., political) calling on their own behalf are exempted from adhering to Do Not Call rules, although if a nonprofit were to contract with a for-profit telemarketing firm, that firm would be subject to Do Not Call restrictions.

National Do Not Call Registry Database:

- Consumers can register online at **www.donotcall.gov**. Consumers may register both their residential telephone numbers and cellular phone numbers (47 C.F.R. § 64.1200(e)). There is no cost for registration. The national do not call registry is administered by the FTC.
  - Consumers need to provide email, and confirm when receiving the registry via email to complete the whole process
  - If a consumer has a complaint about telephone fraud or telemarketers who have disregarded the Do Not Call list, the consumer can file a complaint with the FTC at www. ftccomplaintassistant.gov.
- Marketers can access the national do not call registry database at **https://telemarketing. donotcall.gov**. There is no charge for the first five area codes of data accessed by any person. Data for up to five area codes is free. Beginning October 1, 2021, the annual fee will be $69 per area code of data (after five) up to a maximum annual fee of $19,017.
  - To access the registry, your organization must designate someone as your Authorized Representative and create a profile. You will need to identify your organization as a Seller, Telemarketer, or Service Provider (TM/SP), or as Exempt.
  - Once your organization has created a profile, you can choose which area code subscriptions you want. After you subscribe, your organization will be given a Subscription Account Number (SAN).

Questions and answers

What is a telephone solicitation for purposes of the do-not-call rules?

A "telephone solicitation" is a telephone call that acts as an advertisement. It is very broadly defined by the FCC as the initiation of any telephone call or message, unless exempt, "for the purpose of encouraging the purchase or rental of, or investment in, property, goods, or services, which is transmitted to any person" (47 C.F.R. § 64.1200(f)(9)).

Questions and answers

What about a call made to a place of business?

A telephone call made to a place of business does not fall within the scope of the do-not-call rules. The do-not-call rules only pertain to calls made to residential and wireless telephone numbers to the extent described by the rules (47 C.F.R. § 64.1200(c), (d), and (e)).

Questions and answers

What if I call a place of business, but that business phone number has been inadvertently registered on the do-not-call registry?

A telephone call made to a place of business listed on the do-not-call registry does not violate the do-not-call rules, according to the FCC (70 Federal Register 19330 at 19331 (2005)).

Questions and answers

What about a call made to a home-based business?

A telephone solicitation made to a home-based business is not expressly exempt from the do-not-call rules, according to the FCC. Instead, the FCC has indicated that it will review such calls on a case-by-case basis to determine whether the call was placed to a residential subscriber.

Case Study

FCC v. Dialing Services, 2017

In FCC's order released on July 26, 2017, the order discussed Dialing Services, LLC, a robocalling platform that was fined $2.8 million USD for making $4.7 million calls to wireless phones over a three-month period in 2012.

Case Study

FTC v. DISH Network, 2012

In August 2012, the FTC filed a lawsuit against DISH Network alleging that it illegally called millions of consumers who had previously asked telemarketers from the company or its affiliates not to call them again.

23.8.2.1.2   Robocalls

Robocalls are calls made with an autodialer or that contain a message made with a prerecorded or artificial voice. An autodialer (or "automatic telephone dialing system") is equipment that can generate and dial telephone numbers randomly or sequentially. It becomes more of a problem for consumers, and a more difficult problem to solve as the advances in technology allows illegal and spoofed robocalls to be made from anywhere in the world and more cheaply and easily than ever before.

There are various laws governing the use of autodialers and artificial or prerecorded messages, as set forth in section 227 of Title 47 of the United States Code and section 64.1200 of Title 47 of the Code of Federal Regulation Section (federal law). **The Telephone Consumer Protection Act TCPA 1991 was updated in 2012 to address robocalls.**

- FCC rules require a caller to obtain written consent—on paper or through electronic means, including website forms, a telephone keypress—before it may make a prerecorded telemarketing call to your home or wireless phone number.
- FCC rules also require a caller to obtain your consent, oral or written, before it may make an autodialed or prerecorded call or text to your wireless number. There are exceptions to these rules, such as for emergencies involving danger to life or safety.
  - Informational messages such as school closings or flight information to your home phone are permissible without prior consent.
  - Autodialed or prerecorded calls to wireless phones are prohibited without prior express consent, regardless of the call's content, with a few exceptions such as emergency calls regarding danger to life or safety.
- Telephone solicitation calls to your home are prohibited before 8 am or after 9 pm.
- FCC rules require telemarketers to allow you to opt out of receiving additional telemarketing robocalls immediately during a prerecorded telemarketing call through an automated menu. The opt-out mechanism must be announced at the outset of the message and must be available throughout the duration of the call.
- Telemarketers are no longer able to make telemarketing robocalls to your wireline home telephone based solely on an "established business relationship" that you may have established when purchasing something from a business or contacting the business to ask questions.
- One exception to the new robocall rules is for residential lines made by healthcare-related entities governed by HIPAA.

Under the FCC rules, telemarketers using predictive dialers must ensure that they do not abandon more than 3% of all calls made over a 30-day period. A call is considered "abandoned" if it is not connected to a live sales representative within two seconds of the called person's completed greeting (47 C.F.R. § 64.1200(a)(6)).

Under California law, using auto-dialers to place calls is generally prohibited before 9 am and after 9 pm (Cal. Pub. Util. Code § 2872(c)).

23.8.2.1.3 Do Not Fax Rules

Along with the do not call rules, the FCC has also established rules generally prohibiting the faxing of advertising materials absent the fax recipient's prior permission. Any advertising fax must include an opt-out notice as defined.

23.8.2.2 US State Level Rules

Many states have enacted telemarketing laws as well, creating additional legal requirements for telemarketers. 44 states also have Do Not Call lists. 32 of these states have adopted the National Do Not Call List as their own. The remaining 12 of these 44 states also maintain a state Do Not Call list and residents of these states may want to register their residential telephone numbers on their state's list in addition to the federal list.

In addition to the Do Not Call list, more than half the states require that telemarketers obtain a license or register with the state. Some states require that telemarketers identify themselves at the beginning of the call, or that the telemarketer terminate the call without rebuttal if the recipient of the call desires. Some states may require that a written contract be created for certain transactions.

32 states have adopted the National Do Not Call List since the Federal Trade Commission ("FTC") formed the National Do Not Call Registry in 2003. These states are Alabama, Alaska, Arizona, Arkansas, California, Connecticut, Georgia, Hawaii, Idaho, Illinois, Kansas, Kentucky, Maine, Maryland, Michigan, Minnesota, Montana, Nevada, New Hampshire, New Jersey, New Mexico, New York, North Carolina, North Dakota, Ohio, Oregon, Rhode Island, South Dakota, Utah, Vermont, Virginia, and Wisconsin.[75]

Apart from the National DNC, Table 23.12 lists the 12 states which have their own State Do Not Call lists.

23.8.3 Canada Do Not Call Rules

In Canada, there is a Canadian Radio-television and Telecommunications Commission (CRTC) which is an administrative tribunal that regulates and supervises Canadian broadcasting and telecommunications in the public interest to protect you from unwanted calls, faxes, and email.

Similar to the US National Do Not Call List, in November 2005, the Canadian Parliament amended the Telecommunications Act (section 41) to allow the CRTC to establish a national Do Not Call List (DNCL). Telemarketers are required by law to register and pay fees to download updates from a secure website.

TABLE 23.12
US State Do Not Call Lists

State	Do Not Call Website
Colorado	Colorado No-Call List www.coloradonocall.com/Public/Telemarketers.aspx
Florida	Florida Do Not Call Program www.fdacs.gov/Consumer-Resources/Florida-Do-Not-Call
Indiana	Indiana Do Not Call List www.indonotcall.org/registrations/new
Louisiana	Louisiana Do Not Call Program www.lpsc.louisiana.gov/DNC
Massachusetts	Massachusetts Do Not Call Program www.madonotcall.govconnect.com/welcome.asp
Mississippi	Mississippi No Call Program www.psc.ms.gov/NoCall/home
Missouri	Missouri No Call https://ago.mo.gov/civil-division/consumer/no-call
Oklahoma	Oklahoma Do Not Call Registry www.oag.ok.gov/attorney-generals-telemarketer-restriction-act-consumer-registry
Pennsylvania	Pennsylvania Do Not Call List www.oca.state.pa.us/Industry/TeleCom/other/DoNotCallLists.htm#:~:text=Pennsylvania%20 residents%20can%20register%20home,%2D888%2D777%2D3406.
Tennessee	Tennessee Do Not Call Program www.tn.gov/tpuc/tennessee-do-not-call-program.html
Texas	Texas No Call www.texasnocall.com/subscriberFAQ_TX.asp
Wyoming	Wyoming No Call Law https://ag.wyo.gov/law-office-division/consumer-protection-and-antitrust-unit/telephone-solicitation

- The rules apply to all companies that conduct unsolicited telecommunications, whether for themselves or someone else. Not only are telemarketers required to respect the wishes of consumers who have registered their numbers on the list, but they must also maintain their own internal lists.
- Though there are many restrictions, certain kinds of telemarketing calls and faxes are exempt from the Canadian DNCL, including those made by or on behalf of:
  - Registered charities.
  - Newspapers looking for subscriptions.
  - Political parties and their candidates.
  - Companies with whom you have an existing business relationship.
  - Individuals or organizations made solely for the purpose of market research or surveys (they are not considered to be telemarketing calls because they are not selling a product or service or asking for donations).
  - Debt-collection calls.
  - Persons or entities to whom you have provided express consent to be called.
- If you wish to avoid these telemarketers, you can ask to be put on their Do Not Call Lists.
  - Consumers can register online at https://lnnte-dncl.gc.ca/en/Consumer/Register-your-number/#!/.
  - After you sign up, your numbers will be added to the list within 24 hours. Once a number has been registered on the national DNCL, it is permanent. You can also, at any time, have your number removed. Telemarketers then have 31 days to update their own information and make sure they don't call you in their next round of telemarketing.

23.8.4 Best Practices

The Telemarketing Sales Rule has a "DNC Safe Harbor" that sellers and telemarketers can use to reduce the risk of liability. In order to qualify under the DNC Safe Harbor, the following requirements should be met:

Accountability: You need to have persons or positions that are responsible and accountable for compliance with regulations and do-not-call rules.

Written policy: You need to establish and implement company-specific written procedures for complying with the do-not-call rules.

- You must have a written policy, available on-demand, for maintaining a do-not-call list.
- For instance, in the US, regulations require anyone who initiates a telemarketing call to a residential or cell phone to have, among other things, a written policy, available upon demand, for maintaining the company's do-not-call list (47 C.F.R. § 64.1200(d)(1)).

Accessing: You need to identify how you are going to get the Do Not Call list and ensure compliance. You need to maintain and record a list of telephone numbers that cannot be contacted.

- For covered calls, marketers must access the do-not-call registry.
  - On subsequent visits to the FTC's website, you will be able to download either a complete updated list of telephone numbers from the area codes you have selected or a more limited list showing additions and deletions from when you last downloaded.
- Upon accessing the do-not-call registry, you must update your call list periodically in conjunction with using your own call list and the telephone numbers of people who have registered.

- You must update your call list at least once every 31 days and maintain records documenting this process. This 31-day rule came into effect on January 1, 2005 (47 C.F.R. § 64.1200(c)(2)(i)(D)).
  - Telemarketers are required to keep track of this list, updating their internal list on a monthly basis. In addition to telephone numbers on the Federal list, telemarketers are obligated to maintain lists of individuals who specifically ask them not to call.

Recording: For any residential telephone subscriber who requests not to be called, that person's name, if provided, and telephone number must be placed on a company-specific do-not-call list at the time the request is made.

Training: Your personnel engaged in any aspect of telemarketing must be informed and trained in the existence and use of the do-not-call list. You need to train your personnel in the procedures established pursuant to the do-not-call rules. The general telemarketing requirements are as follows:

- Hours: Do not initiate any telephone solicitation before the hour of 8 am or after 9 pm (local time at the called party's location)
- Stay online: Do not disconnect an unanswered telemarketing call before at least 15 seconds or four rings.
- Identify Yourself: When you call, you must give: (1) your name; (2) your company's name; and (3) your telephone number or address where you may be contacted.

Monitoring and Enforcement: You need to implement a program to monitor and enforce its policies.

24 Workforce Data Protection

This chapter is intended to help readers understand the typical legal obligation for protecting employees' personal data in the workplace environment and implement proper privacy measures to mitigate risks in various domains such as workplace monitoring, processing sensitive personal data, etc.

This chapter covers the following topics:

- *Privacy obligations in the workplace*
- *Typical HR processes and personal data*
- *Background screening*
- *Workplace monitoring*
- *Processing sensitive personal data*
- *Privileged information, legal hold, and eDiscovery*

24.1 PRIVACY OBLIGATIONS IN THE WORKPLACE

An individual's privacy in the workplace is a balance between the employer's need to collect, use, and disclose personal information and the employee's right to ensure the information is accurate and used properly.

Table 24.1 lists EU and US data protection regulations with respect to workplace privacy.

Table 24.2 lists some of the EU members with respect to workplace privacy and data protection requirements.

24.2 TYPICAL HR PROCESSES AND PERSONAL DATA

Table 24.3 lists some examples of HR processes and personal data associated.

24.2.1 TYPICAL LEGAL BASIS

Most organizations usually will deal with the following four lawful bases in their daily operations: legal obligation, contractual obligation, legitimate interest, and consent.

- The legal obligation
  - Processing is necessary for compliance with legal obligations.
  - The legal obligation would be the first basis you should look for as this is necessary for compliance with a legal obligation to which the organization is subject.
- Contractual necessity
  - Processing is necessary to fulfill the employment contract.
  - The contractual obligation falls next as this is necessary to fulfill the employment contract between the employer and employee.
- Legitimate interests
  - Processing is necessary for your legitimate interests
  - Legitimate interest is the most used basis such as moving employee info from one database management system to another. But public authorities can't rely on legitimate interests.

DOI: 10.1201/9781003225089-29

TABLE 24.1

Workplace Privacy Regulations in EU and US

Jurisdiction	Requirements
EU	In the context of workplace data protection, EU members are subject to EU data protection laws, member state data protection laws, and local employment laws.
	An employer may also be obligated to communicate with trade unions and work councils. Local law may require notification of issues concerning the rights of employees.
	GDPR
	Art. 88(3) GDPR: Processing in the context of employment
	1. Member States may, by law or by collective agreements, provide for more specific rules to ensure the protection of the rights and freedoms in respect of the processing of employees' personal data in the employment context, in particular for the purposes of the recruitment, the performance of the contract of employment, including discharge of obligations laid down by law or by collective agreements, management, planning and organization of work, equality and diversity in the workplace, health and safety at work, protection of employer's or customer's property and for the purposes of the exercise and enjoyment, on an individual or collective basis, of rights and benefits related to employment, and for the purpose of the termination of the employment relationship.
	2. Those rules shall include suitable and specific measures to safeguard the data subject's human dignity, legitimate interests, and fundamental rights, with particular regard to the transparency of processing, the transfer of personal data within a group of undertakings, or a group of enterprises engaged in a joint economic activity and monitoring systems at the workplace.
	3. Each Member State shall notify the Commission of those provisions of its law which it adopts pursuant to paragraph 1, by May 25, 2018 and, without delay, any subsequent amendment affecting them.
US	There is no overarching or organized law for employment privacy in the United States.
	US Constitution
	The US Constitution has significant workplace privacy provisions that apply to the federal and state governments, but it does not affect private-sector employment. Notably, the Fourth Amendment prohibits unreasonable searches and seizures by state actors. Courts have interpreted this amendment to place limits on the ability of government employers to search employees' private spaces, such as lockers and desks.
	For private sectors, in general, there is no state action, and no constitutional law governs employment privacy.
	Federal laws
	The United States has a number of federal laws that prohibit discrimination, regulate employee benefits management and regulate data collection and record keeping.
	• Anti-discrimination laws provide employees with some privacy protection—for example, by limiting questioning with respect to what is being protected, such as age, national origin, or disability.
	• Laws regulating employee benefits offer certain privacy and security protections for benefits-related information. They also often mandate the collection of employee medical information. These laws include the following protections:
	• The Health Insurance Portability and Accountability Act of 1996 (HIPAA) contains privacy and security rules that regulate "protected health information" for health insurers, including self-funded health plans.
	• The Consolidated Omnibus Budget Reconciliation Act (COBRA) requires qualified health plans to provide continuous coverage after termination to certain beneficiaries.
	• The Employee Retirement Income Security Act (ERISA) ensures that employee benefits programs are created fairly and administered properly.

- The Family and Medical Leave Act (FMLA) entitles certain employees to leave in the event of birth or illness of self or a family member.
- The laws regulating data collection and record keeping include:
- The Fair Credit Reporting Act (FCRA) regulates the use of "consumer reports" obtained from "consumer reporting agencies" in reference checking and background checks of employees.
- The Fair Labor Standards Act (FLSA) establishes the minimum wage and sets standards for fair pay.
- The Occupational Safety and Health Act (OSHA) regulates workplace safety.
- The Whistleblower Protection Act protects federal employees and applicants for employment who claim to have been subjected to personnel actions because of whistleblowing activities.
- The National Labor Relations Act (NLRA) sets standards for collective bargaining.
- The Immigration Reform and Control Act (IRCA) requires employment eligibility verification.
- Employee privacy is protected by several federal agencies, including the Department of Labor, the Equal Employment Opportunity Commission (EEOC), the Federal Trade Commission (FTC), the Consumer Financial Privacy Board (CFPB) and the National Labor Relations Board (NLRB).

Contract Law

US law looks at the relationship between the employer and employee as fundamentally a matter of contract law.

The general rule in the United States is employment at will, which means that the employer has broad discretion to fire an employee. Employment laws in the United States often provide employers with more discretion than laws in the EU and other countries in the handling of personal information.

That discretion, in turn, has been understood to grant the employer broad latitude in defining other aspects of the employment relationship, such as issues about the employer's knowledge about an employee.

More generally, negotiation of a contract can create binding obligations on the employer. If the employer makes promises in a contract to honor employee privacy, then violations of those promises can constitute an enforceable breach of contract.

The most important contracts concerning employee privacy are collective bargaining agreements. Unions have often negotiated provisions that protect employee privacy, including, for instance, limits on drug testing and monitoring of the workplace by the employer.

Tort

At least three common-law torts—intrusion upon seclusion, publicity was given to private life, and defamation—can be relevant to employee privacy, although US law generally requires a fairly egregious fact pattern before imposing liability on the employer.

A classic example of an intrusion upon seclusion is if the employer puts a camera or peephole in a bathroom or employee changing room—a jury may well find that such surveillance is highly offensive to a reasonable person.

To support a "publicity given to private life" claim, a plaintiff would need to show relatively broad dissemination of the facts involved and that the facts disseminated would be highly offensive to a reasonable person. Courts have been cautious in finding such offensiveness, even for dissemination of a person's salary or other information the employee considers private. Free speech principles under the First Amendment also often provide a defense against such a tort claim.

For employment law, defamation torts can arise if, for instance, a false drug testing report is issued or if a former employer provides a factually incorrect reference to a possible future employer.

Statutory law

Statutes vary enormously state by state, leading to a patchwork of near bewildering complexity and large gaps.

TABLE 24.2

Workplace Privacy Requirements from EU Members

EU Member State	Description
Bulgaria	The Personal Data Protection Act (PDPA) (promulgated in the State Gazette, issue No 17 of 26 February 2019, and entered into force on March 2, 2019) explicitly provides that the retention period for CVs and supporting documentation of job applicants cannot be longer than six months, without the prior express consent of the job applicant. Further, if an employer requests originals or notarized copies of documents, such as diplomas, certificates, etc., these need to be returned within six months of the completion of the respective recruitment campaign. The PDPA furthermore expressly prohibits the production of copies of identity documents, driving licenses, and residence documentation, unless expressly required by the law.
Croatia	Whereas article 23 of the Croatian Implementation Act provides specific rules for personal data processing in an employment context (processing of biometric data of employees and workplace surveillance), no specific rules apply with regards to recruitment.
Cyprus	Cyprus has not included in its national legislation (Law 125(I)/2018) any implementing provisions for the processing of personal data in the employment context. The Cyprus DPA has, however, issued opinions and guidelines on video surveillance at the workplace and the use of biometric systems, access to employees' and former employees' email and general guidance on monitoring in the workplace, but not specifically with regards to recruitment yet.
Finland	The Act on the Protection of Privacy in Working Life (759/2004) provides that data mentioned in a drug testing certificate can be processed during recruitment under certain conditions. An employer cannot, however, require any genetic testing, nor has the right to know whether a (candidate) employee has ever taken part in such testing. Further, under the Workplace Privacy Act, if an employer or a representative of the employer breaches an obligation or a restriction regarding processing personal data in the context of employment, a fine will be imposed on the employer, unless a more severe penalty is provided for in another statute.
France	According to the French Civil Code and Labor Code, an employer is not allowed to ask a candidate for his social security number, information on his parents or siblings, political opinions, or union membership. Only the persons involved in the recruitment process are allowed access to the personal data of the candidates. If a candidate isn't hired, he should be asked for his consent to hold on to his personal data. If he consents, the personal data shall not be retained for longer than 2 years following the last contact, unless the data subject agrees to a longer retention period.
Germany	The key provision is section 26 of the new Data Protection Act (BDSG), but the relevant rules are dispersed over various laws. The Supervisory Authority of Baden-Württemberg (SA) has published a new version of its guidance document on data protection issues in the employment context on March 12, 2019. According to these guidelines, the only information that is necessary to assess a candidate's suitability can be asked and the retention period for CVs and supporting documentation of job applicants should not be longer than four months, without the prior express consent of the job applicant.
Hungary	Employers may only request the presence of an ID card and other personal documents, but no copies can be made, even with the consent of the data subject. Furthermore, the employer cannot request criminal record clearance, unless in very exceptional situations and under strict criteria.
Ireland	The Irish Data Protection Act 2018 (DPA) provides that in the process of recruitment, whether for continued employment of an individual or the contract for the provision of services, individuals will not be compelled to make an access request at the request of the employer/person or supply the employer/person with the data obtained as a result of the access request (Section 4, Chapter 1 Part 1 DPA). There is no other general provision permitting the processing of criminal record background checks by an employer in the context of recruitment/employment.
Italy	The Legislative Decree no. 101 of 10 August 2018 did not repeal the existing Italian Data Protection Act (IDPA), but only amended it. Section 111-bis of the IDPA provides that no consent to the processing of personal data contained in CVs is required.

Lithuania	The Law on Legal Protection of Personal Data in date of 16 July 2018 provides the right for the employer to process personal data submitted by an applicant in the recruitment process (i.e., CV and other related documents) without the consent of the applicant, as well as to use the information available on social media to perform a background check, without the consent of the applicant, provided that such information is publicly available. Prior consent is needed if the employer contacts its friends or current employer to get references/feedback. Finally, it is recommended to determine the retention period to one year in view of possible claims under the Equal Treatment Act. If the retention period would be extended to a longer period consent of the individual is required.
Luxembourg	Whereas article 71 of the Luxembourg Law of 1 August 2018 on the organization of Luxembourg's National Commission for Data Protection provides specific rules for personal data processing in an employment context (regarding workplace surveillance), no specific rules apply with regards to recruitment.
Poland	The Polish Personal Data Protection Act of 10 May 2018 provides a list of employees' and job candidates' personal data which can be processed by employers, as well as a list of data that "must" be requested by employers and provided by candidates and employees. Employers are allowed to collect other personal data on the basis of the job candidates' or employees' consent. The DPA has issued a handbook for employers with answers to frequently asked questions.
Slovakia	Whereas the Slovakian Act no. 18/2018 on Personal Data Protection provides specific rules for personal data processing in an employment context (regarding the publication of employees' personal data: name, title, work address, etc.), no specific rules apply with regards to recruitment.
Spain	Whereas the Organic Law 3/2018 of 5 December, on "Personal Data Protection and guarantee of Digital Rights" provides specific rules for personal data processing in an employment context, no specific rules apply with regards to recruitment in particular.
Sweden	Whereas the Swedish Data Protection Act provides a clause on personal data processing in an employment context (regarding the processing of sensitive personal data), no specific rules apply with regards to recruitment in particular.

TABLE 24.3

Examples of HR Processes and Personal Data Associated

Employment Lifecycle	Process	Personal Data Type (examples)
Attract	Passive talent pool management	Name, email, types of jobs interested in, resume
Recruit	Application	Full Name, Home Address, Phone Number, Email Address, Work Experience, Education, Gender, Minority Status, Disability Status, Veteran Status
	Assessment	Additional test scores and feedback on the candidate
	Standard background check Note: It's common for this to be outsourced to a vendor	References check, Employment verification, Education verification, Professional/certificate verification, social media checks, financial credit, driving records, etc.
	Health Check	Health check results
	Criminal record	Criminal record (driving record, sexual offender)
	Drug testing	Drug testing results
Onboard	Offer and Onboarding	Full Name, Home Address, Phone Number, Email Address, Date of Birth, SSN, Government ID (passport, DL, etc.), Banking Information, Emergency Contact Information, Dependent, and Beneficiary Information
	Payroll/Compensation	Full Name, Employee ID, Banking Information, SSN
	Benefits enrollment and administration	Enrollment info, life events, dependents, disability status
Perform and grow	Basic information updates	Personal info (e.g., name change, address change), title change, comp change, Grievances or complaints
	Time and attendance	Absence, extended leave (medical info), time tracking
	Performance evaluation	Performance metrics, feedback (e.g., 360 feedback), L&D completion/budget (different system), course grades/certificates
	Employee survey	Demographics, medical, preferences, feedback
	Affirmative action reports	Name, address, gender, ethnicity, veteran status, disability status
Exit/ Off-boarding	Termination	Update personal information/banking information, exit survey (could be covered in the survey)
	Retirement plans and management	Full Name, Home Address, Phone Number, Email Address, Date of Birth, Emergency Contact Information, Dependent and Beneficiary Information, Wage Information

- Legitimate interests are often a condition relied upon by employers to process personal data, but employers must be careful to rely on legitimate interests in the right context, and to be able to do so they will need to do a legitimate interest assessment (LIA) conducting assessments for the legality of processing, necessary and proportionate, and balance test.
- Consent
  - The employee has provided consent to the processing.
  - Consent is the hardest basis to use as there is an unequal balance of power between employer and employee dynamics. GDPR makes it clear that consent is valid only where consent is freely given.

- An imbalance of power often exists between the employer and employee. In that situation, the employee may feel pressure to provide consent—so it isn't freely given (Recital 42 of the GDPR).
- An employee might withdraw consent at any time. If you didn't have other grounds on which to process the data, you would need to delete that data, which may be a problem for you.
- This should be used as the last resort.

24.2.2 TYPICAL PROCESSING PURPOSES

- Administering and providing compensation: including administering and providing payroll, bonuses, stock options, and other applicable incentives.
- Administering and providing applicable benefits and other work-related allowances: including reporting of benefit entitlements and use.
- Administering the workforce: including managing work activities, providing performance evaluations and promotions, producing and maintaining corporate organization charts, entity and intra-entity staffing and team management, managing and monitoring business travel, carrying out workforce analysis, conducting talent management and career development, employee training, leave management/approvals, succession planning, providing references as requested, and administering ethics and compliance training.
- Complying with applicable laws and employment-related requirements: along with the administration of those requirements, such as income tax, national insurance deductions, and employment and immigration laws.
- Monitoring and ensuring compliance with applicable laws, regulatory requirements, and applicable Company procedures: by monitoring the use of Company technology resource systems, databases, and property and conducting investigations.
- Performance and administration of the compliance hotline.
- Communicating with you, other Company employees, and third parties (such as existing or potential business partners, suppliers, customers, end-customers, or government officials).
- Communicating with your designated contacts in case of an emergency
- Responding to and complying with requests and legal demands from regulators or other authorities in or outside of your home country.
- Complying with corporate financial responsibilities: including audit requirements (both internal and external), accounting, and cost/budgeting analysis and control.
- Managing corporate information technology: including helpdesk, corporate directory, IT support, and IT security.
- Conducting security screenings: to the extent permitted by law.

24.3 BACKGROUND SCREENING

Before employees are hired, they are often subject to background screening. The type and extent of screening vary depending on the work environment.

Table 24.4 lists some of the requirements in the United States.

Table 24.5 lists some of the requirements in Europe.

24.4 WORKPLACE MONITORING

Each organization is unique and has its reason for whether to monitor employees. Table 24.6 lists some of the common reasons to monitor or not monitor employees.

TABLE 24.4

Examples of Background Screening Requirements in United States

Data Type	Description
Race, genetic, color, religion, national origin, sex, pregnancy, marital status, and age	**Federal-level** • Title VII of the Civil Rights Act of 1964 bars discrimination in employment due to race, color, religion, sex, and national origin. • The Age Discrimination Act bars discrimination against individuals over 40. • The Pregnancy Discrimination Act bars discrimination due to pregnancy, childbirth, and related medical conditions. • The Genetic Information Non-Discrimination Act of 2008 bars discrimination based on individuals' genetic information. **State-level** • Almost half the states currently prohibit sexual preference discrimination in both public- and private-sector jobs, while other states prohibit such discrimination in public workplaces only. • Roughly half the states prohibit discrimination based on marital status.
Disabilities and medical conditions	The Americans with Disabilities Act of 1990 bars discrimination against qualified individuals with disabilities. The law forbids employers with 15 or more employees from discriminating against a "qualified individual with a disability because of the disability of such individual," and specifically covers "medical examinations and inquiries" as grounds for discrimination. • Before an offer of employment is made, the ADA permits such examinations and inquiries only where "job-related and consistent with business necessity." • The ADA generally requires an employer to provide reasonable accommodation to qualified individuals who are employees or applicants for employment, but during the hiring process and before a conditional offer is made, an employer may not ask applicants whether they need a reasonable accommodation for the job, except when the employer knows that an applicant has a disability. • Only after a conditional offer of employment is extended, an employer may inquire whether applicants will need reasonable accommodations if this is asked consistently of all entering employees in the same job category. • Before ADA, it was common for employers to ask about prior injuries or illnesses, including worker compensation claims, but the ADA now effectively prohibits those practices. Employers can no longer routinely ask questions about prior injuries and illnesses, including prior worker compensation claims. • ADA has also limited the use of psychological and personality tests because these may be considered medical examinations.
Credit or financial status	**Federal-level** • The Fair Credit Reporting Act also regulates how employers perform background checks on job applicants. This law goes beyond background credit checks to include any other type of background checks, such as criminal records or driving records. Pre-employment and promotion screening are considered permissible purposes under FCRA, so employers may obtain consumer reports, including investigative consumer reports in the hiring process. But employers must meet the FCRA standards of written notice and consent, the use of a qualified CRA, and certification of the permissible purpose. If a consumer report reveals information that may be used to deny employment, the employer must provide a pre-adverse action notice to the applicant with a copy of the consumer report, to give the applicant an opportunity to dispute the report. And if that adverse action is taken, the employer must provide an adverse action notice. The FCRA does not preempt states from creating stronger legislation in the area of employment credit history checks. • Employers who fail to comply with FCRA requirements may face civil and criminal penalties, including a private right of action. • The Bankruptcy Act provision 11 USC § 525(b) prohibits employment discrimination against persons who have filed for bankruptcy. However, there is some ambiguity as to whether the statute applies to discrimination prior to the extension of an offer of employment, and courts have read the statute both ways.

State-level

- California: Employers operating in California should also be aware of the State's Investigative Consumer Reporting Agencies Act (ICRAA), which was not preempted by the Fair and Accurate Credit Transactions Act (FACTA). Disclosure requirements under the ICRAA are more stringent than under the FCRA. Under the ICRAA, any person who acquires an investigative consumer report for employment purposes must provide separate written disclosure to the applicant or employee before the report is obtained. The written disclosure must include the fact that a report may be obtained; the permissible purpose of the report; the fact that the disclosure may include information on the consumer's character, general reputation, personal characteristics, and mode of living; and the name, address, and telephone number of the investigative consumer reporting agency. As of 2012, the disclosure must also include the web address (or telephone number if the CRA has no website) where the applicant or employee "may find information about the investigative consumer reporting agency's privacy practices, including whether the consumer's personal information will be sent outside the United States or its territories."
- Connecticut, Hawaii, Illinois, Maryland, Oregon, and Washington—currently limit the use of credit information in employment.
- Some states allow credit history checks to be performed if the position applied for fits within predefined occupational categories, generally involving financial or managerial responsibility or exposure to confidential information.

Polygraphs and psychological testing	The Employee Polygraph Protection Act of 1988 (EPPA) is a prominent example of federal protection of privacy in the workplace.
	• Under the act and its regulations, employers are prohibited from using "lie detectors" on incumbent workers or to screen applicants. A "lie detector" is defined to include polygraphs, voice stress analyzers, psychological stress evaluators or any similar device used for the purpose of rendering a diagnostic opinion regarding an individual's honesty. The act prohibits employers from requiring or requesting that a prospective or current employee take a lie detector test. Employers cannot use, accept, refer to or inquire about lie detector test results.
	• The act also prohibits employers from taking adverse action against an employee who refuses to take a test.
	• EPPA has exceptions for certain occupations, including for government employees, employees in certain security services, those engaged in the manufacture of controlled substances, certain defense contractors and those in certain national security functions.
	• Tests are allowed in connection with "an ongoing investigation involving economic loss or injury to the employer's business," such as theft, embezzlement, or industrial espionage. Even for such investigations, there must be reasonable suspicion to test an employee, and other protections for the employee apply. An employee cannot be discharged solely on the basis of the results of a polygraph or for refusing to submit to a polygraph.
	• EPPA requires employers to post the act's essential provisions in a conspicuous location so that employees are aware of its existence.
	• State laws are not preempted, and a large number of states have enacted laws further restricting the use of lie detectors in private employment.
Substance testing	For public-sector employees, there is considerable case law under the Fourth Amendment about when such testing is reasonable. Federal law mandates drug testing for certain positions within the federal sector, including employees of the US Customs and Border Protection. Federal law also creates regulations for drug testing for employees in transportation industries. The rules preempt state laws that would otherwise limit drug testing. The Americans with Disabilities Act prohibits discrimination based on disability, although the application of the ADA varies for illegal drugs and alcohol, for current and past use. The ADA specifically excludes current illegal drug use from its protections, and a test for drug use is not considered a medical examination. By contrast, the responsible federal agencies have stated that "an alcoholic is a person with a disability and is protected by the ADA if s/he is qualified to perform the essential functions of the job." Concerning the history of illegal drug use, the US Department of Justice states that "policies that screen out applicants because of a history of addiction or treatment for addiction must be carefully scrutinized to ensure that the policies are job-related and consistent with business necessity."

(Continued)

TABLE 24.4   (Continued)

Data Type	Description
Drug testing can be used in a variety of settings.	<ul><li>In pre-employment screening, it is generally allowed if not designed to identify legal use of drugs or addiction to illegal drugs.</li><li>When an employer has a reasonable suspicion based on things like appearance, behavior, speech and odors, substance testing is generally allowed as a condition of continued employment.</li><li>Substance testing is generally allowed as a condition of continued employment following a workplace accident if there is "reasonable suspicion" that the employee involved in the accident was under the influence of drugs or alcohol.</li><li>Random testing is acceptable in specific, narrowly defined jobs, such as in highly regulated industries where the employee has a severely diminished expectation of privacy, or where testing is critical to public safety or national security.</li><li>Unless prohibited by state or local law routine substance testing is generally allowed if the employees are notified at the time of hire.</li></ul>

TABLE 24.5

Examples of Background Screening Requirements in Europe

	Employment History and References Check	Education	Credit	Criminal Record
Austria	Employers may verify the employment history provided by the candidate by contacting the candidate's previous employers based on the consent of the candidate. The refusal or withdrawal of the consent, however, must not be the basis for unfavorable treatment and cannot cause any negative consequences for the candidate (such as the refusal to hire). A concrete investigation made of the former employer is permitted, if (i) the applicant has given his consent; or (ii) the Employer has reasonable doubts as to the truth of the information provided by the applicant.	Same as "Employment History and References Check"	Such questions may be permissible if the job applied for demands a high level of trustworthiness in financial matters.	Questions about the criminal record are only permissible, in as much the crime committed may raise serious concerns about the aptitude to fulfill the job's requirements. Under Austrian law, there is a register for criminal records. However, administrative proceedings (e.g., traffic offenses) are not included therein. Criminal convictions, which have been recorded in the criminal register, will be deleted after the expiration of the extinction-time-limit. It will be unacceptable for the employer to ask for information on convictions already extinct from the criminal record.
Bulgaria	Employers are entitled to verify their employment history. In that regard, it would be permissible to review the employment record book or recommendation/performance evaluation by the former employer, as permitted by the Bulgarian Labor Code.	Same as "Employment History and References Check"	Obtaining candidates' credit data would be illegal in Bulgaria.	In Bulgaria, the only option to check candidates' criminal records is to require them to provide an official conviction status certificate. For positions involving liability for monetary or other assets, as determined by their job description, the organization is obligated to collect a conviction status certificate. On the other hand, for positions that are not necessarily liable for monetary or other assets, it would be forbidden to require applicants to share such information.

(Continued)

TABLE 24.5 (Continued)

	Employment History and References Check	Education	Credit	Criminal Record
Croatia	Employers are entitled to verify the employment history provided by the candidate by contacting candidate's previous employers only based on consent.	If there are doubts about the authenticity of the diploma or information provided, verification of diplomas and other documents can be carried out.	Employers are allowed to obtain candidates' credit data, only if this is strictly related to the position the candidate is applying for.	1) Based on the provisions of the Croatian Law on Legal Consequences of the Conviction, Criminal Records and Rehabilitation, the employer would not be entitled to demand that the candidates or its employees submit evidence about criminal convictions and offenses, except for the candidate who is applying for a position involving work with children, and only with the consent of such candidate. 2) In limited cases, the employer would be authorized to ask its employees to provide the clearance certificate which is being issued under Article 159 of the local Administrative Procedure Act. 3) Under the Commercial Companies Act, members of the management board, supervisory board, or liquidators of commercial companies cannot be convicted in a final judgment for specific economic crimes.
Cyprus	The DPA Regulations instruct that collecting data from a previous employer can be done only by having previously notified the employee.	Education documents can be collected during the process of recruitment based on the consent.	Data collected must only be relevant and necessary based on the nature of the employment.	Criminal records are allowed to be obtained by the employer, upon the consent of the employee. The criminal Record can be obtained upon application of the employee to the Police.

Czech Republic	The employer should not verify the employment history provided by the candidate by contacting the candidate's previous employer(s) without the candidate's consent.	Same as "Employment History and References Check"	Under the Labor Code, information related to property situations may be requested by the employer only where there is a cause for it consisting of the nature of work to be performed or where it is specifically laid down in the applicable laws. Without the employee's consent, such information may not be obtained through third parties.	Under the Labor Code, information related to criminal offenses convictions and offenses may be requested by the employer only where there is a cause for it consisting in the nature of work to be performed or where it is specifically laid down in the applicable laws. Without the employee's consent, such information may not be obtained through third parties.
Denmark	Employers are entitled to verify the employment history and reference/ information provided by the candidate by contacting the candidate's previous employers only based on consent. Information on social media: Employers are also entitled to collect and use the information made public on social media based on legitimate interest.	Same as "Employment History and References Check" In Denmark, there are no central databases available to verify education. It is customary to ask candidates to submit documentation for relevant education either as an appendix to the application or at a later interview. Universities/schools have no obligation to reply to a request.	Employers are allowed to collect candidates' credit data if the data is considered reasonably relevant and proportionate for the specific purposes.	1) Employers are allowed to collect candidates' criminal records based on the candidate's consent for certain roles such as the person who will be in a position of trust, etc. (§ 8(3) of the DDPA). 2) Employers may either ask the candidate to provide the criminal record himself or ask for consent to retrieve the criminal record directly from the "public register of criminal records".

(Continued)

TABLE 24.5 (Continued)

	Employment History and References Check	Education	Credit	Criminal Record
Finland	1) All documents and information must be strictly necessary because of the nature of the position (Act on the Protection of Privacy in Working Life, 3 §). 2) When acquiring the documents and information from elsewhere than the applicant, the applicant must be asked for their consent for this.	Same as "Employment History and References Check"	1) No consent is required when obtaining credit information about an employee, but other restrictions apply 2) Credit information can only be obtained regarding employees who will act in a position that requires special trustworthiness and if one of the following applies: a) the employee is allowed to make significant financial commitments on behalf of the employer or may exercise their own discretion when preparing such commitments. b) the employee's specific task is to grant or supervise significant credits. c) the employee has access to the employer's or the employer's clients' essential trade secrets. d) the employee's work tasks require such access rights which allow the employee to transfer the employer's or the employer's clients' assets or modify the information regarding the assets. e) the employee as an essential part of their work tasks and without supervision has access to significant amounts of cash, securities or valuables.	The processing of criminal records by a private employer is very restricted. It can mainly be based on the Security Clearance Act (726/2014, as amended) or the Act on checking the criminal background of persons working with children (504/2002, as amended).

Country				
Greece	When the processing takes place based on consent, that consent must be in writing and the employer must be able to prove that the employee was informed, the consent was freely given and can be revoked at any time without negative repercussions.	Same as "Employment History and References Check"	Credit checks can only be conducted by Bank Institutions which have access to the TEIRESIAS databases, including credit information for their customers.	The employer may process data regarding criminal persecution, security measures and criminal convictions as long as and to the point that it is absolutely necessary to see if the candidate employee is the right person for that particular position or for the work duties or to make decisions in the context of the employment relationship. Furthermore, these criminal records can only be obtained by the employee himself or by authorized third parties and not by the employers.
Hungary	Employers are entitled to verify reference/information provided by the candidate by contacting with candidate's previous employer based on consent (Article 6(1) (a) GDPR).	The verification on the basis of a legitimate interest (Article 6(1)(f) GDPR) is well founded when there are doubts about the authenticity of the diploma or information provided.	Employers are not allowed to obtain candidates' credit data.	1) Under the practice of the Hungarian DPA, the employer may ask for a certification of a clean criminal record only if it is justified by the nature of the position or the tasks to be carried out or if specific laws prescribe such a criminal record check. 2) According to the Hungarian DPA, the employer cannot make a copy of the certification of a clean criminal record, because it is not necessary to copy and store the document to prove the criminal record, so it does not comply with the principle of purpose limitation.

(Continued)

TABLE 24.5   (Continued)

	Employment History and References Check	Education	Credit	Criminal Record
Norway	Employers are entitled to verify the employment history provided by the candidate by contacting the candidate's previous employers only based on consent (Article 6(1)(a) GDPR). If the candidate refuses to give consent or withdraws it, this cannot be the basis for unfavorable treatment and cannot cause any negative consequences for the candidate (such as refusal to hire).	Verification of diplomas and other documents with entities that issued the documents based on a legitimate interest.	Employers are allowed to ask credit reference services (service must be licensed by the Norwegian DPA to conduct credit checks) to check and disclose a potential candidate's credit check if the employer has a justifiable need for such check. According to the Norwegian DPA, there are three criteria that need to be met in order for an employer to ask for a credit check: —the position in question should have a higher function —the position must come with great financial responsibility —credit checks can only be made on the candidates who are relevant in the final phase of the hiring process. Please note that the employer is not allowed to retain such credit checks—they must be deleted once the purpose of asking for such credit check is fulfilled.	Employers are allowed to obtain candidates' criminal record data only when the obligation to do so stems from Norwegian laws or regulations, e.g., provisions establishing specific professional requirements such as security companies, hospitals, schools, kindergartens, and financial entities. Employers are entitled to either ask the candidate for his/her criminal record or apply for the certificate directly from the Norwegian National Register of Criminal Convictions.

Poland	Employers are entitled to verify the employment history provided by the candidate by contacting with candidate's previous employers only based on consent (Article 6(1)(a) GDPR). If the candidate refuses to grant the consent or withdraws it, this cannot be the basis for unfavorable treatment and cannot cause any negative consequences for him (such as the refusal to hire).	If the verification takes place when there are doubts about the authenticity of the diploma or information provided.	Employers are not allowed to obtain candidates' credit data.	Employers are allowed to obtain candidates' criminal record data only when the obligation to do so stems from Polish provisions establishing specific professional requirements, otherwise processing criminal record data is not allowed. Under the Polish Code of Commercial Companies members of the management board, supervisory board, auditors' committee, or liquidators cannot be convicted in a final judgment for specific economic crimes.
Romania	Employers are entitled to verify the employment history provided by the candidate by contacting with candidate's previous employers only on the activities performed and on the duration of the employment and only upon prior notification of the potential employee.	Same as "Employment History and References Check"	Employers are not allowed to obtain candidates' credit data, due to the fact that processing of credit data exceeds the Romanian Labor Code requirements and the purpose of processing.	Employers may process criminal record data based on a legitimate interest (Article 6(1)(f) GDPR) only if criminal record to be requested only for positions for which such document is actually relevant.
Sweden	Data collected from former employers may be collected based on the employer's legitimate interest (GDPR Article 6(1)(f)).	Same as "Employment History and References Check"	Data relating to candidates' credit data may not be collected.	Data relating to criminal convictions and offenses may not be collected.

TABLE 24.6
Common Reasons to and Not to Monitor Employees

Reason to Monitor	Reason Not to Monitor
Protect corporate from any reputation damage or legal liabilities: Employees might incorrectly use email, the Internet, and the telephone in ways that can lead to problems for the employer, such as damage to reputation, and certain liabilities for the employer, such as those relating to defamation, harassment, discrimination copyright infringement, hacking, transmitting viruses, and disclosure of confidential information and trade secrets, etc.	Although monitoring is justified in some settings, there can be serious **privacy concerns** from excessive video monitoring (such as in changing rooms), monitoring of workplace conversations (such as bugs secretly placed by a supervisor to listen to employees) or email and other computer monitoring (such as when emails that an employee believes are personal are reviewed by the employer).
Improving work quality: such as by monitoring service calls with customers; Call centers and firms that do financial transactions over the phone often record telephone conversations for reasons including agent training, quality assurance and security or liability. If a dispute arises with a customer after the fact, the recording can often resolve what was said or agreed upon. However, such recordings must comply with the rules about phone call recording discussed.	Employers often choose not to monitor even where they may have **legal ability** to do so, for reasons including ethics, cost, and morale. Monitoring costs include the legal obligations to detect and act on misconduct revealed by the monitoring program.
Enhance employee performance: trying to keep employees on the task rather than spending time on personal business, such as surfing the web.	**Collective bargaining agreements** can be an additional limiting factor to an employer's ability to monitor the workplace. Many such agreements contain provisions designed to limit workplace monitoring or require that a union representative be informed of an employer's monitoring activities.

24.4.1 Types of Employee Monitoring

Table 24.7 lists some of the typical channels that organizations normally leverage to monitor employees.

24.4.2 General Principles

If you want to carry out workplace monitoring, you should ensure compliance with these principles:

- Necessity: You must be able to show that the monitoring of your employees is truly necessary
  - You need to justify why the organization needs to monitor employees. You need to ask the question: Is there a less intrusive method to achieve the goals instead of monitoring employees?
  - Monitoring must be necessary for employers' purposes and a data privacy impact assessment (DPIA) should be carried out when it is likely to result in a high risk to the rights and freedoms of an individual.
- Legitimacy: You must have lawful grounds for collecting and processing personal data.
  - There should be a lawful basis for monitoring and employers should consider local employment laws, work councils, and other relevant laws. If workplace monitoring is permitted by member state law, for data protection purposes you need to determine your lawful grounds for processing.
  - Consent is rarely an appropriate lawful ground of processing for workplace monitoring because of the imbalance in the employment relationship.

TABLE 24.7

Typical Channels That Organizations Monitor Employees

Types	Description
Email	Computer programs can search across all emails for keywords or email addresses that may pose a threat.
Internet use	Programs can block the use of certain websites, and you can view the employee's browsing history.
Social media	You may monitor employees' social media accounts to ensure that they aren't bringing the organization into disrepute.
	Don't assume, just because somebody's social media profile is public, that you can use this information for your own purposes. You still must have lawful grounds for the processing, such as legitimate interests. It's more likely to be legitimate to inspect social media accounts if they're related to business purposes (such as LinkedIn) rather than to private purposes (such as Facebook).
Telephone use	You may monitor phone calls for quality control, volume, and cost and review employee performance or ensure compliance.
CCTV	This system can be used in the workplace and surrounding areas, generally for security and safety. Security cameras are often used at the perimeter of a business to deter and detect burglary or other unauthorized intrusions.
Vehicle tracking	You may want to monitor your employees' journeys, whether in company cars or on trucks or vans, for example, to ensure compliance with law and productivity.
	Processing location data can be justified where it is done as part of monitoring the transport of people or goods or improving the distribution of resources or services in scattered locations, or where a security objective is being pursued in relation to the employee himself or to the goods or vehicles in his charge.
Fitness tracking	Your health insurance provider may issue Fitbit devices or other fitness tracking devices to employees to monitor movement and process health data.

- An employer has a legitimate interest in protecting your organization from threats, but this must be balanced with each employee's right to privacy. An interest balance test has to be conducted prior to such data collecting and monitoring.
- The following aspects can't be monitored in the EU context in accordance with WP 29 guidance.
  - Employers cannot use keylogging and mouse-movement detection technologies to make sure the remote employees are who they say they are, because such technologies are "disproportionate."
- Employers cannot use an access control system to track when employees come and go as a performance evaluation.
- Proportionality: Your monitoring must be proportionate to the issue you're dealing with.
  - The proposed monitoring should be proportionate to the employer's concern and the concern you're trying to address, and this is linked to the principle of data minimization
  - For example, continuously monitoring all employees' emails to ensure that nobody is disclosing confidential information isn't considered proportionate.
- Transparency: Employers cannot use an access control system to track when employees come and go as a performance evaluation.
  - You must be transparent with employees about what type and amount of work place monitoring is taking place. Merely notifying employees about workplace monitoring isn't the same as receiving consent to the monitoring.
  - To be transparent with employees, you should provide them with the following information in the privacy notice:
    - In the privacy notice of employment monitoring, employees should be informed in advance of the scope and the degree (extent and nature) of the monitoring.

- The standards and rules for using company software and equipment, such as email, Internet, and telephones.
- Explanations of how the usage will be monitored, for what purposes, and to whom it will be disclosed.
- Security Controls
  - Employment monitoring has to be accompanied by "adequate and sufficient safeguards against abuse".

You have a few options for how to conduct less intrusive methods of monitoring. You could limit monitoring to any of these factors:

- Location: Not monitoring changing rooms, toilets, break areas, or places of worship
- Time: Using spot checks rather than continuous monitoring
- Data: Not monitoring employee's personal messages, for example
- Recipient: Allowing only the HR manager to have access to the data
- Data subject: Monitoring only high-risk employees rather than every employee

24.4.3 ELECTRONIC COMMUNICATIONS AND CONTENT

The scenarios in which monitoring may be done are to improve efficiency, investigate employees, or support the employee. There should be alternatives to monitoring as a first resort such as instead of checking if an employee is going on gambling websites, the employer can take pre-emptive action by blocking these kinds of sites.

 Case Study

Monitoring of employees' computer use
Bărbulescu v. Romania, September 5, 2017 (Grand Chamber)[76]
This case concerned the decision of a private company to dismiss an employee—the applicant—after monitoring his electronic communications and accessing their contents. The applicant complained that his employer's decision was based on a breach of his privacy and that the domestic courts had failed to protect his right to respect for his private life and correspondence.
The Grand Chamber held, by 11 votes to 6, that there had been a violation of Article 8 of the Convention, finding that the Romanian authorities had not adequately protected the applicant's right to respect for his private life and correspondence. They had consequently failed to strike a fair balance between the interests at stake. In particular, the national courts had failed to determine whether the applicant had received prior notice from his employer of the possibility that his communications might be monitored; nor had they regarded either the fact that he had not been informed of the nature or the extent of the monitoring or the degree of intrusion into his private life and correspondence. In addition, the national courts had failed to determine, firstly, the specific reasons justifying the introduction of the monitoring measures; secondly, whether the employer could have used measures entailing less intrusion into the applicant's private life and correspondence; and thirdly, whether the communications might have been accessed without his knowledge.

 Case Study

Monitoring of employees' computer use
Libert v. France, February 22, 2018

TABLE 24.8

Examples of Electronic Communications Monitoring Regulations

Jurisdiction	Description
US	Interception
	• Regarding the interception of communications, Federal law is generally strict in prohibiting wiretaps of telephone calls and other aural conversations, such as sound recordings from video cameras. The law also applies to "oral communications," such as hidden bugs or microphones.
	• The Electronic Communications Privacy Act of 1986 (ECPA) extended the ban on the interception to "electronic communications," which essentially are communications, including emails, that are not wire or oral communications.
	• Delaware law prohibits employers from "monitoring or otherwise intercepting any telephone conversation or transmission, electronic mail or transmission, or Internet access or usage" without prior written notice and daily electronic notice.
	• Connecticut law requires that "each employer who engages in any type of electronic monitoring shall give prior written notice to all employees who may be affected, informing them of the types of monitoring which may occur. Each employer shall post, in a conspicuous place which is readily available for viewing by its employees, a notice concerning the types of electronic monitoring which the employer may engage in."
	• Stored communications
	• In general, legal limits on interception are stricter than for access to stored records.
	• The Stored Communications Act (SCA) was enacted as part of ECPA in 1986. It creates a general prohibition against the unauthorized acquisition, alteration, or blocking of electronic communications. For workplace monitoring, the exceptions are simpler than interceptions.
	• In general, legal limits on interception are stricter than for access to stored records.
	• The SCA has an exception for conduct authorized "by the person or entity providing a wire or electronic communications service," which will often be the employer. It also has an exception for conduct authorized "by a user of that service with respect to a communication of or intended for that use."
Norway	Regulation on employers' right to access email and other electronically stored material.
	• The Email Monitoring Regulation outlines that an employer may only access employee emails and personal files when it is necessary for the operation of their business or when the employee is suspected of gross breach of duty. The Regulations enters into force on 20 July 2018.
	https://lovdata.no/dokument/SF/forskrift/2018-07-02-1108
Poland	Email monitoring systems should not violate the confidentiality of correspondence and other personal rights of employees.

This case concerned the dismissal of an SNCF (French national railway company) employee after the seizure of his work computer had revealed the storage of pornographic files and forged certificates drawn up for third persons. The applicant complained in particular that his employer had opened, in his absence, personal files stored on the hard drive of his work computer.

The Court held that there had been no violation of Article 8 of the Convention, finding that in the present case the French authorities had not overstepped the margin of appreciation available to them. The Court noted in particular that the consultation of the files by the applicant's employer had pursued a legitimate aim of protecting the rights of employers, who might legitimately wish to ensure that their employees were using the computer facilities which they had placed at their disposal in line with their contractual obligations and the applicable regulations. The Court also observed that French law comprised a privacy protection mechanism allowing employers to open professional files, although they could not surreptitiously open files identified as being personal. They could only open the latter type of files in the employee's presence. The domestic courts had ruled that the said mechanism would not have prevented the employer from opening the files at issue since they had not been duly identified as being private. Lastly, the Court considered that the domestic courts had properly assessed the applicant's allegation of a violation of his right to respect for his private life and that those courts' decisions had been based on relevant and sufficient grounds.

24.4.4   CCTV AND VIDEO SURVEILLANCE

24.4.4.1   CCTV Data Protection Practices

CCTV surveillance can come in multiple forms, including:

- Covert or overt, depending on whether its use is concealed or made known to the individuals affected by it
- Fixed or mobile, depending on the range of movement available to it through the technology used
- Body-worn cameras and drones
- A combination of video analytics to increase the identifiability of individuals, patterns of behavior, and objects recorded by it.

Table 24.9 lists some of the legal requirements from a few jurisdictions.

An organization that intends to conduct CCTV monitoring activities should consider the following aspects to manage the privacy and data protection risks.

- Lawful basis and purpose
  - CCTV monitoring may be subject to additional local laws like labor law—consult local legal.
  - Use of a surveillance camera system must always be for a specified purpose that is in pursuit of a legitimate aim and necessary to meet an identified pressing need, such as for security purposes or health & safety (no behavior and performance monitoring).
  - The use of a surveillance camera system must take into account its effect on individuals and their privacy, with regular reviews to ensure that its use remains justified.
- DPIA required
  - Trade Union or Workers Representatives may need to be involved/consulted if applicable
  - Review by DPO/PO before going live
- Accountability, policy, and training:
  - There must be clear responsibility and accountability for all surveillance camera system activities, including images and information collected, held, and used.
  - Clear rules, policies, and procedures must be in place before a surveillance camera system is used, and these must be communicated to all who need to comply with them.
  - Conduct staff training on the misuse of CCTV footage and the potential consequences of doing so.
  - Effective review and audit mechanisms should be in place to ensure that legal requirements, policies, and standards are complied with in practice, and regular reports should be published.
- Notification Requirements:
  - Employees need to be informed upfront of CCTV monitoring (in writing/email). There must be as much transparency in the use of a surveillance camera system as possible, including a published contact point for access to information and complaints. Layered Approach of signs (basic notice at all entrances, details at reception)

TABLE 24.9
Examples of CCTV Monitoring Obligations

Jurisdiction	Description

US	• Cameras and video recordings that do not have sound recordings are outside the scope of the federal wiretap and stored-record statutes. Many US employers use closed-circuit television or other video surveillance in the workplace.
	• They are used within a business establishment to deter crimes such as shoplifting and armed robbery, and outside to detect drive-aways from gas stations or other businesses. They are used within warehouses and other parts of a business to reduce the incidence of stealing by employees, and insurance companies may give companies a discount for installing closed-circuit television systems.
	• Although federal law generally does not limit the use of either photography or video cameras, state statutes, and common law creates limits in some settings.
	  • California is similar to other states in forbidding video recording in areas such as restrooms, locker rooms, and places where employees change clothes.
	  • Michigan's statute is broader, forbidding the installation of a device for observing or photographing a "private place" as defined by the statute.

Austria	The use of CCTV to monitor employees **is NOT permitted**. The Data Protection Act contains detailed requirements and safeguards with regard to the lawfulness of the recording and processing of image data, which apply to photographs as well as video recordings (www.whitecase.com/publications/article/gdpr-guide-national-implementation-austria#q1).
Croatia	Biometric data (Art 23 of the Law) Video surveillance of working premises (Art 30 of the Law) 1) Performing video surveillance in the **restroom dressing room or personal hygiene rooms** within the working premises is **prohibited**. 2) Video surveillance of employees can be performed only if all prerequisites related to the video surveillance prescribed by the Law and other regulations related to employee safety are fulfilled and if the employees had been adequately informed of such measure before its commencement. 3) CCTV of public areas can only be carried out by public authorities, entities vested with public powers, and entities performing a public service, provided that such surveillance is prescribed by law and necessary for the performance of tasks and duties of public authorities, or for the protection of the life and health of individuals and property. • Keep recordings for no longer than 6 months, unless the data is necessary for the purposes of judicial, arbitral, or similar proceedings.
Norway	Regulation 1107/2018 on camera surveillance in the workplace ("The Camera Surveillance Regulation"): CCTV monitoring is permitted. Data retention requirements: **7 days** after the recordings have been made and may only be stored for up to **30** days if it is likely that the recordings will be handed to law enforcement agencies in connection with the investigation of criminal offenses.
Poland	The following safeguards apply in order to protect employees' dignity, legitimate interests, and fundamental rights: • CCTV must not be used to monitor rooms made available to trade unions. It must not be used to monitor sanitary rooms, locker rooms, canteens, and smoking areas, unless the use of monitoring in those rooms is necessary to fulfill the objectives specified in Q20(a) above and does not violate the dignity and other personal rights of employees, in particular, by the use of techniques that make it impossible to identify persons present in those rooms. The monitoring of sanitary rooms requires prior consent from the entity's trade union, or if there is no trade union, the consent of employees. • The objectives, the scope, and the manner of use of monitoring systems (CCTV, email monitoring, and other monitoring systems) should be established in a collective labor agreement or in the work regulations, or in an announcement if the employer is not covered by a collective labor agreement or is not obliged to adopt work regulations. An employer must notify employees of the introduction of monitoring no later than two weeks before starting the monitoring. Before permitting an employee to perform their work duties, an employer must provide them with the above information in writing; When monitoring is introduced, the employer must designate monitored rooms and monitored areas in a visible and legible manner, using appropriate signs or sound announcements, no later than one day before starting the monitoring.

(Continued)

TABLE 24.9 (Continued)

Jurisdiction	Description
Portugal	When CCTV is permitted, the recording of sound requires the prior authorization of the DPA if the facilities under surveillance are publicly accessible.

Slovenia	The following safeguards apply in order to protect employees' dignity, legitimate interests, and fundamental rights:
	• CCTV in the workplace is only permitted if it is absolutely necessary for the following purposes, and if such purposes cannot be achieved by any other means:
	  • ensuring the security of people or assets
	  • preventing or identifying violations relating to gambling activities
	  • protecting classified information
	  • protecting business secrets
	• the following additional restrictions apply to CCTV in the workplace:
	  • live monitoring of spaces can only be performed by authorized security personnel or other specifically authorized and trained personnel of the controller
	  • employees should be notified in advance and in writing that CCTV will take place
	  • prior to implementing CCTV, the employer must carry out consultations with the representative of a trade union, a work council, or a worker representative within at least 30 days of the relevant CCTV being implemented.

- Pictogram
- Name of the controller
- Legal Basis
- State purpose
- Retention period
- Recipients/categories of recipients (Portugal requires the name and license number of the operating entity)
- How to contact DPO
- Data subject rights and how to exercise them
- Camera positions:
  - Position cameras so that you narrow the extent of the monitored area to the area of concern in order to minimize the processing that is not necessary for the purpose.
  - Avoid private areas such as toilets and individual workspaces.
  - No video recording of public space (outside of the organization property)—due to local circumstances, public areas outside of the organization property may become part of the monitoring view to fulfill the purpose (e.g., security of the organization buildings) local Privacy Officer, Privacy Interface or DPO should be consulted.
  - No secrete or hidden cameras.
  - If possible, use a fixed camera rather than a mobile camera.
  - Avoid zooming in.
  - No audio recordings.
- Retention:
  - Be mindful of the period of retention of the CCTV footage. It should be retained only as long as necessary for the purpose for which the CCTV was being used. No more images and information should be stored than that which is strictly required for the stated purpose of a surveillance camera system, and such images and information should be deleted after their purposes have been discharged.
  - Generally, CCTV recording should only be stored for 72 hours max unless there is an incident. It could be higher in certain countries. In the case of an incident, related CCTV recordings should be archived until the investigation is closed.

- Security and access to recordings:
  - Surveillance camera system images and information should be subject to appropriate security measures to safeguard against unauthorized access and use.
  - Access to retained images and information should be restricted, and there must be clearly defined rules on who can gain access and for what purpose such access is granted; the disclosure of images and information should take place only when it is necessary for such a purpose or for law enforcement purposes.
  - Only with DPO or PO present, the access needs to be documented (and logged) for audit purposes.

Case Study

López Ribalda and Others v. Spain October 17, 2019[77]

This case concerned the covert video surveillance of employees which led to their dismissal. The applicants complained about the covert video surveillance and the Spanish courts' use of the data obtained to find that their dismissals had been fair. The applicants who signed settlement agreements also complained that the agreements had been made under duress owing to the video material and should not have been accepted as evidence that their dismissals had been fair.

The Grand Chamber held that there had been no violation of Article 8 of the Convention in respect of the five applicants. It found in particular that the Spanish courts had carefully balanced the rights of the applicants—supermarket employees suspected of theft—and those of the employer and had carried out a thorough examination of the justification for the video surveillance. A key argument made by the applicants was that they had not been given prior notification of the surveillance, despite such a legal requirement, but the Court found that there had been a clear justification for such a measure owing to a reasonable suspicion of serious misconduct and to the losses involved, taking account of the extent and the consequences of the measure. In the present case, the domestic courts had thus not exceeded their power of discretion ("margin of appreciation") in finding the monitoring proportionate and legitimate. The Court also held that there had been no violation of Article 6 § 1 (right to a fair trial) of the Convention, finding in particular that the use of the video material as evidence had not undermined the fairness of the trial.

24.4.4.2 Privacy Implication for Facial Recognition

As facial recognition becomes increasingly pervasive, privacy concerns are compounded. For example, the Privacy Commissioner of Canada is open to more limited use of facial recognition technology (FRT) provided privacy regulations are followed (e.g., the organization has employee consent for the use of their personal images for identification in this very specific context, stores the information securely, etc.).[78]

Main concerns of using facial recognition (FR):

- The concern surrounding FR is not just based on the sensitive information that it collects but the way it is deployed and its societal ramifications.
  - Massive deployment
  - Surveillance
- Low accuracy rate and algorithm bias in the technology has shown to produce "false positive" errors, which leads to a face in the system being incorrectly matched to an image in the database. This false identification substantially undermines civil liberties, as an individual may be criminally charged for an act they did not commit, because of an error made by the technology.

- In addition to these concerns, FR technology has even led to the creation of deep fakes, which are manipulated videos, audios, and images of an individual.

Case Study

CNIL v. ITIC, 2018
   CNIL issued compliance decisions on the video surveillance system against ITIC.
   The French data protection authority (CNIL) announced, on July 19, 2018, that it had issued a decision against the Institute of Computer and Commercial Techniques (ITIC) requiring it to comply with the data protection law, within a two-month period, following the results of an investigation conducted into its video surveillance systems. According to CNIL, ITIC did not properly inform individuals that their images had been recorded and that the images had been kept for one month, which was deemed an excessive amount of time by the CNIL. In addition, CNIL deemed that the security measures of ITIC were insufficient. Moreover, CNIL found that the video surveillance system was overly invasive, as there were cameras permanently filming all the classrooms and employees' workstations.

24.4.5 Social Media

Though employers are generally legally permitted to use social media in informing their decisions, they must not violate existing antidiscrimination and privacy laws. Invasive monitoring practices may provide the basis for discrimination lawsuits if the employer accesses and appears to use information that is legally protected. This includes protected classes such as religion, ethnicity, gender or sexual orientation, political affiliations, and other sensitive information, all of which is commonly available on people's social media pages.

Employers should not require prospective or current employees to divulge access information to private networks as a condition of employment. In 2012, Maryland was the first state to ban employers from asking employees or applicants for their social network login information and passwords. Employers have not traditionally had access to an employee's personal email accounts, and a similar analysis applies to gaining access to the private parts of a person's social network activities.

Employers should consider the following factors when they decide to monitor employee's social media.

- The necessity and proportionality of such monitoring must be assessed by the employer, and they should try and find other ways which are less intrusive to carry out the purpose of the monitoring.
- Employers should apply fit-for-purpose IT and monitoring practices to make sure they have adequate safeguards against abuse of the right to respect for private life.
- There should be a DPIA (data protection impact assessment) carried out before monitoring takes place to see if it is acceptable and allowed.

Case Study

Barbulescu v. Romania, 2016[79]
   Mr. Bogdan Mihai Babulescu worked as a sales engineer at a private company in Romania. His employer asked him to create a Yahoo messenger account so that he can

respond to customer inquiries. He signed the company's internal regulations which prohibited employees from using workplace computers for personal purposes.

He was then monitored by the company using Yahoo messenger communications and
was found that he used it for personal communications. The company terminated Mr.
Bogdan's employment contract for violation of internal regulations.

The court found that Romania's restrictive regulations should not restrict Mr. Bogdan's
right to privacy. So, the employer's instructions can't reduce private social life in the
workplace to zero. He should have been informed before the monitoring that such monitoring could take place.

The court said that just because workers are coming to work each day it does not
mean they abandon their right to privacy when they walk through the doors in the
morning. It was said that domestic authorities should make sure that any introduction of
monitoring shall have adequate and sufficient safeguards against abuse.

24.4.6 TELEPHONE

Many companies will record a call between employees and customers. Regardless of the purpose,
it is recommended to obtain the consent of both parties to the call beforehand. Because different
countries have different legal provisions on this, some countries can record as long as one party of
the call agrees, while some countries stipulate that the consent of both parties must be obtained.

 Case Study

HOUZZ is a home improvement company whose business model is to run a home
improvement business through its website and mobile APP. It has some home improvement designers who connect with potential customers through the HOUZZ website or
mobile app. When a home improvement designer registers on the HOUZZ website, a
sales representative of HOUZZ company will contact him by phone to discuss cooperation plans, promote these home improvement designers through cooperation, and let
them get in touch with local potential customers.

On March 29, 2013, for quality assurance and training purposes, HOUZZ began
recording all calls made from the ORANGE County office. But none of the answering
parties (usually home decorators) were told that the call was being recorded.

After July 1, 2013, for quality assurance and training purposes, salespeople in ORANGE
County began recording both incoming and outgoing calls. But none of the non-HOUZZ
personnel were informed that their phone calls were being recorded.

On September 11, 2013, HOUZZ stopped all recordings. HOUZZ claimed that
the recordings were never shared with third parties, that only a small percentage of
employees had access to the recordings, and that very few were reviewed by HOUZZ
employees.

The California Attorney General asked HOUZZ to destroy all recordings, fined
$175,000, and hired a CPO to monitor its privacy law compliance and conduct privacy
risk assessments for HOUZZ.

24.5 PROCESSING SENSITIVE PERSONAL DATA

24.5.1 LAWFUL BASIS FOR SENSITIVE PERSONAL DATA

Processing of special categories of data/Sensitive personal data. By default, sensitive personal data
of data subjects is not collected. Prohibition to process, except the following under the GDPR:

- Explicit consent:
  - Users' explicit consent must be obtained before collecting, using, or disclosing their special categories of data (Russia requires written consent).
  - Processing of sensitive personal data needs to be executed based on the laws and regulations in the target delivery country. (The laws of the EU or its member states may prohibit the processing of preceding personal data, regardless of whether data subjects' explicit consent is obtained.)
- In the context of employment
- Vital interest's data subject
- Legal claims
- Not-for-profit political, philosophical, and religious purposes
- Manifestly made public by data subject
- Substantial public interest laid down in EU/Member State law
- Occupational medicine (by healthcare professional)
- Public health
- Research and statistical purposes
- Scientific research:
  - There is no universally agreed definition of research or scientific research. EDPS opinion 3/2020 *on the European strategy for data* says "It is a common assumption that scientific research is beneficial to the whole of society and that scientific knowledge is a public good to be encouraged and supported."

24.5.2 BIOMETRICS

Biometrics is not only about you but your family.

US

Washington, Texas, and Illinois have passed similar laws governing biometric information, but Illinois' law is distinct in that it contains a provision allowing individuals to file lawsuits for damages from a violation. Should Maryland's and New York's bills pass as mirrors to BIPA, there will likely be similar provisions around the permissibility of litigation in the event of a violation.

Maryland and New York each introduced Biometric Information Privacy bills governing biometric data in their respective legislatures. Each bill has reportedly been drafted similar to the Biometric Information Privacy Act (2008) of Illinois and outlines the regulations around the collection of biometric data. The bills would require companies doing business in each state to comply with requirements around the collection and storage of biometric data. Stipulations include obtaining consent from individuals, destroying biometric identifiers in a timely manner, and securely storing biometric identifiers.

In the United States, the Genetic Information Nondiscrimination Act of 2008 prohibits a health insurer from requiring a genetic test or denying benefits as a result of a pre-existing condition stemming from a genetic test result.

Canada

The OPC has adopted a four-point test for determining whether requesting access to genetic test results goes beyond what is necessary for legitimate business purposes or what a reasonable person would consider appropriate when applying for life or health insurance:

- Is the collection and use of the test results necessary to achieve a legitimate business purpose?
- Are the test results likely to be effective in achieving that purpose?

- Are the collection and use proportionate to the benefits gained?
- Are there less privacy-invasive alternatives to the collection and use of genetic test results?

The OPC has stated that, when applying this four-point test generally, "it is not clear that the collection and use of genetic test results by insurance companies is demonstrably necessary, effective, proportionate or the least intrusive means of achieving the industry's objectives at this time." However, the OPC has stated that it recognizes that rapidly changing medical technology will require its position to be periodically re-examined.

24.6 PRIVILEGED INFORMATION, LEGAL HOLD, AND EDISCOVERY

24.6.1 PRIVILEGED INFORMATION

In general, access is prohibited to the content that is subject to attorney-client privilege. For instance, Canada OPC is prohibited to access to documents that are subject to solicitor-client privilege. The OPC cannot even ask an organization to otherwise prove a document is privileged (Supreme Court Blood Tribe case 2018).

A few things to consider regarding privileged information:

- Legal advice privilege is relevant when personal data is contained in confidential communications between you and your lawyers, where those communications are for the purpose of giving or receiving legal advice. This is relevant only to lawyers and doesn't extend to advice provided by human resources (HR) advisors.
- Alongside legal advice privilege is legal professional privilege, which applies to confidential communications between lawyers and clients where that communication is created for the dominant purpose of ongoing or reasonably contemplated civil or criminal litigation. Again, note that this exemption relates only to advice from lawyers and not from HR advisors.
- Simply copying a lawyer on an email doesn't constitute legal privilege; the lawyer must be providing legal advice, or litigation must be reasonably contemplated.
- Be careful when forwarding emails because legal privilege can be lost when you do so.

24.6.2 LEGAL HOLD PROCESS

Many jurisdictions impose legal hold or eDiscovery obligations. In the European Union, information preservation is governed under Directive 2006/24/EC of the European Parliament and of the Council of 15 March 2006. US Federal Rule of Civil Procedure 37 poses some rules that apply to potential litigants. Japan, South Korea, and Singapore have similar data protection initiatives. In South America, Brazil and Argentina have the Azeredo Bill and the Argentina Data Retention Law of 2004, Law No. 25.873, respectively.

Legal hold and eDiscovery obligations should be considered and integrated into the data retention and depersonalization program, schedule, and process.

Companies must ensure they are in total compliance with data preservation requirements—and with the growing amounts of ESI generated, it is increasingly common for litigation to require access to evidence stored digitally.

A legal hold, also known as a litigation hold, is a process that ensures the preservation of discoverable ESI and relevant information for potential litigation matters, investigations, or other legal disputes. A Legal Hold is used to preserve all forms of electronically stored information (ESI) for potential litigation matters or investigations. A legal hold is a notification sent from the legal department to instruct custodians and data stewards not to delete any ESI or archived documents that

TABLE 24.10
High-Level Legal Hold Process

Step	Description
1. Identify custodians and stewards	You need to identify key custodians and any data stewards who might have access to data related to the anticipated litigation.
2. Issue a Written Legal Hold Notice	You need to ensure that custodians and stewards are aware of the impending litigation and the need for an immediate hold to be placed on ESI. The legal hold notification must be delivered in a written format, either by email or hard copy.
3. Obtain Acknowledgment of the Hold Notice	When issuing your notice, be sure to request a clear acknowledgment of the hold from every recipient. Whilst it is not absolutely required, this step is highly recommended.
4. Document Your Process	Be sure to have a clear record of the steps and measures you took to show the courts, should this ever be required. Your documentation could cover the following: • The date that the hold was initiated • The triggering events • By whom the hold was initiated • The list of personnel involved and the responsibility for the hold • Any changes made throughout the process, such as new custodians, new sources of data, relevant changes in the company • Scope of all the information, custodians, sources, and systems involved • The dates and a record of any notices or reminders sent • Record of the acknowledgment of both notices and reminders sent • Any relevant notes or additional sources of information

might be relevant to an imminent or new legal case. Legal holds certify that the data is secured and available as long as the hold is in place.

Usually, the legal hold notice should be initiated by the team (i.e., legal or HR) that knows the reason/nature of why the legal hold process should be triggered.

Table 24.10 demonstrates the high-level steps.

 Example

Litigation Hold Email Migration vs. In-Place Email Migration

- Litigation Hold migration involves putting a user's entire mailbox on hold for the purpose of retaining it for legal review.
- In-Place Hold migration involves putting a subset of a user's entire mailbox on hold for the purpose of retaining only certain types of email.
- The key difference between these two types of migration is a query. Litigation Hold can be enabled to hold all items that are deleted or modified. In-Place Hold is set up like Litigation Hold but adds a filter query to only retain specific kinds of email.

24.6.3 eDISCOVERY PROCESS

eDiscovery or electronic data discovery is the process of identifying, collecting, and reviewing electronically stored information (ESI) in the initial phase of a litigation or investigation. eDiscovery takes the data from its original source and blows it down to evidence that proves or disproves claims in a case.

Organizations must take proactive and responsive outlooks on eDiscovery, incorporating both information governance as well as technology (and process). To do this, they must understand the major considerations and requirements of an effective upstream information governance program, and then assesses eDiscovery vendors that provide their downstream technology needs.

In today's world, three major forces are driving increased investments in eDiscovery technology and best practices.

1) Electronic Records Are Increasingly Used by Courts and Regulatory Bodies: The significance of written electronic communications and electronic transactions in court proceedings has grown exponentially since the 2000s. This pressure has necessitated the proper management of electronic information.

2) Senior Decision-Makers Increasingly Value Records Management: Poor management of records can exacerbate the already negative impacts of business crises. In addition to being an environmental disaster, the now-famous BP oil spill cost the company in the form of a 20-page court order to freeze all documents that could be associated with the explosion.

3) Electronically Stored Information (ESI) Continues to Grow Exponentially, Senior Decision-Makers Increasingly Value Records Management: The significance of written electronic communications and electronic transactions in court proceedings has grown exponentially since the 2000s. This pressure has necessitated the proper management of electronic information.

The emergence of innovations, from autonomous cars to humanoid robots, and intelligent personal assistants to smart home devices, is introducing new types of ESI—and in exponentially growing amounts. IDC forecasts that by 2025 the global data sphere will grow to 163 zettabytes.[80] The Electronic Discovery Reference Model (EDRM), as described in Figure 24.1, is a conceptual framework that breaks down eDiscovery into nine stages divided across back-end (capture and store) and front-end (retrieve and utilize) processes that are the domain of IT and the business, respectively.[81]

Table 24.11 lists key things to consider when evaluating eDiscovery solutions based on their coverage of the stages within the eDiscovery process.

24.6.4   LEGAL HOLD VS. DATA RETENTION

A litigation hold is typically only triggered when legal or disciplinary action is imminent and tends to be limited to very specific users, data categories, and/or keyword searches. It has to be actioned manually but will trump any applicable retention policies, protecting relevant data even if that data would ordinarily be disposed of during the litigation hold window. Once the litigation hold is lifted, the retention policy will take precedence once again, and any actions (such as automatic deletion) that should have taken place previously will be actioned immediately.

It's important to remember, however, that litigation holds cannot preserve data retroactively. Anything altered or deleted prior to the hold being implemented will not be protected unless it has already been preserved by a pre-existing retention policy.

Both data retention policies and litigation hold have their limitations. Table 24.12 lists the pros and cons of the three models: Reply Solely Data Retention Policy, Reply Solely Litigation Hold Process, and the Hybrid Model.

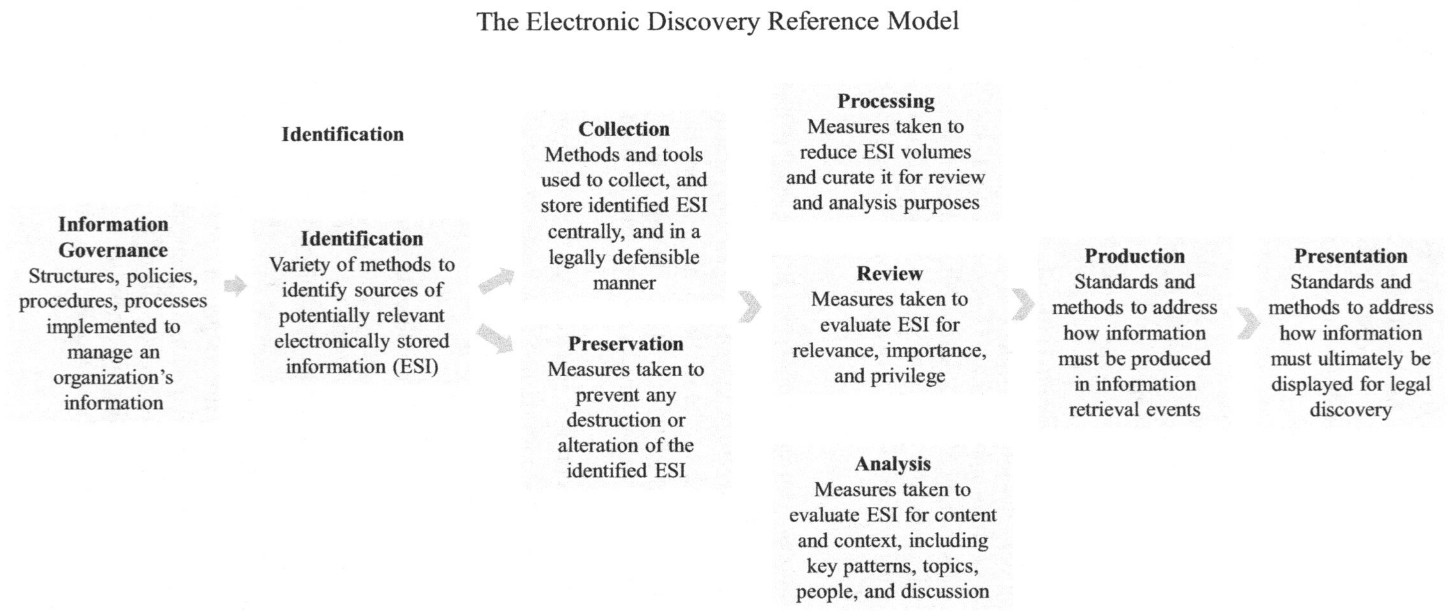

The Electronic Discovery Reference Model

Information Governance
Structures, policies, procedures, processes implemented to manage an organization's information

Identification

Identification
Variety of methods to identify sources of potentially relevant electronically stored information (ESI)

Collection
Methods and tools used to collect, and store identified ESI centrally, and in a legally defensible manner

Preservation
Measures taken to prevent any destruction or alteration of the identified ESI

Processing
Measures taken to reduce ESI volumes and curate it for review and analysis purposes

Review
Measures taken to evaluate ESI for relevance, importance, and privilege

Analysis
Measures taken to evaluate ESI for content and context, including key patterns, topics, people, and discussion

Production
Standards and methods to address how information must be produced in information retrieval events

Presentation
Standards and methods to address how information must ultimately be displayed for legal discovery

FIGURE 24.1 The electronic discovery reference model.

TABLE 24.11

Key Steps and Considerations for eDiscovery

Capability	Description	Things to Consider
Identification	Methods used to identify sources of potentially relevant ESI	Advanced Search; Content/Database Crawlers; Inventory Tools; Content & Data Analytics; Process Management
Preservation	Measures are taken to prevent any destruction or alteration of the identified ESI	Legal Hold; Versioning Controls; Preservation; Repositories; Audit Trails; Encryption; Indexing; Metadata Extraction
Collection	Methods and tools used to gather and store identified ESI centrally and in a legally defensible manner	Culling; Capture; Advanced Capture; OCR, ICR; Bulk Import; Search; Forensic Data Collection; Questionnaires; Mobile Support
Processing	Measures are taken to reduce ESI volume and curate it for review and analysis purposes	Culling; Format Conversion; Deduplication; Categorization; Tagging; Personnel Tracking
Review	Measures are taken to evaluate ESI for relevance, importance, and privilege	First-Pass Review; Early Case Assessment (ECA); Early Data Assessment (EDA); Technology Assisted Review (TAR); Native File Format Review; Translation/Foreign Language Support; Tagging
Analysis	Measures are taken to evaluate ESI for content and context, including key patterns, topics, people, and discussion	Predictive Coding; Visualization; Content Analytics/Semantic Analysis; Process Management

TABLE 24.12

Data Retention vs. Litigation Hold Process

Reply Solely Data Retention Policy	Reply Solely Litigation Hold Process	Hybrid Model
Relying on a retention policy to preserve information pertaining to a legal matter could easily see important data "aging out" and being automatically disposed of during litigation.	Likewise, relying solely on a litigation hold to preserve data, when necessary, means any files or mailbox items deleted before the hold was triggered may be forever out of reach.	Because of this, it's always best to lay a solid data protection foundation using intelligent and justifiable retention policies and save litigation holds for circumstances requiring a more targeted, short-term approach. Separately, these tools are only pieces of the data protection puzzle. Together, they're a powerful force against accidental and malicious data alteration and deletion.

25 Protection of Children's Data

This chapter is intended to help readers understand the risks and consequences of processing children's personal data and to implement proper privacy measures to mitigate the risks.

This chapter covers the following topics:

- *Children's age*
- *Data protection practices*

25.1 CHILDREN'S AGE

Laws raise stricter requirements on the processing of minors' personal data. Children may be less aware of the risks and consequences associated with the processing of personal data. And children may also not understand their rights concerning the processing of personal data. Therefore, children require specific protection which should apply to the use of personal data of children for the purposes of marketing or creating personality or user profiles and the collection of personal data with regard to children when using services offered directly to a child.

The age limit for minors varies according to the laws of different countries. Table 25.1 lists some of the examples.

25.2 DATA PROTECTION PRACTICES

If an organization needs to collect age information, a function needs to be provided to obtain consent from the holders of parental responsibility over minors. Organizations that need to collect children's personal data should take the following three aspects into account.

1) Determine whether a data subject is a minor.
Organizations need to establish methods for identifying data subjects' ages. The organizations should take necessary measures to identify whether the data subject is a minor.

The systems shall strictly identify minors according to the laws of the target delivery country. The systems that are used for collecting minors' personal data shall be properly configured in a way that strictly identifies minors according to the laws of the target delivery country. A minor website needs to require minors to register information; for example, request users to enter their birth years.

You don't need to verify their exact age. However, you must verify that they're at the requisite age or older.

Consent is given or authorized by the holder of parental responsibility over the child
If the system is something that is specifically targeting minors as a target audience, the system must provide a mechanism to obtain consent from the parent. Obtaining consent for processing children's personal data is even more rigorous when information society services are being offered. These include online technologies, such as social media and apps.

- The controller must take appropriate measures to identify whether the consent is provided by the holders of parental responsibility over the children. For instance, GDPR Article 8 and Recital 38 stipulate that the controller shall make reasonable efforts to verify that consent is given or authorized by the holder of parental responsibility over the minor, taking into consideration available technologies.

TABLE 25.1

Examples of Age Limits of Minors in Different Jurisdictions

Region	Age of a Minor	Country
EU	16	The EU GDPR defines children as those under 16, but EU Member States can set the upper age limit to 13 to 16.
		Croatia, Germany, Hungary, Liechtenstein, Luxembourg, the Netherlands, Poland, Romania, and Slovakia.
		In **Ireland**, consent can generally be given at **16 years** of age, but this may vary up to **18 years** of age in some circumstances.
	15	Czech Republic, France, Greece, and Slovenia
	14	Austria, Bulgaria, Cyprus, Italy, Lithuania, Spain
	13	Belgium, Denmark, Estonia, Finland, Iceland, Latvia, Norway, Portugal, Sweden, and the UK
		In Malta, consent can generally be given at 13 years of age, however it can only be given at 16 years of age for students.
North America	14	Bermuda
	13	USA (Children's Online Privacy Protection Rule §312.2), Canada
Asia	18	India, Malaysia, Japan (the Child Welfare Law)
	14	China, South Korea
	13	Singapore PDPC suggests 13
Oceania	18	New Zealand, and Australia: no specific legal requirements, however New Zealand and Australia guidance suggest 18

- The solution must be described to show how the system determines the consent is obtained from the holders of parental responsibility over the children. (For example, require the provisioning of parent accounts for minor accounts and give authorization for minors through corresponding parent accounts.)
- Parental consent doesn't automatically expire when the child reaches the age of consent. You may need to refresh this consent more regularly.

 Example

The organization ID subsystem provides child accounts that have access to all functions and services provided by the accounting system. However, key operations, such as account registration and payment, require the input of parent account passwords to verify the parents' identities and ensure that their consent is obtained.

Do not collect information about the children's parents or relatives

Do not collect information, such as financial information, telephone numbers, home addresses, and health status, about parents or relatives of children.

 Case Study

Spanish DPA v. MAF.com, 2021

The Spanish DPA fines ski club (MAF.COM Esqui Club) €10,000 for publishing video of a minor on website & social media without consent.

The Club offers ski lessons in which the complainant's daughter had participated in the past. By publishing the video, which showed the child practicing the sport, the recipient of the fine wanted to present the courses as more attractive to women and thus increase the number of participants.

For this purpose, the company had previously obtained the consent of the child's father, who had also registered the child for the course, but not of the complainant. The girl's parents were divorced at the time of the incident. The mother of an underage girl filed a complaint with the Spanish Data Protection Authority against the company for posting a video of her daughter on its website and Social Media presence without her consent.

The fact that the parents were divorced doesn't affect directly the consent given by the father. During the civil trial, the Tribunal authorized the consent given by the father for the processing of the daughter's personal data. The consent was limited and valid to the personal data necessary for the inscription to the ski course. What was beyond the consent was the use of the images for promotional videos. The Spanish DPA agrees that that processing was beyond the limited consent given by the father.

 Case Study

FTC v. TikTok, 2019

TikTok was fined $5.7 million in 2019 by the US FTC for violating the Children's Privacy Protection Act

On February 28, 2019, the US Federal Trade Commission (FTC) announced that the investigated company musical.ly (TikTok) agreed to pay a settlement of $5.7 million. The two sides formally reached a settlement. The fine stems from an FTC charge that the company illegally collected information from children.

It was also the agency's largest civil fine in a US children's privacy case. In a statement, the FTC said Musical.ly violated the US Children's Online Privacy Protection Act (COPPA) by illegally collecting children's personal information, including phone numbers, videos, exact location, and biometric data, without sufficient warning, transparency, or the necessary consent required by law, and without children or parents knowing what is being done with that information.

 Case Study

FTC v. Apple, 2014

In 2014, Apple was asked by the FTC to return $32.5M to users because it did not obtain the user's consent to charge in-app fees.

On January 15, 2014, Apple failed to inform parents that entering the password means that they agreed to in-app purchases, and failed to inform parents that Apple would keep the password for 15 minutes, and within these 15 minutes, children may make purchases without entering a password. Since at least March 2011, tens of thousands of consumers complained that children have made in-app purchases without parental authorization, resulting in financial losses to parents, which was identified by the FTC as constituting "Unfair Practices Affecting Commerce," Violating Part 5 of the Federal Trade Commission Act. The FTC required Apple to return $32.5M to users.

 Case Study

Swedish DPA v. The Skellefteå municipality high school board, 2019[82]

In August 2019, the Swedish supervisory authority fined a school in Sweden €18.630 for its trial of facial recognition technology to monitor the attendance of students. The trial only monitored 22 students over a period of 3 weeks. The school did not carry out a risk assessment. Consent was obtained from the guardians of the children participating in the trial, but it was not possible to refuse to participate in the trial.

1) The supervisory authority held that the school had failed to carry out a Data Protection Impact Assessment and that it should have consulted with the supervisory authority in accordance with GDPR Article 36. The supervisory authority considered that the use of facial recognition technology and the processing of biometric data in order to monitor attendance brought a disproportionate risk to the rights and freedoms of the children and that there were less invasive ways to monitor attendance.

2) The supervisory authority noted that any consent to the use of facial recognition software was not valid as the children and their guardians could not freely decide if they or their children wanted to be part of the trial.

3) The school could not demonstrate an exemption for the general prohibition against processing special category data and did not have a sufficient legal basis for the data processing.

 Case Study

Norwegian DPA v. Bergen municipality, 2020[83]

On October 14, 2020, the Norwegian Data Protection Authority gave Bergen municipality a final decision on an administrative fine of approximately EUR 276,000 (3 million NOK). Personal information in the communication system between school and home was not secure enough.

In October 2019, the Data Protection Authority was notified of a personal data breach by Bergen Municipality regarding the municipality's new tool for communication between school and home. Vigilo contains a module where schools and parents can communicate via a portal or app. Files containing personal data were unprotected and openly available.

The fact that the data related to children was considered to be an aggravating factor when setting the fine. The decision emphasized that the municipality had not established nor communicated the necessary guidelines for information about children who have a clear interest in the information about them being processed with the highest degree of confidentiality.

 Case Study

The New York Attorney General v. Oath, 2018

New York Attorney General announces $4.95M settlement with Oath for COPPA violations.

On December 4, 2018, The New York Attorney General (AG) announced a $4.95 million settlement with Oath Inc., formerly known as AOL Inc., for allegedly collecting, using, and disclosing personal information from hundreds of websites it knew were directed to children under the age of 13, without first obtaining parental consent, in violation of the Children's Online Privacy Protection Act of 1998 (COPPA) ("the Settlement").

The oath had collected this personal information to conduct billions of auctions for advertising space on these websites and enable advertisers to track and serve targeted advertisements to children. In particular, the AG noted that Oath had determined that certain websites were directed to children under the age of 13 when it conducted a review of the content and privacy policies of client websites.

As part of the Settlement, Oath agreed to adopt and maintain a comprehensive COPPA compliance program, that includes, among other things, the designation of an executive or officer to oversee the program, annual COPPA training for the relevant Oath personnel, the identification of risks that could result in Oath's violation of COPPA, and the design and implementation of reasonable controls to address the identified risks. The AG observed that the Settlement marks the largest penalty in COPPA enforcement to date.

26 PbD for AI Solutions

This chapter is intended to analyze the privacy and data protection implications of AI solutions and discuss an approach for organizations to implement AI solutions in a responsible way.

This chapter covers the following topics:

- *AI definition and use cases*
- *Privacy and security implications for AI*
- *Guiding principles for responsible AI*
- *AI privacy protection practices*

26.1 AI DEFINITION AND USE CASES

In the age of emerging technologies (i.e., Artificial Intelligence (AI), Big Data, the Internet of Things), it is becoming increasingly difficult for individuals to fully comprehend, let alone control, how and for what purposes organizations collect, use, and disclose their personal information.

Artificial Intelligence (AI), a term coined by emeritus Stanford Professor John McCarthy in 1955, was defined by him as "the science and engineering of making intelligent machines".

While there are many AI definitions from various guidance as listed in Table 26.1, the industry has yet to propose a unified definition of AI.

Basic characteristics of AI include:

- Collecting and combining different amounts of data,
- Extracting information and knowledge
- Learning autonomously
- Making automated decisions at different levels
- Handling complex goals

Table 26.2 demonstrates the differences and relationship among artificial intelligence, machine learning and deep learning.

Technology is neither good nor bad. AI has the ability to profoundly change every industry and every organization, and AI technologies can be used for innovation and enhance our productivity. For instance, AI can replace humans in a dangerous environment (toxic environment, extreme hot/ cold environment, etc.), produce more products with less time and fewer errors, etc.

Examples of identified commercial-level AI applications are listed in Table 26.3 as follows:[88]

26.2 PRIVACY AND SECURITY IMPLICATIONS FOR AI

While bringing substantial opportunities and benefits, this new general-purpose technology also faces significant challenges in security and privacy protection. AI technologies could be very damaging to people's daily lives if they are not used responsibly. For instance, AI technology can be used to judge someone's emotions. Facial Recognition technology's capabilities to judge someone's emotions by reading their facial expressions have moved from being a novelty to reality. Many different industries now use facial recognition to act against individuals who do not seem happy or content.

DOI: 10.1201/9781003225089-31

TABLE 26.1
Examples of AI Definitions

Guidance	Definition
Ethics Guidelines for Trustworthy AI released by the European Commission's High-Level Expert Group on Artificial Intelligence (AI HLEG) in 2019[84]	Artificial Intelligence (AI) systems are software (and possibly also hardware) systems designed by humans that, given a complex goal, act in the physical or digital dimension by perceiving their environment through data acquisition, interpreting the collected structured or unstructured data, reasoning on the knowledge, or processing the information derived from this data and deciding the best action(s) to take to achieve the given goal. AI systems can either use symbolic rules or learn a numeric model, and they can also adapt their behavior by analyzing how the environment is affected by their previous actions.
Ethically Aligned Design First Edition released by IEEE in 2019[85]	The design, development, deployment, decommissioning, and adoption of autonomous or intelligent software when installed into other software and/or hardware systems that can exercise independent reasoning, decision-making, intention forming, and motivating skills according to self-defined principles.
A proposed model AI governance framework by Singapore Personal Data Protection Committee (PDPC)[86]	"Artificial Intelligence (AI)" refers to a set of technologies that seek to simulate human traits such as knowledge, reasoning, problem solving, perception, learning, and planning.
Artificial Intelligence Security White Paper released by the China Academy of Information and Communications Technology (CAICT) in 2018[87]	AI enables intelligent machines or intelligent systems on machines. It studies and develops theories, methods, and technologies for simulating, extending, and expanding human intelligence, perceiving the environment, obtaining knowledge, and using knowledge to reach optimal results.

TABLE 26.2
AI vs. Machine Learning and Deep Learning

	Artificial Intelligence	Machine Learning	Deep Learning
Origination	Artificial intelligence originated around the 1950s (John McCarthy, Stanford University)	Machine learning originated around the 1960s	Deep learning originated around the 1970s
Techniques	AI represents simulated intelligence in machines	Machine learning is the practice of getting machines to make decisions without being programmed	Deep learning is the process of using Artificial Neural Networks to solve complex problems
Relationship	AI is a subset of Data Science	Machine learning is a subset of AI & Data Science	Deep learning is a subset of Machine learning, AI & Data Science
Objectives	The aim is to build machines that are capable of thinking like humans	The aim is to make machines learn through data so that they can solve problems	The aim is to build neural networks that automatically discover patterns for feature detection

TABLE 26.3

Examples of Commercial-Level AI Applications

AI Application Category	AI Use Case
Improving work efficiency	Customer service:

- Customer contact card identification.
- Consumer voice analysis and authentication
- AI integrates with automated hotlines that offer a 24/7 communication channel for customers.
- Consumer profiling: AI systems are able to classify customers, integrate customer data, and manage activities.

Procurement/Contract:
- Automatic contract clause parsing
- Intelligent identification of contract risks
- Intelligent bidding, Intelligent quotation, Intelligent commercial analysis
- Check contract signing and review consistency
- Sensitive words identification

Manufacturing:
- Production line manpower configuration model
- Predictive device maintenance
- Inventory policy for semi-finished goods

R&D
- Smart requirements, Smart documents
- Defective code locating in software development

HR:
- AI assists in the recruitment process to match the supply and demand of candidates, screen candidates' resumes, and intelligently recommend potential candidates.
- Intelligent attendance
- Employee self-service and Q&A
- Employee profiling
- Payroll automation
- Automatic allowance application

Finance:
- Intelligent risk control for employee reimbursement: Reimbursement receipt checking and approval
- Fund planning, Fund transfer, Fund security
- Budgeting and forecasting

Administration and operations:
- Intelligent visa and Intelligent travel request fill-in

IT service monitoring:
- AI can automatically detect system exceptions and determine the optimal solution if IT faults occur, improving the work efficiency of operations personnel.
- Intelligent notetaking
- Automatic translation
- Knowledge search and recommendation

Supply chain management:
- Proactively adjusting inventories to handle issues in the supply chain and sending reminders to supply chain planners
- AI supports predictive resource allocation and scheduling
- Logistics estimation automation

Project management:
- Intelligent scheduling

(Continued)

TABLE 26.3   (Continued)

AI Application Category	AI Use Case
Industry Enablement	Healthcare: AI can be used in medical image recognition, diagnosis using medical images, disease prediction, and risk analysis. Retail: AI optimizes the configuration efficiency of industry chain resources for production, process, and sales via intelligent customer service, intelligent payment systems, unstaffed warehousing, and more. Transportation: AI helps autonomous vehicles establish an accurate location, generate real-time models of the vehicle surroundings, and plan driving routes and strategies by sensing the external environment and reading engine data. Manufacturing: AI improves the productivity of production lines and helps restructure production capacities. By using computer vision and machine learning technologies for mechanical testing, AI reduces machine downtime and consequently lowers the OPEX. Smart City: AI can be used to collect city management data, including information about the atmosphere, water quality, lighting, transportation, schools, communities, and hospitals. This data provides municipal management personnel with valuable insights into city conditions, enabling them to plan and schedule resources more effectively.

Technical reliability, societal applications, and legal requirements and responsibilities are three broad challenges facing the security and privacy protection of AI development. Examples are listed in Table 26.4. We need to think strategically about what we want to accomplish with AI technologies and solutions with appropriate privacy protections.

 Case Study

Various DPAs v. Clearview AI

The Clearview AI has been investigated by many data protection authorities across the globe such as Canada OPC, UK ICO, Australian OACI, the Hamburg DPA, etc.

The Canada OPC found that Clearview engaged in the collection, use and disclosure of personal information through the development and provision of its facial recognition application, without the requisite consent. The OPC also found that Clearview's collection, use and disclosure of personal information through the provision of its facial recognition application was for a purpose that a reasonable person would find to be inappropriate.

The ICO has issued a notice to fine Clearview AI Inc over £17M, including an order to stop processing of personal data of people in the UK and to delete it following alleged serious breaches of data protection laws.

The Australian OAIC ordered to cease to collect and destroy all images and vector of Australians.

The Hamburg DPA has ruled that Clearview AI's searchable database of biometric profiles is illegal under the EU's GDPR and ordered the US company to delete the claimant's biometric profile.

TABLE 26.4
Privacy and Security Implications for AI

Risks	Privacy and Security Implications	Examples
Black-box AI—Technical reliability and explainability	Some machine learning techniques, although very successful from the accuracy point of view, are very opaque in terms of understanding how they make decisions. The notion of black-box AI refers to such scenarios, where it is not possible to trace back the reason for certain decisions. Deep neural networks (DNNs) lack robustness and may therefore be susceptible to evasion attacks. Such attacks will impair the judgment of AI systems and affect business security. Complex systems such as DNNs inherently lack transparency and explainability, which may infringe upon legal or regulatory requirements (such as GDPR in terms of automated decision-making) and may even cause potential unfairness, inaccurate or unidentifiable results, and untraceable or unaccountable consequences. Huge volumes of data may be originated from diversified operating environments. Data breaches, tampering, theft, and misuse may result from the unavailability of comprehensive data security protection.	In the field of autonomous driving, evasion attacks can lead to traffic offenses and even accidents. Attackers can introduce significant errors in the dosage recommended by AI models for nearly 50% of patients by adding only a small amount of malicious data. Although the accuracy rate of cancer screening by AI may be high, doctors agree with about only half of the results because they think the results lack reasoning and logic.
Lack of governance and misuse	The lack of management and control over the purposes of AI may lead to AI being misused. Data quality issues may lead to biased and unfair judgments. Application developers and deployers who have insufficient knowledge and capabilities may misuse AI systems or cause security and privacy incidents.	AI helps people who have difficulty in making sounds create a realistic voice. However, fraudsters may record a person's voice and use AI to generate speech for the purpose of phone fraud. Credit scores are determined by collecting and analyzing a person's network behavior. Immigrants who are not proficient in English were assigned poor credit scores. Facial recognition software incorrectly matched the photos of government officials with criminals' mug shots with a high false match rate due to improper parameter settings. The AI algorithm used to establish a patient's drug dosage can infer the genetic information of the patient according to the drug dosage, breaching the patient's privacy.
Data issues and bias	AI algorithms and datasets can reflect, reinforce, or reduce unfair biases. Since many AI systems, such as those including supervised machine learning components, rely on huge amounts of data to perform well, it is important to understand how data are influencing the behavior of the AI system. If the training data is biased, that is, it is not balanced or inclusive enough, the AI system trained on such data will not be able to generalize well and will possibly make unfair decisions that can favor some groups over others.	Analysis shows bias with AI-powered crime prediction software Potential system bias issues have been found with crime prediction software developed by PredPol, according to an investigation by The Markup and Gizmodo. The specific bias pertained to targeting neighborhoods home to Blacks, Latinos, and low-income families rather than those neighborhoods with greater white or middle-to-upper-income residents.

(Continued)

TABLE 26.4   (Continued)

Risks	Privacy and Security Implications	Examples
Security and privacy protection	There are security vulnerabilities that are prone to attacks on data integrity, model integrity, and model confidentiality. The proliferation of AI solutions that collect and process a large amount of personal data might breach privacy and data protection regulations in various jurisdictions.	Attackers can insert malicious data in the training phase to affect the inference capability of AI models or add a small amount of noise to samples in the judgment phase to change the judgment result. Without proper notification and consent, AI enabled auto-decision making process might violate GDPR's obligations.

26.3   GUIDING PRINCIPLES FOR RESPONSIBLE AI

Various organizations have set forth their AI guiding principles across the globe. Guiding principles are the cornerstone of a responsible and trustworthy approach to AI, especially as intelligent technology becomes more prevalent in the products and services we implement today. We should also acknowledge that the principles are evolving.

Table 26.5 lists some of the examples.

I consider the following five principles in Table 26.6 to be the cornerstone of my responsible AI framework which will be discussed in the next section.

26.4   AI PRIVACY PROTECTION PRACTICES

Although AI brings substantial opportunities and benefits, we need to develop responsible AI frameworks and solutions that can address security and privacy challenges.

The following AI framework in Figure 26.1 can serve as a reference model for your organization in order to design and implement your AI solutions.

AI risk assessment and mitigation

When designing and building AI systems, developers should understand how risks can be introduced and how risks can affect AI-based recommendations.

Organizations should apply systematic risk management (Algorithm Impact Assessment) approach to each phase of the AI system lifecycle on a continuous basis to address risks related to AI systems, including privacy, digital security, safety, bias, etc.

In general, Algorithm Impact Assessment should cover the following factors:

- The assessment should consider various aspects including AI systems design, algorithm, decision type, impact, and data involved.
- A typical algorithm impact assessment should cover the following sections.
  - System Capabilities of the system (that is, image recognition, risk assessment)
  - Algorithm: Transparency of the algorithm, whether it is easily explained
  - Decision-making process
    - Business drivers: Motivation for introducing automation into the decision-making process
    - Classification of the decision being automated
  - Impact: Duration, reversibility and area impacted (freedom, health, economy, or environment)
    - Internal and external stakeholders
    - Data quality: Processes to ensure that data is representative and unbiased, as well as transparency measures related to those processes

TABLE 26.5

Examples of Principles for Responsible AI

Organization	Principles
Government of Canada (5)[89]	Understand and measure
	Be transparent
	Provide meaningful explanations
	Be as open as we can
	Provide sufficient training
Office of the Director of National Intelligence, US (6)[90]	Respect the Law and Act with Integrity
	Transparent and Accountable
	Objective and Equitable
	Human-Centered Development and Use
	Secure and Resilient
	Informed by Science and Technology
Australian Government (8)[91]	Human, societal, and environmental well-being
	Human-centered values
	Fairness
	Privacy protection and security
	Reliability and safety
	Transparency and explainability
	Contestability
	Accountability
EU Commission, High-Level Expert Group (4)[92]	Ethical Principles:
	(i) Respect for human autonomy
	(ii) Prevention of harm
	(iii) Fairness
	(iv) Explicability
OECD (5)[93]	Inclusive growth, sustainable development, and well-being
	Human-centered values and fairness
	Transparency and explainability
	Robustness, security, and safety
	Accountability
Microsoft (6)[94]	Fairness
	Reliability and safety
	Privacy and security
	Inclusiveness
	Transparency
	Accountability
Google (7)[95]	Be socially beneficial
	Avoid creating or reinforcing unfair bias
	Be built and tested for safety
	Be accountable to people
	Incorporate privacy design principles
	Uphold high standards of scientific excellence
	Be made available for uses that accord with these principles

- Procedural fairness: Procedures to audit the system and its decisions, as well as the recourse process
- Privacy and security: Measures to safeguard personal information

Privacy and Securit Protection

Personal information and data should be protected and managed in compliance with the privacy regulations such as GDPR, PIPEDA, PIPL, CPRA, etc. Data and information are shared and AI development is accelerated while privacy is ensured.

TABLE 26.6
Examples of AI Protection Principles

AI Protection Principles	Description
Fairness	To avoid bias and discrimination, and mitigate unfairness caused by procedures, challenge decisions made by AI and seek effective remedies, AI systems should treat everyone fairly and avoid affecting similarly situated groups of people in different ways.
Reliability and safety	These systems should be able to operate as they were originally designed, respond safely to unanticipated conditions, and resist harmful manipulation.
Transparency	Logics generated by the AI system must be explainable and transparent, such as primary purpose and use, nature and uniqueness and Scale, etc. There should be transparency and responsible disclosure so people can understand when they are being significantly impacted by AI, and can find out when an AI system is engaging with them. Disclosure should be made with proportion to the importance of the interaction.
Privacy protection and security	AI systems must comply with privacy laws that require transparency about the collection, use, and storage of data and mandate that consumers have appropriate controls to choose how their data is used.
Accountability	The team that deploys the AI systems must be accountable for how their systems operate througout different phases of the AI system lifecycle, and human oversight of AI systems should be enabled.

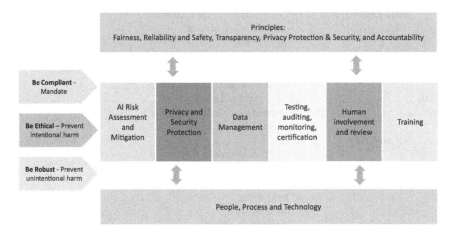

FIGURE 26.1   AI security and privacy protection framework.

AI systems must comply with privacy laws that require transparency about the collection, use, and storage of data and mandate that consumers have appropriate controls to choose how their data is used. An organization should incorporate privacy and data protection principles in the implementation and use of AI technologies. The organization should give opportunity for notice and consent, encourage architecture with privacy safeguards, and provide appropriate transparency and control over the use of data.

An organization should ensure the integrity, accuracy, availability, confidentiality, and comprehensiveness of data. The AI systems should meet the security requirements of robustness, stability, and adaptability and can provide security attestation. AI systems should be robust, secure, and safe throughout their entire lifecycle so that, in conditions of normal use, foreseeable use or misuse, or other adverse conditions, they function appropriately and do not pose an unreasonable safety risk.

The existing security technologies have inherent limitations that leave them unable to cope with new AI security challenges. I propose layers of defense for deploying AI systems in various scenarios:

- Attack defense security: Design targeted defense mechanisms for known attacks.
- Model security: Improve model robustness by means of model verification.
- Architecture security: Design different security mechanisms for services in which AI systems are deployed to ensure business security.

During operations, data and activities that involve security and privacy must be documented based on application scenarios to ensure that the judgment logic and action process are demonstrable and accountable.

Data management
Organizations will seek to avoid unjust impacts on people, particularly those related to sensitive characteristics such as race, ethnicity, gender, nationality, income, sexual orientation, ability, and political or religious beliefs.

Data is critical to AI judgment results and model generation. To help mitigate bias, organizations should use training datasets that reflect the diversity of society. Organizations should also design AI models in ways that allow them to learn and adapt over time without developing biases.

Testing, auditing, monitoring, certification
It's critical that AI systems operate reliably, safely, and consistently under normal circumstances and in unexpected conditions.

It's also important to be able to verify that these systems are behaving as intended under actual operating conditions. Organizations need to test AI technologies in constrained environments and monitor their operation after deployment. Rigorous testing is essential during system development and deployment to ensure AI systems can respond safely in unanticipated situations and edge cases, don't have unexpected performance failures, and don't evolve in ways that are inconsistent with original expectations.

Organizations should ensure traceability, including in relation to datasets, processes, and decisions made during the AI system lifecycle, to enable an analysis of the AI system's outcomes and responses to inquiries, appropriate to the context.

Human involvement
When an AI system significantly impacts a person, community, group or environment, there should be a timely process to allow people to challenge the use or outcomes of the AI system. Organizations should design and implement AI systems in a manner that provides appropriate opportunities for feedback, relevant explanations, and appeal. AI technologies will be subject to appropriate human direction and control.

Organizations should draw upon industry standards to develop accountability norms. These norms can ensure that AI systems are not the final authority on any decision that impacts people's lives and that humans maintain meaningful control over otherwise highly autonomous AI systems.

Ethical and technical review board:

- People need to play a critical role in making decisions about how and when an AI system is deployed, and whether it's appropriate to continue to use it over time. Human judgment will be key to identifying potential blind spots and biases in AI systems.
- Organizations should also consider establishing a dedicated internal review body. This body can provide oversight and guidance to the highest levels of the company on which practices should be adopted to help address the concerns discussed previously and on particularly important questions regarding the development and deployment of AI systems.

- The review body can also help with tasks such as defining best practices for documenting and testing AI systems during development or providing guidance, etc.

Training

- Organizations need to provide sufficient training so that employees developing and using AI solutions have the responsible design, function, and implementation skills needed to make AI-based public services better.
- A crucial part of transparency is intelligibility or the useful explanation of the behavior of AI systems and their components. Improving intelligibility requires that stakeholders comprehend how and why they function so that they can identify potential performance issues, safety, and privacy concerns, biases, exclusionary practices, or unintended outcomes. Those who use AI systems should be honest and forthcoming about when, why, and how they choose to deploy them.

 Case Study

German government supports a ban on AI use in public

The German government signed a coalition deal supporting the ban on facial recognition use in public spaces, Politico reports.

The EU's Artificial Intelligence Act, proposed in April, creates product safety rules for "high risk" AI that is likely to cause harm to humans. It also bans certain "unacceptable" AI uses, such as social scoring, and restricts the use of remote biometric identification in public places from law enforcement, unless it is to fight serious crime, such as terrorism.

The Social Democrats (SPD), Greens, and Free Democrats (FDP) developed the deal calling for the public use ban and "automated state scoring systems by AI are to be excluded under European law". The ban follows the proposed EU Artificial Intelligence Act.

Part 6

Data Breach Handling and DPA Cooperation

This Part Covers the Following Topics:

- Data Subject Rights, Inquires, and Complaints
- Data Breach Handling
- DPA Cooperation

DOI: 10.1201/9781003225089-32

27 Data Subject Rights, Inquiries, and Complaints

This chapter is intended to help readers establish an actionable process to identify, respond and record the DSRs within the required timeframes by security and privacy regulations across the globe.

This chapter covers the following topics:

- *What is a data subject right request*
- *Data subject rights comparison*
- *Core data subject rights and key considerations*
- *Legal basis, applicability, and exceptions*
- *DSR handling workflow*
- *Inquires and complaints handling*

27.1 WHAT IS A DATA SUBJECT RIGHT REQUEST

A Data Subject Request (DSR) is a written or electronic request for personal information made by a data subject to an organization that currently stores information about the individual. These data subjects have the rights such as the right to know, right to access, right to rectification, right to erasure, and so on.

Data subjects have the right to access and ask questions about their personal information. However, organizations have the right to withhold personal data if the act of disclosing it would "adversely affect the rights and freedoms of others."

Requests must be responded to the data subject within the required timeframe or without undue delay. DSRs do not have to be fulfilled by the organization if they are justifiably unfounded or excessive. If a request is refused, the organization must inform the requestor within one month of the request's issue date.

No fee should be charged for a DSR unless it can be justified based on administrative costs. Typically, fees are reasonably charged for requests that are repetitive or excessive.

The general public is much savvier about their data protection rights than they used to be for a few reasons:

- The waves of the introduction of privacy regulations, such as EU GDPR, California CCPA/CPRA, etc. garnered a lot of publicity due to the increased sanctions.
- Supervisory authorities ran various awareness campaigns and published guidelines to ensure that data subjects were aware of their rights.
- Certain high-profile cases, such as the British Airways, Marriott International, Facebook, and Cambridge Analytica cases have received broad coverage in the media.
- This savviness has led to an increase in the number of complaints from data subjects whose personal data hasn't been processed in accordance with privacy laws and regulations. Data subjects are lodging complaints both directly to the data controller and to supervisory authorities.

Data privacy teams have struggled with data subject rights with the privacy regulations for a number of reasons including:

- Manually managing the request workflow across teams
- Difficulty locating PI
- Sifting through excess data to find the relevant information
- Difficulty documenting the response history for compliance auditing
- Managing volume of incoming requests
- Responding to requests on time and in full

All in all, it comes down to the fact that organizations have a lack of knowledge about what data they have, where the data is, how the data has been used, who has access to the data, and what governance policies apply to the data.

27.2 DATA SUBJECT RIGHTS COMPARISON

Different privacy laws and regulations might slightly differ with respect to the types and nature of the data subject rights.

Organizations should design the services, products, or processes that are equipped with the capability to fulfill data subject rights.

For instance, China's PIPL (Art. 44–50) articulates the following core data subjects:

- Right of information and making decisions (i.e., restriction and objection)
- Right of access
- Right to rectification
- Right to erasure
- Right of explanation of processing rules

The EU GDPR (Art. 12–23) articulates the following core data subjects:

- Right of information
- Right of access
- Right to rectification
- Right to erasure (Right to be forgotten)
- Right to restriction of processing
- Right to data portability
- Right to object
- Right not to be subject to automated decision

Table 27.1 provides a high-level comparison regarding data subject rights obligations from various privacy laws and regulations.

Please note:

- Malaysia: Not later than 21 days from the date of receipt of the data access request
- China: Replies or reasonable explanations shall be made within 30 days or within the time limit prescribed by law
- India: 30 days (specified by the Data Protection Authority of India)

TABLE 27.1
Regarding Data Subject Rights Comparison

	GDPR	CCPA	CPRA	LGPD	NZ Privacy Act 2020	Australia Privacy Act 1988	PIPEDA	Canada CPPA	Canada—The Privacy Act	Russia	Japan
	1 month + 2 months extention	10 days confirm of receipt, 45 days (including verification) may extend additional 45 days "Do Not Sell My Personal Information": No later than 15 business days	Same as CCPA	Respond in a simplified format immediately, or up to 15 days in a "clear and complete declaration" format	Within 20 working days with extension of a reasonable period of time	Agencies: 30 calendar days, if needed, explain the delay and provide an expected timeframe Organizations: **reasonable period (should not exceed 30 calendar days)**	30 days, if needed, advise of the new time limit	30 days + 30 days extention	30 days of the request's receipt by the institution, though extensions of time are permitted in certain circumstances.	The right to access (30 days) The right to be adjusted, blocked or deleted —7 days response if confirmed incomplete, incorrect or out of date or illegally received —**Wrongful doing (3 days to stop, 10 days to delete, notify D.S. and DPA if necessary)**	Without delay
Right to be informed	✓	✓ (Right to notice)	✓ (Right to notice)	✓ information about public and private entities with which the controller has shared data information about the possibility of denying consent and the consequences of such denial	✓	✓	✓			✓	✓

(Continued)

TABLE 27.1 (Continued)

	GDPR	CCPA	CPRA	LGPD	NZ Privacy Act 2020	Australia Privacy Act 1988	PIPEDA	Canada CPPA	Canada—The Privacy Act	Russia	Japan
Right of access	✓	✓ (Right to know)	✓ (Expanded Right to know, beyond 12-month look-back)	Two separate rights: —Confirmation of the existence of the processing —Access to the data	✓	✓	✓		✓	✓	✓
Right to rectification	✓	✓	✓ (New, Right to Correct Information)	✓	✓	✓	✓		✓ (Correction or notation)	✓	✓
Right to erasure	✓	✓	✓ (Modified Right to Delete, pass requirements to third parties)	✓					✓	✓	✓
Right of restriction of processing	✓		✓	Anonymization, blocking or deletion of unnecessary or excessive data or data processed in noncompliance with the provisions of this Law					✓	✓	✓

Data subject right						
Right to data portability	✓	✓	✓ (Expanded Right to Data Portability, transmit data to another entity)			
Right to object	✓	✓ (Right to Opt-out, Do Not Sell)	✓ (Expand Right to Opt-out to both selling and sharing)	✓ Revocation of consent	✓ (Opt-out)	✓ (Direct marketing and profiling) ✓ (Opt-out)
Right not to be subject to automated individual decision-making, including profiling		✓	(New, Right to Opt-Out of Automated Decision-Making Technology) (New, Right to Access Information About Automated Decision Making)		✓	
Right to Opt-in	✓ (Consent as a legal basis)	✓ (Children's PD and Financial incentives programs)	✓ (Strengthened Opt-In Rights for Minors, wait 12 months before re-asking, financial incentives programs)	✓ (Consent as a legal basis) (Consent)	✓ (Consent) (Consent)	✓ (Consent) (Consent)

(Continued)

TABLE 27.1 (Continued)

	GDPR	CCPA	CPRA	LGPD	NZ Privacy Act 2020	Australia Privacy Act 1988	PIPEDA	Canada CPPA	Canada— The Privacy Act	Russia	Japan
Right to Limit Sensitive Personal Information Processing	✓ (Article 9)		✓ (new)	✓		✓	✓			✓	✓
Right to communication about PD breach	✓ (Art. 33)	✓ (Leverage state's general breach notification statutes)	✓ (Leverage state's general breach notification statutes)	✓	✓	✓	✓			✓	✓
Right to compensation/ award damages	✓	✓ (non-encrypted or non-redacted PI)	✓ (non-encrypted or non-redacted PI)		✓	✓	✓			✓	✓
Right to Non-Discrimination/ Right not to be subject to discrimination for the exercise of rights	✓ (Inferred Art. 5, 13, 22)	✓	✓	✓							

27.3 CORE DATA SUBJECT RIGHTS AND KEY CONSIDERATIONS

Table 27.2 describes key considerations for each of the data subject rights.

Example

An app is associated with a large amount of personal data and with other services (such as quick payment for bank cards). The account deregistration function provided by the app not only deletes personal data but also disables all associated services. To be specific, the app:

- Allows users to deregister their accounts permanently.
- Promises to safely delete related personal data.
- Disables services such as bank card association after deregistration.

Questions and answers

When does the right to data portability apply?
This new right applies under 3 cumulative conditions.

- Firstly, the personal data requested should be processed, by automatic means (i.e., excluding paper files) on the basis of the data subject's prior consent or on the performance of a contract to which the data subject is a party.
- Secondly, the personal data requested should concern the data subject and be provided by him.
  - WP29 recommends data controllers not take an overly restrictive interpretation of the sentence "personal data concerning the data subject", when third parties' data are contained in a data set relating to the data subject and provided by him and are used by the data subject making the request for personal purposes. Typical examples of data sets including third parties' data are the telephone records (which contain incoming and outgoing calls) a data subject would like to receive, or a bank account history that includes incoming payments from third parties.
  - Personal data can be considered as provided by the data subject when they are **knowingly and actively** "provided by" the data subject, such as account data (e.g., mailing address, username, age) submitted via online forms, **but also when they are generated by and collected from the activities of users, by virtue of the use of the service or the device**. By contrast, personal data that are derived or inferred from the data provided by the data subject, such as a user profile created by analysis of the raw smart metering, are excluded from the scope of the right to data portability, since they are not provided by the data subject, but created by the data controller.
- Last but not least, under the third condition, the exercise of this new right should not affect adversely the rights and freedoms of third parties. For example, if the data set transferred on the data subject request contains personal data relating to other individuals, the new data controller should process these data only if there is an appropriate legal ground to do so. Typically, processing under the sole control of the data subject, as part of purely personal or household activities will be appropriate.

TABLE 27.2
Core Data Subject Rights and Key Considerations

Data Subject Right	Description

Right of access	The data subject shall have the right to obtain from the controller
	1) Confirmation as to whether personal data concerning him or her is being processed, and,
	2) Where that is the case, access to the personal data (free copy of the data), and
	3) Plus, the information relevant to the processing,
	  • Source of the personal data
	  • Purpose of the processing
	  • The data recipients
	  • Confirmation regarding automated decision-making, incl. profiling, its envisioned consequences, and meaningful information about the logic
	  • Rights of the data subject

Right to rectification	The data subject has the right to request the data controller to rectify the inaccurate personal data without undue delay, supplement incomplete personal data, or allow individuals to update or correct the personal data held by the entity.
	With respect to correction, the following two aspects should be considered
	  • Objectively incorrect
	  • Subjectively incorrect (opinions)
	With respect to completion, the following aspect should be considered
	  • As relevant given the purposes of the processing

Right to erasure (Right to be forgotten)	Organizations should provide users with methods and channels for deleting their personal data. When a data subject submits a request for deleting personal data, the organization needs to delete the personal data collected and stored. If the controller has disclosed the information, the controller needs to ask other controllers to delete the information.
	Right to erasure:
	  • The personal data is no longer necessary for the purpose for which it was collected.
	  • The processing is based on consent, and the data subject withdraws that consent.
	  • The processing is based on the controller's legitimate interest, the data subject objects to the processing and the controller is unable to demonstrate that its legitimate interest overrides the interests or the fundamental rights and freedoms of the data subject.
	  • The processing is unlawful.
	  • The personal data must be erased for compliance with EU or member state law.
	  • If consent was given when the data subject was a child (either by the child or a legal guardian); the consent may then be withdrawn, even if the individual is no longer a child.
	Exemptions: national security, crime prevention, and the protection of others' rights and freedoms (including controllers')
	Right to be forgotten:
	The right to be forgotten is an extension of the right to erasure and applies when data has been made public by the controller: for example, posting personal data on a publicly accessible website. If the individual requests erasure, in this case, the original controller must take reasonable steps to "to inform the controllers which are processing such personal data to erase any links to or copies or replications of those personal data".
	Difficulties may include:
	  • Determining all of the data's recipients
	  • Informing all other controllers (which may result in increased exposure)
	  • And objections from controllers based on the fundamental right to freedom of expression and information
	Exception:
	  • Compliance with EU or member state law for a task in the public interest or as part of the controller's official authority
	  • Public health purposes
	  • Archiving in the public interest, scientific or historical research, or statistical purposes (if erasure seriously impairs the objectives)

Data Subject Right	Description
Right to restriction of processing	Restriction provides an alternative to erasure in circumstances where storing personal data is legally required, ensures the protection of another person's rights, or is in the public interest. The controller must inform the data subject before a restriction of processing is lifted. Communicate to each recipient to whom the personal data have been disclosed unless this proves impossible or involves disproportionate effort. The controller shall inform the data subject about those recipients if the data subject requests it. Data subjects may request their personal data to be restricted for the following reasons: • The processing is unlawful, but the data subject prefers restriction to the erasure of personal data. • The accuracy of the data is contested by the data subject, and the controller needs time to verify accuracy. • The controller no longer needs the personal data, but the data subject needs it to be saved for the establishment, exercise, or defense of legal claims. • Or the data subject objects to the processing, pending the controller's attempt to verify legitimate grounds. Once restricted, personal data may only be processed • with new consent from the data subject, • to exercise or defend legal claims, • to protect the rights of another person, • or for important public interest reasons. Open-ended list of possible methods: • Making the personal data temporarily unavailable • Noting the restriction in the system • Moving the data to a separate system • Temporarily blocking a website • Using the data under narrow conditions If data is stored in a system, a robust mechanism must be provided to ensure that the data under restricted processing is no longer processed. That is, personal data under restricted processing needs to be clearly identified. For example, if an attribute is frozen, the system will filter out it during query and processing (e.g., sending marketing emails).

Right to data portability	The data subject shall have the right to receive the personal data concerning him or her, which he or she has provided to a controller, in a structured, commonly used, and machine-readable format and have the right to transmit those data to another controller without hindrance from the controller.
	1) It is similar to Right of Access—Extension to right of access in the new technology time
	• Copy in the structured and machine-readable form: the data provided by users should be extracted from the system or product in a machine-readable format (such as XML, CSV, and plaintext).
	• Interoperability
	• Direct transfer
	2) Narrow applicability (meet all following three conditions)
	• the processing is based on consent or on a contract and the processing is carried out by automated means
	• Personal data concerning him or her, which he or she has provided, which means personal data collected (or observed in some cases) from the data subject, NOT data derived/inferred from data provided
	  • ✓ **Observed**, by tracking people online or by smart devices
	  • ✗ **Derived** from combing other data sets
	  • ✗ **Inferred** by using algorithms to analyze a variety of data, such as social media, location data and records of purchases in order to profile people for example in terms of their credit risk, state of health or suitability for a job.
	• The exercise of this right should not affect adversely the rights and freedoms of others
	Note: Does not create the right to move data from one processor to other processors in B2B services.
	(Continued)

TABLE 27.2   (Continued)

Data Subject Right	Description
Right to object	Data subjects have the right to object to the processing of their personal data that is out of public interests or the legitimate interests of others. Data subjects have the right to object to the processing of their personal data for the purpose of direct marketing. Under the EU GDPR, the right to object is not absolute. This right is only available if the grounds for data processing fall into one of the three categories. • Legitimate interests: A data subject may object at any time to processing based on the public interest or the controller's legitimate interests, based on grounds relating to the individual's particular situation. The controller then has the burden to demonstrate that it has compelling legitimate interests for processing the data that override the individual's interests, rights, and freedoms. To make a decision weighing an objection vs. legitimate interests, the controller could organize a discussion between someone who represents the interests of the organization and an objective individual, such as the data protection officer, who represents the interests of the data subject. • Public interests—Research or statistical purposes: A data subject may object to processing for scientific or historical research purposes or statistical purposes, on grounds relating to his or her particular situation. This right is overridden if the processing is necessary for the performance of a task carried out in the public interest. • Direct marketing: A data subject has the right to object at any time to the processing of his or her personal data for direct marketing purposes. This right is absolute and should cause the controller to cease processing. This right includes profiling.

Right not to be subject to automated decision	The data subject shall have the right not to be subject to a decision based solely on automated processing, including profiling, which produces legal effects concerning him or her or similarly significantly affects him or her.
	It is very relevant in the context of
	• Artificial intelligence
	• Big data
	• Predictive analytics
	• Robotics
	• e-Government
	Things to consider:
	• Identify whether automatic decision-making and profiling exist. If similar functions are available, ensure that users have the right not be subject to the mechanisms.
	  • Give individuals information about the processing.
	    • The usage of such technologies
	    • The significance and envisaged consequences of such processing for the individual
	    • Meaningful information about the logic involved
	  • Introduce simple ways for them to request human intervention or challenge a decision.
	  • Carry out regular checks to make sure that your systems are working as intended.
	• The personal data controller shall provide a complaint method to the personal data subject when a decision that significantly affects the rights of the personal data subject is made according to the automatic decision of the information system (for example, the personal credit and loan amount is determined based on the user profiling, or the user profiling is used for interview screening).

 Questions and answers

Does the exercise of the right to data portability affect the exercise of the other data subject's rights?

When an individual exercises his right to data portability (or other rights within the GDPR) he or she does so without prejudice to any other right. The data subject can exercise his or her rights as long as the data controller is still processing the data. For example, the data subject can continue to use and benefit from the data controller's service even after a data portability operation. Equally, if he or she wants to exercise his or her right to erasure, oppose or access his or her personal data, the previous or subsequent exercise of the right to data portability cannot be used by a data controller as a way of delaying or refusing to answer other data subject's rights. Furthermore, data portability does not automatically trigger the erasure of the data from the data controller's systems and does not affect the original retention period applying to the data which have been transmitted, according to the right to data portability.

Questions and answers

What are the differences between automated decision-making and profiling?
Table 27.3 describes the key differences between automated decision-making and profiling.

Case Study

Italian DPA v. H3G, 2014
H3G user portrait case
In 2012, H3G applied to the Italian data protection agency for a preliminary verification on the processing of user Internet traffic data for the purpose of user profiling and targeted advertising. Traffic data is anonymized before use, so it can be used without user consent, H3G said. However, in the investigation, the Italian data protection agency found that the process of anonymization is reversible, so H3G needs the consent of users to process its traffic data. The data protection authority prohibits H3G from processing its traffic data for the purpose of user profiling without the prior express consent of the user and prior certification by the data protection authority.

After that, on June 12, 2014, the Italian data protection agency found that H3G used users' traffic data to profile users without obtaining the prior consent of all users or notifying the Italian data protection agency.

Questions and answers

What constitutes legal effect with respect to the right not to be subject to automated decisions?
The WP29 clarifies the GDPR's use of "legal" or "similarly significant" effects.

- The guidelines note possible impingements on the freedom to **associate with others**, **vote in an election**, or take **legal action** or an **effect on legal contractual status** or **rights** as examples of "legal effects" under the GDPR.
- "Similarly significant" effects need not necessarily be legal ones. The 29 working party suggests that the threshold is the significance of the decision's impact on the data subject. The decision must have "the potential to significantly influence the circumstances, behavior, or choices of the individuals concerned."
  - The guidance notes the difficulty of drawing a precise boundary for the types of decisions that would qualify as significant, but points to recital 71 of the GDPR, which gives "automatic refusal of **an online credit application**" and "**e-recruiting practices** without any human intervention" as examples. The

TABLE 27.3
Key Differences between Automated Decision-Making and Profiling

Automated Decision-Making	Profiling
These two activities are different; however, automated decision-making could include profiling.	
Definition Making a decision based solely on technical means without human involvement. Examples: • An automatic refusal of an online credit application • E-recruiting practices without any human intervention	Processing of personal data to evaluate certain aspects of an individual. Under GDPR Art. 4, profiling is defined as the following: Any form of automated processing of personal data consisting of the use of personal data to evaluate certain personal aspects relating to a natural person • in particular to analyze or predict aspects concerning that natural person's performance at work, economic situation, health, personal preferences, interests, reliability, behavior, location or movements WP 251 Guide indicates that profiling consists of three elements: • it is an automated form of processing. It concerns personal data and its purpose is to evaluate the personal aspects of a natural person. • The individual has the right to refuse to profile. • There are a few special cases where automated decisioning is permitted, such as when the process is authorized by law or regulation within a Member State or when it is necessary for entering into a contract between the data subject and the data controller, or if it is based on explicit consent. In the case of a contractual agreement, the controller has to implement measures that protect the rights of the individuals. For example, individuals should be allowed to express their point of view, obtain information about the decision that has been reached based on the profiling, and of course, have the right to contest this decision. Example: • For instance, if a video streaming platform collects the watching record and time from the users, automatically analyze what kind of movies or shows they may be more interested in, and then recommend similar movies or shows to the users, which may constitute profiling.
Key Considerations Data subjects have the right to not be subject to a decision that is based solely on automated processing (with no human involvement), including profiling that produces legal effects concerning them or similarly significantly affects them.	Three elements to profiling: • It has to be an automated form of processing. • It has to use personal data. • The purpose of the profiling must be to evaluate the personal aspects of a natural person. Ways profiling may be used: • General profiling • Decision-making based on profiling • A decision solely based on automated decision making, including profiling

guidelines suggest that **online advertising (differential pricing)** may qualify, depending on the following characteristics:

- The intrusiveness of the profiling process.
- The expectations and wishes of the individuals concerned.
- The way the ad is delivered.
- The particular vulnerabilities of the data subjects targeted.
- Significant effects may apply to certain groups when they do not apply to individuals generally. **Differential pricing technology** is specifically mentioned as a potential example.

Case Study

Dutch DPA v. BKR, 2020[96]

National Credit Register (BKR) fined for personal data access charges

In May 2018 the BKR began charging a fee to data subjects for requesting access to their data in a digital format. Furthermore, although data subjects could obtain a paper copy of their data for free, this was only possible once a year. This situation was an infringement of privacy legislation and led to the BKR being fined €830,000.

Following the Dutch DPA's investigation, the BKR has modified its processes. Since April 2019 data subjects have been able to access their data for free. In addition, in March 2019 the BKR changed the number of times a year data subjects can receive a paper copy of their data by post.

Case Study

Danish DPA v. Taxa 4x35, 2019[97]

The Danish Data Protection Authority, Datatilsynet, has recommended fining a taxi company Taxa 4x35 1.2 million kroner ($180,000) for not deleting customers' telephone numbers.

In the autumn of 2018, the Danish Data Protection Agency inspected the Danish taxi company Taxa35. According to Taxa 4x35, personal data used for booking and settlement of the taxi service are made anonymous after two years, since there is no longer a need to identify the customer. However, only the customer's name is deleted after these two years, but not the phone number. Therefore, information on the customer's taxi trip (including addresses) can still be traced to the customer via the phone number, which is not deleted until five years have passed. At the time of the inspection, 8.873.333 personal data records were found for taxi trips older than two years.

It's not enough for companies doing business in Denmark to delete people's names and addresses to satisfy the requirements of the EU General Data Protection Regulation. They must delete all information, including telephone numbers, to avoid potentially high fines.

27.4   LEGAL BASIS, APPLICABILITY AND EXCEPTIONS

Table 27.4 maps the six lawful bases to the data subject rights. Figure 27.1 lists some of the DSR implementation key considerations and exceptions.

TABLE 27.4
Lawful Bases and Data Subject Rights

	Consent	Contract Performance	Legal Obligation	Vital Interests	Public Tasks	Legitimate Interests
Right of Access	✓	✓	✓	✓	✓	✓
Right to Rectification	✓	✓	✓	✓	✓	✓
Right to Erasure	✓	✓	✗	✓	✗	✓
Right to Restriction	✓	✓	✓	✓	✓	✓
Right to Portability	✓	✓	✗	✗	✗	✗
Right to Object	Can withdraw consent	✗	✗	✗	✓	✓

	Apply	Does Not Apply/Exception
Right to be informed	Article 13	• Already has the information
	Article 14	• Already has the information • impossible or disproportionate • Legal obligation (obtaining or disclosure + professional secrecy)
Right of access	1) Confirmation as to **whether** personal data is being processed 2) Where that is the case, **access to** the personal data (free copy) 3) And plus, the **information relevant** to the processing, • Source of the personal data • Purpose of the processing • the data recipients. • Confirmation regarding automated decision-making, incl. profiling, its envisioned consequences and meaningful information about the logic • Rights of data subject	• Adversely affect the rights and freedoms of others
Right to be rectification	• Inaccurate o Objectively incorrect o Subjectively incorrect (opinions) • Incomplete (supplementary statement) o As relevant given the purposes of the processing	X
Right to erasure	Right of erasure (GDPR Art 17.1): Unlawful √; lawful: Legal basis • Consent • Withdraw consent • Article 8.1(child's consent) • Legal obligation; Purpose • No longer necessary; DSR • Object	• Freedom of expression and information • Legal obligation • Public interest • Archiving purposes in the public interest, scientific or historical research purposes or statistical purposes • Establishment, exercise or defense of legal claims
	Erasure of public data (GDPR Art 17.2): ▪ If 17.1 applies ▪ + Data have been made public	
Right to restrict processing	Unlawful & oppose erasure: √; lawful: Purpose • No longer necessary but required by DS for legal claims; Accuracy contested; DSR • Object and verify whether the legitimate grounds of the controller override those of the DS	Such personal data shall, with the exception of storage, only be processed with: • Data subject's consent • Data subject's legal claims • Protection of Other persons' rights • Public interest
Right to data portability	Meet all three • Data provided • Based on consent or contract • By automated data processing means. Note: Does not create right to move data from one processor to other processor in B2B services	• Public interest • Exercise of official authority vested in the controller • Adversely affect the rights and freedoms of others
Right to object	• Based on GDPR Article 6(1) point (e) (public interest) or (f) legitimate interests	• Data controller's interests override data subject interests – requires balancing test • DC's legal claims.
	• Direct marketing	
	• Archive purposes for scientific or historical research purposes or statistical purposes	The processing is necessary for the performance of a task carried out for reasons of public interest.
Right not to be subject to automated decision	• A decision is based solely on automated processing, including profiling • Which produces legal effects or similarly significantly affects him or her	About profiling: • The decision/profiling is not fully automated, or • The decision/profiling does not produce said effects The automated decision is: • Authorized by Union or Member state law applicable to the controller; or • Necessary for the entry into or performance of a contract; or (in this case, data controller has to implement measures that protect the rights of the individuals) • based on the individual's explicit consent. In case of special data • Explicit consent data subject • Substantial public interest laid down in EU/MS law • Suitable safeguards

FIGURE 27.1 DSR implementation key considerations and exceptions.

27.5 DSRS HANDLING WORKFLOW

Organizations should establish and operationalize a process to handle data subject right requests from external and internal data subjects. Usually, the process covers the considerations such as intake triage, identification verification, fulfilling the requests, response to data subjects, case closure, and so on.

Figure 27.2 illustrates an exemplar data subject right request handling process.

Table 27.5 describes the steps and key considerations for a typical DSR handling process.

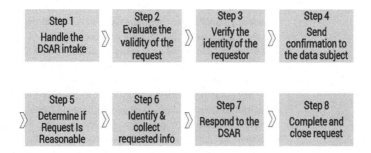

FIGURE 27.2 Subject right request handling process.

TABLE 27.5
DSR Handling Steps and Key Considerations

#	Steps	Key Considerations
1	Handle the data subject right request intake	1) Establish the channels (i.e., web portal, email, phone, physical mail address) for data subjects to submit their requests. 2) Define the information/format that a request from a data subject should contain such as: • The local country or region • Name • Contact information, such as an email address • Request subject • Description of the request
2	Evaluate the validity of the request	Determining whether to accept the request of the data subject. 1) The request information should be clear and valid. When reviewing the request information, pay attention to: • Whether the name and contact information are valid • Whether the request description is related to personal data protection • Whether the request description is consistent with the request subject and the business attribution of the request 2) The requestor's identity shall be consistent with the identity of the personal data subject related to the request unless otherwise specified in the laws and regulations. For example, if a guardian proposes a request on behalf of the person under guardianship and can provide sufficient evidence, the business department concerned can accept the request. 3) If it is confirmed that a request is not accepted, notify the data subject of the rejection in writing form or by other means within five days after receiving the request, provide detailed rejection reasons, and close the data subject's request. 4) If the request is valid, the intake handling team can distribute the data subject's request to the corresponding business department for handling according to the business attribute.

(Continued)

TABLE 27.5   (Continued)

#	Steps	Key Considerations
3	Verify the identity of the requestor	The business department must authenticate requestors to ensure that they are the data subjects of the requested personal data, or they have the request right. • Don't over-collect information from the data subject for the purpose of identity verification. Please see the Spanish AEPD v. Page Group Europe, 2020 case study to follow. • Consider the context and reasonable expectations of data subjects. If some method of verifying identity was good enough when you obtained the data in the first place (e.g., you received them by email), it should be good enough when you receive a request (e.g., email request sent from the same email address). • Use the data you have rather than ask for more new data. • It means that you should try to verify the data subject's knowledge (e.g., by asking some questions) in relation to such data that are subject to the request, or that you hold for related purposes, and consider how the data were obtained in the first place. If your method of authentication was previously nickname and password, the very nickname and password should enable you to process the request. If nicknames or passwords were lost, of course, asking for name and surname will not make sense if they were not linked to the profile. • Where the controller has reasonable doubts concerning the identity of the natural person making the request, the controller may request the provision of additional information necessary to confirm the identity of the data subject. However, you need to take the following things into consideration: • By the minimum data necessary • If you actually need some additional information, it should be the minimum amount and only what is relevant in the given context. • Avoid asking for sensitive data • Asking for sensitive data usually is disproportionate and not always relevant. And by collecting such information, you will create additional risks for data subjects, as such data may be used, for identity theft or fraud. • Asking for a copy of an ID document, passport, or other officials, government-issued document, such as a birth certificate, as a standard way of verifying the identity of data subjects should be definitely avoided. • It is highly recommended that you do not obtain clearly more sensitive or potentially more harmful data, for the purpose of authentication, than the data that is subject to the request. • If the process is facilitated by the system automatically, the system should verify the data subjects' identities before allowing the data subjects to perform any actions (i.e., update, delete, etc.). For example, using activation links in emails and verification codes in text messages, during registration. • In the online context, the GDPR explicitly says that identification should include the digital identification of a data subject, for example, through an authentication mechanism, such as the same credentials, used by the data subject to log in to the online service offered by the data controller. • If a data subject fails the identity authentication due to insufficient information provided by him/her, the business department has the right to reject his/her request and request him/her to provide further information.
4	Send confirmation to the data subject	The request handling team sends the confirmation back to the data subject to the knowledge of the recipient of the request.
5	Determine Whether the Request Is Reasonable	In any of the following conditions, the business department has the right to reject the request but needs to provide the requestor with rejection reasons: • The organization does not have the personal data of the data subject. • The organization is not a controller of the data subject's personal data.

#	Steps	Key Considerations
		• The data subject's request may have an adverse impact on others' rights and freedom, for example, adversely affecting other individuals' personal data protection, freedom of speech, trade secrets, or legal intellectual property rights.
		• The data subject's request conflicts with the obligations that the organization must fulfill according to applicable laws or regulations. For example, a data subject requests to delete his/her personal data; however, according to applicable law or regulation, the organization must retain his/her personal data.
		• The data subject's request is beyond the applicable laws and regulations.
		If the business department determines that the request of a data subject is unreasonable, it should consult with the privacy officer and determine whether to reject or continue handling the request referring to the privacy officer's guidance.
6	Identify and collect requested information	If the request is reasonable, the corresponding business team should identify and collect the requested information within the legally required timeframe.
		The business department must use a standard template to provide handling results in a clear, concise, and easy-to-understand language.
		If the country/region where data subjects are located has specific requirements (for example, language requirements) on the resulting feedback, the business department should customize the content of the provided information.
		When handling portability requests, the business department should provide personal data in a structured, universal, and machine-readable form (such as the XML format).
7	Respond to the request	**Response:** The request handling team sends the handling result of the business department to the data subject and closes the data subject's request.
		• The information shall be provided in writing, or by other means, including, where appropriate, by electronic means. When requested by the data subject, the information may be provided orally, provided that the identity of the data subject is proven by other means.
		• Sending only the information and documentation you're legally obliged to disclose is extremely important. Don't over-send the information to the data subjects
		Extension: If the controller does not act on the request of the data subject, the controller shall inform the data subject without delay and at the latest within one month of receipt of the request of the reasons for not taking action and the possibility of lodging a complaint with a supervisory authority and seeking a judicial remedy.
		Rejection: Rejection of data subjects' requests and dispute mechanism. Notify the reason why the data subjects' requests are rejected, the legal basis for the rejection (if any), and the right to raise an objection (if any) according to the laws and regulations in written forms. Notify the reasons for rejection of personal data rectification requests and how individuals can appeal in written form.
8	Complete and close request	The request handling team completes and closes the request if the response has been provided to the data subject and no further questions are raised.
		Your organization needs to document the following information regarding the requests:
		• The date you received the DSAR
		• Who the DSAR was received from
		• Whether the data subject was an employee, a client, or another type of data subject
		• Whether the DSAR was made by a Third Party on behalf of the data subject
		• Form of the DSAR
		• Whether a form of identity was provided
		• Date of your response to the DSAR
		• Nature of your response to the DSAR
		• Whether any further action was taken by the data subject

 **Case Study**

Spanish AEPD v. Page Group Europe, 2020[98]

Spanish DPA AEPD fined Page Group Europe €240,000 for requesting unnecessary copies of IDs and other docs from customers who made access requests.

The controller is Michael Page International, a company based in the United Kingdom, and the parent company of the PageGroup business group. It is an employment agency and operates under various brands, including "Michael Page".

A data subject complained to the Dutch Data Protection authority that Michael Page, a recruitment agency belonging to PAGE GROUP EUROPE, had required the submission of several documents in order to respond to requests for information to prove identity. Since the decisions to respond to requests for information were made in the Spanish branch of Michael Page, the responsibility fell to the Spanish data protection authority, which carried out the investigation in close cooperation with the Dutch DPA.

The complainant, registered through the recruitment agency's Dutch website, had asked Michael Page what personal data about him the agency held. However, Michael Page would not grant the Dutchman access to his data until he proved his identity by sending a complete copy of his identity card and insurance card. The fine recipient also requested a copy of the data subject's current energy or water bill in order to verify the accuracy of his address.

According to the Spanish Data Protection Authority, the recipient of the fine had unnecessarily requested the production of the documents because the documents were not needed to verify the identity of the applicant. The authority clarified that the fact that the complainant was registered with an account in Michael Page's online portal, to which he was the only one with access, was already sufficient as proof.

27.6   INQUIRIES AND COMPLAINTS HANDLING

Organizations should establish a process to address privacy-related inquiries, complaints, and disputes from internal and external stakeholders to ensure the inquiries or complaints are handled properly in a timely manner.

The submitted inquiries, complaints, and disputes might touch on various aspects such as privacy process discrepancies, policy violations, or any concerns. Some organizations may consider integrating the complaint handling process with the data subject rights request handling process. With respect to internal complaint handling, some jurisdictions may require that any employee who reports the discrepancy, violation or concerns should be protected from retaliation and the communication should be kept confidential.

Some privacy regulations (i.e., HIPAA) may require organizations to designate a contact person or privacy officer handling complaints or inquiries.

- Organizations need to appoint designated contact in handling complaints or inquiries if required by law or necessary for the business operations.
- Internal-facing process: Organizations need to establish a discrepancy reporting mechanism to take intakes and manage the reporting about privacy discrepancies or policy violations, or any concerns in an appropriate manner (confidential communications, etc.). Any employees who report the discrepancy, violation, or concerns should be protected from retaliation.
- External-facing process: An organization must make readily available information about the process for making a complaint or request. An organization must investigate any

complaint that it receives and make any necessary changes to its policies, practices, and procedures as a result of the investigation.

• Organizations should incorporate lessons learned from problematic data actions.

 Case Study

Spain AEPD v. Vodafone, 2019

Spanish DPA fined Vodafone €40,000 for sending two invoices to an incorrect recipient by email.

A Data Subject filed a complaint with the Spanish Data Protection authority (APED) against the telecommunications company for sending two invoices from another person to her via email. The complainant received the bills in June and July 2019. She then initially contacted VODAFONE España by telephone in this regard, but her concerns were not addressed there. None of the connected employees knew anything about the incorrect mailing or were able to correct the problem underlying it.

The data protection authority considered the incident to be a violation of the duty of the recipient of the fine to implement technical and organizational measures to ensure a level of security appropriate to the risk to the data subjects. In this context, it also found a violation of the principle of integrity and confidentiality on the part of other consumers' personal information which was collected and stored by Vodafone.

28 Data Breach Handling

This chapter is intended to help readers understand the data breach notification obligations across various jurisdictions and to embed data breach handling requirements into the broader security incident handling process.

This chapter covers the following topics:

- *What is a data breach*
- *Data breach notification obligations*
- *Data breach handling process*

28.1 WHAT IS A DATA BREACH

On the one hand, the driving and empowering effect of data capitalization on technological innovation, economic development, and public governance have become increasingly prominent, and various organizations such as governments and enterprises are increasingly relying on data under the accelerated digital transformation, and development, circulation, and utilization. On the other hand, the situation of data security and personal information protection is becoming more and more severe. IDC research shows that 3,932 data security breaches were publicly reported worldwide in 2020, and the number of personal information breaches reached 37 billion, while IBM research shows that the average cost of data breaches to enterprises in 2020 is $3.86 million, especially as the cost of a large data breach has skyrocketed into the millions.

High-profile cyberattacks and data breaches, such as Capitol One in 2019, have brought the issue of privacy to the forefront of executives' minds. For instance, Equifax's data breach expenses reach $242.7M. Senior management and executives now acknowledge privacy and security as some of the biggest risks to the business. Previously, the entire scope of privacy would fall upon IT professionals to manage and control. Regulatory obligations to notify the public of breaches and pay significant fines for noncompliance have also pushed executives to be more concerned than ever before.

However, a report by Stericycle's information security service Shred-it found that 63% of high-ranking executives and 67% of small US businesses do not have an incident response plan, while 75% of large US businesses have experienced a data breach.[99]

Implications of data breach:

- Hefty fines and reputational damage are two of the primary setbacks incurred following a publicized data breach.
- Data breaches cause tremendous problems, not only for the company affected but also for its clients. Depending on the company, stolen data can range from relatively benign information to extremely personal details. In any case, a breach can cost a lot of money for remediation and cause significant damage to a company's image.

A data breach is when unauthorized access, collection, use, or disclosure of personal information occurs. Privacy breaches commonly happen when personal information is hacked, stolen, lost, or inadvertently disclosed to the wrong people.

Table 28.1 provides data breach definitions from some regulations.

TABLE 28.1

Examples of Data Breach Definitions

Regulation	Definition
GDPR	Article 4(12) of the GDPR defines a "personal data breach" as "a breach of security leading to the accidental or unlawful destruction, loss, alteration, unauthorized disclosure of, or access to, personal data transmitted, stored or otherwise processed."
EU ePrivacy Directive	A personal data breach means a breach of security leading to the accidental or unlawful destruction, loss, alteration, unauthorized disclosure of, or access to personal data transmitted, stored or otherwise processed in connection with the provision of a publicly available electronic communications service in the Community.
US HITECH (HIPAA) Act	A breach is an unauthorized acquisition, access, use, or disclosure of protected health information, which compromises the security or privacy of such information.
California CPRA	The definition of a data breach under CCPA covers scenarios where: (1) "unencrypted personal information was, or is reasonably believed to have been, acquired by an unauthorized person," or "(2) whose encrypted personal information was or is reasonably believed to have been, acquired by an unauthorized person and the encryption key or security credential was, or is reasonably believed to have been, acquired by an unauthorized person and the agency that owns or licenses the encrypted information has a reasonable belief that the encryption key or security credential could render that personal information readable or usable."
Canada PIPEDA	A breach of security safeguards is defined in PIPEDA as: the loss of, unauthorized access to or unauthorized disclosure of personal information resulting from a breach of an organization's security safeguards

 Case Study

China authorities v. China Mobile and China Unicom, 2010

In 2010, three employees of China Mobile and China Unicom were charged with the crime of selling and illegally providing citizens' personal information for taking advantage of the convenience of work to obtain user information and illegally provide it to others for profit. Because their illegal acts occurred before the promulgation of new crimes such as the crime of illegally obtaining citizens' personal information, the court finally determined that the three persons were accomplices in the crime of illegal business operations and were sentenced to fixed-term imprisonment ranging from two years and two months to two years and nine months, and corresponding penalties.

28.2 DATA BREACH NOTIFICATION OBLIGATIONS

Data breach notification laws, primarily enacted over concerns about identity theft, create incentives to implement effective controls because they expose companies to the financial and reputational harm associated with the public disclosure of their failure to adequately protect their sensitive personal information.

28.2.1 NATIONAL LEVEL

Different jurisdictions may pose very different legal obligations to organizations with respect to data breach reporting to data protection authorities and data subjects. The organization should identify, document, and maintain corresponding requirements in each jurisdiction in which your organization operates.

Table 28.2 illustrates some of the regulatory requirements with respect to data breach notification obligations.

 Case Study

Ireland DPC v. Twitter, 2021

The Irish Data Protection Commission (DPC) imposed an administrative fine on Twitter International Company confirmed in the Dublin Circuit Court on October 18, 2021. The application to confirm the decision to impose an administrative fine of €450,000 was made pursuant to Section 143 of the Data Protection Act 2018.

The DPC inquiry examined Twitter's notification of a breach to the DPC, as distinct from examining the breach itself. Twitter was found to have infringed GDPR Articles 33(1) and 33(5)—failure to notify the breach on time to the DPC and to adequately document the breach.

 Case Study

Dutch DPA v. Booking.com, 2021

The Dutch data protection authority imposed a fine of 475,000 euros on Booking.com failing to report a major data breach to the regulator in a timely manner on April 2, 2021. The fine was imposed by the Dutch DPA as the company's global headquarters are legally established in Amsterdam.

The online travel company formally learned of the data breach on January 13, 2019, but only notified the Dutch DPA the following month on February 7. As per GDPR provisions, the incident should have been notified within 72 hours.

TABLE 28.2

Examples of Data Breach Notification Obligations

Regulation	Requirement
EU GDPR	Notify the corresponding supervisory authority within 72 hours; When the personal data breach is likely to result in a high risk to the rights and freedoms of natural persons, the controller shall communicate the personal data breach to the data subject without undue delay.
	Data processors are also obligated to notify data controllers of any data breach incidents.
US HIPAA	Covered entities must notify the following stakeholders "without reasonable delay" and no later than 60 days after discovering the breach.
	• Affected patients (written or electronic notice if not withdrawn)
	• Prominent media outlets (>500 residents affected)
	• HHS: >= 500 residents
	For HHS, when <500 residents, maintain a log and provide notice, not later than 60 days after the end of each calendar year
US-DOT	The US Department of the Treasury's Office of the Comptroller of the Currency announced the approval of final rulemaking for improving cyber incident reporting affecting the US bank system. The rule calls for mandatory reporting of an incident within 36 hours of determining an incident occurred. Bank service providers are also required to inform potentially affected customers immediately following an incident that lasts 4 hours or longer within a system.
PCI-DSS	Applies to organizations that handle credit card payments. It is a contractual obligation rather than a federally mandated regulation.
	Notify the payment card company of the breach within allotted timelines using the phone numbers provided.

(Continued)

TABLE 28.2   (Continued)

Regulation	Requirement
California CPRA	Under CCPA and CPRA, businesses must notify any California resident whose personal information was compromised as a result of a data breach.
	Any business that is required to notify more than 500 California residents as a result of a single breach must also submit a single sample copy of that notification to California's Attorney General.
	The disclosure "shall be made in the most expedient time possible and without unreasonable delay, consistent with the legitimate needs of law enforcement."
	The CCPA regulation also provides a data breach notification template that organizations should follow (798.29). The security breach notification "shall be written in plain language" and should include the following sections:
	• Title: Notice of Data Breach
	• "What Happened"
	• "What Information Was Involved"
	• "What We Are Doing"
	• "What You Can Do"
	• "For More Information"
Canada— PIPEDA	Report to Commissioner:
	• Report to the Commissioner of any breach of security safeguards involving personal information
	• As soon as feasible after the organization determines that the breach has occurred.
	Notification to individuals:
	• Shall notify an individual of any breach of security safeguards if it is reasonable to believe that the breach creates a real risk of significant harm to an individual
	• As soon as feasible after the organization determines that the breach has occurred
	Record Keeping:
	• Maintain a record of every breach of security safeguards for 24 months after the day on which the organization determines the breach has occurred
Canada— provincial	Ontario—the Health Information Protection Act (HIPA) 2016
	The bill included making breach reporting mandatory
	Newfoundland and Labrador
	In Newfoundland and Labrador, in situations where a custodian reasonably believes there has been a material breach involving the unauthorized collection, use or disclosure of personal health information, that custodian is required to notify the commissioner of the breach.

Booking.com was initially alerted by email on January 9, 2019, by one of the concerned UAE hotels to suspicious activity following a customer complaint about a call regarding their reservation. This isolated incident alone did not necessarily constitute awareness of a breach. However, when Booking.com received a second email on January 13 over a similar incident from the same hotel, the company should have realized that it had an issue on its hands. The Dutch DPA concluded that the company should have been "aware" of a breach as of January 13.

Booking.com, however, took the position that it had to conduct an internal security investigation in the first instance to conclude that a breach had, in fact, occurred. That investigation was concluded on February 4. The notification to the Dutch DPA followed February 7, and in doing so, Booking. com was of the view that they fulfilled their obligation within the 72-hour time frame. However, in their notification filing, they stated they had become aware of the incident on January 10. This is what triggered the regulatory investigation.

28.2.2   US STATE SECURITY BREACH NOTIFICATION LAWS

As of May 2022, all 50 states, the District of Columbia, Guam, Puerto Rico, and the Virgin Islands have laws requiring private businesses, and in most states, governmental entities as well, to notify individuals of security breaches of information involving personally identifiable information.

In 2003, California became the first state to pass such a law, known as SB 1386.92. This law provides that California government agencies and commercial entities that do business in California must, except in a few circumstances, disclose the breach of any computer system that contains unencrypted personal information of California residents.

Security breach laws typically have provisions regarding who must comply with the law (e.g., businesses, data or information brokers, government entities, etc.); definitions of "personal information" (e.g., name combined with SSN, driver's license or state ID, account numbers, etc.); what constitutes a breach (e.g., unauthorized acquisition of data); requirements for notice (e.g., timing or method of notice, who must be notified); and exemptions (e.g., for encrypted information).

Table 28.3 provides a summary of US State Data Breach Notification Statutes from the information provided by the National Conference of State Legislatures (NCSL).[100]

TABLE 28.3
US State Data Breach Notification Statutes

State	Statute	Applicability—Private Sector	Applicability—Government
Alabama	Ala. Code § 8–38–1 *et seq.*	✓	✓
Alaska	Alaska Stat. § 45.48.010 *et seq.*	✓	✓
Arizona	Ariz. Rev. Stat. § 18–551 to -552	✓	✓
Arkansas	Ark. Code §§ 4–110–101 *et seq.*	✓	✓
California	Cal. Civ. Code § 1798.82	✓	
	Cal. Civ. Code § 1798.29		✓
Colorado	Colo. Rev. Stat. § 6–1–716	✓	
	Colo. Rev. Stat. § 24–73–103		✓
Connecticut	Conn. Gen Stat. §§ 36a-701b, 4e-70	✓	✓
Delaware	Del. Code tit. 6, § 12B-101 *et seq.*	✓	✓
Florida	Fla. Stat. § 501.171	✓	✓
Georgia	Ga. Code §§ 10–1–910 to -912	✓	✓
Hawaii	Haw. Rev. Stat. § 487N-1 *et seq.*	✓	✓
Idaho	Idaho Stat. §§ 28–51–104 to -107	✓	✓
Illinois	815 ILCS §§ 530/1 to 530/25, 815 ILCS 530/	✓	✓
Indiana	Ind. Code § 24–4.9 *et seq.*	✓	
	Ind. Code § 4–1–11 *et seq.*		✓
Iowa	Iowa Code §§ 715C.1, 715C.2	✓	✓
Kansas	Kan. Stat. § 50–7a01 et seq.	✓	✓
Kentucky	KRS § 365.732	✓	
	KRS § 365.732, KRS § 61.931 to .934		✓
Louisiana	La. Rev. Stat. §§ 51:3071 *et seq.*	✓	✓
Maine	Me. Rev. Stat. tit. 10 § 1346 *et seq.*	✓	✓
Maryland	Md. Code Com. Law § 14–3504	✓	
	Md. State Govt. Code § 10–1305		✓
Massachusetts	Mass. Gen. Laws § 93H-1 *et seq.*	✓	✓
Michigan	Mich. Comp. Laws §§ 445.63, 445.72	✓	✓
Minnesota	Minn. Stat. §§ 325E.61, 325E.64	✓	
	Minn. Stat. § 13.055		✓
Mississippi	Miss. Code § 75–24–29	✓	✗
Missouri	Mo. Rev. Stat. § 407.1500	✓	✓

(Continued)

TABLE 28.3 (Continued)

State	Statute	Applicability—Private Sector	Applicability—Government
Montana	Mont. Code §§ 30–14–1704, 33–19–321	✓	
	Mont. Code §§ 2–6–1501 to -1503		✓
Nebraska	Neb. Rev. Stat. §§ 87–801 *et seq.*	✓	✓
Nevada	Nev. Rev. Stat. §§ 603A.010 *et seq.*	✓	
	Nev. Rev. Stat. §§ 603A.010 *et seq.*, 242.183		✓
New Hampshire	N.H. Rev. Stat. §§ 359-C:19, 359-C:20, 359-C:21	✓	✓
New Jersey	N.J. Stat. § 56:8–161, 163	✓	✓
New Mexico	N.M. Stat. §§ 57–12C-1	✓	✗
New York	N.Y. Gen. Bus. Law § 899-AA	✓	
	NY CLS State Tech. Law § 208		✓
North Carolina	N.C. Gen. Stat § 75–61, § 75–65	✓	✗
North Dakota	N.D. Cent. Code §§ 51–30–01 *et seq.*	✓	
	N.D. Cent. Code §§ 54–59.1–01 *et seq.*		✓
Ohio	Ohio Rev. Code §§ 1349.19, 1349.191, 1345.01 *et seq.*	✓	
	Ohio Rev. Code §§ 1347.12, 1349.192		✓
Oklahoma	Okla. Stat. §§ 24–161 to -166	✓	
	Okla. Stat. § 74–3113.1		✓
Oregon	Oregon Rev. Stat. §§ 646A.600 to .628	✓	✗
Pennsylvania	73 Pa. Stat. §§ 2301 *et seq.*	✓	✓
Rhode Island	R.I. Gen. Laws §§ 11–49.3–1 *et seq.*	✓	✓
South Carolina	S.C. Code § 39–1–90	✓	
	S.C. Code § 1–11–490		✓
South Dakota	S.D. Cod. Laws §§ 20–40–19 to -26	✓	✗
Tennessee	Tenn. Code §§ 47–18–2107	✓	
	Tenn. Code §§ 47–18–2107; 8–4–119		✓
Texas	Tex. Bus. & Com. Code §§ 521.002, 521.053	✓	
	Tex. Govt. Code § 2054.1125		✓
Utah	Utah Code §§ 13–44–101 *et seq.*, 80 78B-4–701 *et seq.*	✓	✗
Vermont	Vt. Stat. tit. 9 §§ 2430, 2435	✓	✓
Virginia	Va. Code §§ 18.2–186.6, 32.1–127.1:05	✓	✓
Washington	Wash. Rev. Code §§ 19.255.010	✓	
	Wash. Rev. Code § 42.56.590		✓
West Virginia	W.V. Code §§ 46A-2A-101 et seq.	✓	✓
Wisconsin	Wis. Stat. § 134/98	✓	✓
Wyoming	Wyo. Stat. §§ 40–12–501 to -502	✓	✗
District of Columbia	D.C. Code §§ 28–3851 *et seq.*	✓	✓
Guam	9 GCA §§ 48–10 *et seq.*	✓	✓
Puerto Rico	10 LRPA §§ 4051 *et seq.*	✓	✓
Virgin Islands	V.I. Code tit. 14 § 2209	✓	
	V.I. Code tit. 14 § 2208		✓

Table 28.4 provides a quick summary of some of key considerations of data breach notification obligations from various States.

Case Study

FCC v. AT&T, 2015

The Federal Communications Commission reached a $25 million settlement with AT&T Inc. over a consumer data breach at call centers in Mexico, Colombia, and the Philippines. The breaches occurred in 2013 and 2014.

Employees of all three locations have unauthorized access to consumers' names, phone numbers, Social Security numbers, and other account-related information to obtain AT&T cell phone unlock codes and provide this information to a third party, which holds a large number of stolen or second-hand phones require this information to unlock the phone. AT&T failed to take effective measures to avoid such behaviors and failed to notify the FCC in a timely manner after the customer's proprietary network information was leaked.

Case Study

SEC v. Yahoo, 2018 (SECURITIES ACT OF 1933, Release No. 10485/April 24, 2018)

Yahoo was fined $35M for failing to disclose 2014 breach

The US Securities and Exchange Commission announced Yahoo will pay $35 million to settle charges for failing to properly disclose its 2014 data breach, MediaPost reports.

TABLE 28.4

Key Considerations of Data Breach Notification Obligations

Consideration	Description
Whom to notify	• At least 14 states require entities who detected a data breach to notify the state attorney general and/or other state agencies: • California, Idaho: notify the AGs • At least 27 states require that entities notify nationwide CRAs—consumer reporting agencies • The Texas law requires Texas companies that experience a data breach to notify not only Texas residents, but also residents of states lacking a data protection notification law.

When to notify	• The most common phrase used in conjunction with timing is "the most expeditious time possible and without unreasonable delay."
	• Timing
	  • Most stringent is Idaho, where state agencies suffering a data breach must notify the AG within 24 hours of incident detection.
	  • Puerto Rico is interesting in this regard, requiring notification to the territorial Department of Consumer Affairs within 10 days of detection, and the department will make the breach public within 24 hours of receipt.
	  • Florida and Ohio specify a limit—45 days—to "expeditious time."
	• Number of individuals impacted
	  • California entities must notify the AG if more than 500 California residents are affected, and other states have a number affected threshold.
	• Most states also allow delays "for a reasonable period of time" a law enforcement agency determines that the notification will impede a criminal investigation and that law enforcement agency has made a request that the notification be delayed.

(Continued)

TABLE 28.4   (Continued)

Consideration	Description

What to include in the notification letter	• Most states do not specify the contents of the notification to the data subject,
	• California, Iowa, Michigan, New Hampshire, New York, North Carolina, Oregon, Vermont, Virginia, and West Virginia do specify the contents.
	• North Carolina's requirements, for example, are among the most extensive, including:
	  • A description of the incident in general terms
	  • A description of the type of personal information that was subject to the unauthorized access and acquisition
	  • A description of what the business has done to prevent further unauthorized access
	  • Who in the business affected individual can call for further information and assistance
	  • A warning that the person should remain vigilant by reviewing account statements and monitoring free credit reports
	  • The toll-free numbers and addresses for the major consumer reporting agencies
	  • The toll-free numbers, addresses and website addresses for the Federal Trade Commission and the North Carolina attorney general's office, telling the individual that he or she can obtain information from these sources about preventing identity theft
	• Oregon's requirements include "advice to the individual to report suspected identity theft to law enforcement."
	• Virginia and Massachusetts require the notification to tell people how they can obtain a police report and request a credit freeze.
	• Massachusetts law was unique in specifically prohibiting the notice from including a description of the nature of the breach in the notification or the number of residents affected by the breach, while laws in other states require the notification to include a general description of the incident.

How to notify	• To data subject
	  • States generally provide notification options, but a written notice to the data subject is always the first option.
	  • Telephonic and electronic messages are typical alternatives, but usually only if the data subject has previously explicitly chosen one of those as the preferred communication method.
	  • Most legislation recognizes that data breach notifications involving thousands of impacted data subjects could place an undue financial burden on the organization and therefore allow substitute notification methods. In Connecticut, for example, "Substitute notice shall consist of the following:
	    • (A) Electronic mail notice when the person, business or agency has an electronic mail address for the affected persons.
	    • (B) conspicuous posting of the notice on the web site of the person, business, or agency if the person maintains one; and
	    • (C) Notification to major state-wide media, including newspapers, radio, and television."
	• Notification to attorneys general and regulators may be sent via letter or email. Some states—notably New York and North Carolina—have specific online forms that must be used for this reporting.
	• The CRAs have established email addresses to receive breach notification reports.

Exceptions	• The first and most common exception allowed by states is for entities subject to other, more stringent data breach notification laws. This includes HIPAA- and GLBA-covered entities and financial institutions subject to and in compliance with the GLBA Safeguards Rule. • Most states allow exceptions for entities that already follow breach notification procedures as part of their own information security policies as long as these are compatible with the requirements of the state law. • Many states also have an exception for data protected by encrypted and other technical controls. Typically, an incident is not considered a breach if the data was encrypted or redacted and the key remains secure, although the District of Columbia, Hawaii, Illinois, Iowa, Louisiana, Nevada, and Ohio do not make such a distinction. Most states make this explicit by stating that the exception does not apply when the decryption key is breached along with the encrypted data.
Penalties and rights of action	• The Connecticut law reserves enforcement, as many states do, to the state attorney general, and some states specify penalties. • The data breach notification laws of several states also grant a private right of action to individuals harmed by disclosure of their personal information in order to recover damages.

The 2014 data breach affected 500 million users, as hackers were able to steal email addresses, phone numbers and dates of birth. Yahoo did not disclose the breach until it was going to be purchased by Verizon in September 2016. "Yahoo senior management and relevant legal staff did not properly assess the scope, business impact, or legal implications of the breach," the SEC wrote in its order. "Furthermore, Yahoo's senior management and legal teams did not share information regarding the breach with Yahoo's auditors or outside counsel in order to assess the company's disclosure obligations in its public filings."

28.3 DATA BREACH HANDLING PROCESS

To protect the best interest of your organization, data breaches should be handled properly in a timely manner. Data breaches shouldn't just concern senior leadership and management. A robust data breach handling process should involve stakeholders at all levels. The personal data breach handling process should be properly established, exercised, and executed.

A key component of a successful privacy program involves a well-developed set of incident response and management procedures. Organizations should establish a consistent data breach handling process that includes the handling requirements, procedure, and responsibilities throughout various phases such as preparation, detection, investigation and triage, containment, eradication and recovery, reporting, improvements, and so on. It is crucial that a breach response process is developed and documented prior to an incident.

It is not an uncommon practice for organizations to integrate the personal data breach handling process into the security incident handling process. To be productive, the team who is responsible for creating the data breach handling process should take the following aspects into account.

- Use relevant regulatory timeframes as a guideline. Align incident management to relevant regulations. Language within privacy regulations is explicit in requiring notification to the supervisory authority and data subjects in the instance of a data breach.
- Involve business unit privacy champions when creating the response plan.
- Identify all interdependencies and map them out as a part of the validation process.

Organizations should conduct regular data breach drills to evaluate the effectiveness of the data breach handling process and make updates and improvements accordingly. Usually, the cadence of data breach drills is once a year or less depending on the specific business context.

Figure 28.1 illustrates a 6-step data breach handling process.

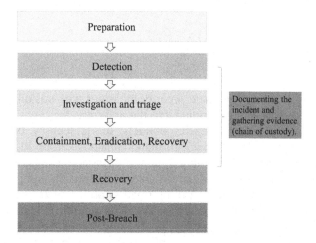

FIGURE 28.1 Data breach handling process.

Table 28.5 lists some of the key considerations throughout various phases of the data breach handling process.

 Questions and answers

Ransomware scenario: if an organization gets hit with something like ransomware which means that they no longer have access to their customer contact database, they would not be able to notify their customers immediately. If Article 34 stipulates "without undue delay", how would that be interpreted in this scenario?

- In most cases, the data protection authorities (regulators) want to know what kind of due diligence an organization has done to protect and notify the impacted data subjects. For instance, is there a backup that has customers' contact information? Or are there any other means to gather the information (i.e., looking into the email communications, etc.)?
- The bottom line is that the organization needs to demonstrate it has undertaken **all possible and reasonable efforts** to gather the information before it declares that there is no way to notify the data subjects. And if it IS the case that the organization can't notify the data subjects, it should **document that and communicate with the DPA**. The DPA might require the organization to issue a public notice regarding the breach on its website or through other means (i.e., via media, etc.)
- And whenever the database gets recovered later, the organization should notify the impacted data subjects as soon as feasible.

 Questions and answers

Ransomware scenario: Do I need to consider keeping a separate backup of customer contact information for just reporting purposes?

- There are no specific legal requirements for organizations to keep a backup for just this purpose.
- However, based on ARTICLE 29's official guide (page 31) Guidelines on Personal data breach notification under Regulation 2016/679, it did mention the ransomware and backup scenario as shown to follow in Table 28.6.

 Case Study

Spanish DPA v. Real Madrid Club, 2021[101]
The Spanish DPA decided not to fine a football club that suffered a data breach because it had implemented adequate security measures and was diligent in mitigating the breach's consequences and reporting it to the authority.

Real Madrid suffered a Data Breach: contracts, sports licenses, budgets, and other types of identifying data and economic information related to around 1,000 persons were affected. This was done by a hacker that accessed the system with stolen credentials.

The club diligently informed the Spanish DPA of the breach and proceeded to scan the Deep Web and regular Real Madrid information on the web to verify whether the information had been made public or was for sale. There was no evidence that the hacked information had been used, nor received the DPA any complaints regarding it. After the breach, the controller installed additional measures to prevent it from happening again,

TABLE 28.5

Key Considerations of Data Breach Handling

Data Breach Handling Phase	Objective	Key Considerations
Preparation	Ensure the appropriate resources are available to best handle an incident.	• Procedures and responsibilities, including internal reporting procedure, etc. • Handler communications and facilities • Incident analysis tools/checklist • Internal documentation (port lists, asset lists, network diagrams, current baselines of network traffic) • Data breach awareness and training • Incident drills/exercises
Detection	Leverage monitoring controls to actively detect threats	• Detection and identification: Alerts and validation, the timeline of the attack
Investigation and triage	Distill real events from false positives	• Investigation and classification (type of data, affected systems, affected users, overall impact, and level, etc.) • Incident triage: assign the handling to the proper teams
Containment, Eradication, Recovery	Isolate the threat before it can cause additional damage Eliminate the threat from your operating environment	• Containment: discontinue the affected systems • Eradication: identification of root causes, remediation, escalation path
Recovery	Restore impacted systems to a normal state of operations	• Recovery: restoration to operation, change management

Post-Breach	Conduct a lessons-learned post-mortem analysis
	Define and uphold your post-incident record-keeping requirements
		• Data Breach Records: The GDPR, in Article 33(5), dictates that you must keep a record of any data breach that takes place relating to your organization. The following list, which isn't exhaustive, shows what a data breach record should, ideally, include:
		  • Date of the data breach
		  • Number of people affected by the breach
		  • Nature of the breach
		  • Description of the breach
		  • The date you became aware of the breach
		  • How you become aware of the breach
		  • Description of the data involved in the breach
		  • Likely consequences of the breach
		  • Actual consequences of the breach
		  • Whether all affected data subjects have been informed
		  • Whether you have informed your data protection supervisory authority and, if so, on what date
		  • What remedial action has been taken
		• Lessons learned & Further improvements
		• Notifying/Reporting/Disclosing/Sharing Information with Outside Parties (i.e., DPA, data subjects, media) if required or considered necessary
		  • When it is required to notify either the data protection authorities or data subjects, usually the organization should include the following content (Not an exhaustive list)
		    • The types of personal data impacted, causes, and possible harm caused by the leak, distortion, or loss that occurred or might have occurred
		    • The mitigation measures taken by the personal information handler and measures individuals can adopt to mitigate harm
		    • Contact method of the personal information handler

TABLE 28.6

Data Breach Notification—Ransomware and Backup Scenario

Example	Notify the Supervisory Authority?	Notify the Data Subject?	Notes/Recommendations
iv. A controller suffers a ransomware attack which results in all data being encrypted. No backups are available, and data cannot be restored. On investigation it becomes clear that the ransomware's only functionality was to encrypt the data, and that there was no other malware present in the system.	Yes, report to the supervisory authority, if there are likely consequences to individuals as this is a loss of availability.	Yes, report to individuals, depending on the nature of the personal data affected and the possible effect of the lack of availability of the data, as well as other likely consequences.	If there was a backup available and data could be restored in good time, this would not need to be reported to the supervisory authority or individuals as there would have been no permanent loss of availability or confidentiality. However, if the supervisory authority became aware of the incident by other means, it may consider an investigation to assess compliance with the broader security requirements of article 32.

among other new cyber security measures, new laptop security protocols and blocking the IPs from which the attack came. The controller issued a report considering that the stolen information would not affect the reputation of the people involved, nor pose any kind of risk to them. Therefore, they decided not to communicate the breach to the Data Subjects.

   Questions and answers

What are the differences between computer forensics and eDiscovery?

Table 28.7 illustrates some of the key differences between computer forensics and eDiscovery.

TABLE 28.7

Key Differences between Computer Forensics and eDiscovery

Factors	Computer Forensics	Electronic Discovery (eDiscovery)
Primary Purpose	Incident response	HR or legal purpose
The respective timelines	A full forensic investigation may be tied to incident response, requiring rapid action to acquire a "snapshot" of systems and data. This incident response may be measured in minutes or hours.	An eDiscovery process is likely to be slower. The need to preserve and collect information is in response to a legal requirement, a slower process than incident response, measured in the weeks and months if not years.
Type of data	Live, resurrected, reconstructed fragments	Live or stored data (such as email and email achieve)
Recover deleted or temporary data	Yes	No (unless provided by forensics process)

Factors	Computer Forensics	Electronic Discovery (eDiscovery)
Type of collection	Bit image only	Bit image and/or copy
Downtime of client computers	Usually	No
Scope of data	The entire universe of data stored on a targeted device (i.e., a hard disk drive)	Usually only focuses on a smaller grouping of data stored on the targeted device/folder/group
Chain of custody forms	Yes	Yes
Scope of work	Forensic experts can partner with attorneys to pinpoint keywords related to the case, and then cross-reference those keywords against the collected data.	eDiscovery experts typically do not analyze the data they collect. Additionally, they usually do not clarify the intent of a computer user and they generally don't provide clients with legal advice.
Testimony	Opinion (expert)	Fact (protocol)

 Questions and answers

What are the differences between cloning vs. imaging?

Cloning and imaging are similar in that they can both make exact copies of your hard drive's contents. When you clone a drive, you turn a second drive into a copy of the first. With imaging, you create a very large backup file from which you can recreate the drive's contents later, either onto the original drive or another one.

Cloning and imaging do not require the disks to be identical or even the same size.

29 DPA Cooperation

This chapter is intended to help readers understand the powers and data protection authorities and identify main establishment and lead authority as well as cooperate with the relevant data protection authorities.

This chapter covers the following topics:

- *DPA powers*
- *Identifying ME and lead SA*
- *Cooperation with DPAs*

29.1 DPA POWERS

Under the GDPR, supervisory authorities are the regulatory authorities (often known as data protection authorities, or DPAs) within individual EU member states that are responsible for the member state enforcement of the GDPR.

DPAs may have different powers (i.e., investigative powers, corrective powers, authorization, and advisory powers) in different jurisdictions. For instance, DPAs have several powers to perform the tasks entrusted by the privacy regulations under the GDPR.

In general, the powers can be categorized into three types: investigative power, corrective power, and authorization and advisory power, as described in Table 29.1 in accordance with the GDPR.

 Questions and answers

What are the factors considered when a DPA issue a fine under GDPR?

1) When it comes to deciding on an appropriate fine, each case will be carefully assessed, and a range of factors will be taken into account:
   - the nature, gravity/duration of the violation
   - the number of data subjects affected, and the level of damage suffered by them;
   - the intentional character of the infringement
   - degree of responsibility
   - any relevant previous infringements
   - any actions are taken to mitigate the damage
   - any other aggravating or mitigating factor
   - **the degree of cooperation** with the supervisory authority
     - knuddels.de got reduced fines (20k Euros) because it actively cooperated with the Germany Baden-Württemberg DPA.
2) Some DPAs set forth a more detailed GDPR Fine Structure as guidance.

For instance, the Dutch Data Protection Authority Sets GDPR Fines Structure.[102]

- On March 14, 2019, the Dutch data protection authority (*Autoriteit Persoonsgegevens*, DPA) announced its fining structure for violations of the European General Data Protection Regulation (GDPR) and the Dutch law implementing the GDPR (Implementation Act).

TABLE 29.1
Examples of DPA Powers

Category	Powers

Investigative	• Order the controller and the processor to provide any information it requires for the performance of its tasks
	• Carry out a review on certifications
	• Carry out **investigations** in the form of data protection **audits**
	  • To obtain, from the controller and the processor, access to all personal data and to all information necessary for the performance of its tasks
	  • To obtain access to any premises of the controller and the processor, including to any data processing equipment and means, in accordance with Union or Member State procedural law
	  • Possible investigation format
	    • Investigations based on documents
	    • Investigations based on hearings
	    • Online investigations
	    • Onsite investigations
	• Notify the controller or the processor of an alleged infringement of this Regulation

Corrective	• In case of a data controller and processor infringement
	  • To issue warnings
	  • To issue reprimands
	  • To order the controller or processor to bring processing operations into compliance with the provisions of the Regulation, where appropriate, in a specified manner and within a specified period
	  • To order the suspension of data flows to a recipient in a third country or to an international organization.
	  • To impose a temporary or definitive limitation including a ban on processing
	  • To impose an administrative fine
	• Data controller and processor certification
	  • To withdraw a certification or to order the certification body to withdraw a certification, or to order the certification body not to issue certification if the requirements for the certification are not or are no longer met
	• Data subject related
	  • To order the controller or the processor to comply with the data subject's requests to exercise his or her rights pursuant to this Regulation
	  • To order the rectification or erasure of personal data or restriction of processing and the notification of such actions to recipients to whom the personal data have been disclosed
	  • To order the controller to communicate a personal data breach to the data subject

Authorization and advisory	• Legal basis—public interest
	  • To authorize processing referred to in Article 36(5)—public interest
	• DPIA consultation
	  • In case of Consultation with the supervisory authority is required prior to processing when the DPIA indicates a high risk to data subjects that are not mitigated. Supervisory authorities have the power to approve or reject it.
	• Data transfers
	  • To adopt standard data protection clauses—own version of standard contractual clauses (Ad hoc contractual clauses)
	  • To authorize contractual clauses
	  • To authorize administrative arrangements
	  • To approve binding corporate rules pursuant
	• Approve code of conduct and certification program
	• Advise the national parliament, Member State government, other institutions, and bodies, as well as the public

TABLE 29.2
Dutch DPA Fine Schedule

Category of Fines	Range	Default Fine
Category I	€0—€200,000	€100,000
Category II	€120,000—€500,000	€310,000
Category III	€300,000—€750,000	€525,000
Category IV	€450,000—€1,000,000	€725,000

- The GDPR sets two levels of administrative fines that may apply depending on which GDPR provisions have been infringed: The higher of €10 million or 2% of global revenue and the higher of €20 million or 4% of global revenue. At both levels, the GDPR sets maximums for administrative fines and calls on member state authorities to determine what fine is appropriate in individual cases.
- The Dutch DPA has introduced the four categories as set out in Table 29.2. While the Dutch DPA has set default fines for violations in each category, it also has set a range to be applied depending on the specifics of a violation.
- The first category is reserved for simple violations such as not sufficiently keeping records of the responsibilities of processors or joint controllers, and not publishing the contact details of the Data Protection Officer (DPO).
- The second category is reserved for not fulfilling certain requirements for processing such as not concluding data processing agreements with processors, not securing personal data well enough, not conducting impact assessments, or guaranteeing the DPO's independence.
- Examples of the third category include violations of the transparency requirement, failure to notify of data breaches, and not cooperating with the Dutch DPA.
- The fourth category is reserved for the unlawful processing of special categories of data (including the national identification number) unlawful profiling, and not complying with specific orders from the Dutch DPA.
- Interestingly, categories I and II do not correspond to violations that are punishable by the lower GDPR fine of €10 million, nor do categories III and IV solely correspond to violations that are punishable by the GDPR fine of €20 million.
- The Dutch DPA will diverge from the default amount listed if there are either mitigating or aggravating circumstances, such as the nature, severity, and duration of the violation, amount of affected individuals, and the scope of the damages. Most importantly, if the amount is deemed not to be fitting, the Dutch DPA can still impose the maximum fine of €20 million or 4% of revenue.

29.2   IDENTIFYING ME AND LEAD SA

Main establishment
Under the GDPR (recital 36)
The main establishment of a controller in the Union should be determined according to objective criteria and should imply the effective and real exercise of management activities determining the main decisions as to the purposes and means of processing through stable arrangements.

- That criterion should not depend on whether the processing of personal data is carried out at that location.

- The presence and use of technical means and technologies for processing personal data or processing activities do not, in themselves, constitute a main establishment and are therefore not determining criteria for the main establishment.

The main establishment of the processor should be the place of its central administration in the Union or if it has no central administration in the Union, the place where the main processing activities take place in the Union.

- In cases involving both the controller and the processor, the competent lead supervisory authority should remain the supervisory authority of the Member State where the controller has its main establishment, but the supervisory authority of the processor should be considered to be a supervisory authority concerned and that supervisory authority should participate in the cooperation procedure provided for by this Regulation.
- In any case, the supervisory authorities of the Member State or the Member States where the processor has one or more establishments should not be considered to be supervisory authorities concerned where the draft decision concerns only the controller.
- Where the processing is carried out by a group of undertakings, the main establishment of the controlling undertaking should be considered to be the main establishment of the group of undertakings, except where the purposes and means of processing are determined by another undertaking.

The One-Stop Mechanism and Lead Authority
Organizations should identify concerned DPAs in applicable jurisdictions and document the contact information. Also, organizations should monitor and follow the guidelines published by DPAs.

One-stop-shop: Within a single market for data, identical rules on paper are not enough. The rules must be applied in the same way everywhere. The "one-stop-shop" will streamline cooperation between the data protection authorities on issues with implications for all of Europe. Companies will only have to deal with one authority, not 28 authorities. It will ensure legal certainty for businesses. Businesses will profit from faster decisions, from one single interlocutor (eliminating multiple contact points). They will benefit from the consistency of decisions where the same processing activity takes place in the several Member States.

- The one-stop-shop mechanism is facilitated mainly by the European Data Protection Board (EDPB). The GDPR replaces Article 29 Working Party with the EPDB. It comprises a representative of every member state's supervisory authority.

A lead supervisory authority is a primary regulator responsible for dealing with the cross-border processing activities of a controller or processor. This includes coordinating operations of all supervisory authorities concerned.

- According to GDPR Article 4(23), cross-border processing is defined as "processing of personal data which takes place in the context of the activities of establishments in more than one Member State of a controller or processor in the Union where the controller or processor is established in more than one Member State" or "processing of personal data which takes place in the context of the activities of a single establishment of a controller or processor in the Union but which substantially affects or is likely to substantially affect data subjects in more than one Member State."
- In terms of the meaning of "substantially affects," the Article 29 Working Party states that "Supervisory Authorities will interpret substantially affects' on a case-by-case basis."

Lead DPA cannot be randomly chosen. It depends on where the main establishment or controller is located. If the processing is in fact cross-border processing, how does the controller identify the lead supervisory authority?

- If the organization has a single establishment in the EU, then the lead supervisory authority will simply be that of the place of establishment.
- If the organization has more than one establishment in the EU, then the lead supervisory authority will be that of the place of central administration. That is, unless decisions about purposes, means and implementation of processing take place at a different location. If this is the case, then the SA of that location where the processing decisions take place will be the lead. This makes it possible for a company to have more than one lead SAs. If it conducts several cross-border activities whose related decisions take place in more than one location.
- The same criteria apply for identifying a processor's lead supervisory authority unless the controller is also involved in the processing-in which case, the controller's lead supervisory authority would be the processor's lead as well. The processor's supervisory authority would then be considered the supervisory authority concerned.

List of examples of DPAs

Throughout the European Union and in many other countries, there is a single agency responsible for the enforcement of information privacy laws. These are often referred to as Data Protection Agencies (DPAs). However, there is a different situation in the United States. There is no single DPA. There are a number of agencies that regulate privacy depending on the jurisdiction and the industry sector.

Table 29.3 provides a list of some data protection authorities in different regions (the US is in a separate list).

Table 29.4 provides a list of some data protection authorities in the US across various sectors.

TABLE 29.3

Examples of Data Protection Authorities in Different Regions

Region	Country/Agency	DPA	Website
Europe	Austria	Österreichische Datenschutzbehörde	www.dsb.gv.at/
	Belgium	Autorité de la protection des données— Gegevensbeschermingsautoriteit (APD-GBA)	www.autoriteprotectiondonnees. be
	Bulgaria	Commission for Personal Data Protection	www.cpdp.bg/
	Croatia	Croatian Personal Data Protection Agency	www.azop.hr/
	Cyprus	Commissioner for Personal Data Protection	www.dataprotection.gov.cy/
	Czech Republic	Office for Personal Data Protection	www.uoou.cz/
	Denmark	Datatilsynet	www.datatilsynet.dk/
	EDPB	European Data Protection Board	https://edpb.europa.eu/
	EDPS	European Data Protection Supervisor	https://edps.europa.eu/
	Estonia	Estonian Data Protection Inspectorate (Andmekaitse Inspektsioon)	www.aki.ee/
	Finland	Office of the Data Protection Ombudsman	www.tietosuoja.fi/en/
	France	Commission Nationale de l'Informatique et des Libertés—CNIL	www.cnil.fr/
	Germany	Der Bundesbeauftragte für den Datenschutz und die Informationsfreiheit	www.bfdi.bund.de/
	Greece	Hellenic Data Protection Authority	www.dpa.gr/

(Continued)

TABLE 29.3 (Continued)

Region	Country/Agency	DPA	Website
	Hungary	Hungarian National Authority for Data Protection and Freedom of Information	www.naih.hu/
	Ireland	Data Protection Commission	www.dataprotection.ie/
	Italy	Garante per la protezione dei dati personali	www.garanteprivacy.it/
	Latvia	Data State Inspectorate	www.dvi.gov.lv/
	Lithuania	State Data Protection Inspectorate	https://vdai.lrv.lt/
	Luxembourg	Commission Nationale pour la Protection des Données	www.cnpd.lu/
	Malta	Office of the Information and Data Protection Commissioner	www.idpc.org.mt/
	Netherlands	Autoriteit Persoonsgegevens	https://autoriteitpersoonsgegevens.nl/
	Poland	Urząd Ochrony Danych Osobowych (Personal Data Protection Office)	https://uodo.gov.pl/
	Portugal	Comissão Nacional de Proteção de Dados—CNPD	www.cnpd.pt/
	Romania	The National Supervisory Authority for Personal Data Processing	www.dataprotection.ro/
	Slovakia	Office for Personal Data Protection of the Slovak Republic	www.dataprotection.gov.sk/
	Slovenia	Information Commissioner of the Republic of Slovenia	www.ip-rs.si/
	Spain	Agencia Española de Protección de Datos (AEPD)	www.aepd.es/
	Sweden	Integritetsskyddsmyndigheten	www.imy.se/
	Iceland	Persónuvernd	www.dpa.is
	Liechtenstein	Data Protection Authority, Principality of Liechtenstein	www.datenschutzstelle.li
	Norway	Datatilsynet	www.datatilsynet.no
APAC	China-HK	Office of the Privacy Commissioner for Personal Data	www.pcpd.org.hk
	China-Macau	Office for Personal Data Protection	www.gpdp.gov.mo/
	Israel	The Privacy Protection Authority	www.gov.il/en
	Japan	Personal Data Protection Commission	www.ppc.go.jp/en/
	Korea, South	The Personal Information Protection Commission (PIPC)	www.pipc.go.kr/
		The PIPC is an independent body established under the Personal Information Protection Act (PIPA) to protect the privacy rights of individuals. The key role of PIPC is to deliberate on and resolve personal data-related policies, coordinate difference opinions among other government agencies on the processing of personal data.	
		Ministry of the Interior and Safety	www.mois.go.kr/eng/a01/engMain.do
		As a competent authority of Personal Information Protection Act, MOIS is responsible for personal data policy development and investigation, and the enforcement of personal data protection legislation.	

Region	Country/Agency	DPA	Website
		Korea Communications Commission	https://eng.kcc.go.kr/user/
		As a competent authority of Act on Promotion of Information and Communications Network Utilization and Information Protection, ETC, KCC regulates broadcasting and communication service providers, protects users of broadcasting and communications services, and establish and implement personal data protection policies related to broadcasting and communications.	ehpMain.do
		Financial Services Commission	www.fsc.go.kr/eng/index
		As a competent authority of Use and Protection of Credit Information Act, FSC is responsible for credit information protection.	
		National Human Rights Commission	www.humanrights.go.kr/site/
		The Commission was established as a national advocacy institution for human rights protection. The key role of the commission is to ensure that inviolable, fundamental human rights of all individuals are protected and the standards of human rights are improved.	main/index002
		Korea Internet & Security Agency	www.kisa.or.kr/EN
		As a statutory organization, set by the of Act on Promotion of Information and Communications Network Utilization and Information Protection, ETC, KISA's role in relation to personal data protection is to provide support and assistance to the Government and local government agencies to remedy data breaches and research and provide advice on personal data protection security standards and policies.	
	Philippines	National Privacy Commission	www.privacy.gov.ph/
	Russian Federation	Federal Service for Supervision of Communications, Information Technology and Mass Media (Roskomnadzor)	http://government.ru/en/ department/58/
	Australia	Office of the Australian Information Commissioner	www.oaic.gov.au/
	New Zealand	Office of the Privacy Commissioner of New Zealand	www.privacy.org.nz/
North America	Canada	The Office of Privacy Commissioner of Canada (OPC)	www.priv.gc.ca/en/
	Mexico	National Institute of Transparency, Access to Information and Protection of Personal Data (INAI)	https://networkforintegrity.org/ continents/america/ instituto-nacional-de-transparencia-acceso-a-la-informacion-y-proteccion-de-datos-personales-inai/
South America	Argentina	The National Directorate for Personal Data Protection	www.jus.gob.ar/datos-personales/
	Brazil	The Brazilian National Data Protection Authority (ANPD)	www.gov.br/anpd/pt-br
Africa	South Africa	Information regulator	https://inforegulator.org.za/
	Nigeria	Nigeria Data Protection Bureau (NDPB)	https://ndpr.nitda.gov.ng/
	Egypt	the Data Protection Centre (DPC)	-

TABLE 29.4
Data Protection Authorities in the US

Legislation/Domain	Authority
Health Insurance Portability and Accountability Act (HIPAA)	Civil enforcement by the Office for Civil Rights (OCR) at the Department of Health and Human Services (HHS)
	Criminal sanctions will be enforced by the Department of Justice
The Gramm-Leach-Bliley Act (GLBA)	The Federal Trade Commission (FTC)
Children's Online Privacy Protection Act (COPPA)	FTC
Telemarketing Sales Rule and the CAN-SPAM Act	The FTC shares the authority with the Federal Communications Commission (FCC)
Data breaches related to medical records	The FTC shares the authority with HHS
Fair Credit Reporting Act (FCRA) as amended by the Fair and Accurate Credit Transactions Act (FACTA)	The FTC shares the authority with the Consumer Financial Protection Bureau (CFPB)
Disposal Rule under the Fair and Accurate Credit Transactions Act (FACTA)	The FTC shares the authority with CFPB and The Office of the Comptroller of the Currency.
Dodd-Frank Wall Street Reform and Consumer Protection Act of 2010	CFPB
Workplace—labor laws	The Department of labor: <ul><li>The US Department of Labor oversees "the welfare of the job seekers, wage earners, and retirees of the United States by improving their working conditions, advancing their opportunities for profitable employment, protecting their retirement and health care benefits, helping employers find workers, strengthening free collective bargaining, and tracking changes in employment, prices, and other national economic measurements."</li><li>Each state has an agency, often called the Department of Labor, to oversee the state's labor laws. These laws include state minimum wage laws and laws limiting work by minors. The same department in most states may administer state unemployment insurance programs and employee rehabilitation programs. Some departments also conduct safety inspections of worker conditions.</li></ul>
Workplace—Title VII of the Civil Rights Act, the Age Discrimination in Employment Act of 1967 (ADEA) and Titles I and V of the Americans with Disabilities Act of 1990 (ADA)	The Equal employment opportunity commission (EEOC) <ul><li>The Equal Employment Opportunity Commission (EEOC) works to prevent discrimination in the workplace.</li></ul>
Workplace—The National Labor Relations Act	National Labor Relations Board (NLRB)
	The National Labor Relations Board administers the National Labor Relations Act. The board conducts elections to determine if employees want union representation and investigates and remedies unfair labor practices by employers and unions.
Workplace—receive an employee's or applicant's information obtained from a consumer reporting agency	Federal Trade Commission (FTC)
	The Federal Trade Commission regulates unfair and deceptive commercial practices and enforces a variety of laws, including the Fair Credit Reporting Act, which limits employers' ability to receive an employee's or applicant's credit report, driving records, criminal records and other "consumer reports" obtained from a "consumer reporting agency."
E-Verify program for new employees	The Department of Homeland Security (DHS)
Rules for air traveler records (through TSA)	The Department of Homeland Security (DHS)
State laws	State Attorneys General

29.3 COOPERATION WITH DPAS

The controller and the processor and, where applicable, their representatives, shall cooperate, on request, with the supervisory authority in the performance of its tasks.

Organizations should establish and implement an internal procedure with respect to response to DPAs' inquiries and/or investigations. The procedure may include setting up a contact point (i.e., a liaison) and protocols of proper interactions with the DPAs.

- Reactive interaction: The controller and the processor and, where applicable, their representatives, shall cooperate, on request, with the supervisory authority in the performance of its tasks.
- Proactive interaction: To act as the contact point for the supervisory authority on issues relating to processing, including the prior consultation referred to in Article 36, and to consult, where appropriate, with regard to any other matter.
  - Note: Some organizations may also intend to build an ongoing communication channel with DPAs.

Case Study

CNIL closes notice against DIRECT ENERGIE about obtaining consent from customers

On October 25, 2018, The French data protection authority (CNIL) issued a decision closing the formal notice proceedings against DIRECT ENERGIE Société Anonyme, regarding failures in obtaining consent for the collection of customer usage data from smart meters.

In this decision, CNIL held that DIRECT ENERGIE was able to demonstrate compliance with obligations imposed by CNIL, including providing consumers with a clear choice in relation to the data they wish to share and informing consumers of their right to withdraw their consent at any time.

Case Study

CNIL closes notices against Fidzup and Singlespot

On November 29, 2018, the French data protection authority (CNIL) issued two decisions closing its formal notice proceedings against Fidzup SAS and Singlespot SAS, regarding their initial failures to obtain consent for the processing of geolocation data for marketing purposes.

In these two decisions, CNIL found that Fidzup and Singlespot were able to demonstrate that data subjects were informed of the purpose of the data processing, and the identity of the data controllers and had provided information on the data collection, including geolocation data. Furthermore, CNIL stated that the free, specific and informed consent of data subjects was collected prior to the processing of their data. Finally, CNIL held that Fidzup and Singlespot were in compliance with the General Data Protection Regulation (Regulation (EU) 2016/679) (GDPR).

Appendix A: EU GDPR One-Pager Summary

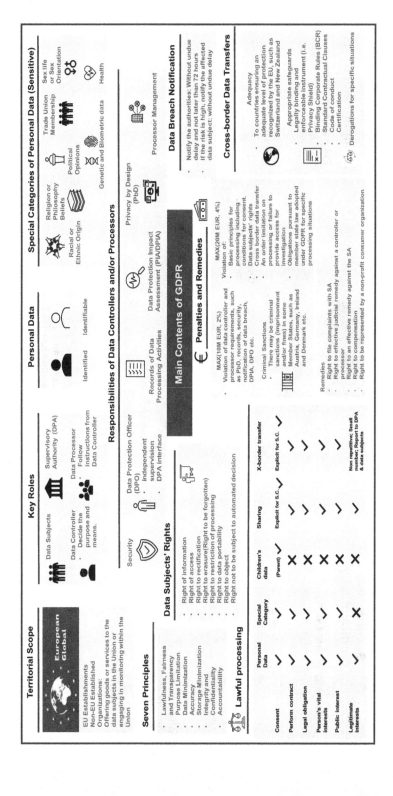

Appendix B: EU ePrivacy One-Pager Summary

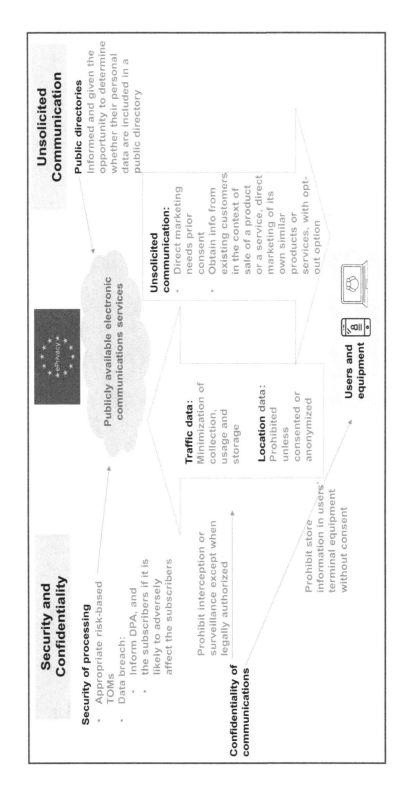

Security and Confidentiality

Security of processing
- Appropriate risk-based TOMs
- Data breach:
  - Inform DPA, and
  - the subscribers if it is likely to adversely affect the subscribers

Confidentiality of communications

Prohibit interception or surveillance except when legally authorized

Prohibit store information in users' terminal equipment without consent

Publicly available electronic communications services

ePrivacy

Traffic data: Minimization of collection, usage and storage

Location data: Prohibited unless consented or anonymized

Unsolicited communication:
- Direct marketing needs prior consent
- Obtain info from existing customers in the context of sale of a product or a service, direct marketing of its own similar products or services, with opt-out option

Users and equipment

Unsolicited Communication

Public directories
Informed and given the opportunity to determine whether their personal data are included in a public directory

Appendix C: FTC Act Section 5

FTC Act
Section 5

Scope

- Prohibits "unfair or deceptive acts or practices (UDAP) in or affecting commerce."
- This prohibition applies to all persons engaged in commerce, including banks.

Definition of Unfairness

Unfairness (Section 5(a) and 5(n)):

- Causes or likely to cause substantial injury to consumers
- Not reasonably avoidable by consumers
- Not outweighed by countervailing benefit to consumers or to competition

Examination Objectives and Procedures
(From the joint statement of the Board and FDIC*)

Definition of Deception

Deception (Section 5(a)(1)):

- A representation, omission, or practice misleads or is likely to mislead the consumer;
- A consumer's interpretation of the representation, omission, or practice is considered reasonable under the circumstances; and
- the misleading representation, omission, or practice is material.

Enforcement

Year of 2019
The maximum civil penalty amount has increased from $41,484 to $42,530

Examination procedures

- Review previous examinations reports, including consumer compliance, and safety and soundness examination reports;
- Review current and prior examination findings regarding the institution's involvement in acts or practices that violate or may violate section 5 of the FTC Act;
- Review the bank's policies, procedures, and internal controls;
- Review a sample of consumer complaints, advertisements and promotional materials, disclosures, customer agreements, and third-party contracts and instructions;
- Interview management and staff about the bank's acts and practices; and
- Discuss any examiner concerns with bank management.

Examination Objectives

1) Evaluating Compliance Management Programs

2) Evaluating Advertising and Promotional Materials

3) Evaluating Initial and Subsequent Disclosures

4) Evaluating Servicing and Collections

5) Monitoring the Conduct of Employees and Third Parties

Appendix D: US HIPAA One-Pager Summary

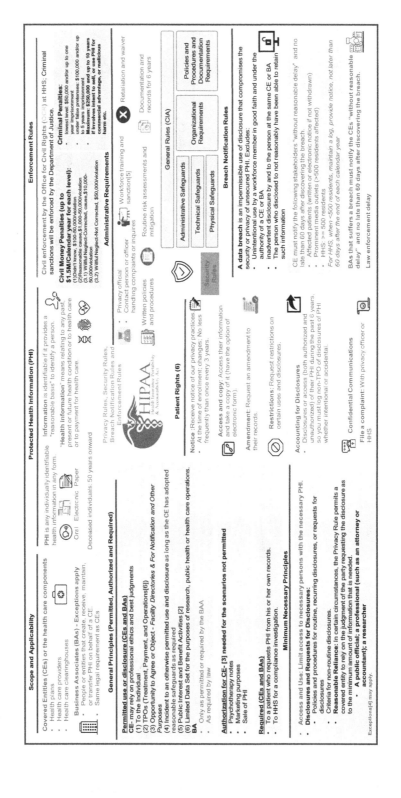

Appendix E: US GLBA One-Pager Summary

Scope

GLBA applies to "financial institutions."

- While these "financial institutions" would include traditional banks, credit unions, and savings and loans the law's definition of "financial institution" encompasses all entities that are "significantly engaged" in providing financial products or services — including student loans which means education institutes might be subject to GLBA

Material Scope

Scope: Nonpublic personal information" means personally identifiable financial information

Exceptions: Does not include publicly available information

- According to 17 CFR 160.3, publicly available information means "any information that you reasonably believe is lawfully made available to the general public from:
  - (i) Federal, state or local government records;
  - (ii) Widely distributed media; or
  - (iii) Disclosures to the general public that are required to be made by federal, state or local law."

Enforcement (Title 18, United States Code)

	Infraction	Class B or C	Class A	Resulting in death	Felony
Individual	$5,000	$5,000	$100,000	$250,000	$250,000
Org	$10,000	$10,000	$200,000	$500,000	$500,000

Criminal charges:
- Level 1:
  - Up to 5 years imprisonment
- Level 2: Involving more than $100,000 in a 12-month period
  - Double fine
  - 10 years

For education institutes (From U.S. Department of Education):
- Cybersecurity breaches are at risk of restricted or complete loss of Title IV funding, making them ineligible to participate in federally funded financial aid programs.

GLBA

Gramm-Leach-Bliley Act

Pretext Rule: Fraudulent access to financial information

(A) Prohibition on obtaining customer information by false pretenses.
(B) Prohibition on solicitation of a person to obtain customer information from financial institution under false pretenses.

Non applicability
(C) Non applicability to law enforcement agencies.
(D) Non applicability to financial institutions in certain cases. (performance of the official duties)
(E) Non applicability to insurance institutions for investigation of insurance fraud.
(F) Non applicability to certain types of customer information of financial institutions. (Publically available information)
(G) Non applicability to collection of child support judgments.

Privacy Rule: collection and disclosure

Privacy notice: Financial institutions must provide their customers a privacy notice that details what data the company gathers about the client, where this data is shared, and how the company safeguards that data.

Disclose to a nonaffiliated 3rd is not allowed unless

- Privacy policy provided and Opt out
  - Exception for Non sensitive data (account number, access code for credit card, deposit account or transaction account are considered sensitive data): Fin institution has NDA agreement with 3rd parties.
- General exceptions (Legal Basis)
  - Consent
  - Customer Authorization for transactions
  - Legitimate interest
  - Legal requirements
  - Proposed or actual sale, merger or transfer of business

Safeguards Rule: security programs

Develop a written information security plan that describes how the company protects clients' nonpublic personal information. This security plan must:

- Designate at least one employee to manage the safeguards (Administrative, technical, and physical safeguards
  - **For traditional financial institutions-** reference FFIEC (Federal Financial Institutions Examination Council) information security handbook
  - For education institutions- reference NIST SP800-171 (U.S. Department of Education)
- Develop a risk management methodology for areas handling customer data
- Develop, monitor, and test a program to secure the information
- Change the safeguards as needed with the changes in how information is collected, stored and used.

Appendix F: US FERPA One-Pager Summary

FERPA

Family Educational Rights & Privacy Act

Scope	Education Records	Personally Identifiable Information	Enforcement
Educational agency or institution receiving funds	The term means those records that are: (1) Directly related to a student; and (2) Maintained by an educational agency or institution or by a party acting for the agency or institution. Exceptions mentioned in the ACT.	The term includes, but is not limited to— (a) The student's name; (b) The name of the student's parent or other family members; (c) The address of the student or student's family; (d) A personal identifier, such as the student's social security number, student number, or biometric record; (e) Other indirect identifiers, such as the student's date of birth, place of birth, and mother's maiden name; (f) Other information that, alone or in combination, is linked or linkable to a specific student that would allow a reasonable person in the school community, who does not have personal knowledge of the relevant circumstances, to identify the student with reasonable certainty; or (g) Information requested by a person who the educational agency or institution reasonably believes knows the identity of the student to whom the education record relates.	Authority: U.S. Department of Education **Penalties** (1) Withhold further payments under any applicable program; (2) Issue a complaint to compel compliance through a cease and desist order; or (3) Terminate eligibility to receive funding under any applicable program.

Annual Notification

Parents and Students' Rights	Reasonable Means	Obligations on Data Disclosure

(1) Inspect and review the student's education records
· Inspect and review
  · Not more than 45 days
  · May provide a copy
· Limitation:
  · more than one student, only about that student
  · Financial records of his or her parents
  · Some confidential letters and confidential statements
(2) The right to prevent disclosure of education records
(3) The right to Seek amendment of education records if believed to be inaccurate or misleading
· within a reasonable time
· inform the decision and rights
(4) The right to hearing:
· hold the hearing within a reasonable time
· make its decision in writing within a reasonable period of time after the hearing
(5) The right to be notified of their privacy rights under FERPA;
(6) The right to file a complaint with the U.S. Department of Education.
	· Notify parents or eligible students who are disabled
	· Notify parents who have a primary or home language other than English
	
	① **Full rights to either parent**
	② **Transfer from the parents to the eligible student**
		· Consent required: In general consent is required
		  · Signed and dated written consent
		· Consent not required (permitted disclosures)
		  · School officials with legitimate educational interest
		  · Other schools to which a student is transferring
		  · Specified officials for audit or evaluation purposes
		  · Appropriate parties in connection with financial aid to a student
		  · Organizations conducting certain studies for, or on behalf of, the school
		  · Accrediting organizations
		  · Appropriate officials in cases of health and safety emergencies
		  · State and local authorities, within a juvenile justice system, pursuant to specific state law
		  · To comply with a judicial order or lawfully issued subpoena
		· **Reasonable controls(Section 99.31 - Security)**
		  · Reasonable access controls (physical and technical) around education records
		  · Identify and authenticate the identity of parents, students, school officials, and any other parties to whom the agency or institution discloses personally identifiable information from education records.
		· Recordkeeping (Section 99.32)
		  · Maintain a record of each request for access to and each disclosure as long as the education records
		· Re-disclosure of information (Section 99.33)
		  · Should not disclose without prior consent or to authority representatives
		  · Only used for the authorized purposes

Key Roles

Child <13 · Operator · Parent · FTC

COPPA — Children's Online Privacy Protection Act

Scope and Applicability

The Rule implements the COPPA 1998, which prohibits unfair or deceptive acts or practices in connection with the collection, use, and/or disclosure of personal information from and **about children on the Internet**. **Operators** of commercial websites and online services (especially those directed to children under the age of 13), though it also applies to general-audience websites and online services if they have **actual knowledge that they are collecting personal information from children under the age of 13**.

General requirements

Notice
- **General principles of notice**
  - Operator's obligation to provide direct notice to the parent
  - Notice must be clearly and understandably written, complete, and must contain no unrelated, confusing, or contradictory materials
  - Obtain verifiable parental consent
  - Notice on the Web site or online service
- **4 types of direct notice to the parent**
  - Notice to obtain parental consent
  - Voluntary notice
  - Intent to communicate with the Child Multiple Times
  - Protect the safety of a child

Parental consent
- Option to consent to the collection and use without consenting to disclosure
- **Methods for verifiable parental consent, Existing methods:**
  - Consent form signed and returned by postal mail, facsimile, or electronic scan
  - Connection with a monetary transaction
  - Parent call a toll-free telephone number
  - parent connect via video-conference
  - Checking a form of government-issued identification against databases
  - Use an email coupled with additional steps
- **Exceptions to prior parental consent**
  - Name or online contact information
    - Sole purpose to provide notice and obtain parental consent
      - purpose to provide voluntary notice
    - Sole purpose to respond directly on a one-time basis
    - purpose to respond directly more than once to the child's specific request
    - Legitimate interest: 1) Security or integrity of its Web site; 2) Precautions against liability; 3) Respond to judicial process; 4) Under law
  - Persistent identifier
    - Support for the internal operations of the Web site or online service
    - User is not a child

Personal Information and Online Contact Information

Personal information means individually identifiable information about an individual collected online, including:
(1) A first and last name;
(2) A home or other physical address including street name and name of a city or town;
(3) Online contact information
(Screen name or user name that functions in the same manner as online contact information);
(4) A screen or user name where it functions in the same manner as online contact information, as defined in this section;
(5) A telephone number;
(6) A Social Security number;
(7) A persistent identifier that can be used to recognize a user over time and across different Web sites or online services. Such persistent identifier includes, but is not limited to, a customer number held in a cookie, an Internet Protocol (IP) address, a processor or device serial number, or unique device identifier;
(8) A photograph, video, or audio file where such file contains a child's image or voice;
(9) Geolocation information sufficient to identify street name and name of a city or town; or
(10) Information concerning the child or the parents of that child that the operator collects online from the child and combines with an identifier described in this definition.

Online contact information means an email address or any other substantially similar identifier that permits direct contact with a person online, including but not limited to, an instant messaging user identifier, a voice over internet protocol (VOIP) identifier, or a video chat user identifier.

Right of parent to review
- **Specific types or categories of personal information**
- **Opportunity to refuse the collection and use and direct the operator to delete**
- **A means of reviewing**

Prohibition against conditioning

Confidentiality, security, and integrity
- **Reasonable procedures to protect confidentiality, security, and integrity**
- **Release children's personal information only to service providers and third parties who are capable and provide assurances**

Data retention and deletion: Storage minimization

Safe harbor programs

FTC may approve self-regulatory program guidelines

Voluntary Commission Approval

FTC may approve
- Parental consent methods
- Activities defined as support for internal operations of the Web site or online service

Enforcement

Violation of a rule defining an unfair or deceptive act under FTC Act

Appendix H: US FACTA One-Pager Summary

FACTA
Fair Accurate Credit Transactions Act

Scope

① Consumer reporting agencies
② And any of the following capacities:
- Procurers and users of information (i.e. credit grantors)
- Furnishers and transmitters of information
- Marketers of credit or insurance products and
- Employers

Module 1 Purposes

Permissible Purposes
- Legally Permissible Purposes (i.e. Investigative reports)
- Consumers can obtain a free copy of consumer file once during a 12 month period.

Procedures
- Employ procedures, controls, or other safeguards to ensure that consumer reports only obtained and used with permissible purposes

Module 4 Duties of Users and Furnishers

- Address Discrepancies - NCRA provide a notice of address discrepancy to the users
- Accuracy and integrity of furnished information - Written policies and procedures
- Consumer direct dispute - Conduct a reasonable investigation of a direct dispute (unless exceptions)

Consumer Report

A "consumer report" is any written, oral, or other communication of any information by a consumer reporting agency that bears on a consumer's creditworthiness, credit standing, credit capacity, character, general reputation, personal characteristics, or mode of living that is used or expected to be used or collected, in whole or in part, for the purpose of serving as a factor in establishing the consumer's eligibility for any of the following:
1. Credit or insurance to be used primarily for personal, family, or household purposes;
2. Employment purposes; or
3. Any other purpose authorized under Section 604 (15 U.S.C. 1681b).

Module 2 Sharing Among Affiliates

Consumer Report and Information Sharing Among Affiliates
- Transaction or experience information – OK
- Other information (i.e. credit score) – Notice with opt out

Affiliate Marketing Opt-Out Requirement
- Entity may not use information received from an affiliate unless Notice and opt out

Medical Information
- generally prohibited in connection with determination of the consumer's eligibility, or continued eligibility, for credit
- Limits on re-disclosure of information

Module 5 Consumer Alerts and Identity Theft Protections

1) Fraud and Active Duty Alerts
- Initial Fraud and Active Duty Alerts (no less than 90 days, Active duty alerts no less than 12 months)
- Extended Alerts (lasts seven years)
2) Information Available to Victims
- provide records of fraudulent transactions to victims within 30 days after the receipt of a request
3) Duties Regarding the Detection, Prevention, and Mitigation of Identity Theft (Red Flags rule)
- On November 9, 2007, the Agencies published final rules and guidelines in the Federal Register implementing this section
4) Secure Disposal of Consumer Information
- On December 28, 2004, the federal banking agencies published final rules and guidelines in the Federal Register implementing this section (69 FR 77610).

Enforcement

Up to $3,500 per violation (year of 2009)

Module 3 Disclosures and Miscellaneous Requirements

1) Use of Consumer Reports for Employment Purposes
- Written permission for "employment purposes"
- Prior to taking any adverse action involving employment:
  - A copy of the report.
  - A description in writing of the rights of the consumer under
2) Prescreened Consumer Reports
- Only contain:
  - name and address
  - An identifier that is not unique and solely for verifying identity
  - Info does not identify the relationship or experience
- Notice and Opt-Out Requirements - Short and Long Notice
2) Truncation of Credit and Debit Card Account Numbers
- For electronically developed receipts (i.e. POS): No more than last five digits
3) Adverse Action Disclosures - disclosure required/Risk-Based Pricing Notice
- Take adverse actions
- Deny credit or increase the charge for credit
- Take certain adverse action based on info from an affiliate

Appendix I: California CCPA One-Pager Summary

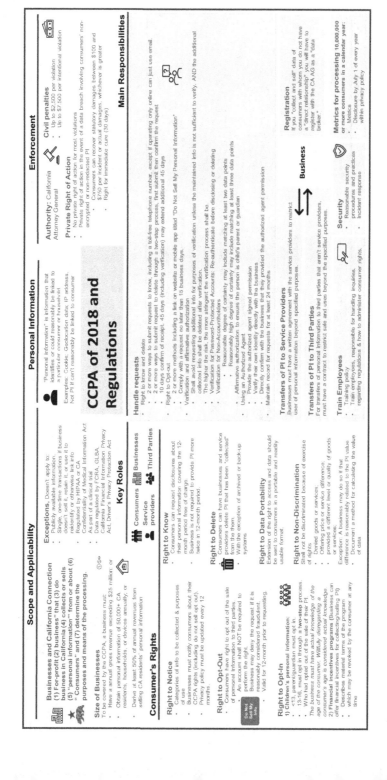

Appendix J: Canada PIPEDA One-Pager Summary

PIPEDA

Personal Information Protection and Electronic Documents Act

Personal Data

Personal information includes any factual or subjective information, recorded or not, about an identifiable individual. This includes information in any form.

Territory and Material Scope

	Apply			Does NOT Apply
	Personal data relating to commercial activities[4]	Employee information	Business contact[2]	
Private-sector (no cross-provincial or national border transfer) Exemption[3]: -Alberta's Personal Information Protection Act ("Alberta PIPA") -British Columbia's Personal Information Protection Act ("BC PIPA") -Quebec's Act Respecting the Protection of Personal Information in the Private Sector ("the Quebec Act")	✓	✗ PIPEDA NOT ✓ Alberta and BC's PIPA apply to employee information	✗	**Orgs:** • Government institution to which the Privacy Act applies • Provincial or territorial governments and their agents • Not-for-profit and charity groups; or • Political parties and associations. **Activities:** • An individual's collection, use or disclosure of personal information strictly for personal purposes (e.g. greeting card list) • An organization's collection, use or disclosure of personal information solely for journalistic, artistic or literary purposes
Private-sector (involving cross-provincial or national border transfer) No exemption	✓	✗	✗	
Federally regulated organizations[1]	✓	✓	✗	

Remedies

OPC Power:
• The OPC is NOT empowered to impose fines or award damages
• Commissioner can conduct an investigatory audit and issue recommendations
  • Conduct investigation that include the power to subpoena and compel the giving of evidence, may enter any premises.
  • Recommend that an organization take an action (and later can take the organization to federal court if the organization refuses to implement the recommendation)
  • OPC is NOT granted the power to initiate an application in federal court if an organization refuses to implement the recommendations contained in an audit report.
• OPC can enter into a compliance agreement with organizations

Fine:
• Obstruct an OPC investigation, or fails to retain personal information that is the subject of an access request is guilty of (a) an offence punishable on summary conviction and liable to a fine not exceeding $10,000; or (b) an indictable offence and liable to a fine not exceeding $100,000.
• Fail to report to the OPC or notify affected individuals of a breach that poses a real risk of significant harm, or knowingly fail to maintain a record of all breaches, could face fines of up to $100,000.

Individual Rights

• Right to be informed
• Right of access
  • Respond to an individual's request within a reasonable time and at minimal or no cost
• Right to rectification
  • Respond to an individual's request within a reasonable time and at minimal or no cost
• Right of challenging compliance
  • Complaint to the designated individual or individuals
  • Put procedures in place to receive and respond to complaints or inquiries
  • Inform individuals who make inquiries or lodge complaints of the existence of relevant complaint procedures (external, to authorities)

Data Breach Notification

Report to Commissioner
• Report to the Commissioner of any breach of security safeguards involving personal information
• As soon as feasible after the organization determines that the breach has occurred

Notification to individual
• Shall notify an individual of any breach of security safeguards if it is reasonable to believe that the breach creates a real risk of significant harm to an individual
• As soon as feasible after the organization determines that the breach has occurred

Record Keeping:
• Maintain a record of every breach of security safeguards for 24 months after the day on which the organization determines the breach has occurred

10 Principles

1. Accountability
2. Identifying Purposes
3. Consent
4. Limiting Collection
5. Limiting Use, Disclosure and Retention
6. Accuracy
7. Safeguards
8. Openness
9. Individual Access
10. Challenging Compliance

Appendix K: Canada Anti-Spam Law One-Pager Summary

CASL
Canada's Anti-Spam Law

Territory Scope	Material Scope	Enforcement and Penalties

CASL applies to senders of CEMs from Canada, as well as to those who send messages into Canada from other countries.	• All forms of electronic messaging, including email, SMS text messages, and messages sent via social networking.
	• Installation of Computer Programs
	• Amendments to the Competition Act: false and misleading misrepresentations in electronic messages
		• CASL is enforced by the Canadian Radio-television and Telecommunications Commission (CRTC), with related amendments to the Competition Act and PIPEDA enforced by the Competition Bureau and the OPC respectively.
		• Administrative Monetary Penalties (AMPs) - AMPs are not generally reviewable by courts:
		  • up to $1 million per violation for individuals and
		  • $10 million per violation for other persons (or businesses)
		  • Directors, officers and agents can be held personally liable in the event of a violation
		• the private right of action (has not yet come into force)

Main Obligations

Commercial Electronical Messages (CEMs)

Consent
- Default rule: The default rule is that consent from the recipient must be obtained before a CEM is sent.
- Express consent (explicit)
- Implied consent: Consent may be implied in any of the following four circumstances
  - The sender and recipient have an existing business relationship
  - The sender and recipient have an existing nonbusiness relationship
  - The recipient has conspicuously published their electronic address (e.g., on a website) and has not expressly stated that they do not wish to receive unsolicited messages.
  - The message must be related to the recipient's professional capacity.
  - The recipient has disclosed their electronic address directly to the sender and has not expressly stated that they do not wish to receive unsolicited messages. The message must be related to the recipient's professional capacity.
- Exceptions for consent:
  - Is sent to someone with whom the sender has a personal or family relationship
  - Is an inquiry about a product or service offered by the recipient
  - Provides a quote or estimate, if requested
  - Facilitates a commercial transaction
  - Provides warranty or safety information
  - Provides information about, for example, an ongoing subscription or membership
  - Provides information related to an employment relationship or benefit plan
  - Delivers a good or service

Identification
- Senders are required to clearly identify themselves.
- If the message is sent on behalf of another person, that person must be identified as well.

Unsubscribing
- Every CEM must contain a functional unsubscribe mechanism that enables the recipient to unsubscribe at no cost.
- This must include an unsubscribe link that is functional for a minimum of 60 days.
- Unsubscribe requests must be processed without delay, and in no event, more than 10 days after the request has been made.
- An unsubscribe mechanism must be "readily performed," "It should be simple, quick and easy for the end user.

Record Keeping
- All evidence of express and implied consent (e.g., audio recordings, copies of signed consent forms, completed electronic forms) from consumers who agree to receive CEMs
- Documented methods through which consent was collected
- Policies and procedures regarding CASL compliance
- All unsubscribe requests and resulting actions

Installation of computer programs

- Express (explicit) consent required
- Exceptions for consent
  - Cookies (small text files stored on a client machine that may later be retrieved by a web server from the machine)
  - HTML
  - JavaScript
  - An operating system
  - Any other program executable through another program to which the end user already consented
  - Software installed solely to correct a failure in a computer system (i.e., bug fixes)
  - Telecommunications service providers (as defined in CASL) installing software to protect the security of all or part of an end-user's network from a current and identifiable threat or updating or upgrading all or part of the network
- **To ensure that automatic downloads do not violate CASL, vendors have several options:**
  - They can implement user-installed updates (i.e., the user must click "install"), likely avoiding CASL altogether
  - If the vendor chooses to implement automatic downloads, it must obtain consent from the individual at the point of initial installation of the program
  - Vendors can allow automatic updates to be activated and deactivated via a user setting, thereby avoiding CASL completely by making the automatic downloads a user-activated function

Amendments to the Competition Act

- Sender information
- Subject matter information ((e.g., an email subject line))
- locator information, (e.g., a URL)
- the contents of an electronic message.

Appendix L: China PIPL One-Pager Summary

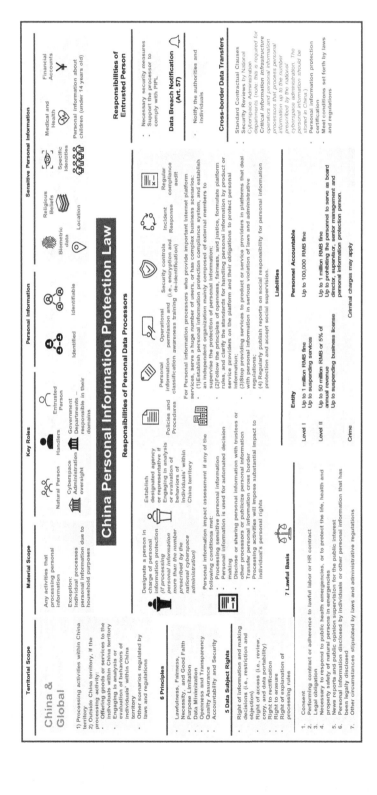

China Personal Information Protection Law

Territorial Scope

China & Global

1) Processing activities within China territory
2) Outside China territory, if the processing activity:
- Offering goods or services to the individuals within China territory
- Engaging in analysis or evaluation of behaviors of individuals' within China territory
- Other scenarios regulated by laws and regulations

Material Scope

Any activities that processing personal information

Exception:
Individual processes personal information due to household purposes

Key Roles

- Natural Person
- Cyberspace Administration oversight
- Handlers
- Government Departments — responsible in their domains
- Entrusted Person

Personal Information

- Identified
- Identifiable

Sensitive Personal Information

- Biometric data
- Religious Beliefs
- Specific Identities
- Medical and Health
- Financial Accounts
- Location
- Personal Information about children (under 14 years old)

6 Principles

- Lawfulness, Fairness, Necessity, and Good Faith
- Purpose Limitation
- Data Minimization
- Openness and Transparency
- Quality Assurance
- Accountability and Security

5 Data Subject Rights

- Right of information and making decisions (i.e., restriction and objection)
- Right of access (i.e., review, copy, and data portability)
- Right to rectification
- Right to erasure
- Right of explanation of processing rules

7 Lawful Basis

1. Consent
2. Performing contract or adherence to lawful labor or HR contract
3. Legal obligation
4. Necessary to respond to public health emergencies, or to protect the life, health and property safety of natural persons in emergencies
5. News reports and public opinion supervision for the public interest
6. Personal information disclosed by individuals or other personal information that has been legally disclosed
7. Other circumstances stipulated by laws and administrative regulations

Responsibilities of Personal Data Processors

- Designate a person in charge of personal information protection (if processing personal information more than the number prescribed by the national cyberspace administration)
- Personal information impact assessment if any of the following conditions met:
  - Processing sensitive personal information
  - Personal information is used for automated decision making
  - Disclose or sharing personal information with trustees or other processors or publicize personal information
  - Transfer personal information cross border
  - Processing activities will impose substantial impact to individual's personal rights

- Establish designated agency or representative if Engaging in analysis or evaluation of behaviors of Individuals' within China territory
- Policies and Procedures
- Personal Information classification awareness training
- Operational permission and (i.e. encryption and de-identification)
- Security controls
- Incident Response
- Regular compliance audit

For Personal information processors who provide important Internet platform services, serve a huge number of users, or has complex business scenarios:
(1)Establish personal information protection compliance system, and establish an independent organization mainly composed of external members to supervise the protection of personal information;
(2)Follow the principles of openness, fairness, and justice, formulate platform rules, and clarify the standards for handling personal information by product or service providers on the platform and their obligations to protect personal information;
(3)Stop providing services to product or service providers in platforms that deal with personal information in serious violation of laws and administrative regulations;
(4)Regularly publish reports on social responsibility for personal information protection and accept social supervision.

Responsibilities of Entrusted Person

- Necessary security measures
- Support the processor to comply with PIPL

Data Breach Notification (Art. 57)

- Notify the authorities and individuals

Cross-border Data Transfers

- Standard Contractual Clauses
- Security Reviews by National Cyberspace Administration departments (note: this is required for Critical Information infrastructure operators and personal information processors that process personal information up to the number prescribed by the national cyberspace administration. The personal information should be stored in China.)
- Personal information protection certification
- Meet conditions set forth by laws and regulations

Liabilities

	Entity	Personnel Accountable
Level I	Up to 1 million RMB fine Up to suspending services	Up to 100,000 RMB fine
Level II	Up to 50 million RMB or 5% of annual revenue Up to suspending business license	Up to 1 million RMB fine Up to prohibiting the personnel to serve as board director, supervisor, senior management and personal information protection person.
Crime	Criminal charges may apply	

Appendix M: China Data Security Law One-Pager Summary

China Data Security Law

Purpose

- Regulate data processing activities
- Ensure data security
- Protect the legitimate rights and interests of individuals and organizations
- Protect national sovereignty, security, and development interests

Key Definition

- Data: Refers to any electronic or other recording of information
- Data Security: It means to take necessary measures to ensure that the data is in a state of effective protection and legal use, as well as the ability to ensure a continuous security state

General principles

- Adhere to the overall national security framework
- Establish a sound data security governance system
- Improve data security assurance capabilities

Authority and Responsibilities

- Overall authority: Central National Security Leadership Agency
- National Cyberspace Administration: responsible for network data security
- Other government departments and agencies: responsible for the data security in their own industry or domain

Territorial Scope

- China and outside of China

Classification

- National core data
- Important data
- General data

Data Security and Development

- Implement big data strategy and build data infrastructure
- Data security should safeguard data development and utilization
- Establish a data transaction management system to regulate data transaction behavior

Data Security Mechanisms

- Establish a data classification, categorization, and graded protection system
- Establish a centralized, unified, efficient and authoritative data security risk assessment, reporting, information sharing, monitoring and early warning mechanism
- Establish a data security emergency response mechanism
- Establish a data security review system
- Implement export controls on data in accordance with the law
- Take reciprocal measures to address discriminatory prohibitions and restrictions from other nations

Data security obligations

- Data shall be collected in a lawful and fair manner
- Data brokers shall require data providers to explain the source of the data, review the identities of both parties to the transaction, and keep records of the review and transaction
- Organizations shall establish and improve an end-to-end security management system, take corresponding technical measures and other necessary measures
- Network data shall be protected in accordance with the network security graded protection system
- Establish and enhance data security risk monitoring and incident management and reporting
- For critical data, risk assessments shall be carried out on a regular basis, and risk assessment reports should be submitted to relevant competent authorities.
- The cross-border transfer of data of Critical Information Infrastructure shall adhere to the Cybersecurity Law. The requirements of cross-border transfer of other data should be formulated by the State Cyberspace Administration in conjunction with relevant departments
- To protect national security or investigating crimes, authorities can retrieve data after approval
- Without approval, organizations and individuals shall not provide data stored in the territory of China to foreign judicial or law enforcement agencies

Security and openness of government data

- State agencies should follow the principles of justice, fairness, and convenience for the people, and disclose government affairs data in a timely and accurate manner in accordance with regulations
- State agencies shall establish and improve data security management systems, implement data security protection responsibilities, and ensure the security of government data
- State agencies shall protect personal privacy, personal information, trade secrets, and confidential business information
- The use of third parties by state agencies shall undergo strict approval procedures. Agencies shall supervise the third parties to perform corresponding data security protection obligations.

Penalties

- Up to 10 Million RMB administrative fine and/or revoke of business license and/or criminal charges

Appendix N: Australia Privacy Act One-Pager Summary

Key Roles

- Individual
- APP entity
- Office of the Privacy Commissioner

Personal Data

- Identified
- Identifiable

Sensitive Information

- Racial or Ethnic Origin
- Religion or Philosophy Beliefs
- Political Opinions
- Genetic and Biometric data/templates
- Membership of Political association, professional/trade association, trade union
- Sex life or Sex Orientation
- Health
- Criminal Records

Scope

Covered APP entity:
- **Most Australian Government agencies**
- **All private sector and not-for-profit organizations with an annual turnover of more than AUS $3 million**
- **All private health service providers,** and
- **Some small businesses (i.e., that trade in personal information for a benefit, are a contracted service provider to the Australian Government, or are a credit reporting body**

Territory:
- **Orgs in Australia**
- **Other orgs doing business and collect personal data from Australians**

Exception: Employment related employee data not covered

Individuals' Rights

Core rights:
- **Right to be informed**
- **Right of access**
- **Right of correction**

Other rights:
- **Have the option of not identifying yourself, or of using a pseudonym in certain circumstances**
- **Stop receiving unwanted direct marketing**
- **Make a complaint about an organization or agency the Privacy Act covers, if you think they've mishandled your personal information**

Main Contents of Privacy Act 1988

13 APPs

APP	Non-sensitive data	Sensitive data
APP 1: Open and transparent management of personal information		
APP 2: Anonymity and pseudonymity		
APP 3: Collection of solicited personal information	Reasonably necessary	Consent, or exceptions law enforcement, etc.
APP 4: Dealing with unsolicited personal information		
APP 5: Notification of the collection of personal information		
APP 6: Use or disclosure of personal information	Not use or disclose for another purpose unless consented	
APP 7: Direct marketing	Opt-out	Consent
APP 8: Cross-border disclosure of personal information		
APP 9: Adoption, use or disclosure of government related identifiers		
APP 10: Quality of personal information		
APP 11: Security of personal information		
APP 12: Access to personal information		
APP 13: Correction of personal information		

Penalties and Remedies

Up to AUD $2.3 million for companies

Data Breach Notification

For eligible data breaches (that generate a "likely risk of serious harm" to affected individuals)
- the Privacy Commissioner as soon as practicable
- If it is unclear whether a breach is eligible, APP entities must conduct an assessment within 30 days of becoming aware of the breach

Cross-border Data Transfers

- Take reasonable steps to ensure that the recipient does not breach the APPs.
- An APP entity that discloses personal information to an overseas recipient is accountable for a breach of the APPs by the recipient.
- Derogations for specific situations

Appendix O: New Zealand Privacy Act 2020 One-Pager Summary

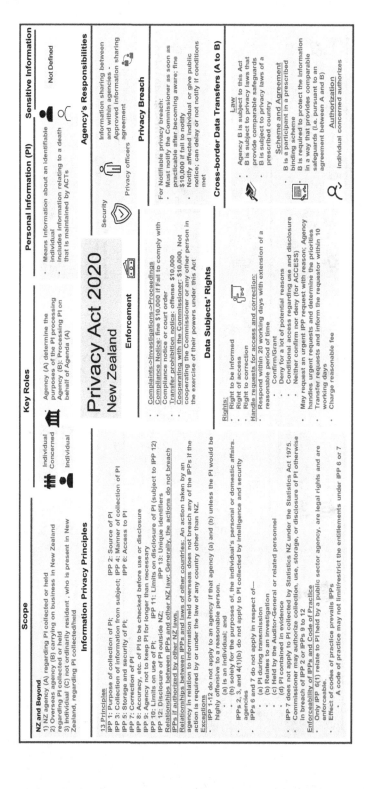

Appendix P: Brazil LGPD One-Pager Summary

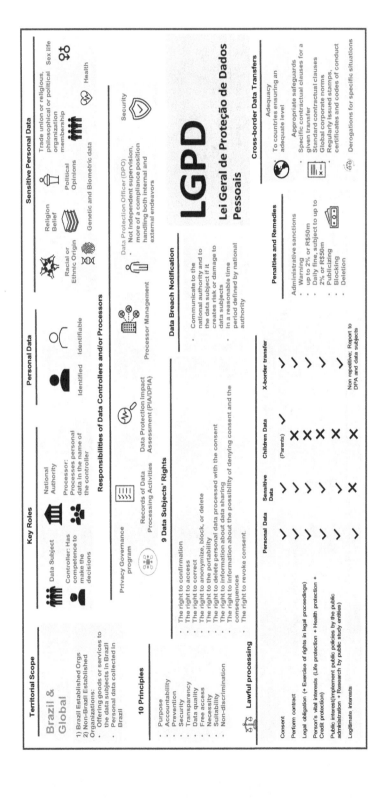

Appendix Q: Argentina PDPA One-Pager Summary

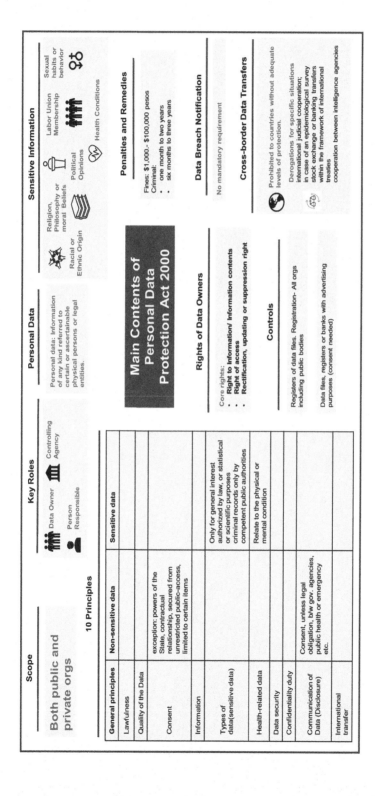

Scope

Both public and private orgs

10 Principles

General principles	Non-sensitive data	Sensitive data
Lawfulness		
Quality of the Data		
Consent	exception: powers of the State, contractual relationship, secured from unrestricted public-access, limited to certain items	
Information		
Types of data(sensitive data)		Only for general interest authorized by law, or statistical or scientific purposes criminal records only by competent public authorities
Health-related data		Relate to the physical or mental condition
Data security		
Confidentiality duty		
Communication of Data (Disclosure)	Consent, unless legal obligation, b/w gov. agencies, public health or emergency etc.	
International transfer		

Key Roles

Data Owner

Person Responsible

Controlling Agency

Personal Data

Personal data: Information of any kind referred to certain or ascertainable physical persons or legal entities.

Sensitive Information

Racial or Ethnic Origin

Religion, Philosophy or moral Beliefs

Political Opinions

Labor Union Membership

Health Conditions

Sexual habits or behavior

Main Contents of Personal Data Protection Act 2000

Rights of Data Owners

Core rights:
- **Right to information/ Information contents**
- **Right of access**
- **Rectification, updating or suppression right**

Controls

Registers of data files. Registration- All orgs including public bodies

Data files, registers or banks with advertising purposes (consent needed)

Penalties and Remedies

Fines: $1,000.- $100,000 pesos
Criminal:
- one month to two years
- six months to three years

Data Breach Notification

No mandatory requirement

Cross-border Data Transfers

Prohibited to countries without adequate levels of protection.

Derogations for specific situations: international judicial cooperation; in case of an epidemiological survey stock exchange or banking transfers within the framework of international treaties cooperation between intelligence agencies

References

[1] Perkins, Kleiner. *IDC White Paper Sponsored by Seagate: Data Age 2025. The Digitization of the World from Edge to Core.* Statista Digital Market Outlook. November 2018.

[2] Altman, Irwin. *The Environment and Social Behavior.* Brooks/Cole. 1975.

[3] IAPP. *IAPP Glossary on the Website.* 2022.

[4] Klein, Kris. *CIPP/C, CIPM, FIP: Canadian Privacy,* Fourth Edition, IAAP. 2020.

[5] Judgment of the Court. *EU Judgment of the Court,* Second Chamber. October 19, 2016.

[6] Clegg, Michael, Katherine Ellena, David Ennis and Chad Vickery. *The Hierarchy of Laws: Understanding and Implementing the Legal Frameworks that Govern Elections,* ACI. 2016.

[7] European Union. *Types of Legislation.* May 2022.

[8] UNCTAD. *United Nations Conference on Trade and Development.* February 27, 2022.

[9] Cisco. *2022 Data Privacy Benchmark Study.* February 1, 2022.

[10] EDPB. *Guidelines 1/2018 on Certification and Identifying Certification Criteria in Accordance with Articles 42 and 43 of the Regulation.* June 4, 2019.

[11] European Commission. *Data Protection Certification Mechanisms-Study on Articles 42 and 43 of the Regulation (EU) 2016/679.* February 2019.

[12] CMS. *GDPR Enforcement Tracker.* May 2022.

[13] Völkel, Christian. *Privacy as a Competitive Advantage.* March 12, 2021.

[14] Data & Marketing Association and Acxiom. *Data Privacy: What the Consumer Really Thinks.* June 2018.

[15] Chiavetta, Ryan. *2021 Privacy Tech Vendor Report 5.2.01.* 2021.

[16] Judgment of the Court. *European Court Reports 2003 I-12971.* November 2003.

[17] Judgment of the Court. *Official Journal of the European Union.* October 2015.

[18] Judgment of the Court. *Court of Justice of the European Union,* Press Release No 81/18. June 2018.

[19] Judgment of the Court (Grand Chamber). *Digital Reports (Court Reports—General) ECLI Identifier: ECLI:EU:C:2014:317.* May 13, 2014.

[20] Hatmaker, Taylor. *US News Sites are Ghosting European Readers on GDPR Deadline.* May 25, 2018.

[21] Cisco. *Privacy Maturity Benchmark Study.* 2018.

[22] IAPP. *Data Protection Officer Requirements by Country.* 2021.

[23] Hanratty, Carissa. *Legal Risks to Being a DPO.* 2021.

[24] MediaPRO. *2020 State of Privacy and Security Awareness Report.* February 25, 2020.

[25] Solove, Daniel J. and Danielle Keats Citron. *Privacy Harms.* GW Law Faculty Publications & Other Works. 2021.

[26] IMY. *Penalty Fee Against Klarna After Review.* March 29, 2022.

[27] European Court of Human Rights. *Factsheet—Personal Data Protection.* January 2022.

[28] Center for Internet Security, Inc. *CIS Controls V7 Implementation Guide for Industrial Controls Systems.* March 19, 2018.

[29] OCEG. *Managing Third-Party InfoSec Risk.* 2017.

[30] Educause. *Higher Education Cloud Vendor Assessment Tool.* October 25, 2017.

[31] Cloud Security Alliance. *Consensus Assessments Initiative Questionnaire.* Cloud Security Alliance. 2017.

[32] Haist, Dennis. *Is Effective Third-Party Due Diligence Possible Under GDPR?* Steele Compliance Solutions, Inc. May 25, 2018.

[33] Ross, Alexandra. *A Strategic Approach to Vendor-Management Under the GDPR.* The International Association of Privacy Professionals. February 28, 2017.

[34] US Department of Health & Human Services. *HIPAA for Professionals.* HHS. June 16, 2017.

[35] Vendor Security Alliance. *2018 Questionnaire.* December 22, 2017.

[36] New York Department of Financial Services. *Cybersecurity Requirements for Financial Services Companies.* 2017.

[37] Ponemon Institute. *Data Risk in the Third-Party Ecosystem: Second Annual Study.* Ponemon Institute LLC. September 2017.

[38] Office of the Superintendent of Financial Institutions. *Cyber Security Self-Assessment Guidance.* September 24, 2018.

[39] National Institute of Standards and Technology. *NIST Special Publication 800–53 Revision 4: Security and Privacy Controls for Federal Information Systems and Organizations.* NIST. April 2013.

[40] National Institute of Standards and Technology. *Framework for Improving Critical Infrastructure Cybersecurity.* NIST. April 16, 2018.

[41] PCI Security Standards Council. *Payment Card Industry (PCI) Data Security Standard Requirements and Security Assessment Procedures Version 3.2.* PCI Security Standards Council Document Library. April 2016.

[42] International Organization for Standardization. *ISO/IEC 27002: Information Technology—Security Techniques—Code of Practice for Information Security Controls.* ISO. October 1, 2013.

[43] Cisco Systems, Inc. *Cisco Study Finds Privacy Is Now Mission Critical for Organizations Worldwide.* January 26, 2022.

[44] European Commission. *Adequacy Decisions-How the EU Determines if a Non-EU Country Has an Adequate Level of Data Protection.* May 2022.

[45] Court of Justice of the European Union. *Judgment in Case C-311/18 Data Protection Commissioner v Facebook Ireland and Maximillian Schrems.* July 16, 2020.

[46] Morton, Carol Cruzan and Hakon Heimer. *INTERVIEW: Health Research Stymied by Legal Barriers to Safe and Effective Data Sharing.* October 2021.

[47] Datenschutzkonferenz (DSK). *100th Conference the Independent Data Protection Supervisory aAuthorities of the Federal and State Governments Video Conference on November 25th and 26th, 2020.* January 14, 2021.

[48] Feustel, Alina. *Senate Chancellery Formally Warned Against Using "Zoom".* August 16, 2021.

[49] NOBY. *Next Steps for EU Companies and FAQs.* July 20, 2020.

[50] EDPB. *Guidelines 05/2021 on the Interplay Between the Application of Article 3 and the Provisions on International Transfers as Per Chapter V of the GDPR.* November 18, 2022.

[51] Asia-Pacific Economic Cooperation. *What Is the Cross-Border Privacy Rules System.* October 2021.

[52] National Conference of State Legislatures. *Data Disposal Laws.* August 21, 2021.

[53] EU EDPB. *Opinion 3/2020 on the European Strategy for Data.* June 16, 2020.

[54] UK ICO. *Anonymization: Managing Data Protection Risk Code of Practice.* November 2012.

[55] Federal Trade Commission. *Equifax Data Breach Settlement.* July 11, 2019.

[56] Canada OPC. *PIPEDA Report of Findings #2019–001.* April 9, 2019.

[57] UK ICO. *ICO Fines British Airways £20m for Data Breach Affecting More Than 400,000 Customers.* October 16, 2020.

[58] UK ICO. *ICO Fines Marriott International Inc £18.4 million for Failing to Keep Customers' Personal Data Secure.* October 30, 2020.

[59] Singapore PDPC. *Breach of Protection Obligation by Flight Raja Travels.* June 11, 2018.

[60] Google, Ipsos. *Privacy by Design: Exceeding Customer Expectations.* 2020.

[61] Ipsos, the Netherlands. *Data Privacy Study: Consumer Model of Data Privacy.* 2020.

[62] Ipsos, UK, Germany, France, the Netherlands. *Data Ethics Study: Data Ethics and Effectiveness, Part 1—Ethics (n=6,000).* 2021.

[63] Ipsos, Global. *Global Trends 2020.* 2020.

[64] Ipsos, UK. *Responsible Marketing Deep Dive.* 2020.

[65] ICO, CMA. *Competition and Data Protection in Digital Markets: A Joint Statement Between the CMA and the ICO.* May 19, 2021.

[66] Microsoft. *Microsoft Edge is Committed to Helping you Stay Safe on the Web.* May 20, 2022.

[67] Brave Software. *Advanced Privacy A Long List of Brave's Behind-the-scenes Protections and Commitments.* May 20, 2022.

[68] Huang, Tim, Johann Hofmann and Arthur Edelstein. *Firefox 86 Introduces Total Cookie Protection.* February 23, 2021.

[69] Chromium.org. *The Privacy Sandbox.* May 20, 2022.

[70] RESPECTeD Project. *Advanced Data Protection Control (ADPC).* May 20, 2022.

[71] W3C Working Group. *Tracking Compliance and Scope.* January 22, 2019.

[72] NOYB. *NOYB Files 422 Formal GDPR Complaints on Nerve-Wrecking "Cookie Banners".* August 10, 2021.

[73] Graham, Kean. *First Party Cookies vs. Third Party Cookies: WTF Is the Difference?* October 5, 2021.

[74] FTC. *Q&A for Telemarketers & Sellers About DNC Provisions in TSR.* May 18, 2022.

[75] Petersen, Donald E. *State Do Not Call Lists.* September 6, 2017.

[76] EU Grande Chamber. *Case of Bărbulescu V. Romania.* September 5, 2017.

[77] Council of Europe/European Court of Human Rights. *Information Note on the Court's Case-Law 233*. October 2019.

[78] Lamb, Scott and Lauren Zeleschuk. *Facial Recognition Technology: The Privacy Commissioner Responds in Canada*. July 01, 2021.

[79] European Court of Human Rights. *Case of Bărbulescu V. Romania*. January 12, 2016.

[80] Reinsel, David, John Gantz and John Rydning. *The Digitization of the World from Edge to Core*. November 2018.

[81] EDRM.NET. *EDRM Model*. January 2020.

[82] Gaidis, Alexander J. *Case Study of the GDPR Violation by the Skellefteå Municipality School Board*. 2019.

[83] EDPB. *Norwegian Data Protection Authority: Decision to Fine Bergen Municipality*. October 14, 2020.

[84] Europe Commission's AI HLEG. *Ethics Guidelines for Trustworthy AI*. 2019.

[85] IEEE Standards Association. *Ethically Aligned Design*, First Edition, IEEE. 2019.

[86] Singapore PDPC. *A Proposed Model AI Governance Framework*. 2019.

[87] CAICT. *Artificial Intelligence Security White Paper*. 2018.

[88] Huawei GSPO Office. *Thinking Ahead About AI Security and Privacy Protection*. 2019.

[89] Government of Canada. *Responsible Use of Artificial Intelligence (AI)*. May 2022.

[90] Office of the Director of National Intelligence. *Principles of Artificial Intelligence Ethics for the Intelligence Community*. May 2022.

[91] Australian Government. *Australia's Artificial Intelligence Ethics Framework*. May 2022.

[92] EU Commission. *High-Level Expert Group on Artificial Intelligence*. April 2019.

[93] OECD. *OECD AI Principles Overview*. May 2022.

[94] Microsoft. *Identify Guiding Principles for Responsible AI*. May 2022.

[95] Google. *Artificial Intelligence at Google: Our Principles*. May 2022.

[96] Dutch DPA. *National Credit Register (BKR) Fined for Personal Data Access Charge*. July 6, 2020.

[97] EDPB. *The Danish Data Protection Agency Proposes a DKK 1,2 Million Fine for Danish Taxi Company*. March 25, 2019.

[98] EDPB. *Spanish Data Protection Authority (AEPD) Imposes Fine on Company for Not Complying with Advertisement Exclusion*. August 18, 2020.

[99] Venturebeat. *Report: 63% of C-suite Execs do not have an Incident Response Plan*. December 2, 2021.

[100] US National Conference of State Legislatures. *Security Breach Notification Laws*. January 17, 2022.

[101] Spain AEPD. *National Case Number/Name: E/07796/2020*. April 16, 2021.

[102] Dutch DPA. *AP Adjusts Fine Policy Rules*. March 14, 2019.

[103] Article 29 Data Protection Working Party. *Opinion 4/2007 on the Concept of Personal Data*. 2007.

[104] Sullivan, John V. *How Our Laws Are Made*, 110th Congress 1st Session. July 24, 2007.

[105] Microsoft. *Where Your Microsoft 365 Customer Data Is Stored*. April 26, 2022.

[106] US DoE Privacy Technical Assistance Center. *Data Security Checklist*. July 2015.

[107] UK ICO. *Information Commissioner's Opinion: Data Protection and Privacy Expectations for Online Advertising Proposals*. November 25, 2021.

Glossary

Anonymization: A process that strips out any information that can identify a particular person, by means of encryption or another method. For data to be truly anonymized, the process must be irreversible. See also pseudonymization

Automated decision-making: The process of making a decision by automated means without any human involvement.

Binding corporate rules: Internal rules approved on an individual basis by supervisory authorities for data transfers within multinational organizations that allow such organizations to transfer personal data within the same group of companies to countries that do not provide an adequate level of protection without any further safeguards.

Biometric data: Personal data resulting from specific technical processing relating to the physical, physiological, or behavioral characteristics of a natural person which allow or confirm the unique identification of that natural person, such as facial images or fingerprint data.

Consent: Any freely given, specific, informed, and unambiguous indication of the data subject's wishes by which the person, by way of a statement or clear affirmative action signifies agreement to the processing of their personal data.

Controller (or data controller): The natural or legal person, public authority, agency, or other body that, alone or jointly with others, determines the purposes of the processing of personal data.

Cookie: A small text file generated by the website on which the user is browsing which is then stored on the user's computer by the website browser, with the aim of identifying the user.

Criminal convictions data: Data about criminal allegations. proceedings, or conviction and personal data linked to related security measures.

Cross-border processing: 1) The processing of personal data which takes place in the context of the activities of establishments in more than one EU member state of a controller or processor in the EU where the controller or processor is established in more than on member state: 2) the processing of personal data which takes place in the context of the activities of a single establishment of a controller or processor in the EU but which substantially affects or is likely to substantially affect, data subjects in more than one EU member state.

Data Processing Agreement: A legally binding agreement in writing between the data controller and data processor that contains the mandatory terms for the processing set out in the GDPR. It is often referred to as a DPA.

Data protection by design and by default: The concept requiring data controllers to put in place appropriate technical and organizational measures to implement data protection principles and safeguard data subjects' rights.

Data subject: An individual whose personal data is collected, held, and/or processed by a data controller for varying purposes and who can be identified, directly or indirectly, by reference to such personal data.

Direct marketing: The communication (by whatever means) of advertising or marketing material which is directed to individuals.

ePrivacy Directive: The Privacy and Electronic Communications Directive 2002/58/EC, an EU directive on data protection and privacy in the digital age (as amended by Directive 2009/136).

European Data Protection Board (EDPB): An independent EU body that contributes to the consistent application of the GDPR and other data protection rules throughout the EL and promotes cooperation between supervisory authorities.

European Economic Area (EEA): An area uniting the EU member states and Iceland Liechtenstein, and Norway—three countries that have adopted a national law implementing the GDPR.

European Union (EU): A political and economic union of 28 member states located.

Filing system: Any structured set of personal data which is accessible according to specific criteria, whether centralized, decentralized, or dispersed on a functional or geographical basis.

Genetic data: Personal data relating to the inherited or acquired genetic characteristics of a natural person which give unique information about the physiology or health of that natural person and which result, in particular, from an analysis of a biological sample from the natural person in question.

Individual subscriber: A living individual, including an unincorporated body of individuals that subscribes to a service for electronic communications services, such as email. This definition is relevant to the UK's PECR.

Identifiable natural person: A person who can be identified, directly or indirectly, in particular by reference to an identifier such as a name, an identification number, location data, or an online identifier or to one or more factors specific to the physical, physiological, genetic, mental, economic, cultural, or social identity of that natural person. See also data subject, personal data, sensitive data.

Information society service: A service as defined in point(b) of Article 1(1) of Directive (EU)2015/1535 of the European Parliament and of the Council—any service provided for renumeration, at a distance, by electronic means and at the individual request of a recipient of services.

International organization: An organization and its subordinate bodies governed by public international law, or any other body which is set up by, or on the basis of an agreement between two or more countries.

International transfer: When personal data that is being processed (or will be processed) is sent to a third country or an international organization (see also third country international organization).

Joint controller: A data controller that acts together with at least one other data controller to determine the purposes and manner of the processing of certain personal data.

Just-in-time notices: A notice that can consist of text, video messages, or other forms of communication that appears at the point that data subjects input their personal data (for example, on an organization's website), providing a brief message explaining how their information will be used and typically linking to a Privacy Notice.

Lead authority: The supervisory authority that has primary responsibility for matters arising out of cross border processing.

Legal person: An entity that has a separate legal status to an individual, such as a company, a Limited Liability Partnership, or a government organization.

Main establishment: 1) As regards a controller with establishments in more than one EU member state, the place of its central administration in the EU, unless the decisions on the purposes and of the processing of personal data are taken in another establishment of the controller in the EU and the latter establishment has the power to have such decisions implemented, in which case the establishment having taken such decisions is to be considered to be the main establishment. 2) As regards a processor with establishments in more than one EU member state, the place of its central administration in the EU, or, if the processor has no central administration in the EU, the establishment of the processor in the EU where the main processing activities in the context of the activities of an establishment of the processor take place to the extent that the processor is subject to specific obligations under this regulation.

Natural person: A living human being

Personal data: Any information relating to an identified or identifiable natural person, including a name, an identification number, location data, an online identifier or to one or more factors specific to the physical, physiological, genetic, mental, economic, cultural, or social identity of that natural person. See also data subject, identifiable natural person, special-category data.

Personal data breach: A breach of security leading to the accidental or unlawful destruction, loss, alteration, unauthorized disclosure of, or access to personal data transmitted, stored, or otherwise processed.

Privacy Notice: A notice providing certain information to data subjects about the use of their personal data, as required by the GDPR.

Processing: Any operation or set of operations which is performed on personal data or on sets of personal data, such as collection, recording, organization, structuring storage adaptation or alteration, retrieval, consultation, use, disclosure by transmission, dissemination, or otherwise making available, alignment or combination, restriction, erasure, or destruction.

Processor (or data processor): A natural or legal person, public authority, agency. or other body that processes personal data on behalf of and under the instructions of the controller.

Profiling: Any form of automated processing of personal data consisting of the use of personal data to evaluate certain personal aspects relating to a natural person—in particular, to analyze or predict aspects concerning that natural person's performance a work, economic situation, health, personal preferences, interests, reliability, behavior, location, or movements.

Pseudonymization: The processing of personal data in such a manner that the personal data can no longer be attributed to a specific data subject without the use of additional information, provided that such additional information is kept separately and is subject to technical and organizational measures to ensure that the personal data aren't attributed to an identified or identifiable natural person. See also anonymization.

Recipient: A natural or legal person, public authority, agency, or another body to which the personal data are disclosed, whether a Third Party or not. However, public authorities that may receive personal data in the framework of a particular inquiry in accordance with EU or member state law shall not be regarded as recipients; the processing of those data by those public authorities shall be in compliance with the applicable data protection rules according to the purposes of the processing.

Regulation: A legal act of the EU that becomes immediately enforceable as law in all EU member states. See also directive.

Representative: A natural or legal person established in the EU who, designated by the controller or processor in writing, represents the controller or processor with regard to their respective obligations under the GDPR.

Restriction of processing: The marking of stored personal data with the aim of limiting their processing in the future.

Special category data: Personal data which includes racial or ethnic origin; political opinions; religious or philosophical beliefs; trade union membership; the processing of genetic data; biometric data for the purpose of uniquely identifying a natural person; or data concerning a natural person's sex life or sexual orientation.

Supervisory authority: An independent public entity in each EU member state responsible for monitoring the application of the GOPR and contributing to the consistent application of the GDPR throughout the EU, bestowed with certain tasks and powers under the GDPR such as providing advice on data protection issues, investigating complaints of violations, and levying fines and other sanctions for noncompliance with the GDPR. Also known as a "data protection authority."

Supervisory authority concerned: A supervisory authority that is concerned by the processing of personal data for one of these reasons.

Printed in the United States
by Baker & Taylor Publisher Services